GEOMETRY AND COMPLEXITY THEORY

Two central problems in computer science are P versus NP and the complexity of matrix multiplication. The first is also a leading candidate for the greatest unsolved problem in mathematics. The second is of enormous practical and theoretical importance. Algebraic geometry and representation theory provide fertile ground for advancing work on these problems and others in complexity.

This introduction to algebraic complexity theory for graduate students and researchers in computer science and mathematics features concrete examples that demonstrate the application of geometric techniques to real-world problems. Written by a noted expert in the field, it offers numerous open questions to motivate future research. Complexity theory has rejuvenated classical geometric questions and brought different areas of mathematics together in new ways. This book shows the beautiful, interesting, and important questions that have arisen as a result.

J. M. Landsberg is Professor of Mathematics at Texas A&M University. He is a leading geometer working in complexity theory, with research interests in differential geometry, algebraic geometry, representation theory, the geometry and application of tensors, and, most recently, algebraic complexity theory. The author of more than 60 research articles and 4 books, he has given numerous intensive research courses and lectures at international conferences. He co-organized the Fall 2014 semester "Algorithms and Complexity in Algebraic Geometry" at the Simons Institute for the Theory of Computing and served as the UC Berkeley Chancellor's professor during the program.

Geometry and Complexity Theory

J. M. LANDSBERG
Texas A&M University

CAMBRIDGE
UNIVERSITY PRESS

University Printing House, Cambridge CB2 8BS, United Kingdom

One Liberty Plaza, 20th Floor, New York, NY 10006, USA

477 Williamstown Road, Port Melbourne, VIC 3207, Australia

4843/24, 2nd Floor, Ansari Road, Daryaganj, Delhi - 110002, India

79 Anson Road, #06-04/06, Singapore 079906

Cambridge University Press is part of the University of Cambridge.

It furthers the University's mission by disseminating knowledge in the pursuit of
education, learning, and research at the highest international levels of excellence.

www.cambridge.org
Information on this title: www.cambridge.org/9781107199231
DOI: 10.1017/9781108183192

© J. M. Landsberg 2017

First published 2017

Printed in the United States of America by Sheridan Books, Inc.

A catalogue record for this publication is available from the British Library.

Library of Congress Cataloging-in-Publication Data
Names: Landsberg, J. M., author.
Title: Geometry and complexity theory / J.M. Landsberg, Texas A&M University.
Description: New York, NY, USA : Cambridge University Press, [2017] |
Includes bibliographical references and index.
Identifiers: LCCN 2017020187 | ISBN 9781107199231 (hardback : alk. paper)
Subjects: LCSH: Computational complexity. | Geometry, Algebraic.
Classification: LCC QA267.7 .L35 2017 | DDC 516.3/5–dc23
LC record available at https://lccn.loc.gov/2017020187

ISBN 978-1-107-19923-1 Hardback

Contents

Preface

This book describes recent applications of algebraic geometry and representation theory to complexity theory. I focus on two central problems: *the complexity of matrix multiplication* and *Valiant's algebraic variants of* **P** *versus* **NP**.

I have attempted to make this book accessible to both computer scientists and geometers and the exposition as self-contained as possible. Two goals are to convince computer scientists of the utility of techniques from algebraic geometry and representation theory and to show geometers beautiful, interesting, and important geometry questions arising in complexity theory.

Computer scientists have made extensive use combinatorics, graph theory, probability, and linear algebra. I hope to show that even elementary techniques from algebraic geometry and representation theory can substantially advance the search for lower bounds, and even upper bounds, in complexity theory. I believe such additional mathematics will be necessary for further advances on questions discussed in this book as well as related complexity problems. Techniques are introduced as needed to deal with concrete problems.

For geometers, I expect that complexity theory will be as good a source for questions in algebraic geometry as has been modern physics. Recent work has indicated that subjects such as Fulton-McPherson intersection theory, the Hilbert scheme of points, and the Kempf-Weyman method for computing syzygies all have something to add to complexity theory. In addition, complexity theory has a way of rejuvenating old questions that had been nearly forgotten but remain beautiful and intriguing: questions of Hadamard, Darboux, Lüroth, and the classical Italian school. At the same time, complexity theory has brought different areas of mathematics together in new ways: for instance, combinatorics, representation theory, and algebraic geometry all play a role in understanding the coordinate ring of the orbit closure of the determinant.

This book evolved from several classes I have given on the subject: a spring 2013 semester course at Texas A&M; summer courses at Scuola Matematica Inter-universitaria, Cortona (July 2012), CIRM, Trento (June 2014), the University of Chicago (IMA sponsored) (July 2014), KAIST, Deajeon (August 2015), and Obergurgul, Austria (September 2016); a fall 2016 semester course at Texas A&M; and, most importantly, a fall 2014 semester course at the University of California, Berkeley, as part of the semester-long program Algorithms and Complexity in Algebraic Geometry at the Simons Institute for the Theory of Computing.

Since I began writing this book, even since the first draft was completed in fall 2014, the research landscape has shifted considerably: the two paths toward Valiant's conjecture that had been considered the most viable have been shown to be unworkable, at least as originally proposed. On the other hand, there have been significant advances in our understanding of the matrix multiplication tensor. The contents of this book are the state of the art as of January 2017.

Prerequisites

Chapters 1–8 only require a solid background in linear algebra and a willingness to accept several basic results from algebraic geometry that are stated as needed. Nothing beyond [Sha07] is used in these chapters. Because of the text [Lan12], I am sometimes terse regarding basic properties of tensors and multilinear algebra. Chapters 9 and 10 contain several sections requiring further background.

Layout

All theorems, propositions, remarks, examples, etc., are numbered together within each section; for example, Theorem 1.3.2 is the second numbered item in Section 1.3. Equations are numbered sequentially within each chapter. I have included hints for selected exercises, those marked with the symbol ⊙ at the end, which is meant to be suggestive of a life preserver. Exercises are marked with (1), (2), or (3), indicating the level of difficulty. Important exercises are also marked with an exclamation mark, sometimes even two, e.g., (1!!) is an exercise that is easy and very important.

Acknowledgments

Numerous people have given me help with this book over the years. These include Malek Abdesselam, Harold Boaz, Emmanuel Briand, Michel Brion, Peter Bürgisser, Klim Efremenko, Skip Garibaldi, Josh Grochow, Jesko Hüttenhain, Anthony Iarrobino, Suil Kang, Pascal Koiran, Shrawan Kumar, Laurent Manivel, Maximilliano Mella, Ketan Mulmuley, Giorgio Ottaviani, Victor Pan,

Gregory Pearlstein, Kristian Ranestad, Nick Ryder, Anna Seigal, Anne Shiu, Alistair Sinclair, Les Valient, Jerzy Weyman, Avi Wigderson, Ryan Williams, and Virginia Vassilevaska Williams. I am especially indebted to Markus Bläser, Jarek Buczynski and Mateusz Michalek, Michael Forbes and Amir Shpilka, and Christian Ikenmeyer, respectively, for help with Chapters 5, 10, 7, and 9. The book was helped tremendously by Fulvio Gesmundo, who gave a careful reading and corrections to the entire text.

I also thank all the students in the classes I have given, the organizers of the various summer courses, as well as my collaborators. Finally, I thank the Simons Center for hosting the fall 2014 semester-long program Algorithms and Complexity in Algebraic Geometry, for an inspiring semester where the first draft of this book was completed.

1

Introduction

A dramatic leap for signal processing occurred in the 1960s with the implementation of the fast Fourier transform, an algorithm that surprised the engineering community with its efficiency.[1] Is there a way to predict the existence of such fast unexpected algorithms? Can we determine when they do not exist? *Complexity theory* addresses these questions.

This book is concerned with the use of *geometry* toward these goals. I focus primarily on two central questions: the complexity of matrix multiplication and algebraic variants of the famous **P** versus **NP** problem. In the first case, a surprising algorithm exists, and it is conjectured that even better algorithms exist. In the second case, it is conjectured that no surprising algorithm exists.

In this chapter I introduce the main open questions discussed in this book, establish notation that is used throughout the book, and introduce fundamental geometric notions.

1.1 Matrix Multiplication

Much of scientific computation amounts to linear algebra, and the basic operation of linear algebra is matrix multiplication. All operations of linear algebra – solving systems of linear equations, computing determinants, etc. – use matrix multiplication.

1.1.1 The Standard Algorithm

The standard algorithm for multiplying matrices is row-column multiplication: let A, B be 2×2 matrices

$$A = \begin{pmatrix} a_1^1 & a_2^1 \\ a_1^2 & a_2^2 \end{pmatrix}, \quad B = \begin{pmatrix} b_1^1 & b_2^1 \\ b_1^2 & b_2^2 \end{pmatrix}.$$

---

[1] To this day, it is not known if there is an even more efficient algorithm than the FFT. See [Val77, Lok08, KLPSMN09, GHIL16].

Remark 1.1.1.1 While computer scientists generally keep all indices down (to distinguish from powers), I use the convention from differential geometry that in a matrix X, the entry in the ith row and jth column is labeled x^i_j.

The usual algorithm to calculate the matrix product $C = AB$ is

$$c^1_1 = a^1_1 b^1_1 + a^1_2 b^2_1,$$

$$c^1_2 = a^1_1 b^1_2 + a^1_2 b^2_2,$$

$$c^2_1 = a^2_1 b^1_1 + a^2_2 b^2_1,$$

$$c^2_2 = a^2_1 b^1_2 + a^2_2 b^2_2.$$

It requires 8 multiplications and 4 additions to execute, and applied to $\mathbf{n} \times \mathbf{n}$ matrices, it uses $\mathbf{n}^3$ multiplications and $\mathbf{n}^3 - \mathbf{n}^2$ additions.

This algorithm has been around for about two centuries.

In 1968, V. Strassen set out to prove the standard algorithm was optimal in the sense that no algorithm using fewer multiplications exists (personal communication). Since that might be difficult to prove, he set out to show it was true at least for 2×2 matrices – at least over $\mathbb{Z}_2$. His spectacular failure opened up a whole new area of research.

1.1.2 Strassen's Algorithm for Multiplying 2 × 2 Matrices using 7 Scalar Multiplications [Str69]

Set

$$I = \left(a^1_1 + a^2_2\right)\left(b^1_1 + b^2_2\right), \qquad (1.1.1)$$

$$II = \left(a^2_1 + a^2_2\right)b^1_1,$$

$$III = a^1_1\left(b^1_2 - b^2_2\right),$$

$$IV = a^2_2\left(-b^1_1 + b^2_1\right),$$

$$V = \left(a^1_1 + a^1_2\right)b^2_2,$$

$$VI = \left(-a^1_1 + a^2_1\right)\left(b^1_1 + b^2_1\right),$$

$$VII = \left(a^1_2 - a^2_2\right)\left(b^2_1 + b^2_2\right).$$

Exercise 1.1.2.1 (1) Show that if $C = AB$, then

$$c^1_1 = I + IV - V + VII,$$

$$c^2_1 = II + IV,$$

$$c^1_2 = III + V,$$

$$c^2_2 = I + III - II + VI.$$

This raises questions:

1. Can one find an algorithm that uses just six multiplications?
2. Could Strassen's algorithm have been predicted in advance?
3. Since it uses more additions, is it actually better in practice?
4. This algorithm was found by accident and looks ad hoc. Is there any way to make sense of it? For example, is there any way to see that it is correct other than a brute force calculation?
5. What about algorithms for **n** × **n** matrices?

I address question 4 in §1.1.15 and the others below, with the last question first.

1.1.3 Fast Multiplication of n × n Matrices

In Strassen's algorithm, the entries of the matrices need not be scalars – they could themselves be matrices. Let A, B be 4×4 matrices, and write

$$A = \begin{pmatrix} a_1^1 & a_2^1 \\ a_1^2 & a_2^2 \end{pmatrix}, \quad B = \begin{pmatrix} b_1^1 & b_2^1 \\ b_1^2 & b_2^2 \end{pmatrix}.$$

where a_j^i, b_j^i are 2×2 matrices. One may apply Strassen's algorithm to get the blocks of $C = AB$ in terms of the blocks of A, B by performing seven multiplications of 2×2 matrices. Since one can apply Strassen's algorithm to each block, one can multiply 4×4 matrices using $7^2 = 49$ multiplications instead of the usual $4^3 = 64$.

If A, B are $2^k \times 2^k$ matrices, one may multiply them using 7^k multiplications instead of the usual 8^k. If **n** is not a power of 2, enlarge the matrices with blocks of zeros to obtain matrices whose size is a power of 2. Asymptotically, by recursion and block multiplication, one can multiply **n** × **n** matrices using approximately $\mathbf{n}^{\log_2(7)} \simeq \mathbf{n}^{2.81}$ multiplications. To see this, let $\mathbf{n} = 2^k$ and write $7^k = (2^k)^a$, so $a = \log_2 7$.

1.1.4 Regarding the Number of Additions

The number of additions in Strassen's algorithm also grows like $\mathbf{n}^{2.81}$, so this algorithm *is* more efficient in practice when the matrices are large. For any efficient algorithm for matrix multiplication, the total complexity is governed by the number of multiplications; see [BCS97, Proposition 15.1]. This is fortuitous because there is a geometric object, *tensor rank*, discussed in §1.1.11, that counts the number of multiplications in an optimal algorithm (within a factor of 2), and thus provides a geometric measure of the complexity of matrix multiplication.

Just how large a matrix must be in order to obtain a substantial savings with Strassen's algorithm (a size of about 2,000 suffices) and other practical matters are addressed in [BB].

1.1.5 An Even Better Algorithm?

Regarding question (1) above, one cannot improve upon Strassen's algorithm for 2×2 matrices. This was first shown in [Win71]. I will give a proof, using geometry and representation theory, of a stronger statement in §8.3.2. However, for $\mathbf{n} > 2$, very little is known, as discussed below and in Chapters 2–5. What is known is that better algorithms than Strassen's exist for $\mathbf{n} \times \mathbf{n}$ matrices when $\mathbf{n}$ is large.

1.1.6 How to Predict in Advance?

The answer to question (2) is yes! In fact, it could have been predicted 100 years ago.

Had someone asked Terracini in 1913, he would have been able to predict the existence of something like Strassen's algorithm from geometric considerations alone. Matrix multiplication is a bilinear map (see §1.1.9). Terracini would have been able to tell you, thanks to a simple parameter count (see §2.1.6), that even a general bilinear map $\mathbb{C}^4 \times \mathbb{C}^4 \to \mathbb{C}^4$ can be executed using seven multiplications, and thus, fixing any $\epsilon > 0$, one can perform any bilinear map $\mathbb{C}^4 \times \mathbb{C}^4 \to \mathbb{C}^4$ within an error of ϵ using seven multiplications.

1.1.7 Big/Little O, etc., Notation

For functions f, g of a real variable (or integer) x,

$f(x) = O(g(x))$ if there exists a constant $C > 0$ and x_0 such that $|f(x)| \leq C|g(x)|$ for all $x \geq x_0$,

$f(x) = o(g(x))$ if $\lim_{x \to \infty} \frac{|f(x)|}{|g(x)|} = 0$,

$f(x) = \Omega(g(x))$ if there exists a constant $C > 0$ and x_0 such that $C|f(x)| \geq |g(x)|$ for all $x \geq x_0$,

$f(x) = \omega(g(x))$ if if $\lim_{x \to \infty} \frac{|g(x)|}{|f(x)|} = 0$, and

$f(x) = \Theta(g(x))$ if $f(x) = O(g(x))$ and $f(x) = \Omega(g(x))$.

1.1.8 The Exponent of Matrix Multiplication

The following quantity is the standard measure of the complexity of matrix multiplication.

Definition 1.1.8.1 The *exponent* ω of matrix multiplication is

$$\omega := \inf\{h \in \mathbb{R} \mid \mathbf{n} \times \mathbf{n} \text{ matrices can be multiplied using}$$
$$O(\mathbf{n}^h) \text{ arithmetic operations}\},$$

where inf denotes the infimum.

By Theorem 1.1.11.3, Strassen's algorithm shows $\omega \leq \log_2(7) < 2.81$, and it is easy to prove $\omega \geq 2$. Determining ω is a central open problem in complexity theory. After Strassen's work, it was shown in 1978 that $\omega \leq 2.7962$ [Pan78], then $\omega \leq 2.7799$ [Bin80] in 1979, then $\omega \leq 2.55$ [Sch81] in 1981, then $\omega \leq 2.48$ [Str87] in 1987, and then $\omega \leq 2.38$ [CW90] in 1989, which might have led people in 1990 to think a resolution was near. However, then nothing happened for more than 20 years, and the current "world record" of $\omega < 2.373$ [Wil, LG14, Sto] is not much of an improvement since 1990. These results are the topic of Chapter 3.

If one is interested in multiplying matrices of reasonable size, only the algorithms in [Pan78, Smi13] are known to beat Strassen's. This "practical" exponent is discussed in Chapter 4.

The above work has led to the following astounding conjecture.

Conjecture 1.1.8.2 $\omega = 2$.

That is, *it is conjectured that, asymptotically, it is nearly just as easy to multiply matrices as it is to add them!*

Although I am unaware of anyone taking responsibility for the conjecture, most computer scientists I have discussed it with expect it to be true. (For example, it is possible to multiply $\mathbf{n}$-bit integers in near-linear time $O(\mathbf{n}\log(\mathbf{n}))$, which is almost as efficient as adding them.)

I have no opinion on whether the conjecture should be true or false and thus discuss both upper and lower bounds for the complexity of matrix multiplication, focusing on the role of geometry. Chapters 2 and 5 are dedicated to lower bounds and Chapters 3 and 4 to upper bounds.

1.1.9 Matrix Multiplication as a Bilinear Map

I will use the notation

$$M_{\langle \mathbf{n}, \mathbf{m}, \mathbf{l} \rangle} : \mathbb{C}^{\mathbf{n} \times \mathbf{m}} \times \mathbb{C}^{\mathbf{m} \times \mathbf{l}} \to \mathbb{C}^{\mathbf{n} \times \mathbf{l}}$$

for matrix multiplication of an $\mathbf{n} \times \mathbf{m}$ matrix with an $\mathbf{m} \times \mathbf{l}$ matrix, and write $M_{\langle \mathbf{n} \rangle} = M_{\langle \mathbf{n}, \mathbf{n}, \mathbf{n} \rangle}$.

Matrix multiplication is a *bilinear map*; that is, for all $X_j, X \in \mathbb{C}^{\mathbf{n} \times \mathbf{m}}, Y_j, Y \in \mathbb{C}^{\mathbf{m} \times \mathbf{l}}$, and $a_j, b_j \in \mathbb{C}$:

$$M_{\langle \mathbf{n},\mathbf{m},\mathbf{l} \rangle}(a_1 X_1 + a_2 X_2, Y) = a_1 M_{\langle \mathbf{n},\mathbf{m},\mathbf{l} \rangle}(X_1, Y) + a_2 M_{\langle \mathbf{n},\mathbf{m},\mathbf{l} \rangle}(X_2, Y) \text{ and}$$

$$M_{\langle \mathbf{n},\mathbf{m},\mathbf{l} \rangle}(X, b_1 Y_1 + b_2 Y_2) = b_1 M_{\langle \mathbf{n},\mathbf{m},\mathbf{l} \rangle}(X, Y_1) + b_2 M_{\langle \mathbf{n},\mathbf{m},\mathbf{l} \rangle}(X, Y_2).$$

The set of all bilinear maps $\mathbb{C}^{\mathbf{a}} \times \mathbb{C}^{\mathbf{b}} \to \mathbb{C}^{\mathbf{c}}$ is a vector space. (In our case, $\mathbf{a} = \mathbf{nm}, \mathbf{b} = \mathbf{ml}$, and $\mathbf{c} = \mathbf{ln}$.) Write $a_1, \dots, a_{\mathbf{a}}$ for a basis of $\mathbb{C}^{\mathbf{a}}$ and similarly for $\mathbb{C}^{\mathbf{b}}, \mathbb{C}^{\mathbf{c}}$. Then $T : \mathbb{C}^{\mathbf{a}} \times \mathbb{C}^{\mathbf{b}} \to \mathbb{C}^{\mathbf{c}}$ is uniquely determined by its action on basis vectors:

$$T(a_i, b_j) = \sum_{k=1}^{\mathbf{c}} t^{ijk} c_k. \tag{1.1.2}$$

That is, the vector space of bilinear maps $\mathbb{C}^{\mathbf{a}} \times \mathbb{C}^{\mathbf{b}} \to \mathbb{C}^{\mathbf{c}}$, which I will denote by $\mathbb{C}^{\mathbf{a}*} \otimes \mathbb{C}^{\mathbf{b}*} \otimes \mathbb{C}^{\mathbf{c}}$, has dimension $\mathbf{abc}$. (The notation $\mathbb{C}^{\mathbf{a}*} \otimes \mathbb{C}^{\mathbf{b}*} \otimes \mathbb{C}^{\mathbf{c}}$ is motivated in §2.1.) If we represent a bilinear map by a three-dimensional matrix, it may be thought of as taking two column vectors and returning a third column vector.

1.1.10 Ranks of Linear Maps

I use the notation $\mathbb{C}^{\mathbf{a}}$ for the column vectors of height $\mathbf{a}$ and $\mathbb{C}^{\mathbf{a}*}$ for the row vectors.

Definition 1.1.10.1 A linear map $f : \mathbb{C}^{\mathbf{a}} \to \mathbb{C}^{\mathbf{b}}$ has *rank one* if there exist $\alpha \in \mathbb{C}^{\mathbf{a}*}$ and $w \in \mathbb{C}^{\mathbf{b}}$ such that $f(v) = \alpha(v)w$. (In other words, every rank one matrix is the product of a row vector with a column vector.) In this case I write $f = \alpha \otimes w$. The *rank* of a linear map $h : \mathbb{C}^{\mathbf{a}} \to \mathbb{C}^{\mathbf{b}}$ is the smallest r such that h may be expressed as a sum of r rank one linear maps.

Given an $\mathbf{a} \times \mathbf{b}$ matrix X, one can always change bases, i.e., multiply X on the left by an invertible $\mathbf{a} \times \mathbf{a}$ matrix and on the right by an invertible $\mathbf{b} \times \mathbf{b}$ matrix, to obtain a matrix with some number of 1s along the diagonal and zeros elsewhere. The number of 1s appearing is called the *rank* of the matrix, and it is the rank of the linear map X determines. In other words, the only property of a linear map $\mathbb{C}^{\mathbf{a}} \to \mathbb{C}^{\mathbf{b}}$ that is invariant under changes of bases is its rank, and for each rank, we have a normal form. This is not surprising, because the dimension of the space of such linear maps is $\mathbf{ab}$, we have $\mathbf{a}^2$ parameters of changes of bases in $\mathbb{C}^{\mathbf{a}}$ that we can make in a matrix representing the map, and $\mathbf{a}^2 + \mathbf{b}^2 > \mathbf{ab}$.

1.1.11 Tensor Rank

For bilinear maps $\mathbb{C}^{\mathbf{a}} \times \mathbb{C}^{\mathbf{b}} \to \mathbb{C}^{\mathbf{c}}$ we are not so lucky as with linear maps, as usually $\mathbf{abc} > \mathbf{a}^2 + \mathbf{b}^2 + \mathbf{c}^2$, i.e., there are fewer free parameters of changes of bases than the number of parameters needed to describe the map. This indicates why the study of bilinear maps is vastly more complicated than the study of linear maps.

Nonetheless, there are properties of a bilinear map that will not change under a change of basis. The most important properties for complexity are *tensor rank* and *tensor border rank*. Tensor border rank is defined in §1.1.12. Tensor rank is a generalization of the rank of a linear map. Tensor rank is defined properly in §2.1.3. Informally, a bilinear map T has *tensor rank one* if it can be computed with one multiplication. More precisely, T has tensor rank one if, in some coordinate system, the multidimensional matrix representing it has exactly one nonzero entry. This may be expressed without coordinates:

Definition 1.1.11.1 $T \in \mathbb{C}^{\mathbf{a}*} \otimes \mathbb{C}^{\mathbf{b}*} \otimes \mathbb{C}^{\mathbf{c}}$ has *tensor rank one* if there exist row vectors $\alpha \in \mathbb{C}^{\mathbf{a}*}$, $\beta \in \mathbb{C}^{\mathbf{b}*}$ and a column vector $w \in \mathbb{C}^{\mathbf{c}}$ such that $T(u, v) = \alpha(u)\beta(v)w$. T has *tensor rank* r if it can be written as the sum of r rank one tensors but no fewer, in which case we write $\mathbf{R}(T) = r$. Let $\hat{\sigma}_r^0 = \hat{\sigma}_{r,\mathbf{a},\mathbf{b},\mathbf{c}}^0$ denote the set of bilinear maps in $\mathbb{C}^{\mathbf{a}*} \otimes \mathbb{C}^{\mathbf{b}*} \otimes \mathbb{C}^{\mathbf{c}}$ of tensor rank at most r.

Remark 1.1.11.2 The peculiar notation $\hat{\sigma}_r^0$ will be explained in §4.7.1. For now, to give an idea where it comes from, $\sigma_r = \sigma_r(Seg(\mathbb{P}^{\mathbf{a}-1} \times \mathbb{P}^{\mathbf{b}-1} \times \mathbb{P}^{\mathbf{c}-1}))$ is standard notation in algebraic geometry for the rth secant variety of the Segre variety, which is the object we will study. The hatted object $\hat{\sigma}_r$ denotes its cone in affine space, and the 0 indicates the subset of this set consisting of tensors of rank at most r.

The following theorem shows that tensor rank is a legitimate measure of complexity.

Theorem 1.1.11.3 *(Strassen [Str69]; also see [BCS97, §15.1])*

$$\omega = \inf\{\tau \in \mathbb{R} \mid \mathbf{R}(M_{\langle \mathbf{n} \rangle}) = O(\mathbf{n}^{\tau})\}.$$

That is, $\mathbf{n} \times \mathbf{n}$ *matrices may be multiplied using* $O(\mathbf{n}^{\omega+\epsilon})$ *arithmetic operations if and only if the tensor rank of* $M_{\langle \mathbf{n} \rangle}$ *is* $O(\mathbf{n}^{\omega+\epsilon})$.

Our goal is thus to determine, for a given r, whether or not matrix multiplication lies in $\hat{\sigma}_r^0$.

1.1.12 How to Use Algebraic Geometry to Prove Lower Bounds for the Complexity of Matrix Multiplication

Algebraic geometry deals with the study of zero sets of polynomials. By a polynomial on the space of bilinear maps $\mathbb{C}^{\mathbf{a}*} \otimes \mathbb{C}^{\mathbf{b}*} \otimes \mathbb{C}^{\mathbf{c}}$, I mean a polynomial in the coefficients t^{ijk}, i.e., in **abc** variables. In §1.1.14 I describe a plan to use algebraic geometry to prove upper complexity bounds. A plan to use algebraic geometry for lower bounds is as follows.

Plan to Show $M_{\langle n,m,l \rangle} \notin \hat{\sigma}_r^0$ via Algebraic Geometry

- Find a polynomial P on the space of bilinear maps $\mathbb{C}^{nm} \times \mathbb{C}^{ml} \to \mathbb{C}^{nl}$, such that $P(T) = 0$ for all $T \in \hat{\sigma}_r^0$.
- Show that $P(M_{\langle n,m,l \rangle}) \neq 0$.

Chapters 2 and 5 discuss techniques for finding such polynomials, using algebraic geometry and *representation theory*, the study of symmetry in linear algebra.

1.1.13 Representation Theory

Representation theory is the systematic study of symmetry. We will primarily be concerned with properties of bilinear maps, tensors, polynomials, etc., that are invariant under changes of bases. Representation theory will facilitate the study of these properties. It has been essential for proving lower bounds for the complexity of $M_{\langle n \rangle}$.

Let V be a complex vector space of dimension $\mathbf{v}$. (I reserve the notation $\mathbb{C}^{\mathbf{v}}$ for the column vectors with their standard basis.) Let $GL(V)$ denote the group of invertible linear maps $V \to V$, and I write $GL_{\mathbf{v}}$ for $GL(\mathbb{C}^{\mathbf{v}})$. If we have fixed a basis of V, this is the group of invertible $\mathbf{v} \times \mathbf{v}$ matrices. If G is a group and $\mu : G \to GL(V)$ is a group homomorphism, we will say G *acts on* V and that V is a G-*module*. The image of μ is called a *representation* of G.

For example, the *permutation group* on n elements $\mathfrak{S}_n$ acts on $\mathbb{C}^n$ by

$$\sigma \begin{pmatrix} v_1 \\ \vdots \\ v_n \end{pmatrix} = \begin{pmatrix} v_{\sigma^{-1}(1)} \\ \vdots \\ v_{\sigma^{-1}(n)} \end{pmatrix},$$

where $\sigma \in \mathfrak{S}_n$ is a permutation. That is, the image of $\mathfrak{S}_n$ in GL_n is the set of permutation matrices. (The inverse is used so that for a vector $\overline{v}$, $\sigma(\tau \overline{v}) = (\sigma \tau) \overline{v}$.)

A group action is *irreducible* if there does not exist a proper subspace $U \subset V$ such that $\mu(g)u \in U$ for all $u \in U$ and $g \in G$.

The action of $\mathfrak{S}_n$ on $\mathbb{C}^n$ is not irreducible since the line spanned by $e_1 + \cdots + e_n$ is preserved by $\mathfrak{S}_n$. Note that the subspace spanned by $e_1 - e_2, \ldots, e_1 - e_n$ is also preserved by $\mathfrak{S}_n$. Both these subspaces are irreducible $\mathfrak{S}_n$-modules.

The essential point is that the sets X, such as $X = \hat{\sigma}_r^0 \subset \mathbb{C}^{\mathbf{abc}}$, for which we want polynomials that are zero at the points of X are *invariant* under the action of groups.

Definition 1.1.13.1 A set $X \subset V$ is *invariant* under a group $G \subset GL(V)$ if, for all $x \in X$ and all $g \in G$, $g(x) \in X$. Let $G_X \subset GL(V)$ denote the *group preserving* X, the largest subgroup of $GL(V)$ under which X is invariant.

When one says that an object has symmetry, it means the object is invariant under the action of a group.

In the case at hand, $X = \hat{\sigma}_r^0 \subset V = A \otimes B \otimes C$. Then $\hat{\sigma}_r^0$ is invariant under the action of the subgroup $GL(A) \times GL(B) \times GL(C)$ of $GL(V)$, i.e., this subgroup lies in $G_{\hat{\sigma}_r^0}$.

Recall that an ideal I in a ring R is a vector subspace such that for all $P \in I$ and $Q \in R$, $PQ \in I$.

Definition 1.1.13.2 For a set $X \subset V$, we will say a polynomial P *vanishes* on X if $P(x) = 0$ for all $x \in X$. The set of all polynomials vanishing on X forms an ideal in the space of polynomials on V, called the *ideal* of X and denoted $I(X)$.

If a polynomial P is in the ideal of X, then the polynomial $g(P)$ will also be in the ideal of X for all $g \in G_X$. That is,

The ideal of polynomials vanishing on X is a G_X-module.

The systematic exploitation of symmetry is used throughout this book: to study the ideals of varieties such as $\hat{\sigma}_r$ via their irreducible components in Chapter 2, to find new decompositions of the matrix multiplication tensor in Chapter 4, to find normal forms, e.g., in order to prove the state of the art lower bound for the complexity of matrix multiplication in Chapter 5, and to define the only restricted model where an exponential separation of the permanent from the determinant is known in Chapter 7. Chapter 8 is dedicated to representation theory, and Chapters 9 and 10 approach problems in algebraic geometry using representation theory.

1.1.14 How to Use Algebraic Geometry to Prove upper Bounds for the Complexity of Matrix Multiplication

Based on the above discussion, one could try the following strategy.

Plan to show $M_{\langle n,m,l \rangle} \in \hat{\sigma}_r^0$ with algebraic geometry.

- Find a set of polynomials $\{P_j\}$ on the space of bilinear maps $\mathbb{C}^{nm} \times \mathbb{C}^{ml} \to \mathbb{C}^{nl}$ such that $T \in \hat{\sigma}_r^0$ if and only if $P_j(T) = 0$ for all j.
- Show that $P_j(M_{\langle n,m,l \rangle}) = 0$ for all j.

This plan has a problem: consider the set $S = \{(w,z) \in \mathbb{C}^2 \mid z = 0, w \neq 0\}$, whose real picture looks like the z-axis with the origin removed:

Any polynomial $P \in I(S)$, i.e., any P that evaluates to zero at all points of S, will also be zero at the origin:

Exercise 1.1.14.1 (1!) Prove the above assertion.

Just as in this example, the zero set of the polynomials vanishing on $\hat{\sigma}_r^0$ is larger than $\hat{\sigma}_r^0$ when $r > 1$ (see §2.1.5), so one cannot certify membership in $\hat{\sigma}_r^0$ via polynomials, but rather its *Zariski closure*, which I now define.

Definition 1.1.14.2 The *Zariski closure* of a set $S \subset V$, denoted $\overline{S}$, is the set of $u \in V$ such that $P(u) = 0$ for all $P \in I(S)$. A set S is said to be *Zariski closed* or an *algebraic variety* if $S = \overline{S}$, i.e., S is the common zero set of a collection of polynomials.

In the example above, $\overline{S} = \{(w, z) \in \mathbb{C}^2 \mid z = 0\}$.

When $U = \mathbb{C}^{a*} \otimes \mathbb{C}^{b*} \otimes \mathbb{C}^{c}$, let $\hat{\sigma}_r := \overline{\hat{\sigma}_r^0}$ denote the Zariski closure of the set of bilinear maps of tensor rank at most r.

We will see that for almost all **a**, **b**, **c**, and r, $\hat{\sigma}_r^0 \subsetneq \hat{\sigma}_r$. The problem with the above plan is that it would only show $M_{\langle \mathbf{n} \rangle} \in \hat{\sigma}_r$.

Definition 1.1.14.3 $T \in \mathbb{C}^{a} \otimes \mathbb{C}^{b} \otimes \mathbb{C}^{c}$ has *border rank* r if $T \in \hat{\sigma}_r$ and $T \notin \hat{\sigma}_{r-1}$. In this case we write $\underline{\mathbf{R}}(T) = r$.

For the study of the exponent of matrix multiplication, we have good luck:

Theorem 1.1.14.4 (Bini [Bin80], see §3.2)

$$\omega = \inf\{\tau \in \mathbb{R} \mid \underline{\mathbf{R}}(M_{\langle \mathbf{n} \rangle}) = O(n^\tau)\}.$$

That is, although we may have $\underline{\mathbf{R}}(M_{\langle \mathbf{n} \rangle}) < \mathbf{R}(M_{\langle \mathbf{n} \rangle})$, they are not different enough to affect the exponent. In other words, as far as the exponent is concerned, the plan does *not* have a problem.

For $\mathbf{n} = 2$, we will see that $\underline{\mathbf{R}}(M_{\langle 2 \rangle}) = \mathbf{R}(M_{\langle 2 \rangle}) = 7$. It is expected that for $\mathbf{n} > 2$, $\underline{\mathbf{R}}(M_{\langle \mathbf{n} \rangle}) < \mathbf{R}(M_{\langle \mathbf{n} \rangle})$. For $\mathbf{n} = 3$, we only know $16 \leq \underline{\mathbf{R}}(M_{\langle 3 \rangle}) \leq 20$ and $19 \leq \mathbf{R}(M_{\langle 3 \rangle}) \leq 23$. In general, we know $\mathbf{R}(M_{\langle \mathbf{n} \rangle}) \geq 3\mathbf{n}^2 - o(\mathbf{n})$ (see §2.6), and $\underline{\mathbf{R}}(M_{\langle \mathbf{n} \rangle}) \geq 2\mathbf{n}^2 - \lceil \log_2(\mathbf{n}) \rceil - 1$ (see §5.4.5).

1.1.15 Symmetry and Algorithms

In this subsection I mention three uses of symmetry groups in the study of algorithms.

I first address the question raised in §1.1.2: can we make sense of Strassen's algorithm (1.1.1)? Just as the set $\hat{\sigma}_r$ has a symmetry group, the point $M_{\langle \mathbf{l}, \mathbf{m}, \mathbf{n} \rangle}$

also has a symmetry group that includes $GL_l \times GL_m \times GL_n$. (Do not confuse this with $GL_{lm} \times GL_{mn} \times GL_{nl}$ acting on $\mathbb{C}^{lm} \otimes \mathbb{C}^{mn} \otimes \mathbb{C}^{nl}$, which preserves $\hat{\sigma}_r^0$.) If we let this group act on Strassen's algorithm for $M_{(2)}$, in general we get a new algorithm that also computes $M_{(2)}$. But perhaps the algorithm itself has symmetry.

It does, and the first step to seeing the symmetry is to put all three vector spaces on an equal footing. A linear map $f : A \to B$ determines a bilinear form $A \times B^* \to \mathbb{C}$ by $(a, \beta) \mapsto \beta(f(a))$. Similarly, a bilinear map $A \times B \to C$ determines a trilinear form $A \times B \times C^* \to \mathbb{C}$.

Exercise 1.1.15.1 (2!) Show that $M_{(n)}$, considered as a trilinear form, is $(X, Y, Z) \mapsto \text{trace}(XYZ)$ ⊚

Since $\text{trace}(XYZ) = \text{trace}(YZX)$, we see that $G_{M_{(n)}}$ also includes a cyclic $\mathbb{Z}_3$-symmetry. In Chapter 4 we will see that *Strassen's algorithm is invariant under this $\mathbb{Z}_3$-symmetry*!

This hints that we might be able to use geometry to help *find* algorithms. This is the topic of Chapter 4.

For tensors or polynomials with continuous symmetry, their algorithms come in *families*. So to prove lower bounds, i.e., nonexistence of a family of algorithms, one can just prove nonexistence of a special member of the family. This idea is used to prove the state-of-the-art lower bound for matrix multiplication presented in §5.4.5.

1.2 Separation of Algebraic Complexity Classes

In 1955, John Nash (see [NR16, Chapter 1]) sent a letter to the NSA regarding cryptography, conjecturing an exponential increase in mean key computation length with respect to the length of the key. In a 1956 letter to von Neumann (see [Sip92, appendix]) Gödel tried to quantify the apparent difference between intuition and systematic problem solving. Around the same time, researchers in the Soviet Union were trying to determine if "brute force search" was avoidable in solving problems like the famous traveling salesman problem, where there seems to be no fast way to find a solution but any proposed solution can be easily checked (see [Tra84]). (The problem is to determine if there exists a way to visit, say, 20 cities traveling less than a thousand miles. If I claim to have an algorithm to do so, you just need to look at my plan and check the distances.) These discussions eventually gave rise to the complexity classes **P**, which models problems admitting a fast algorithm to produce a solution, and **NP**, which models problems admitting a fast algorithm to verify a proposed solution. The famous conjecture **P** $\neq$ **NP** of Cook, Karp, and Levin is that these two classes are distinct. Many important problems are complete in **NP**, and hence resolving the **P** versus **NP** question has practical importance for understanding whether these problems can be routinely computed. See [Sip92] for a history of the problem and [NR16, Chapter 1] for an up-to-date survey.

The transformation of this conjecture to a conjecture in geometry goes via algebra:

1.2.1 From Complexity to Algebra

The **P** versus **NP** conjecture is generally believed to be out of reach at the moment, so there have been weaker conjectures proposed that might be more tractable. One such comes from a standard counting problem discussed in §6.1.1. This variant has the advantage that it admits a clean algebraic formulation that I now discuss.

L. Valiant [Val79] conjectured that a sequence of polynomials for which there exists an "easy" recipe to write down its coefficients should not necessarily admit a fast evaluation. He defined algebraic complexity classes that are now called **VP** and **VNP**, respectively, the sequences of polynomials that are "easy" to evaluate and the sequences whose coefficients are "easy" to write down (see §6.1.3 for their definitions) and conjectured:

Conjecture 1.2.1.1 (Valiant [Val79]) $\mathbf{VP} \neq \mathbf{VNP}$.

For the precise relationship between this conjecture and the $\mathbf{P} \neq \mathbf{NP}$ conjecture, see [BCS97, Chapter 21]. As with the original conjecture, many natural polynomials are complete in **VNP**, and hence resolving **VP** versus **VNP** is important for understanding the computability of these natural polynomials in practice.

Many problems from graph theory, combinatorics, and statistical physics (partition functions) are in **VNP**. A good way to think of **VNP** is as the class of sequences of polynomials that can be written down "explicitly."

Most problems from linear algebra (e.g., inverting a matrix, computing its determinant, multiplying matrices) are in **VP**.

Valiant also showed that a particular polynomial sequence, the *permanent* (perm_n), is *complete* for the class **VNP** in the sense that $\mathbf{VP} \neq \mathbf{VNP}$ if and only if $(\mathrm{perm}_n) \notin \mathbf{VP}$. As explained in §6.1.1, the permanent is natural for computer science. Although it is not immediately clear, the permanent is also natural to geometry (see §6.6.2). The formula for the permanent of an $n \times n$ matrix $x = (x_j^i)$ is

$$\mathrm{perm}_n(x) := \sum_{\sigma \in \mathfrak{S}_n} x_{\sigma(1)}^1 \cdots x_{\sigma(n)}^n. \qquad (1.2.1)$$

Here $\mathfrak{S}_n$ denotes the group of permutations of $\{1, \ldots, n\}$.

How would one show there is no fast algorithm for the permanent? First we need a precise class of algorithms to consider. To this end, in §6.1.3, I define *algebraic circuits*, the standard class of algorithms for computing a polynomial studied in algebraic complexity theory, and their *size*, which is a measure of the complexity of the algorithm. Let circuit-size(perm_n) denote the size of the smallest algebraic circuit computing perm_n. Valiant's hypothesis 1.2.1.1 may be rephrased as follows:

Conjecture 1.2.1.2 (Valiant [Val79]) circuit-size(perm_n) *grows faster than any polynomial in n.*

1.2.2 From Algebra to Algebraic Geometry

As with our earlier discussion, to prove lower complexity bounds for the permanent, one could work as follows:

Let $S^n \mathbb{C}^N$ denote the vector space of all homogeneous polynomials of degree n in N variables, so perm_n is a point of the vector space $S^n \mathbb{C}^{n^2}$. If we write an element of $S^n \mathbb{C}^N$ as $p(y_1, \dots, y_N) = \sum_{1 \le i_1 \le \dots \le i_n \le N} c^{i_1, \dots, i_n} y_{i_1} \cdots y_{i_n}$, then we may view the coefficients $c^{i_1, \dots, i_n}$ as coordinates on the vector space $S^n \mathbb{C}^N$. We will look for polynomials on our space of polynomials, that is, polynomials in the coefficients $c^{i_1, \dots, i_n}$.

Plan to show (perm_n) $\notin$ **VP, or at least bound its circuit size by** r, **with algebraic geometry.**

- Find a polynomial P on the space $S^n \mathbb{C}^{n^2}$ such that $P(p) = 0$ for all $p \in S^n \mathbb{C}^{n^2}$ with circuit-size(p) $\le r$.
- Show that $P(\text{perm}_n) \ne 0$.

By the discussion above on Zariski closure, this may be a more difficult problem than Valiant's original hypothesis: we are not just trying to exclude perm_n from having a circuit, but we are also requiring that it not be "near" to having a small circuit. I return to this issue in §1.2.5.

1.2.3 Benchmarks and Restricted Models

Valiant's hypothesis is expected to be extremely difficult, so it is reasonable to work toward partial results. Two types of partial results are as follows. First, one could attempt to prove the conjecture under additional hypotheses. In the complexity literature, a conjecture with supplementary hypotheses is called a *restricted model*. For an example of a restricted model, one could restrict to circuits that are *formulas* (the underlying graph is a tree; see Remark 6.1.5.2). The definition of a formula coincides with our usual notion of a formula. Restricted models are discussed in Chapter 7. Second, one can fix a complexity measure, e.g., circuit-size(perm$_n$), and prove lower bounds for it. I will refer to such progress as improving *benchmarks*.

1.2.4 Another Path to Algebraic Geometry

The permanent resembles one of the most, perhaps *the* most, studied polynomial, the *determinant* of an $n \times n$ matrix $x = (x_j^i)$:

$$\det_n(x) := \sum_{\sigma \in \mathfrak{S}_n} \text{sgn}(\sigma) x_{\sigma(1)}^1 \cdots x_{\sigma(n)}^n. \tag{1.2.2}$$

Here sgn(σ) denotes the sign of the permutation σ. The determinant, despite its enormous formula of $n!$ terms, can be computed very quickly, e.g., by Gaussian elimination. (See §6.1.3 for a division-free algorithm.) In particular, (det$_n$) $\in$ **VP**. It is not known if det$_n$ is *complete* for **VP**, that is, whether or not a sequence of polynomials is in **VP** if and only if it can be *reduced* to the determinant in the sense made precise below.

Although

$$\text{perm}_2 \begin{pmatrix} a & b \\ c & d \end{pmatrix} = \det_2 \begin{pmatrix} a & -b \\ c & d \end{pmatrix},$$

Marcus and Minc [MM61], building on work of Pólya and Szegö (see [Gat87]), proved that one could not express perm$_m(y)$ as a size m determinant of a matrix whose entries are affine linear functions of the x_j^i when $m > 2$. This raised the question that perhaps the permanent of an $m \times m$ matrix could be expressed as a slightly larger determinant, which would imply **VP** = **VNP**. More precisely, we say $p(y^1, \ldots, y^M)$ is an *affine linear projection* of $q(x^1, \ldots, x^N)$ if there exist affine linear functions $x^\alpha(y) = x^\alpha(y^1, \ldots, y^M)$ such that $p(y) = q(x(y))$. For example,

$$\text{perm}_3(y) = \det_7 \begin{pmatrix} 0 & 0 & 0 & 0 & y_3^3 & y_2^3 & y_1^3 \\ y_1^1 & 1 & & & & & \\ y_2^1 & & 1 & & & & \\ y_3^1 & & & 1 & & & \\ & y_2^2 & y_1^2 & 0 & 1 & & \\ & y_3^2 & 0 & y_1^2 & & 1 & \\ & 0 & y_3^2 & y_2^2 & & & 1 \end{pmatrix}. \tag{1.2.3}$$

This formula is due to B. Grenet [Gre11], who also generalized it to express perm$_m$ as a determinant of size $2^m - 1$ (see §6.6.3).

Valiant conjectured that one cannot do much better than this:

Definition 1.2.4.1 Let p be a polynomial. Define the *determinantal complexity* of p, denoted $\mathrm{dc}(p)$, to be the smallest n such that p is an affine linear projection of the determinant.

Valiant showed that for any polynomial p, $\mathrm{dc}(p)$ is finite but possibly larger than circuit-size(p), so the following conjecture is possibly weaker than Conjecture 1.2.1.2.

Conjecture 1.2.4.2 (Valiant [Val79]) $\mathrm{dc}(\mathrm{perm}_m)$ *grows faster than any polynomial in m.*

The state of the art, obtained with classical differential geometry, is $\mathrm{dc}(\mathrm{perm}_m) \geq \frac{m^2}{2}$, due to Mignon and Ressayre [MR04]. An exposition of their result is given in §6.4.

1.2.5 Geometric Complexity Theory

The "Zariski closed" version of Conjecture 1.2.4.2 is the flagship conjecture of *Geometric Complexity Theory* (GCT) and is discussed in Chapters 6 and 8. To state it in a useful form, first rephrase Valiant's hypothesis as follows:

Let $\mathrm{End}(\mathbb{C}^{n^2})$ denote the space of all linear maps $\mathbb{C}^{n^2} \to \mathbb{C}^{n^2}$, which acts on $S^n \mathbb{C}^{n^2}$ under the action $L \cdot p(x) := p(L^T(x))$, where x is viewed as a column vector of size n^2, L is an $n^2 \times n^2$ matrix, and T denotes the transpose. (The transpose is used so that $L_1 \cdot (L_2 \cdot p) = (L_1 L_2) \cdot p$.) Let

$$\mathrm{End}(\mathbb{C}^{n^2}) \cdot p = \{L \cdot p \mid L \in \mathrm{End}(\mathbb{C}^{n^2})\}.$$

Define an auxiliary variable $\ell \in \mathbb{C}^1$ so $\ell^{n-m} \mathrm{perm}_m \in S^n \mathbb{C}^{m^2+1}$. Consider any linear inclusion $\mathbb{C}^{m^2+1} \to \mathbb{C}^{n^2}$ (e.g., with the $Mat_{m \times m}$ in the upper left-hand corner and ℓ in the $(m+1) \times (m+1)$ slot and zeros elsewhere in the space of $n \times n$ matrices), so we may consider $\ell^{n-m} \mathrm{perm}_m \in S^n \mathbb{C}^{n^2}$. Then

$$\mathrm{dc}(\mathrm{perm}_m) \leq n \iff \ell^{n-m} \mathrm{perm}_m \in \mathrm{End}(\mathbb{C}^{n^2}) \cdot \det{}_n . \qquad (1.2.4)$$

This situation begins to resemble our matrix multiplication problem: we have an ambient space $S^n \mathbb{C}^{n^2}$ (resp. $(\mathbb{C}^{n^2})^{\otimes 3}$ for matrix multiplication), a subset $\mathrm{End}(\mathbb{C}^{n^2}) \cdot \det{}_n$ (resp. $\hat{\sigma}_r^0$, the tensors of rank at most r), and a point $\ell^{n-m} \mathrm{perm}_m$ (resp. $M_{\langle \mathbf{n} \rangle}$) and we want to show the point is not in the subset. Note one difference here: the dimension of the ambient space is exponentially large with respect to the dimension of our subset. As before, if we want to separate the point from the subset with polynomials, we are attempting to prove a stronger statement.

Definition 1.2.5.1 For $p \in S^d\mathbb{C}^M$, let $\overline{dc}(p)$ denote the smallest n such that $\ell^{n-d}p \in \overline{\mathrm{End}(\mathbb{C}^{n^2})} \cdot \det_n$, the Zariski closure of $\mathrm{End}(\mathbb{C}^{n^2}) \cdot \det_n$. Call $\overline{dc}$ the *border determinantal complexity* of p.

Conjecture 1.2.5.2 [MS01] $\overline{dc}(\mathrm{perm}_m)$ *grows faster than any polynomial in* m.

For this problem, we do not have an analog of Bini's theorem 1.1.14.4 that promises similar asymptotics for the two complexity measures. In this situation Mulmuley [Mul14] conjectures that there exist sequences of polynomials (p_m) such that $\overline{dc}(p_m)$ grows like a polynomial in m but $dc(p_m)$ grows faster than any polynomial. Moreover, he speculates that this gap explains why Valiant's hypothesis is so difficult.

Representation theory indicates a path toward solving Conjecture 1.2.5.2. To explain the path, I introduce the following terminology:

Definition 1.2.5.3 A polynomial $p \in S^n\mathbb{C}^N$ is *characterized by its symmetries* if, letting $G_p := \{g \in GL_N \mid g \cdot p = p\}$, for any $q \in S^n\mathbb{C}^N$ with $G_q \supseteq G_p$, one has $p = \lambda q$ for some $\lambda \in \mathbb{C}$.

There are two essential observations:

- $\overline{\mathrm{End}(\mathbb{C}^{n^2})} \cdot \det_n = \overline{GL_{n^2} \cdot \det_n}$, that is, the variety $\overline{\mathrm{End}(\mathbb{C}^{n^2})} \cdot \det_n$ is an *orbit closure*.
- $\det_n$ and perm_n are characterized by their symmetries.

In principle representation theory (more precisely, the *Peter-Weyl Theorem*; see §8.6) gives a description of the polynomials vanishing on an orbit closure modulo the effect of the boundary. (It describes the ring of regular functions on the orbit.) Unfortunately for the problem at hand, the approach to Valiant's conjecture via the Peter-Weyl theorem, outlined in [MS01, MS08], was recently shown [IP15, BIP16] not to be viable as proposed. Nevertheless, the approach suggests several alternative paths that could be viable. For this reason, I explain the approach and the proof of its nonviability in Chapter 8.

Unlike matrix multiplication, progress on Valiant's hypothesis and its variants is in its infancy. To gain insight as to what techniques might work, it will be useful to examine "toy" versions of the problem – these questions are of mathematical significance in their own right and lead to interesting connections between combinatorics, representation theory, and geometry. Chapter 9 is dedicated to one such problem, dating back to Hermite and Hadamard, to determine the ideal of the *Chow variety* of polynomials that decompose into a product of linear forms.

1.3 How to Find Hay in a Haystack: The Problem of Explicitness

A "random" bilinear map $b : \mathbb{C}^{\mathbf{m}} \times \mathbb{C}^{\mathbf{m}} \to \mathbb{C}^{\mathbf{m}}$ will have tensor rank around $\frac{\mathbf{m}^2}{3}$ (see §4.7 for the precise rank). (In particular, the standard algorithm for matrix multiplication already shows that it is pathological as a tensor as $\mathbf{n}^3 \ll \frac{(\mathbf{n}^2)^2}{3}$.) On the other hand, how would one find an *explicit* tensor of tensor rank around $\frac{\mathbf{m}^2}{3}$? This is *the problem of finding hay in a haystack.*[2] Our state of the art for this question is so dismal that there is no known explicit bilinear map of tensor rank $3\mathbf{m}$; in fact, the highest rank of an explicit tensor known (modulo the error term) is for matrix multiplication [Lan14]: $\mathbf{R}(M_{\langle \mathbf{n} \rangle}) \geq 3\mathbf{n}^2 - o(\mathbf{n}^2)$. Other explicit sequences $T_{\mathbf{m}} : \mathbb{C}^{\mathbf{m}} \times \mathbb{C}^{\mathbf{m}} \to \mathbb{C}^{\mathbf{m}}$ with $\mathbf{R}(T_{\mathbf{m}}) \geq 3\mathbf{m} - o(\mathbf{m})$ were found in [Zui15], and the largest known rank tensor, from [AFT11], has $\mathbf{R}(T_{\mathbf{m}}) \geq 3\mathbf{m} - o(\log(\mathbf{m}))$. It is a frequently stated open problem to find explicit bilinear maps $T_{\mathbf{m}} : \mathbb{C}^{\mathbf{m}} \times \mathbb{C}^{\mathbf{m}} \to \mathbb{C}^{\mathbf{m}}$ with $\mathbf{R}(T_{\mathbf{m}}) \geq (3 + \epsilon)\mathbf{m}$. In Chapter 5, I discuss the state of the art of this problem and the related border rank problem, where no explicit tensor $T \in \mathbb{C}^{\mathbf{m}} \otimes \mathbb{C}^{\mathbf{m}} \otimes \mathbb{C}^{\mathbf{m}}$ with $\underline{\mathbf{R}}(T) > 2\mathbf{m}$ is known. Valiant's hypothesis may also be phrased in this language: exhibiting an explicit polynomial sequence that is provably difficult to compute would be sufficient to prove Valiant's hypothesis (a random sequence is provably difficult).

1.4 The Role of Algebraic Geometry

Recent research (e.g., [Gal17, BB14]) has shown that to prove superlinear lower bounds on tensor rank or border rank, thanks to the *cactus variety*, one must deal with subtle questions regarding zero-dimensional schemes. The work [GKKS13a] indicates that questions regarding the *geometry of syzygies* could play a role in the resolution of Valiant's hypothesis. Chapter 10 introduces these topics and others from algebraic geometry and representation theory and explains their role in complexity theory. It is written as an invitation to algebraic geometers with expertise in these areas to work on questions in complexity theory.

---

[2] This phrase is due to Howard Karloff.

2

The Complexity of Matrix Multiplication I:
First Lower Bounds

In this chapter I discuss lower complexity bounds for tensors in general and matrix multiplication in particular. The two basic measures of complexity are *rank* and *border rank*. I begin, in §2.1, by defining tensors and their rank. I motivate the definition of border rank with the story of the discovery by Bini et al. of approximate algorithms for a reduced matrix multiplication tensor and then give its definition. Next, in §2.2, I present Strassen's equations. In order to generalize them, I present elementary definitions and results from mutli-linear algebra and representation theory in §2.3, including the essential *Schur's Lemma*. I then, in §2.4, give Ottaviani's derivation of Strassen's equations that generalizes to *Koszul flattenings*, which are also derived. In §2.5, I show a $2\mathbf{n}^2 - \mathbf{n}$ lower bound for the border rank of $M_{\langle \mathbf{n} \rangle}$. This border rank lower bound is exploited to prove a $3\mathbf{n}^2 - o(\mathbf{n}^2)$ rank lower bound for $M_{\langle \mathbf{n} \rangle}$ in §2.6. The current state of the art is a $2\mathbf{n}^2 - \lceil \log_2(\mathbf{n}) \rceil - 1$ lower bound for the border rank of $M_{\langle \mathbf{n} \rangle}$, which is presented in §5.4.5, as it requires more geometry and representation theory than what is covered in this chapter.

2.1 Matrix Multiplication and Multilinear Algebra

To better understand matrix multiplication as a bilinear map, I first review basic facts from multilinear algebra. For more details on this topic, see [Lan12, Chapter 2].

2.1.1 Linear Algebra without Coordinates

In what follows it will be essential to work without bases, so instead of writing $\mathbb{C}^\mathbf{v}$, I use V to denote a complex vector space of dimension $\mathbf{v}$.

The *dual space* V^* to a vector space V is the vector space whose elements are linear maps from V to $\mathbb{C}$:

$$V^* := \{\alpha : V \to \mathbb{C} \mid \alpha \text{ is linear}\}.$$

This notation is consistent with the notation of $\mathbb{C}^v$ for column vectors and $\mathbb{C}^{v*}$ for row vectors because if in bases elements of V are represented by column vectors, then elements of V^* are naturally represented by row vectors and the map $v \mapsto \alpha(v)$ is just row-column matrix multiplication. Given a basis $v_1, \ldots, v_v$ of V, it determines a basis $\alpha^1, \ldots, \alpha^v$ of V^* by $\alpha^i(v_j) = \delta_{ij}$, called the *dual basis*.

Let $V^* \otimes W$ denote the vector space of all linear maps $V \to W$. Given $\alpha \in V^*$ and $w \in W$, define a linear map $\alpha \otimes w : V \to W$ by $\alpha \otimes w(v) := \alpha(v)w$. In bases, if α is represented by a row vector and w by a column vector, $\alpha \otimes w$ will be represented by the matrix $w\alpha$. Such a linear map is said to have *rank one*. Define the *rank* of an element $f \in V^* \otimes W$ to be the smallest r such f may be expressed as a sum of r rank one linear maps.

Recall from Definition 1.1.14.2 that a variety is the common zero set of a collection of polynomials.

Definition 2.1.1.1 A variety $Z \subset V$ is *reducible* if it is possible to write $Z = Z_1 \cup Z_2$ with Z_1, Z_2 nonempty varieties. Otherwise, it is *irreducible*.

Definition 2.1.1.2 A property of points of an irreducible variety $Z \subset W$ is *general* or *holds generally* if the property holds on the complement of a proper subvariety of Z.

A *general point* of a variety $Z \subset V$ is a point not lying on some explicit Zariski closed subset of Z. This subset is often understood from the context and so is not mentioned.

The complement to the zero set of any polynomial over the complex numbers has full measure, so properties that hold at general points hold with probability one for a randomly chosen point in Z.

Theorem 2.1.1.3 (Fundamental theorem of linear algebra) *Let V, W be finite-dimensional vector spaces, let $f : V \to W$ be a linear map, and let A_f be a matrix representing f. Then*

1 $\text{rank}(f) = \dim f(V)$
   $$= \dim(\text{span}\{\text{columns of } A_f\})$$
   $$= \dim(\text{span}\{\text{rows of } A_f\})$$
   $$= \dim V - \dim \ker f.$$

   In particular, $\text{rank}(f) \leq \min\{\dim V, \dim W\}$.
2 *For general $f \in V^* \otimes W$,* $\text{rank}(f) = \min\{\dim V, \dim W\}$.

    3 *If a sequence of linear maps f_t of rank r has a limit f_0, then* rank(f_0) $\leq r$.

    4 rank(f) $\leq r$ *if and only if, in any choice of bases, the determinants of all size $r + 1$ submatrices of the matrix representing f are zero.*

Note that assertion 4 shows that the set of linear maps of rank at most r forms an algebraic variety. Although we take it for granted, it is really miraculous that the fundamental theorem of linear algebra is true. I explain why in §2.1.5.

Exercise 2.1.1.4 (1!) Prove the theorem. ⊙

Exercise 2.1.1.5 (1) Assuming V is finite-dimensional, write down a canonical isomorphism $V \to (V^*)^*$. ⊙

Many standard notions from linear algebra have coordinate-free definitions. For example, a linear map $f : V \to W$ determines a linear map $f^T : W^* \to V^*$ defined by $f^T(\beta)(v) := \beta(f(v))$ for all $v \in V$ and $\beta \in W^*$. Note that this is consistent with the notation $V^* \otimes W \simeq W \otimes V^*$, being interpreted as the space of all linear maps $(W^*)^* \to V^*$; that is, the order in which we write the factors does not matter. If we work in bases and insist that all vectors are column vectors, the matrix of f^T is just the transpose of the matrix of f.

Exercise 2.1.1.6 (1) Show that we may also consider an element $f \in V^* \otimes W$ as a bilinear map $b_f : V \times W^* \to \mathbb{C}$ defined by $b_f(v, \beta) := \beta(f(v))$.

2.1.2 Multilinear Maps and Tensors

The space $V \otimes W$ is called the *tensor product* of V with W. More generally, for vector spaces $A_1, \ldots, A_n$, define their tensor product $A_1 \otimes \cdots \otimes A_n$ to be the space of n-linear maps $A_1^* \times \cdots \times A_n^* \to \mathbb{C}$, equivalently the space of $(n - 1)$-linear maps $A_1^* \times \cdots \times A_{n-1}^* \to A_n$, etc. When $A_1 = \cdots = A_n = V$, write $V^{\otimes n} = V \otimes \cdots \otimes V$.

    Let $a_j \in A_j$ and define an element $a_1 \otimes \cdots \otimes a_n \in A_1 \otimes \cdots \otimes A_n$ to be the n-linear map

$$a_1 \otimes \cdots \otimes a_n(\alpha^1, \ldots, \alpha^n) := \alpha^1(a_1) \cdots \alpha^n(a_n).$$

Exercise 2.1.2.1 (1) Show that if $\{a_j^{s_j} \mid 1 \leq s_j \leq \mathbf{a}_j\}$ is a basis of A_j, then $\{a_1^{s_1} \otimes \cdots \otimes a_n^{s_n} \mid 1 \leq s_j \leq \mathbf{a}_j\}$ is a basis of $A_1 \otimes \cdots \otimes A_n$. In particular, $\dim(A_1 \otimes \cdots \otimes A_n) = \mathbf{a}_1 \cdots \mathbf{a}_n$. ⊙

Remark 2.1.2.2 One may identify $A_1 \otimes \cdots \otimes A_n$ with any reordering of the factors. When I need to be explicit about this, I will call the identification the *reordering isomorphism*.

Example 2.1.2.3 (Matrix multiplication) Let $x_\alpha^i, y_u^\alpha, z_i^u$ be, respectively, bases of $A = \mathbb{C}^{nm}$, $B = \mathbb{C}^{ml}$, $C = \mathbb{C}^{ln}$; then the standard expression of matrix multiplication as a tensor is

$$M_{\langle \mathbf{l},\mathbf{m},\mathbf{n}\rangle} = \sum_{i=1}^{n}\sum_{\alpha=1}^{m}\sum_{u=1}^{l} x_\alpha^i \otimes y_u^\alpha \otimes z_i^u. \qquad (2.1.1)$$

Exercise 2.1.2.4 (2) Write out Strassen's algorithm as a tensor. ⊚

2.1.3 Tensor Rank

An element $T \in A_1 \otimes \cdots \otimes A_n$ is said to have *rank one* if there exist $a_j \in A_j$ such that $T = a_1 \otimes \cdots \otimes a_n$.

I will use the following measure of complexity:

Definition 2.1.3.1 Let $T \in A_1 \otimes \cdots \otimes A_n$. Define the *rank* (or *tensor rank*) of T to be the smallest r such that T may be written as the sum of r rank one tensors. Write $\mathbf{R}(T) = r$. Let $\hat{\sigma}_r^0 \subset A_1 \otimes \cdots \otimes A_n$ denote the set of tensors of rank at most r.

For bilinear maps, tensor rank is comparable to all other standard measures of complexity on the space of bilinear maps, see (e.g., [BCS97, §14.1]).

By (2.1.1), we conclude $\mathbf{R}(M_{\langle \mathbf{n},\mathbf{m},\mathbf{l}\rangle}) \leq \mathbf{nml}$. Strassen's algorithm shows that $\mathbf{R}(M_{\langle 2,2,2\rangle}) \leq 7$. Shortly afterward, Winograd [Win71] showed that $\mathbf{R}(M_{\langle 2,2,2\rangle}) = 7$.

2.1.4 Another Spectacular Failure

After Strassen's failure to prove the standard algorithm for matrix multiplication was optimal, Bini et al. [BLR80] considered the *reduced matrix multiplication operator*

$$M_{\langle 2\rangle}^{red} := x_1^1 \otimes \left(y_1^1 \otimes z_1^1 + y_2^1 \otimes z_1^2\right) + x_2^1 \otimes \left(y_1^2 \otimes z_1^1 + y_2^2 \otimes z_1^2\right) \\ + x_1^2 \otimes \left(y_1^1 \otimes z_2^1 + y_2^1 \otimes z_2^2\right) \in \mathbb{C}^3 \otimes \mathbb{C}^4 \otimes \mathbb{C}^4$$

obtained by setting the x_2^2 entry for $M_{\langle 2\rangle}$ to zero. The standard presentation shows $\mathbf{R}(M_{\langle 2\rangle}^{red}) \leq 6$. Bini et al. attempted to find a rank five expression for $M_{\langle 2\rangle}^{red}$. They searched for such an expression by computer. Their method was to minimize the norm of $M_{\langle 2\rangle}^{red}$ minus a rank five tensor that varied (see §4.6 for a description of the method), and their computer kept on producing rank five tensors with the norm of the difference getting smaller and smaller, but with larger and larger coefficients. Bini (personal communication) told me about how he lost sleep trying to understand what was wrong with his computer code. This went on for some time, when finally he realized *there was nothing wrong with the code*: the output it produced was a manifestation of the phenomenon Bini named *border rank* [Bin80], which was mentioned in the introduction in the context of finding polynomials for upper rank bounds.

The expression for the tensor $M_{\langle 2 \rangle}^{red}$ that their computer search found was essentially

$$
\begin{aligned}
M_{\langle 2 \rangle}^{red} = \lim_{t \to 0} \frac{1}{t} \big[& \big(x_2^1 + t x_1^1\big) \otimes \big(y_2^1 + t y_2^2\big) \otimes z_1^2 \qquad\qquad (2.1.2) \\
& + \big(x_1^2 + t x_1^1\big) \otimes y_1^1 \otimes \big(z_1^1 + t z_2^1\big) \\
& - x_2^1 \otimes y_2^1 \otimes \big((z_1^1 + z_1^2) + t z_2^2\big) \\
& - x_1^2 \otimes \big((y_1^1 + y_2^1) + t y_1^2\big) \otimes z_1^1 \\
& + \big(x_2^1 + x_1^2\big) \otimes \big(y_2^1 + t y_1^2\big) \otimes \big(z_1^1 + t z_2^2\big) \big].
\end{aligned}
$$

The rank five tensors found by Bini et al. were the right-hand side of (2.1.2) (without the limit) for particular small values of t.

In what follows I first explain why border rank is needed in the study of tensors, and then I properly define it.

2.1.5 The Fundamental Theorem of Linear Algebra is False for Tensors

Recall the fundamental theorem of linear algebra from §2.1.1.3.

Theorem 2.1.5.1 *If $T \in \mathbb{C}^m \otimes \mathbb{C}^m \otimes \mathbb{C}^m$ is general, i.e., outside the zero set of a certain finite collection of polynomials (in particular, outside a certain set of measure zero), then $\mathbf{R}(T) \geq \lceil \frac{m^3-1}{3m-2} \rceil$.*
Tensor rank can jump up (or down) under limits.

The first assertion is proved in §4.7.1. To see the second assertion, at least when $r = 2$, consider

$$
T(t) := \frac{1}{t} [a_1 \otimes b_1 \otimes c_1 - (a_1 + t a_2) \otimes (b_1 + t b_2) \otimes (c_1 + t c_2)]
$$

and note that

$$
\lim_{t \to 0} T(t) = a_1 \otimes b_1 \otimes c_2 + a_1 \otimes b_2 \otimes c_1 + a_2 \otimes b_1 \otimes c_1,
$$

which has rank three.

Exercise 2.1.5.2 (1) Prove $\mathbf{R}(a_1 \otimes b_1 \otimes c_2 + a_1 \otimes b_2 \otimes c_1 + a_2 \otimes b_1 \otimes c_1) = 3$. ◎

Remark 2.1.5.3 Physicists call the tensor $a_1 \otimes b_1 \otimes c_2 + a_1 \otimes b_2 \otimes c_1 + a_2 \otimes b_1 \otimes c_1$ the *W-state*, so I will sometimes denote it T_{WState}.

To visualize why rank can jump up while taking limits, consider the following picture, where the curve represents the points of $\hat{\sigma}_1^0$. Points of $\hat{\sigma}_2^0$ (e.g., the dots limiting to the dot labeled T) are those on a secant line to $\hat{\sigma}_1^0$, and the points where the rank jumps up, such at the dot labeled T, are those that lie on a tangent line to $\hat{\sigma}_1^0$. This phenomenon fails to occur for matrices because for matrices, every point on a tangent line is also on an honest secant line. Thus, in some sense, it is a miracle that rank is semicontinuous for matrices.

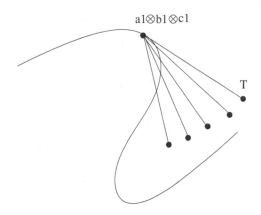

Our situation regarding tensor rank may be summarized as follows:

- The set $\hat{\sigma}_r^0$ is not closed under taking limits. I will say a set that is closed under taking limits is *Euclidean closed*.
- It is also not *Zariski closed*, i.e., the zero set of all polynomials vanishing on $\hat{\sigma}_r^0$ includes tensors that are of rank greater than r.

Exercise 2.1.5.4 (2) Show that the Euclidean closure (i.e., closure under taking limits) of a set is always contained in its Zariski closure. ⊚

The tensors that are honestly "close" to tensors of rank r would be the Euclidean closure, but to deal with polynomials as proposed in §1.1.12–1.1.14, we need to work with the potentially larger Zariski closure.

Often the Zariski closure is much larger than the Euclidean closure. For example, the Zariski closure of $\mathbb{Z} \subset \mathbb{C}$ is $\mathbb{C}$, while $\mathbb{Z}$ is already closed in the Euclidean topology.

For the purposes of proving lower bounds, none of this is an issue, but when we discuss upper bounds, we will need to deal with these problems. For now, I mention that with $\hat{\sigma}_r^0$, we have good luck: the Zariski and Euclidean closures of $\hat{\sigma}_r^0$ coincide, so our apparently different informal uses of the term border rank coincide. I present the proof in §3.1.6.

Remark 2.1.5.5 This coincidence is a consequence of a standard result in algebraic geometry that the computer science community was unaware of. As a result, it ended up being reproven in special cases, e.g., in [Lic84].

2.1.6 Border Rank

Generalizing the discussion in §1.1.11, $\hat{\sigma}_r = \hat{\sigma}_{r,A_1 \otimes \cdots \otimes A_n}$ denotes the Zariski (and by the above discussion Euclidean) closure of $\hat{\sigma}_r^0$, and the *border rank* of $T \in A_1 \otimes \cdots \otimes A_n$, denoted $\underline{\mathbf{R}}(T)$, is the smallest r such that $T \in \hat{\sigma}_r$. By the above discussion, border rank is semicontinuous.

Exercise 2.1.6.1 (1) Write down an explicit tensor of border rank r in $\mathbb{C}^r \otimes \mathbb{C}^r \otimes \mathbb{C}^r$ with rank greater than r. ⊙

Border rank is easier to work with than rank for several reasons. For example, the maximal rank of a tensor in $\mathbb{C}^m \otimes \mathbb{C}^m \otimes \mathbb{C}^m$ is not known in general. In contrast, the maximal border rank is known to be $\lceil \frac{m^3-1}{3m-2} \rceil$ for all $m \neq 3$, and is 5 when $m = 3$ [Lic85]. In particular, Strassen's algorithm could have been predicted in advance with this knowledge. The method of proof is a differential-geometric calculation that dates back to Terracini in the 1900s [Ter11]; see §4.7.1 for a discussion.

Exercise 2.1.6.2 (1) Prove that if $T \in A \otimes B \otimes C$ and $T' := T|_{A' \times B' \times C'}$ (here T is being considered as a trilinear form) for some $A' \subseteq A^*, B' \subseteq B^*, C' \subseteq C^*$, then $\mathbf{R}(T) \geq \mathbf{R}(T')$ and $\underline{\mathbf{R}}(T) \geq \underline{\mathbf{R}}(T')$. ⊙

Exercise 2.1.6.3 (1) Let $T_j \in A_j \otimes B_j \otimes C_j$, $1 \leq j, k, l \leq s$. Consider $T_1 \oplus \cdots \oplus T_s \in (\oplus_j A_j) \otimes (\oplus_k B_k) \otimes (\oplus_l C_l)$. Show that $\mathbf{R}(\oplus_j T_j) \leq \sum_{i=1}^s \mathbf{R}(T_i)$ and $\underline{\mathbf{R}}(\oplus_j T_j) \leq \sum_{i=1}^s \underline{\mathbf{R}}(T_i)$.

Exercise 2.1.6.4 (1) Let $T_j \in A_j \otimes B_j \otimes C_j$, $1 \leq j, k, l \leq s$. Let $A = \otimes_j A_j$, $B = \otimes_k B_k$, and $C = \otimes_l C_l$; consider $T_1 \otimes \cdots \otimes T_s \in A \otimes B \otimes C$. Show that $\mathbf{R}(\otimes_{i=1}^s T_i) \leq \Pi_{i=1}^s \mathbf{R}(T_i)$ and that $\underline{\mathbf{R}}(\otimes_{i=1}^s T_i) \leq \Pi_{i=1}^s \underline{\mathbf{R}}(T_i)$.

2.1.7 Our First Lower Bound

Given $T \in A \otimes B \otimes C$, write $T \in A \otimes (B \otimes C)$ and think of T as a linear map $T_A : A^* \to B \otimes C$. I will write $T(A^*) \subset B \otimes C$ for the image.

Proposition 2.1.7.1 $\underline{\mathbf{R}}(T) \geq \operatorname{rank}(T_A)$.

Exercise 2.1.7.2 (1!) Prove Proposition 2.1.7.1. ⊙

Say dimensions $\mathbf{a}, \mathbf{b}, \mathbf{c}$ are *unbalanced* if any of the inequalities $\mathbf{a} > \mathbf{bc}, \mathbf{b} > \mathbf{ac}, \mathbf{c} > \mathbf{ab}$ hold, and otherwise that they are *balanced*.

Permuting the three factors, and assuming the dimensions are balanced, we have equations for $\hat{\sigma}_{r,A\otimes B\otimes C}$ for $r \leq \max\{\mathbf{a}-1, \mathbf{b}-1, \mathbf{c}-1\}$, namely, the size $r+1$ minors of the linear maps T_A, T_B, T_C.

Definition 2.1.7.3 A tensor $T \in A\otimes B\otimes C$ is *concise* if the maps T_A, T_B, and T_C are all injective.

Exercise 2.1.7.4 (2!) Find a choice of bases such that

$$M_{\langle \mathbf{n} \rangle_A}(A^*) = \begin{pmatrix} x & & \\ & \ddots & \\ & & x \end{pmatrix}$$

where $x = (x_j^i)$ is $\mathbf{n} \times \mathbf{n}$, i.e., the image in the space of $\mathbf{n}^2 \times \mathbf{n}^2$ matrices is block diagonal with all blocks the same.

Exercise 2.1.7.5 (1) Show that $\underline{\mathbf{R}}(M_{\langle \mathbf{n} \rangle}) \geq \mathbf{n}^2$.

Exercise 2.1.7.6 (1) Show $\underline{\mathbf{R}}(M_{\langle \mathbf{m},\mathbf{n},1 \rangle}) = \mathbf{R}(M_{\langle \mathbf{m},\mathbf{n},1 \rangle}) = \mathbf{mn}$ and $\underline{\mathbf{R}}(M_{\langle \mathbf{m},1,1 \rangle}) = \mathbf{R}(M_{\langle \mathbf{m},1,1 \rangle}) = \mathbf{m}$.

Exercise 2.1.7.7 (1!) Let $\mathbf{b} = \mathbf{c}$ and assume T_A is injective. Show that if $T(A^*)$ is simultaneously diagonalizable under the action of $GL(B) \times GL(C)$ (i.e., there exists $g \in GL(B) \times GL(C)$ such that for any basis $\alpha^1, \ldots, \alpha^{\mathbf{a}}$ of A^*, the elements $g \cdot T(\alpha^1), \ldots, g \cdot T(\alpha^{\mathbf{a}})$ are all diagonal), then $\mathbf{R}(T) \leq \mathbf{b}$, and therefore if $T(A^*)$ is the limit of simultaneously diagonalizable subspaces, then $\underline{\mathbf{R}}(T) \leq \mathbf{b}$.

2.2 Strassen's Equations

It wasn't until 1983 [Str83] that the first nonclassical equations were found for tensor border rank. These equations had been found in the related settings of partially symmetric tensors in 1877 by Fram-Toeplitz and in 1977 by Barth [Toe77, Bar77], and in the completely symmetric case in 1858 by Aronhold [Aro58]. See [Ott07] for a history. They are as follows.

2.2.1 A Test Beyond the Classical Equations

The classical equations just used that $B\otimes C$ is a vector space. To extract more information from T_A, we examine its image in $B\otimes C$, which we will view as a space of linear maps $C^* \to B$. If dimensions are balanced and if T is concise and has minimal border rank $\max\{\mathbf{a}, \mathbf{b}, \mathbf{c}\}$, the image should be special in some way, but how? Assume $\mathbf{b} = \mathbf{c}$ so the image is a space of linear maps between two vector spaces of the same dimension. (If $\mathbf{b} < \mathbf{c}$, just restrict to some $\mathbb{C}^{\mathbf{b}} \subset C^*$.) If $\mathbf{R}(T) = \mathbf{b}$, then $T(A^*)$ will be spanned by $\mathbf{b}$ rank one linear maps.

Lemma 2.2.1.1 *If $\mathbf{a} = \mathbf{b} = \mathbf{c}$ and T_A is injective, then $\mathbf{R}(T) = \mathbf{a}$ if and only if $T(A^*)$ is spanned by $\mathbf{a}$ rank one linear maps.*

Exercise 2.2.1.2 (2!) Prove Lemma 2.2.1.1. ⊙

How can we test if the image is spanned by $\mathbf{b}$ rank one linear maps? If $T = a_1 \otimes b_1 \otimes c_1 + \cdots + a_{\mathbf{a}} \otimes b_{\mathbf{a}} \otimes c_{\mathbf{a}}$ with each set of vectors a basis, then

$$T(A^*) = \left\{ \begin{pmatrix} x_1 & & & \\ & x_2 & & \\ & & \ddots & \\ & & & x_{\mathbf{a}} \end{pmatrix} \mid x_j \in \mathbb{C} \right\},$$

and this is the case for a general rank $\mathbf{a}$ tensor in $\mathbb{C}^{\mathbf{a}} \otimes \mathbb{C}^{\mathbf{a}} \otimes \mathbb{C}^{\mathbf{a}}$. That is, the space $T(A^*) \subset B \otimes C$, when T has border rank $\mathbf{a}$, lies in the Zariski closure of the subspaces that, under the action of $GL(B) \times GL(C)$, are simultaneously *diagonalizable* in the sense of Exercise 2.1.7.7. From this perspective our problem becomes to determine polynomials on $A \otimes B \otimes C$ that vanish of the set of T such that $T(A^*)$ is diagonalizable. (The problem is more naturally defined using the Grassmanian of Definition 2.3.3.1.)

A set of equations whose zero set is exactly the Zariski closure of the set of tensors giving rise to diagonalizable spaces of matrices is not known! What follows are *some* equations. (More are given in Chapter 5.) Recall that $B \otimes C = \mathrm{Hom}(C^*, B)$, the space of linear maps from C^* to B. If instead we were in the case of $\mathrm{Hom}(B, B) = \mathrm{End}(B)$, the space of linear maps from B to itself, a necessary condition for endomorphisms to be simultaneously diagonalizable is that they must commute, and the algebraic test for a subspace $U \subset \mathrm{End}(B)$ to be abelian is simple: the commutators $[X_i, X_j] := X_i X_j - X_j X_i$ must vanish on a basis $X_1, \ldots, X_{\mathbf{u}}$ of U. (I emphasize that commutators only make sense for maps from a vector space to itself.) These degree two equations exactly characterize abelian subspaces. We do not have maps from a vector space to itself, but we can fix the situation if there exists $\alpha \in A^*$ such that $T(\alpha) : C^* \to B$ is invertible, as then we could test if the commutators $[T(\alpha_1)T(\alpha)^{-1}, T(\alpha_2)T(\alpha)^{-1}]$ are zero. So we now have a test, but it is not expressed in terms of polynomials on $A \otimes B \otimes C$, and we cannot apply it to all tensors. These problems are fixed in §2.4.1. For now I record what we have so far:

Proposition 2.2.1.3 *Let $\mathbf{b} = \mathbf{c}$ and let $T \in A \otimes B \otimes C$ be such that there exists $\alpha \in A^*$ with $\mathrm{rank}(T(\alpha)) = \mathbf{b}$, so $\underline{\mathbf{R}}(T) \geq \mathbf{b}$. If $\underline{\mathbf{R}}(T) = \mathbf{b}$, then for all $X_1, X_2 \in T(A^*)T(\alpha)^{-1} \subset \mathrm{End}(B)$, $[X_1, X_2] = 0$.*

2.2.2 Strassen's Equations: Original Formulation

If $T \in A \otimes B \otimes C$ is "close to" having rank $\mathbf{a} = \mathbf{b} = \mathbf{c}$, one expects, using α with $T(\alpha)$ invertible, that $T(A^*)T(\alpha)^{-1} \subset \text{End}(B)$ will be "close to" being abelian. The following theorem makes this precise:

Theorem 2.2.2.1 (Strassen) [Str83] *Let $T \in A \otimes B \otimes C$ and assume $\mathbf{b} = \mathbf{c}$. Assume that there exists $\alpha \in A^*$ such that $\text{rank}(T(\alpha)) = \mathbf{b}$. Then, for all $X_1, X_2 \in T(A^*)T(\alpha)^{-1} \subset \text{End}(B)$,*

$$\underline{\mathbf{R}}(T) \geq \frac{1}{2}\text{rank}([X_1, X_2]) + \mathbf{b}.$$

I prove Theorem 2.2.2.1 for the case of the determinant of $[X_1, X_2]$ in §2.4.1 and in general in §5.2.2.

We now have potential tests for border rank for tensors in $\mathbb{C}^m \otimes \mathbb{C}^m \otimes \mathbb{C}^m$ up to $r = \frac{3}{2}\mathbf{m}$ – in fact tests for border rank for tensors in $\mathbb{C}^3 \otimes \mathbb{C}^m \otimes \mathbb{C}^m$ up to $r = \frac{3}{2}\mathbf{m}$ – since our test only used three vectors from A^*. (I write "potential tests" rather than "polynomial tests" because to write down the commutator, we must be able to find an invertible element in $T(A^*)$.)

Strassen uses Theorem 2.2.2.1 to show that $\underline{\mathbf{R}}(M_{\langle \mathbf{n} \rangle}) \geq \frac{3}{2}\mathbf{n}^2$:

Exercise 2.2.2.2 (2!) Prove $\underline{\mathbf{R}}(M_{\langle \mathbf{n} \rangle}) \geq \frac{3}{2}\mathbf{n}^2$. ⊚

Exercise 2.2.2.3 (2) Show that $\underline{\mathbf{R}}(M_{\langle 2 \rangle}^{red}) = 5$ and for $\mathbf{m} > 2$ that $\underline{\mathbf{R}}(M_{\langle \mathbf{m},2,2 \rangle}^{red}) \geq 3\mathbf{m} - 1$, where $M_{\langle \mathbf{m},2,2 \rangle}^{red}$ is $M_{\langle \mathbf{m},2,2 \rangle}$ with x_1^1 set to zero.

A natural question arises: exchanging the roles of A, B, C, we obtain three sets of such equations – are the three sets of equations the same or different? We should have already asked this question for the three types of usual flattenings: are the equations coming from the minors of T_A, T_B, T_C the same or different? It is easy to write down tensors where $\text{rank}(T_A), \text{rank}(T_B)$, and $\text{rank}(T_C)$ are distinct; however, for 2×2 minors, two sets of them vanishing implies that the third does as well (see §8.3.1, where these questions are answered with the help of representation theory).

One can generalize Strassen's equations by taking higher order commutators (see [LM08b]). These generalizations do give new equations, but they do not give equations for border rank beyond the $\frac{3}{2}\mathbf{b}$ of Strassen's equations.

An extensive discussion of Strassen's equations and generalizations appears in [Lan12, §7.6].

2.2.3 Coming Attractions: Border Rank Bounds Beyond Strassen's Equations

The following, more complicated expression gives equations for $\hat{\sigma}_r$ for $r > \frac{3}{2}\mathbf{b}$.

Let $T \in \mathbb{C}^5 \otimes \mathbb{C}^\mathbf{b} \otimes \mathbb{C}^\mathbf{b}$; write $T = a_0 \otimes X_0 + \cdots a_4 \otimes X_4$ with $X_j \in B \otimes C$. Assume that rank$(X_0) = \mathbf{b}$ and choose bases such that $X_0 = \mathrm{Id}$. Consider the following $5\mathbf{b} \times 5\mathbf{b}$ matrix:

$$T_A^{\wedge 2} = \begin{pmatrix} 0 & [X_1, X_2] & [X_1, X_3] & [X_1, X_4] \\ [X_2, X_1] & 0 & [X_2, X_3] & [X_2, X_4] \\ [X_3, X_1] & [X_3, X_2] & 0 & [X_3, X_4] \\ [X_4, X_1] & [X_4, X_2] & [X_4, X_3] & 0 \end{pmatrix}. \tag{2.2.1}$$

The name $T_A^{\wedge 2}$ is explained in §2.4.2, where the proof of the following proposition also appears.

Proposition 2.2.3.1 [LO15] *Let $T \in \mathbb{C}^5 \otimes \mathbb{C}^\mathbf{b} \otimes \mathbb{C}^\mathbf{b}$ be as written above. Then* $\underline{\mathbf{R}}(T) \geq \frac{\mathrm{rank} T_A^{\wedge 2}}{3}$. *If $T \in A \otimes \mathbb{C}^\mathbf{b} \otimes \mathbb{C}^\mathbf{b}$ with $\mathbf{a} > 5$, one obtains the same result for all restrictions of T to $\mathbb{C}^5 \otimes \mathbb{C}^\mathbf{b} \otimes \mathbb{C}^\mathbf{b}$ for any $\mathbb{C}^5 \subset A^*$.*

In particular, the minors of (2.2.1) give equations up to border rank $\frac{5}{3}\mathbf{b}$ for tensors in $\mathbb{C}^\mathbf{a} \otimes \mathbb{C}^\mathbf{b} \otimes \mathbb{C}^\mathbf{c}$ for $\mathbf{a} \geq 5$ and $\mathbf{b} \leq \mathbf{c}$.

I do not know how anyone would have found (2.2.1) without using the theory discussed in the next section. Hopefully this will motivate the theory-adverse reader to persevere through it.

2.3 Theory Needed for the Generalization of Strassen's Equations

The matrices $[X_1, X_2]$ and the right-hand side of (2.2.1) are part of a sequence of constructions giving better lower bounds for border rank for tensors. The limits of this method are lower bounds of $2\mathbf{b} - 3$. To describe them, we will need more language from multilinear algebra. Our first task will be to generalize the space of skew-symmetric matrices. It will be convenient to generalize symmetric matrices at the same time. Before that, I present a fundamental result in representation theory.

2.3.1 Schur's Lemma

I take a short detour into elementary representation theory to prove a lemma everyone should know. Recall the definition of a G-module from §1.1.13.

Definition 2.3.1.1 Let W_1, W_2 be vector spaces, let G be a group, and let $\rho_j : G \to GL(W_j)$, $j = 1, 2$ be representations. A G *module homomorphism*, or G *module map*, is a linear map $f : W_1 \to W_2$ such that $f(\rho_1(g) \cdot v) = \rho_2(g) \cdot f(v)$ for all $v \in W_1$ and $g \in G$. One also says that f is G-*equivariant*. For a group G and G-modules V and W, let $\mathrm{Hom}_G(V, W) \subset V^* \otimes W$ denote the vector space of G-module homomorphisms $V \to W$.

One says W_1 and W_2 are *isomorphic G-modules* if there exists a G-module homomorphism $W_1 \to W_2$ that is a linear isomorphism.

Exercise 2.3.1.2 (1!!) Show that the image and kernel of a G-module homomorphism are G-modules.

The following easy lemma is central to representation theory:

Lemma 2.3.1.3 (Schur's Lemma) *Let G be a group, let V and W be irreducible G-modules, and let $f : V \to W$ be a G-module homomorphism. Then either $f = 0$ or f is an isomorphism. If, further, $V = W$, then $f = \lambda \operatorname{Id}_V$ for some constant λ.*

Exercise 2.3.1.4 (1!!) Prove Schur's Lemma.

We will see numerous examples illustrating the utility of Schur's Lemma. I cannot overemphasize the importance of this simple lemma. I use it every day of my mathematical life.

For any group G, G-module M, and irreducible G-module V, the *isotypic component* of V in M is the largest subspace of M isomorphic to $V^{\oplus m_V}$ for some m_V. The integer m_V is called the *multiplicity* of V in M.

2.3.2 Symmetric and Skew-Symmetric Tensors

Exercise 2.3.2.1 (1) Let X be a matrix representing a bilinear form on $\mathbb{C}^m$ by $X(v, w) = v^T X w$. Show that if X is a symmetric matrix, then $X(v, w) = X(w, v)$, and if X is a skew-symmetric matrix, then $X(v, w) = -X(w, v)$.

Recall that $\mathfrak{S}_d$ denotes the permutation group on d elements.

Definition 2.3.2.2 A tensor $T \in V^{\otimes d}$ is said to be *symmetric* if $T(\alpha_1, \ldots, \alpha_d) = T(\alpha_{\sigma(1)}, \ldots, \alpha_{\sigma(d)})$ for all $\alpha_1, \ldots, \alpha_d \in V^*$ and all permutations $\sigma \in \mathfrak{S}_d$ and *skew-symmetric* if $T(\alpha_1, \ldots, \alpha_d) = \operatorname{sgn}(\sigma) T(\alpha_{\sigma(1)}, \ldots, \alpha_{\sigma(d)})$ for all $\alpha_1, \ldots, \alpha_d \in V^*$ and all $\sigma \in \mathfrak{S}_d$. Let $S^d V \subset V^{\otimes d}$ (resp. $\Lambda^d V \subset V^{\otimes d}$) denote the space of symmetric (resp. skew-symmetric) tensors.

The spaces $\Lambda^d V$ and $S^d V$ are independent of a choice of basis in V. In particular, the splitting

$$V^{\otimes 2} = S^2 V \oplus \Lambda^2 V \tag{2.3.1}$$

of the space of matrices into the direct sum of symmetric and skew-symmetric matrices is invariant under the *action* of $GL(V)$ given by the following: for $g \in GL(V)$ and $v \otimes w \in V \otimes V$, $v \otimes w \mapsto gv \otimes gw$.

Introduce the notations

$$x_1 x_2 \cdots x_k := \sum_{\sigma \in \mathfrak{S}_k} x_{\sigma(1)} \otimes x_{\sigma(2)} \otimes \cdots \otimes x_{\sigma(k)} \in S^k V$$

and

$$x_1 \wedge x_2 \wedge \cdots \wedge x_k := \sum_{\sigma \in \mathfrak{S}_k} \mathrm{sgn}(\sigma) x_{\sigma(1)} \otimes x_{\sigma(2)} \otimes \cdots \otimes x_{\sigma(k)} \in \Lambda^k V,$$

called the *symmetric product* (or simply *product*) of $x_1, \ldots, x_k$ and the *wedge product* of $x_1, \ldots, x_k$, respectively

The space $S^k V^*$ may be thought of as the space of homogeneous polynomials of degree k on V (to a symmetric tensor T associate the polynomial P_T where $P_T(v) := T(v, \ldots, v)$). Thus $x_1 \cdots x_k$ may also be read as the multiplication of $x_1, \ldots, x_k$.

If $v_1, \ldots, v_\mathbf{v}$ is a basis of V, then $v_{i_1} \otimes \cdots \otimes v_{i_d}$ with $i_j \in [\mathbf{v}] := \{1, \ldots, \mathbf{v}\}$ is a basis of $V^{\otimes d}$, $v_{i_1} \cdots v_{i_d}$ with $1 \leq i_1 \leq \cdots \leq i_d \leq \mathbf{v}$ is a basis of $S^d V$ and $v_{i_1} \wedge \cdots \wedge v_{i_d}$ with $1 \leq i_1 < \cdots < i_d \leq \mathbf{v}$ is a basis of $\Lambda^d V$. Call these bases *induced bases*. If $x_j = (x_j^1, \ldots, x_j^\mathbf{v})^T$ in the basis $v_1, \ldots, v_\mathbf{v}$, then the expression of $x_1 \wedge \cdots \wedge x_k$ in the induced basis is such that the coefficient of $v_{i_1} \wedge \cdots \wedge v_{i_k}$ is

$$\det \begin{pmatrix} x_1^{i_1} & \cdots & x_1^{i_k} \\ & \vdots & \\ x_k^{i_1} & \cdots & x_k^{i_k} \end{pmatrix}.$$

For example, if $V = \mathbb{C}^4$ with basis $e_1, \ldots, e_4$, then $\Lambda^2 V$ inherits a basis $e_1 \wedge e_2, \ldots, e_3 \wedge e_4$. If

$$v = \begin{pmatrix} v_1 \\ v_2 \\ v_3 \\ v_4 \end{pmatrix}, \quad w = \begin{pmatrix} w_1 \\ w_2 \\ w_3 \\ w_4 \end{pmatrix}, \quad \text{then } v \wedge w = \begin{pmatrix} v_1 w_2 - v_2 w_1 \\ v_1 w_3 - v_3 w_1 \\ v_1 w_4 - v_4 w_1 \\ v_2 w_3 - v_3 w_2 \\ v_2 w_4 - v_4 w_2 \\ v_3 w_4 - v_4 w_3 \end{pmatrix}.$$

Exercise 2.3.2.3 (1) Show that there is a $GL(V)$-module map $\Lambda^k V \otimes V \to \Lambda^{k+1} V$ and, more generally, that there are $GL(V)$-module maps $\Lambda^k V \otimes \Lambda^l V \to \Lambda^{k+l} V$ and $S^k V \otimes S^l V \to S^{k+l} V$, the latter of which may be interpreted as multiplication of polynomials.

Exercise 2.3.2.4 (1) Let $k \geq t$, and show that there is a $GL(V)$-module map $S^k V^* \otimes S^t V \to S^{k-t} V^*$. This map has the following interpretation: $S^t V$ may be interpreted as the homogeneous linear differential operators of order t on the space of polynomials $S^k V^*$. The map is then $P \otimes D \mapsto D(P)$. Sometimes $D(P)$ is denoted $D \lrcorner P$.

Exercise 2.3.2.5 (1) Show that for $k < l$, there is a $GL(V)$-module map, $\Lambda^k V^* \otimes \Lambda^l V \to \Lambda^{l-k} V$. This map is often denoted $\beta \otimes Y \mapsto \beta \lrcorner Y$.

Exercise 2.3.2.6 (1) Let $Sym(V) = \oplus_{j=0}^\infty S^j V$, $\Lambda^\bullet V = \oplus_{j=0}^\mathbf{v} \Lambda^j V$, and $V^{\otimes \bullet} = \oplus_{j=0}^\infty V^{\otimes j}$. Show that these spaces are all naturally algebras with the above defined products, called the *symmetric, exterior,* and *tensor* algebras, respectively.

2.3.3 The Grassmannian

Before returning to border rank, I define an important algebraic variety that we will need for the proof of tensor rank lower bounds:

Definition 2.3.3.1 *Projective space* is the most important special case of a Grassmannian $\mathbb{P}V = G(1, V)$. $\mathbb{P}V := (V \backslash 0)/ \sim$, where $v \sim w$ if and only if $v = \lambda w$ for some $\lambda \in \mathbb{C} \backslash 0$. For $S \subset V$, the image of its projection to $\mathbb{P}V$ is denoted $\mathbb{P}S$. The *Grassmannian* of k-planes through the origin in V is

$$G(k, V) := \mathbb{P}\{T \in \Lambda^k V \mid \exists v_1, \ldots, v_k \in V \text{ such that}$$
$$T = v_1 \wedge \cdots \wedge v_k\} \subset \mathbb{P}\Lambda^k V. \tag{2.3.2}$$

The interpretation of the Grassmannian as the space parameterizing the k-planes through the origin in V is via the correspondence $[v_1 \wedge \cdots \wedge v_k] \leftrightarrow \text{span}\{v_1, \ldots, v_k\}$.

The following exercise shows that the Grassmannian is indeed an algebraic variety. It can be safely skipped on a first reading.

Exercise 2.3.3.2 (3) The Grassmannian is the zero set of equations parametrized by $\Lambda^{k-2j} V^* \otimes \Lambda^{k+2j} V^*$ for $1 \leq j \leq \min\{\lfloor \frac{\mathbf{v}-k}{2} \rfloor, \lfloor \frac{k}{2} \rfloor\}$ as follows: for $\mu \in \Lambda^{k-2j} V^*$ and $\zeta \in \Lambda^{k+2j} V^*$, recall Exercise 2.3.2.5, and consider $T \lrcorner \zeta \in \Lambda^{2j} V^*$ and $\mu \lrcorner T \in \Lambda^{2j} V$. Define $P_{\mu \otimes \zeta}(T) := \langle T \lrcorner \zeta, \mu \lrcorner T \rangle$, the evaluation of an element of $\Lambda^{2j} V^*$ on an element of $\Lambda^{2j} V$. Note that these are quadratic equations in the coefficients of T. Show that the zero set of these equations is the Grassmannian. ◎

2.4 Koszul Flattenings

2.4.1 Reformulation and Proof of Strassen's Equations

Augment the linear map $T_B : B^* \to A \otimes C$ by tensoring it with Id_A to obtain a linear map

$$\text{Id}_A \otimes T_B : A \otimes B^* \to A \otimes A \otimes C.$$

So far this is not interesting, but by (2.3.1) the target of this map decomposes as a $GL(A) \times GL(C)$-module as $(\Lambda^2 A \otimes C) \oplus (S^2 A \otimes C)$, and we may project onto these factors. Write the projections as

$$T_{BA}^{\wedge} = T_A^{\wedge} : A \otimes B^* \to \Lambda^2 A \otimes C \text{ and } T_{BA}^{\circ} : A \otimes B^* \to S^2 A \otimes C. \quad (2.4.1)$$

Exercise 2.4.1.1 (1) Show that if $T = a \otimes b \otimes c$ is a rank one tensor, then $\text{rank}(T_A^{\wedge}) = \mathbf{a} - 1$ and $\text{rank}(T_{BA}^{\circ}) = \mathbf{a}$.

Exercise 2.4.1.1 implies the following:

Proposition 2.4.1.2 *If* $\underline{\mathbf{R}}(T) \leq r$, *then* $\text{rank}(T_A^{\wedge}) \leq r(\mathbf{a} - 1)$ *and* $\text{rank}(T_{BA}^{\circ}) \leq r\mathbf{a}$.

The second map will not give border rank lower bounds better than the classical equations, but the first, e.g., when $\mathbf{a} = 3$, is a map from a $2\mathbf{b}$-dimensional vector space to a $2\mathbf{c}$-dimensional vector space, so if $\mathbf{b} \leq \mathbf{c}$, we can get border rank bounds up to $\frac{3}{2}\mathbf{b}$.

The first set is equivalent to Strassen's equations, as I now show. If $\mathbf{a} > 3$, one can choose a three-dimensional subspace $A' \subset A^*$ and consider T restricted to $A' \times B^* \times C^*$ to obtain equations. (This is what we did in the case of Strassen's equations where A' was spanned by $\alpha, \alpha', \alpha''$.)

Let a_1, a_2, a_3 be a basis of A, with dual basis $\alpha^1, \alpha^2, \alpha^3$ of A^* so $T \in A \otimes B \otimes C$ may be written as $T = a_1 \otimes X_1 + a_2 \otimes X_2 + a_3 \otimes X_3$, where $X_j = T(\alpha_j)$. Then $T_A^{\wedge}$ will be expressed by a $3\mathbf{b} \times 3\mathbf{b}$ matrix. Ordering the basis of $A \otimes B^*$ by $a_3 \otimes \beta^1, \dots, a_3 \otimes \beta^{\mathbf{b}}, a_2 \otimes \beta^1, \dots, a_2 \otimes \beta^{\mathbf{b}}, a_1 \otimes \beta^1, \dots, a_1 \otimes \beta^{\mathbf{b}}$, and that of $\Lambda^2 A \otimes C$ by $(a_1 \wedge a_2) \otimes c_1, \dots, (a_1 \wedge a_2) \otimes c_{\mathbf{b}}, (a_1 \wedge a_3) \otimes c_1, \dots, (a_1 \wedge a_3) \otimes c_{\mathbf{b}}, (a_2 \wedge a_3) \otimes c_1, \dots, (a_2 \wedge a_3) \otimes c_{\mathbf{b}}$, we obtain the block matrix

$$T_A^{\wedge} = \begin{pmatrix} 0 & X_1 & -X_2 \\ X_2 & X_3 & 0 \\ X_1 & 0 & X_3 \end{pmatrix}. \quad (2.4.2)$$

Recall the following basic identity about determinants of blocked matrices (see, e.g., [Pra94, Theorem 3.1.1]), assuming the block W is invertible:

$$\det \begin{pmatrix} X & Y \\ Z & W \end{pmatrix} = \det(W) \det(X - YW^{-1}Z). \quad (2.4.3)$$

Block (2.4.2) $X = 0$, $Y = (X_1, -X_2)$, $Z = \begin{pmatrix} X_2 \\ X_1 \end{pmatrix}$, $W = \begin{pmatrix} X_3 & 0 \\ 0 & X_3 \end{pmatrix}$. Assume $X_3 = T(\alpha^3)$ is invertible to obtain

$$\det T_A^{\wedge} = \det(X_3)^2 \det \left(X_1 X_3^{-1} X_2 - X_2 X_3^{-1} X_1 \right). \quad (2.4.4)$$

Equation (2.4.4) shows the new formulation is equivalent to the old, at least in the case of maximal rank. (We are only interested in the nonvanishing of the polynomial, not its values, so we can multiply the inner matrix on the right by X_3^{-1}.) Equation (2.4.4) combined with Proposition 2.4.1.2 proves Theorem 2.2.2.1 in this case.

Note that here we have actual polynomials on $A \otimes B \otimes C$ (the minors of (2.4.2)), whereas in our original formulation of Strassen's equations we did not. To obtain polynomials in the original formulation, one uses the adjugate matrix instead of the inverse (see [Lan12, §3.8]).

Remark 2.4.1.3 Both the classical equations and Strassen's equations are obtained by taking minors of a matrix whose entries are linear combinations of the coefficients of our tensor. Such constructions are part of a long tradition of finding *determinantal equations* for algebraic varieties discussed further in Chapters 8 and 10. For the experts, given a variety X and a subvariety $Y \subset X$, one way to find defining equations for Y is to find vector bundles E, F over X and a vector bundle map $\phi : E \to F$ such that Y is realized as the *degeneracy locus* of ϕ, that is, the set of points $x \in X$ such that ϕ_x drops rank. Strassen's equations in the partially symmetric case had been discovered by Barth [Bar77] in this context.

Remark 2.4.1.4 In §8.2 and §8.3.1, we will see two different ways of deriving Strassen's equations via representation theory.

2.4.2 Definition of Koszul Flattenings

The reformulation of Strassen's equations suggests the following generalization: let $\dim A = 2p + 1$ and consider

$$T_A^{\wedge p} : B^* \otimes \Lambda^p A \to \Lambda^{p+1} A \otimes C \tag{2.4.5}$$

obtained by first taking $T_B \otimes \mathrm{Id}_{\Lambda^p} A : B^* \otimes \Lambda^p A \to \Lambda^p A \otimes A \otimes C$ and then projecting to $\Lambda^{p+1} A \otimes C$ as in Exercise 2.3.2.3.

If $\{a_i\}$, $\{b_j\}$, $\{c_k\}$ are bases of A, B, C and $T = \sum_{i,j,k} t^{ijk} a_i \otimes b_j \otimes c_k$, then

$$T_A^{\wedge p}(\beta \otimes f_1 \wedge \cdots \wedge f_p) = \sum_{i,j,k} t^{ijk} \beta(b_j) a_i \wedge f_1 \wedge \cdots \wedge f_p \otimes c_k. \tag{2.4.6}$$

The map $T_A^{\wedge p}$ is called a *Koszul flattening*. Note that if $T = a \otimes b \otimes c$ has rank one, then $\mathrm{rank}(T_A^{\wedge p}) = \binom{2p}{p}$ as the image is $a \wedge \Lambda^p A \otimes c$. By linearity of the map $T \mapsto T_A^{\wedge p}$, we conclude the following:

Proposition 2.4.2.1 [LO15] *Let* $T \in A \otimes B \otimes C$ *with* $\dim A = 2p + 1$. *Then*

$$\underline{\mathbf{R}}(T) \geq \frac{\mathrm{rank}(T_A^{\wedge p})}{\binom{2p}{p}}.$$

Since the source (resp. target) has dimension $\binom{2p+1}{p} \mathbf{b}$ (resp. $\binom{2p+1}{p+1} \mathbf{c}$), assuming $\mathbf{b} \leq \mathbf{c}$, we potentially obtain equations for $\hat{\sigma}_r$ up to

$$r = \frac{\binom{2p+1}{p} \mathbf{b}}{\binom{2p}{p}} - 1 = \frac{2p+1}{p+1} \mathbf{b} - 1.$$

Just as with Strassen's equations (case $p = 1$), if $\dim A > 2p + 1$, one obtains the best bound for these equations by restricting to subspaces of A^* of dimension $2p + 1$.

Exercise 2.4.2.2 (2) Show that if $T_A^{\wedge p} : \Lambda^p A \otimes B^* \to \Lambda^{p+1} A \otimes C$ is injective, then $T_A^{\wedge q} : \Lambda^q A \otimes B^* \to \Lambda^{q+1} A \otimes C$ is injective for all $q < p$. ⊚

2.4.3 Koszul Flattenings in Coordinates

To prove lower bounds on the rank of matrix multiplication, and to facilitate a comparison with Griesser's equations discussed in §5.2.2, it will be useful to view $T_A^{\wedge p}$ in coordinates. Let $\dim A = 2p + 1$. Write $T = a_0 \otimes X_0 + \cdots + a_{2p} \otimes X_{2p}$, where a_j is a basis of A with dual basis α^j and $X_j = T(\alpha^j)$. An expression of $T_A^{\wedge p}$ in bases is as follows: write $a_I := a_{i_1} \wedge \cdots \wedge a_{i_p}$ for the induced basis elements of $\Lambda^p A$, require that the first $\binom{2p}{p-1}$ basis vectors of $\Lambda^p A$ have $i_1 = 0$, that the second $\binom{2p}{p}$ do not, and call these multi-indices $0J$ and K. Order the bases of $\Lambda^{p+1} A$ such that the first $\binom{2p}{p+1}$ multi-indices do not have 0, and the second $\binom{2p}{p}$ do, and furthermore that the second set of indices is ordered the same way as K is ordered, only we write $0K$ since a zero index is included. The resulting matrix is of the form

$$\begin{pmatrix} 0 & Q \\ \tilde{Q} & R \end{pmatrix}, \tag{2.4.7}$$

where this matrix is blocked $((\binom{2p}{p+1}) \mathbf{b}, (\binom{2p}{p}) \mathbf{b}) \times ((\binom{2p}{p+1}) \mathbf{b}, (\binom{2p}{p}) \mathbf{b})$,

$$R = \begin{pmatrix} X_0 & & \\ & \ddots & \\ & & X_0 \end{pmatrix},$$

and $Q, \tilde{Q}$ have entries in blocks consisting of $X_1, \ldots, X_{2p}$ and zero. Thus if X_0 is of full rank and we change coordinates such that it is the identity matrix, then R

becomes the size $\binom{2p}{p}\mathbf{b}$ identity matrix and the determinant equals the determinant of $Q\tilde{Q}$ by (2.4.3). If we order the appearances of the K multi-indices such that the jth K is the complement of the jth J in $[2p]$, then $Q\tilde{Q}$ will be block skew-symmetric. When $p = 1$, $Q\tilde{Q} = [X_1, X_2]$, and when $p = 2$, we recover the matrix (2.2.1).

In general, $Q\tilde{Q}$ is a block skew-symmetric $\binom{2p}{p-1}\mathbf{b} \times \binom{2p}{p-1}\mathbf{b}$ matrix whose block entries are either zero or commutators $[X_i, X_j]$. Each $[X_i, X_j]$ appears (up to sign) $\binom{2p-1}{2}$ times, and each block row and column contain exactly $\binom{2p-1}{2}$ nonzero blocks, so the resulting matrix is very sparse.

2.5 Matrix Multiplication and Koszul Flattenings

We would like to apply our new equations to matrix multiplication. In order to do so, we first must understand the matrix multiplication tensor better from a geometric perspective.

2.5.1 The Matrix Multiplication Tensor from an Invariant Perspective

In the vector space $V^* \otimes V$, there is a unique line such that every vector on the line has the same matrix representative for any choice of basis (and corresponding choice of dual basis). This line is of course $\mathbb{C}\{\mathrm{Id}_V\}$, the scalar multiples of the identity map. We say $\mathbb{C}\{\mathrm{Id}_V\}$ is the unique line in $V^* \otimes V$ *invariant* under the action of $GL(V)$.

We have

$$M_{\langle U,V,W \rangle} \in (U^* \otimes V) \otimes (V^* \otimes W) \otimes (W^* \otimes U) \simeq U^* \otimes U \otimes V^* \otimes V \otimes W^* \otimes W.$$

Moreover, we know $M_{\langle U,V,W \rangle}$ is invariant under the action of $GL(U) \times GL(V) \times GL(W)$. The only element of $U^* \otimes U \otimes V^* \otimes V \otimes W^* \otimes W$ that is invariant under $GL(U) \times GL(V) \times GL(W)$ is up to scale $\mathrm{Id}_U \otimes \mathrm{Id}_V \otimes \mathrm{Id}_W$. Checking the scale, we conclude the following:

Proposition 2.5.1.1 $M_{\langle U,V,W \rangle}$, *after applying the reordering isomorphism, is* $\mathrm{Id}_U \otimes \mathrm{Id}_V \otimes \mathrm{Id}_W$.

Exercise 2.5.1.2 (1) If $v_1, \ldots, v_\mathbf{v}$ is a basis of V and $\alpha^1, \ldots, \alpha^\mathbf{v}$ is the dual basis of V^*, show that the identity map on V is $\mathrm{Id}_V = \sum_j \alpha^j \otimes v_j$.

Exercise 2.5.1.3 (1) Use Exercise 2.5.1.2 and the coordinate presentation of matrix multiplication to get a second proof of Proposition 2.5.1.1. This proof also shows that $M_{\langle U,V,W \rangle}$ is invariant under the action of the image of $GL(U) \times GL(V) \times GL(W)$ in $GL(A) \times GL(B) \times GL(C)$.

Exercise 2.5.1.4 (1) Show that there is a canonical isomorphism $(V^* \otimes W)^* \rightarrow V \otimes W^*$ where $\alpha \otimes w(v \otimes \beta) := \alpha(v)\beta(w)$. Now let $V = W$ and let $\mathrm{Id}_V \in V^* \otimes V \simeq (V^* \otimes V)^*$ denote the identity map. What is $\mathrm{Id}_V(f)$ for $f \in V^* \otimes V$? ◉

Exercise 2.5.1.5 (1!) Show that $M_{\langle U,V,W \rangle}$ when viewed as a trilinear map

$$M_{\langle U,V,W \rangle} : (U^* \otimes V)^* \times (V^* \otimes W)^* \times (W^* \otimes U)^* \rightarrow \mathbb{C}$$

is $(X, Y, Z) \mapsto \mathrm{trace}(XYZ)$. ◉

Exercise 2.5.1.6 (1!) Using Exercise 2.5.1.5, show that $M_{\langle \mathbf{n} \rangle} \in \mathbb{C}^{\mathbf{n}^2} \otimes \mathbb{C}^{\mathbf{n}^2} \otimes \mathbb{C}^{\mathbf{n}^2}$ is preserved by the cyclic permutation of the factors.

Exercise 2.5.1.7 (1!) Using Exercise 2.5.1.5, show that $M_{\langle \mathbf{n} \rangle} \in \mathbb{C}^{\mathbf{n}^2} \otimes \mathbb{C}^{\mathbf{n}^2} \otimes \mathbb{C}^{\mathbf{n}^2}$ is preserved by action $x \otimes y \otimes z \mapsto x^T \otimes z^T \otimes y^T$, where x^T is the transpose of the $\mathbf{n} \times \mathbf{n}$ matrix x.

Exercise 2.5.1.8 (1) Show that $\mathrm{Id}_V \otimes \mathrm{Id}_W \in V \otimes V^* \otimes W \otimes W^* = (V \otimes W) \otimes (V \otimes W)^*$, after reordering, equals $\mathrm{Id}_{V \otimes W}$.

Exercise 2.5.1.9 (1!) Using Exercise 2.5.1.8, show that $M_{\langle \mathbf{n},\mathbf{m},\mathbf{l} \rangle} \otimes M_{\langle \mathbf{n}',\mathbf{m}',\mathbf{l}' \rangle} = M_{\langle \mathbf{nn}',\mathbf{mm}',\mathbf{ll}' \rangle}$.

A fancy proof that $\underline{\mathbf{R}}(M_{\langle \mathbf{n} \rangle}) \geq \mathbf{n}^2$, which will be useful for proving further lower bounds, is as follows: write $A = U^* \otimes V$, $B = V^* \otimes W$, $C = W^* \otimes U$, so $(M_{\langle \mathbf{n} \rangle})_A : A^* \rightarrow B \otimes C$ is a map $U \otimes V^* \rightarrow V^* \otimes W \otimes W^* \otimes U$. This map is, for $f \in A^*$, $f \mapsto f \otimes \mathrm{Id}_W$ and thus is clearly injective. In other words, the map is $u \otimes v \mapsto \sum_k (v \otimes w_k) \otimes (w^k \otimes u)$, where $w_1, \dots, w_{\mathbf{w}}$ is a basis of W with dual basis $w^1, \dots, w^{\mathbf{w}}$.

2.5.2 Koszul Flattenings and Matrix Multiplication

When $T = M_{\langle U,V,W \rangle}$, the Koszul flattening map is

$$(M_{\langle U,V,W \rangle})_A^{\wedge p} : V \otimes W^* \otimes \Lambda^p(U^* \otimes V) \rightarrow \Lambda^{p+1}(U^* \otimes V) \otimes (W^* \otimes U).$$

The presence of $\mathrm{Id}_W = \mathrm{Id}_{W^*}$ implies the map factors as $(M_{\langle U,V,W \rangle})_A^{\wedge p} = (M_{\langle \mathbf{u},\mathbf{v},1 \rangle})_A^{\wedge p} \otimes \mathrm{Id}_{W^*}$, where

$$(M_{\langle \mathbf{u},\mathbf{v},1 \rangle})_A^{\wedge p} : V \otimes \Lambda^p(U^* \otimes V) \rightarrow \Lambda^{p+1}(U^* \otimes V) \otimes U \qquad (2.5.1)$$

$$v \otimes (\xi^1 \otimes e_1) \wedge \cdots \wedge (\xi^p \otimes e_p) \mapsto \sum_{s=1}^{\mathbf{u}} u_s \otimes (u^s \otimes v) \wedge (\xi^1 \otimes c_1) \wedge \cdots \wedge (\xi^p \otimes e_p),$$

where $u_1, \dots, u_{\mathbf{u}}$ is a basis of U with dual basis $u^1, \dots, u^{\mathbf{u}}$ of U^*, so $\mathrm{Id}_U = \sum_{s=1}^{\mathbf{u}} u^s \otimes u_s$.

As discussed above, Koszul flattenings could potentially prove a border rank lower bound of $2\mathbf{n}^2 - 3$ for $M_{\langle \mathbf{n} \rangle}$. However, this does not happen, as there is a large kernel for the maps $M_{\langle \mathbf{n} \rangle}^{\wedge p}$ when $p \geq \mathbf{n}$: let $\mathbf{u} = \mathbf{v} = \mathbf{n}$, and let $p = \mathbf{n}$. Then

$$v \otimes (u^1 \otimes v) \otimes \cdots \otimes (u^\mathbf{n} \otimes v) \mapsto \sum_j (u^j \otimes v) \wedge (u^1 \otimes v) \otimes \cdots \otimes (u^\mathbf{n} \otimes v) \otimes u_j = 0,$$

so $M_{\langle \mathbf{n} \rangle}^{\wedge \mathbf{n}}$ is not injective. Since $M_{\langle \mathbf{u}, \mathbf{v}, 1 \rangle)_A^{\wedge p}$ is a $GL(U) \times GL(V)$-module map, by Schur's Lemma 2.3.1.3, $\ker(M_{\langle \mathbf{n} \rangle}^{\wedge \mathbf{n}}) \subset V \otimes \Lambda^\mathbf{n}(U^* \otimes V) \subset V^{\otimes \mathbf{n}+1} \otimes U^{* \otimes \mathbf{n}}$ must be a submodule. It is clearly symmetric in V and skew in U^*, so the kernel must contain the irreducible submodule $\Lambda^\mathbf{n} U^* \otimes S^{\mathbf{n}+1} V$.

Now consider the case $p = \mathbf{n} - 1$. I claim $(M_{\langle \mathbf{n}, \mathbf{n}, 1 \rangle})_A^{\wedge \mathbf{n}-1}$ is injective. The following argument is due to L. Manivel. Say $X_1 \otimes v_1 + \cdots + X_\mathbf{n} \otimes v_\mathbf{n} \in \ker(M_{\langle \mathbf{n}, \mathbf{n}, 1 \rangle})_A^{\wedge \mathbf{n}-1}$, i.e.,

$$\sum_s [X_1 \wedge (u^s \otimes v_1) + \cdots + X_\mathbf{n} \wedge (u^s \otimes v_\mathbf{n})] \otimes u_s = 0.$$

Then, for each s, each term in the brackets must be zero.

Lemma 2.5.2.1 *Let A be a vector space, let $X_1, \ldots, X_k \in \Lambda^q A$, and let $a_1, \ldots, a_k \in A$ be linearly independent. Then, if $X_1 \wedge a_1 + \cdots + X_k \wedge a_k = 0$, we may write each $X_j = \sum_{i=1}^k Y_{ij} \wedge a_i$ for some $Y_{ij} \in \Lambda^{q-1} A$.*

Exercise 2.5.2.2 (2) Prove Lemma 2.5.2.1. ⊚

Exercise 2.5.2.3 (2) Show that $\ker(M_{\langle \mathbf{n}, \mathbf{n}, 1 \rangle})_A^{\wedge \mathbf{n}} = \Lambda^\mathbf{n} U^* \otimes S^{\mathbf{n}+1} V$. ⊚

Remark 2.5.2.4 This is a special case of the generalized *Cartan Lemma* (see [IL16b, §A.1]). With the aid of representation theory, one can more precisely describe the Y_{ji}. (For those familiar with the notation, use the sequence $0 \to S_{2,1^{q-1}} A \to \Lambda^q A \otimes A \to \Lambda^{q+1} A \to 0$.)

Returning to the proof of injectivity, when $p = \mathbf{n} - 1$, taking $s = 1$, we have $X_j = \sum Y_{j,(1,i)} \wedge (u^1 \otimes a_i)$, so each term in X_j is divisible by $(u^1 \otimes a_i)$ for some i, but then taking $s = 2$, each term in X_j is divisible by $(u^2 \otimes a_l)$ for some l. Continuing, if $p < \mathbf{n}$, we run out of factors, so there cannot be a kernel. In summary:

Proposition 2.5.2.5 *When $p < \mathbf{n}$, the map $(M_{\langle \mathbf{n}, \mathbf{n}, 1 \rangle})_A^{\wedge p}$ is injective.*

At this point, one would like to say that if some $T^{\wedge p}$ is injective, then restricting to a generic $A' \subset A^*$, the map $T^{\wedge p}|_{\Lambda^p A' \otimes B^*} : \Lambda^p A' \otimes B^* \to \Lambda^{p+1} A' \otimes C$ would still be injective. Unfortunately, I do not know how to prove this, because a priori $T^{\wedge p}|_{\Lambda^p A' \otimes B^*}$ injects into $[\Lambda^{p+1} A' \otimes C] \oplus [\Lambda^p A' \otimes (A/A') \otimes C]$, and it is not clear to me whether for generic A' it must remain injective when one projects to the first factor. What follows are two proofs that this is indeed the case for $(M_{\langle \mathbf{n,n},1\rangle})_A^{\wedge \mathbf{n}-1}$. The first is combinatorial. It has the advantages that it is elementary and will be used to prove the $2\mathbf{n}^2 - \lceil \log_2 \mathbf{n} \rceil - 1$ lower bound of §5.4.5. The second is geometrical. It has the advantage of being shorter and more elegant.

Theorem 2.5.2.6 [LO15] *Let* $\mathbf{n} \le \mathbf{m}$. *Then*

$$\underline{\mathbf{R}}(M_{\langle \mathbf{m,n},1\rangle}) \ge \frac{\mathbf{nl}(\mathbf{n} + \mathbf{m} - 1)}{\mathbf{m}}.$$

In particular, $\underline{\mathbf{R}}(M_{\langle \mathbf{n}\rangle}) \ge 2\mathbf{n}^2 - \mathbf{n}$.

I prove the case $\mathbf{n} = \mathbf{m}$ and leave the general case to the reader. We need to find $A' \subset A^*$ of dimension $2\mathbf{n} - 1$ such that, setting $\tilde{A} = A/A'^{\perp} \simeq A'^*$, $(M_{\langle \mathbf{n,n},1\rangle}|_{A'\otimes B^*\otimes C^*})_{\tilde{A}}^{\wedge \mathbf{n}-1}$ is injective.

First proof. Define the projection

$$\phi : A \to \mathbb{C}^{2\mathbf{n}-1} \tag{2.5.2}$$

$$x_j^i \mapsto e_{i+j-1}. \tag{2.5.3}$$

Let $e_S := e_{s_1} \wedge \cdots \wedge e_{s_{\mathbf{n}-1}}$, where $S = \{s_1, \dots, s_{\mathbf{n}-1}\} \subset [2\mathbf{n} - 1]$. The map $(M_{\langle \mathbf{n,n},1\rangle}|_{A'\otimes B^*\otimes C^*})_{\tilde{A}}^{\wedge \mathbf{n}-1}$ is

$$e_S \otimes v_k \mapsto \sum_j \phi(u^j \otimes v_k) \wedge e_S \otimes u_j = \sum_j e_{j+k-1} \wedge e_S \otimes u_j.$$

Index a basis of the source by pairs (S, k), with $k \in [\mathbf{n}]$, and the target by (P, l), where $P \subset [2\mathbf{n} - 1]$ has cardinality $\mathbf{n}$ and $l \in [\mathbf{n}]$.

What follows is an ordering of the basis vectors in the target such that the resulting matrix is upper-triangular. Then we just need to show that each diagonal element of the matrix is nonzero to conclude. Unfortunately, the order on (P, l) is a little complicated, because, e.g., if the ls are ordered sequentially, then to get a diagonal matrix, the Ps must be given an order in the opposite direction.

Define an order relation on the target basis vectors as follows: for (P_1, l_1) and (P_2, l_2), set $l = \min\{l_1, l_2\}$, and declare $(P_1, l_1) < (P_2, l_2)$ if and only if

1 in lexicographic order, the set of l minimal elements of P_1 is strictly after the set of l minimal elements of P_2 (i.e., the smallest element of P_2 is smaller than the smallest of P_1 or they are equal and the second smallest of P_2 is smaller or equal etc. up to lth), or

2 the l minimal elements in P_1 and P_2 are the same, and $l_1 < l_2$, or

3 the l minimal elements in P_1 and P_2 are the same, $l_1 = l_2$, and the set of $\mathbf{n} - l$ tail elements of P_1 are after the set of $\mathbf{n} - l$ tail elements of P_2.

The third condition is irrelevant – any breaking of a tie for the first two will lead to an upper-triangular matrix. Note that $(\{\mathbf{n}, \ldots, 2\mathbf{n} - 1\}, 1)$ is the minimal element for this order and that $([\mathbf{n}], \mathbf{n})$ is the maximal element. Note further that

$$e_{\mathbf{n}+1} \wedge \cdots \wedge e_{2\mathbf{n}-1} \otimes u_\mathbf{n} \mapsto e_\mathbf{n} \wedge \cdots \wedge e_{2\mathbf{n}-1} \otimes v_1,$$

i.e., that

$$(\{\mathbf{n} + 1, \ldots, 2\mathbf{n} - 1\}, \mathbf{n}) \mapsto (\{\mathbf{n}, \ldots, 2\mathbf{n} - 1\}, 1),$$

so $(\{\mathbf{n} + 1, \ldots, 2\mathbf{n} - 1\}, \mathbf{n})$ will be our first basis element for the source. The order for the source is implicitly described in the proof.

Work by induction: the base case that $(\{\mathbf{n}, \ldots, 2\mathbf{n} - 1\}, 1)$ is in the image has been established. Let (P, l) be any basis element, and assume all (P', l') with $(P', l') < (P, l)$ have been shown to be in the image. Write $P = (p_1, \ldots, p_\mathbf{n})$ with $p_i < p_{i+1}$. Consider the image of $(P\backslash\{p_l\}, 1 + p_l - l)$, which is

$$\sum_j \phi(u^j \otimes v_{1+p_l-l}) \wedge e_{P\backslash\{p_l\}} \otimes u_j = \sum_{\{j \mid j-l+p_l \notin P\backslash\{p_l\}\}} e_{p_l-l+j} \wedge e_{P\backslash\{p_l\}} \otimes u_j.$$

Taking $j = l$, we see (P, l) is among the summands. If $j < l$, the contribution to the summand is a (P', j), where the first j terms of P' equal the first of P, so by condition (2), $(P', j) < (P, l)$. If $j > l$, the summand is a (P'', j), where the first $l - 1$ terms of P and P'' agree, and the lth terms are, respectively, p_l and $p_l - l + j$, so by condition (1), $(P'', j) < (P, l)$. $\qquad\square$

To illustrate, consider the first seven terms when $\mathbf{n} = 3$:

$$(345, 1), (345, 2), (345, 3), (245, 1), (235, 1), (234, 1), (245, 2),$$

where the order did not matter for the triple $(245, 1), (235, 1), (234, 1)$. We have

$$(45, 3) \mapsto (345, 1)$$
$$(35, 2) \mapsto (345, 2)$$
$$(34, 3) \mapsto (345, 3)$$
$$(45, 2) \mapsto (245, 1) + (345, 2)$$
$$(35, 2) \mapsto (235, 1) + (345, 3)$$
$$(34, 2) \mapsto (234, 1)$$
$$(25, 3) \mapsto (245, 2).$$

Second proof. For this proof, take $\mathbf{u} = \mathbf{n} \leq \mathbf{v} = \mathbf{m}$. Take a vector space E of dimension 2, and fix isomorphisms $U \simeq S^{\mathbf{n}-1}E$, $V \simeq S^{\mathbf{m}-1}E^*$. Let $A' = S^{\mathbf{m}+\mathbf{n}-2}E^* \subset S^{\mathbf{n}-1}E^* \otimes S^{\mathbf{m}-1}E^* = U \otimes V^*$, and set $\tilde{A} = A/A'^{\perp}$. This turns out to be the same projection operator as in the previous proof.

Our map is

$$\Lambda^{\mathbf{n}-1}(S^{\mathbf{m}+\mathbf{n}-2}E) \otimes S^{\mathbf{n}-1}E \rightarrow \Lambda^{\mathbf{n}}(S^{\mathbf{m}+\mathbf{n}-2}E) \otimes S^{\mathbf{m}-1}E^*$$

$$Q_1 \wedge \cdots \wedge Q_{\mathbf{n}-1} \otimes f \mapsto \sum_{j=0}^{\mathbf{m}-1} (fh^j) \wedge Q_1 \wedge \cdots \wedge Q_{\mathbf{n}-1} \otimes h_j,$$

where $h^j = x^j y^{\mathbf{m}-j-1}$ and h_j is the dual basis vector.

Recall the contraction map from Exercise 2.3.2.4, for $\alpha \geq \beta$:

$$S^{\alpha}E \times S^{\beta}E^* \rightarrow S^{\alpha-\beta}E$$

$$(f, g) \mapsto g \lrcorner f.$$

In the case $f = l^{\alpha}$ for some $l \in E$, $g \lrcorner l^{\alpha} = g(l)l^{\alpha-\beta}$ (here $g(l)$ denotes g, considered as a polynomial, evaluated at the point l), so that $g \lrcorner l^{\alpha} = 0$ if and only if l is a root of g.

Consider the transposed map, and relabel E as E^* (they are isomorphic as $SL(E) \simeq SL_2$ modules):

$$((M_{\langle 1, \mathbf{m}, \mathbf{n} \rangle}|_{A' \otimes U^* \otimes V^*})^{\wedge p}_{\tilde{A}})^T :$$

$$S^{\mathbf{m}-1}E^* \otimes \Lambda^{\mathbf{n}} S^{\mathbf{m}+\mathbf{n}-2}E \rightarrow S^{\mathbf{n}-1}E \otimes \Lambda^{\mathbf{n}-1} S^{\mathbf{m}+\mathbf{n}-2}E$$

$$g \otimes (f_1 \wedge \cdots \wedge f_{\mathbf{n}}) \mapsto \sum_{i=1}^{\mathbf{n}} (-1)^{i-1} (g \lrcorner f_i) \otimes f_1 \wedge \cdots \hat{f_i} \cdots \wedge f_{\mathbf{n}}.$$

The map $((M_{\langle 1, \mathbf{m}, \mathbf{n} \rangle}|_{A' \otimes U^* \otimes V^*})^{\wedge p}_{\tilde{A}})^T$ is surjective: let $l^{\mathbf{n}-1} \otimes (l_1^{\mathbf{m}+\mathbf{n}-2} \wedge \cdots \wedge l_{\mathbf{n}-1}^{\mathbf{m}+\mathbf{n}-2}) \in S^{\mathbf{n}-1}E \otimes \Lambda^{\mathbf{n}-1} S^{\mathbf{m}+\mathbf{n}-2}E$ with $l, l_i \in E$. Such elements span the target, so it will be sufficient to show any such element is in the image. Assume first that l is distinct from the l_i. Since $\mathbf{n} \leq \mathbf{m}$, there is a polynomial $g \in S^{\mathbf{m}-1}E^*$ which vanishes on $l_1, \ldots, l_{\mathbf{n}-1}$ and is nonzero on l. Then, up to a nonzero scalar, $g \otimes (l_1^{\mathbf{m}+\mathbf{n}-2} \wedge \cdots \wedge l_{\mathbf{n}-1}^{\mathbf{m}+\mathbf{n}-2} \wedge l^{\mathbf{m}+\mathbf{n}-2})$ maps to our element.

The condition that l is distinct from the l_i may be removed by taking limits, as the image of a linear map is closed. $\qquad\square$

In §2.6.2 we will need the following extension:

Proposition 2.5.2.7 *For $2p < \mathbf{n} - 1$, there exist $A' \subset U \otimes V^*$ of dimension $2p + 1$ such that, setting $\tilde{A} = A/(A')^{\perp}$,*

$$(M_{\langle \mathbf{n}, \mathbf{n}, 1 \rangle}|_{A' \otimes V \otimes U^*})^{\wedge p}_{\tilde{A}} : V \otimes \Lambda^p \tilde{A} \rightarrow \Lambda^{p+1} \tilde{A} \otimes U$$

is injective. A general choice of A' will have this property.

Proof. Consider A' as a subspace of $S^{2n-2}E \subset A^*$ as in the proof above. Take A' spanned by $\ell_1^{2n-2-\alpha} m_1^\alpha, \dots, \ell_{2p+1}^{2n-2-\alpha} m_{2p+1}^\alpha$, where all the $4p+2$ points ℓ_k, m_j are in general position, and $\alpha < n-1$ will be chosen below. I show the transposed map is surjective. The target of the transposed map is spanned by vectors of the form $h \otimes \ell_{s_1}^{2n-2-\alpha} m_{s_1}^\alpha \wedge \cdots \wedge \ell_{s_p}^{2n-2-\alpha} m_{s_p}^\alpha$, where $\{s_1, \dots, s_p\} = S \subset [2p+1]$. The kernel of the map $(\ell_{s_i}^{2n-2-\alpha} m_{s_i}^\alpha)_{n-1,n-1} : S^{n-1}E^* \to S^{n-1}E$ has dimension $n - \alpha - 1$. Since the points were chosen in general linear position, the intersection of the p kernels will have codimension $p(\alpha+1)$. In order to imitate the proof above, we need this intersection to be nonempty and so require $p(\alpha+1) < n$. Now consider some $(\ell_j^{2n-2-\alpha} m_j^\alpha)_{n-1,n-1}$ for $j \notin S$ restricted to the intersection of the kernels. Again, since the points were chosen in general linear position, it will be injective, so its image will have dimension $n - p(\alpha+1)$. We have $p+1$ such maps, and again by general position arguments, the images will be transverse. Thus, as long as $(p+1)(n - p(\alpha+1)) \geq n$, the span of these $p+1$ images will be all of $S^n E$. Thanks to the hypothesis on p, the three inequalities on α are compatible, and we can select any α in the admissible range. Thus every $h \otimes \ell_{s_1}^{2n-2-\alpha} m_{s_1}^\alpha \wedge \cdots \wedge \ell_{s_1}^{2n-2-\alpha} m_{s_1}^\alpha$ will be the image under $(M_{\langle n,n,1 \rangle}|_{A' \otimes V \otimes U^*})_{\tilde A}^{\wedge p}$ of

$$\sum_{j \notin S} g_j \otimes \ell_j^{2n-2-\alpha} m_j^\alpha \wedge \ell_{s_1}^{2n-2-\alpha} m_{s_1}^\alpha \wedge \cdots \wedge \ell_{s_1}^{2n-2-\alpha} m_{s_1}^\alpha$$

for some $g_j \in S^{n-1}E^*$.

Write $\tilde A = A/A'^\perp$. Define

$$P_{2p+1} : G(2p+1, A^*) \to \mathbb{C}$$

$$A' \mapsto \det((M_{\langle n,n,m \rangle}|_{A' \otimes B^* \otimes C^*})_{\tilde A}^{\wedge p} : \Lambda^p \tilde A \otimes B^* \to \Lambda^{p+1} \tilde A \otimes C). \quad (2.5.4)$$

The above argument shows that P_{2p+1} is not identically zero for all $2p \leq n-1$, but since it is a polynomial, it is not zero on a general A'. $\qquad\square$

2.5.3 Why didn't We Get a Better Bound?

The above result begs the question, did we fail to get a better bound because this is the best bound Koszul flattenings can give, or is there something pathological about matrix multiplication that prevented the full power of Koszul flattenings? That is, perhaps the Koszul flattenings for $\mathbb{C}^m \otimes \mathbb{C}^m \otimes \mathbb{C}^m$ could be trivial beyond border rank $2m - \sqrt{m}$. This is not the case:

Theorem 2.5.3.1 [Lan15b] *The maximal minors of the Koszul flattening* $T_A^{\wedge p} : \Lambda^p \mathbb{C}^{2p+1} \otimes (\mathbb{C}^{2p+2})^* \to \Lambda^{p+1} \mathbb{C}^{2p+1} \otimes \mathbb{C}^{2p+2}$ *give nontrivial equations for* $\hat\sigma_r \subset \mathbb{C}^{2p+1} \otimes \mathbb{C}^{2p+2} \otimes \mathbb{C}^{2p+2}$, *the tensors of border rank at most r in* $\mathbb{C}^{2p+1} \otimes \mathbb{C}^{2p+2} \otimes \mathbb{C}^{2p+2}$, *up to $r = 4p+1$.*

For $\mathbb{C}^m \otimes \mathbb{C}^m \otimes \mathbb{C}^m$, *this implies that when* $\mathbf{m}$ *is even (resp. odd), the equations are nontrivial up to* $r = 2\mathbf{m} - 3$ *(resp.* $r = 2\mathbf{m} - 5$*).*

Exercise 2.5.3.2 (2!) Prove the theorem. ⊚

2.6 Lower Bounds for the Rank of Matrix Multiplication

2.6.1 The Results

Most tensors have rank equal to border rank, in the sense that the set of tensors of rank greater than r in $\hat{\sigma}_r$ is a proper subvariety, in particular, a set of measure zero in $\hat{\sigma}_r$. I expect matrix multiplication to have larger rank than border rank when $\mathbf{n} > 2$ because of its enormous symmetry group, as explained in Chapter 4.

The key to the rank lower bound is that our proof of the border rank lower bound used equations of relatively low degree because of the factorization $(M_{\langle \mathbf{n} \rangle})_A^{\wedge p} = (M_{\langle \mathbf{n}, \mathbf{n}, 1 \rangle})_A^{\wedge p} \otimes \mathrm{Id}_W$, so we were considering minors of a size $\binom{2\mathbf{n}-1}{\mathbf{n}}\mathbf{n}$ matrix instead of a size $\binom{2\mathbf{n}-1}{\mathbf{n}}\mathbf{n}^2$ matrix. I will show that if a low-degree polynomial is nonzero on $M_{\langle \mathbf{n} \rangle}$, and $M_{\langle \mathbf{n} \rangle}$ has an optimal rank decomposition $M_{\langle \mathbf{n} \rangle} = \sum_{j=1}^r a_j \otimes b_j \otimes c_j$, then the polynomial is already zero on a subset of the summands. This is a variant of the *substitution method* discussed in §5.3.

Theorem 2.6.1.1 [MR13] *Let* $p \le \mathbf{n}$ *be a natural number. Then*

$$\mathbf{R}(M_{\mathbf{n},\mathbf{n},\mathbf{m}}) \ge \left(1 + \frac{p}{p+1}\right)\mathbf{nm} + \mathbf{n}^2 - \left(2\binom{2p}{p+1} - \binom{2p-2}{p-1} + 2\right)\mathbf{n}.$$

$$(2.6.1)$$

When $\mathbf{n} = \mathbf{m}$,

$$\mathbf{R}(M_{\langle \mathbf{n} \rangle}) \ge \left(3 - \frac{1}{p+1}\right)\mathbf{n}^2 - \left(2\binom{2p}{p+1} - \binom{2p-2}{p-1} + 2\right)\mathbf{n}. \quad (2.6.2)$$

For example, when $p = 1$, one recovers Bläser's bound of $\frac{5}{2}\mathbf{n}^2 - 3\mathbf{n}$. When $p = 3$, the bound (2.6.2) becomes $\frac{11}{4}\mathbf{n}^2 - 26\mathbf{n}$, which improves Bläser's for $\mathbf{n} \ge 132$. A modification of the method also yields $\mathbf{R}(M_{\langle \mathbf{n} \rangle}) \ge \frac{8}{3}\mathbf{n}^2 - 7\mathbf{n}$. See [MR13, Lan14] for proofs of the modifications of the error terms.

I give a proof of a $3\mathbf{n}^2 - o(\mathbf{n}^2)$ lower bound for $\mathbf{R}(M_{\langle \mathbf{n} \rangle})$:

Theorem 2.6.1.2 [Lan14] *Let* $2p < \mathbf{n} - 1$. *Then*

$$\mathbf{R}(M_{\langle \mathbf{n},\mathbf{n},\mathbf{m} \rangle}) \ge \frac{2p+1}{p+1}\mathbf{nm} + \mathbf{n}^2 - (2p+1)\binom{2p+1}{p}\mathbf{n}.$$

To see this implies $\mathbf{R}(M_{\langle \mathbf{n} \rangle}) \ge 3\mathbf{n}^2 - o(\mathbf{n}^2)$, take $p = \log(\log(\mathbf{n}))$.

2.6.2 Proof of Theorem 2.6.1.2

We will need a few facts from algebraic geometry before the proof.

The following standard lemma, also used in [Blä03], appears in this form in [Lan12, Lemma 11.5.0.2]:

Lemma 2.6.2.1 *Given a polynomial P of degree d on $\mathbb{C}^{\mathbf{a}}$, there exists a subset of basis vectors $\{e_{i_1}, \ldots, e_{i_d}\}$ such that $P\mid_{\langle e_{i_1}, \ldots, e_{i_d}\rangle}$ is not identically zero.*

In other words, there exists a coordinate subspace $\mathbb{C}^d \subset \mathbb{C}^{\mathbf{a}}$ such that $\mathbb{C}^d \not\subset$ Zeros(P).

The lemma follows by simply choosing the basis vectors from a degree d monomial that appears in P. For example, Lemma 2.6.2.1 implies that a surface in $\mathbb{P}^3$ defined by a degree two equation cannot contain six lines whose pairwise intersections span $\mathbb{P}^3$.

Recall the Grassmannian $G(k, A)$ from Definition 2.3.3.1.

Lemma 2.6.2.2 *Let A be given a basis. For k, d satisfying $dk < \dim A$ and a nonzero homogeneous polynomial P of degree d on $\Lambda^k A$ that is not in $I(G(k, A))$, there exist dk basis vectors of A such that, denoting their dk-dimensional span by $\tilde{A}$, P restricted to $G(k, \tilde{A})$ is not identically zero.*

Proof. Consider the map $f : A^{\times k} \rightarrow \hat{G}(k, A)$ given by $(a_1, \ldots, a_k) \mapsto a_1 \wedge \cdots \wedge a_k$. Then f is surjective. Take the polynomial P and pull it back by f. Here the *pullback* $f^*(P)$ is defined by $f^*(P)(a_1, \ldots, a_k) := P(f(a_1, \ldots, a_k))$. The pullback is of degree d in each copy of A. (That is, fixing $k - 1$ of the a_j, it becomes a degree d polynomial in the kth.) Now apply Lemma 2.6.2.1 k times to obtain dk basis vectors such that the pulled-back polynomial is not identically zero restricted to their span $\tilde{A}$, and thus P restricted to $\hat{G}(k, \tilde{A})$ is not identically zero. $\qquad\square$

Remark 2.6.2.3 The bound in Lemma 2.6.2.2 is sharp: give A a basis $a_1, \ldots, a_{\mathbf{a}}$ and consider the polynomial on $\Lambda^k A$ with coordinates $x^I = x^{i_1} \cdots x^{i_k}$ corresponding to the vector $\sum_I x^I a_{i_1} \wedge \cdots \wedge a_{i_k}$:

$$P = x^{1,\ldots,k} x^{k+1,\ldots,2k} \cdots x^{(d-1)k+1,\ldots,dk}.$$

Then P restricted to $G(k, \langle a_1, \ldots, a_{dk}\rangle)$ is nonvanishing, but there is no smaller subspace spanned by basis vectors on which it is nonvanishing.

Proof of Theorem 2.6.1.2. Say $\mathbf{R}(M_{\langle \mathbf{n,n,m}\rangle}) = r$ and write an optimal expression

$$M_{\langle \mathbf{n,n,m}\rangle} = \sum_{j=1}^{r} a_j \otimes b_j \otimes c_j. \qquad (2.6.3)$$

I will show that the Koszul-flattening equation is already nonzero restricted to a subset of this expression for a judicious choice of $\tilde{A} \subset A$ of dimension $2p + 1$ with $p < \mathbf{n} - 1$. Then the rank will be at least the border rank bound plus the number of terms not in the subset. Here are the details:

Recall the polynomial P_{2p+1} from (2.5.4). It is a polynomial of degree $\binom{2p+1}{p}\mathbf{nm} > \mathbf{nm}$, so at first sight, e.g., when $\mathbf{m} \sim \mathbf{n}$, Lemma 2.6.2.2 will be of no help because $dk > \dim A = \mathbf{n}^2$, but since

$$(M_{\langle \mathbf{n},\mathbf{n},\mathbf{m}\rangle}|_{A' \otimes B^* \otimes C^*})_{\tilde{A}}^{\wedge p} = (M_{\langle \mathbf{n},\mathbf{n},1\rangle}|_{A' \otimes V \otimes U^*})_{\tilde{A}}^{\wedge p} \otimes \mathrm{Id}_{W^*},$$

we actually have $P = \tilde{P}^{\mathbf{m}}$, where

$$\tilde{P} : G(2p+1, A) \to \mathbb{C}$$
$$\tilde{A} \mapsto \det((M_{\langle \mathbf{n},\mathbf{n},1\rangle}|_{A' \otimes V \otimes U^*})_{\tilde{A}}^{\wedge p} : \Lambda^p \tilde{A} \otimes V \to \Lambda^{p+1} \tilde{A} \otimes U).$$

Hence we may work with $\tilde{P}$, which is of degree $\binom{2p+1}{p}\mathbf{n}$, which will be less than $\mathbf{n}^2$ if p is sufficiently small. Since $(M_{\langle \mathbf{n},\mathbf{n},\mathbf{m}\rangle})_A : A^* \to B \otimes C$ is injective, some subset of the a_j forms a basis of A. Lemma 2.6.2.2 implies that there exists a subset of those basis vectors of size $dk = \binom{2p+1}{p}\mathbf{n}(2p+1)$ such that if we restrict to terms of the expression (2.6.3) that use only a_j whose expansion in the fixed basis has nonzero terms from that subset of dk basis vectors, calling the sum of these terms M', we have $\underline{\mathbf{R}}(M') \geq \frac{2p+1}{p+1}\mathbf{nm}$. Let M'' be the sum of the remaining terms in the expression. There are at least $\mathbf{a} - dk = \mathbf{n}^2 - \binom{2p+1}{p}\mathbf{n}(2p+1)$ of the a_j appearing in M'' (the terms corresponding to the complementary basis vectors). Since we assumed we had an optimal expression for $M_{\langle \mathbf{n},\mathbf{n},\mathbf{m}\rangle}$, we have

$$\mathbf{R}(M_{\langle \mathbf{n},\mathbf{n},\mathbf{m}\rangle}) = \mathbf{R}(M') + \mathbf{R}(M'')$$
$$\geq \frac{2p+1}{p+1}\mathbf{nm} + \left[\mathbf{n}^2 - (2p+1)\binom{2p+1}{p}\mathbf{n}\right]. \qquad \square$$

The further lower bounds are obtained by lowering the degree of the polynomial by localizing the equations. An easy such localization is to set $X_0 = \mathrm{Id}$, which reduces the determinant of (2.4.7) to that of (2.2.1) when $p = 2$ and yields a similar reduction of degree in general. Further localizations reduce both the degree and the size of the Grassmannian, each of which improves the error term.

3

The Complexity of Matrix Multiplication II:
Asymptotic Upper Bounds

This chapter discusses progress toward the astounding conjecture that asymptotically, the complexity of multiplying two $\mathbf{n} \times \mathbf{n}$ matrices is nearly the same as the complexity of adding them. I cover the main advances in upper bounds for the exponent of matrix multiplication beyond Strassen's original discovery in 1969: the 1979 upper bound $\omega < 2.78$ of Bini et al., the 1981 bound $\omega \leq 2.55$ of Schönhage, the 1987 bound $\omega < 2.48$ of Strassen, and the Coppersmith-Winograd 1990 bound $\omega < 2.38$, emphasizing a geometric perspective. I mention recent "explanations" as to why progress essentially stopped in 1990 from [AFLG15]. In Chapter 4, I discuss other potential paths for upper bounds and present Pan's 1978 $\omega < 2.79$ [Pan78], which was the first bound to beat Strassen's. It, along with the recent bounds of [Smi13] are the only decomposition other than Strassen's implementable in practice.

The exponent ω of matrix multiplication is naturally defined in terms of tensor rank:

$$\omega := \inf\{\tau \in \mathbb{R} \mid \mathbf{R}(M_{\langle \mathbf{n} \rangle}) = O(\mathbf{n}^{\tau})\}.$$

See [BCS97, §15.1] for the proof that tensor rank yields the same exponent as other complexity measures.

The above-mentioned conjecture is that $\omega = 2$. One does not need to work asymptotically to get upper bounds on ω: Proposition 3.2.1.1 states that for all $\mathbf{n}$, $\mathbf{R}(M_{\langle \mathbf{n} \rangle}) \geq \mathbf{n}^{\omega}$. The only methods for proving upper bounds on $\mathbf{R}(M_{\langle \mathbf{n} \rangle})$ for any fixed $\mathbf{n}$ that have been used effectively are to find explicit rank decompositions, and very few of these are known.

As I explain in §3.2, Bini et al. showed that one may also define the exponent in terms of border rank, namely (see Proposition 3.2.1.10),

$$\omega = \inf\{\tau \in \mathbb{R} \mid \underline{\mathbf{R}}(M_{\langle \mathbf{n} \rangle}) = O(\mathbf{n}^{\tau})\}.$$

Again, we do not need to work asymptotically to get upper bounds on ω using border rank. Theorem 3.2.1.10 states that for all $\mathbf{n}$, $\underline{\mathbf{R}}(M_{\langle \mathbf{n} \rangle}) \geq \mathbf{n}^{\omega}$. In order to make the transition from rank to border rank, we will need a basic result in algebraic geometry. Because of this, I begin, in §3.1, with some basic facts from the subject. Just as with rank, the only methods for proving upper bounds on $\underline{\mathbf{R}}(M_{\langle\mathbf{n}\rangle})$ for any fixed $\mathbf{n}$ that have been used effectively are to find explicit border rank decompositions, and very few of these are known.

A small help is that we may also use rectangular matrix multiplication to prove upper bounds on ω: Proposition 3.2.1.10 states that for all $\mathbf{l}, \mathbf{m}, \mathbf{n}$,

$$\underline{\mathbf{R}}(M_{\langle\mathbf{m},\mathbf{n},\mathbf{l}\rangle}) \geq (\mathbf{lmn})^{\frac{\omega}{3}}.$$

But again, our knowledge of border rank is scant.

To improve the situation, one needs techniques that enable one to avoid dealing with tensors beyond the small range we have results in. After the work of Bini et al., *all upper bounds on ω are obtained via tensors other than* $M_{\langle\mathbf{l},\mathbf{m},\mathbf{n}\rangle}$.

The next advance in upper bounds, due to Schönhage (Theorem 3.3.3.1) and described in §3.3, is more involved: it says it is sufficient to prove upper bounds on sums of *disjoint* matrix multiplications.

To go beyond this, Strassen had the idea to look for a tensor $T \in A \otimes B \otimes C$ that has special combinatorial structure rendering it easy to study and that can be *degenerated* into a collection of disjoint matrix multiplications.

The inequalities regarding ω above are strict, e.g., there does not exist $\mathbf{n}$ with $\underline{\mathbf{R}}(M_{\langle\mathbf{n}\rangle})$ equal to $\mathbf{n}^\omega$. (This does not rule out $\underline{\mathbf{R}}(M_{\langle\mathbf{n}\rangle})$ equal to $2\mathbf{n}^\omega$ for all $\mathbf{n}$.) Strassen looked for *sequences* $T_N \in A_N \otimes B_N \otimes C_N$ that could be degenerated into sums $\bigoplus_{i=1}^{s(N)} M_{\langle\mathbf{l}_i(N),\mathbf{m}_i(N)\mathbf{n}_i(N)\rangle}$ with the border rank of the sums giving upper bounds on ω. This is Strassen's "laser method" described in §3.4.

More precisely, to obtain a sequence of disjoint matrix multiplication tensors, one takes a base tensor T and degenerates the tensor powers $T^{\otimes N} \in (A^{\otimes N}) \otimes (B^{\otimes N}) \otimes (C^{\otimes N})$. Strassen's degeneration is in the sense of points in the $GL(A^{\otimes N}) \times GL(B^{\otimes N}) \times GL(C^{\otimes N})$-orbit closure of $T^{\otimes N}$.

After Strassen, all other subsequent upper bounds on ω use what I will call *combinatorial restrictions* of $T^{\otimes N}$ for some "simple" tensor T, where entries of a coordinate presentation of $T^{\otimes N}$ are just set equal to zero. The choice of entries to zero out is subtle. I describe these developments in §3.4.

In addition to combinatorial restrictions, Cohn et al. exploit a geometric change of basis when a tensor is the multiplication tensor of an algebra (or even more general structures). They use the discrete Fourier transform for finite groups (and more general structures) to show that the multiplication tensor in the Fourier basis (and thus in any basis) has "low" rank but nevertheless in the standard basis admits a combinatorial restriction to a "large" sum of matrix multiplication tensors. I discuss this approach in §3.5.

The proofs in this chapter make essential use of the property from Exercise 2.5.1.9:

$$M_{\langle l,m,n \rangle} \otimes M_{\langle l',m',n' \rangle} = M_{\langle ll',mm',nn' \rangle}, \tag{3.0.1}$$

where, for tensors $T \in A \otimes B \otimes C$ and $T' \in A' \otimes B' \otimes C'$, $T \otimes T'$ is considered as a tensor in the triple tensor product $(A \otimes A') \otimes (B \otimes B') \otimes (C \otimes C')$.

3.1 Facts and Definitions from Algebraic Geometry

Standard references for this material are [Har95, Mum95, Sha07]. The first is very good for examples, while the second and third have clean proofs, with the proofs in the second more concise.

Several results from this section will be used repeatedly in this book: that the linear projection of a projective variety is a projective variety (Theorem 3.1.4.1), that projective varieties of complementary dimension must intersect (Theorem 3.1.5.1), and that the Zariski and Euclidean closures of certain sets agree (Theorem 3.1.6.1).

3.1.1 Projective Varieties

Varieties in a vector space V defined by homogeneous polynomials are invariant under rescaling. For this and other reasons, it will be convenient to work in projective space (Definition 2.3.3.1). Write $\pi : V \backslash 0 \to \mathbb{P}V$ for the projection map. For $X \subset \mathbb{P}V$, write $\pi^{-1}(X) \cup \{0\} =: \hat{X} \subset V$ and $\pi(y) = [y]$. If $\hat{X} \subset V$ is a variety, I will also refer to $X \subset \mathbb{P}V$ as a variety. The zero set in V of a collection of polynomials on V is called an *affine variety*, and the image in $\mathbb{P}V$ of the zero set of a collection of homogeneous polynomials on V is called a *projective variety*. For subsets $Z \subset V$, $\mathbb{P}Z \subset \mathbb{P}V$ denotes its image under π. If $P \in S^d V^*$ is an irreducible polynomial, then its zero set $\mathrm{Zeros}(P) \subset \mathbb{P}V$ is an irreducible variety, called a *hypersurface of degree d*. For a variety $X \subset \mathbb{P}V$, $I_d(X) := \{P \in S^d V^* \mid X \subset \mathrm{Zeros}(P)\}$ denotes the ideal of X in degree d, and $I(X) = \oplus_d I_d(X) \subset Sym(V^*)$ is the ideal of X.

We will be mostly concerned with varieties in spaces of tensors (for the study of matrix multiplication) and spaces of polynomials (for geometric complexity theory).

3.1.2 Examples of Varieties

1 Projective space $\mathbb{P}V \subseteq \mathbb{P}V$.

2 The *Segre variety* of rank one tensors

$$\sigma_1 = Seg(\mathbb{P}A_1 \times \cdots \times \mathbb{P}A_n)$$
$$:= \mathbb{P}\{T \in A_1 \otimes \cdots \otimes A_n \mid \exists a_j \in A_j \text{ such that }$$
$$T = a_1 \otimes \cdots \otimes a_n\} \subset \mathbb{P}(A_1 \otimes \cdots \otimes A_n).$$

3 The *Veronese variety*

$$v_d(\mathbb{P}V) = \mathbb{P}\{P \in S^d V \mid P = x^d \text{ for some } x \in V\} \subset \mathbb{P}S^d V.$$

4 The *Grassmannian*

$$G(k, V) := \mathbb{P}\{T \in \Lambda^k V \mid \exists v_1, \ldots, v_k \in V \text{ such that}$$
$$T = v_1 \wedge \cdots \wedge v_k\} \subset \mathbb{P}\Lambda^k V.$$

5 The *Chow variety*

$$Ch_d(V) := \overline{\mathbb{P}\{P \in S^d V \mid \exists v_1, \ldots, v_d \in V \text{ such that } P = v_1 \cdots v_d\}} \subset \mathbb{P}S^d V.$$

By definition, projective space is a variety (the zero set of no equations).

Exercise 3.1.2.1 (2) Show that $Seg(\mathbb{P}A_1 \times \cdots \times \mathbb{P}A_n)$ is the zero set of the size two minors of the *flattenings* $A_j^* \rightarrow A_1 \otimes \cdots \otimes \hat{A}_j \otimes \cdots \otimes A_n$, for $1 \leq j \leq n$.

To get equations for $v_d(\mathbb{P}V)$, given $P \in S^d V$, consider the *flattening* $P_{1,d-1}$: $V^* \rightarrow S^{d-1}V$ defined by $\frac{\partial}{\partial v} \mapsto \frac{\partial P}{\partial v}$. For example when $d = 4$, $\mathbf{v} = 2$, and $P = \sum_{i=0}^4 p_i x^i y^{4-i}$, the matrix representing $P_{1,3}$ is

$$\begin{pmatrix} p_4 & p_3 & p_2 & p_1 \\ p_3 & p_2 & p_1 & p_0 \end{pmatrix} \tag{3.1.1}$$

and $v_4(\mathbb{P}^1)$ is the zero set of the six size two minors of this matrix.

Exercise 3.1.2.2 (1) Show that $v_d(\mathbb{P}V)$ is the zero set of the size two minors of the flattening $V^* \rightarrow S^{d-1}V$.

We saw equations for the Grassmannian in §2.6.2.

Exercise 3.1.4.2 will show that it is not necessary to take the Zariski closure when defining the Chow variety. Equations for the Chow variety are known (see §9.6). However, generators of the ideal of the Chow variety are not known explicitly – what is known is presented in Chapter 9.

3.1.3 Dimension via Tangent Spaces

Informally, the dimension of a variety is the number of parameters needed to describe it locally. For example, the dimension of $\mathbb{P}V$ is $\mathbf{v} - 1$ because in coordinates on the open neighborhood where $x_1 \neq 0$, points of $\mathbb{P}V$ have a unique expression as $[1, x_2, \ldots, x_\mathbf{v}]$, where $x_2, \ldots, x_\mathbf{v}$ are free parameters.

I first define dimension of a variety via dimensions of vector spaces. Define the *affine tangent space* to $X \subset \mathbb{P}V$ at $[x] \in X$, $\hat{T}_x \hat{X} = \hat{T}_{[x]} X \subset V$ to be the span of the tangent vectors $x'(0)$ to analytic curves $x(t)$ on $\hat{X}$ with $x(0) = x$, and note that this is independent of the choice of (nonzero) $x \in [x]$. A point $x \in \hat{X}$ is defined to be a *smooth* point if $\dim \hat{T}_y \hat{X}$ is constant for all y in some neighborhood of x.

The *dimension* of an irreducible variety $\hat{X} \subset V$ is the dimension of the tangent space at a smooth point of $\hat{X}$. If x is a smooth point, $\dim X = \dim \hat{X} - 1 = \dim \hat{T}_x \hat{X} - 1$. If x is not a smooth point, it is called a *singular point*, and we let $X_{\text{sing}} \subset X$ denote the singular points of X. A variety of dimension one is called a *curve*.

Remark 3.1.3.1 The above definitions of smooth points and dimension implicitly assume that X is a *reduced* variety. A hypersurface $\{P = 0\}$ is reduced if under a decomposition of P into irreducible factors $P = p_1^{a_1} \cdots p_r^{a_r}$, all $a_j = 1$. For example, $\{\ell^{n-m} \text{perm}_m = 0\}$ is not reduced when $n - m > 1$. The definition of dimension in §3.1.5 avoids this problem. For a definition of singular points that avoids this problem, see §6.3.1.

Exercise 3.1.3.2 (2) Show that $\dim\{\det_n = 0\}_{\text{sing}} = n^2 - 4$.

If a Zariski open subset of a variety is given parametrically, then one can calculate the tangent space to the variety via the parameter space. For example, $\hat{Seg}(\mathbb{P}A \times \mathbb{P}B \times \mathbb{P}C)$ may be thought of as the image of the map

$$A \times B \times C \to A \otimes B \otimes C$$
$$(a, b, c) \mapsto a \otimes b \otimes c,$$

so to compute $\hat{T}_{[a \otimes b \otimes c]} Seg(\mathbb{P}A \times \mathbb{P}B \times \mathbb{P}C)$, take curves $a(t) \subset A$ with $a(0) = a$ and similarly for B, C, and then $\frac{d}{dt}|_{t=0} a(t) \otimes b(t) \otimes c(t) = a' \otimes b \otimes c + a \otimes b' \otimes c + a \otimes b \otimes c'$ by the Leibnitz rule. Since a' can be any vector in A and similarly for b', c', we conclude

$$\hat{T}_{[a \otimes b \otimes c]} Seg(\mathbb{P}A \times \mathbb{P}B \times \mathbb{P}C) = A \otimes b \otimes c + a \otimes B \otimes c + a \otimes b \otimes C.$$

The right-hand side spans a space of dimension $\mathbf{a} + \mathbf{b} + \mathbf{c} - 2$, so $\dim(Seg(\mathbb{P}A \times \mathbb{P}B \times \mathbb{P}C)) = \mathbf{a} + \mathbf{b} + \mathbf{c} - 3$.

I can now pay off two debts: in §2.1.1, I asserted that the fundamental theorem of linear algebra is something of a miracle, and in Theorem 2.1.5.1, I asserted that a general tensor in $\mathbb{C}^{\mathbf{m}} \otimes \mathbb{C}^{\mathbf{m}} \otimes \mathbb{C}^{\mathbf{m}}$ has tensor rank around $\frac{\mathbf{m}^2}{3}$.

A general point of σ_2 is of the form $[a_1 \otimes b_1 \otimes c_1 + a_2 \otimes b_2 \otimes c_2]$, and a general tangent vector at that point is of the form $a_1 \otimes b_1 \otimes c_1' + a_1 \otimes b_1' \otimes c_1 + a_1' \otimes b_1 \otimes c_1 + a_2 \otimes b_2 \otimes c_2' + a_2 \otimes b_2' \otimes c_2 + a_2' \otimes b_2 \otimes c_2$; hence

$$\hat{T}_{[a_1 \otimes b_1 \otimes c_1 + a_2 \otimes b_2 \otimes c_2]} \sigma_2 = a_1 \otimes b_1 \otimes C + a_1 \otimes B \otimes c_1 + A \otimes b_1 \otimes c_1$$
$$+ a_2 \otimes b_2 \otimes C + a_2 \otimes B \otimes c_2 + A \otimes b_2 \otimes c_2$$

so that $\dim \sigma_2 \leq 2(\dim(Seg(\mathbb{P}A \times \mathbb{P}B \times \mathbb{P}C))) + 2 - 1$ (and equality clearly holds if $\mathbf{a}, \mathbf{b}, \mathbf{c} \geq 3$) and similarly $\dim \sigma_r \leq r(\dim(Seg(\mathbb{P}A \times \mathbb{P}B \times \mathbb{P}C))) + r - 1$. The first chance this has to be the entire ambient space is when this number is $\mathbf{abc} - 1$. When $\mathbf{a} = \mathbf{b} = \mathbf{c} = \mathbf{m}$, this means $r \geq \frac{\mathbf{m}^3}{3\mathbf{m}-2}$, paying the second debt.

For the first,

$$\hat{T}_{[a_1 \otimes b_1 + a_2 \otimes b_2]} \sigma_{2,A \otimes B} = \mathrm{span}\{a_1 \otimes b_1' + a_1' \otimes b_1 + a_2 \otimes b_2' + a_2' \otimes b_2\}$$
$$= A \otimes \mathrm{span}\{b_1, b_2\} + \mathrm{span}\{a_1, a_2\} \otimes B,$$

and this space has dimension $2 \dim Seg(\mathbb{P}A \times \mathbb{P}B)$, instead of the expected $2 \dim Seg(\mathbb{P}A \times \mathbb{P}B) + 1$. This accounts for the upper semicontinuity of matrix rank, which fails for tensor rank: any point on a tangent line, i.e., a point of the form $a' \otimes b + a \otimes b'$, is also transparently on a secant line, i.e., the sum of two rank one matrices.

Exercise 3.1.3.3 (1) Compute $\hat{T}_{[x^d]} v_d(\mathbb{P}V)$.

3.1.4 Noether Normalization

Consider the curve $\{xy = 1\} \subset \mathbb{C}^2$:

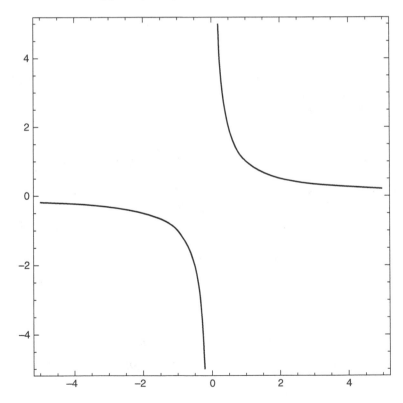

If we project the curve onto the x-axis, we get the set $\{x \in \mathbb{C} \mid x \neq 0\}$, which, as was discussed in §1.1.14, is not Zariski closed.

One of the many wonderful things about projective space is that the projection of an algebraic variety to a hyperplane is still an algebraic variety. I remind the reader that unless mentioned otherwise, I work exclusively over the complex numbers, because the next theorem is false over $\mathbb{R}$:

Theorem 3.1.4.1 *If $X \subset \mathbb{P}W$ is a variety, $L \subset W$ is a subspace with $\mathbb{P}L \cap X = \emptyset$, and one considers the projection map $p : W \to W/L$, then $\mathbb{P}p(\hat{X}) \subset \mathbb{P}(W/L)$ is also a variety.*

Theorem 3.1.4.1 is part of the *Noether normalization* theorem (see, e.g., [Sha07, §1.5.4] or [Mum95, §2C]). It is proved via elimination theory. In addition to failing in affine space, this projection property fails over $\mathbb{R}$: the curve in $\mathbb{R}\mathbb{P}^2$ given by $x^2 + z^2 - y^2 = 0$, when projected from $[1, 0, 0]$, is not a real algebraic variety. (It consists of $\mathbb{R}\mathbb{P}^1 \backslash \{[0, 1]\}$.)

Exercise 3.1.4.2 (1) Show that if $W = V^{\otimes d}$ and L is the $GL(V)$-complement to $S^d V$ in $V^{\otimes d}$, taking $p : V^{\otimes d} \to V^{\otimes d}/L \simeq S^d V$, then $p(Seg(\mathbb{P}V \times \cdots \times \mathbb{P}V)) = Ch_d(V)$. Conclude the closure is not needed in the definition of the Chow variety. ⊚

The ideal of the projection of a variety from a coordinate point is obtained by eliminating that coordinate from the equations in the ideal. For example, give $S^4 \mathbb{C}^2$ coordinates $(p_4, p_3, p_2, p_1, p_0)$ as above and project from p_2. Eliminating p_2 from the equations

$$p_4 p_2 - p_3^2, \ p_4 p_1 - p_2 p_3, \ p_4 p_0 - p_1 p_3, \ p_3 p_1 - p_2^2, \ p_2 p_0 - p_1^2,$$

gives the ideal generated by

$$p_4 p_0 - p_1 p_3, \ p_3^3 - p_4^2 p_1, \ p_1^3 - p_0^2 p_3.$$

Exercise 3.1.4.3 (2) What equations does one get when projecting from p_3? Give a geometric explanation why the answer is different. (A complete answer to this question is beyond what we have covered; I am just asking for some equations.) ⊚

Remark 3.1.4.4 Since elimination theory doesn't care which point one projects from, one can even project from a point on a variety. The resulting "map" is not defined at the point one projects from, but the Zariski closure of the image of the points where it is defined at is well defined. This is an example of a *rational map*.

Exercise 3.1.4.5 (2) What ideal does one get when projecting $v_4(\mathbb{P}^1)$ from p_4? (A complete answer to this question is beyond what we have covered; I am just asking for some equations.) ⊚

As long as X does not surject onto $\mathbb{P}V/L$, we can continue projecting it to smaller and smaller projective spaces.

If $X \subset \mathbb{P}V$ is a projective variety and $f : X \to Y \subset \mathbb{P}^N$ is given by $N + 1$ homogeneous polynomials on V, then f is an example of a *regular map*. If $X \subset \mathbb{C}^M$ and $Y \subset \mathbb{C}^N$ are affine varieties, a regular map $f : X \to Y$ is one given by N polynomials $p_1, \dots, p_N$ on $\mathbb{C}^M$, such that $(p_1(x), \dots, p_N(x)) \in Y$ for all $x \in X$. For the definition of a regular map, see e.g., [Sha07, §1.2.3]. If $X \subset \mathbb{C}^N$ is an affine variety, $\mathbb{C}[X] := \mathbb{C}[x_1, \dots, x_N]/I(X)$ denotes the space of *regular functions* on X.

Exercise 3.1.4.6 (1) If X, Y are affine varieties and $f : X \to Y$ is a regular map, show that one gets a map $f^* : \mathbb{C}[Y] \to \mathbb{C}[X]$, called the induced *pullback map*, and that f^* is injective if f is surjective.

Theorem 3.1.4.1 generalizes to the following:

Theorem 3.1.4.7 *(see, e.g., [Sha07, §5.2, Theorem 1.10]) If X is a projective variety and $f : X \to Y$ is a regular map, then $f(X)$ is Zariski closed.*

Exercise 3.1.4.8 (1) Show that if X is irreducible and $f : X \to Y$ is regular, then $f(X)$ is irreducible. ⊚

3.1.5 Dimension via Projection

The dimension of $X \subset \mathbb{P}V$ is also the largest integer n such that there exists a surjective linear projection onto a $\mathbb{P}^n$. In this case the surjective projection $X \to \mathbb{P}(V/\mathbb{C}^c)$ may be chosen to be finite to one. The integer $c = \mathbf{v} - 1 - n$ is called the *codimension* of X in $\mathbb{P}V$. Noether normalization implies that a general linear space $\mathbb{P}L$ will satisfy $\dim(X \cap \mathbb{P}L) = \mathbf{v} - 1 - n - \dim \mathbb{P}L$. In particular, the intersection of X with a general linear space of dimension $c + 1$ will be a finite number of points. This number of points is called the *degree* of X.

A consequence of this more algebraic definition of dimension is the following result:

Theorem 3.1.5.1 *Let $X, Y \subset \mathbb{P}^N$ (resp. $X, Y \subset \mathbb{C}^N$) be irreducible projective (resp. affine) varieties.*

Then any nonempty component Z of $X \cap Y$ has $\dim Z \geq \dim X + \dim Y - N$.

Moreover, in the projective case, if $\dim X + \dim Y - N > 0$, then $X \cap Y \neq \emptyset$.

For the proof, see, e.g., [Sha07, §1.6.4].

3.1.6 Zariski and Euclidean Closure

Recall from §1.1.14.2 that the Zariski closure of a set can be larger than the Euclidean closure. Nevertheless, the following theorem, proved using Noether normalization, shows that in our situation, the two closures agree:

Theorem 3.1.6.1 *Let $Z \subset \mathbb{P}V$ be a subset. Then the Euclidean closure of Z is contained in the Zariski closure of Z. If Z contains a Zariski open subset of its Zariski closure, and $\overline{Z}$ is irreducible, then the two closures coincide. The same assertions hold for subsets $Z \subset V$.*

A proof that uses nothing but Noether normalization is given in [Mum95, Theorem 2.33]. I present a proof using the following basic fact: for every irreducible algebraic curve $C \subset \mathbb{P}V$, there exists a smooth algebraic curve $\tilde{C}$ and a surjective algebraic map $\pi : \tilde{C} \to C$ that is one-to-one over the smooth points of C. (More precisely, π is a *finite map* as defined in §9.5.1.) See, e.g., [Sha07, §1.2.5.3] for a proof. The curve $\tilde{C}$ is called the *normalization* of C.

The theorem will follow immediately from the following lemma:

Lemma 3.1.6.2 *Let $Z \subset \mathbb{P}V$ be an irreducible variety and let $Z^0 \subset Z$ be a Zariski open subset. Let $p \in Z \backslash Z^0$. Then there exists an analytic curve $C(t)$ such that $C(t) \in Z^0$ for all $t \neq 0$ and $\lim_{t \to 0} C(t) = p$.*

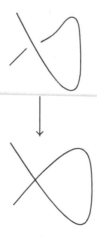

Proof. Let c be the codimension of Z and take a general linear space $\mathbb{P}L \subset \mathbb{P}V$ of dimension $c + 1$ that contains p. Then $\mathbb{P}L \cap Z$ will be a possibly reducible algebraic curve containing p. Take a component C of the curve that contains p. If p is a smooth point of the curve, we are done, as we can expand a Taylor series about p. Otherwise, take the normalization $\pi : \tilde{C} \to C$ and a point of $\pi^{-1}(p)$, expand a Taylor series about that point, and compose with π to obtain the desired analytic curve. $\square$

3.2 The Upper Bounds of Bini, Capovani, Lotti, and Romani

3.2.1 Rank, Border Rank, and the Exponent of Matrix Multiplication

Proposition 3.2.1.1 [Bin80] *For all* $\mathbf{n}$, $R(M_{\langle \mathbf{n} \rangle}) \geq \mathbf{n}^{\omega}$, *i.e.*, $\omega \leq \frac{\log R(M_{\langle \mathbf{n} \rangle})}{\log(\mathbf{n})}$.

Proof. By the definitions of the exponent and O, there exists a constant C such that $CR(M_{\langle \mathbf{n} \rangle}) \geq \mathbf{n}^{\omega}$ for all $\mathbf{n}$. By (3.0.1) and Exercise 2.1.6.3, $R(M_{\langle \mathbf{n}^k \rangle}) \leq R(M_{\langle \mathbf{n} \rangle})^k$. Say $R(M_{\langle \mathbf{n} \rangle}) = r$. Then $Cr^k \geq (\mathbf{n}^k)^{\omega}$, i.e., $C^{\frac{1}{k}} r \geq \mathbf{n}^{\omega}$. Now let k go to infinity; we get $r \geq \mathbf{n}^{\omega}$. $\square$

Remark 3.2.1.2 The calculation in the proof of Proposition 3.2.1.1 is typical in the upper bound literature and will show up several times in this chapter: one has an initially hazardous constant (in this case, C) that gets washed out asymptotically by taking high tensor powers of $M_{\langle \mathbf{n} \rangle}$.

Proposition 3.2.1.3 *For all* $\mathbf{l}, \mathbf{m}, \mathbf{n}$, $(\mathbf{lmn})^{\frac{\omega}{3}} \leq R(M_{\langle \mathbf{m}, \mathbf{n}, \mathbf{l} \rangle})$, *i.e.*, $\omega \leq \frac{3 \log R(M_{\langle \mathbf{m}, \mathbf{n}, \mathbf{l} \rangle})}{\log(\mathbf{mnl})}$.

Exercise 3.2.1.4 (2) Prove Proposition 3.2.1.3. ⊚

Remark 3.2.1.5 The inequalities in Propositions 3.2.1.1 and 3.2.1.3 are strict; see Theorem 3.3.3.5.

To show that ω may also be defined in terms of border rank, introduce a sequence of ranks that interpolate between rank and border rank.

We say $R_h(T) \leq r$ if there exists an expression

$$T = \lim_{\epsilon \to 0} \frac{1}{\epsilon^h} (a_1(\epsilon) \otimes b_1(\epsilon) \otimes c_1(\epsilon) + \cdots + a_r(\epsilon) \otimes b_r(\epsilon) \otimes c_r(\epsilon)) \qquad (3.2.1)$$

where $a_j(\epsilon), b_j(\epsilon), c_j(\epsilon)$ are analytic functions of ϵ.

Proposition 3.2.1.6 $\underline{R}(T) \leq r$ *if and only if there exists an* h *such that* $R_h(T) \leq r$.

Proof. We need to show $\underline{R}(T) \leq r$ implies there exists an h with $R_h(T) \leq r$. Since $Seg(\mathbb{P}A \times \mathbb{P}B \times \mathbb{P}C)$ is just the product of three projective spaces, every curve in $Seg(\mathbb{P}A \times \mathbb{P}B \times \mathbb{P}C)$ is of the form $[a(t) \otimes b(t) \otimes c(t)]$ for some curves $a(t) \subset A$, etc., and if the curve is analytic, the functions $a(t), b(t), c(t)$ can be taken to be analytic as well. Thus every analytic curve in $\sigma_r^0(Seg(\mathbb{P}A \times \mathbb{P}B \times \mathbb{P}C))$ may be written as $[\sum_{j=1}^{r} a_j(t) \otimes b_j(t) \otimes c_j(t)]$ for some analytic curves

$a_j(t) \subset A$, etc. Since the Euclidean and Zariski closures of $\hat{\sigma}_r^0$ agree by Theorem 3.1.6.1, we conclude that if $T \in \hat{\sigma}_r$, then $\mathbf{R}_h(T) \le r$ for h equal to the order of first nonzero term in the Taylor expansion of $\sum_{j=1}^{r} a_j(t) \otimes b_j(t) \otimes c_j(t)$. $\qquad\square$

Proposition 3.2.1.7 *If* $\mathbf{R}_h(T) \le r$, *then* $\mathbf{R}(T) \le r\binom{h+2}{2} < rh^2$.

Proof. Write T as in (3.2.1). Then T is the coefficient of the ϵ^h term of the expression in parentheses. For each summand, there is a contribution of $\sum_{\alpha+\beta+\gamma=h}(\epsilon^\alpha a_\alpha) \otimes (\epsilon^\beta b_\beta) \otimes (\epsilon^\gamma c_\gamma)$ that consists of $\binom{h+2}{2}$ terms. $\qquad\square$

Remark 3.2.1.8 In fact, $\mathbf{R}(T) \le r(h+1)$; see Exercise 3.5.3.3.

Exercise 3.2.1.9 (1) Show that for $T \in A \otimes B \otimes C$, if $\mathbf{R}_h(T) \le r$, then $\mathbf{R}_{Nh}(T^{\otimes N}) \le r^N$, where $T^{\otimes N}$ is considered as an element of the triple tensor product $(A^{\otimes N}) \otimes (B^{\otimes N}) \otimes (C^{\otimes N})$.

Theorem 3.2.1.10 [Bini, [Bin80]] *For all* $\mathbf{l}, \mathbf{m}, \mathbf{n}$, $\omega \le \frac{3\log \mathbf{R}(M_{\langle \mathbf{m},\mathbf{n},\mathbf{l}\rangle})}{\log(\mathbf{mnl})}$.

Proof. Write $r = \underline{\mathbf{R}}(M_{\langle \mathbf{m},\mathbf{n},\mathbf{l}\rangle})$. Set $N = \mathbf{mnl}$. We have $\mathbf{R}_h(M_{\langle N\rangle}) \le r^3$ for some h and thus $\mathbf{R}(M_{\langle N^k\rangle}) \le r^{3k}(hk)^2$, which implies

$$(N^k)^\omega \le r^{3k}(hk)^2,$$

so

$$N^\omega \le r^3 (hk)^{\frac{2}{k}}.$$

Letting $k \to \infty$ gives the result. $\qquad\square$

3.2.2 Bini et al.'s Algorithm

Recall from §2.1.4 that $\underline{\mathbf{R}}(M_{\langle 2\rangle}^{red}) \le 5$.

Exercise 3.2.2.1 (1) Use that $\underline{\mathbf{R}}(M_{\langle 2\rangle}^{red}) \le 5$ to show $\underline{\mathbf{R}}(M_{\langle 2,2,3\rangle}) \le 10$. More generally, show that if $\underline{\mathbf{R}}(M_{\langle \mathbf{m},2,2\rangle}^{red}) = r$ and $\underline{\mathbf{R}}(M_{\langle \mathbf{m}',2,2\rangle}^{red}) = r'$, then setting $n = m + m' - 1$, $\underline{\mathbf{R}}(M_{\langle n,2,2\rangle}) \le r + r'$. $\circledcirc$

Using Proposition 3.2.1.10, we conclude the following:

Theorem 3.2.2.2 [BCRL79] $\omega < 2.78$.

3.3 Schönhage's Upper Bounds

The next contribution to upper bounds for the exponent of matrix multiplication was Schönhage's discovery that the border rank of the sum of two tensors in disjoint spaces can be smaller than the sum of the border ranks and that this failure could be exploited to prove further upper bounds on the exponent. This result enables one to prove upper bounds with tensors that are easier to analyze because of their low border rank. Before giving Schönhage's bounds, I begin with geometric preliminaries on orbit closures.

3.3.1 Orbit Closures

Orbit closures will play a central role in our study of GCT. They also play a role in the work of Schönhage and Strassen on matrix multiplication.

When $r \leq \mathbf{a}_i$ for $1 \leq i \leq n$, $\sigma_r(Seg(\mathbb{P}A_1 \times \cdots \times \mathbb{P}A_n))$ is an *orbit closure*: let $a_j^{\alpha_j}$, $1 \leq \alpha_j \leq \mathbf{a}_j$, be a basis of A_j; then

$$\sigma_r(Seg(\mathbb{P}A_1 \times \cdots \times \mathbb{P}A_n))$$
$$= \overline{GL(A_1) \times \cdots \times GL(A_n) \cdot [a_1^1 \otimes \cdots \otimes a_n^1 + \cdots + a_1^r \otimes \cdots \otimes a_n^r]}$$
$$\subset \mathbb{P}(A_1 \otimes \cdots \otimes A_n).$$

Write $M_{\langle 1 \rangle}^{\oplus r} = \sum_{j=1}^r a_j \otimes b_j \otimes c_j \in \mathbb{C}^r \otimes \mathbb{C}^r \otimes \mathbb{C}^r$, where $\{a_j\}, \{b_j\}, \{c_j\}$ are bases. This tensor is sometimes called the *unit tensor*. Then

$$\sigma_r(Seg(\mathbb{P}^{r-1} \times \mathbb{P}^{r-1} \times \mathbb{P}^{r-1})) = \overline{GL_r \times GL_r \times GL_r \cdot [M_{\langle 1 \rangle}^{\oplus r}]}. \quad (3.3.1)$$

Exercise 3.3.1.1 (2) Let V be a G-module and let $v, w \in V$. Show that $w \in \overline{G \cdot v}$ if and only if $\overline{G \cdot w} \subseteq \overline{G \cdot v}$.

Proposition 3.3.1.2 *If $T' \in \overline{GL(A) \times GL(B) \times GL(C) \cdot T} \subset A \otimes B \otimes C$, then $\underline{\mathbf{R}}(T') \leq \underline{\mathbf{R}}(T)$.*

Exercise 3.3.1.3 (1) Prove Proposition 3.3.1.2. ⊙

Definition 3.3.1.4 If $T' \in \overline{GL(A) \times GL(B) \times GL(C) \cdot T} \subset A \otimes B \otimes C$, we say T' is a *degeneration* of T.

Consider the orbit closure of the matrix multiplication tensor

$$\overline{GL(A) \times GL(B) \times GL(C) \cdot [M_{\langle U,V,W \rangle}]} \subset \mathbb{P}(A \otimes B \otimes C).$$

By Exercise 3.3.1.1, we may rephrase our characterization of border rank as, taking inclusions $A, B, C \subset \mathbb{C}^r$,

$$\underline{\mathbf{R}}(M_{\langle \mathbf{n} \rangle}) \leq r \Leftrightarrow [M_{\langle \mathbf{n} \rangle}] \in \sigma_r(Seg(\mathbb{P}A \times \mathbb{P}B \times \mathbb{P}C))$$
$$\Leftrightarrow \overline{GL_r \times GL_r \times GL_r \cdot [M_{\langle \mathbf{n} \rangle}]} \subset \sigma_r(Seg(\mathbb{P}^{r-1} \times \mathbb{P}^{r-1} \times \mathbb{P}^{r-1}))$$
$$\Leftrightarrow \overline{GL_r \times GL_r \times GL_r \cdot [M_{\langle \mathbf{n} \rangle}]} \subset \overline{GL_r \times GL_r \times GL_r \cdot [M_{\langle 1 \rangle}^{\oplus r}]}.$$

3.3.2 Schönhage's Example

Recall from Exercise 2.1.7.6 that $\underline{\mathbf{R}}(M_{\langle 1,\mathbf{m},\mathbf{n} \rangle}) = \mathbf{mn}$ and $\underline{\mathbf{R}}(M_{\langle N,1,1 \rangle}) = N$. Recall the notation from §2.1.6 that if $T_1 \in A_1 \otimes B_1 \otimes C_1$ and $T_2 \in A_2 \otimes B_2 \otimes C_2$, we define the tensor $T_1 \oplus T_2 \in (A_1 \oplus A_2) \otimes (B_1 \oplus B_2) \otimes (C_1 \oplus C_2)$. (In Exercise 5.3.1.6 you will show that $\underline{\mathbf{R}}(M_{\langle 1,\mathbf{m},\mathbf{n}\rangle} \oplus M_{\langle N,1,1\rangle}) = \mathbf{mn} + N$.)

Theorem 3.3.2.1 (Schönhage [Sch81]) *Set* $N = (\mathbf{n} - 1)(\mathbf{m} - 1)$. *Then*

$$\underline{\mathbf{R}}(M_{\langle 1,\mathbf{m},\mathbf{n}\rangle} \oplus M_{\langle N,1,1\rangle}) = \mathbf{mn} + 1.$$

Proof. By conciseness, we only need to show $\underline{\mathbf{R}}(M_{\langle 1,\mathbf{m},\mathbf{n}\rangle} \oplus M_{\langle N,1,1\rangle}) \le \mathbf{mn} + 1$. Write

$$M_{\langle 1,\mathbf{m},\mathbf{n}\rangle} = \sum_{i=1}^{\mathbf{m}} \sum_{j=1}^{\mathbf{n}} x_i \otimes y_j \otimes z_{i,j},$$

$$M_{\langle N,1,1\rangle} = \sum_{u=1}^{\mathbf{m}-1} \sum_{v=1}^{\mathbf{n}-1} x_{u,v} \otimes y_{u,v} \otimes z.$$

Then

$$M_{\langle 1,\mathbf{m},\mathbf{n}\rangle} \oplus M_{\langle N,1,1\rangle} = \lim_{t \to 0} \frac{1}{t^2} \Bigg[\sum_{u=1}^{\mathbf{m}-1} \sum_{v=1}^{\mathbf{n}-1} (x_u + tx_{uv}) \otimes (y_v + ty_{uv}) \otimes (z + t^2 z_{uv})$$

$$+ \sum_{u=1}^{\mathbf{m}-1} x_u \otimes \left(y_{\mathbf{n}} + t\left(-\sum_v y_{uv} \right) \right) \otimes (z + t^2 z_{u\mathbf{n}})$$

$$+ \sum_{v=1}^{\mathbf{n}-1} \left(x_{\mathbf{m}} + t\left(-\sum_u x_{uv} \right) \right) \otimes y_v \otimes (z + t^2 z_{\mathbf{m}v})$$

$$+ x_{\mathbf{m}} \otimes y_{\mathbf{n}} \otimes \left(z + t^2 z_{\mathbf{mn}} \right) - \left(\sum_i x_i \right) \otimes \left(\sum_s y_s \right) \otimes z \Bigg].$$

$\square$

For a discussion of the geometry of this limit, see [Lan12, §11.2.2].

3.3.3 Schönhage's Asymptotic Sum Inequality

To develop intuition how an upper bound on a sum of matrix multiplications could give an upper bound on a single matrix multiplication, say we knew $\underline{\mathbf{R}}(M_{\langle \mathbf{n}\rangle}^{\oplus s}) \le r$ with $s \le \mathbf{n}^3$. Then, to compute $M_{\langle \mathbf{n}^2\rangle}$, we could write $M_{\langle \mathbf{n}^2\rangle} = M_{\langle \mathbf{n}\rangle} \otimes M_{\langle \mathbf{n}\rangle}$. At worst, this is evaluating $\mathbf{n}^3$ disjoint copies of $M_{\langle \mathbf{n}\rangle}$. Now group these $\mathbf{n}^3$ disjoint copies in groups of s and apply the bound to obtain a savings.

Here is the precise statement:

Theorem 3.3.3.1 [Sch81] *[Schönhage's asymptotic sum inequality] For all* $l_i, m_i, n_i,$ *with* $1 \leq i \leq s,$

$$\sum_{i=1}^{s} (\mathbf{m}_i \mathbf{n}_i \mathbf{l}_i)^{\frac{\omega}{3}} \leq \underline{\mathbf{R}}\left(\bigoplus_{i=1}^{s} M_{\langle \mathbf{m}_i, \mathbf{n}_i, \mathbf{l}_i \rangle}\right).$$

The main step of the proof, and an outline of the rest of the argument, is given below.

Remark 3.3.3.2 A similar result (also proven in [Sch81]) holds for the border rank of the multiplication of matrices with some entries equal to zero, where the product $\mathbf{m}_i \mathbf{n}_i \mathbf{l}_i$ is replaced by the number of multiplications in the naïve algorithm for the matrices with zeros.

Here is a special case that isolates the new ingredient (following [Blä13]):

Lemma 3.3.3.3

$$\mathbf{n}^{\omega} \leq \left\lceil \frac{\underline{\mathbf{R}}(M_{\langle \mathbf{n} \rangle}^{\oplus s})}{s} \right\rceil.$$

In particular, $s\mathbf{n}^{\omega} \leq \underline{\mathbf{R}}(M_{\langle \mathbf{n} \rangle}^{\oplus s}).$

Proof. Let $r = \underline{\mathbf{R}}(M_{\langle \mathbf{n} \rangle}^{\oplus s}).$ It is sufficient to show that for all $N,$

$$\underline{\mathbf{R}}\left(M_{\langle \mathbf{n}^N \rangle}^{\oplus s}\right) \leq \left\lceil \frac{r}{s} \right\rceil^{N} s \qquad (3.3.2)$$

as then, since trivially $\underline{\mathbf{R}}(M_{\langle \mathbf{n}^N \rangle}^{\oplus s}) \geq \underline{\mathbf{R}}(M_{\langle \mathbf{n}^N \rangle}) \geq (\mathbf{n}^N)^{\omega},$ we have

$$(\mathbf{n}^N)^{\omega} \leq \left\lceil \frac{r}{s} \right\rceil^{N} s,$$

i.e.,

$$\mathbf{n}^{\omega} \leq \left\lceil \frac{r}{s} \right\rceil s^{\frac{1}{N}}$$

and the result follows by letting $N \to \infty.$

I prove (3.3.2) by induction on N. The hypothesis is the case $N = 1$. Assume (3.3.2) holds up to N and observe that

$$M_{\langle \mathbf{n}^{N+1} \rangle}^{\oplus s} = M_{\langle \mathbf{n} \rangle}^{\oplus s} \otimes M_{\langle \mathbf{n}^N \rangle}$$

Now $\underline{\mathbf{R}}(M_{\langle \mathbf{n} \rangle}^{\oplus s}) \leq r$ implies $M_{\langle \mathbf{n} \rangle}^{\oplus s} \in \overline{GL_r^{\times 3} \cdot M_{\langle 1 \rangle}^{\oplus r}}$ by Equation (3.3.1), so $M_{\langle \mathbf{n} \rangle}^{\oplus s} \otimes M_{\langle \mathbf{n}^N \rangle} \in \overline{GL_r^{\times 3} \cdot M_{\langle 1 \rangle}^{\oplus r} \otimes M_{\langle \mathbf{n}^N \rangle}}.$ Thus $\underline{\mathbf{R}}(M_{\langle \mathbf{n}^{N+1} \rangle}^{\oplus s}) \leq \underline{\mathbf{R}}(M_{\langle 1 \rangle}^{\oplus r} \otimes M_{\langle \mathbf{n}^N \rangle}).$ Recall that $M_{\langle 1 \rangle}^{\oplus t} \otimes M_{\langle \mathbf{n}^N \rangle} = M_{\langle \mathbf{n}^N \rangle}^{\oplus t}$. Now

$$\underline{\mathbf{R}}\left(M_{\langle \mathbf{n}^{N+1} \rangle}^{\oplus s}\right) \leq \underline{\mathbf{R}}\left(M_{\langle \mathbf{n}^N \rangle}^{\oplus r}\right)$$

$$\leq \underline{\mathbf{R}}\left(M_{\langle \mathbf{n}^N \rangle}^{\oplus \lceil \frac{r}{s} \rceil s}\right)$$

$$\leq \underline{\mathbf{R}}\left(M_{\langle 1 \rangle}^{\oplus \lceil \frac{r}{s} \rceil} \otimes M_{\langle \mathbf{n}^N \rangle}^{\oplus s}\right)$$

$$\leq \underline{\mathbf{R}}\left(M_{\langle 1 \rangle}^{\oplus \lceil \frac{r}{s} \rceil}\right) \underline{\mathbf{R}}\left(M_{\langle \mathbf{n}^N \rangle}^{\oplus s}\right)$$

$$\leq \left\lceil \frac{r}{s} \right\rceil \left(\left\lceil \frac{r}{s} \right\rceil^N s\right)$$

where the last inequality follows from the induction hypothesis. □

The general case of Theorem 3.3.3.1 essentially follows from the above lemma and arguments used previously: one first takes a high tensor power of the sum, then switches to rank at the price of introducing an h that washes out in the end. The new tensor is a sum of products of matrix multiplications that one converts to a sum of matrix multiplications. One then takes the worst term in the summation and estimates with respect to it (multiplying by the number of terms in the summation) and applies the lemma to conclude.

Corollary 3.3.3.4 [Sch81] $\omega < 2.55$.

Proof. Applying Theorem 3.3.3.1 to $\underline{\mathbf{R}}(M_{\langle 1, \mathbf{m}, \mathbf{n} \rangle} \oplus M_{\langle (\mathbf{m}-1)(\mathbf{n}-1), 1, 1 \rangle}) = \mathbf{mn} + 1$ gives

$$(\mathbf{mn})^{\frac{\omega}{3}} + ((\mathbf{m} - 1)(\mathbf{n} - 1))^{\frac{\omega}{3}} \leq \mathbf{mn} + 1,$$

and taking $\mathbf{m} = \mathbf{n} = 4$ gives the result. □

In [CW82] the authors prove that for any tensor T that is a direct sum of disjoint matrix multiplications, if $\mathbf{R}(T) \leq r$, then there exists N such that $\underline{\mathbf{R}}(T \oplus M_{\langle N, 1, 1 \rangle}) \leq r + 1$. This, combined with our earlier arguments using $\mathbf{R}_h$ to bridge the gap between rank and border rank asymptotically, implies that the inequality in Theorem 3.3.3.1 is strict:

Theorem 3.3.3.5 [CW82] *For all* $\mathbf{l}_i, \mathbf{m}_i, \mathbf{n}_i,$ *with* $1 \leq i \leq s,$

$$\sum_{i=1}^{s} (\mathbf{m}_i \mathbf{n}_i \mathbf{l}_i)^{\frac{\omega}{3}} < \underline{\mathbf{R}}\left(\bigoplus_{i=1}^{s} M_{\langle \mathbf{m}_i, \mathbf{n}_i, \mathbf{l}_i \rangle}\right).$$

In particular, for all $\mathbf{n}$, $\underline{\mathbf{R}}(M_{\langle \mathbf{n} \rangle}) > \mathbf{n}^{\omega}$, so one cannot determine ω from $M_{\langle \mathbf{n} \rangle}$ for any fixed $\mathbf{n}$.

3.4 Strassen's Laser Method

3.4.1 Introduction

Recall our situation: we don't understand rank or even border rank in the range we would need to prove upper bounds on ω via $M_{\langle \mathbf{n} \rangle}$, so we showed that upper bounds on ω could be proved first with rectangular matrix multiplication, then with sums of disjoint matrix multiplications that had the property that the border rank of the sum was less than the sum of the border ranks and the border rank in each case was determined via an explicit decomposition.

We also saw that to determine the exponent by such methods, one would need to deal with sequences of tensors. Strassen's laser method is based on taking high tensor powers of a fixed tensor and then degenerating it to a disjoint sum of matrix multiplication tensors. Because it deals with sequences, there is no known obstruction to determining ω exactly via Strassen's method.

Starting with Strassen's method, all attempts to determine ω aim at best for a Pyrrhic victory in the sense that even if ω were determined by these methods, they would not give any indication as to what would be optimally fast matrix multiplication for any given size matrix.

3.4.2 Strassen's Tensor

Consider the following tensor:

$$T_{STR} = \sum_{j=1}^{q} a_0 {\otimes} b_j {\otimes} c_j + a_j {\otimes} b_0 {\otimes} c_j \in \mathbb{C}^{q+1} {\otimes} \mathbb{C}^{q+1} {\otimes} \mathbb{C}^q. \quad (3.4.1)$$

Exercise 5.3.1.7 will show that $\mathbf{R}(T_{STR}) = 2q$, so (3.4.1) is an optimal rank expression. Nevertheless, $\underline{\mathbf{R}}(T_{STR}) = q + 1$. To see why one could expect this, consider the q points $a_0 {\otimes} b_0 {\otimes} c_j$. The tensor T_{STR} is a sum of tangent vectors to these q points:

$$T_{STR} = \sum_{j=1}^{q} \lim_{t \to 0} \frac{1}{t} [(a_0 + t a_j) {\otimes} (b_0 + t b_j) {\otimes} c_j - a_0 {\otimes} b_0 {\otimes} c_j].$$

Note that the sum $\sum_j a_0 {\otimes} b_0 {\otimes} c_j$ is also a rank one tensor, which leads one to the expression

$$\lim_{t \to 0} \frac{1}{t} \left[\sum_{j=1}^{q} (a_0 + t a_j) {\otimes} (b_0 + t b_j) {\otimes} c_j - a_0 {\otimes} b_0 {\otimes} (c_1 + \cdots + c_q) \right],$$

showing the border rank is at most $q + 1$, but since the tensor is concise, we obtain equality. Geometrically, the original $q + 1$ points all lie on the linear space $[a_0 {\otimes} b_0 {\otimes} \mathbb{C}^q] \subset Seg(\mathbb{P}A \times \mathbb{P}B \times \mathbb{P}C)$.

Now consider $\tilde{T}_{STR} := T_{STR} \otimes \sigma(T_{STR}) \otimes \sigma^2(T_{STR})$, where σ is a cyclic permutation of the three factors. Group triples of spaces together to consider $\tilde{T}_{STR} \in \mathbb{C}^{q(q+1)^2} \otimes \mathbb{C}^{q(q+1)^2} \otimes \mathbb{C}^{q(q+1)^2}$. We have the upper bound $\underline{\mathbf{R}}(\tilde{T}_{STR}) \leq (q+1)^3$.

Write $a_{\alpha\beta\gamma} := a_\alpha \otimes a_\beta \otimes a_\gamma$ and similarly for bs and cs. Then, omitting the $\otimes$s,

$$\tilde{T}_{STR} = \sum_{i,j,k=1}^{q} (a_{ij0}b_{0jk}c_{i0k} + a_{ijk}b_{0jk}c_{i00} + a_{ij0}b_{00k}c_{ijk} + a_{ijk}b_{00k}c_{ij0}$$
$$+ a_{0j0}b_{ijk}c_{i0k} + a_{0jk}b_{ijk}c_{i00} + a_{0j0}b_{i0k}c_{ijk} + a_{0jk}b_{i0k}c_{ij0}). \quad (3.4.2)$$

We may think of $\tilde{T}_{STR}$ as a sum of eight terms, each of which is a $M_{\langle \mathbf{l,m,n} \rangle}$ with $\mathbf{lmn} = q^3$, e.g., the first is $\sum_{i,j,k=1}^{q} a_{ij0}b_{0jk}c_{i0k} = M_{\langle q,q,q \rangle}$, the second $M_{\langle q^2,q,1 \rangle}$, etc. (I will say terms of *volume* q^3.) Were they all disjoint expressions, we could use the asymptotic sum inequality to conclude $8q^\omega \leq (q+1)^3$, and for small q we would see $\omega < 2$. Of course, this is not the case, but we can try to zero out some of the variables to keep as many of these eight terms as possible. For example, if we set c_{i00}, b_{00k}, b_{ijk}, c_{ijk} all to zero, we are left with two disjoint matrix multiplications, and we conclude $2q^\omega \leq (q+1)^3$. This is best when $q = 15$, giving $\omega < 2.816$, which is not so interesting.

At this point enters a new idea: since we are dealing with border rank, we have greater flexibility in degeneration than simply zeroing out terms. By taking limits, we will be able to keep three terms! To explain this, I need to take another detour regarding orbit closures.

3.4.3 All Tensors of Border Rank $\lfloor \frac{3}{4}\mathbf{n}^2 \rfloor$ are Degenerations of $M_{\langle \mathbf{n} \rangle}$

Theorem 3.4.3.1 (Strassen [Str87]) *Set $r = \lfloor \frac{3}{4}\mathbf{n}^2 \rfloor$ and choose a linear embedding $\mathbb{C}^r \subset \mathbb{C}^{\mathbf{n}^2}$. Then*

$$\sigma_r(Seg(\mathbb{P}^{r-1} \times \mathbb{P}^{r-1} \times \mathbb{P}^{r-1})) \subset \overline{GL_{\mathbf{n}^2} \times GL_{\mathbf{n}^2} \times GL_{\mathbf{n}^2} \cdot [M_{\langle \mathbf{n} \rangle}]},$$

i.e.,

$$\overline{GL_r \times GL_r \times GL_r \cdot [M_{\langle 1 \rangle}^{\oplus r}]} \subset \overline{GL_{\mathbf{n}^2} \times GL_{\mathbf{n}^2} \times GL_{\mathbf{n}^2} \cdot [M_{\langle \mathbf{n} \rangle}]}.$$

Proof. The proof will be by a very simple degeneration: let $T^A \subset GL(A) = GL_{\mathbf{n}^2}$ denote the diagonal $\mathbf{n}^2 \times \mathbf{n}^2$ matrices. I will show

$$M_{\langle 1 \rangle}^{\oplus r} \subset \overline{T^A \times T^B \times T^C \cdot M_{\langle \mathbf{n} \rangle}}.$$

Write x_{ij} for a basis of A, etc., so $M_{\langle \mathbf{n} \rangle} = \sum_{i,j,k} x_{ij} \otimes y_{jk} \otimes z_{ki}$. We want to kill off as few terms as possible such that in the remaining terms, each basis vector appears in at most one monomial. That is, if we have x_{ij} appearing, then there should be a unique $k_0 = k(i,j)$ such that the only term surviving in

$\sum_k x_{ij} \otimes y_{jk} \otimes z_{ki}$ is $x_{ij} \otimes y_{jk_0} \otimes z_{k_0 i}$. We should view this more symmetrically, fixing some integer h and requiring that the only terms appearing are of the form $x_{ij} \otimes y_{jk} \otimes z_{ki}$, where $i + j + k = h$. To do this, look for curves

$$x_{ij} \mapsto t^{\alpha(i,j)} x_{ij},$$

$$y_{jk} \mapsto t^{\beta(j,k)} y_{jk},$$

$$z_{ki} \mapsto t^{\gamma(k,i)} z_{ki}$$

so that $\alpha + \beta + \gamma = 0$ when $i + j + k = h$ and $\alpha + \beta + \gamma > 0$ when $i + j + k \neq h$, as then

$$\lim_{t \to 0} \sum_{i,j,k=1}^{\mathbf{n}} t^{\alpha(i,j)+\beta(j,k)+\gamma(k,i)} x_{ij} \otimes y_{jk} \otimes z_{ki} = \sum_{i+j+k=h} x_{ij} \otimes y_{jk} \otimes z_{ki}.$$

Set $\lambda = i + j + k$. We could satisfy the requirements on α, β, γ by requiring

$$\alpha + \beta + \gamma = (h - \lambda)^2 = h^2 - 2\lambda h + \lambda^2.$$

Take

$$\alpha = \frac{1}{2}(i^2 + j^2) + 2ij + \left(\frac{h}{3} - i - j\right)h,$$

$$\beta = \frac{1}{2}(k^2 + j^2) + 2kj + \left(\frac{h}{3} - k - j\right)h,$$

$$\gamma = \frac{1}{2}(i^2 + k^2) + 2ik + \left(\frac{h}{3} - i - k\right)h.$$

Exercise 3.4.3.2 (1) Verify that $\alpha + \beta + \gamma = (h - \lambda)^2$.

Exercise 3.4.3.3 (2) Show that the best value of h is $h = \lceil \frac{3\mathbf{n}}{2} \rceil + 1$, which yields $r = \lfloor \frac{3}{4}\mathbf{n}^2 \rfloor$ to finish the proof. □

Remark 3.4.3.4 This degeneration is more complicated than setting linear combinations of variables to zero because there are values of i, j, k where one of α, β, γ is negative. To avoid negative terms for the curves in A, B, C, we could add r to each of α, β, γ and then divide the entire entire expression by t^{3r}.

Call degenerations that only use the diagonal matrices *toric degenerations*.

Corollary 3.4.3.5 *Every tensor in* $\mathbb{C}^{\frac{3}{2}\mathbf{n}} \otimes \mathbb{C}^{\frac{3}{2}\mathbf{n}} \otimes \mathbb{C}^{\frac{3}{2}\mathbf{n}}$ *arises as a toric degeneration of* $M_{\langle \mathbf{n} \rangle}$.

Proof. As mentioned in §2.1.6, the maximum border rank of any tensor in $\mathbb{C}^{\frac{3}{2}\mathbf{n}} \otimes \mathbb{C}^{\frac{3}{2}\mathbf{n}} \otimes \mathbb{C}^{\frac{3}{2}\mathbf{n}}$ is at most $\frac{3}{4}\mathbf{n}^2$, and any tensor of border rank $\frac{3}{4}\mathbf{n}^2$ is a degeneration of $M_{\langle \mathbf{n} \rangle}$. □

Remark 3.4.3.6 Theorem 3.4.3.1 may be interpreted as saying that one can degenerate $M_{\langle \mathbf{n} \rangle}$ to a tensor that computes $\lfloor \frac{3}{4} \mathbf{n}^2 \rfloor$ independent scalar multiplications. If we have any tensor realized as $M_{\langle \mathbf{n} \rangle} \otimes T$, the same degeneration procedure works to degenerate it to $M_{\langle 1 \rangle}^{\oplus \lfloor \frac{3}{4} \mathbf{n}^2 \rfloor} \otimes T$.

3.4.4 A Better Bound using the Toric Degeneration

Now we return to the expression (3.4.2). There are four kinds of A-indices: $ij0$, ijk, $0j0$, and $0jk$. To emphasize this, and to suggest what kind of degeneration to perform, label these with superscripts [11], [21], [12], and [22]. Label each of the B and C indices (which come in four types as well) similarly to obtain

$$
\tilde{T}_{STR} = \sum_{i,j,k=1}^{q} \left(a_{ij0}^{[11]} b_{0jk}^{[11]} c_{i0k}^{[11]} + a_{ijk}^{[21]} b_{0jk}^{[11]} c_{i00}^{[12]} + a_{ij0}^{[11]} b_{00k}^{[12]} c_{ijk}^{[21]} + a_{ijk}^{[21]} b_{00k}^{[12]} c_{ij0}^{[22]} \right.
$$
$$
\left. + a_{0j0}^{[12]} b_{ijk}^{[21]} c_{i0k}^{[11]} + a_{0jk}^{[22]} b_{ijk}^{[21]} c_{i00}^{[12]} + a_{0j0}^{[12]} b_{i0k}^{[22]} c_{ijk}^{[21]} + a_{0jk}^{[22]} b_{i0k}^{[22]} c_{ij0}^{[22]} \right).
$$

This expression has the structure of block 2×2 matrix multiplication. Think of it as a sum of q^3 2×2 matrix multiplications. Now use Theorem 3.4.3.1 to degenerate each 2×2 matrix multiplication to a sum of three disjoint terms. Namely, following the recipe that the three indices must add to 4, we keep all terms $a^{[s,t]} b^{[t,u]} c^{[u,s]}$ where $s + t + u = 4$, namely, we degenerate $\tilde{T}_{STR}$ to

$$
\sum_{i,j,k=1}^{q} a_{ijk}^{[21]} b_{0jk}^{[11]} c_{i00}^{[12]} + a_{ij0}^{[11]} b_{00k}^{[12]} c_{ijk}^{[21]} + a_{0j0}^{[12]} b_{ijk}^{[21]} c_{i0k}^{[11]}.
$$

The asymptotic sum inequality implies $3q^{\omega} \leq (q+1)^3$, which gives the best bound on ω when $q = 7$, namely, $\omega < 2.642$, which is still not as good as Schönhage's bound.

3.4.5 Strassen's Bound

We do better by using the standard trick of this chapter: taking a high tensor power of $\tilde{T}_{STR}$, as $\tilde{T}_{STR}^{\otimes N}$ contains $(2^N)^2$ matrix multiplications $M_{\langle \mathbf{l}, \mathbf{m}, \mathbf{n} \rangle}$, all with $\mathbf{lmn} = q^{3N}$, and again by Theorem 3.4.3.1, we may keep $\frac{3}{4} 2^{2N}$ of them. The asymptotic sum inequality applied to the degenerated tensor gives

$$
\frac{3}{4} 2^{2N} q^{N\omega} \leq (q+1)^{3N}.
$$

Taking Nth roots and letting N tend to infinity, the $\frac{3}{4}$ goes away and we obtain

$$
2^2 q^{\omega} \leq (q+1)^3.
$$

Finally, the case $q = 5$ implies the following:

Theorem 3.4.5.1 [Str87] $\omega < 2.48$.

3.4.6 Asymptotic Rank

The above discussion suggests the introduction of yet another complexity measure for tensors: given $T \in A \otimes B \otimes C$, we can consider $T^{\otimes N} \in A^{\otimes N} \otimes B^{\otimes N} \otimes C^{\otimes N}$, and this construction played a central role in Strassen's laser method to prove upper bounds for the complexity of matrix multiplication via auxiliary tensors.

Definition 3.4.6.1 The *asymptotic rank* $\tilde{\mathbf{R}}(T)$ of a tensor $T \in A \otimes B \otimes C$ is

$$\tilde{\mathbf{R}}(T) := \inf_N [\mathbf{R}(T^{\otimes N})]^{\frac{1}{N}}.$$

Exercise 3.4.6.2 (1) Show that in the definition, one can replace the infimum by $\lim_{N \to \infty}$ by using Lemma 3.4.7.2.

Exercise 3.4.6.3 (2) Show that $\tilde{\mathbf{R}}(T) \leq \underline{\mathbf{R}}(T)$. ⊙

Since $M_{(2)}^{\otimes k} = M_{(2^k)}$, we have $\tilde{\mathbf{R}}(M_{(2)}) = 2^\omega$.

Conjecture 3.4.6.4 [Str91] *Let $T \in \mathbb{C}^{\mathbf{m}} \otimes \mathbb{C}^{\mathbf{m}} \otimes \mathbb{C}^{\mathbf{m}}$ be concise. Then* $\tilde{\mathbf{R}}(T) = $ **m**.

Note that if Conjecture 3.4.6.4 holds for $T = M_{(2)}$, this would imply $\omega = 2$.
More subtly, if the conjecture holds for $T_{cw,2}$ introduced in §3.4.9, then $\omega = 2$ ([BCS97, Rem. 15.44]).

3.4.7 Degeneracy Value

I now formalize what we did to get Strassen's bound. The starting point is if a tensor T degenerates to $\bigoplus_{i=1}^{s} M_{\langle l_i, m_i, n_i \rangle}$, then $\sum_{i=1}^{s} (l_i m_i n_i)^{\frac{\omega}{3}} \leq \underline{\mathbf{R}}(T)$, and more generally we worked with degenerations of $T^{\otimes N}$ as well. Informally define the *degeneracy value* of T to be the best upper bound on ω we can get in this manner. More precisely:

Definition 3.4.7.1 Let $T \in A \otimes B \otimes C$. Fix $N \geq 1$ and $\rho \in [2, 3]$. Define $V_{\rho,N}^{degen}(T)$ to be the maximum of $\sum_{i=1}^{s} (l_i m_i n_i)^{\frac{\rho}{3}}$ over all degenerations of $T^{\otimes N}$ to $\bigoplus_{i=1}^{s} M_{\langle l_i, m_i, n_i \rangle}$ over all choices of s, l_i, m_i, n_i, and define the *degeneracy value* of T to be $V_{\rho}^{degen}(T) := \sup_N V_{\rho,N}^{degen}(T)^{\frac{1}{N}}$.

The asymptotic sum inequality implies $V_{\omega}^{degen}(T) \leq \underline{\mathbf{R}}(T)$, or in other words, if $V_{\rho}^{degen}(T) \geq \underline{\mathbf{R}}(T)$, then $\omega \leq \rho$.

The supremum in the definition can be replaced by a limit, thanks to *Fekete's Lemma*, since the sequence $\log(V^{degen}_{\rho,N}(T))$ is superadditive:

Lemma 3.4.7.2 (Fekete's Lemma) *For every superadditive sequence* $\{a_n\}^{\infty}_{n=1}$ *(i.e.,* $a_{n+m} \geq a_n + a_m$*), the limit* $\lim_{n \to \infty} \frac{a_n}{n}$ *exists (possibly* $+\infty$*) and is equal to* $\sup \frac{a_n}{n}$*.*

Exercise 3.4.7.3 (3) Prove Fekete's Lemma.

Fekete's Lemma implies that $\frac{1}{N} \log V^{degen}_{\rho,N}(T)$ tends to a limit. See [AFLG15] for details.

There is also an analogue of the asymptotic sum inequality for degeneracy value:

Theorem 3.4.7.4 $\sum^{s}_{i=1} V^{degen}_{\omega}(T_i) \leq \underline{\mathbf{R}}(\oplus^{s}_{i=1} T_i)$.

The proof is similar to the proof of the asymptotic sum inequality. It is clear that $V^{degen}_{\omega}(T_1 \otimes T_2) \geq V^{degen}_{\omega}(T_1) \otimes V^{degen}_{\omega}(T_2)$. To show $V^{degen}_{\omega}(T_1 \oplus T_2) \geq V^{degen}_{\omega}(T_1) + V^{degen}_{\omega}(T_2)$, one expands out $V^{degen}_{\omega,N}(T_1 \oplus T_2)$: the result is a sum of products with coefficients, but as with the asymptotic sum inequality, one can essentially just look at the largest term, and as N tends to infinity, the coefficient becomes irrelevant after taking Nth roots.

Thus tensors of low border rank with high degeneracy value give upper bounds on ω. The problem is that we have no systematic way of estimating degeneracy value. For an extreme example, the tensor of border rank r with the highest degeneracy value is $M^{\oplus r}_{\langle 1 \rangle}$, as all border rank r tensors are degenerations of it.

In subsequent work, researchers restrict to a special type of value that is possible to estimate.

3.4.8 The Value of a Tensor

Let $\mathrm{End}(A) \times \mathrm{End}(B) \times \mathrm{End}(C)$ act on $A \otimes B \otimes C$ by the action inherited from the $GL(A) \times GL(B) \times GL(C)$ action (not the Lie algebra action). Then, for all $X \in \mathrm{End}(A) \times \mathrm{End}(B) \times \mathrm{End}(C)$ and $T \in A \otimes B \otimes C$, we have $\mathbf{R}(X \cdot T) \leq \mathbf{R}(T)$ and $\underline{\mathbf{R}}(X \cdot T) \leq \underline{\mathbf{R}}(T)$ by Exercise 2.1.6.2.

Definition 3.4.8.1 One says T *restricts to* T' if $T' \in \mathrm{End}(A) \times \mathrm{End}(B) \times \mathrm{End}(C) \cdot T$.

Definition 3.4.8.2 For $T \in A \otimes B \otimes C$, $N \geq 1$ and $\rho \in [2, 3]$ define $V^{restr}_{\rho,N}(T)$ to be the maximum of $\sum^{s}_{i=1} (\mathbf{l}_i \mathbf{m}_i \mathbf{n}_i)^{\frac{\rho}{3}}$ over all restrictions of $T^{\otimes N}$ to $\oplus^{s}_{i=1} M_{\langle \mathbf{l}_i, \mathbf{m}_i, \mathbf{n}_i \rangle}$ and define the *restriction value* of T to be $V^{restr}_{\rho}(T) := \sup_N V^{restr}_{\rho,N}(T)^{\frac{1}{N}}$.

I emphasize that the degeneration used by Strassen is more general than restriction.

Coppersmith-Winograd and all subsequent work use only the following type of restriction:

Definition 3.4.8.3 Let A, B, C be given bases, so write them as $\mathbb{C}^{\mathbf{a}}, \mathbb{C}^{\mathbf{b}}, \mathbb{C}^{\mathbf{c}}$. We say $T \in \mathbb{C}^{\mathbf{a}} \otimes \mathbb{C}^{\mathbf{b}} \otimes \mathbb{C}^{\mathbf{c}}$ *combinatorially restricts to* T' if T restricts to T' by setting some of the coordinates of T to zero.

The condition that $T \in \mathbb{C}^{\mathbf{a}} \otimes \mathbb{C}^{\mathbf{b}} \otimes \mathbb{C}^{\mathbf{c}}$ admits a combinatorial restriction to the matrix multiplication tensor $M_{\langle \mathbf{l}, \mathbf{m}, \mathbf{n} \rangle}$ may be phrased as follows (following [CU03]): write $a_\alpha, b_\beta, c_\gamma$ for the given bases of A, B, C and write $T = \sum_{\alpha=1}^{\mathbf{a}} \sum_{\beta=1}^{\mathbf{b}} \sum_{\gamma=1}^{\mathbf{c}} t^{\alpha,\beta,\gamma} a_\alpha \otimes b_\beta \otimes c_\gamma$. Then $T \in \mathbb{C}^{\mathbf{a}} \otimes \mathbb{C}^{\mathbf{b}} \otimes \mathbb{C}^{\mathbf{c}}$ combinatorially restricts to $M_{\langle \mathbf{l}, \mathbf{m}, \mathbf{n} \rangle}$ means that there exist injections

$$\alpha : [\mathbf{l}] \times [\mathbf{m}] \to [\mathbf{a}],$$
$$\beta : [\mathbf{m}] \times [\mathbf{n}] \to [\mathbf{b}],$$
$$\gamma : [\mathbf{n}] \times [\mathbf{l}] \to [\mathbf{c}]$$

such that

$$t^{\alpha(i,j'),\beta(j,k'),\gamma(k,i')} = \begin{cases} 1 & \text{if } i = i', \ j = j', \ k = k' \\ 0 & \text{otherwise} \end{cases}. \tag{3.4.3}$$

One can similarly phrase combinatorial restriction to a sum of disjoint matrix multiplication tensors.

Definition 3.4.8.4 For $T \in \mathbb{C}^{\mathbf{a}} \otimes \mathbb{C}^{\mathbf{b}} \otimes \mathbb{C}^{\mathbf{c}}, N \geq 1$, and $\rho \in [2, 3]$ define $V_{\rho,N}(T)$ to be the maximum of $\sum_{i=1}^{s} (\mathbf{l}_i \mathbf{m}_i \mathbf{n}_i)^{\frac{\rho}{3}}$ over all combinatorial restrictions of $T^{\otimes N}$ to $\oplus_{i=1}^{s} M_{\langle \mathbf{l}_i, \mathbf{m}_i, \mathbf{n}_i \rangle}$ and define the *combinatorial value* (or *value* for short, since it is the value used in the literature) of T to be $V_\rho(T) := \lim_{N \to \infty} V_{\rho,N}(T)^{\frac{1}{N}}$. (The limit is shown to exist in [DS13].)

Note that the values satisfy $V_\rho^{degen} \geq V_\rho^{restr} \geq V_\rho$. As with all the values, we have that

- $V_\rho(T)$ is a nondecreasing function of ρ and,
- $V_\omega(T) \leq \underline{\mathbf{R}}(T)$.

Thus, if $V_\rho(T) \geq \underline{\mathbf{R}}(T)$, then $\omega \leq \rho$.

Combinatorial value can be estimated in principle, as for each N, there are only a finite number of combinatorial restrictions. In practice, the tensor is presented in such a way that there are "obvious" combinatorial degenerations to disjoint matrix multiplication tensors, and at first, one optimizes just among these obvious combinatorial degenerations. However, it may be that there are matrix multiplication tensors of the form $\sum_j a_0 \otimes b_j \otimes c_j$ as well as tensors of the form $a_0 \otimes b_k \otimes c_k$ where k is not in the range of j. Then one can *merge* these tensors to $a_0 \otimes (\sum_j b_j \otimes c_j + b_k \otimes c_k)$ to increase value, because although, formally speaking, they were not disjoint, they do not interfere with each other. (The value increases as, e.g., $q^\omega + r^\omega < (q+r)^\omega$.) So the actual procedure is to optimize among combinatorial restrictions with merged tensors.

3.4.9 The Coppersmith-Winograd Tensors

Coppersmith and Winograd apply Strassen's laser method, enhanced with merging, using combinatorial restrictions to the tensors (3.4.4) and (3.4.5):

The "easy Coppersmith-Winograd tensor", is as follows:

$$T_{q,cw} := \sum_{j=1}^{q} a_0 \otimes b_j \otimes c_j + a_j \otimes b_0 \otimes c_j + a_j \otimes b_j \otimes c_0 \in \mathbb{C}^{q+1} \otimes \mathbb{C}^{q+1} \otimes \mathbb{C}^{q+1}.$$

(3.4.4)

Proposition 5.5.1.1 will imply $\mathbf{R}(T_{q,cw}) = 2q + 1$, so the above expression is not optimal. We also have

Proposition 3.4.9.1 $\underline{\mathbf{R}}(T_{q,cw}) = q + 2.$

Proof. Consider the second derivatives of a curve in the Segre: let $x(t) = a(t) \otimes b(t) \otimes c(t)$, write x' for $x'(0)$, and similarly for all derivatives. Then

$$x'' = (a'' \otimes b \otimes c + a \otimes b'' \otimes c + a \otimes b \otimes c'') + 2(a' \otimes b' \otimes c + a' \otimes b \otimes c' + a \otimes b' \otimes c'),$$

so if we begin with the base point $a_0 \otimes b_0 \otimes c_0$, each term in the summand for $T_{q,cw}$ is a term of the second kind. The terms in the first parentheses are ordinary tangent vectors. Thus, taking q curves beginning at $a_0 \otimes b_0 \otimes c_0$, we can cancel out all the terms of the first type with a single vector to obtain the resulting border rank $q + 2$ expression:

$$T_{q,cw} = \lim_{t \to 0} \frac{1}{t^2} \left[\sum_{j=1}^{q} (a_0 + t a_j) \otimes (b_0 + t b_j) \otimes (c_0 + t c_j) \right.$$
$$\left. - \left(a_0 + t \sum_j a_j \right) \otimes \left(b_0 + t \sum_j b_j \right) \otimes \left(c_0 + t \sum_j c_j \right) \right.$$
$$- (q-1) a_0 \otimes b_0 \otimes c_0.$$

Exercise 3.4.9.2 (2) Show that $\underline{\mathbf{R}}(T_{q,cw}) \geq q + 2$ so that equality holds. □

A slightly more complicated tensor yields even better results: let

$$T_{q,CW} := \sum_{j=1}^{q} (a_0 \otimes b_j \otimes c_j + a_j \otimes b_0 \otimes c_j + a_j \otimes b_j \otimes c_0) + a_0 \otimes b_0 \otimes c_{q+1}$$

$$+ a_0 \otimes b_{q+1} \otimes c_0 + a_{q+1} \otimes b_0 \otimes c_0 \in \mathbb{C}^{q+2} \otimes \mathbb{C}^{q+2} \otimes \mathbb{C}^{q+2} \quad (3.4.5)$$

and call $T_{q,CW}$ the *Coppersmith-Winograd tensor*.

Exercise 3.4.9.3 (2) Show the Coppersmith-Winograd tensor also has border rank $q + 2$ by modifying the curves used to obtain $T_{q,cw}$. ⊙

Now suggestively relabel $T_{q,CW}$ as we did with Strassen's tensor,

$$T_{q,CW} := \sum_{j=1}^{q} \left(a_0^{[0]} \otimes b_j^{[1]} \otimes c_j^{[1]} + a_j^{[1]} \otimes b_0^{[0]} \otimes c_j^{[1]} + a_j^{[1]} \otimes b_j^{[1]} \otimes c_0^{[0]} \right)$$

$$+ a_0^{[0]} \otimes b_0^{[0]} \otimes c_{q+1}^{[2]} + a_0^{[0]} \otimes b_{q+1}^{[2]} \otimes c_0^{[0]}$$

$$+ a_{q+1}^{[2]} \otimes b_0^{[0]} \otimes c_0^{[0]} \in \mathbb{C}^{q+2} \otimes \mathbb{C}^{q+2} \otimes \mathbb{C}^{q+2}, \quad (3.4.6)$$

to see that $T_{q,CW}$ is the sum of three matrix multiplications of volume q^2, and three of volume 1, all nondisjoint. To get more interesting matrix multiplications, consider $T_{q,CW}^{\otimes 2}$, but this time, instead of double superscripts, simply add the superscripts:

$$T_{q,CW}^{\otimes 2} = \sum_{i,j=1}^{q} \left[a_{00}^{[0]} \otimes b_{ij}^{[2]} \otimes c_{ij}^{[2]} + a_{0j}^{[1]} \otimes b_{i0}^{[0]} \otimes c_{ij}^{[2]} + a_{0j}^{[1]} \otimes b_{ij}^{[2]} \otimes c_{i0}^{[1]} \right.$$

$$+ a_{i0}^{[1]} \otimes b_{0j}^{[1]} \otimes c_{ij}^{[2]} + a_{i0}^{[1]} \otimes b_{ij}^{[2]} \otimes c_{0j}^{[1]} + a_{ij}^{[2]} \otimes b_{i0}^{[1]} \otimes c_{0j}^{[1]}$$

$$\left. + a_{ij}^{[2]} \otimes b_{00}^{[0]} \otimes c_{ij}^{[2]} + a_{ij}^{[2]} \otimes b_{ij}^{[2]} \otimes c_{00}^{[1]} + a_{ij}^{[2]} \otimes b_{0j}^{[1]} \otimes c_{i0}^{[1]} \right]$$

$$+ \sum_{j=1}^{q} \left[a_{0,q+1}^{[2]} \otimes b_{j0}^{[1]} \otimes c_{j0}^{[1]} + a_{q+1,0}^{[2]} \otimes b_{0j}^{[1]} \otimes c_{0j}^{[1]} + a_{q+1,j}^{[3]} \otimes b_{0j}^{[1]} \otimes c_{00}^{[0]} \right.$$

$$\left. + a_{j,q+1}^{[3]} \otimes b_{j0}^{[1]} \otimes c_{00}^{[0]} + a_{q+1,j}^{[3]} \otimes b_{00}^{[0]} \otimes c_{0j}^{[1]} + a_{j,q+1}^{[3]} \otimes b_{00}^{[0]} \otimes c_{j0}^{[1]} \right]$$

$$+ a_{q+1,q+1}^{[4]} \otimes b_{00}^{[0]} \otimes c_{00}^{[0]} + a_{00}^{[0]} \otimes b_{q+1,j}^{[3]} \otimes c_{0j}^{[1]} + a_{00}^{[0]} \otimes b_{0j}^{[1]} \otimes c_{q+1,j}^{[3]}$$

$$+ a_{00}^{[0]} \otimes b_{q+1,q+1}^{[4]} \otimes c_{00}^{[0]} + a_{00}^{[0]} \otimes b_{00}^{[0]} \otimes c_{q+1,q+1}^{[4]}.$$

Now we have nondisjoint matrix multiplications of volumes q^2, q, and 1. Thus, when we zero out terms to get disjoint matrix multiplications in $(T_{q,CW}^{\otimes 2})^{\otimes N}$, in order to optimize value, we need to weight the q^2 terms more than the q terms, etc.

As mentioned above, one can obtain better upper bounds with merging. One needs to make a choice how to merge. Coppersmith and Winogrand group the $\mathbb{C}^{a^2}$-variables as

$$\mathcal{A}^{[0]} = \left\{ a_{00}^{[0]} \right\},$$
$$\mathcal{A}^{[1]} = \left\{ a_{i0}^{[1]}, a_{0j}^{[1]} \right\},$$
$$\mathcal{A}^{[2]} = \left\{ a_{q+1,0}^{[2]}, a_{ij}^{[2]}, a_{0,q+1}^{[2]} \right\},$$
$$\mathcal{A}^{[3]} = \left\{ a_{q+1,j}^{[3]}, a_{i,q+1}^{[3]} \right\},$$
$$\mathcal{A}^{[4]} = \left\{ a_{q+1,q+1}^{[4]} \right\},$$

and similarly for bs and cs. Then

$$T_{q,CW}^{\otimes 2} = \sum_{I+J+K=4} \mathcal{A}^{[I]} \otimes \mathcal{B}^{[J]} \otimes \mathcal{C}^{[K]},$$

where, e.g., $\mathcal{A}^{[I]}$ is to be interpreted as the sum of all elements of $\mathcal{A}^{[I]}$. Most of these terms are just matrix multiplications, however, terms with $1 + 1 + 2$ are not:

$$\mathcal{A}^{[1]} \otimes \mathcal{B}^{[1]} \otimes \mathcal{C}^{[2]} = \sum_{i=1}^{q} a_{i0}^{[1]} \otimes b_{i0}^{[1]} \otimes c_{0,q+1}^{[2]} + \sum_{j=1}^{q} a_{0j}^{[1]} \otimes b_{0j}^{[1]} \otimes c_{q+1,0}^{[2]}$$
$$+ \sum_{i,j=1}^{q} \left[a_{i0}^{[1]} \otimes b_{0j}^{[1]} \otimes c_{ij}^{[2]} + a_{0j}^{[1]} \otimes b_{i0}^{[1]} \otimes c_{ij}^{[2]} \right].$$

To this term, we estimate value using the laser method, i.e., we degenerate tensor powers of $\mathcal{A}^{[1]} \otimes \mathcal{B}^{[1]} \otimes \mathcal{C}^{[2]}$ to disjoint matrix multiplication tensors. Coppersmith and Winograd show that it has value at least $2^{\frac{2}{3}} q^{\omega} (q^{3\omega} + 2)^{\frac{1}{3}}$.

Now there is an optimization problem to solve, which I briefly discuss in §3.4.10.

Coppersmith and Winograd get their best result of $\omega < 2.3755$ by merging $T_{q,CW}^{\otimes 2}$ and then optimizing over the various combinatorial restrictions. In subsequent work, Stothers [Sto], resp. Williams [Wil], resp. LeGall [LG14] used merging with $T_{q,CW}^{\otimes 4}$, resp. $T_{q,CW}^{\otimes 8}$, resp. $T_{q,CW}^{\otimes 16}$ and $T_{q,CW}^{\otimes 32}$, leading to the current "world record":

Theorem 3.4.9.4 [LG14] $\omega < 2.3728639$.

Ambainis, Filmus, and LeGall [AFLG15] showed that taking higher powers of $T_{q,CW}$ when $q \geq 5$ cannot be used to prove $\omega < 2.30$ by this method alone. Their argument avoids higher powers by more sophisticated methods to account for when potential merging in higher tensor powers can occur.

Thus one either needs to develop new methods or find better base tensors. I discuss the search for better base tensors.

3.4.10 How One Optimizes in Practice

To get an idea of how the optimization procedure works, start with some base tensor T that contains a collection of matrix multiplication tensors $M_{\langle \mathbf{l}_i, \mathbf{m}_i, \mathbf{n}_i \rangle}$, $1 \leq i \leq x$ that are not disjoint. Then $T^{\otimes N}$ will contain matrix multiplication tensors of the form $M_{\langle \mathbf{l}_\mu, \mathbf{m}_\mu, \mathbf{n}_\mu \rangle}$, where $\mathbf{l}_\mu = \mathbf{l}_{\mu_1} \cdots \mathbf{l}_{\mu_N}$, and similarly for $\mathbf{m}_\mu$, $\mathbf{n}_\mu$, where $\mu_j \in [x]$.

Each matrix multiplication tensor will occur with a certain multiplicity and certain variables. The problem becomes to zero out variables in a way that maximizes the value of what remains. More precisely, for large N, one wants to maximize the sum $\sum_j K_j (\mathbf{l}_{\mu_j} \mathbf{m}_{\mu_j} \mathbf{n}_{\mu_j})^{\frac{\rho}{3}}$ where the surviving matrix multiplication tensors are $M^{\oplus K_j}_{\langle \mathbf{l}_{\mu_j} \mathbf{m}_{\mu_j} \mathbf{n}_{\mu_j} \rangle}$ and disjoint. One then takes the smallest ρ such that $\sum_j K_j (\mathbf{l}_{\mu_j} \mathbf{m}_{\mu_j} \mathbf{n}_{\mu_j})^{\frac{\rho}{3}} \geq \underline{\mathbf{R}}(T)$ and concludes $\omega \leq \rho$. One ingredient is the Salem-Spencer Theorem:

Theorem 3.4.10.1 (Salem and Spencer [SS42]) *Given $\epsilon > 0$, there exists $M_\epsilon \simeq 2^{\frac{c}{\epsilon^2}}$ such that for all $M > M_\epsilon$, there is a set B of $M' > M^{1-\epsilon}$ distinct integers $0 < b_1 < b_2 < \cdots < b_{M'} < \frac{M}{2}$ with no three terms in an arithmetic progression, i.e., for $b_i, b_j, b_k \in B$, $b_i + b_j = 2b_k$ if and only if $b_i = b_j = b_k$. In fact, no three terms form an arithmetic progression mod M.*

This theorem ensures that one can get away with only zeroing out a relatively small number of terms, so in some sense it plays the role of Strassen's degeneration theorem. I state it explicitly to emphasize that it is an existence result, not an algorithm. In the general case, one assigns probability distributions and optimizes using techniques from probability to determine what percentage of each type gets zeroed out. See [CW82] for the basic idea and [AFLG15] for the state of the art regarding this optimization.

3.5 The Cohn-Umans Program

A conceptually appealing approach to proving upper bounds on ω was initiated by H. Cohn and C. Umans.

Imagine a tensor that comes presented in two different bases. In one, the *cost* of the tensor is clear: it may be written as a sum of small disjoint matrix multiplication tensors. On the other hand, in the other, its *value* (in the sense discussed above) is high, because it may be seen to degenerate to good matrix multiplication tensors. Such a situation does arise in practice! It occurs for *structure tensors* for the group algebra of a finite group, as defined below. In one (the "matrix coefficient basis"), one gets an upper bound on the rank of the tensor, and in the other (the "standard basis"), there are many potential combinatorial degenerations, and one gets a lower bound on the value.

I state the needed representation theory now and defer proofs of the statements to §8.6. In §3.5.4 I present their method.

3.5.1 Structure Tensor of an Algebra

Let $\mathcal{A}$ be a finite-dimensional *algebra*, i.e., a vector space with a multiplication operation, with basis $a_1, \ldots, a_{\mathbf{a}}$ and dual basis $\alpha^1, \ldots, \alpha^{\mathbf{a}}$. Write $a_i a_j = \sum_k A_{ij}^k a_k$ for the multiplication in $\mathcal{A}$, where the A_{ij}^k are constants. The multiplication $\mathcal{A} \times \mathcal{A} \to \mathcal{A}$ is a bilinear map, and one defines the corresponding *structure tensor of $\mathcal{A}$* as

$$T_{\mathcal{A}} := \sum_{i,j,k} A_{ij}^k \alpha^i \otimes \alpha^j \otimes a_k \in \mathcal{A}^* \otimes \mathcal{A}^* \otimes \mathcal{A}. \tag{3.5.1}$$

For example, $M_{\langle \mathbf{n} \rangle}$ is the structure tensor for the algebra of $\mathbf{n} \times \mathbf{n}$-matrices with operation matrix multiplication.

The Group Algebra of a Finite Group

Let G be a finite group and let $\mathbb{C}[G]$ denote the vector space of complex-valued functions on G, called the *group algebra* of G. The following exercise justifies the name:

Exercise 3.5.1.1 (1) Show that if the elements of G are $g_1, \ldots, g_r$, then $\mathbb{C}[G]$ has a basis indexed $\delta_{g_1}, \ldots, \delta_{g_r}$, where $\delta_{g_i}(g_j) = \delta_{ij}$. Show that $\mathbb{C}[G]$ may be given the structure of an algebra by defining $\delta_{g_i} \delta_{g_j} := \delta_{g_i g_j}$ and extending linearly.

Thus, if G is a finite group, then $T_{\mathbb{C}[G]} = \sum_{g,h \in G} \delta_g^* \otimes \delta_h^* \otimes \delta_{gh}$.

Example 3.5.1.2

$$T_{\mathbb{C}[\mathbb{Z}_m]} = \sum_{0 \le i,j < m} \delta_i^* \otimes \delta_j^* \otimes \delta_{i+j \bmod m}.$$

Notice that, introducing coordinates $x_0, \ldots, x_{m-1}$ on $\mathbb{C}[\mathbb{Z}_m]$, so $v \in \mathbb{C}[\mathbb{Z}_m]$ may be written $\sum x_s \delta_s$, one obtains a circulant matrix for $T_{\mathbb{C}[\mathbb{Z}_m]}(\mathbb{C}[\mathbb{Z}_m]^*) \subset \mathbb{C}[\mathbb{Z}_m]^* \otimes \mathbb{C}[\mathbb{Z}_m]^*$:

$$T_{\mathbb{C}[\mathbb{Z}_m]}(\mathbb{C}[\mathbb{Z}_m]^*) = \left\{ \begin{pmatrix} x_0 & x_1 & \cdots & x_{m-1} \\ x_{m-1} & x_0 & x_1 & \cdots \\ \vdots & & \ddots & \\ x_1 & x_2 & \cdots & x_0 \end{pmatrix} \,\Big|\, x_j \in \mathbb{C} \right\}. \tag{3.5.2}$$

In what follows I slightly abuse notation and write the matrix with entries x_j rather than in the form above. Note that all entries of the matrix are nonzero and filled with basis vectors. This holds in general for the presentation of $\mathbb{C}[G]$ in the standard basis, which makes it useful for combinatorial restrictions.

What are $\underline{\mathbf{R}}(T_{\mathbb{C}[\mathbb{Z}_m]})$ and $\mathbf{R}(T_{\mathbb{C}[\mathbb{Z}_m]})$? The space of circulant matrices forms an abelian subspace, which indicates that the rank and border rank might be minimal or nearly minimal among concise tensors. We will determine the rank and border rank of $T_{\mathbb{C}[\mathbb{Z}_m]}$ momentarily via the discrete Fourier transform.

3.5.2 The Structure Theorem of $\mathbb{C}[G]$

I give a proof of the following theorem and an explanation of the $G \times G$-module structure on $\mathbb{C}[G]$ in §8.6.5.

Theorem 3.5.2.1 *Let G be a finite group; then, as a $G \times G$-module,*

$$\mathbb{C}[G] = \bigoplus_i V_i^* {\otimes} V_i, \tag{3.5.3}$$

where the sum is over all the distinct irreducible representations of G. In particular, if $\dim V_i = d_i$, then as an algebra,

$$\mathbb{C}[G] \simeq \bigoplus_i Mat_{d_i \times d_i}(\mathbb{C}). \tag{3.5.4}$$

3.5.3 The (Generalized) Discrete Fourier Transform

We have two natural expressions for $T_{\mathbb{C}[G]}$, the original presentation in terms of the algebra multiplication in terms of delta functions, the *standard basis*, and the *matrix coefficient basis*, in terms of the entries of the matrices in (3.5.4). The change of basis matrix from the standard basis to the matrix coefficient basis is called the (generalized) *Discrete Fourier Transform* (DFT).

Example 3.5.3.1 The classical DFT is the case $G = \mathbb{Z}_m$. The irreducible representations of $\mathbb{Z}_m$ are all one-dimensional: $\rho_k : \mathbb{Z}_m \to GL_1$. Let $\sigma \in \mathbb{Z}_m$ be a generator; then $\rho_k(\sigma)v = e^{\frac{2\pi i k}{m}} v$ for $0 \le k \le m$. The DFT matrix is

$$\left(e^{\frac{2\pi i (j+k)}{m}} \right)_{0 \le j, k \le m-1}$$

Proposition 3.5.3.2 $\underline{\mathbf{R}}(T_{\mathbb{C}[\mathbb{Z}_m]}) = \mathbf{R}(T_{\mathbb{C}[\mathbb{Z}_m]}) = m$.

Proof. Theorem 3.5.2.1 implies $T_{\mathbb{C}[\mathbb{Z}_m]} = M_{\langle 1 \rangle}^{\oplus m}$. □

Compared with (3.5.2), in the matrix coefficient basis, the image $T_{\mathbb{C}[\mathbb{Z}_m]}(\mathbb{C}[\mathbb{Z}_m]^*)$ is the set of diagonal matrices

$$T_{\mathbb{C}[\mathbb{Z}_m]}(\mathbb{C}[\mathbb{Z}_m]^*) = \begin{pmatrix} y_0 & & & \\ & y_1 & & \\ & & \ddots & \\ & & & y_{m-1} \end{pmatrix}.$$

Exercise 3.5.3.3 (2) Show that if $T \in \hat{\sigma}_r^{0,h}$, then $\mathbf{R}(T) \leq r(h+1)$. ⊙

Exercise 3.5.3.4 (2) Obtain a fast algorithm for multiplying two polynomials in one variable by the method you used to solve the previous exercise. ⊙

Example 3.5.3.5 Consider $\mathfrak{S}_3$. In the standard basis,

$$T_{\mathbb{C}[\mathfrak{S}_3]}(\mathbb{C}[\mathfrak{S}_3]^*) = \begin{pmatrix} x_0 & x_1 & x_2 & x_3 & x_4 & x_5 \\ x_1 & x_0 & x_4 & x_5 & x_2 & x_3 \\ x_2 & x_5 & x_0 & x_4 & x_3 & x_1 \\ x_3 & x_4 & x_5 & x_0 & x_1 & x_2 \\ x_4 & x_3 & x_1 & x_2 & x_5 & x_0 \\ x_5 & x_2 & x_3 & x_1 & x_0 & x_4 \end{pmatrix}.$$

Here I have written an element of $\mathbb{C}[\mathfrak{S}_3]$ as $x_0 \delta_{\mathrm{Id}} + x_1 \delta_{(12)} + x_2 \delta_{(13)} + x_3 \delta_{(23)} + x_4 \delta_{(123)} + x_5 \delta_{(132)}$. The irreducible representations of $\mathfrak{S}_3$ are the trivial, denoted [3], the sign, denoted [1, 1, 1], and the two-dimensional standard representation (the complement of the trivial in $\mathbb{C}^3$), which is denoted [2, 1]. (See §8.6.5 for an explanation of the notation.) Since $\dim[3] = 1$, $\dim[1, 1, 1] = 1$, and $\dim[2, 1] = 2$, by Theorem 3.5.2.1, $T_{\mathbb{C}[\mathfrak{S}_3]} = M_{\langle 1 \rangle}^{\oplus 2} \oplus M_{\langle 2 \rangle}$, and in the matrix coefficient basis,

$$T_{\mathbb{C}[\mathfrak{S}_3]}(\mathbb{C}[\mathfrak{S}_3]^*) = \begin{pmatrix} y_0 & & & & & \\ & y_1 & & & & \\ & & y_2 & y_3 & & \\ & & y_4 & y_5 & & \\ & & & & y_2 & y_3 \\ & & & & y_4 & y_5 \end{pmatrix}.$$

where the blank entries are zero. We conclude that $\mathbf{R}(T_{\mathbb{C}[\mathfrak{S}_3]}) \leq 1 + 1 + 7 = 9$.

3.5.4 Upper Bounds via Finite Groups

Here is the main idea:

Use the standard basis to get a lower bound on the value of $T_{\mathbb{C}[G]}$ and the matrix coefficient basis to get an upper bound on its cost.

Say $T_{\mathbb{C}[G]}$ expressed in its standard basis combinatorially restricts to a sum of matrix multiplications, say, $\oplus_{j=1}^{s} M_{\langle \mathbf{l}_j, \mathbf{m}_j, \mathbf{n}_j \rangle}$. The standard basis is particularly well suited to combinatorial restrictions because all the coefficients of the tensor in this basis are zero or one, and all the entries of the matrix $T_{\mathbb{C}[G]}(\mathbb{C}[G]^*)$ are nonzero and coordinate elements. (Recall that all the entries of the matrix $M_{\langle \mathbf{l}, \mathbf{m}, \mathbf{n} \rangle}(A^*)$ are either zero or coordinate elements.) Using the matrix coefficient basis, we see $T_{\mathbb{C}[G]} = \oplus_{u=1}^{q} M_{\langle d_u \rangle}$, where d_u is the dimension of the uth irreducible representation of G. Thus $\underline{\mathbf{R}}(\oplus_{j=1}^{s} M_{\langle \mathbf{l}_j, \mathbf{m}_j, \mathbf{n}_j \rangle}) \leq \underline{\mathbf{R}}(\oplus_{u=1}^{q} M_{\langle d_u \rangle})$ and $\mathbf{R}(\oplus_{j=1}^{s} M_{\langle \mathbf{l}_j, \mathbf{m}_j, \mathbf{n}_j \rangle}) \leq \mathbf{R}(\oplus_{u=1}^{q} M_{\langle d_u \rangle})$.

The asymptotic sum inequality implies the following:

Proposition 3.5.4.1 [CU03, CU13] *If $T_{\mathbb{C}[G]}$ degenerates to $\oplus_{j=1}^{s} M_{\langle \mathbf{l}_j, \mathbf{m}_j, \mathbf{n}_j \rangle}$ and d_u are the dimensions of the irreducible representations of G, then $\sum_{j=1}^{s} (\mathbf{l}_j \mathbf{m}_j \mathbf{n}_j)^{\frac{\omega}{3}} \leq \mathbf{R}(\oplus_{u=1}^{q} M_{\langle d_u \rangle}) \leq \sum d_u^3$. In fact, $\sum_{j=1}^{s} (\mathbf{l}_j \mathbf{m}_j \mathbf{n}_j)^{\frac{\omega}{3}} \leq \sum d_u^\omega$.*

In this section I will denote the standard basis for $\mathbb{C}[G]$ given by the group elements (which I have been denoting δ_{g_i}) simply by g_i.

Basis elements of $\mathbb{C}[G]$ are indexed by elements of G, so our sought-after combinatorial restriction is of the form

$$\alpha : [\mathbf{l}] \times [\mathbf{m}] \to G,$$
$$\beta : [\mathbf{m}] \times [\mathbf{n}] \to G,$$
$$\gamma : [\mathbf{n}] \times [\mathbf{l}] \to G.$$

Recall the requirement that $t^{\alpha(i,j'), \beta(j,k'), \gamma(k,i')}$ is one if and only if $i = i'$, $j = j'$, and $k = k'$, and is otherwise zero. Here, when considering $T_{\mathbb{C}[G]}$ as a trilinear map, we have

$$t^{\alpha, \beta, \gamma} = \begin{cases} 1 & \alpha\beta\gamma = \mathrm{Id} \\ 0 & \text{otherwise.} \end{cases}$$

We want that $\alpha(i, j')\beta(j, k')\gamma(k, i') = \mathrm{Id}$ if and only if $i = i'$, $j = j'$, $k = k'$. To simplify the requirement, assume the maps factor to $s_1 : [\mathbf{l}] \to G$, $s_2 : [\mathbf{m}] \to G$, $s_3 : [\mathbf{n}] \to G$, and that $\alpha(i, j') = s_1^{-1}(i)s_2(j')$, $\beta(j, k') = s_2^{-1}(j)s_3(k')$, and $\gamma(k, i') = s_3^{-1}(k)s_1(i')$. Our requirement becomes

$$s_1^{-1}(i)s_2(j')s_2^{-1}(j)s_3(k')s_3^{-1}(k)s_1(i') = \mathrm{Id} \Leftrightarrow i = i', \; j = j', \; k = k'.$$

Let S_j denote the image of s_j. Our requirement is summarized in the following definition:

Definition 3.5.4.2 [CU03] *A triple of subsets $S_1, S_2, S_3 \subset G$ satisfies the* triple product property *if, for any $s_j, s_j' \in S_j$, $s_1' s_1^{-1} s_2' s_2^{-1} s_3' s_3^{-1} = \mathrm{Id}$ implies $s_1' = s_1$, $s_2' = s_2$, $s_3' = s_3$.*

There is a corresponding simultaneous triple product property when there is a combinatorial restriction to a collection of disjoint matrix multiplication tensors.

Example 3.5.4.3 [CKSU05] Let $G = (\mathbb{Z}_N^{\times 3} \times \mathbb{Z}_N^{\times 3}) \rtimes \mathbb{Z}_2$, where $\mathbb{Z}_2$ acts by switching the two factors, so $|G| = 2N^6$. Write elements of G as $[(\omega^i, \omega^j, \omega^k)(\omega^l, \omega^s, \omega^t)\tau^\epsilon]$, where $0 \leq i, j, k, l, s, t \leq N - 1$, ω is a primitive Nth root of unity, τ is a generator of $\mathbb{Z}_2$, and $\epsilon \in \{0, 1\}$. Set $\mathbf{l} = \mathbf{m} = \mathbf{n} = 2N(N-1)$. Label the elements of $[\mathbf{n}] = [2N(N-1)]$ by a triple (a, b, ϵ) where $1 \leq a \leq N - 1$, $0 \leq b \leq N - 1$ and $\epsilon \in \{0, 1\}$, and define

$$s_1 : [\mathbf{l}] \to G$$
$$(a, b, \epsilon) \mapsto [(\omega^a, 1, 1)(1, \omega^b, 1)\tau^\epsilon],$$

$$s_2 : [\mathbf{m}] \to G$$
$$(a, b, \epsilon) \mapsto [(1, \omega^a, 1)(1, 1, \omega^b)\tau^\epsilon],$$

$$s_3 : [\mathbf{n}] \to G$$
$$(a, b, \epsilon) \mapsto [(1, 1, \omega^a)(\omega^b, 1, 1)\tau^\epsilon].$$

As explained in [CKSU05], the triple product property indeed holds (there are several cases), so $T_{\mathbb{C}[G]}$ combinatorially restricts to $M_{\langle 2N(N-1)\rangle}$. Now G has $2N^3$ irreducible one-dimensional representations and $\binom{N^3}{2}$ irreducible two-dimensional representations (see [CKSU05]). Thus $\mathbf{R}(M_{\langle 2N(N-1)\rangle}) \leq 2N^3 + 8\binom{N^3}{2}$, which is less than $\mathbf{n}^3 = [2N(N-1)]^3$ for all $N \geq 5$. Asymptotically, this is about $\frac{7}{16}\mathbf{n}^3$. If one applies Proposition 3.5.4.1 with $N = 17$ (which is optimal), one obtains $\omega < 2.9088$. Note that this does not even exploit Strassen's algorithm, so one actually has $\mathbf{R}(M_{\langle \mathbf{n}\rangle}) \leq 2N^3 + 7\binom{N^3}{2}$; however, this does not affect the asymptotics. If one could use the failure of additivity for border rank, one potentially could do better.

While this is worse than what one would obtain just using Strassen's algorithm (writing $40 = 32 + 8$ and using Strassen in blocks), the algorithm is *different*. In [CKSU05] the authors obtain a bound of $\omega < 2.41$ by such methods, but key lemmas in their proof are almost the same as the key lemmas used by Coopersmith-Winograd in their optimizations.

3.5.5 Further Ideas Toward Upper Bounds

The structure tensor of $\mathbb{C}[G]$ had the convenient property that in the standard basis, all the coefficients of the tensor are zero or one, and all entries of the matrix $T_{\mathbb{C}[G]}(\mathbb{C}[G]^*)$ are basis vectors. In [CU13] the authors propose looking at combinatorial restrictions of more general structure tensors, where the coefficients can be more general, but vestiges of these properties are preserved. They make the following definition, which is very particular to matrix multiplication:

Definition 3.5.5.1 We say $T \in A{\otimes}B{\otimes}C$, given in bases a_α, b_β, c_γ of A, B, C, *combinatorially supports* $M_{\langle \mathbf{l},\mathbf{m},\mathbf{n}\rangle}$, if such that, writing $T = \sum t^{\alpha,\beta,\gamma} a_\alpha{\otimes}b_\beta{\otimes}c_\gamma$, there exist injections

$$\alpha : [\mathbf{l}] \times [\mathbf{m}] \to [\mathbf{a}],$$
$$\beta : [\mathbf{m}] \times [\mathbf{n}] \to [\mathbf{b}],$$
$$\gamma : [\mathbf{n}] \times [\mathbf{l}] \to [\mathbf{c}]$$

such that $t^{\alpha(i,j'),\beta(j,k')\gamma(k,i')} \neq 0$ if and only if $i = i'$, $j = j'$, and $k = k'$. (Recall that T combinatorially restricts to $M_{\langle \mathbf{l},\mathbf{m},\mathbf{n}\rangle}$ if, moreover, $t^{\alpha(i,j),\beta(j,k)\gamma(k,i)} = 1$ for all i, j, k.)

T combinatorially supports $M_{\langle \mathbf{m},\mathbf{n},\mathbf{l}\rangle}$ if there exists a coordinate expression of T such that, upon setting some of the coefficients in the multidimensional matrix representing T to zero, one obtains $\mathbf{mnl}$ nonzero entries such that in that coordinate system, matrix multiplication is supported on exactly those $\mathbf{mnl}$ entries. They then proceed to define the *s-rank* of a tensor T', which is the lowest rank of a tensor T that combinatorially supports it. This is a strange concept, because *the s-rank of a generic tensor is one*: a generic tensor is combinatorially supported by $T = (\sum_j a_j){\otimes}(\sum_k b_k){\otimes}(\sum_l c_l)$, where $\{a_j\}$ is a basis of A, etc.

Despite this, they show that $\omega \leq \frac{3}{2}\omega_s - 1$, where ω_s is the analog of the exponent of matrix multiplication for s-rank. In particular, $\omega_s = 2$ would imply $\omega = 2$. The idea of the proof is that if T combinatorially supports $M_{\langle \mathbf{n}\rangle}$, then $T^{\otimes 3}$ combinatorially degenerates to $M_{\langle \mathbf{n}\rangle}^{\oplus t}$ with $t = O(\mathbf{n}^{2-o(1)})$. Compare this with the situation when T combinatorially restricts to $M_{\langle \mathbf{n}\rangle}$, then $T^{\otimes 3}$ combinatorially restricts to $M_{\langle \mathbf{n}\rangle}{\otimes}M_{\langle \mathbf{n}^2\rangle}$, and thus toric degenerates to $M_{\langle \mathbf{n}\rangle}^{\oplus\lfloor \frac{3}{4}\mathbf{n}^2\rfloor}$ by Theorem 3.4.3.1.

4

The Complexity of Matrix Multiplication III: Explicit Decompositions via Geometry

One might argue that the exponent of matrix multiplication is unimportant for the world we live in, since ω might not be relevant until the sizes of the matrices are on the order of the number of atoms in the known universe. For implementation, it is more important to develop explicit decompositions that provide a savings for matrices of sizes that need to be multiplied in practice. One purpose of this chapter is to discuss such decompositions. Another is to gain insight into the asymptotic situation by studying the symmetry groups that occur in the known decompositions of $M_{\langle n \rangle}$. I begin, in §4.1, by discussing generalities about decompositions: the generalized Comon conjecture positing that optimal decompositions with symmetry exist, a review of Strassen's original decomposition of $M_{\langle 2 \rangle}$ that hints that this is indeed the case, and defining symmetry groups of decompositions. In particular, I point out that decompositions come in *families* essentially parametrized by $G_{M_{\langle n \rangle}}$, and one gains insight studying the entire family rather than individual members. In §4.2, I describe two decompositions of $M_{\langle n \rangle}$ that have appeared in the literature, a recent one by Grochow-Moore and Pan's 1978 decomposition that held the world record for practical matrix multiplication from 1978 to 2013 in a sense I now make precise.

Introduce $\omega_{prac,k}$ to be the smallest τ such that there exists $\mathbf{n} \leq k$ with $\mathbf{R}(M_{\langle n \rangle}) \leq \mathbf{n}^\tau$. In contrast to the exponent, there is no hidden constant. By definition, $\omega_{prac,k} \geq \omega_{prac,k'}$ for all $k' > k$ and for all k, $\omega_{prac,k} > \omega$. If we decide that we want to multiply unstructured matrices of size, say, $10,000$ but no larger, then $\omega_{prac,10,000}$ will be a more useful quantity than ω. In this regard, the best result is Smirnov's 2013 $\omega_{prac,54} \leq 2.77$ [Smi13] which comes from his rank 40 decomposition of $M_{\langle 3,3,6 \rangle}$. Previous to that was Pan's 1978 decomposition (Theorem 4.2.1.1), which implied $\omega_{prac,70} \leq 2.79512$. In comparison, using Schönhage's order two border rank 21 decomposition of $M_{\langle 3 \rangle}$, converted to a rank decomposition of a $M_{\langle 3^k \rangle}$ (as discussed in §3.2.1), one needs matrices on the order of 10^{35} before one beats Strassen's 2.81. Using Bini et al's order one border rank 10 decomposition for $M_{\langle 2,2,3\rangle}$ converted to a rank decomposition of $M_{\langle 12^k\rangle}$, one needs matrices of size on the order of 10^{40}. In order to make, e.g., Coppersmith-Winograd's method viable, one needs matrices of size larger than the number of atoms in the known universe (larger than 10^{81}).

Problem 4.0.1 Prove upper bounds on $\omega_{prac,1,000}$ or $\omega_{prac,10,000}$.

This is currently an active area of research.

In §4.3, I revisit Strassen's decomposition and give a proof of Burichenko's theorem [Bur14] that its symmetry group is as large as one could naïvely hope it to be. In order to determine symmetry groups and determine if different decompositions are in the same family, one needs invariants of decompositions. These are studied in §4.4. Two interesting examples of decompositions of $M_{\langle 3\rangle}$ are given in §4.5, a variant of Laderman's decomposition and decomposition with $\mathbb{Z}_4 \times \mathbb{Z}_3$-symmetry from [BILR]. In §4.6 I briefly describe the alternating least squares method that has been used to find decompositions numerically. Border rank decompositions also have geometry associated with them. In order to describe the geometry, I give some geometric preliminaries, including the definition of secant varieties in §4.7. I conclude with two examples of border rank decompositions and their geometry in §4.8 from [LR17].

4.1 Symmetry and Decompositions

4.1.1 Warm-up: Strassen's Decomposition

Strassen's algorithm, written as a tensor, is

$$
M_{(2)} = \begin{pmatrix} 1 & 0 \\ 0 & 1 \end{pmatrix}^{\otimes 3} + \begin{pmatrix} 1 & 0 \\ 0 & 0 \end{pmatrix} \otimes \begin{pmatrix} 0 & 0 \\ 1 & -1 \end{pmatrix} \otimes \begin{pmatrix} 0 & 1 \\ 0 & 1 \end{pmatrix} + \begin{pmatrix} 0 & 0 \\ 1 & -1 \end{pmatrix} \otimes \begin{pmatrix} 0 & 1 \\ 0 & 1 \end{pmatrix} \otimes \begin{pmatrix} 1 & 0 \\ 0 & 0 \end{pmatrix}
$$

$$
+ \begin{pmatrix} 0 & 1 \\ 0 & 1 \end{pmatrix} \otimes \begin{pmatrix} 1 & 0 \\ 0 & 0 \end{pmatrix} \otimes \begin{pmatrix} 0 & 0 \\ 1 & -1 \end{pmatrix} - \begin{pmatrix} 0 & 0 \\ 0 & 1 \end{pmatrix} \otimes \begin{pmatrix} 1 & -1 \\ 0 & 0 \end{pmatrix} \otimes \begin{pmatrix} 1 & 0 \\ 1 & 0 \end{pmatrix}
$$

$$
- \begin{pmatrix} 1 & -1 \\ 0 & 0 \end{pmatrix} \otimes \begin{pmatrix} 1 & 0 \\ 1 & 0 \end{pmatrix} \otimes \begin{pmatrix} 0 & 0 \\ 0 & 1 \end{pmatrix} - \begin{pmatrix} 1 & 0 \\ 1 & 0 \end{pmatrix} \otimes \begin{pmatrix} 0 & 0 \\ 0 & 1 \end{pmatrix} \otimes \begin{pmatrix} 1 & -1 \\ 0 & 0 \end{pmatrix}. \qquad (4.1.1)
$$

A first observation is that the $\mathbb{Z}_3$-symmetry of $M_{(2)}$ (see Exercise 2.5.1.6), which I will call the *standard cyclic symmetry*, also occurs in Strassen's decomposition: the $\mathbb{Z}_3$ action fixes the first term and permutes the other two triples of terms. This motivates the study of *symmetry groups of rank decompositions*.

Exercise 4.1.1.1 (2) Show that if we change bases by

$$g_U = \begin{pmatrix} 1 & -1 \\ 0 & -1 \end{pmatrix} \in GL(U), \, g_V = \begin{pmatrix} -1 & 0 \\ -1 & 1 \end{pmatrix} \in GL(V), \, g_W = \begin{pmatrix} 0 & 1 \\ 1 & 0 \end{pmatrix} \in GL(W),$$

then the new decomposition of $M_{(2)}$ has four terms fixed by the standard cyclic $\mathbb{Z}_3$. ⊚

4.1.2 Symmetry Groups of Tensors and their Rank Decompositions

Consider $Seg(\mathbb{P}A_1 \times \cdots \times \mathbb{P}A_d) \subset \mathbb{P}(A_1 \otimes \cdots \otimes A_d)$. If all the vector spaces have different dimensions, consider the symmetry group of the cone over the Segre as a subgroup of $GL(A_1) \times \cdots \times GL(A_d)$ (more precisely of $GL(A_1) \times \cdots \times GL(A_d)/(\mathbb{C}^*)^{d-1}$, because if $\lambda_1 \cdots \lambda_d = 1$, then $(\lambda_1 \, \mathrm{Id}_{A_1}, \ldots, \lambda_d \, \mathrm{Id}_{A_d}) \in GL(A_1) \times \cdots \times GL(A_d)$ acts trivially). If all dimensions are the same, consider the symmetry group as a subgroup of $(GL(A_1) \times \cdots \times GL(A_d)/(\mathbb{C}^*)^{\times d-1}) \rtimes \mathfrak{S}_d$, where the $\mathfrak{S}_d$ acts by permuting the factors after isomorphisms of the A_j have been chosen. One can also consider intermediate cases. For $T \in (\mathbb{C}^N)^{\otimes d}$, let

$$G_T := \left\{ g \in \left(GL_N^{\times d}/(\mathbb{C}^*)^{\times d-1} \right) \rtimes \mathfrak{S}_d \mid gT = T \right\},$$

and for $T \in A_1 \otimes \cdots \otimes A_d$ with different dimensions, define

$$G_T := \{ g \in GL(A_1) \times \cdots \times GL(A_d)/(\mathbb{C}^*)^{\times d-1} \mid gT = T \}.$$

For a polynomial $P \in S^d V$, write

$$G_P := \{ g \in GL(V) \mid gP = P \}.$$

For a rank decomposition $T = \sum_{j=1}^{r} t_j$, define the set $\mathcal{S} := \{t_1, \ldots, t_r\}$, which I also call the decomposition. If T has a rank decomposition $\mathcal{S}$ and a nontrivial symmetry group G_T, then given $g \in G_T$, $g \cdot \mathcal{S} := \{gt_1, \ldots, gt_r\}$ is also a rank decomposition of T.

Definition 4.1.2.1 The *symmetry group of a decomposition* $\mathcal{S}$ is $\Gamma_{\mathcal{S}} := \{g \in G_T \mid g \cdot \mathcal{S} = \mathcal{S}\}$. Let $\Gamma_{\mathcal{S}}' = \Gamma_{\mathcal{S}} \cap (\Pi_j GL(A_j))$.

A guiding principle of this chapter (for which there is no theoretical justification but which holds in several situations; see §7.1.2 and §6.6.3) is that if T has a large symmetry group, then there will exist optimal decompositions of T with symmetry. This even extends to border rank decompositions, as we will see in §4.7.4.

Naïvely, one might think that some decompositions in a family have better symmetry groups than others. Strictly speaking, this is not correct:

Proposition 4.1.2.2 [CILO16] *For $g \in G_T$, $\Gamma_{g \cdot S} = g\Gamma_S g^{-1}$.*

Proof. Let $h \in \Gamma_S$, then $ghg^{-1}(gt_j) = g(ht_j) \in g \cdot S$, so $\Gamma_{g \cdot S} \subseteq g\Gamma_{S,} g^{-1}$, but the construction is symmetric in $\Gamma_{g \cdot S}$ and Γ_S. $\qquad\qquad\qquad\square$

As explained below, there may be preferred decompositions in a family where certain symmetries take a particularly transparent form.

For a polynomial $P \in S^d V$ and a symmetric rank decomposition $P = \ell_1^d + \cdots + \ell_r^d$ for some $\ell_j \in V$ (also called a *Waring decomposition*), and $g \in G_P \subset GL(V)$, the same result holds with $S = \{\ell_1^d, \ldots, \ell_r^d\}$.

In summary, decompositions come in $\dim(G_T)$-dimensional families, and each member of the family has the same abstract symmetry group.

4.1.3 Symmetries of $M_{\langle \mathbf{n} \rangle}$

Let $PGL(U)$ denote $GL(U)/\mathbb{C}^*$, where $\mathbb{C}^* = \{\lambda \operatorname{Id}_U \mid \lambda \in \mathbb{C}^*\}$. This group acts on $\mathbb{P}U$, as well as on $U^* \otimes U$. The first action is clear, the second because the action of $GL(U)$ on $\alpha \otimes u$ is $\alpha g^{-1} \otimes gu$, so the scalars times the identity will act trivially.

In §2.5.1 we saw that $PGL_{\mathbf{n}}^{\times 3} \rtimes (\mathbb{Z}_3 \rtimes \mathbb{Z}_2) \subseteq G_{M_{\langle \mathbf{n} \rangle}}$. I emphasize that this $\mathbb{Z}_2$ is not contained in either the $\mathfrak{S}_3$ permuting the factors or the $PGL(A) \times PGL(B) \times PGL(C)$ acting on them.

Proposition 4.1.3.1 [dG78, Theorems 3.3, 3.4] $G_{M_{\langle \mathbf{n} \rangle}} = PGL_{\mathbf{n}}^{\times 3} \rtimes (\mathbb{Z}_3 \rtimes \mathbb{Z}_2)$.

A proof is given in §8.12.4.

4.1.4 The Comon Conjecture and Its Generalization

Conjecture 4.1.4.1 (P. Comon [Com02]) *If $T \in S^d \mathbb{C}^N \subset (\mathbb{C}^N)^{\otimes d}$, then there exists an optimal rank decomposition of T made from symmetric tensors.*

After being initially greeted with skepticism by algebraic geometers (Comon is an engineer), the community has now embraced this conjecture and generalized it.

Question 4.1.4.2 [Generalized Comon Conjecture] [BILR] Let $T \in (\mathbb{C}^N)^{\otimes d}$ be invariant under some $\Gamma \subset \mathfrak{S}_d$. Does there exist an optimal rank decomposition S of T satisfying $\Gamma \subseteq \Gamma_S$?

I use the following special case as a working hypothesis:

Conjecture 4.1.4.3 [BILR] *If $\mathbf{R}(M_{\langle \mathbf{n} \rangle}) = r$, then there exists a rank r decomposition of $M_{\langle \mathbf{n} \rangle}$ that has standard cyclic symmetry.*

4.1.5 Decomposition of $A^{\otimes 3}$ under $\mathbb{Z}_3$

In order to search for standard cyclic $\mathbb{Z}_3$ decompositions of $M_{\langle n \rangle}$, we need to understand the $GL(A)$-decomposition of $A^{\otimes 3}$.

Exercise 4.1.5.1 (1!) Verify that the cyclic $\mathbb{Z}_3$ acts trivially on both $S^3 A$ and $\Lambda^3 A$.

Proposition 4.1.5.2 *Let $\mathbb{Z}_3 \subset \mathfrak{S}_3$ act on $A^{\otimes 3}$ by cyclically permuting factors. Then*

$$(A^{\otimes 3})^{\mathbb{Z}_3} = S^3 A \oplus \Lambda^3 A.$$

Proposition 4.1.5.2 is proved in Exercise 8.7.2.4.

Thus, if we are searching for cyclic $\mathbb{Z}_3$-invariant decompositions for $M_{\langle n \rangle}$, the size of our search space is cut down from $\mathbf{n}^6$ dimensions to $\frac{\mathbf{n}^6 + 2\mathbf{n}^2}{3}$ dimensions.

It is easy to write down the decomposition of $M_{\langle n \rangle} \in S^3 A \oplus \Lambda^3 A$ into its symmetric and skew-symmetric components:

$$\text{trace}(XYZ) = \frac{1}{2}[\text{trace}(XYZ) + \text{trace}(YXZ)] + \frac{1}{2}[\text{trace}(XYZ) - \text{trace}(YXZ)]$$
$$= : M^S_{\langle n \rangle}(X, Y, Z) + M^\Lambda_{\langle n \rangle}(X, Y, Z).$$

Exercise 4.1.5.3 (1) Verify that the first term in brackets lives in $S^3 A$ and that the second lives in $\Lambda^3 A$.

Remark 4.1.5.4 In [CHI+] we show that the exponent of $M^S_{\langle n \rangle}$ is the same as that of $M_{\langle n \rangle}$. Since $M^S_{\langle n \rangle}$ is a polynomial, this suggests one can use further tools from algebraic geometry (study of cubic hypersurfaces) in the attempt to determine the exponent.

4.2 Two Decomposition Families of $M_{\langle n \rangle}$ of Rank $< n^3$

Call a subset of points $\{[a_1], \ldots, [a_r]\}$ of $\mathbb{P}A$ a *pinning set* if the stabilizer of this set in $PGL(A)$ is finite and no subset of the points has a finite stabilizer. If we choose vector representatives for the $[a_j]$, call it a *framed pinning*. For example, if the subset contains a collection of $\mathbf{a} + 1$ elements in general linear position, it is a pinning set, and $\mathbf{a} + 1$ is the minimal cardinality of a pinning set. Call such a pinning set a *standard pinning*.

A standard pinning determines $\binom{a+1}{2}$ points in $\mathbb{P}A^*$ obtained by intersecting sets of $\mathbf{a} - 1$ hyperplanes coming from the standard pinning points.

4.2.1 Pan's Decomposition Family

Let $\mathbf{n} = 2\mathbf{m}$. Let $\mathbb{Z}_3$ denote the standard cyclic permutation of factors. Introduce the notation $\bar{\imath} = i + \mathbf{m}$, $\bar{\jmath} = j + \mathbf{m}$. Write $x_j^i = u^i \otimes v_j$, $y_j^i = v^i \otimes w_j$, $z_j^i = w^i \otimes u_j$. Let $\mathbb{Z}_2^U$ be generated by σ_U, which is the exchange $u^i \leftrightarrow u^{\bar{\imath}}$ (which also sends $u_i \leftrightarrow u_{\bar{\imath}}$), and define $\mathbb{Z}_2^V$ and $\mathbb{Z}_2^W$ similarly, with generators σ_V, σ_W. Let $\mathbb{Z}_2^\sigma$ be generated by the product of the generators, so σ acts by $x_j^i \leftrightarrow x_{\bar{\jmath}}^{\bar{\imath}}, y_j^i \leftrightarrow y_{\bar{\jmath}}^{\bar{\imath}}$, $z_j^i \leftrightarrow z_{\bar{\jmath}}^{\bar{\imath}}$.

Because of the cyclic $\mathbb{Z}_3$ symmetry, it will be convenient to identify the three spaces, and I will use x_j^i for all three. In what follows, indices are to be considered mod $\mathbf{n}$.

For a finite group $\Gamma \subset GL_N \times GL_N \times GL_N \rtimes \mathfrak{S}_3$, introduce the notation

$$\langle x \otimes y \otimes z \rangle_\Gamma := \sum_{g \in \Gamma} g \cdot (x \otimes y \otimes z). \tag{4.2.1}$$

Let $\mathbb{Z}_2^\tau$ denote the standard transpose $x \otimes y \otimes z \mapsto y^T \otimes x^T \otimes z^T$, and let $\mathbb{Z}_2^{\tau'}$ denote the transpose-like symmetry obtained by composing the standard transpose symmetry with σ_V.

Theorem 4.2.1.1 [Pan78] *With notations as above, $M_{\langle \mathbf{n} \rangle}$ equals*

$$\sum_{(i,j,k)|0 \leq i < j < k \leq \mathbf{m}-1} \left\langle \left(x_j^i + x_k^j + x_i^k\right)^{\otimes 3} \right\rangle_{\mathbb{Z}_2^\sigma} \tag{4.2.2}$$

$$- \sum_{(i,j,k)|0 \leq i < j < k \leq \mathbf{m}-1} \left\langle \left(x_j^i - x_k^{\bar{\imath}} + x_{\bar{\imath}}^k\right) \otimes \left(-x_{\bar{\jmath}}^i + x_k^j + x_i^k\right)\left(x_{\bar{\jmath}}^i + x_k^j - x_i^{\bar{k}}\right) \right\rangle_{\mathbb{Z}_2^\sigma \times \mathbb{Z}_3} \tag{4.2.3}$$

$$+ \sum_{i,j=0}^{\mathbf{m}-1} \left\langle x_j^i \otimes x_j^i \otimes \left[(\mathbf{m} - \delta_{ij}) x_j^i + \sum_{k=0}^{\mathbf{m}-1} \left[\left(x_k^k + x_k^j\right) - \delta_{ij}\left(x_i^k + x_k^i\right)\right] \right] \right\rangle_{\mathbb{Z}_2^\sigma \times \mathbb{Z}_3 \times \mathbb{Z}_2^{\tau'}} \tag{4.2.4}$$

$$+ \sum_{i,j=0}^{\mathbf{m}-1} \left\langle x_j^i \otimes x_j^{\bar{\imath}} \otimes \left[(\mathbf{m} - \delta_{ij}) x_{\bar{\jmath}}^i + \sum_{k=0}^{\mathbf{m}-1} \left[\left(x_k^{\bar{k}} + x_k^j\right) - \delta_{ij}\left(x_i^{\bar{k}} + x_k^i\right)\right] \right] \right\rangle_{\mathbb{Z}_2^\sigma \times \mathbb{Z}_3 \times \mathbb{Z}_2^\tau}. \tag{4.2.5}$$

Note that the terms (4.2.2), (4.2.4), and (4.2.5) are $M_{\langle \mathbf{n} \rangle}$ plus "garbage" terms. The term (4.2.3) eliminates the garbage terms. Call the decomposition S_{Pan}.

Remark 4.2.1.2 According to Burichenko (announced in [Bur15, Theorem 1.1]), $\Gamma_{S_{Pan}} = \mathfrak{S}_{\mathbf{m}} \times \mathbb{Z}_2 \times \mathfrak{S}_3$.

Exercise 4.2.1.3 (2) Show that the number of triples (i, j, k) with $0 \le i \le j < k \le \mathbf{m} - 1$ is $\frac{2}{3}(\mathbf{m}^3 - \mathbf{m})$ and conclude that Pan's decomposition is of rank $\frac{1}{3}\mathbf{n}^3 + 6\mathbf{n}^2 - \frac{4}{3}\mathbf{n}$.

Exercise 4.2.1.4 (1) Show that when $\mathbf{n} = 70$, Pan's decomposition has rank 143, 240, and conclude that $\omega_{prac,70} \le 2.79512$.

4.2.2 The Grochow-Moore Decompositions

The group $\mathfrak{S}_{\mathbf{n}+1}$ acts irreducibly on $\mathbb{C}^{\mathbf{n}}$ (see §1.1.13 for the action and §8.7.2 for the proof), and the induced action on $\mathbb{C}^{\mathbf{n}*} \otimes \mathbb{C}^{\mathbf{n}}$ has a unique trivial representation, namely, $\mathrm{Id}_{\mathbb{C}^{\mathbf{n}}}$ (see Exercise 8.6.8.3).

Exercise 4.2.2.1 (1) Show that any $T \in (U^* \otimes V) \otimes (V^* \otimes W) \otimes (W^* \otimes U)$ that is acted on trivially by $\mathfrak{S}_{\mathbf{n}+1}^{\times 3}$, where the first copy acts on U, U^*, the second on V, V^*, and the third on W, W^*, is up to scale $M_{\langle \mathbf{n} \rangle}$.

Let $u^1, \dots, u^{\mathbf{n}+1} \in U^*$ be a framed pinning normalized so that $u^1 + \cdots + u^{\mathbf{n}+1} = 0$, with $\binom{\mathbf{n}+1}{2}$ induced points $u_{ij} := u_{[\mathbf{n}+1] \setminus \{i,j\}}$ for $i < j$, with normalizations $\sum_j u^j = 0$, and $u^i(u_{ik}) = 1, u^i(u_{ki}) = -1$. Adopt the notation $u_{ji} := -u_{ij}$, so $u_{ii} = 0$.

Given a framed pinning, define a dual framed pinning $u_1, \dots, u_{\mathbf{n}+1}$ of U by requiring

$$u^i(u_j) = \left\{ \begin{matrix} 1 & i = j \\ -\frac{1}{\mathbf{n}} & i \ne j \end{matrix} \right\}.$$

Exercise 4.2.2.2 (1) When $\mathbf{n} = 2$, compute the dual pinning to $\begin{pmatrix} 1 \\ 0 \end{pmatrix}, \begin{pmatrix} 0 \\ 1 \end{pmatrix}, \begin{pmatrix} -1 \\ -1 \end{pmatrix}$. ⊚

Exercise 4.2.2.3 (1) Show that with the above normalizations, $u_{ij} = u_i - u_j$.

Exercise 4.2.2.4 (1) Show that with the above normalizations, $\mathrm{Id}_U = \frac{\mathbf{n}}{\mathbf{n}+1} \sum_{i=1}^{\mathbf{n}+1} u^i \otimes u_i$.

Proposition 4.2.2.5 [GM16] *Notations as above. Then*

$$M_{\langle \mathbf{n} \rangle} = \left(\frac{\mathbf{n}}{\mathbf{n}+1} \right)^3 \sum_{i,j,k=1}^{\mathbf{n}+1} u^i v_j \otimes v^j w_k \otimes w^k u_i.$$

Proof. Note that the right-hand side is invariant under $\mathfrak{S}_{\mathbf{n}+1}^{\times 3}$, so it is some constant times $M_{\langle \mathbf{n} \rangle}$. To check that the constant is correct, evaluate the right-hand side on, e.g., $\mathrm{Id}_{\mathbf{n}}^{\otimes 3}$. □

Proposition 4.2.2.5 gives a rank $(\mathbf{n}+1)^3$ decomposition of $M_{\langle \mathbf{n} \rangle}$, so at first glance, it does not appear interesting. However, it is used to prove the following theorem:

Theorem 4.2.2.6 [GM16] *Let $u^1, \dots, u^{\mathbf{n}+1} \in U^*$ be a framed pinning with induced vectors $u_{ij} \in U$ as above, and choose identifications $U \simeq V \simeq W$ to obtain inherited pinnings and induced vectors. The following is a rank $\mathbf{n}^3 - \mathbf{n}+1$ decomposition of $M_{\langle \mathbf{n} \rangle}$, call it $\mathcal{S}_{GM}$, with $\Gamma_{\mathcal{S}_{GM}} \supset \mathfrak{S}_{\mathbf{n}+1} \rtimes \mathbb{Z}_3$:*

$$M_{\langle \mathbf{n} \rangle} = \mathrm{Id}_{\mathbf{n}}^{\otimes 3} - \left(\frac{\mathbf{n}}{\mathbf{n}+1} \right)^3 \sum_{i,j,k \in [\mathbf{n}+1] \text{ and distinct}} u^i v_{ij} \otimes v^j w_{jk} \otimes w^k u_{ki}.$$

Proof. First, notice that

$$\sum_{i,j,k \in [\mathbf{n}+1] \text{ and distinct}} u^i v_{ij} \otimes v^j w_{jk} \otimes w^k u_{ki} = \sum_{i,j,k \in [\mathbf{n}+1]} u^i v_{ij} \otimes v^j w_{jk} \otimes w^k u_{ki}$$

because $v_{ii} = 0$. By Exercise 4.2.2.3, we may write $v_{ij} = v_i - v_j$. One then expands out, using Exercise 4.2.2.4 and Proposition 4.2.2.5, to conclude. $\square$

Theorem 4.2.2.6 gives another perspective on Strassen's decomposition family for $M_{\langle 2 \rangle}$.

4.3 Strassen's Decomposition Revisited

Let $\mathcal{S}tr$ denote the Strassen decomposition of $M_{\langle 2 \rangle}$.

4.3.1 The Strassen Family

As discussed above, decompositions are best studied in families. In the case of $M_{\langle 2 \rangle}$, there is a unique family:

Theorem 4.3.1.1 [dG78] *The set of rank seven decompositions of $M_{\langle 2 \rangle}$ is the orbit $G_{M_{\langle 2 \rangle}} \cdot \mathcal{S}tr$.*

The proof follows from a careful analysis of every possible decomposition, taking into account that an element $a \otimes b \otimes c$ is not just a triple of vectors, but a triple of endomorphisms $\mathbb{C}^2 \to \mathbb{C}^2$, and the analysis is via the possible triples of ranks that can appear.

In preparation for studying the Strassen family of decompositions, write

$$u_1 = \begin{pmatrix} 1 \\ 0 \end{pmatrix}, \ u_2 = \begin{pmatrix} 0 \\ 1 \end{pmatrix}, \ u^1 = (1, 0), \ u^2 = (0, 1) \qquad (4.3.1)$$

and set $v_j = w_j = u_j$ and $v^j = w^j = u^j$.

Strassen's decomposition becomes

$$
\begin{aligned}
M_{(2)} = {} & (v_1 u^1 + v_2 u^2) \otimes (w_1 v^1 + w_2 v^2) \otimes (u_1 w^1 + u_2 w^2) \\
& + \langle v_1 u^1 \otimes w_2 (v^1 - v^2) \otimes (u_1 + u_2) w^2 \rangle_{\mathbb{Z}_3} \\
& + \langle v_2 u^2 \otimes w_1 (v^2 - v^1) \otimes (u_1 + u_2) w^1 \rangle_{\mathbb{Z}_3}.
\end{aligned}
\tag{4.3.2}
$$

From this presentation we transparently recover much of the entire Strassen family, namely, by letting u_1, u_2, v_1, v_2, and w_1, w_2 be arbitrary bases, with dual basis vectors denoted with superscripts. We obtain a family parametrized by $PGL(U) \times PGL(V) \times PGL(W)$, and since the decomposition (4.3.2) is manifestly $\mathbb{Z}_3$-invariant, the only potential additional decompositions arise from applying a transpose symmetry such as $x \otimes y \otimes z \mapsto x^T \otimes z^T \otimes y^T$. Call such a transpose symmetry *convenient*.

Exercise 4.3.1.2 (1) Show that if we set $u_3 = \begin{pmatrix} -1 \\ -1 \end{pmatrix}$ and $u^3 = (1, -1)$, and similarly for v, w, then the matrices in Exercise 4.1.1.1 correspond to the permutations $(2, 3)$, $(1, 3)$, and $(1, 2)$, respectively. The matrix in the first term of the decomposition that one obtains from Exercise 4.1.1.1 also corresponds to a permutation. Which one?

Exercise 4.3.1.3 (2) Find a change of basis such that the first term in the decomposition of Exercise 4.1.1.1 becomes $\begin{pmatrix} \omega & 0 \\ 0 & \omega^2 \end{pmatrix}^{\otimes 3}$, where $\omega = e^{\frac{2\pi i}{3}}$, and write out the decomposition in this basis.

Under $x \otimes y \otimes z \mapsto x^T \otimes z^T \otimes y^T$, Strassen's decomposition is mapped to

$$
\begin{aligned}
M_{(2)} = {} & \begin{pmatrix} 1 & 0 \\ 0 & 1 \end{pmatrix}^{\otimes 3} + \left\langle \begin{pmatrix} 1 & 0 \\ 0 & 0 \end{pmatrix} \otimes \begin{pmatrix} 0 & 0 \\ 1 & 1 \end{pmatrix} \otimes \begin{pmatrix} 0 & 1 \\ 0 & -1 \end{pmatrix} \right\rangle_{\mathbb{Z}_3} \\
& - \left\langle \begin{pmatrix} 0 & 0 \\ 0 & 1 \end{pmatrix} \otimes \begin{pmatrix} 1 & 1 \\ 0 & 0 \end{pmatrix} \otimes \begin{pmatrix} 1 & 0 \\ -1 & 0 \end{pmatrix} \right\rangle_{\mathbb{Z}_3}.
\end{aligned}
\tag{4.3.3}
$$

Notice that this is almost Strassen's decomposition (4.1.1) – just some of the signs are wrong. We can "fix" the problem by conjugating all the matrices with

$$
g_0 := \begin{pmatrix} 0 & -1 \\ 1 & 0 \end{pmatrix}.
$$

Exercise 4.3.1.4 (1) Verify that acting by $g_0^{\times 3} \in PGL(U) \times PGL(V) \times PGL(W)$ takes (4.3.3) to Strassen's decomposition.

Exercise 4.3.1.4 shows that there is a nonstandard $\mathbb{Z}_2 \subset PGL_2^{\times 3} \rtimes (\mathbb{Z}_3 \rtimes \mathbb{Z}_2)$ contained in Γ_{Str}, namely, the convenient transpose symmetry composed with $g_0^{\times 3}$. It also implies a refinement of deGroote's theorem:

Proposition 4.3.1.5 [Bur14, CILO16] *The set of rank seven decompositions of $M_{\langle 2 \rangle}$ is $PGL_2^{\times 3} \cdot Str$.*

With the expression (4.3.2), notice that if we exchange $u_1 \leftrightarrow u_2$ and $u^1 \leftrightarrow u^2$, the decomposition is also preserved by this $\mathbb{Z}_2 \subset PGL_2^{\times 3}$, with orbits (4.3.2) and the exchange of the triples. So we see $\Gamma_{Str} \supseteq \mathbb{Z}_2 \rtimes (\mathbb{Z}_3 \rtimes \mathbb{Z}_2)$, where the first $\mathbb{Z}_2$ is diagonally embedded in $PGL_2^{\times 3}$.

Although the above description of the Strassen family of decompositions for $M_{\langle 2 \rangle}$ is satisfying, it becomes even more transparent with a projective perspective. With the projective perspective, we will see that Γ_{Str} is even larger.

4.3.2 $M_{\langle 2 \rangle}$ Viewed Projectively

That all rank seven decompositions of $M_{\langle 2 \rangle}$ are obtained via $PGL_2^{\times 3}$ suggests using a projective perspective. The group PGL_2 acts simply transitively on triples of distinct points of $\mathbb{P}^1$. So to fix a decomposition in the family, select a pinning (triple of points) in each space. I focus on $\mathbb{P}U$. Call the points $[u_1], [u_2], [u_3]$. Then these determine three points in $\mathbb{P}U^*$, $[u^{1\perp}], [u^{2\perp}], [u^{3\perp}]$. Choose representatives u_1, u_2, u_3 satisfying $u_1 + u_2 + u_3 = 0$. I could have taken any linear relation, it just would introduce coefficients in the decomposition. I take the most symmetric relation to keep all three points on an equal footing. Similarly, fix the scales on the $u^{j\perp}$ by requiring $u^{j\perp}(u_{j-1}) = 1$ and $u^{j\perp}(u_{j+1}) = -1$, where indices are considered mod $\mathbb{Z}_3$, so $u_{3+1} = u_1$ and $u_{1-1} = u_3$.

In comparison with what we had before, letting the old vectors be hatted, $\hat{u}_1 = u_1$, $\hat{u}_2 = u_2$, $\hat{u}^1 = u^{2\perp}$, and $\hat{u}^2 = -u^{1\perp}$. The effect is to make the symmetries of the decomposition more transparent. Our identifications of the ordered triples $\{u_1, u_2, u_3\}$ and $\{v_1, v_2, v_3\}$ determines a linear isomorphism $a_0 : U \to V$, and similarly for the other pairs of vector spaces. Note that $a_0 = v_j \otimes u^{j+1\perp} + v_{j+1} \otimes u^{j+2\perp}$ for any $j = 1, 2, 3$.

Then

$$M_{\langle 2 \rangle} = a_0 \otimes b_0 \otimes c_0 + \langle (v_1 u^{2\perp}) \otimes (w_3 v^{1\perp}) \otimes (u_2 w^{3\perp}) \rangle_{\mathbb{Z}_3} \qquad (4.3.4)$$
$$+ \langle (n_1 u^{3\perp}) \otimes (m_2 n^{1\perp}) \otimes (u_3 w^{2\perp}) \rangle_{\mathbb{Z}_3}.$$

Here, to make the terms shifted by $\mathbb{Z}_3$ live in the proper space, one must act by a_0, b_0, c_0 appropriately, e.g., to shift $v_1 u^{2\perp}$ to the second slot, one takes $b_0 v_1 u^{2\perp} a_0^{-1}$.

With this presentation, taking $a_0 = b_0 = c_0 = \mathrm{Id}$, the diagonally embedded $\mathfrak{S}_3 \subset PGL_2^{\times 3}$ acting by permuting the indices transparently preserves the decomposition, with two orbits, the fixed point $a_0 \otimes b_0 \otimes c_0$ and the orbit of $(v_1 u^{2\perp}) \otimes (w_3 v^{1\perp}) \otimes (u_2 w^{3\perp})$. The action on each of U, V, W is the standard irreducible two-dimensional representation.

We now see $\Gamma_{Str} \supseteq \mathfrak{S}_3 \ltimes (\mathbb{Z}_3 \rtimes \mathbb{Z}_2)$, with $\mathfrak{S}_3 \subset \Gamma'_{Str}$. With a little more work, one sees that the equality holds:

Theorem 4.3.2.1 [Bur14] *The symmetry group Γ_{Str} of Strassen's decomposition of $M_{\langle 2 \rangle}$ is $(\mathfrak{S}_3 \times \mathbb{Z}_3) \rtimes \mathbb{Z}_2 \subset PGL_2^{\times 3} \rtimes (\mathbb{Z}_3 \rtimes \mathbb{Z}_2) = G_{M_{\langle 2 \rangle}}$.*

Remark 4.3.2.2 One can prove that Strassen's decomposition is indeed matrix multiplication simply by the group invariance (see [CILO16]).

4.4 Invariants Associated to a Decomposition of $M_{\langle \mathbf{n} \rangle}$

Given two decompositions of $M_{\langle \mathbf{n} \rangle}$, how can we determine if they are in the same family? Given one, how can we determine its symmetry group? These questions are related, as a necessary condition for two decompositions to be in the same family is that they have isomorphic symmetry groups. I first define invariants $\mathcal{S}_{s,t,u}$ that are subsets of points in $\mathbb{P}(A \otimes B \otimes C)$. Keeping track of the cardinalities of these sets dates at least back to [JM86]. I then further define subsets $\mathcal{S}_U \subset \mathbb{P}U, \mathcal{S}_{U^*} \subset \mathbb{P}U^*$ that give more information. I describe further invariants associated to a decomposition via graphs. I then discuss the sets $\mathcal{S}_U, \mathcal{S}_U^*$ in more detail: it turns out that the collection of points themselves has geometry that is also useful for distinguishing decompositions and determining symmetry groups.

4.4.1 Invariants of Decompositions of $M_{\langle \mathbf{n} \rangle}$

Let $M_{\langle \mathbf{n} \rangle} = \sum_{j=1}^{r} t_j$ be a rank decomposition for $M_{\langle \mathbf{n} \rangle}$ and write $t_j = a_j \otimes b_j \otimes c_j$. Let $\mathbf{r}_j := (\mathrm{rank}(a_j), \mathrm{rank}(b_j), \mathrm{rank}(c_j))$, and let $\tilde{\mathbf{r}}_j$ denote the unordered triple. The following proposition is clear:

Proposition 4.4.1.1 [BILR] *Let $\mathcal{S}$ be a rank decomposition of $M_{\langle \mathbf{n} \rangle}$. Partition $\mathcal{S}$ by unordered rank triples into disjoint subsets: $\{\tilde{\mathcal{S}}_{1,1,1}, \tilde{\mathcal{S}}_{1,1,2}, \ldots, \tilde{\mathcal{S}}_{n,n,n}\}$. Write the corresponding ordered triplets as $\{\mathcal{S}_{1,1,1}, \mathcal{S}_{1,1,2}, \mathcal{S}_{1,2,1}, \ldots, \mathcal{S}_{n,n,n}\}$. Then $\Gamma_{\mathcal{S}}$ preserves each $\tilde{\mathcal{S}}_{s,t,u}$ and $\Gamma'_{\mathcal{S}}$ preserves each $\mathcal{S}_{s,t,u}$.*

We can say more about rank one elements: if $a \in U^* \otimes V$ and $\mathrm{rank}(a) = 1$, then there are unique points $[\mu] \in \mathbb{P}U^*$ and $[v] \in \mathbb{P}V$ such that $[a] = [\mu \otimes v]$. So given a decomposition $\mathcal{S}$ of $M_{\langle \mathbf{n} \rangle}$, define $\mathcal{S}_{U^*} \subset \mathbb{P}U^*$ and $\mathcal{S}_U \subset \mathbb{P}U$ to correspond to the U^* and U elements appearing in $\mathcal{S}_{1,1,1}$. Then $\Gamma'_{\mathcal{S}}$ preserves the sets $\mathcal{S}_U$ and $\mathcal{S}_{U^*}$ up to projective equivalence.

I will say a decomposition has a *transpose-like $\mathbb{Z}_2$ invariance* if it is invariant under a $\mathbb{Z}_2$ such as $x \otimes y \otimes z \mapsto x^T \otimes z^T \otimes y^T$ composed with an element of $PGL(U) \times PGL(V) \times PGL(W)$.

Exercise 4.4.1.2 (1) Show that if a decomposition of $M_{\langle \mathbf{n} \rangle}$ is cyclic $\mathbb{Z}_3$-invariant and also has a transpose-like $\mathbb{Z}_2$-invariance, then $\mathcal{S}_U$ and $\mathcal{S}_{U^*}$ have the same cardinality.

4.4.2 A Graph

Define a bipartite graph $\mathcal{IG}_{\mathcal{S}}$, the *incidence graph* where the top vertex set is given by elements in $\mathcal{S}_{U^*}$ and the bottom vertex set by elements in $\mathcal{S}_U$. Draw an edge between elements $[\mu]$ and $[v]$ if they are *incident*, i.e., $\mu(v) = 0$. Geometrically, $[v]$ belongs to the hyperplane determined by $[\mu]$ (and vice versa). One can weight the vertices of this graph in several ways; the simplest (and in practice this has been enough) is just by the number of times the element appears in the decomposition. Let $\Gamma_{\mathcal{IG}_{\mathcal{S}}} \subset G_{M_{\langle \mathbf{n} \rangle}}$ denote the automorphism group of $\mathcal{IG}_{\mathcal{S}}$, so $\Gamma'_{\mathcal{S}} \subseteq \Gamma_{\mathcal{IG}_{\mathcal{S}}}$, and if we take the triple of incidence graphs, we get a similar inclusion for $\Gamma_{\mathcal{S}}$. See the examples in §4.5.1 and §4.5.2.

If a decomposition is $\mathbb{Z}_3$ invariant, the incidence graphs form V, V^* and from W, W^* are isomorphic; otherwise, they give additional information.

Given a $\mathbb{Z}_3$-invariant decomposition, a necessary condition for it to also have a transpose-like $\mathbb{Z}_2$ symmetry is that there is an isomorphism of the bipartite graph swapping the sets of (weighted) vertices.

In practice (see the examples below) the incidence graph has been enough to determine the symmetry group $\Gamma_{\mathcal{S}}$, in the sense that it cuts the possible size of the group down and it becomes straightforward to determine $\Gamma_{\mathcal{S}}$ from $\Gamma_{\mathcal{IG}_{\mathcal{S}}}$.

Remark 4.4.2.1 In [BILR] a second graph, called the *pairing graph*, is defined that gives further information about $\Gamma'_{\mathcal{S}}$.

4.4.3 Configurations of Points in Projective Space

In practice, perhaps because of the numerical methods used, the sets $\mathcal{S}_U$, and $\mathcal{S}_{U^*}$ have been relatively small. It is not surprising that they each are spanning sets. Usually they have come from *configurations* in a sense I now describe. For $\mathbb{P}^1$, a configuration is simply a triple of points and the triple of points they determine in the dual vector space. For example, Strassen's decomposition is built from a configuration. The higher-dimensional analog of such pairs of triples is more complicated.

I emphasize that the decompositions of [BILR] were found by numerical searches, without distinguishing any configurations. However, in most cases, we were able to give a simple description of the vectors appearing in the decomposition in terms of a configuration. This bodes well for future work.

I restrict the discussion to $\mathbb{P}^2$; see [BILR] for the general case. The group PGL_3 acts simply transitively on the set of 4-ples of points in general linear position (i.e., such that any three of them span $\mathbb{P}^2$).

Start with any 4-ple of points in general linear position. In the decomposition, actual vectors will appear. Even in the decomposition, since what will appear are vectors tensored with each other, there is only a "global scale" for each term. Take the simplest (to write down) 4-ple, choosing the fourth vector in order to have the linear relation $u_1 + u_1 + u_3 + u_4 = 0$. I'll call this the *default configuration*. That is, the default configuration starts with

$$u_1 = \begin{pmatrix} 1 \\ 0 \\ 0 \end{pmatrix}, \quad u_2 = \begin{pmatrix} 0 \\ 1 \\ 0 \end{pmatrix}, \quad u_3 = \begin{pmatrix} 0 \\ 0 \\ 1 \end{pmatrix}, \quad u_4 = \begin{pmatrix} -1 \\ -1 \\ -1 \end{pmatrix}.$$

The $\{[u_j]\}$ determine points in the dual space by taking pairwise intersections of the lines (hyperplanes) that they determine in $\mathbb{P}U^*$:

$$v_{12} = (0,0,1), \quad v_{13} = (0,1,0), \quad v_{14} = (0,1,-1),$$
$$v_{23} = (-1,0,0), \quad v_{24} = (-1,0,1), \quad v_{34} = (1,-1,0).$$

Here $[v_{ij}]$ is the line in $\mathbb{P}^2$ (considered as a point in the dual space $\mathbb{P}^{2*}$) through the points $[u_i]$ and $[u_j]$ in $\mathbb{P}^2$ (or dually, the point of intersection of the two lines $[u_i]$, $[u_j]$ in $\mathbb{P}^{2*}$). Here choices of representatives are being made. I have made choices that will be useful for the decomposition $\mathcal{S}_{BILR,\mathbb{Z}_4 \times \mathbb{Z}_3}$ of §4.5.1.

The $v_{i,j}$ in turn determine new points of intersection,

$$u_{12,34} = \begin{pmatrix} 1 \\ 1 \\ 0 \end{pmatrix}, \quad u_{13,24} = \begin{pmatrix} 1 \\ 0 \\ 1 \end{pmatrix}, \quad u_{14,23} = \begin{pmatrix} 0 \\ 1 \\ 1 \end{pmatrix},$$

which determine new points

$$v_{(12,34),(13,24)} = (-1,1,1), \quad v_{(12,34),(14,23)} = (1,-1,1),$$
$$v_{(13,24),(14,23)} = (1,1,-1),$$

which determine new points in U, etc. (see [BILR] for details). In practice, only vectors from the first three sets of a configuration (7 for U, 6 for V, or vice versa) have been useful.

4.5 Cyclic $\mathbb{Z}_3$-Invariant Rank 23 Decompositions of $M_{(3)}$

In [BILR], new standard cyclic families of decompositions were found, as well as a standard cyclic variant of Laderman's decomposition. What follows is one of the new decompositions and the standard cyclic variant of Laderman's decomposition.

4.5.1 A Rank 23 Decomposition of $M_{(3)}$ with $\mathbb{Z}_4 \times \mathbb{Z}_3$ Symmetry

Take a configuration and let $a_0 : U \to V$ send u_j to v_{j+1}. In the default configuration,

$$a_0 = \begin{pmatrix} 0 & 0 & -1 \\ 1 & 0 & -1 \\ 0 & 1 & -1 \end{pmatrix}$$

corresponds to the generator of $\mathbb{Z}_4$ that cyclically permutes indices.

Theorem 4.5.1.1 [BILR] *Let* u_{ij}, v_i, $v_{ij|kl}$ *be as in §4.4.3. Then*

$$M_{(3)} = - a_0^{\otimes 3} + \langle (u_{24}v_{12|34})^{\otimes 3} \rangle_{\mathbb{Z}_2 \subset \mathbb{Z}_4} + \langle -[u_{24}v_4 + u_{12}v_3]^{\otimes 3} \rangle_{\mathbb{Z}_4}$$
$$+ \langle (u_{12}v_3)^{\otimes 3} \rangle_{\mathbb{Z}_4} + \langle (u_{12}v_1) \otimes (u_{23}v_3) \otimes (u_{24}v_4) \rangle_{\mathbb{Z}_4 \times \mathbb{Z}_3}.$$

Here is the incidence graph:

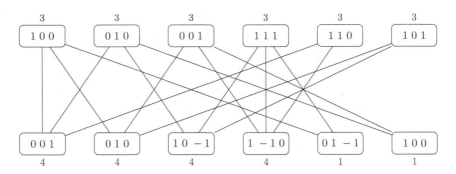

Given the distribution of the frequencies of the points – $(4, 4, 4, 4, 1, 1)$ in V, $(3, 3, 3, 3, 3, 3)$ in U^* – a transpose-like symmetry is not possible. Moreover, it is clear one cannot upgrade the $\mathbb{Z}_4$ to $\mathfrak{S}_4$ since only two of the three $v_{ij|kl}$ appear in the decomposition: $v_{12|34}$, $v_{14|23}$ ($v_{13|24}$ is omitted). So, e.g., the transposition $(2, 3)$ takes $\mathcal{S}_{BILR, \mathbb{Z}_4 \times \mathbb{Z}_3}$ to a different decomposition in the family.

Proposition 4.5.1.2 [BILR] $\Gamma_{\mathcal{S}_{BILR, \mathbb{Z}_4 \times \mathbb{Z}_3}} = \mathbb{Z}_4 \times \mathbb{Z}_3$.

Exercise 4.5.1.3 (2) Use the incidence graph to prove Proposition 4.5.1.2.

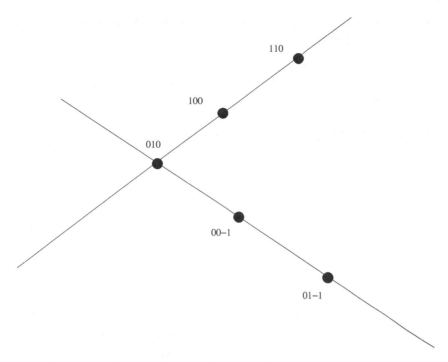

Figure 4.5.1 Configuration from the symmetric Laderman decomposition.

4.5.2 Laderman's Decomposition

I now discuss a variant of Laderman's rank 23 decomposition of $M_{\langle 3 \rangle}$, which I denote $\mathcal{L}ad$. According to Burichenko [Bur15], one has a $\mathbb{Z}_2 \times \mathbb{Z}_2 \subset PGL(U) \times PGL(V) \times PGL(W)$ contained in $\Gamma_{\mathcal{L}ad}$ and the full cyclic permutation and a transpose-like $\mathbb{Z}_3 \rtimes \mathbb{Z}_2$ also in $\Gamma_{\mathcal{L}ad}$, acting in a twisted way. Thanks to the transpose-like symmetry, it is better to label points in the dual space by their image under the transpose-like symmetry rather than annihilators, to make the symmetry more transparent. Here it is:

Points:

$$u_1 = \begin{pmatrix} 1 \\ 0 \\ 0 \end{pmatrix}, \; u_2 = \begin{pmatrix} 0 \\ 1 \\ 0 \end{pmatrix}, \; u_3 = \begin{pmatrix} 0 \\ 0 \\ 1 \end{pmatrix}, \; u_{12} = \begin{pmatrix} 1 \\ -1 \\ 0 \end{pmatrix}, \; u_{23} = \begin{pmatrix} 0 \\ 1 \\ -1 \end{pmatrix}.$$

$$v_1 = (1, 0, 0), \; v_2 = (0, 1, 0), \; v_3 = (0, 0, 1),$$
$$v_{12} = (1, 1, 0), \; v_{23} = (0, 1, 1).$$

Note that the configuration of points in $\mathbb{P}U$ is as in Figure 4.5.1.

Exercise 4.5.2.1 (1) Determine the subgroup of PGL_3 fixing the configuration of two lines in the plane. ⊙

Exercise 4.5.2.2 (2) What is the subgroup of your answer to Exercise 4.5.2.1 that preserves the full configuration in $\mathbb{P}^2$ (i.e., two lines, intersecting in a point, each with two additional marked points).

Theorem 4.5.2.3 [BILR, Lad76] *Notations as above. Then*

$$M_{\langle 3 \rangle} = (u_2 v_2)^{\otimes 3} \tag{4.5.1}$$

$$+ (u_3 v_3)^{\otimes 3} \tag{4.5.2}$$

$$+ (u_{12} v_1)^{\otimes 3} \tag{4.5.3}$$

$$+ (u_1 v_{12})^{\otimes 3} \tag{4.5.4}$$

$$+ (u_2 v_1 - u_1 v_{12})^{\otimes 3} \tag{4.5.5}$$

$$+ \langle (u_1 v_3) \otimes (u_3 v_1) \otimes (u_1 v_1) \rangle_{\mathbb{Z}_3} \tag{4.5.6}$$

$$+ \langle (u_{23} v_1) \otimes (u_{12} v_3) \otimes (u_{23} v_3) \rangle_{\mathbb{Z}_3} \tag{4.5.7}$$

$$+ \langle (u_3 v_{12}) \otimes (u_1 v_{23}) \otimes (u_3 v_{23}) \rangle_{\mathbb{Z}_3} \tag{4.5.8}$$

$$+ \langle (u_2 v_3 - u_{23} v_1) \otimes (u_1 v_2 - u_{12} v_3) \otimes (u_3 v_2 - u_{23} v_3) \rangle_{\mathbb{Z}_3} \tag{4.5.9}$$

$$+ \langle (u_{23} v_{12} + u_2 v_3 - u_1 v_{23}) \otimes (u_2 v_3) \otimes (u_3 v_2) \rangle_{\mathbb{Z}_3} \tag{4.5.10}$$

$$+ \langle (u_{12} v_{12} + u_2 v_3 - u_3 v_2) \otimes (u_2 v_1) \otimes (u_1 v_2) \rangle_{\mathbb{Z}_3}. \tag{4.5.11}$$

The transpose-like $\mathbb{Z}_2$ is $x \otimes y \otimes z \mapsto (\epsilon_2 y \epsilon_2)^T \otimes (\epsilon_2 x \epsilon_2)^T \otimes (\epsilon_2 z \epsilon_2)^T$, where $\epsilon_2 = \begin{pmatrix} 1 & \\ & -1 \\ & & 1 \end{pmatrix}$. (Note the similarities with Strassen's decomposition.) In other words send $u_1 \leftrightarrow v_1$, $u_2 \leftrightarrow -v_2$, $u_3 \leftrightarrow v_3$ and then switch the first two factors in $A \otimes B \otimes C$. This action performs the exchanges (4.5.3) ↔ (4.5.4) and (4.5.7) ↔ (4.5.8), and fixes all other terms in the decomposition.

Here is the incidence graph:

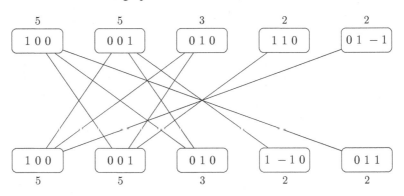

4.6 Alternating Least Squares (ALS) Method for Decompositions

I now explain the method used to numerically find decompositions.

Let A, B, C respectively have bases $\{e_i\}$, $\{f_j\}$, $\{g_k\}$. Given a tensor $T = \sum_{i=1}^{\mathbf{a}} \sum_{j=1}^{\mathbf{b}} \sum_{k=1}^{\mathbf{c}} t^{ijk} e_i \otimes f_j \otimes g_k \in A \otimes B \otimes C$, say we have reason to believe it has rank at most r. To find a rank r expression we could work as follows: For $1 \leq u \leq r$, write $a_u = \sum_i X_u^i e_i$, $b_u = \sum_j Y_u^j f_j$, and $c_u = \sum_k Z_u^k g_k$ where the X_u^i, Y_u^j, Z_u^k are constants to be determined. We want $\sum_{u=1}^{r} a_u \otimes b_u \otimes c_u = T$, i.e.,

$$\sum_{u=1}^{r} X_u^i Y_u^j Z_u^k = t^{ijk} \tag{4.6.1}$$

for all i, j, k. If we restrict ourselves to real coefficients, we want

$$\text{objfn}_1 := \sum_{i,j,k} \left(\sum_{u=1}^{r} X_u^i Y_u^j Z_u^k - t^{ijk} \right)^2 , \tag{4.6.2}$$

called the *objective function*, to be zero. (One can obtain a similar equation for complex coefficients by splitting all complex numbers into their real and imaginary parts. I stick to the real presentation for simplicity of exposition.) Now (4.6.2) is a degree six polynomial, but it is quadratic in each of the unknown quantities. To solve in practice, one begins with an initial "guess" of the X_u^i, Y_u^j, Z_u^k, e.g., chosen at random. Then one tries to minimize (4.6.2) e.g., as a function of the X_u^i while holding the Y_u^j, Z_u^k fixed. This is a linear problem. Once one obtains a solution, one starts again, holding the X_u^i and Z_u^k fixed and solving for the Y_u^j. Then one repeats, minimizing for the Z_u^k, and then cycling around again and again until the result converges (or fails to, in which case one can start again with different initial points). This algorithm was first written down in [Bre70].

Now this procedure could "attempt" to find a border rank solution, that is, the coefficients could go off to infinity. If one wants a rank decomposition, one can add a penalty term to (4.6.2), instead minimizing

$$\text{objfn}_2 := \sum_{i,j,k} \left(\sum_{u=1}^{r} X_u^i Y_u^j Z_u^k - t^{ijk} \right)^2 + \epsilon \left(\sum_{u,i,j,k}^{r} \left(X_u^i \right)^2 + \left(Y_u^j \right)^2 + \left(Z_u^k \right)^2 \right) \tag{4.6.3}$$

for some ϵ that in practice is found by trial and error.

In the literature (e.g. [Lad76, JM86, Smi13, AS13]) they prefer coefficient values to be from a small list of numbers, ideally confined to something like $0, \pm 1$ or $0, \pm 1, \pm \frac{1}{2}$. If the tensor in question has a large symmetry group (as does matrix multiplication), one can use the group action to fix some of the coefficients to these desired values.

According to Smirnov, in [Smi13], for $T = M_{\langle \mathbf{n} \rangle}$ (but not rectangular matrix multiplication) the critical points of $objfn_1$ are integers in practice, although he does not give an explanation why one would expect this to be the case. Thus, by these heuristics, if one can obtain a decomposition with $objfn_1 < 1$, then it will converge to zero by the ALS process, producing either a decomposition or limit to a border rank decomposition.

4.7 Secant Varieties and Additional Geometric Language

To better discuss border rank decompositions in §4.8, I now introduce the language of *secant varieties*. This language will also enable us to discuss rank decompositions in a larger context and will arise in the study of Valiant's conjecture and its variants.

4.7.1 Secant Varieties

Given a variety $X \subset \mathbb{P}V$, define the *X-rank* of $[p] \in \mathbb{P}V$, $\mathbf{R}_X([p])$, to be the smallest r such that there exist $x_1, \ldots, x_r \in \hat{X}$ such that p is in the span of $x_1, \ldots, x_r$, and the *X-border rank* $\underline{\mathbf{R}}_X([p])$ is defined to be the smallest r such that there exist curves $x_1(t), \ldots, x_r(t) \in \hat{X}$ such that p is in the span of the limiting plane $\lim_{t \to 0} \langle x_1(t), \ldots, x_r(t) \rangle$, where $\langle x_1(t), \ldots, x_r(t) \rangle \subset G(r, V)$ is viewed as a curve the Grassmannian. Here and in what follows, I am assuming that for $t \neq 0, x_1(t), \ldots, x_r(t)$ are linearly independent (otherwise we are really dealing with a decomposition of lower border rank).

Let $\sigma_r(X) \subset \mathbb{P}V$ denote the set of points of X-border rank at most r, called the *rth secant variety of X*. (Theorem 3.1.6.1 assures us that $\sigma_r(X)$ is indeed a variety.) In other words

$$\sigma_r(X) = \overline{\bigcup_{x_1, \ldots, x_r \in X} \langle x_1, \ldots, x_r \rangle}$$

where $\langle x_1, \ldots, x_r \rangle$ denotes the linear span in projective space and the overline denotes Zariski closure. The notation is such that $\sigma_1(X) = X$. When $X = Seg(\mathbb{P}A_1 \times \cdots \times \mathbb{P}A_n)$ is the set of rank one tensors, $\sigma_r(X) = \sigma_r$.

Let $X \subset \mathbb{P}V$ be a smooth variety, and let $p \in \sigma_2(X)$. If p is not a point of X, nor a point on an honest secant line, then p must line on some tangent line to X, where here I take the naïve definition of tangent line, namely a point on a limit of secant lines.

Terracini's lemma (see, e.g., [Lan12, §5.3]) generalizes our caculation of $\hat{T}_{[a_1 \otimes b_1 \otimes c_1 + a_2 \otimes b_2 \otimes c_2]} Seg(\mathbb{P}A \times \mathbb{P}B \times \mathbb{P}C)$ of §3.1.3: if $z = [x_1 + \cdots + x_r]$ with

$[x_j] \in X$ general points, then $\hat{T}_z \sigma_r(X) = \sum_{j=1}^r \hat{T}_{[x_j]} X$. In particular $\dim \sigma_r(X) \le r \dim X + r - 1$.

Thus $\dim \sigma_r(X) \le \min\{r \dim X + r - 1, \mathbf{v} - 1\}$, and when equality holds we will say $\sigma_r(X)$ is of the *expected dimension*. The expected dimension is indeed what occurs "most" of the time. For example, $\dim \sigma_r(\mathbb{P}^N \times \mathbb{P}^N \times \mathbb{P}^N)$ is the expected dimension $\min\{3Nr + r - 1, N^3 - 1\}$ for all (r, N) except $(r, N) = (4, 2)$ [Lic85].

4.7.2 Homogeneous Varieties, Orbit Closures, and *G*-Varieties

The Segre, Veronese and Grassmannian of §3.1.2 are examples of *homogeneous varieties*:

Definition 4.7.2.1 A subvariety $X \subset \mathbb{P}V$, is *homogeneous* if it is a closed orbit of some point $x \in \mathbb{P}V$ under the action of some group $G \subset GL(V)$. If $P \subset G$ is the subgroup fixing x, write $X = G/P$.

A variety $X \subset \mathbb{P}V$ is called a *G-variety* for a group $G \subset GL(V)$, if for all $g \in G$ and $x \in X$, $g \cdot x \in X$.

Orbit closures (see §3.3.1) and homogeneous varieties are G-varieties.

Exercise 4.7.2.2 (1) What are the points in $\overline{GL_n \cdot (x_1 \cdots x_n)}$ that are not in $GL_n \cdot (x_1 \cdots x_n)$?

4.7.3 The Abstract Secant Variety

Given projective varieties $Y_j \subset \mathbb{P}V_j$, one can define their Segre product $Y_1 \times \cdots \times Y_r \subset Seg(\mathbb{P}V_1 \times \cdots \times \mathbb{P}V_r) \subset \mathbb{P}(V_1 \otimes \cdots \otimes V_r)$. Let $X \subset \mathbb{P}V$ be a variety. Consider the set

$$S_r(X)^0 := \{(x_1, \ldots, x_r, z) \in X^{\times r} \times \mathbb{P}V \mid z \in \mathrm{span}\{x_1, \ldots, x_r\}\}$$
$$\subset Seg(X^{\times r} \times \mathbb{P}V) \subset \mathbb{P}V^{\otimes r+1}$$

and let $S_r(X) := \overline{S_r(X)^0}$ denote its Zariski closure. (For those familiar with quotients, it would be more convenient to deal with $X^{(\times r)} := X^{\times r}/\mathfrak{S}_r$.) We have a map $\pi^0 : S_r(X)^0 \to \mathbb{P}V$, extending to a map $\pi : S_r(X) \to \mathbb{P}V$, given by projection onto the last factor and the image is $\sigma_r^0(X)$ (resp. $\sigma_r(X)$). Call $S_r(X)$ the *abstract rth secant variety of X*. As long as $r < \rho_{max}$, where $\sigma_{r_{max}}(X) = \mathbb{P}V$, but $\sigma_{r_{max}-1}(X) \neq \mathbb{P}V$ and X is not contained in a linear subspace of $\mathbb{P}V$, $\dim S_r(X) = r \dim X + r - 1$ because $\dim X^{\times r} = r \dim X$ and a general set of r points on X will span a $\mathbb{P}^{r-1}$.

If $\sigma_r(X)$ is of the expected dimension and is not all of $\mathbb{P}V$, so its dimension equals that of $S_r(X)$, then for general points $z \in \sigma_r(X)^0$, $(\pi^0)^{-1}(z)$ will consist of a finite number of points and each point will correspond to a decomposition $\overline{z} = \overline{x_1} + \cdots + \overline{x_r}$ for $\overline{x_j} \in \hat{x}_j$, $\overline{z} \in \hat{z}$. In summary:

Proposition 4.7.3.1 *If $X^n \subset \mathbb{P}^N$ and $\sigma_r(X)$ is of (the expected) dimension $rn + r - 1 < N$, then each of the points of a Zariski dense subset of $\sigma_r(X)$ has a finite number of decompositions into a sum of r elements of X.*

If the fiber of π^0 over $z \in \sigma_r^0(X)$ is k-dimensional, then there is a k-parameter family of decompositions of z as a sum of r rank one tensors. This occurs, for example if $z \in \sigma_{r-1}^0(X)$, but it can also occur for points in $\sigma_r(X)\backslash\sigma_{r-1}(X)$.

For example, every point of $\sigma_7(Seg(\mathbb{P}^3 \times \mathbb{P}^3 \times \mathbb{P}^3)) = \mathbb{P}^{63}$ has a five-dimensional family of points in the fiber, but $M_{\langle 2 \rangle}$ has a nine-dimensional family. A general point of $\sigma_{23}(Seg(\mathbb{P}^8 \times \mathbb{P}^8 \times \mathbb{P}^8))$ will have a finite number of points in the fiber, but $M_{\langle 3 \rangle}$ has at least a 24-dimensional fiber, in fact by [JM86], at least a 27-dimensional fiber.

If X is a G-variety, then $\sigma_r(X)$ is also a G-variety, and if $z \in \sigma_r^0(X)$ is fixed by $G_z \subset G$, then G_z will act (possibly trivially) on $(\pi^0)^{-1}(z)$, and every distinct (up to reordering if one is not working with $X^{(\times r)}$) point in its orbit will correspond to a distinct decomposition of z. Let $q \in (\pi^0)^{-1}(x)$. If $\dim(G_z \cdot q) = d_z$, then there is at least a d_z parameter family of decompositions of z as a sum of r elements of X.

Remark 4.7.3.2 Note that $\mathrm{codim}(S_{r-1}(X), S_r(X)) \leq \dim X - 1$, where the inclusion is just by adding any point of X to a border rank $r - 1$ decomposition. In particular, in the case of the Segre relevant for matrix multiplication, this codimension is at most $3(\mathbf{n}^2 - 1)$. On the other hand $\dim G_{M_{\langle \mathbf{n} \rangle}} = 3(\mathbf{n}^2 - 1)$, so by a dimension count, one might "expect" $\pi_r^{-1}(M_{\langle \mathbf{n} \rangle})$ to intersect $S_{r-1}(X)$, meaning that we could keep reducing the border rank of $M_{\langle \mathbf{n} \rangle}$ all the way down to one. Of course since $S_r(Seg(\mathbb{P}A \times \mathbb{P}B \times \mathbb{P}C))$ is not a projective space, Theorem 3.1.5.1 does not apply, but this dimension count illustrates the pathology of the tensor $M_{\langle \mathbf{n} \rangle}$.

4.7.4 What is a Border Rank Decomposition?

Usually an X-border rank decomposition of some $v \in V$ is presented as $v = \lim_{t \to 0}(x_1(t) + \cdots + x_r(t))$ where $[x_j(t)]$ are curves in X. In order to discuss border rank decompositions geometrically, it will be useful to study the corresponding curve in the Grassmannian $\langle x_1(t), \ldots, x_r(t) \rangle \subset G(r, V)$. The geometry of the intersection of the limiting r plane that contains v with X has useful information.

To better understand this geometry, consider

$$\tilde{S}_r^0(X) := \{([v], ([x_1], \ldots, [x_r]), E) \mid v \in \langle x_1, \ldots, x_r \rangle \subseteq E\}$$
$$\subset \mathbb{P}V \times X^{\times r} \times G(r, V)$$

and $\tilde{S}_r(X) := \overline{\tilde{S}_r^0(X)}$.

We can stratify $\sigma_r(X)$ and $\tilde{S}_r(X)$ by the h's of the intermediate ranks $\mathbf{R}_h$ of §3.2.1. The case $h = 0$ is rank. The next case $h = 1$ has a straightforward geometry.

To understand the $h = 1$ case, first consider the case $r = 2$, so $v = \lim_{t \to 0} \frac{1}{t}(x_1(t) + x_2(t))$ for curves $[x_j(t)] \subset X$. Then we must have $\lim_{t \to 0}[x_1(t)] = \lim_{t \to 0}[x_2(t)]$, letting $[x]$ denote this limiting point, we obtain an element of $\hat{T}_x X$. In the case of $\sigma_r(X)$, one needs r curves such that the points are linearly independent for $t \neq 0$ and such that they become dependent when $t = 0$. This is most interesting when no subset of $r - 1$ points becomes linearly dependent. Then one may obtain an arbitrary point of $\hat{T}_{x_1} X + \cdots + \hat{T}_{x_r} X$ (see [Lan12, §10.8.1]). For some varieties there may not exist r distinct points on them that are linearly dependent (e.g., $v_d(\mathbb{P}^1)$ when $d > r$). An easy way for such sets of points to exist is if there is a $\mathbb{P}^{r-1}$ on the variety, as was the case for T_{STR} of §5.6. The decompositions for $M_{\langle \mathbf{m}, 2, 2 \rangle}^{red}$ I discuss in the next section are not quite from such simple configurations, but nearly are. Because of this I next discuss the geometry of linear spaces on the Segre.

4.7.5 Lines on Segre Varieties

There are three types of lines on $Seg(\mathbb{P}A \times \mathbb{P}B \times \mathbb{P}C)$: α-lines, which are of the form $\mathbb{P}(\langle a_1, a_2 \rangle \otimes b \otimes c)$ for some $a_j \in A$, $b \in B$, $c \in C$, and the other two types are defined similarly and called β and γ lines.

Exercise 4.7.5.1 (2) Show that all lines on $Seg(\mathbb{P}A \times \mathbb{P}B \times \mathbb{P}C)$ are one of these types. ⊙

Given two lines $L_\beta, L_\gamma \subset Seg(\mathbb{P}A \times \mathbb{P}B \times \mathbb{P}C)$ respectively of type β, γ, if they do not intersect, then $\langle L_\beta, L_\gamma \rangle = \mathbb{P}^3$ and if the lines are general, furthermore $\langle L_\beta, L_\gamma \rangle \cap Seg(\mathbb{P}A \times \mathbb{P}B \times \mathbb{P}C) = L_\beta \sqcup L_\gamma$.

However if $L_\beta = \mathbb{P}(a \otimes \langle b_1, b_2 \rangle \otimes c)$ and $L_\gamma = \mathbb{P}(a' \otimes b \otimes \langle c_1, c_2 \rangle)$ with $b \in \langle b_1, b_2 \rangle$ and $c \in \langle c_1, c_2 \rangle$, then they still span a $\mathbb{P}^3$ but $\langle L_\beta, L_\gamma \rangle \cap Seg(\mathbb{P}A \times \mathbb{P}B \times \mathbb{P}C) = L_\beta \sqcup L_\gamma \sqcup L_\alpha$, where $L_\alpha = \mathbb{P}(\langle a, a' \rangle \otimes b \otimes c)$, and L_α intersects both L_β and L_γ.

Let $x, y, z \in Seg(\mathbb{P}A \times \mathbb{P}B \times \mathbb{P}C)$ be distinct points that all lie on a line $L \subset Seg(\mathbb{P}A \times \mathbb{P}B \times \mathbb{P}C)$. Then

$$\hat{T}_x Seg(\mathbb{P}A \times \mathbb{P}B \times \mathbb{P}C) \subset \langle \hat{T}_y Seg(\mathbb{P}A \times \mathbb{P}B \times \mathbb{P}C), \hat{T}_z Seg(\mathbb{P}A \times \mathbb{P}B \times \mathbb{P}C) \rangle.$$
$$(4.7.1)$$

The analogous statement is true for lines on any cominuscule variety, see [BL14, Lemma 3.3]. Because of this, it will be more geometrical to refer to $\hat{T}_L Seg(\mathbb{P}A \times \mathbb{P}B \times \mathbb{P}C) := \langle \hat{T}_y Seg(\mathbb{P}A \times \mathbb{P}B \times \mathbb{P}C), \hat{T}_z Seg(\mathbb{P}A \times \mathbb{P}B \times \mathbb{P}C) \rangle$, as the choice of $y, z \in L$ is irrelevant.

Exercise 4.7.5.2 (1) Verify (4.7.1).

The matrix multiplication tensor $M_{\langle U, V, W \rangle}$ endows A, B, C with additional structure, e.g., $B = V^* \otimes W$, so there are two types of distinguished β-lines (corresponding to lines of rank one matrices), call them (β, v^*)-lines and (β, ω)-lines, where, e.g., a v^*-line is of the form $\mathbb{P}(a \otimes (\langle v^1, v^2 \rangle \otimes w) \otimes c)$, and among such lines there are further distinguished ones where moreover both a and c also have rank one. Call such further distinguished lines *special* (β, v^*)-lines.

4.8 Border Rank Decompositions

4.8.1 $M_{\langle 2 \rangle}^{red}$

Here $A \subset U^* \otimes V$ has dimension three.

What follows is a slight modification of the decomposition of $M_{\langle 2 \rangle}^{red}$ from [BCRL79] that appeared in [LR17]. Call it the *BCLR*-decomposition. I label the points such that x_1^1 is set equal to zero. The main difference is that in the original all five points moved, but here one is stationary.

$$p_1(t) = x_2^1 \otimes \left(y_2^2 + y_1^2 \right) \otimes \left(z_2^2 + t z_1^1 \right)$$
$$p_2(t) = - \left(x_1^1 - t x_2^2 \right) \otimes y_2^2 \otimes \left(z_2^2 + t \left(z_1^1 + z_1^2 \right) \right)$$
$$p_3(t) = x_1^2 \otimes \left(y_1^2 + t y_2^1 \right) \otimes \left(z_2^2 + z_2^1 \right)$$
$$p_4(t) = \left(x_1^2 - t x_2^2 \right) \otimes \left(-y_1^2 + t \left(y_1^1 - y_2^1 \right) \right) \otimes z_2^1$$
$$p_5(t) = - \left(x_1^2 + x_2^1 \right) \otimes y_1^2 \otimes z_2^2$$

and

$$M_{\langle 2 \rangle}^{red} = \lim_{t \to 0} \frac{1}{t} [p_1(t) + \cdots + p_5(t)].$$
$$(4.8.1)$$

Use the notation $x_j^i = u^i \otimes v_j$, $y_k^j = v^j \otimes w_k$ and $z_i^k = w^k \otimes u_i$.

Theorem 4.8.1.1 [LR17] *Let* $E^{BCLR} = \lim_{t \to 0} \langle p_1(t), \ldots, p_5(t) \rangle \in G(5, A \otimes B \otimes C)$. *Then* $E^{BCLR} \cap Seg(\mathbb{P}A \times \mathbb{P}B \times \mathbb{P}C)$ *is the union of three lines:*

$$L_{12,(\beta,\omega)} = x_2^1 \otimes (v^2 \otimes W) \otimes z_2^1,$$

$$L_{21,(\gamma,\omega^*)} = x_1^2 \otimes y_2^2 \otimes (W^* \otimes u_2),$$

$$L_\alpha = \langle x_1^2, x_2^1 \rangle \otimes y_2^2 \otimes z_2^1.$$

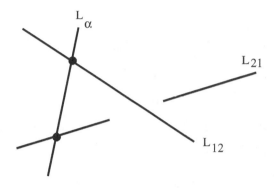

Here $L_{12,(\beta,\omega)}$ *is a special* (β, ω)-*line,* $L_{21,(\gamma,\omega^*)}$, *is a special* (γ, ω^*)-*line, and* L_α, *is an* α-*line with rank one B and C points. Moreover, the C-point of* $L_{12,(\beta,\omega)}$ *lies in the* ω^*-*line of* $L_{21,(\gamma,\omega^*)}$, *the B-point of* $L_{21,(\gamma,\omega^*)}$ *lies in the* ω-*line of* $L_{12,(\beta,\omega)}$ *and* L_α *is the unique line on the Segre intersecting* $L_{12,(\beta,\omega)}$ *and* $L_{21,(\gamma,\omega^*)}$ *(and thus it is contained in their span).*
Furthermore, $E^{BCLR} = \langle M_{(2)}^{red}, L_{12,(\beta,\omega)}, L_{21,(\gamma,\omega^*)} \rangle$ *and*

$$M_{(2)}^{red} \in \langle \hat{T}_{L_{12,(\beta,\omega)}} Seg(\mathbb{P}A \times \mathbb{P}B \times \mathbb{P}C), \hat{T}_{L_{21,(\gamma,\omega^*)}} Seg(\mathbb{P}A \times \mathbb{P}B \times \mathbb{P}C) \rangle.$$

Proof. Write $p_j = p_j(0)$. Then (up to sign, which is irrelevant for geometric considerations)

$$p_1 = x_2^1 \otimes \left(y_2^2 + y_1^2 \right) \otimes z_2^2,$$

$$p_2 = x_2^1 \otimes y_2^2 \otimes z_2^2,$$

$$p_3 = x_1^2 \otimes y_1^2 \otimes \left(z_2^2 + z_2^1 \right),$$

$$p_4 = x_1^2 \otimes y_1^2 \otimes z_2^1,$$

$$p_5 = \left(x_1^2 + x_2^1 \right) \otimes y_1^2 \otimes z_2^2.$$

Then $L_{12,(\beta,\omega)} = \langle p_1, p_2 \rangle$, $L_{21,(\gamma,\omega^*)} = \langle p_3, p_4 \rangle$, and $p_5 \in L_\alpha$.

To see there are no other points in $E^{BCLR} \cap Seg(\mathbb{P}A \times \mathbb{P}B \times \mathbb{P}C)$, first note that any such point would have to lie on $Seg(\mathbb{P}\langle x_2^1, x_1^2 \rangle \times \mathbb{P}\langle y_1^2, y_2^2 \rangle \times \mathbb{P}\langle z_2^1, z_2^2 \rangle)$ because there is no way to eliminate the rank two $x_2^2 \otimes (y_1^2 \otimes z_2^1 + y_2^2 \otimes z_2^2)$ term in $M_{(2)}^{red}$ with a linear combination of $p_1, \ldots, p_4$. Let $[(sx_2^1 + tx_1^2) \otimes (uy_2^2 + vy_1^2) \otimes (pz_2^2 + qz_2^1)]$ be an arbitrary point on this variety. To have it be in the span of $p_1, \ldots, p_4$ it must satisfy the equations $suq = 0$, $svq = 0$, $tuq = 0$, $tup = 0$. Keeping in mind that one cannot have $(s, t) = (0, 0)$, $(u, v) = (0, 0)$, or $(p, q) = (0, 0)$, we conclude the only solutions are the three lines already exhibited.

We have

$$p_1(0)' = x_2^1 \otimes (y_2^2 + y_1^2) \otimes z_1^1,$$

$$p_2(0)' = x_2^1 \otimes y_2^2 \otimes z_2^2 - x_2^1 \otimes y_2^2 \otimes (-z_1^2 + z_1^1),$$

$$p_3(0)' = x_1^2 \otimes y_2^2 \otimes (z_2^2 + z_1^1),$$

$$p_4(0)' = x_2^2 \otimes y_1^2 \otimes z_2^1 + x_1^2 \otimes (y_1^1 - y_2^1) \otimes z_2^1,$$

$$p_5(0)' = 0.$$

Then $M_{(2)}^{red} = (p_1' + p_2') + (p_3' + p_4')$ where $p_1' + p_2' \in T_{L_{12,(\beta,\omega)}} Seg(\mathbb{P}A \times \mathbb{P}B \times \mathbb{P}C)$ and $p_3' + p_4' \in T_{L_{21,(\gamma,\omega^*)}} Seg(\mathbb{P}A \times \mathbb{P}B \times \mathbb{P}C)$. $\qquad\square$

Remark 4.8.1.2 By removing x_1^1 from our tensor, we lose the cyclic $\mathbb{Z}_3$-symmetry but retain a standard transpose symmetry $x \otimes y \otimes z \mapsto x^T \otimes z^T \otimes y^T$. Similarly we lose the $GL(U) \times GL(V)$ symmetry but retain the $GL(W)$ action. By composing the standard transpose symmetry with another $\mathbb{Z}_2$ action which switches the basis vectors of W, the action swaps $p_1(t) + p_2(t)$ with $p_3(t) + p_4(t)$ and $L_{12,(\beta,\omega)}$ with $L_{21,(\gamma,\omega^*)}$. This action fixes p_5.

Remark 4.8.1.3 Note that it is important that p_5 lies neither on $L_{12,(\beta,\omega)}$ nor on $L_{21,(\gamma,\omega^*)}$, so that no subset of the five points lies in a linearly degenerate position to enable us to have tangent vectors coming from all five points, but I emphasize that any point on the line L_α not on the original lines would have worked equally well, so the geometric object is this configuration of lines.

4.8.2 $M_{\langle 3,2,2 \rangle}^{red}$

Here is the decomposition in [AS13, Theorem 2] due to Alexeev and Smirnov, only changing the element set to zero in their decomposition to x_1^1. The decomposition is order two and the only nonzero coefficients appearing are $\pm 1, \pm\frac{1}{2}$.

$$p_1(t) = \left(\frac{-1}{2}t^2 x_2^3 - \frac{1}{2}tx_1^2 + x_1^2\right) \otimes \left(-y_1^2 + y_2^2 + ty_1^1\right) \otimes \left(z_3^1 + tz_2^1\right),$$

$$p_2(t) = \left(x_1^2 + \frac{1}{2}x_2^1\right) \otimes \left(y_1^2 - y_2^2\right) \otimes \left(z_3^1 + z_3^2 + tz_2^1 + tz_2^2\right),$$

$$p_3(t) = \left(t^2 x_2^3 + tx_1^3 - \frac{1}{2}tx_2^2 - x_1^2\right) \otimes \left(y_1^2 + y_2^2 + ty_2^1\right) \otimes z_3^2,$$

$$p_4(t) = \left(\frac{1}{2}t^2 x_2^3 - tx_1^3 - \frac{1}{2}tx_2^2 + x_1^2\right) \otimes \left(y_1^2 + y_2^2 - ty_1^1\right) \otimes z_3^1,$$

$$p_5(t) = \left(-t^2 x_2^3 + tx_2^2 - x_2^1\right) \otimes y_1^2 \otimes \left(z_3^2 + \frac{1}{2}tz_2^1 + \frac{1}{2}tz_2^2 - t^2 z_1^1\right),$$

$$p_6(t) = \left(\frac{1}{2}tx_2^2 + x_1^2\right) \otimes \left(-y_1^2 + y_2^2 + ty_2^1\right) \otimes \left(z_3^2 + tz_2^2\right),$$

$$p_7(t) = \left(-tx_1^3 + x_1^2 + \frac{1}{2}x_2^1\right) \otimes \left(y_1^2 + y_2^2\right) \otimes \left(-z_3^1 + z_3^2\right),$$

$$p_8(t) = \left(tx_2^2 + x_2^1\right) \otimes y_2^2 \otimes \left(z_3^1 + \frac{1}{2}tz_2^1 + \frac{1}{2}tz_2^2 + t^2 z_1^2\right).$$

Then

$$M^{red}_{\langle 3,2,2\rangle} = \frac{1}{t^2}[p_1(t) + \cdots + p_8(t)].$$

Remark 4.8.2.1 In [BDHM15] they prove $\underline{\mathbf{R}}(M^{red}_{\langle 3,2,2\rangle}) = 8$.

Theorem 4.8.2.2 [LR17] *Let* $E^{AS,3} = \lim_{t\to 0}\langle p_1(t), \ldots, p_8(t)\rangle \in G(8, A\otimes B\otimes C)$. *Then* $E^{AS,3} \cap Seg(\mathbb{P}A \times \mathbb{P}B \times \mathbb{P}C)$ *is the union of two irreducible algebraic surfaces, both abstractly isomorphic to* $\mathbb{P}^1 \times \mathbb{P}^1$: *The first is a sub-Segre variety:*

$$Seg_{21,(\beta,\omega),(\gamma,\omega^*)} := [x_1^2] \times \mathbb{P}(v^2\otimes W) \times \mathbb{P}(W^*\otimes u_3),$$

The second, $\mathbb{L}_\alpha$ *is a one-parameter family of lines passing through a parametrized curve in* $Seg_{21,(\beta,\omega),(\gamma,\omega^*)}$ *and the plane conic curve (which has the same parametrization):*

$$C_{12,(\beta,\omega),(\gamma,\omega^*)} := \mathbb{P}\left(\cup_{[s,t]\in\mathbb{P}^1} x_2^1\otimes\left(sy_1^2 - ty_2^2\right)\otimes\left(sz_3^2 + tz_3^1\right)\right).$$

The three varieties $C_{12,(\beta,\omega),(\gamma,\omega^*)}$, $Seg_{21,(\beta,\omega),(\gamma,\omega^*)}$, *and* $\mathbb{L}_\alpha$ *respectively play roles analogous to the lines* $L_{12,(\beta,\omega)}$, $L_{21,(\gamma,\omega^*)}$, *and* L_α, *as described in Figure 4.8.1 and the proof.*

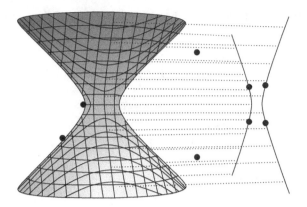

Figure 4.8.1 The curve $C_{12,(\beta,\omega),(\gamma,\omega^*)}$ with its four points, the surface $Seg_{21,(\beta,\omega),(\gamma,\omega^*)}$ with its four points (only two of which are visible), and the surface $\mathbb{L}_\alpha$ with its two points, which don't lie on either the curve or surface $Seg_{21,(\beta,\omega),(\gamma,\omega^*)}$.

Proof. The limit points are (up to sign)

$$p_1 = x_1^2 \otimes \left(y_1^2 - y_2^2\right) \otimes z_3^1,$$

$$p_3 = x_1^2 \otimes \left(y_1^2 + y_2^2\right) \otimes z_3^2,$$

$$p_4 = x_1^2 \otimes \left(y_1^2 + y_2^2\right) \otimes z_3^1,$$

$$p_6 = x_1^2 \otimes \left(y_1^2 - y_2^2\right) \otimes z_3^2,$$

$$p_5 = x_2^1 \otimes y_1^2 \otimes z_3^2,$$

$$p_8 = x_2^1 \otimes y_2^2 \otimes z_3^1,$$

$$p_2 = \left(x_1^2 + \frac{1}{2}x_2^1\right) \otimes \left(y_1^2 - y_2^2\right) \otimes \left(z_3^1 + z_3^2\right),$$

$$p_7 = \left(x_1^2 + \frac{1}{2}x_2^1\right) \otimes \left(y_1^2 + y_2^2\right) \otimes \left(z_3^1 - z_3^2\right).$$

Just as with $M_{(2)}^{red}$, the limit points all lie on a $Seg(\mathbb{P}^1 \times \mathbb{P}^1 \times \mathbb{P}^1)$, in fact the "same" $Seg(\mathbb{P}^1 \times \mathbb{P}^1 \times \mathbb{P}^1)$. Pictorially the Segres are

$$\begin{pmatrix} 0 & * \\ & * \end{pmatrix} \times \begin{pmatrix} & \\ * & * \end{pmatrix} \times \begin{pmatrix} * \\ * \end{pmatrix}$$

for $M_{(2,2,2)}^{red}$ and

$$\begin{pmatrix} 0 & * \\ & * \end{pmatrix} \times \begin{pmatrix} & \\ * & * \end{pmatrix} \times \begin{pmatrix} & * \\ & * \end{pmatrix}$$

for $M^{red}_{(3,2,2)}$. Here $E^{AS,3} \cap Seg(\mathbb{P}A \times \mathbb{P}B \times \mathbb{P}C)$ is the union of a one-parameter family of lines $\mathbb{L}_\alpha$ passing through a plane conic and a special $\mathbb{P}^1 \times \mathbb{P}^1$: $Seg_{21,(\beta,\omega),(\gamma,\omega^*)} := [x_1^2] \times \mathbb{P}(v^2 \otimes W) \times \mathbb{P}(W^* \otimes u_3)$ (which contains p_1, p_3, p_4, p_6). To define the family and make the similarity with the BCLR case clearer, first define the plane conic curve

$$C_{12,(\beta,\omega),(\gamma,\omega^*)} := \mathbb{P}\big(\cup_{[s,t] \in \mathbb{P}^1} x_2^1 \otimes (sy_1^2 - ty_2^2) \otimes (sz_3^2 + tz_3^1) \big).$$

The points p_5, p_8 lie on this conic (respectively the values $(s,t) = (1,0)$ and $(s,t) = (0,1)$). Then define the variety

$$\mathbb{L}_\alpha := \mathbb{P}\big(\cup_{[\sigma,\tau] \in \mathbb{P}^1} \cup_{[s,t] \in \mathbb{P}^1} (\sigma x_2^1 + \tau x_1^2) \otimes (sy_1^2 - ty_2^2) \otimes (sz_3^2 + tz_3^1) \big),$$

which is a one-parameter family of lines intersecting the conic and the special $\mathbb{P}^1 \times \mathbb{P}^1$. The points p_2, p_7 lie on $\mathbb{L}_\alpha$ but not on the conic. Explicitly p_2 (resp. p_7) is the point corresponding to the values $(\sigma, \tau) = (1, \frac{1}{2})$ and $(s,t) = (1,1)$ (resp. $(s,t) = (1,-1)$).

The analog of L_α in the $M^{red}_{(2)}$ decomposition is $\mathbb{L}_\alpha$, and $C_{12,(\beta,\omega),(\gamma,\omega^*)}$ and $Seg_{21,(\beta,\omega),(\gamma,\omega^*)}$ are the analogs of the lines $L_{12,(\beta,\omega)}$, $L_{21,(\gamma,\omega^*)}$. (A difference here is that $C_{12,(\beta,\omega),(\gamma,\omega^*)} \subset \mathbb{L}_\alpha$.)

The span of the configuration is the span of a $\mathbb{P}^2$ (the span of the conic) and a $\mathbb{P}^3$ (the span of the $\mathbb{P}^1 \times \mathbb{P}^1$), i.e., a $\mathbb{P}^6$.

The proof that these are the only points in the intersection is similar to the BCLR case. □

More decompositions are described geometrically in [LR17].

It would be reasonable to expect that the BCLR and Alekseev-Smirnov decompositions generalize to all **m**, so that $\underline{\mathbf{R}}(M^{red}_{(\mathbf{m},2,2)}) \leq 3\mathbf{m} - 1$, which would imply that $\underline{\mathbf{R}}(M_{\langle \mathbf{n},2,2 \rangle}) \leq 3\mathbf{n} + 1$ for all **n**.

5

The Complexity of Matrix Multiplication IV: The Complexity of Tensors and More Lower Bounds

In Chapter 2 we developed equations to test the border rank of tensors. In this chapter I explain further techniques for proving lower and upper bounds for border rank and rank. I also discuss geometric properties that could be useful for future investigations.

I begin, in §5.1, by making explicit the dictionary between (1_A-generic) tensors in $\mathbb{C}^a \otimes \mathbb{C}^m \otimes \mathbb{C}^m$ and linear subspaces of $\mathrm{End}(\mathbb{C}^m)$. This enables one both to find new ways to bound rank and border rank via linear algebra, and to use knowledge of tensors to make progress on classical questions in linear algebra.

While up until now I have emphasized the use of explicit polynomials to test membership in varieties, sometimes varieties satisfy Zariski closed conditions that are easy to describe but difficult to write as polynomials. Some such are discussed in §5.1. Two more such conditions are discussed in §5.2. One particularly useful such technique, the *border substitution method*, is discussed in detail in §5.4. In particular, it enables the $2\mathbf{n}^2 - \log_2(\mathbf{n}) - 1$ lower bound for $\underline{\mathbf{R}}(M_{\langle \mathbf{n} \rangle})$ presented in §5.4.5.

Regarding tensor rank, the only general method for proving tensor rank lower bounds I am aware of is the *substitution* method discussed in §5.3.

The best upper bounds for the exponent ω were obtained with T_{STR}, $T_{cw,q}$, and $T_{CW,q}$. What makes these tensors special? It is clear they have nice combinatorial properties, but do they have distinguishing geometric features? I discuss several such geometric properties in §5.5. If such features could be identified, one could in principle look for other tensors with the same properties and apply the laser method to those tensors, as was proposed in [AFLG15].

Several tensors that have been studied arise naturally as structure tensors of algebras. I discuss rank and border rank lower bounds for structure tensors of algebras in §5.6. In particular, I present Bläser's and Zuiddam's sequences of tensors with rank to border rank ratio approaching three.

5.1 Tensors and Classical Linear Algebra

This section follows [LM15].

5.1.1 1-Genericity

How good are Strassen's equations? We have seen that unless there exists $\alpha \in A^*$ with $T(\alpha) \subset B{\otimes}C$ of maximal rank (or $\beta \in B^*$, resp. $\gamma \in C^*$ with $T(\beta)$, resp. $T(\gamma)$, of maximal rank), they are essentially useless. The following definition names the class of tensors they are useful for.

Definition 5.1.1.1 A tensor $T \in A{\otimes}B{\otimes}C$ is 1_A-*generic* if there exists $\alpha \in A^*$ with $T(\alpha) \subset B{\otimes}C$ of maximal rank, and T is 1-generic if it is 1_A, 1_B and 1_C-generic.

Fortunately, $M_{\langle \mathbf{n} \rangle}$ and all tensors used to study the exponent of matrix multiplication are 1-generic.

The 1-genericity of $M_{\langle \mathbf{n} \rangle}$ has the consequence that for the purpose of proving $\underline{\mathbf{R}}(M_{\langle \mathbf{n} \rangle}) \leq r$, it would be sufficient to find a collection of polynomials such that their common zero set simply contains $\sigma_r(Seg(\mathbb{P}^{\mathbf{n}^2-1} \times \mathbb{P}^{\mathbf{n}^2-1} \times \mathbb{P}^{\mathbf{n}^2-1}))$ as an irreducible component, as long as all other components of the zero set are contained in the set of non-1-generic tensors.

Say a tensor T is 1_A-generic, $\mathbf{b} = \mathbf{c}$, and Strassen's commutators are identically zero – can we conclude $\underline{\mathbf{R}}(T) = \mathbf{b}$?

I address this question in this section and the next. I first show that the properties of tensor rank and border rank of tensors in $A{\otimes}B{\otimes}C$ can be studied as properties of **a**-dimensional linear subspaces of $B{\otimes}C$.

5.1.2 The Dictionary

The following standard result shows that the rank and border rank of a tensor $T \in A{\otimes}B{\otimes}C$ may be recovered from the subspace $T(A^*) \subset B{\otimes}C$. I present a version of it from [LM15].

Proposition 5.1.2.1 *For a tensor* $T \in A{\otimes}B{\otimes}C$, $\mathbf{R}(T)$ *equals the minimal number of rank one elements of* $B{\otimes}C$ *needed to span (a space containing)* $T(A^*)$, *and similarly for the permuted statements.*

Say $\dim T(A^*) = k$. *Let* $Z_r \subset G(k, B{\otimes}C)$ *denote the set of k-planes in* $B{\otimes}C$ *that are contained in the span of r rank one elements, so* $\mathbf{R}(T) \leq r$ *if and only if* $T(A^*) \in Z_r$. *Then* $\underline{\mathbf{R}}(T) \leq r$ *if and only if* $T(A^*) \in \overline{Z_r}$.

Proof. Let T have rank r so there is an expression $T = \sum_{i=1}^{r} a_i{\otimes}b_i{\otimes}c_i$. (The vectors a_i need not be linearly independent, and similarly for the b_i and c_i.) Then $T(A^*) \subseteq \langle b_1{\otimes}c_1, \ldots, b_r{\otimes}c_r \rangle$ shows that the number of rank one matrices needed to span $T(A^*) \subset B{\otimes}C$ is at most $\mathbf{R}(T)$.

For the other inequality, say $T(A^*)$ is contained in the span of rank one elements $b_1 \otimes c_1, \ldots, b_r \otimes c_r$. Let $\alpha^1, \ldots, \alpha^{\mathbf{a}}$ be a basis of A^*, with dual basis $e_1, \ldots, e_{\mathbf{a}}$ of A. Then $T(\alpha^i) = \sum_{s=1}^{r} x_s^i b_s \otimes c_s$ for some constants x_s^i. But then $T = \sum_{s,i} e_i \otimes (x_s^i b_s \otimes c_s) = \sum_{s=1}^{r} (\sum_i x_s^i e_i) \otimes b_s \otimes c_s$, proving $\mathbf{R}(T)$ is at most the number of rank one matrices needed to span $T(A^*) \subset B \otimes C$. $\square$

Exercise 5.1.2.2 (1) Prove the border rank assertion.

5.1.3 Equations via Linear Algebra

All the equations we have seen so far arise as Koszul flattenings, which all vanish if Strassen's equations for minimal border rank are zero, as can be seen by the coordinate expressions (2.2.1) and the discussion in §2.4.3. Thus we have robust equations only if T is 1_A, 1_B or 1_C-generic, because otherwise the presence of $T(\alpha)^{\wedge \mathbf{a}-1}$ in the expressions make them likely to vanish. When T is 1_A-generic, the Koszul flattenings $T_A^{\wedge p} : \Lambda^p A \otimes B^* \to \Lambda^{p+1} A \otimes C$ provide measures of the failure of $T(A^*) T(\alpha)^{-1} \subset \mathrm{End}(B)$ to be an abelian subspace.

A first concern is that perhaps the choice of $\alpha \in A^*$ effects this failure. The following lemma addresses that concern, at least in the case of minimal border rank:

Lemma 5.1.3.1 [LM15] *Let $T \in A \otimes B \otimes C = \mathbb{C}^{\mathbf{a}} \otimes \mathbb{C}^{\mathbf{a}} \otimes \mathbb{C}^{\mathbf{a}}$ be 1_A-generic and assume* $\mathrm{rank}(T(\alpha_0)) = \mathbf{a}$. *If $T(A^*) T(\alpha_0)^{-1}$ is abelian, then $T(A^*) T(\alpha_0')^{-1}$ is abelian for any $\alpha_0' \in A^*$ such that $\mathrm{rank}(T(\alpha_0')) = \mathbf{a}$.*

Proof. Say $T(A^*) T(\alpha_0)^{-1}$ is abelian, and set $X_i = T(\alpha_i) T(\alpha_0)^{-1}$, so $[X_1, X_2] = 0$. Set $X_i' = T(\alpha_i) T(\alpha_0')^{-1}$ and $X' = T(\alpha_0') T(\alpha_0)^{-1}$, so $[X_i, X'] = 0$ as well, which implies $[X_i, (X')^{-1}] = 0$. We want to show $[X_1', X_2'] = 0$. But $X_j' = X_j (X')^{-1}$, so

$$
\begin{aligned}
X_1' X_2' - X_2' X_1' &= X_1 (X')^{-1} X_2 (X')^{-1} - X_2 (X')^{-1} X_1 (X')^{-1} \\
&= X_1 X_2 (X')^{-1} (X')^{-1} - X_2 X_1 (X')^{-1} (X')^{-1} \\
&= [X_1, X_2] (X')^{-1} (X')^{-1} \\
&= 0.
\end{aligned}
$$
                                   $\square$

Definition 5.1.3.2 Let $\mathbf{a} = \mathbf{b} = \mathbf{c}$ and let $\mathrm{Abel}_A \subset A \otimes B \otimes C$ denote the set of concise, 1_A-generic tensors such that for some (and hence any) $\alpha \in A^*$ with $T(\alpha)$ of maximal rank, $T(A^*) T(\alpha)^{-1} \subset \mathrm{End}(B)$ is abelian. Note that Abel_A is not Zariski closed.

Let $\mathrm{Diag}_{\mathrm{End}(B)}^0 \subset G(\mathbf{b}, \mathrm{End}(B))$ denote the set of $\mathbf{b}$-dimensional subspaces that are simultaneously diagonalizable under the action of $GL(B)$, and let

$\mathrm{Diag}_{\mathrm{End}(B)} = \overline{\mathrm{Diag}^0_{\mathrm{End}(B)}}$ denote its Zariski closure. Let $\alpha \in A^*$ be such that $T(\alpha)$ is of maximal rank, and let

$$\mathrm{Diag}_A := \overline{\{T \in \mathrm{Abel}_A \mid T(A^*)T(\alpha)^{-1} \in \mathrm{Diag}_{\mathrm{End}(B)}\}} \cap \mathrm{Abel}_A .$$

By definition, $\mathrm{Diag}_A \subseteq \mathrm{Abel}_A$. To what extent does equality hold? The following proposition gives a necessary algebraic condition to be in Diag_A:

Proposition 5.1.3.3 [Ger61] *The set*

$$\{U \in G(\mathbf{a}, \mathrm{End}(B)) \mid U \text{ is closed under composition}\}$$

is Zariski closed.

In particular, if $T \in A \otimes B \otimes C = \mathbb{C}^{\mathbf{a}} \otimes \mathbb{C}^{\mathbf{a}} \otimes \mathbb{C}^{\mathbf{a}}$ is 1_A-generic with $\underline{R}(T) = \mathbf{a}$, then for all $\alpha \in A^*$ with $T(\alpha)$ invertible, $T(A^*)T(\alpha)^{-1}$ is closed under composition.

Proof. If $u_1, \ldots, u_{\mathbf{a}}$ is a basis of U, then U is closed under composition if and only if, for all $u \in U$,

$$(uu_j) \wedge u_1 \wedge \cdots \wedge u_{\mathbf{a}} = 0 \ \forall 1 \le j \le \mathbf{a}.$$

Let $(Abel_A \times A^*)^0 = \{(T, \alpha) \mid \mathrm{rank}(T(\alpha)) = \mathbf{b}\}$, and note that the map $(Abel_A \times A^*)^0 \to G(\mathbf{a}, \mathrm{End}(B))$, given by $(T, \alpha) \mapsto T(A^*)T(\alpha)^{-1}$, is continuous. The "in particular" assertion follows from this continuity because if $U \in \mathrm{Diag}^0_{\mathrm{End}(B)}$, then U is closed under composition. $\qquad\square$

Exercise 5.1.3.4 (2) Show that if $T(\alpha)$, $T(\alpha')$ are invertible and $T(A^*)T(\alpha)^{-1}$ is closed under composition, then $T(A^*)T(\alpha')^{-1}$ is closed under composition.

Let $\mathrm{End}\,\mathrm{Abel}_A \subseteq \mathrm{Abel}_A$ denote the subset of tensors with $T(A)T(\alpha)^{-1}$ closed under composition for some (and hence all) $\alpha \in A^*$ with $T(\alpha)$ invertible. We have

$$\mathrm{Diag}_A \subseteq \mathrm{End}\,\mathrm{Abel}_A \subseteq \mathrm{Abel}_A, \tag{5.1.1}$$

where the first inclusion is Proposition 5.1.3.3 and the second is by definition. Are these containments strict?

A classical theorem states that when $\mathbf{a} = 3$, the three sets are equal. Moreover:

Theorem 5.1.3.5 [IM05] *When $\mathbf{a} \le 4$, $\mathrm{Diag}_A = \mathrm{End}\,\mathrm{Abel}_A = \mathrm{Abel}_A$.*

See [IM05] for the proof, which has numerous cases.
What happens when $\mathbf{a} = 5$?

Proposition 5.1.3.6 [Lei16] *Let* $T_{Leit,5} = a_1 \otimes (b_1 \otimes c_1 + b_2 \otimes c_2 + b_3 \otimes c_3 + b_4 \otimes c_4 + b_5 \otimes c_5) + a_2 \otimes (b_1 \otimes c_3 + b_3 \otimes c_5) + a_3 \otimes b_1 \otimes c_4 + a_4 \otimes b_2 \otimes c_4 + a_5 \otimes b_2 \otimes c_5$, *which gives rise to the linear space*

$$T_{Leit,5}(A^*) = \begin{pmatrix} x_1 & & & & \\ & x_1 & & & \\ x_2 & & x_1 & & \\ x_3 & x_4 & & x_1 & \\ & x_5 & x_2 & & x_1 \end{pmatrix}. \tag{5.1.2}$$

Then $T_{Leit,5}(A^*)T(\alpha^1)^{-1}$ *is an abelian Lie algebra, but not* End-*closed. That is,* $T_{Leit,5} \in \text{Abel}_A$, *but* $T_{Leit,5} \notin \text{End Abel}_A$.

Throughout this chapter, an expression of the form (5.1.2) is to be read as $T(x_1\alpha^1 + \cdots + x_a\alpha^a)$, where $\alpha^1, \ldots, \alpha^a$ is a basis of A^*.

Exercise 5.1.3.7 (1) Verify that $T_{Leit,5}(A^*)T(\alpha^1)^{-1}$ is not closed under composition.

Thus, when $\mathbf{a} \geq 5$, End Abel$_A \subsetneq$ Abel$_A$. The following proposition shows that the first containment in (5.1.1) is also strict when $\mathbf{a} \geq 7$:

Proposition 5.1.3.8 [LM15] *The tensor corresponding to*

$$T_{end,7}(A^*) = \begin{pmatrix} x_1 & & & & & & \\ & x_1 & & & & & \\ & & x_1 & & & & \\ & & & x_1 & & & \\ & x_2 + x_7 & x_3 & x_4 & x_1 & & \\ x_2 & x_3 & x_5 & x_6 & & x_1 & \\ x_4 & x_5 & x_6 & x_7 & & & x_1 \end{pmatrix}$$

is in End Abel$_A$, *but has border rank at least* 8.

The proof is given in §5.2.1.

We have seen that set-theoretic equations for End Abel$_A$ are easy, whereas set-theoretic equations for Diag$_A$ are not known. One might hope that if $T \in$ End Abel$_A$, at least $\underline{\mathbf{R}}(T)$ should be *close* to $\mathbf{a}$. This hope fails miserably:

Proposition 5.1.3.9 [LM15] *There exist* 1_A-*generic tensors in* $\mathbb{C}^{\mathbf{a}} \otimes \mathbb{C}^{\mathbf{a}} \otimes \mathbb{C}^{\mathbf{a}}$ *in* End Abel$_A$ *of border rank greater than* $\frac{\mathbf{a}^2}{8}$.

Proof. Consider T such that

$$
T(A^*) \subset \begin{pmatrix} x_1 & & & & & \\ & \ddots & & & & \\ & & x_1 & & & \\ * & \cdots & * & x_1 & & \\ \vdots & \vdots & \vdots & & \ddots & \\ * & \cdots & * & & & x_1 \end{pmatrix}, \qquad (5.1.3)
$$

and set $x_1 = 0$. We obtain a generic tensor in $\mathbb{C}^{\mathbf{a}-1} \otimes \mathbb{C}^{\lfloor \frac{\mathbf{a}}{2} \rfloor} \otimes \mathbb{C}^{\lceil \frac{\mathbf{a}}{2} \rceil}$, which will have border greater than $\frac{\mathbf{a}^2}{8}$. Conclude by applying Exercise 2.1.6.2. $\qquad\square$

Tensors of the form (5.1.3) expose a weakness of Strassen's equations that I discuss further in §5.4.2. Variants of the tensors of the form (5.1.3) are 1-generic and still exhibit the same behavior.

5.1.4 Sufficient Conditions for a Concise Tensor to be of Minimal Border Rank

A classical result in linear algebra says a subspace $U \subset \text{End}(B)$ is diagonalizable if and only if U is abelian and every $x \in U$ (or equivalently for each x_j in a basis of U) is diagonalizable. This implies:

Proposition 5.1.4.1 *A necessary and sufficient condition for a concise 1_A-generic tensor $T \in A \otimes B \otimes C$ with $\mathbf{a} = \mathbf{b} = \mathbf{c}$ to be of minimal rank $\mathbf{a}$ is that for some basis $\alpha_1, \ldots, \alpha_{\mathbf{a}}$ of A^* with $\text{rank}(T(\alpha_1)) = \mathbf{b}$, the space $T(A)T(\alpha_1)^{-1} \subset \text{End}(B)$ is abelian and each $T(\alpha_j)T(\alpha_1)^{-1}$ is diagonalizable.*

Although we have seen several necessary conditions to be of minimal border rank, the question is open in general:

Problem 5.1.4.2 [BCS97, Prob. 15.2] Classify concise tensors of minimal border rank.

Below is a sufficient condition to be of minimal border rank.

For $x \in \text{End}(B)$, define the *centralizer* of x, denoted $C(x)$, by

$$
C(x) := \{ y \in \text{End}(B) \mid [y, x] = 0 \}.
$$

Definition 5.1.4.3 An element $x \in \text{End}(B)$ is *regular* if $\dim C(x) = \mathbf{b}$, and it is *regular semi-simple* if x is diagonalizable with distinct eigenvalues.

Exercise 5.1.4.4 (2) An $\mathbf{m} \times \mathbf{m}$ matrix is *regular nilpotent* if it is zero, except for the super diagonal, where the entries are all 1s. Show that a regular nilpotent element is indeed regular and that its centralizer is the space of upper-triangular matrices where the entries on each (upper) diagonal are the same, e.g., when $\mathbf{m} = 3$, the centralizer is

$$\left\{ \begin{pmatrix} x & y & z \\ & x & y \\ & & x \end{pmatrix} \mid x, y, z \in \mathbb{C} \right\}.$$

Exercise 5.1.4.5 (2) Show that $\dim C(x) \geq \mathbf{b}$ with equality if and only if the minimal polynomial of x equals the characteristic polynomial. ⊚

Note that x is regular semi-simple if and only if $C(x) \subset \mathrm{End}(B)$ is a diagonalizable subspace. In this case the eigenvalues of x are distinct.

Proposition 5.1.4.6 *(L. Manivel [LM15]) Let $U \subset \mathrm{End}(B)$ be an abelian subspace of dimension $\mathbf{b}$ such that there exists $x \in U$ that is regular. Then $U \in \mathrm{Diag}_{\mathrm{End}(B)} \subset G(\mathbf{b}, \mathrm{End}(B))$.*

Proof. Since the Zariski closure of the set of regular semi-simple elements is all of $\mathrm{End}(B)$, for any $x \in \mathrm{End}(B)$, there exists a curve x_t of regular semi-simple elements with $\lim_{t \to 0} x_t = x$. Consider the induced curve in the Grassmannian $C(x_t) \subset G(\mathbf{b}, \mathrm{End}(B))$. Then $C_0 := \lim_{t \to 0} C(x_t)$ exists and is contained in $C(x) \subset \mathrm{End}(B)$, and since U is abelian, we also have $U \subseteq C(x)$. But if x is regular, then $\dim C(x) = \dim(U) = \mathbf{b}$, so $\lim_{t \to 0} C(x_t)$, C_0 and U must all be equal, and thus U is a limit of diagonalizable subspaces. □

Proposition 5.1.4.6 applied to $T(A)T(\alpha)^{-1}$ provides a sufficient condition for a concise 1_A-generic tensor $T \in A \otimes B \otimes C$ to be of minimal border rank. The condition is not necessary, even for 1-generic tensors, e.g., the Coppersmith-Winograd tensor $T_{q,CW}$ of (3.4.5) is 1-generic of minimal border rank but $T_{q,CW}(A^*)T_{q,CW}(\alpha)^{-1}$ does not contain a regular element for any $\alpha \in A^*$.

Exercise 5.1.4.7 (2) Show that the centralizer of $T_{\mathbb{C}[\mathbb{Z}_m]}(x_1)$ from Example 3.5.1.2 is $T_{\mathbb{C}[\mathbb{Z}_m]}(\mathbb{C}[\mathbb{Z}_m])$ to obtain a second proof that $\underline{\mathbf{R}}(T_{\mathbb{C}[\mathbb{Z}_m]}) = m$.

Problem 5.1.4.8 Determine a criterion for $U \in G(\mathbf{b}, \mathrm{End}(B))$ to be in the closure of the diagonalizable $\mathbf{b}$-planes, when U does not contain a regular element.

5.1.5 Strassen's Equations and Symmetric Tensors

Proposition 5.1.5.1 [LM15] *Let $T \in A \otimes B \otimes C = \mathbb{C}^m \otimes \mathbb{C}^m \otimes \mathbb{C}^m$ be 1_A and 1_B generic and satisfy the A-Strassen equations. Then, after a suitable choice of identification of A with B via bases, T is isomorphic to a tensor in $S^2 A \otimes C$.*

In particular:

1 *After making choices of general $\alpha \in A^*$ and $\beta \in B^*$, $T(A^*)$ and $T(B^*)$ are GL_m-isomorphic subspaces of* $\mathrm{End}(\mathbb{C}^m)$.
2 *If T is 1-generic, then T is isomorphic to a tensor in $S^3\mathbb{C}^m$.*

Proof. Let $\{a_i\}, \{b_j\}, \{c_k\}$ respectively be bases of A, B, C, with dual bases $\{\alpha_i\}, \{\beta_j\}, \{\gamma_k\}$. Write $T = \sum t^{ijk} a_i \otimes b_j \otimes c_k$. After a change of basis in A so that $\mathrm{rank}(T(\alpha_1)) = \mathbf{m}$ and in B, C, so that it is the identity matrix, we obtain that $t^{1jk} = \delta_{jk}$, and after a change of basis B so that $T(\beta_1)$ is of full rank and further changes of bases in A, B, C, we may assume $t^{i1k} = \delta_{ik}$ as well. (To obtain $t^{i1k} = \delta_{ik}$ only requires changes of bases in A, C, but a further change in B may be needed to preserve $t^{1jk} = \delta_{jk}$.) Identify $T(A^*) \subset \mathrm{End}(\mathbb{C}^m)$ via α^1. Strassen's A-equations then say

$$0 = [T(\alpha^{i_1}), T(\alpha^{i_2})]_{(j,k)} = \sum_l t^{i_1 jl} t^{i_2 lk} - t^{i_2 jl} t^{i_1 lk} \ \forall i_1, i_2, j, k.$$

Consider when $j = 1$:

$$0 = \sum_l t^{i_1 1l} t^{i_2 lk} - t^{i_2 1l} t^{i_1 lk} = t^{i_2 i_1 k} - t^{i_1 i_2 k} \ \forall i_1, i_2, k,$$

because $t^{i1l} = \delta_{i,l}$. But this says $T \in S^2\mathbb{C}^m \otimes \mathbb{C}^m$.

For the last assertion, say $L_B : B \to A$ is such that $\mathrm{Id}_A \otimes L_B \otimes \mathrm{Id}_C(T) \in S^2 A \otimes C$ and $L_C : C \to A$ is such that $\mathrm{Id}_A \otimes \mathrm{Id}_B \otimes L_C \in S^2 A \otimes B$. Then $\mathrm{Id}_A \otimes L_B \otimes L_C(T)$ is in $A^{\otimes 3}$, symmetric in the first and second factors as well as the first and third. But $\mathfrak{S}_3$ is generated by two transpositions, so $\mathrm{Id}_A \otimes L_B \otimes L_C(T) \in S^3 A$. $\qquad \square$

Thus the A, B, and C-Strassen equations for minimal border rank, despite being nonisomorphic modules (see [LM08a]), when restricted to 1-generic tensors, all have the same zero sets.

5.2 Indirectly Defined Equations

This section and §5.4.1 discuss Zariski closed conditions that in principle give rise to equations, but they are difficult to write down explicitly – to do so systematically, one would need to use elimination theory, which is impossible to implement in practice other than in very small cases. Nonetheless, for certain tensors, these conditions can be used to prove lower bounds on border rank, e.g., the lower bound on $\underline{\mathbf{R}}(M_{\langle \mathbf{n} \rangle})$ via Griesser's equations in §5.2.2 and the state-of-the-art lower bound on $\underline{\mathbf{R}}(M_{\langle \mathbf{n} \rangle})$ of Theorem 5.4.5.1.

5.2.1 Intersection Properties

Exercise 5.2.1.1 (2) [BCS97, Example 15.14] Given $T \in \mathbb{C}^{\mathbf{a}} \otimes \mathbb{C}^{\mathbf{a}} \otimes \mathbb{C}^{\mathbf{a}} = A \otimes B \otimes C$ that is concise, show that $\mathbb{P}T(A^*) \cap Seg(\mathbb{P}B \times \mathbb{P}C) = \emptyset$ implies $\underline{\mathbf{R}}(T) > \mathbf{a}$. ⊚

Proof of Proposition 5.1.3.8. The fact that $T_{end,7}(A^*)$ is End-closed follows by inspection. The tensor has border rank at least 8 by Exercise 5.2.1.1 as $T_{end,7}(A^*)$ does not intersect the Segre. Indeed, if it intersected the Segre, the vanishing of size two minors implies $x_1 = x_4 = 0$, $(x_2 + x_7)x_2 = 0$, and $(x_2 + x_7)x_7 = 0$. If $x_2 + x_7 = 0$, then $x_3 = 0$, and $x_7^2 = (x_2 + x_7)x_7 = 0$, and hence $x_2 = 0$ as well, and we are done. If $x_2 = 0$, analogously, we obtain $x_7 = 0$ and $x_3 = x_5 = x_6 = 0$. □

A *complete flag* in a vector space V is a sequence of subspaces $0 \subset V_1 \subset V_2 \subset \cdots \subset V_{\mathbf{v}}$ with $\dim V_j = j$.

Proposition 5.2.1.2 [Lei16, LM15] *Let* $T \in \mathbb{C}^{\mathbf{a}} \otimes \mathbb{C}^{\mathbf{a}} \otimes \mathbb{C}^{\mathbf{a}} = A \otimes B \otimes C$ *be concise. If* $\underline{\mathbf{R}}(T) = \mathbf{a}$, *then there exists a complete flag* $A_1 \subset \cdots \subset A_{\mathbf{a}-1} \subset A_{\mathbf{a}} = A^*$, *with* $\dim A_j = j$, *such that* $\mathbb{P}T(A_j) \subset \sigma_j(Seg(\mathbb{P}B \times \mathbb{P}C))$.

Proof. Write $T = \lim_{t \to 0} \sum_{j=1}^{\mathbf{a}} a_j(t) \otimes X_j(t)$, where $X_j(t) \in B \otimes C$ have rank one. Since T is concise, we may assume without loss of generality that $a_1(t), \ldots, a_{\mathbf{a}}(t)$ is a basis of A for $t \neq 0$. Let $\alpha^1(t), \ldots, \alpha^{\mathbf{a}}(t) \in A^*$ be the dual basis. Then take $A_k(t) = \text{span}\{\alpha^1(t), \ldots, \alpha^k(t)\} \in G(k, A^*)$ and $A_k = \lim_{t \to 0} A_k(t)$. Since $\mathbb{P}T^*(A_k(t)) \subset \sigma_k(Seg(\mathbb{P}B \times \mathbb{P}C))$, the same must be true in the limit. □

One can say even more. For example:

Proposition 5.2.1.3 [LM15] *Let* $T \in \mathbb{C}^{\mathbf{a}} \otimes \mathbb{C}^{\mathbf{a}} \otimes \mathbb{C}^{\mathbf{a}} = A \otimes B \otimes C$. *If* $\underline{\mathbf{R}}(T) = \mathbf{a}$ *and* $T(A^*) \cap Seg(\mathbb{P}B \times \mathbb{P}C) = [X_0]$ *is a single point, then* $\mathbb{P}(T(A^*) \cap \hat{T}_{[X_0]} Seg(\mathbb{P}B \times \mathbb{P}C))$ *must contain a* $\mathbb{P}^1$.

Proof. Say $T(A^*)$ were the limit of $\text{span}\{X_1(t), \ldots, X_{\mathbf{a}}(t)\}$ with each $X_j(t)$ of rank one. Then since $\mathbb{P}T(A^*) \cap Seg(\mathbb{P}B \times \mathbb{P}C) = [X_0]$, we must have each $X_j(t)$ limiting to X_0. But then $\lim_{t \to 0} \text{span}\{X_1(t), X_2(t)\}$, which must be two-dimensional, must be contained in $\hat{T}_{[X_0]} Seg(\mathbb{P}B \times \mathbb{P}C)$ and $T(A^*)$. □

5.2.2 Griesser's Equations

The following theorem describes potential equations for $\sigma_r(Seg(\mathbb{P}A \times \mathbb{P}B \times \mathbb{P}C))$ in the range $\mathbf{b} < r \leq 2\mathbf{b} - 1$.

Theorem 5.2.2.1 [Gri86] *Let* $\mathbf{b} = \mathbf{c}$. *Given a* 1_A-*generic tensor* $T \in A \otimes B \otimes C$ *with* $\underline{\mathbf{R}}(T) \leq r$, *let* $\alpha_0 \in A^*$ *be such that* $T(\alpha_0)$ *is invertible. For* $\alpha' \in A^*$, *let* $X(\alpha') = T(\alpha')T(\alpha_0)^{-1} \in \text{End}(B)$. *Fix* $\alpha_1 \in A^*$. *Consider the space of endomorphisms* $U := \{[X(\alpha_1), X(\alpha')] : B \to B \mid \alpha' \in A^*\} \subset \mathfrak{sl}(B)$. *Then there exists* $E \in G(2\mathbf{b} - r, B)$ *such that* $\dim(U.E) \le r - \mathbf{b}$.

Remark 5.2.2.2 Compared with the minors of $T_A^{\wedge p}$, here one is just examining the first block column of the matrix appearing in the expression $Q\tilde{Q}$ in (2.4.7), but one is apparently extracting more refined information from it.

Proof. For the moment, assume $\mathbf{R}(T) = r$ and $T = \sum_{j=1}^{r} a_j \otimes b_j \otimes c_j$. Let $\hat{B} = \mathbb{C}^r$ be equipped with basis $e_1, \ldots, e_r$. Define $\pi : \hat{B} \to B$ by $\pi(e_j) = b_j$. Let $i : B \to \hat{B}$ be such that $\pi \circ i = \text{Id}_B$. Choose $B' \subset \hat{B}$ of dimension $r - \mathbf{b}$ such that $\hat{B} = i(B) \oplus B'$, and denote the inclusion and projection as $i' : B' \to \hat{B}$ and $\pi' : \hat{B} \to B'$, respectively. Pictorially,

$$\hat{B}$$
$$i \nearrow \swarrow \pi \quad \pi' \searrow \nwarrow i'$$
$$B \qquad\qquad B'$$

Let $\alpha_0, \alpha_1, \ldots, \alpha_{\mathbf{a}-1}$ be a basis of A^*. Let $\hat{T} = \sum_{j=1}^{r} a_j \otimes e_j \otimes e_j^* \in A \otimes \hat{B} \otimes \hat{B}^*$ and let $\hat{X}_j := \hat{T}(\alpha_j)\hat{T}(\alpha_0)^{\wedge r-1}$. (Recall that the matrix of $\hat{T}(\alpha_0)^{\wedge r-1}$ is the cofactor matrix of $\hat{T}(\alpha_0)$.) Now in $\text{End}(\hat{B})$, all the commutators $[\hat{X}_i, \hat{X}_j]$ are zero because $\mathbf{R}(\hat{T}) = r$. For all $2 \le s \le \mathbf{a} - 1$, $[\hat{X}_1, \hat{X}_s] = 0$ implies

$$0 = \pi[\hat{X}_1, \hat{X}_s]i$$
$$= [X_1, X_s] + (\pi\hat{X}_1 i')(\pi'\hat{X}_s i) - (\pi\hat{X}_s i')(\pi'\hat{X}_1 i). \qquad (5.2.1)$$

Now take $E \subseteq \ker \pi'\hat{X}_1 i \subset B$ of dimension $2\mathbf{b} - r$. Then, for all s, $[X_1, X_s] \cdot E \subset \text{Image } \pi\hat{X}_1 i'$, which has dimension at most $r - \mathbf{b}$ because $\pi\hat{X}_1 i' : B' \to B$ and $\dim B' = r - \mathbf{b}$. The general case follows because these conditions are all Zariski closed. $\square$

Proof of Theorem 2.2.2.1. Here there is just one commutator $[X_1, X_2]$ and its rank is at most the sum of the ranks of the other two terms in (5.2.1). But each of the other two terms is a composition of linear maps, including i'' which can have rank at most $r - \mathbf{b}$, so their sum can have rank at most $2(r - \mathbf{b})$. $\square$

Remark 5.2.2.3 It is not known to what extent Griesser's equations are nontrivial. Proving nontriviality of equations, even when the equations can be written down explicitly, is often more difficult than finding the equations. For example, it took several years after Koszul flattenings were discovered to prove they were nontrivial to almost the full extent possible. Regarding Griesser's equations, it is known they are nontrivial up to $r \le \frac{3}{2}\mathbf{m} + \frac{\sqrt{\mathbf{m}}}{2} - 2$ when $\mathbf{m}$ is odd and a similar, slightly smaller bound when $\mathbf{m}$ is even by Proposition 5.2.2.5.

On the other hand, the equations are trivial when $r = 2\mathbf{b} - 1$ and all $\mathbf{a}$, and when $r = 2\mathbf{b} - 2$, and $\mathbf{a} \leq \frac{\mathbf{b}}{2} + 2$, in particular $\mathbf{a} = \mathbf{b} = 4$ by [Lan15b]. I do not know whether the equations are trivial for $r = 2\mathbf{b} - 2$, $\mathbf{a} = \mathbf{b}$, and $\mathbf{b} > 4$.

Griesser's equations are most robust when $T(\alpha_1)T(\alpha_0)^{-1}$ is a generic endomorphism, which motivates the following definition:

Definition 5.2.2.4 For a 1_A-generic tensor $T \in A \otimes B \otimes C$, define T to be 2_A-*generic* if there exist $\alpha \in A^*$ such that $T(\alpha) : C^* \to B$ is of maximal rank and $\alpha' \in A^*$ such that $T(\alpha')T(\alpha)^{-1} : B \to B$ is regular semi-simple.

Proposition 5.1.4.6 implies that when $T \in \mathbb{C}^m \otimes \mathbb{C}^m \otimes \mathbb{C}^m$ is concise, is 2_A-generic, and satisfies Strassen's equations, $\underline{\mathbf{R}}(T) = \mathbf{m}$.

Unfortunately for proving lower bounds, $M_{\langle \mathbf{n} \rangle}$ is not 2_A-generic. The equations coming from Koszul flattenings, and even more so Griesser's equations, are less robust for tensors that fail to be 2_A-generic. This partially explains why $M_{\langle \mathbf{n} \rangle}$ satisfies some of the Koszul-flattening equations and Griesser's equations (as shown below). Thus an important problem is to identify modules of equations for σ_r that are robust for non-2-generic tensors.

Proposition 5.2.2.5 [Lan15b] *Matrix multiplication* $M_{\langle \mathbf{n} \rangle}$ *fails to satisfy Griesser's equations for* $r \leq \frac{3}{2}\mathbf{n}^2 - 1$ *when* $\mathbf{n}$ *is even and* $r \leq \frac{3}{2}\mathbf{n}^2 + \frac{\mathbf{n}}{2} - 2$ *when* $\mathbf{n}$ *is odd and satisfies the equations for all larger* r.

Proof. Consider matrix multiplication $M_{\langle \mathbf{n} \rangle} \in \mathbb{C}^{\mathbf{n}^2} \otimes \mathbb{C}^{\mathbf{n}^2} \otimes \mathbb{C}^{\mathbf{n}^2} = A \otimes B \otimes C$. Recall from Exercise 2.1.7.4 that with a judicious ordering of bases, $M_{\langle \mathbf{n} \rangle}(A^*)$ is block diagonal:

$$\begin{pmatrix} x & & \\ & \ddots & \\ & & x \end{pmatrix}, \tag{5.2.2}$$

where $x = (x_j^i)$ is $\mathbf{n} \times \mathbf{n}$. In particular, the image is closed under brackets. Choose $X_0 \in M_{\langle \mathbf{n} \rangle}(A^*)$ to be the identity. It is not possible to have $X_1 \in M_{\langle \mathbf{n} \rangle}(A^*)$ diagonal with distinct entries on the diagonal; the most generic choice for X_1 is to be block diagonal, with each block having the same $\mathbf{n}$ distinct entries. For a subspace E of dimension $2\mathbf{n}^2 - r = d\mathbf{n} + e$ with $0 \leq e \leq \mathbf{n} - 1$, the image of a generic choice of $[X_1, X_2], \ldots, [X_1, X_{\mathbf{n}^2-1}]$ applied to E is of dimension at least $(d+1)\mathbf{n}$ if $e \geq 2$, at least $(d+1)\mathbf{n} - 1$ if $e = 1$, and $d\mathbf{n}$ if $e = 0$, and equality will hold if we choose E to be, e.g., the span of the first $2\mathbf{n}^2 - r$ basis vectors of B. (This is because the $[X_1, X_s]$ will span the entries of type (5.2.2) with zeros on the diagonal.) If $\mathbf{n}$ is even, taking $2\mathbf{n}^2 - r = \frac{\mathbf{n}^2}{2} + 1$, so $r = \frac{3\mathbf{n}^2}{2} - 1$, the image occupies a space of dimension $\frac{\mathbf{n}^2}{2} + \mathbf{n} - 1 > \frac{\mathbf{n}^2}{2} - 1 = r - \mathbf{n}^2$. If one takes $2\mathbf{n}^2 - r = \frac{\mathbf{n}^2}{2}$, so $r = \frac{3\mathbf{n}^2}{2}$, the image occupies a space of dimension $\frac{\mathbf{n}^2}{2} = r - \mathbf{n}^2$, showing Griesser's equations cannot do better for $\mathbf{n}$ even. If $\mathbf{n}$ is odd, taking $2\mathbf{n}^2 - r = \frac{\mathbf{n}^2}{2} - \frac{\mathbf{n}}{2} + 2$, so $r = \frac{3\mathbf{n}^2}{2} + \frac{\mathbf{n}}{2} - 2$, the image will have dimension $\frac{\mathbf{n}^2}{2} + \frac{\mathbf{n}}{2} > r - \mathbf{n}^2 = \frac{\mathbf{n}^2}{2} + \frac{\mathbf{n}}{2} - 1$, and taking $2\mathbf{n}^2 - r = \frac{\mathbf{n}^2}{2} - \frac{\mathbf{n}}{2} + 1$, the image can have dimension $\frac{\mathbf{n}^2}{2} - \frac{\mathbf{n}}{2} + (\mathbf{n} - 1) = r - \mathbf{n}^2$, so the equations vanish for this and all larger r. Thus Griesser's equations for $\mathbf{n}$ odd give Lickteig's bound $\underline{\mathbf{R}}(M_{\langle \mathbf{n} \rangle}) \geq \frac{3\mathbf{n}^2}{2} + \frac{\mathbf{n}}{2} - 1$. $\qquad\qquad\square$

5.3 The Substitution Method

The following method has a long history dating back to [Pan66] (see [BCS97, Chapter 6] and [Blä14, Chapter 6] for a history and many applications). It is the only general technique available for proving lower bounds on tensor rank that I am aware of. However, the limit of the method is at most tensor rank lower bounds of $3\mathbf{m} - 1$ in $\mathbb{C}^\mathbf{m} \otimes \mathbb{C}^\mathbf{m} \otimes \mathbb{C}^\mathbf{m}$. (In §10.1 I will describe a powerful method for proving lower bounds on symmetric rank.)

5.3.1 Lower Bounds on Tensor Rank via the Substitution Method

Proposition 5.3.1.1 [AFT11, Appendix B] *Let $T \in A \otimes B \otimes C$. Fix a basis $a_1, \ldots, a_\mathbf{a}$ of A, with dual basis $\alpha^1, \ldots, \alpha^\mathbf{a}$. Write $T = \sum_{i=1}^{\mathbf{a}} a_i \otimes M_i$, where $M_i \in B \otimes C$. Let $\mathbf{R}(T) = r$ and $M_1 \neq 0$. Then there exist constants $\lambda_2, \ldots, \lambda_\mathbf{a}$, such that the tensor*

$$\tilde{T} := \sum_{j=2}^{\mathbf{a}} a_j \otimes (M_j - \lambda_j M_1) \in \mathrm{span}\{a_2, \ldots, a_\mathbf{a}\} \otimes B \otimes C$$

has rank at most $r - 1$. Moreover, if $\mathrm{rank}(M_1) = 1$, then for any choice of λ_j, $\mathbf{R}(\tilde{T})$ is either r or $r - 1$.

The same assertions hold exchanging the role of A with that of B or C.

Proof. (Following [LM15]) By Proposition 5.1.2.1, there exist $X_1, \ldots, X_r \in \hat{S}eg(\mathbb{P}B \times \mathbb{P}C)$ and scalars d_j^i such that

$$M_j = \sum_{i=1}^{r} d_j^i X_i.$$

Since $M_1 \neq 0$, we may assume $d_1^1 \neq 0$ and define $\lambda_j = \frac{d_j^1}{d_1^1}$. Then the subspace $\tilde{T}(\langle \alpha^2, \ldots, \alpha^\mathbf{a} \rangle)$ is spanned by $X_2, \ldots, X_r$, so Proposition 5.1.2.1 implies $\mathbf{R}(\tilde{T}) \leq r - 1$. The last assertion holds because if $\mathrm{rank}(M_1) = 1$, then we may assume $X_1 = M_1$, so we cannot lower the rank by more than one. $\qquad\square$

In practice, the method is used iteratively, with each of A, B, C playing the role of A above, to reduce T to a smaller and smaller tensor, at each step gaining one in the lower bound for the rank of T. At some steps one may project T to a smaller space to simplify the calculation.

Example 5.3.1.2 [AFT11] Let $T_{aft,3} \in A \otimes B \otimes C$ have an expression in bases such that, letting the columns of the following matrix correspond to B-basis vectors and the rows to C basis vectors,

$$T_{aft,3}(A^*) = \begin{pmatrix} x_1 & & & & & & & \\ & x_1 & & & & & & \\ & & x_1 & & & & & \\ & & & x_1 & & & & \\ x_2 & & & & x_1 & & & \\ & x_2 & & & & x_1 & & \\ x_3 & & x_2 & & & & x_1 & \\ x_4 & x_3 & & x_2 & & & & x_1 \end{pmatrix}.$$

For the first iteration of the substitution method, start with $b_8 \in B$ in the role of a_1 in the proposition. Write

$$\begin{aligned} T_{aft,3} = {} & b_1 \otimes (a_1 \otimes c_1 + a_2 \otimes c_5 + a_3 \otimes c_7 + a_4 \otimes c_8) \\ & + b_2 \otimes (a_1 \otimes c_2 + a_2 \otimes c_6 + a_3 \otimes c_8) + b_3 \otimes (a_1 \otimes c_3 + a_2 \otimes c_7) \\ & + b_4 \otimes (a_1 \otimes c_4 + a_2 \otimes c_8) + b_5 \otimes a_1 \otimes c_5 + b_6 \otimes a_1 \otimes c_6 \\ & + b_6 \otimes a_1 \otimes c_6 + b_7 \otimes a_1 \otimes c_7 + b_8 \otimes a_1 \otimes c_8. \end{aligned}$$

Then there exist $\lambda_1, \ldots, \lambda_7$ and a new tensor $T' \in A \otimes \mathbb{C}^7 \otimes C$ with $\mathbf{R}(T) \geq \mathbf{R}(T') + 1$ where

$$T'(A^*) = \begin{pmatrix} x_1 & & & & & & \\ & x_1 & & & & & \\ & & x_1 & & & & \\ & & & x_1 & & & \\ x_2 & & & & x_1 & & \\ & x_2 & & & & x_1 & \\ x_3 & & x_2 & & & & x_1 \\ x_4 & x_3 & & x_2 & & & \end{pmatrix} + \begin{pmatrix} & & & & & & \\ & & & & & & \\ & & & & & & \\ & & & & & & \\ & & & & & & \\ & & & & & & \\ & & & & & & \\ \lambda_1 x_1 & \lambda_2 x_1 & \cdots & & & & \lambda_7 x_1 \end{pmatrix}.$$

Continue removing the last three columns until we get a tensor $T'' \in A \otimes \mathbb{C}^4 \otimes C$ with

$$
T''(A^*) =
\begin{pmatrix}
x_1 & & & \\
& x_1 & & \\
& & x_1 & \\
& & & x_1 \\
x_2 & & & \\
& x_2 & & \\
x_3 & & x_2 & \\
x_4 & x_3 & & x_2
\end{pmatrix}
+
\begin{pmatrix}
& & & \\
& & & \\
& & & \\
& & & \\
\mu_{1,1}x_1 & \mu_{2,1}x_1 & \mu_{3,1}x_1 & \mu_{4,1}x_1 \\
\mu_{1,2}x_1 & \mu_{2,2}x_1 & \mu_{3,2}x_1 & \mu_{4,2}x_1 \\
\mu_{1,3}x_1 & \mu_{2,3}x_1 & \mu_{3,3}x_1 & \mu_{4,3}x_1 \\
\mu_{1,4}x_1 & \mu_{2,4}x_1 & \mu_{3,4}x_1 & \mu_{4,4}x_1
\end{pmatrix}.
$$

Now apply the method successively to $c_1, \ldots, c_4$ to obtain a tensor T'''' with $T''''(A^*) \in \mathbb{C}^4 \otimes \mathbb{C}^4$ such that $\mathbf{R}(T_{aft,3}) \geq 8 + \mathbf{R}(T''')$. Now project T'''' to the space given by $x_1 = 0$, so all the unknown constants disappear. The new tensor cannot have rank or border rank greater than that of T''''. Iterate the method with the projection of T'''' until one arrives at $\tilde{T}(A^*) \in \mathbb{C}^1 \otimes \mathbb{C}^1$ and the bound $\mathbf{R}(T_{aft,3}) \geq 8 + 4 + 2 + 1 = 15$. In fact $\mathbf{R}(T_{aft,3}) = 15$: observe that $T_{aft,3}(A^*)T_{aft,3}(\alpha^1)^{-1}$ is a projection of the centralizer of a regular nilpotent element as in Exercise 5.3.1.8, which implies $\mathbf{R}(T_{aft,3}) \leq 15$.

On the other hand, $\underline{\mathbf{R}}(T_{aft,3}) = 8$, again because $T_{aft,3}(A^*)T_{aft,3}(\alpha^1)^{-1}$ is a projection of the centralizer of a regular nilpotent element, so Proposition 5.1.4.6 applies.

This example generalizes to $T_{aft,k} \in \mathbb{C}^{k+1} \otimes \mathbb{C}^{2^k} \otimes \mathbb{C}^{2^k}$ of rank $2 \cdot 2^k - 1$ and border rank 2^k. The tensor T'''' above is $T_{aft,2}$.

Example 5.3.1.3 [AFT11] Let $T_{AFT,3} = a_1 \otimes (b_1 \otimes c_1 + \cdots + b_8 \otimes c_8) + a_2 \otimes (b_1 \otimes c_5 + b_2 \otimes c_6 + b_3 \otimes c_7 + b_4 \otimes c_8) + a_3 \otimes (b_1 \otimes c_7 + b_2 \otimes c_8) + a_4 \otimes b_1 \otimes c_8 + a_5 \otimes b_8 \otimes c_1 + a_6 \otimes b_8 \otimes c_2 + a_7 \otimes b_8 \otimes c_3 + a_8 \otimes b_8 \otimes c_4$, so

$$
T_{AFT,3}(A^*) =
\begin{pmatrix}
x_1 & & & & & & & x_5 \\
& x_1 & & & & & & x_6 \\
& & x_1 & & & & & x_7 \\
& & & x_1 & & & & x_8 \\
x_2 & & & & x_1 & & & \\
& x_2 & & & & x_1 & & \\
x_3 & & x_2 & & & & x_1 & \\
x_4 & x_3 & & x_2 & & & & x_1
\end{pmatrix}.
$$

Begin the substitution method with b_8 in the role of a_1 in the proposition, then project to $\langle \alpha^8, \ldots, \alpha^5 \rangle^\perp$ to obtain a tensor $\tilde{T}$ represented by the matrix

$$
\begin{pmatrix}
x_1 & & & & & & & \\
& x_1 & & & & & & \\
& & x_1 & & & & & \\
& & & x_1 & & & & \\
x_2 & & & & x_1 & & & \\
& x_2 & & & & x_1 & & \\
x_3 & & x_2 & & & & x_1 & \\
x_4 & x_3 & & x_2 & & & & x_1
\end{pmatrix},
$$

and $\mathbf{R}(T_{AFT,3}) \geq 4 + \mathbf{R}(\tilde{T})$. The substitution method then gives $\mathbf{R}(\tilde{T}) \geq 14$ by Example 5.3.1.2, and thus $\mathbf{R}(T_{AFT,3}) \geq 18$. This example generalizes to $T_{AFT,k} \in \mathbb{C}^{2^k+1} \otimes \mathbb{C}^{2^k} \otimes \mathbb{C}^{2^k+1}$ of rank at least $3(2^k + 1) - k - 4$. In fact, equality holds: in the case of $T_{AFT,3}$, it is enough to consider 17 matrices with just one nonzero entry corresponding to all nonzero entries of $T_{AFT,3}(A^*)$, apart from the top left and bottom right corner and one matrix with 1 at each corner and all other entries equal to 0. Moreover, as observed in [Lan15b], for these tensors, $(2^k + 1) + 1 \leq \mathbf{R}(T_{AFT,k}) \leq 2^{k+1} - k$.

Exercise 5.3.1.4 (2) Prove $(2^k + 1) + 1 \leq \underline{\mathbf{R}}(T_{AFT,k}) \leq 2^{k+1} - k$. ⊚

In summary:

Proposition 5.3.1.5 *The tensors* $T_{AFT,k} \in \mathbb{C}^{2^k+1} \otimes \mathbb{C}^{2^k} \otimes \mathbb{C}^{2^k+1}$ *of* [AFT11] *satisfy* $(2^k + 1) + 1 \leq \underline{\mathbf{R}}(T_{AFT,k}) \leq 2(2^k + 1) - 2 - k < 3(2^k + 1) - k - 4 = \mathbf{R}(T_{AFT,k})$.

Exercise 5.3.1.6 (2) Show that for all $\mathbf{m}, \mathbf{n}, N$, $\mathbf{R}(M_{\langle 1, \mathbf{m}, \mathbf{n}\rangle} \oplus M_{\langle N,1,1\rangle}) = \mathbf{mn} + N$.

Exercise 5.3.1.7 (2) Show that Strassen's tensor from §5.6, $T_{STR,q} = \sum_{j=1}^q (a_0 \otimes b_j \otimes c_j + a_j \otimes b_0 \otimes c_j) \in \mathbb{C}^{q+1} \otimes \mathbb{C}^{q+1} \otimes \mathbb{C}^q$ satisfies $\mathbf{R}(T_{STR,q}) = 2q$.

Exercise 5.3.1.8 (3) Show that a tensor $T \in \mathbb{C}^{\mathbf{m}} \otimes \mathbb{C}^{\mathbf{m}} \otimes \mathbb{C}^{\mathbf{m}}$ corresponding to the centralizer of a regular nilpotent element satisfies $\mathbf{R}(T) = 2\mathbf{m} - 1$. ⊚

To date, $T_{AFT,k}$ and its cousins are the only known examples of explicit tensors $T \in \mathbb{C}^{\mathbf{m}} \otimes \mathbb{C}^{\mathbf{m}} \otimes \mathbb{C}^{\mathbf{m}}$ satisfying $\mathbf{R}(T) \geq 3\mathbf{m} - O(\log(\mathbf{m}))$. There are several known to satisfy $\mathbf{R}(T) \geq 3\mathbf{m} - O(\mathbf{m})$, e.g., $M_{\langle \mathbf{n}\rangle}$, as was shown in §2.6, and $T_{WState}^{\otimes n} \in \mathbb{C}^{2^n} \otimes \mathbb{C}^{2^n} \otimes \mathbb{C}^{2^n}$, discussed in §5.6.

Problem 5.3.1.9 [Blä14] Find an explicit tensor $T \in \mathbb{C}^{\mathbf{m}} \otimes \mathbb{C}^{\mathbf{m}} \otimes \mathbb{C}^{\mathbf{m}}$ satisfying $\mathbf{R}(T) \geq (3 + \epsilon)\mathbf{m}$ for any $\epsilon > 0$.

Remark 5.3.1.10 Proposition 5.3.1.1 holds with any choice of basis, so we get to pick $[\alpha^1] \in \mathbb{P}A^*$, as long as $M_1 \neq 0$ (which is automatic if T is A-concise). On the other hand, there is no choice of the λ_j, so when dealing with $\tilde{T}$, one has to assume the λ_j are as bad as possible for proving lower bounds. For this reason, it is easier to implement this method on tensors with simple combinatorial structure or tensors that are sparse in some basis.

From a geometric perspective, we are restricting T, considered as a trilinear form $A^* \times B^* \times C^* \to \mathbb{C}$, to the hyperplane $A' \subset A^*$ defined by $\alpha^1 + \sum_{j=2}^{\mathbf{a}} \lambda_j \alpha^j = 0$, and our condition is that $\mathbf{R}(T|_{A' \otimes B^* \otimes C^*}) \leq \mathbf{R}(T) - 1$. Our freedom is the choice of $\langle a_2, \dots, a_{\mathbf{a}} \rangle \subset A$, and then A' (which we do not get to choose) is any hyperplane satisfying the open condition $\langle a_2, \dots, a_{\mathbf{a}} \rangle^\perp \not\subset A'$.

5.3.2 Strassen's Additivity Conjecture

Given $T_1 \in A_1 \otimes B_1 \otimes C_1$ and $T_2 \in A_2 \otimes B_2 \otimes C_2$, if one considers $T_1 + T_2 \in (A_1 \oplus A_2) \otimes (B_1 \oplus B_2) \otimes (C_1 \oplus C_2)$, where each $A_j \otimes B_j \otimes C_j$ is naturally included in $(A_1 \oplus A_2) \otimes (B_1 \oplus B_2) \otimes (C_1 \oplus C_2)$, we saw that $\mathbf{R}(T_1 + T_2) \leq \mathbf{R}(T_1) + \mathbf{R}(T_2)$. Also recall Schönhage's example §3.3.2 that $\underline{\mathbf{R}}(M_{\langle 1,\mathbf{m},\mathbf{n}\rangle} \oplus M_{\langle(\mathbf{n}-1)(\mathbf{m}-1),1,1\rangle}) = \mathbf{mn} + 1 < 2\mathbf{mn} - \mathbf{m} - \mathbf{n} + 1 = \underline{\mathbf{R}}(M_{\langle 1,\mathbf{m},\mathbf{n}\rangle}) + \underline{\mathbf{R}}(M_{\langle(\mathbf{n}-1)(\mathbf{m}-1),1,1\rangle})$. Before this example was known, Strassen made the following conjecture:

Conjecture 5.3.2.1 [Str73] *With the above notation,* $\mathbf{R}(T_1 + T_2) = \mathbf{R}(T_1) + \mathbf{R}(T_2)$.

Exercise 5.3.1.6 shows that despite the failure of a border rank analog of the conjecture for $M_{\langle 1,\mathbf{m},\mathbf{n}\rangle} \oplus M_{\langle(\mathbf{n}-1)(\mathbf{m}-1),1,1\rangle}$, the rank version does hold in this case.

While this conjecture has been studied from several different perspectives (e.g., [FW84, JT86, Bsh98, CCC15b, BGL13]), very little is known about it, and experts are divided as to whether it should be true or false.

In many cases of low rank the substitution method provides the correct rank. In light of this, the following theorem indicates why providing a counter example to Strassen's conjecture would need new techniques for proving rank lower bounds.

Theorem 5.3.2.2 [LM15] *Let $T_1 \in A_1 \otimes B_1 \otimes C_1$ and $T_2 \in A_2 \otimes B_2 \otimes C_2$ be such that $\mathbf{R}(T_1)$ can be determined by the substitution method applied to two of A_1, B_1, C_1. Then Strassen's additivity conjecture holds for $T_1 \oplus T_2$, i.e., $\mathbf{R}(T_1 \oplus T_2) = \mathbf{R}(T_1) + \mathbf{R}(T_2)$.*

Proof. With each application of the substitution method to elements of A_1, B_1, and C_1, T_1 is modified to a tensor of lower rank living in a smaller space, and

T_2 is unchanged. After all applications, T_1 has been modified to zero and T_2 is still unchanged.   □

The rank of any tensor in $\mathbb{C}^2 \otimes B \otimes C$ can be computed using the substitution method as follows: by dimension count, we can always find either $\beta \in B^*$ or $\gamma \in C^*$, such that $T(\beta)$ or $T(\gamma)$ is a rank one matrix. In particular, Theorem 5.3.2.2 provides an easy proof of Strassen's additivity conjecture if the dimension of any of A_1, B_1, or C_1 equals 2. This was first shown in [JT86] by other methods.

5.4 The Border Substitution Method

What follows are indirectly defined equations for border rank, in other words, indirectly defined algebraic varieties that contain $\sigma_r(Seg(\mathbb{P}A \times \mathbb{P}B \times \mathbb{P}C))$. While we don't have equations for these varieties, sometimes one can prove membership or nonmembership by direct arguments. The method is primarily useful for tensors with symmetry, as there border rank decompositions come in families, and it suffices to prove nonmembership for a convenient member of a putative family.

5.4.1 The Border Substitution Method

The substitution method may be restated as follows:

Proposition 5.4.1.1 *Let* $T \in A \otimes B \otimes C$ *be A-concise. Fix and* $\tilde{A} \subset A$ *of dimension* $\mathbf{a}'$. *Then*

$$\mathbf{R}(T) \geq \min_{\{A' \in G(\mathbf{a}', A^*) | A' \cap \tilde{A}^\perp = 0\}} \mathbf{R}(T|_{A' \otimes B^* \otimes C^*}) + (\mathbf{a} - \mathbf{a}').$$

Here $\tilde{A}$ in the case $\mathbf{a}' = \mathbf{a} - 1$ plays the role of $\langle a_2, \ldots, a_{\mathbf{a}} \rangle$ in Proposition 5.3.1.1. Recall that $T|_{A' \otimes B^* \otimes C^*} \in (A/(A')^\perp) \otimes B \otimes C$.

More generally,

Proposition 5.4.1.2 *Let* $T \in A \otimes B \otimes C$ *be concise. Fix* $\tilde{A} \subset A$, $\tilde{B} \subset B$, *and* $\tilde{C} \subset C$ *respectively of dimensions* $\mathbf{a}'$, $\mathbf{b}'$, *and* $\mathbf{c}'$. *Then*

$$\mathbf{R}(T) \geq (\mathbf{a} - \mathbf{a}') + (\mathbf{b} - \mathbf{b}') + (\mathbf{c} - \mathbf{c}')$$
$$+ \min \begin{Bmatrix} A' \in G(\mathbf{a}', A^*) \mid A' \cap \tilde{A}^\perp = 0 \\ B' \in G(\mathbf{b}', B^*) \mid B' \cap \tilde{B}^\perp = 0 \\ C' \in G(\mathbf{c}', C^*) \mid A' \cap \tilde{C}^\perp = 0 \end{Bmatrix} \mathbf{R}(T|_{A' \otimes B' \otimes C'}).$$

A border rank version is as follows:

Proposition 5.4.1.3 [BL16, LM17b] *Let* $T \in A \otimes B \otimes C$ *be A-concise. Fix* $\mathbf{a}' < \mathbf{a}$. *Then*

$$\underline{\mathbf{R}}(T) \geq \min_{A' \in G(\mathbf{a}', A^*)} \underline{\mathbf{R}}(T|_{A' \otimes B^* \otimes C^*}) + (\mathbf{a} - \mathbf{a}').$$

Proof. Say $\underline{\mathbf{R}}(T) = r$, so $T = \lim_{t \to 0} T_t$, for some tensors $T_t = \sum_{j=1}^{r} a_j(t) \otimes b_j(t) \otimes c_j(t)$. Without loss of generality, we may assume $a_1(t), \ldots, a_{\mathbf{a}}(t)$ form a basis of A. Let $A'_t = \langle a_{\mathbf{a}'+1}, \ldots, a_{\mathbf{a}} \rangle^{\perp} \subset A^*$. Then $\mathbf{R}(T_t \mid_{A'_t \otimes B^* \otimes C^*}) \leq r - (\mathbf{a} - \mathbf{a}')$ by Proposition 5.4.1.1. Let $A' = \lim_{t \to 0} A'_t \in G(\mathbf{a}', A^*)$. Then $T \mid_{A' \otimes B^* \otimes C^*} = \lim_{t \to 0} T_t \mid_{A'_t \otimes B^* \otimes C^*}$ so $\underline{\mathbf{R}}(T \mid_{A' \otimes B^* \otimes C^*}) \leq r - (\mathbf{a} - \mathbf{a}')$, i.e., $r \geq \underline{\mathbf{R}}(T \mid_{A' \otimes B^* \otimes C^*}) + (\mathbf{a} - \mathbf{a}')$. $\square$

Corollary 5.4.1.4 [BL16] *Let $T \in A \otimes B \otimes C$ be A-concise. Then $\underline{\mathbf{R}}(T) \geq \mathbf{a} - 1 + \min_{\alpha \in A^* \setminus \{0\}} \text{rank}(T(\alpha))$.*

The corollary follows because for matrices, rank equals border rank and $\mathbb{C}^1 \otimes B \otimes C = B \otimes C$.

Although our freedom in the substitution method was minor (a restriction to a Zariski open subset of the Grassmannian determined by $\tilde{A}^{\perp}$), it is still useful for tensors with simple combinatorial structure. With the border substitution method we have no freedom at all, but nevertheless it will be useful for tensors with symmetry, as the symmetry group will enable us to restrict to special A'.

As was the case for the substitution method, this procedure can be iterated: write $T_1 = T \mid_{A' \otimes B^* \otimes C^*}$. If T_1 is B-concise, apply the proposition again with B; if not, let $B_1 \subset B$ be maximal such that T_1 is B_1-concise and then apply the proposition. By successive iterations, one finds the following:

Corollary 5.4.1.5 [LM17a] *If, for all $A' \subset A^*, B' \subset B^*, C' \subset C^*$, respectively of dimensions $\mathbf{a}', \mathbf{b}', \mathbf{c}'$, one has $T \mid_{A' \otimes B' \otimes C'} \neq 0$, then $\underline{\mathbf{R}}(T) > \mathbf{a} + \mathbf{b} + \mathbf{c} - (\mathbf{a}' + \mathbf{b}' + \mathbf{c}')$.*

It is obvious this method cannot prove border rank bounds better than $\mathbf{a} + \mathbf{b} + \mathbf{c} - 3$. The actual limit of the method is even less, as I now explain.

5.4.2 Limits of the Border Substitution Method

Definition 5.4.2.1 A tensor $T \in A \otimes B \otimes C$ is $(\mathbf{a}', \mathbf{b}', \mathbf{c}')$-*compressible* if there exist subspaces $A' \subset A^*, B' \subset B^*, C' \subset C^*$ of respective dimensions $\mathbf{a}', \mathbf{b}', \mathbf{c}'$ such that $T \mid_{A' \otimes B' \otimes C'} = 0$, i.e., there exists $(A', B', C') \in G(\mathbf{a}', A^*) \times G(\mathbf{b}', B^*) \times G(\mathbf{c}', C^*)$, such that $A' \otimes B' \otimes C' \subset T^{\perp}$, where $T^{\perp} \subset (A \otimes B \otimes C)^*$ is the hyperplane annihilating T. Otherwise, one says T is $(\mathbf{a}', \mathbf{b}', \mathbf{c}')$-*compression generic*.

Let $X(\mathbf{a}', \mathbf{b}', \mathbf{c}')$ be the set of all tensors that are $(\mathbf{a}', \mathbf{b}', \mathbf{c}')$-compressible.

Corollary 5.4.1.5 may be rephrased as

$$\sigma_{\mathbf{a}+\mathbf{b}+\mathbf{c}-(\mathbf{a}'+\mathbf{b}'+\mathbf{c}')} Seg(\mathbb{P}A \times \mathbb{P}B \times \mathbb{P}C) \subset X(\mathbf{a}', \mathbf{b}', \mathbf{c}').$$

Proposition 5.4.2.2 [LM17a] *The set* $X(\mathbf{a}', \mathbf{b}', \mathbf{c}') \subseteq \mathbb{P}(A \otimes B \otimes C)$ *is Zariski closed of dimension at most*

$$\min\{\mathbf{abc} - 1, (\mathbf{abc} - \mathbf{a}'\mathbf{b}'\mathbf{c}' - 1) + (\mathbf{a} - \mathbf{a}')\mathbf{a}' + (\mathbf{b} - \mathbf{b}')\mathbf{b}' + (\mathbf{c} - \mathbf{c}')\mathbf{c}'\}.$$

In particular, if

$$\mathbf{aa}' + \mathbf{bb}' + \mathbf{cc}' < (\mathbf{a}')^2 + (\mathbf{b}')^2 + (\mathbf{c}')^2 + \mathbf{a}'\mathbf{b}'\mathbf{c}'', \qquad (5.4.1)$$

then $X(\mathbf{a}', \mathbf{b}', \mathbf{c}') \subsetneq \mathbb{P}(A \otimes B \otimes C)$, *so in this range the border substitution method may be used to prove nontrivial lower bounds for border rank.*

Proof. The following is a standard construction in algebraic geometry called an *incidence correspondence* (see, e.g., [Har95, §6.12] for a discussion): let

$$\mathcal{I} := \{((A', B', C'), [T]) \in [G(\mathbf{a}', A^*) \times G(\mathbf{b}', B^*) \times G(\mathbf{c}', C^*)]$$
$$\times \mathbb{P}(A \otimes B \otimes C) \mid A' \otimes B' \otimes C' \subset T^{\perp}\},$$

and note that the projection of $\mathcal{I}$ to $\mathbb{P}(A \otimes B \otimes C)$ has image $X(\mathbf{a}', \mathbf{b}', \mathbf{c}')$. A fiber of the other projection $\mathcal{I} \to G(\mathbf{a}', A^*) \times G(\mathbf{b}', B^*) \times G(\mathbf{c}', C^*)$ is $\mathbb{P}((A' \otimes B' \otimes C')^{\perp})$, a projective space of dimension $\mathbf{abc} - \mathbf{a}'\mathbf{b}'\mathbf{c}' - 1$. Hence

$$\dim \mathcal{I} := (\mathbf{abc} - \mathbf{a}'\mathbf{b}'\mathbf{c}' - 1) + (\mathbf{a} - \mathbf{a}')\mathbf{a}' + (\mathbf{b} - \mathbf{b}')\mathbf{b}' + (\mathbf{c} - \mathbf{c}')\mathbf{c}'.$$

Since the map $\mathcal{I} \to X$ is surjective, this proves the dimension assertion. Since the projection to $\mathbb{P}(A \otimes B \otimes C)$ is a regular map, the Zariski closed assertion also follows.   □

The proof and examples show that beyond this bound, one expects $X(\mathbf{a}', \mathbf{b}', \mathbf{c}') = \mathbb{P}(A \otimes B \otimes C)$, so that the method cannot be used. Also note that tensors could be quite compressible and still have near-maximal border rank, a weakness we already saw with the tensor of (5.1.3) (which also satisfies Strassen's equations).

The inequality in Proposition 5.4.2.2 may be sharp or nearly so. For tensors in $\mathbb{C}^{\mathbf{m}} \otimes \mathbb{C}^{\mathbf{m}} \otimes \mathbb{C}^{\mathbf{m}}$ the limit of this method alone would be a border rank lower bound of $3(\mathbf{m} - \sqrt{3\mathbf{m} + \frac{9}{4}} + \frac{3}{2})$.

5.4.3 How to Exploit Symmetry

As mentioned above, the border substitution method is particularly useful for tensors T with a large symmetry group G_T, as one can replace the unknown A' by representatives of the closed G_T-orbits in the Grassmannian. For matrix multiplication, one obtains the following:

Theorem 5.4.3.1 [LM17b]

$$M_{\langle \mathbf{n} \rangle} \in \sigma_r(Seg(\mathbb{P}^{\mathbf{n}^2-1} \times \mathbb{P}^{\mathbf{n}^2-1} \times \mathbb{P}^{\mathbf{n}^2-1}))$$

if and only if there exist curves $p_j(t) \subset Seg(\mathbb{P}^{\mathbf{n}^2-1} \times \mathbb{P}^{\mathbf{n}^2-1} \times \mathbb{P}^{\mathbf{n}^2-1})$ *such that for* $2 \leq j \leq r$, $\lim_{t\to 0} p_j(t) = x_2^1 \otimes y_2^1 \otimes z_2^1$ *and* $M_{\langle \mathbf{n} \rangle} \in \lim_{t\to 0} \langle x_2^1 \otimes y_2^1 \otimes z_2^1$, $p_2(t), \ldots, p_r(t)\rangle$.

In §5.4.5, Theorem 5.4.3.1 is used to improve the lower bounds for border rank.

In this section and the next, I explain the theory. One can also use these methods when attempting to search for new decompositions to limit one's searches for decompositions with certain normal forms. To discuss these methods, I first develop language to discuss the G_T orbit closures in the Grassmannian.

To simplify notation, for a tensor $T \in A_1 \otimes \ldots \otimes A_k$, and $\tilde{A} \subset A_1$, write

$$T/\tilde{A} := T \mid_{\tilde{A}^\perp \otimes A_2^* \otimes \cdots \otimes A_k^*} \in (A_1/\tilde{A}) \otimes A_2 \otimes \ldots \otimes A_k.$$

Define

$$B_{\rho, \mathbf{a}'}(T) := \{\tilde{A} \in G(\mathbf{a}', A_1) \mid \underline{\mathbf{R}}(T/\tilde{A}) \leq \rho\}.$$

Proposition 5.4.3.2 [LM17a] *The set* $B_{\rho, \mathbf{a}'}(T)$ *is Zariski closed.*

The proof requires some standard notions from geometry and can be skipped on a first reading.

A *vector bundle* $\mathcal{V}$ on a variety X is a variety $\mathcal{V}$ equipped with a surjective regular map $\pi : \mathcal{V} \to X$ such that for all $x \in X$, $\pi^{-1}(x)$ is a vector space of dimension $\mathbf{v}$, satisfying certain compatibility conditions (in particular, local triviality: for all $x \in X$, there exists an open subset U containing x such that $\mathcal{V}|_U \simeq \mathbb{C}^{\mathbf{v}} \times U$). See [Sha13, §6.1.2] for an algebraic definition or [Spi79, Chapter 3, p. 71] for a differential-geometric definition. A *section* of $\mathcal{V}$ is a regular map $s : X \to \mathcal{V}$ such that $\pi \circ s = \mathrm{Id}_X$.

Two vector bundles over the Grassmannian $G(k, V)$ are ubiquitous: first the *tautological subspace bundle* $\pi_{\mathcal{S}} : \mathcal{S} \to G(k, V)$ where $\pi_{\mathcal{S}}^{-1}(E) = E$. This is a vector subbundle of the trivial bundle with fiber V, which I denote $\underline{V}$. The *tautological quotient bundle* $\pi_{\mathcal{Q}} : \mathcal{Q} \to G(k, V)$ has fiber $\pi_{\mathcal{Q}}^{-1}(E) = V/E$, so we have an exact sequence of vector bundles

$$0 \to \mathcal{S} \to \underline{V} \to \mathcal{Q} \to 0.$$

All three bundles are $GL(V)$-homogeneous. See, e.g., [Wey03, §3.3] for more details.

For any vector bundle over a projective variety, the corresponding bundle of projective spaces is a projective variety, and a subfiber bundle defined by homogeneous equations is also projective.

Proof. Consider the bundle $\pi : \mathcal{Q} \otimes A_1 \otimes \cdots \otimes A_k \to G(\mathbf{a}', A_1)$, where $\pi^{-1}(\tilde{A}) = (A_1/\tilde{A}) \otimes A_2 \otimes \cdots \otimes A_k$. Given T, define a natural section $s_T : G(\mathbf{a}', A_1) \to \mathcal{Q} \otimes A_1 \otimes \cdots \otimes A_k$ by $s_T(\tilde{A}) := T/\tilde{A}$. Let $X \subset \mathbb{P}(\mathcal{Q} \otimes A_2 \otimes \cdots \otimes A_k)$ denote the subvariety (that is also a subfiber bundle) defined by $X \cap \mathbb{P}((A_1/\tilde{A}) \otimes A_2 \otimes \cdots \otimes A_k) = \sigma_\rho(Seg(\mathbb{P}((A_1/\tilde{A}) \times \mathbb{P}A_2 \times \cdots \times \mathbb{P}A_k))$. By the discussion above, X is realizable as a projective variety. Let $\tilde{\pi} : X \to G(\mathbf{a}', A_1)$ denote the projectivization of π restricted to X. Then $B_{\rho,\mathbf{a}'}(T) = \tilde{\pi}(X \cap \mathbb{P}s_T(G(\mathbf{a}', A_1)))$. Since the intersection of two projective varieties is a projective variety, as is the image of a projective variety under a regular map (see Theorem 3.1.4.7), we conclude. $\square$

Lemma 5.4.3.3 [LM17a] *Let $T \in A_1 \otimes \ldots \otimes A_k$ be a tensor, let $G_T \subset GL(A_1) \times \cdots \times GL(A_k)$ denote its stabilizer and let $G_1 \subset GL(A_1)$ denote its projection to $GL(A_1)$. Then $B_{\rho,\mathbf{a}'}(T)$ is a G_1-variety.*

Proof. Let $g = (g_1, \ldots, g_k) \in G_T$. Then $\underline{\mathbf{R}}(T/\tilde{A}) = \underline{\mathbf{R}}(g \cdot T/g \cdot \tilde{A}) = \underline{\mathbf{R}}(T/g_1\tilde{A})$. $\square$

Recall the definition of a homogeneous variety $X = G/P \subset \mathbb{P}V$ from Definition 4.7.2.1.

Lemma 5.4.3.4 [BL14] *Let $X = G/P \subset \mathbb{P}V$ be a homogeneous variety and let $p \in \sigma_r(X)$. Then there exist a point $x_0 \in \hat{X}$ and $r - 1$ curves $z_j(t) \in \hat{X}$ such that $p \in \lim_{t \to 0} \langle x_0, z_1(t), \ldots, z_{r-1}(t) \rangle$.*

Proof. Since $p \in \sigma_r(X)$, there exist r curves $x(t), y_1(t), \ldots, y_{r-1}(t) \in \hat{X}$ such that

$$p \in \lim_{t \to 0} \mathbb{P}\langle x(t), y_1(t), \ldots, y_{r-1}(t) \rangle.$$

Choose a curve $g_t \in G$, such that $g_t(x(t)) = x_0 = x(0)$ for all t and $g_0 = \mathrm{Id}$. We have

$$\langle x(t), y_1(t), \ldots, y_{r-1}(t) \rangle = g_t^{-1} \cdot \langle x_0, g_t \cdot y_1(t), \ldots, g_t \cdot y_{r-1}(t) \rangle \text{ and}$$

$$\lim_{t \to 0} \langle x(t), y_1(t), \ldots, y_{r-1}(t) \rangle = \lim_{t \to 0} \left(g_t^{-1} \cdot \langle x_0, g_t \cdot y_1(t), \ldots, g_t \cdot y_{r-1}(t) \rangle \right)$$

$$= \lim_{t \to 0} \langle x_0, g_t \cdot y_1(t), \ldots, g_t \cdot y_{r-1}(t) \rangle.$$

Set $z_j(t) = g_t \cdot y_j(t)$ to complete the proof. $\square$

Exercise 5.4.3.5 (1) Show that if X is a G-variety, then any orbit $G \cdot x$ for $x \in X$ of minimal dimension must be Zariski closed. ⊙

The following lemma applies both to $M_{\langle \mathbf{n} \rangle}$ and to the determinant polynomial:

Lemma 5.4.3.6 (Normal form lemma) [LM17b] *Let $X = G/P \subset \mathbb{P}V$ be a homogeneous variety and let $v \in V$ be such that $G_v := \{g \in G \mid g[v] = [v]\}$ has a single closed orbit $\mathcal{O}_{min}$ in X. Then any border rank r decomposition of v may be modified using G_v to a border rank r decomposition with limit plane $\lim_{t \to 0} \langle x_1(t), \dots, x_r(t) \rangle$ such that there is a stationary point $x_1(t) \equiv x_1$ lying in $\mathcal{O}_{min}$.*

If, moreover, every orbit of $G_v \cap G_{x_1}$ contains x_1 in its closure, we may further assume that all other $x_j(t)$ limit to x_1.

Proof. I prove the second statement. By Lemma 5.4.3.4, it is sufficient to show that we can have all points limiting to the same point $x_1(0)$.

Work by induction. Say we have shown that $x_1(t), \dots, x_q(t)$ all limit to the same point $x_1 \in \mathcal{O}_{min}$. It remains to show that our curves can be modified so that the same holds for $x_1(t), \dots, x_{q+1}(t)$. Take a curve $g_\epsilon \in G_v \cap G_{x_1}$ such that $\lim_{\epsilon \to 0} g_\epsilon x_{q+1}(0) = x_1$. For each fixed ϵ, acting on the $x_j(t)$ by g_ϵ, we obtain a border rank decomposition for which $g_\epsilon x_i(t) \to g_\epsilon x_1(0) = x_1(0)$ for $i \leq q$ and $g_\epsilon x_{q+1}(t) \to g_\epsilon x_{q+1}(0)$. Fix a sequence $\epsilon_n \to 0$. Claim: we may choose a sequence $t_n \to 0$ such that

- $\lim_{n \to \infty} g_{\epsilon_n} x_{q+1}(t_n) = x_1(0)$,
- $\lim_{n \to \infty} < g_{\epsilon_n} x_1(t_n), \dots, g_{\epsilon_n} x_r(t_n) >$ contains v, and
- $\lim_{n \to \infty} g_{\epsilon_n} x_j(t_n) = x_1(0)$ for $j \leq q$.

The first point holds as $\lim_{\epsilon \to 0} g_\epsilon x_{q+1}(0) = x_1$. The second follows as for each fixed ϵ_n, taking t_n sufficiently small we may assure that a ball of radius $1/n$ centered at v intersects $< g_{\epsilon_n} x_1(t_n), \dots, g_{\epsilon_n} x_r(t_n) >$. In the same way we may assure that the third point is satisfied. Considering the sequence $\tilde{x}_i(t_n) := g_{\epsilon_n} x_i(t_n)$, we obtain the desired border rank decomposition. □

Exercise 5.4.3.7 (1) Write out a proof of the first assertion in the normal form lemma.

Applying the normal form lemma to matrix multiplication, in order to prove $[M_{\langle \mathbf{n} \rangle}] \notin \sigma_r(Seg(\mathbb{P}A \times \mathbb{P}B \times \mathbb{P}C))$, it is sufficient to prove it is not contained in a smaller variety. This variety, called the *greater areole*, is discussed in the next section.

5.4.4 Larger Geometric Context

Recall that for $X \subset \mathbb{P}V$, $\sigma_r(X)$ may be written as

$$\sigma_r(X) = \bigcup_{x_j(t) \subset X, \, 1 \leq j \leq r} \{z \in \mathbb{P}V \mid z \in \lim_{t \to 0} \langle x_1(t), \ldots, x_r(t) \rangle\},$$

where the union is over all curves $x_j(t)$ in X, including stationary ones. (One can take algebraic or analytic curves.) Remarkably, for the study of certain points such as $M_{\langle \mathbf{n} \rangle}$ and $\det_n$ with large symmetry groups, it is sufficient to consider "local" versions of secant varieties.

It is better to discuss Theorem 5.4.3.1 in the larger context of secant varieties, so make the following definition:

Definition 5.4.4.1 (Greater Areole) [LM17b] Let $X \subset \mathbb{P}V$ be a projective variety and let $p \in X$. The *r*th **greater areole** at p is

$$\tilde{\mathfrak{a}}_r(X, p) := \bigcup_{\substack{x_j(t) \subset X \\ x_j(t) \to p}} \lim_{t \to 0} \langle x_1(t), \ldots, x_r(t) \rangle \subset \mathbb{P}V.$$

Then Theorem 5.4.3.1 may be restated as follows:

Theorem 5.4.4.2 [LM17b]

$$M_{\langle \mathbf{n} \rangle} \in \sigma_r(Seg(\mathbb{P}^{\mathbf{n}^2-1} \times \mathbb{P}^{\mathbf{n}^2-1} \times \mathbb{P}^{\mathbf{n}^2-1}))$$

if and only if

$$M_{\langle \mathbf{n} \rangle} \in \tilde{\mathfrak{a}}_r\big(Seg(\mathbb{P}^{\mathbf{n}^2-1} \times \mathbb{P}^{\mathbf{n}^2-1} \times \mathbb{P}^{\mathbf{n}^2-1}), [x_2^1 \otimes y_2^1 \otimes z_2^1]\big).$$

Exercise 5.4.4.3 (2) Show that when $G/P = v_n(\mathbb{P}^{n^2-1})$ is the Veronese variety and $v = \det_n$, $\mathcal{O}_{min} = v_n(Seg(\mathbb{P}E \times \mathbb{P}F))$ is the unique closed $G_{\det_n}$-orbit, and every orbit of $G_{\det_n,(x_1^1)^n}$ contains $(x_1^1)^n$ in its closure, so the normal form lemma applies. ⊚

Exercise 5.4.4.4 (2) When $G/P = Seg(\mathbb{P}(U^* \otimes V) \times \mathbb{P}(V^* \otimes W) \times \mathbb{P}(W^* \otimes U))$ $\subset \mathbb{P}(\mathbb{C}^{n^2} \otimes \mathbb{C}^{n^2} \otimes \mathbb{C}^{n^2})$ and $v = M_{\langle \mathbf{n} \rangle}$, let

$$\mathcal{K} := \{[\mu \otimes v \otimes v \otimes w \otimes \omega \otimes u] \in Seg(\mathbb{P}U^* \times \mathbb{P}V \times \mathbb{P}V^* \times \mathbb{P}W \times \mathbb{P}W^* \times \mathbb{P}U) \mid \mu(u)$$
$$= \omega(w) = v(v) = 0\}.$$

Show that $\mathcal{K}$ is the unique closed $G_{M_{\langle U,V,W \rangle}}$-orbit in $Seg(\mathbb{P}A \times \mathbb{P}B \times \mathbb{P}C)$, and every orbit of $G_{M_{\langle U,V,W \rangle}, x_2^1 \otimes y_2^1 \otimes z_2^1}$ contains $x_2^1 \otimes y_2^1 \otimes z_2^1$ in its closure. (Of course, the same is true for any $k \in \mathcal{K}$.) ⊚

5.4.5 The Border Rank Bound $\underline{R}(M_{\langle n \rangle}) \geq 2n^2 - \lceil \log_2(n) \rceil - 1$

Theorem 5.4.5.1 [LM17a] *Let* $0 < m < n$. *Then*

$$\underline{R}(M_{\langle n,n,w \rangle}) \geq 2nw - w + m - \left\lfloor \frac{w\binom{n-1+m}{m-1}}{\binom{2n-2}{n-1}} \right\rfloor.$$

In particular, taking $w = n$ *and* $m = n - \lceil \log_2(n) \rceil - 1$,

$$\underline{R}(M_{\langle n \rangle}) \geq 2n^2 - \lceil \log_2(n) \rceil - 1.$$

Proof. First observe that the "in particular" assertion follows from the main assertion because, taking $m = n - c$, we want c such that

$$\frac{n\binom{2n-1-c}{n}}{\binom{2n-2}{n-1}} < 1.$$

This ratio is

$$\frac{(n-1)\cdots(n-c)}{(2n-2)(2n-3)\cdots(2n-c)} = \frac{n-c}{2^{c-1}} \frac{n-1}{n-\frac{2}{2}} \frac{n-2}{n-\frac{3}{2}} \frac{n-3}{n-\frac{4}{2}} \cdots \frac{n-c+1}{n-\frac{c}{2}},$$

so if $c - 1 \geq \log_2(n)$, it is less than one.

For the rest of the proof, introduce the following notation: a *Young diagram* associated to a partition $\lambda = (\lambda_1, \ldots, \lambda_\ell)$ is a collection of left aligned boxes, with λ_j boxes in the jth row. Label it with the upside-down convention as representing entries in the southwest corner of an $n \times n$ matrix. More precisely, for $(i, j) \in \lambda$, number the boxes of λ by pairs (row,column), however, number the rows starting from n, i.e., $i = n$ is the first row. For example,

$$\begin{array}{|c|c|} \hline x & y \\ \hline z & \\ \cline{1-1} w & \\ \cline{1-1} \end{array}$$

(5.4.2)

is labeled $x = (n, 1), y = (n, 2), z = (n - 1, 1), w = (n - 2, 1)$. Let $\tilde{A}_\lambda := \operatorname{span}\{u^i \otimes v_j \mid (i, j) \in \lambda\}$ and write $M_{\langle n,n,w \rangle}^\lambda := M_{\langle n,n,w \rangle}/\tilde{A}_\lambda$.

The proof consists of two parts. The first is to show that for any $k < n$, there exists a Young diagram λ with k boxes such that $\underline{R}(M_{\langle n,n,w \rangle}^\lambda) \leq \underline{R}(M_{\langle n,n,w \rangle}) - k$, and this is done by induction on k. The second is to use Koszul flattenings to obtain a lower bound on $\underline{R}(M_{\langle n,n,w \rangle}^\lambda)$ for any λ.

As usual, write $M_{\langle n,n,w \rangle} \in A \otimes B \otimes C = (U^* \otimes V) \otimes (V^* \otimes W) \otimes (W^* \otimes U)$ where $u = v = n$.

Part 1. First consider the case $k = 1$. By Proposition 5.4.1.3, there exists $[a] \in B_{\underline{R}(M_{\langle n,n,w \rangle})-1, n^2-1}(M_{\langle n,n,w \rangle})$ such that the reduced tensor drops border rank. The group $GL(U) \times GL(V) \times GL(W)$ stabilizes $M_{\langle n,n,w \rangle}$. Lemma 5.4.3.3

applies with $G_1 = GL(U) \times GL(V) \subset GL(A)$. Since the $GL(U) \times GL(V)$-orbit closure of any $[a] \in \mathbb{P}A$ contains $[u^n \otimes v_1]$, we may replace $[a]$ by $[u^n \otimes v_1]$.

Now assume that $\underline{\mathbf{R}}(M^{\lambda'}_{\langle \mathbf{n,n,w} \rangle}) \leq \underline{\mathbf{R}}(M_{\langle \mathbf{n,n,w} \rangle}) - k + 1$, where λ' has $k-1$ boxes. Again by Proposition 5.4.1.3, there exists $[a'] \in B_{\underline{\mathbf{R}}(M_{\langle \mathbf{n,n,w} \rangle})-k,}$ $\mathbf{n}^2 - k(M^{\lambda'}_{\langle \mathbf{n,n,w} \rangle})$ such that when we reduce by $[a']$, the border rank of the reduced tensor drops. We no longer have the full action of $GL(U) \times GL(V)$. However, the product of *parabolic subgroups* of $GL(U) \times GL(V)$, which by definition are the subgroups that stabilize the flags in U^* and V induced by λ', stabilizes $M^{\lambda'}_{\langle \mathbf{n,n,w} \rangle}$. In particular, all parabolic groups are contained in the *Borel* subgroup of upper-triangular matrices. By the diagonal (torus) action and Lemma 5.4.3.3, we may assume that a has just one nonzero entry outside of λ. Furthermore, using the upper-triangular (Borel) action, we can move the entry southwest to obtain the Young diagram λ.

For example, when the Young diagram is (5.4.2) with $\mathbf{n} = 4$, and we want to move x_4^1 into the diagram, we may multiply it on the left and right, respectively, by

$$\begin{pmatrix} \epsilon & & & \\ 1 & 1 & & \\ & & 1 & \\ & & & 1 \end{pmatrix} \text{ and } \begin{pmatrix} \epsilon & & & 1 \\ & \epsilon & & \\ & & 1 & \\ & & & 1 \end{pmatrix},$$

where blank entries are zero. Then $x_4^1 \mapsto \epsilon^2 x_4^1 + \epsilon(x_4^2 + x_1^4) + x_1^2$, and we let $\epsilon \to 0$.

Part 2. Recall that for the matrix multiplication operator, the Koszul flattening of §2.4 factors as $M_{\langle \mathbf{n,n,w} \rangle} = M_{\langle \mathbf{n,n,1} \rangle} \otimes \mathrm{Id}_W$, so it will suffice to apply the Koszul flattening to $M^{\lambda}_{\langle \mathbf{n,n,1} \rangle} \in [(U^* \otimes V)/A_\lambda] \otimes V^* \otimes U$. We need to show that for all λ of size m,

$$\underline{\mathbf{R}}(M^{\lambda}_{\langle \mathbf{n,n,1} \rangle}) \geq 2\mathbf{n} - 1 - \frac{\binom{\mathbf{n}-1+m}{m-1}}{\binom{2\mathbf{n}-1}{\mathbf{n}-1}}.$$

This will be accomplished by restricting to a suitable $A' \subset [(U^* \otimes V)/A_\lambda]^*$ of dimension $2\mathbf{n} - 1$, such that, setting $\hat{A} = (A')^*$,

$$\mathrm{rank}\left(M^{\lambda}_{\langle \mathbf{n,n,1} \rangle} |_{A' \otimes V \otimes U^*}\right)^{\wedge \mathbf{n}-1}_{\hat{A}} \geq \binom{2\mathbf{n}-1}{\mathbf{n}-1} \mathbf{n} - \binom{\mathbf{n}-1+m}{m-1},$$

i.e.,

$$\dim \ker \left(M^{\lambda}_{\langle \mathbf{n,n,1} \rangle} |_{A' \otimes V \otimes U^*}\right)^{\wedge \mathbf{n}-1}_{\hat{A}} \leq \binom{\mathbf{n}-1+m}{m-1},$$

and applying Proposition 2.4.2.1. Since we are working in bases, we may consider $M^\lambda_{\langle \mathbf{n},\mathbf{n},1\rangle} \in (A/A_\lambda) \otimes B \otimes C$ in $A \otimes B \otimes C$, with specific coordinates set equal to 0.

Recall the map $\phi : A \to \mathbb{C}^{2\mathbf{n}-1} = \hat{A}$ given by $u^i \otimes v_j \mapsto e_{i+j-1}$ from (2.5.2) and the other notations from the proof of Theorem 2.5.2.6. The crucial part is to determine how many zeros are added to the diagonal when the entries of λ are set to zero. The map $(M^\lambda_{\langle \mathbf{n},\mathbf{n},1\rangle}|_{A' \otimes V \otimes U^*})^{\wedge \mathbf{n}-1}_{\hat{A}}$ is

$$(S, j) := e_{s_1} \wedge \cdots \wedge e_{s_{\mathbf{n}-1}} \otimes v_j \mapsto \sum_{\{k \in [\mathbf{n}] | (i,j) \notin \lambda\}} e_{j+i-1} \wedge e_{s_1} \wedge \cdots \wedge e_{s_{\mathbf{n}-1}} \otimes u^i.$$

Recall that when working with $M_{\langle \mathbf{n},\mathbf{n},1\rangle}$, the diagonal terms in the matrix were indexed by pairs $[(S, j) = (P\backslash p_l, 1 + p_l - l), (P, l)]$, in other words that $(P\backslash p_l, 1 + p_l - l)$ mapped to (P, l) plus terms that are lower in the order. So fix $(i, j) \in \lambda$, we need to count the number of terms (P, i) that will not appear anymore as a result of (i, j) being in λ. That is, fixing (i, j), we need to count the number of $(p_1, \ldots, p_{i-1})$ with $p_1 < \cdots < p_{i-1} < i + j - 1$, of which there are $\binom{i+j-2}{i-1}$, and multiply this by the number of $(p_{i+1}, \ldots, p_{\mathbf{n}})$ with $i + j - 1 < p_{i+1} < \cdots < p_{\mathbf{n}} \leq 2\mathbf{n} - 1$, of which there are $\binom{2\mathbf{n}-1-(i+j-1)}{\mathbf{n}-i}$. In summary, each $(i, j) \in \lambda$ kills $g(i, j) := \binom{i+j-1}{i-1}\binom{2\mathbf{n}-i-j}{\mathbf{n}-i}$ terms on the diagonal. Hence, it is enough to prove that $\sum_{(i,j) \in \lambda} g(i, j) \leq \binom{\mathbf{n}-1+m}{m-1}$.

Exercise 5.4.5.2 (1) Show that $\sum_{j=1}^{m} \binom{\mathbf{n}+j-2}{j-1} = \binom{m+\mathbf{n}-2}{m-1}$. ◎

By Exercise 5.4.5.2 and a similar calculation, we see $\sum_{i=\mathbf{n}}^{\mathbf{n}-m+1} g(i, 1) = \sum_{j=1}^{m} g(\mathbf{n}, j) = \binom{\mathbf{n}-2+m}{m-1}$. So it remains to prove that the Young diagram that maximizes $f_\lambda := \sum_{(i,j) \in \lambda} g(i, j)$ has one row or column. Use induction on the size of λ, the case $|\lambda| = 1$ being trivial. Note that $g(\mathbf{n} - i, j) = g(\mathbf{n} - j, i)$. Moreover, $g(i, j + 1) \geq g(i, j)$.

Say $\lambda = \lambda' \cup \{(i, j)\}$. By induction, it is sufficient to show that

$$g(\mathbf{n}, ij) = \binom{\mathbf{n}-1+ij-1}{\mathbf{n}-1} \geq \binom{\mathbf{n}+i-j-1}{i-1}\binom{\mathbf{n}-i+j}{j-1} = g(i, j), \tag{5.4.3}$$

where $\mathbf{n} > ij$.

Exercise 5.4.5.3 (3) Prove the estimate. ◎   □

5.4.6 The Boundary Case

The proof of Corollary 5.4.6.1 below uses elementary properties of Chern classes and can be skipped by readers unfamiliar with them. Let $\pi_A :$

$G(\mathbf{a}', A^*) \times G(\mathbf{b}', B^*) \times G(\mathbf{c}', C^*) \to G(\mathbf{a}', A^*)$ denote the projection and similarly for π_B, π_C. Let $\mathcal{E} = \mathcal{E}(\mathbf{a}', \mathbf{b}', \mathbf{c}') := \pi_A^*(\mathcal{S}_A) \otimes \pi_B^*(\mathcal{S}_B) \otimes \pi_C^*(\mathcal{S}_C)$ be the vector bundle that is the tensor product of the pullbacks of tautological subspace bundles $\mathcal{S}_A, \mathcal{S}_B, \mathcal{S}_C$. In each particular case, it is possible to explicitly compute how many different $A' \otimes B' \otimes C'$ a generic hyperplane may contain, as follows:

Corollary 5.4.6.1 [LM17a]

1. *If (5.4.1) holds, then a generic tensor is* $(\mathbf{a}', \mathbf{b}', \mathbf{c}')$-*compression generic.*
2. *If (5.4.1) does not hold, then* rank $\mathcal{E}^* \le$ dim $(G(\mathbf{a}', A^*) \times G(\mathbf{b}', B^*) \times G(\mathbf{c}', C^*))$. *If the top Chern class of* $\mathcal{E}^*$ *is nonzero, then no tensor is* $(\mathbf{a}', \mathbf{b}', \mathbf{c}')$-*compression generic.*

Proof. The first assertion is a restatement of Proposition 5.4.2.2.

For the second, notice that T induces a section $\tilde{T}$ of the vector bundle $\mathcal{E}^* \to G(\mathbf{a}', A^*) \times G(\mathbf{b}', B^*) \times G(\mathbf{c}', C^*)$ defined by $\tilde{T}(A' \otimes B' \otimes C') = T|_{A' \otimes B' \otimes C'}$. The zero locus of $\tilde{T}$ is $\{(A', B', C') \in G(\mathbf{a}', A^*) \times G(\mathbf{b}', B^*) \times G(\mathbf{c}', C^*) \mid A' \otimes B' \otimes C' \subset T^{\perp}\}$. In particular, $\tilde{T}$ is nonvanishing if and only if T is $(\mathbf{a}', \mathbf{b}', \mathbf{c}')$-compression generic. If the top Chern class is nonzero, there cannot exist a nonvanishing section. $\square$

5.5 Geometry of the Coppersmith-Winograd Tensors

As we saw in Chapter 3, in practice, only tensors of minimal, or near-minimal, border rank have been used to prove upper bounds on the exponent of matrix multiplication. Call a tensor that gives a "good" upper bound for the exponent via the methods of [Str87, CW90] of *high Coppersmith-Winograd value* or *high CW-value* for short. Ambainis, Filmus, and LeGall [AFLG15] showed that taking higher powers of $T_{CW,q}$ when $q \ge 5$ cannot prove $\omega < 2.30$ by this method alone. They posed the problem of finding additional tensors of high value. The work in this section was motivated by their problem – to isolate geometric features of the Coppersmith-Winograd tensors and find other tensors with such features. However, it turned out that the features described here, with the exception of a large rank/border rank ratio, actually characterize them. The study is incomplete because the CW-value of a tensor also depends on its presentation, and in different bases a tensor can have quite different CW-values. Moreover, even determining the value in a given presentation still involves some "art" in the choice of a good decomposition, choosing the correct tensor power, estimating the value and probability of each block [Wil].

5.5.1 The Coppersmith-Winograd Tensors

Recall the Coppersmith-Winograd tensors

$$T_{q,cw} := \sum_{j=1}^{q} a_0 \otimes b_j \otimes c_j + a_j \otimes b_0 \otimes c_j + a_j \otimes b_j \otimes c_0 \in \mathbb{C}^{q+1} \otimes \mathbb{C}^{q+1} \otimes \mathbb{C}^{q+1}$$

$$(5.5.1)$$

and

$$T_{q,CW} := \sum_{j=1}^{q}(a_0 \otimes b_j \otimes c_j + a_j \otimes b_0 \otimes c_j + a_j \otimes b_j \otimes c_0) + a_0 \otimes b_0 \otimes c_{q+1}$$

$$+ a_0 \otimes b_{q+1} \otimes c_0 + a_{q+1} \otimes b_0 \otimes c_0 \in \mathbb{C}^{q+2} \otimes \mathbb{C}^{q+2} \otimes \mathbb{C}^{q+2}, \quad (5.5.2)$$

both of which have border rank $q + 2$.

Written as symmetric tensors (polynomials): $T_{q,cw} = x_0\left(\sum_{j=1}^{q} x_j^2\right)$ and $T_{q,CW} = x_0\left(\sum_{j=1}^{q} x_j^2 + x_0 x_{q+1}\right)$.

Proposition 5.5.1.1 [LM15] $\mathbf{R}(T_{q,cw}) = 2q + 1$, $\mathbf{R}(T_{q,CW}) = 2q + 3$.

Proof. I first prove the lower bound for $T_{q,cw}$. Apply Proposition 5.3.1.1 to show that the rank of the tensor is at least $2q - 2$ plus the rank of $a_0 \otimes b_1 \otimes c_1 + a_1 \otimes b_0 \otimes c_1 + a_1 \otimes b_1 \otimes c_0$, which is 3. An analogous estimate provides the lower bound for $\mathbf{R}(T_{q,CW})$. To show that $\mathbf{R}(T_{q,cw}) \leq 2q + 1$, consider the following rank 1 matrices, whose span contains $T(A^*)$:

1. $q + 1$ matrices with all entries equal to 0 apart from one entry on the diagonal equal to 1 and,
2. q matrices indexed by $1 \leq j \leq q$, with all entries equal to zero apart from the four entries $(0, 0)$, $(0, j)$, $(j, 0)$, (j, j) equal to 1. $\qquad\square$

~~Exercise 5.5.1.2~~ (2) Using the lower bound for $T_{q,cw}$, prove the lower bound for $T_{q,CW}$.

In §5.6, we saw that $\underline{\mathbf{R}}(T_{STR,q}) = q + 1$, and by Exercise 5.3.1.7, $\mathbf{R}(T_{STR,q}) = 2q$. Strassen's tensor has rank nearly twice the border rank, like the Coppersmith-Winograd tensors. So one potential source of high CW-value tensors are tensors with a large gap between rank and border rank.

5.5.2 Extremal Tensors

Let $A, B, C = \mathbb{C}^{\mathbf{a}}$. There are normal forms for curves in $Seg(\mathbb{P}A \times \mathbb{P}B \times \mathbb{P}C)$ up to order $\mathbf{a} - 1$, namely,

$$T_t = (a_1 + ta_2 + \cdots + t^{\mathbf{a}-1}a_{\mathbf{a}} + O(t^{\mathbf{a}})) \otimes (b_1 + tb_2 + \cdots + t^{\mathbf{a}-1}b_{\mathbf{a}}$$

$$+ O(t^{\mathbf{a}})) \otimes (c_1 + tc_2 + \cdots + t^{\mathbf{a}-1}c_{\mathbf{a}} + O(t^{\mathbf{a}})),$$

and if the a_j, b_j, c_j are each linearly independent sets of vectors, call the curve *general to order* $\mathbf{a} - 1$.

Proposition 5.5.2.1 [LM15] *Let* $T \in A \otimes B \otimes C = \mathbb{C}^{\mathbf{a}} \otimes \mathbb{C}^{\mathbf{a}} \otimes \mathbb{C}^{\mathbf{a}}$. *If there exists a curve* T_t *that is general to order* $\mathbf{a}$ *such that*

$$T(A^*) = \frac{d^{\mathbf{a}-1} T_t(A^*)}{(dt)^{\mathbf{a}-1}}\Big|_{t=0},$$

then, for suitably chosen $\alpha \in A^*$ *and bases,* $T(A^*)T(\alpha)^{-1}$ *is the centralizer of a regular nilpotent element.*

Proof. Note that $\frac{d^q T_t}{(dt)^q}\big|_{t=0} = q! \sum_{i+j+k=q+3} a_i \otimes b_j \otimes c_k$, i.e.,

$$\frac{d^q T_t(A^*)}{(dt)^q}\Big|_{t=0} = \begin{pmatrix} x_{q-2} & x_{q-3} & \cdots & \cdots & x_1 & 0 & \cdots \\ x_{q-3} & x_{q-4} & \cdots & x_1 & 0 & \cdots & \cdots \\ \vdots & & & & & & \\ \vdots & & \ddots & & & & \\ x_1 & 0 & \cdots & & & & \\ 0 & 0 & \cdots & & & & \\ \vdots & \vdots & & & & & \\ 0 & 0 & \cdots & & & & \end{pmatrix}.$$

In particular, each space contains the previous, and the last equals

$$\begin{pmatrix} x_{\mathbf{a}} & x_{\mathbf{a}-1} & \cdots & & x_1 \\ x_{\mathbf{a}-1} & x_{\mathbf{a}-2} & \cdots & x_1 & 0 \\ \vdots & \vdots & \ddots & & \\ \vdots & & x_1 & & \\ x_1 & 0 & & & \end{pmatrix},$$

which is isomorphic to the centralizer of a regular nilpotent element. □

This provides another, explicit proof that the centralizer of a regular nilpotent element belongs to the closure of diagonalizable algebras.

Note that the Coppersmith-Winograd tensor $T_{\mathbf{a}-2,CW}$ satisfies $\mathbb{P}T(A^*) \cap Seg(\mathbb{P}B \times \mathbb{P}C) = [X]$ is a single point, and $\mathbb{P}\hat{T}_{[X]}Seg(\mathbb{P}B \times \mathbb{P}C) \cap \mathbb{P}T(A^*)$ is a $\mathbb{P}^{\mathbf{a}-2}$. It turns out these properties characterize it among 1_A-generic tensors:

Theorem 5.5.2.2 [LM15] *Let* $T \in A \otimes B \otimes C = \mathbb{C}^{\mathbf{a}} \otimes \mathbb{C}^{\mathbf{a}} \otimes \mathbb{C}^{\mathbf{a}}$ *be of border rank* $\mathbf{a} > 2$. *Assume* $\mathbb{P}T(A^*) \cap Seg(\mathbb{P}B \times \mathbb{P}C) = [X]$ *is a single point, and* $\mathbb{P}\hat{T}_{[X]}Seg(\mathbb{P}B \times \mathbb{P}C) \supset \mathbb{P}T(A^*)$. *Then* T *is not* 1_A-generic.

If

    i $\mathbb{P}T(A^*) \cap Seg(\mathbb{P}B \times \mathbb{P}C) = [X]$ *is a single point,*
   ii $\mathbb{P}\hat{T}_{[X]}Seg(\mathbb{P}B \times \mathbb{P}C) \cap \mathbb{P}T(A^*)$ *is a* $\mathbb{P}^{a-2}$, *and*
  iii T *is* 1_A-*generic,*

then T *is isomorphic to the Coppersmith-Winograd tensor* $T_{a-2,CW}$.

Proof. For the first assertion, no element of $\mathbb{P}\hat{T}_{[X]}Seg(\mathbb{P}B \times \mathbb{P}C)$ has rank greater than two.

For the second, I first show that T is 1-generic. Choose bases such that $X = b_1 \otimes c_1$, then, after modifying the bases, the $\mathbb{P}^{a-2}$ must be the projectivization of

$$
E := \begin{pmatrix} x_1 & x_2 & \cdots & x_{a-1} & 0 \\ x_2 & & & & \\ \vdots & & & & \\ x_{a-1} & & & & \\ 0 & & & & \end{pmatrix}. \tag{5.5.3}
$$

(Rank one tangent vectors cannot appear by property (i).)

Write $T(A^*) = \mathrm{span}\{E, M\}$ for some matrix M. As T is 1_A-generic, we can assume that M is invertible. In particular, the last row of M must contain a nonzero entry. In the basis order where M corresponds to $T(\alpha^a)$, the space of matrices $T(B^*)$ has triangular form and contains matrices with nonzero diagonal entries. The proof for $T(C^*)$ is analogous, hence T is 1-generic.

By Proposition 5.1.5.1, we may assume that $T(A^*)$ is contained in the space of symmetric matrices. Hence, we may assume that E is as above and M is a symmetric matrix. By further changing the bases, we may assume that M has

   1   the first row and column equal to zero, apart from their last entries that are nonzero (we may assume they are equal to 1) and
   2   the last row and column equal to zero apart from their first entries.

Hence the matrix M is determined by a submatrix M' of rows and columns 2 to $a - 1$. As $T(A^*)$ contains a matrix of maximal rank, the matrix M' must have rank $a - 2$. We can change the basis $\alpha^2, \dots, \alpha^{a-1}$ in such a way that the quadric corresponding to M' equals $x_2^2 + \cdots + x_{a-1}^2$. This will also change the other matrices, which correspond to quadrics $x_1 x_i$ for $1 \le i \le a - 1$, but will not change the space that they span. We obtain the tensor $T_{a-2,CW}$.   □

5.5.3 Compression Extremality

In this subsection I discuss tensors for which the border substitution method fails miserably. In particular, although the usual substitution method correctly determines the rank of the Coppersmith-Winograd tensors, the tensors are special in that they are nearly characterized by the failure of the border substitution method to give lower border rank bounds.

Definition 5.5.3.1 A 1-generic, tensor $T \in A \otimes B \otimes C$ is said to be *maximally compressible* if there exists hyperplanes $H_A \subset A^*, H_B \subset B^*, H_C \subset C^*$ such that $T |_{H_A \times H_B \times H_C} = 0$.

If $T \in S^3 A \subset A \otimes A \otimes A$, T is *maximally symmetric compressible* if there exists a hyperplane $H_A \subset A^*$ such that $T |_{H_A \times H_A \times H_A} = 0$.

Recall from Proposition 5.1.5.1 that a tensor $T \in \mathbb{C}^{\mathbf{a}} \otimes \mathbb{C}^{\mathbf{a}} \otimes \mathbb{C}^{\mathbf{a}}$ that is 1-generic and satisfies Strassen's equations with suitable choices of bases becomes a tensor in $S^3 \mathbb{C}^{\mathbf{a}}$.

Theorem 5.5.3.2 [LM15] *Let $T \in S^3 \mathbb{C}^{\mathbf{a}}$ be 1-generic and maximally symmetric compressible. Then T is one of*

1 $T_{\mathbf{a}-1,cw}$,
2 $T_{\mathbf{a}-2,CW}$,
3 $T = a_1 (a_1^2 + \cdots a_{\mathbf{a}}^2)$.

In particular, the only 1-generic, maximally symmetric compressible, minimal border rank tensor in $\mathbb{C}^{\mathbf{a}} \otimes \mathbb{C}^{\mathbf{a}} \otimes \mathbb{C}^{\mathbf{a}}$ is isomorphic to $T_{\mathbf{a}-2,CW}$.

Proof. Let a_1 be a basis of the line $H_A^{\perp} \subset \mathbb{C}^{\mathbf{a}}$. Then $T = a_1 Q$ for some $Q \in S^2 \mathbb{C}^{\mathbf{a}}$. By 1-genericity, the rank of Q is either $\mathbf{a}$ or $\mathbf{a} - 1$. If the rank is $\mathbf{a}$, there are two cases, either the hyperplane H_A is tangent to Q, or it intersects it transversely. The second is case 3. The first has a normal form $a_1 (a_1 a_{\mathbf{a}} + a_2^2 + \cdots + a_{\mathbf{a}-1}^2)$, which, when written as a tensor, is $T_{\mathbf{a}-2,CW}$. If Q has rank $\mathbf{a} - 1$, by 1-genericity, $\ker(Q_{1,1})$ must be in H_A, and thus we may choose coordinates such that $Q = (a_2^2 + \cdots + a_{\mathbf{a}}^2)$, but then T, written as a tensor, is $T_{\mathbf{a}-1,cw}$. $\square$

Proposition 5.5.3.3 [LM15] *The Coppersmith-Winograd tensor $T_{\mathbf{a}-2,CW}$ is the unique up to isomorphism 1-generic tensor in $\mathbb{C}^{\mathbf{a}} \otimes \mathbb{C}^{\mathbf{a}} \otimes \mathbb{C}^{\mathbf{a}}$ that is maximally compressible and satisfies any of the following:*

1 *Strassen's equations,*
2 *cyclic $\mathbb{Z}_3$-invariance,*
3 *has border rank $\mathbf{a}$.*

Proof. Let $a_1, \ldots, a_{\mathbf{a}}$ be a basis of A with $H_A = a_1^{\perp}$ and similarly for $H_B = b_1^{\perp}$ and $H_C = c_1^{\perp}$. Thus (allowing reordering of the factors A, B, C) $T = a_1 \otimes X + b_1 \otimes Y + c_1 \otimes Z$, where $X \in B \otimes C, Y \in A \otimes C, Z \in A \otimes B$. Now no $\alpha \in H_A$ can be such that $T(\alpha)$ is of maximal rank, as for any $\beta_1, \beta_2 \in H_B$, $T(\alpha, \beta_j) \subset \mathbb{C}\{c_1\}$. So $T(a^1)$, $T(b^1)$, $T(c^1)$ are all of rank **a**, where a^1 is the dual basis vector to a_1, etc. After a modification, we may assume X has rank **a**.

Let $(g, h, k) \in GL(A) \times GL(B) \times GL(C)$. We may normalize $X = \mathrm{Id}$, which forces $g = h$. We may then rewrite X, Y, Z such that Y is full rank and renormalize

$$X = Y = \begin{pmatrix} \frac{1}{3} & \\ & \mathrm{Id}_{\mathbf{a}-1} \end{pmatrix},$$

which forces $h = k$ and uses up our normalizations.

Now we use any of the above three properties. The weakest is the second, but by $\mathbb{Z}_3$-invariance, if $X = Y$, we must have $Z = X = Y$ as well, and T is the Coppersmith-Winograd tensor. The other two imply the second by Proposition 5.1.5.1. $\qquad\square$

5.6 Ranks and Border Ranks of Structure Tensors of Algebras

In this section I discuss ranks and border ranks of a class of tensors that appear to be more tractable than arbitrary tensors: structure tensors of algebras. It turns out this class is larger than appears at first glance: as explained in §5.6.1, all tensors in $A \otimes B \otimes C = \mathbb{C}^{\mathbf{m}} \otimes \mathbb{C}^{\mathbf{m}} \otimes \mathbb{C}^{\mathbf{m}}$ that are 1_A and 1_B-generic are equivalent to structure tensors of algebras with unit. In §5.6.2, I show structure tensors corresponding to algebras of the form $\mathbb{C}[x_1, \ldots, x_n]/\mathcal{I}$, where $\mathcal{I}$ is an ideal whose zero set is finite, are equivalent to symmetric tensors and give several examples. (For those familiar with the language, these are structure tensors of coordinate rings of zero-dimensional affine schemes, see §10.1.1.) The algebra structure can facilitate the application of the substitution and border substitution methods, as is illustrated in §5.6.3 and §5.6.4, respectively. In particular, using algebras of the form $\mathbb{C}[x_1, \ldots, x_n]/\mathcal{I}$, I present examples of tensors with rank to border rank ratio approaching three. I conclude with Bläser and Lysikov's study of structure tensors of algebras that have minimal border rank.

Throughout this section, $\mathcal{A}$ denotes a finite-dimensional associative algebra and $T_\mathcal{A} \in \mathcal{A}^* \otimes \mathcal{A}^* \otimes \mathcal{A}$ denotes its structure tensor, as discussed in §3.5.1.

5.6.1 Algebras and Minimal Border Rank Tensors

The following reduction theorem is due to Bläser and Lysikov:

Theorem 5.6.1.1 [BL16] *Let $\mathcal{A}$, $\mathcal{A}_1$ be algebras of dimension* **m** *with structure tensors $T_\mathcal{A}, T_{\mathcal{A}_1}$. Then $T_\mathcal{A} \subset \overline{GL_{\mathbf{m}}^{\times 3} \cdot T_{\mathcal{A}_1}}$ if and only if $T_\mathcal{A} \subset \overline{GL_{\mathbf{m}} \cdot T_{\mathcal{A}_1}}$.*

Proof. Write $\mathbb{C}^{\mathbf{m}} \simeq \mathcal{A} \simeq \mathcal{A}_1$ as a vector space, so $T_\mathcal{A}, T_{\mathcal{A}_1} \in \mathbb{C}^{\mathbf{m}*} \otimes \mathbb{C}^{\mathbf{m}*} \otimes \mathbb{C}^{\mathbf{m}}$. Write $T_\mathcal{A} = \lim_{t\to 0} T_t$, where $T_t := (f_t, g_t, h_t) \cdot T_{\mathcal{A}_1}$, with f_t, g_t, h_t curves in $GL_{\mathbf{m}}$. Let $e \in \mathcal{A}$ denote the identity element. Then $T_t(e, y) = h_t T_{\mathcal{A}_1}$ $(f_t^{-1}e, g_t^{-1}y) = y + O(t)$. Write $L_{f_t^{-1}e} : \mathcal{A} \to \mathcal{A}$ for $f_t^{-1}e$ considered as a linear map. Then $h_t L_{f_t^{-1}e} g_t^{-1} = \mathrm{Id} + O(t)$, so we may replace g_t by $\tilde{g}_t :=$ $h_t L_{f_t^{-1}e}$. Similarly, using that $T_t(y, e) = y + O(t)$, we may replace f_t by $\tilde{f}_t := h_t R_{\tilde{g}_t^{-1}e}$, where R is used to remind us that it corresponds to right multiplication in the algebra, so our new curve is $T_A = \lim_{t \to 0}((R_{\tilde{g}_t^{-1}e})^{-1} h_t^{-1},$ $(L_{f_t^{-1}e})^{-1} h_t^{-1}, h_t) \cdot T_{\mathcal{A}_1}$. Finally, noting that for any linear maps $X, Y \in$ $\mathrm{End}(\mathbb{C}^{\mathbf{m}})$, $T_A(Xy, Yz) = X T_A(y, z)Y$, and taking $X_t = L_{f_t^{-1}e}^{-1}$, $Y_t = R_{\tilde{g}_t^{-1}e}^{-1}$, our new action is by $h_t L_{f_t^{-1}e} R_{\tilde{g}_t^{-1}e} \in GL_{\mathbf{m}} \subset GL_{\mathbf{m}}^{\times 3}$. $\qquad\square$

Proposition 5.6.1.2 [BL16] *Let* $T \in A \otimes B \otimes C = \mathbb{C}^{\mathbf{m}} \otimes \mathbb{C}^{\mathbf{m}} \otimes \mathbb{C}^{\mathbf{m}}$ *be* 1_A *and* 1_B *generic. Then there exists an algebra* $\mathcal{A}$ *with unit such that* T *is equivalent to* T_A, *i.e., they are in the same* $GL_{\mathbf{m}}^{\times 3}$-*orbit.*

Proof. Take $\alpha \in A^*$, $\beta \in B^*$ with $T(\alpha) : B^* \to C$ and $T(\beta) : A^* \to C$ of full rank. Give C the algebra structure $c_1 \cdot c_2 := T(T(\beta)^{-1}c_1, T(\alpha)^{-1}c_2)$ and note that the structure tensor of this algebra is in the same $GL_{\mathbf{m}}^{\times 3}$-orbit as T. $\qquad\square$

Exercise 5.6.1.3 (1) Verify that the product above indeed gives C the structure of an algebra with unit.

Combining Theorem 5.6.1.1 and Proposition 5.6.1.2, we obtain the following:

Theorem 5.6.1.4 [BL16] *Let* $T \in A \otimes B \otimes C = \mathbb{C}^{\mathbf{m}} \otimes \mathbb{C}^{\mathbf{m}} \otimes \mathbb{C}^{\mathbf{m}}$ *be* 1_A *and* 1_B *generic. Take* $\alpha \in A^*$, $\beta \in B^*$ *with* $T(\alpha) \in B \otimes C$, $T(\beta) \in A \otimes C$ *of full rank, and use them to construct an equivalent tensor* $\tilde{T} \in C^* \otimes C^* \otimes C$. *Then* $\underline{\mathbf{R}}(T) = \mathbf{m}$, *i.e.,* $T \in \overline{GL(A) \times GL(B) \times GL(C) \cdot M_{\langle 1 \rangle}^{\oplus \mathbf{m}}}$ *if and only if* $\tilde{T} \in \overline{GL(C) \cdot M_{\langle 1 \rangle}^{\oplus \mathbf{m}}}$.

Recall the Comon conjecture from §4.1.4 that posits that for symmetric tensors, $\mathbf{R}(T) = \mathbf{R}_S(T)$. One can define a border rank version:

Conjecture 5.6.1.5 *[Border rank Comon conjecture]*[BGL13] *Let* $T \in$ $S^3 \mathbb{C}^{\mathbf{m}} \subset (\mathbb{C}^{\mathbf{m}})^{\otimes 3}$. *Then* $\underline{\mathbf{R}}(T) = \underline{\mathbf{R}}_S(T)$.

Theorem 5.6.1.4 combined with Proposition 5.1.5.1, which says that minimal border rank 1-generic tensors are symmetric, implies the following:

Proposition 5.6.1.6 *The border rank Comon conjecture holds for 1-generic tensors of minimal border rank.*

5.6.2 Structural Tensors of Algebras of the Form $\mathbb{C}[x_1, \ldots, x_n]/\mathcal{I}$

Let $\mathcal{I} \subset \mathbb{C}[x_1, \ldots, x_n]$ be an ideal whose zero set in affine space is finite, so that $\mathcal{A}_{\mathcal{I}} := \mathbb{C}[x_1, \ldots, x_n]/\mathcal{I}$ is a finite-dimensional algebra. Let $\{p_I\}$ be a basis of $\mathcal{A}_{\mathcal{I}}$ with dual basis $\{p_I^*\}$. We can write the structural tensor of $\mathcal{A}_{\mathcal{I}}$ as

$$T_{\mathcal{A}_{\mathcal{I}}} = \sum_{p_I, p_J \in \mathcal{A}_{\mathcal{I}}} p_I^* \otimes p_J^* \otimes (p_I p_J \bmod \mathcal{I}).$$

This tensor is transparently in $S^2 \mathcal{A}^* \otimes \mathcal{A}$.

Consider an algebra $\mathcal{A} = \mathcal{A}_{\mathcal{I}} \in S^2 \mathcal{A}^* \otimes \mathcal{A}$ defined by an ideal as above. Note that since $T_{\mathcal{A}}(1, \cdot) \in \mathrm{End}(\mathcal{A})$ and $T_{\mathcal{A}}(\cdot, 1) \in \mathrm{End}(\mathcal{A})$ have full rank and that the induced isomorphism $B^* \to C$ is just $(\mathcal{A}^*)^* \to \mathcal{A}$, and similarly for the isomorphism $A^* \to C$. Since the algebra is abelian, Strassen's equations are satisfied, so by Proposition 5.1.5.1, there exists a choice of bases such that $T_{\mathcal{A}} \in S^3 \mathcal{A}$.

Proposition 5.6.2.1 *[Michalek and Jelisiejew, personal communication] Structural tensors of algebras of the form $\mathcal{A} = \mathbb{C}[x_1, \ldots, x_n]/\mathcal{I}$ are symmetric if either of the following equivalent conditions hold:*

- $\mathcal{A}^* = \mathcal{A} \cdot f$ *for some* $f \in \mathcal{A}^*$*, where for* $a, b \in \mathcal{A}$*,* $(a \cdot f)(b) := f(ab)$*;*
- $T_{\mathcal{A}}$ *is 1-generic.*

Proof. We have already seen that if $T_{\mathcal{A}}$ is 1-generic and satisfies Strassen's equations, then $T_{\mathcal{A}}$ is symmetric.

The following are clearly equivalent for an element $f \in \mathcal{A}^*$:

1 $T_{\mathcal{A}}(f) \in \mathcal{A}^* \otimes \mathcal{A}^*$ is of full rank;
2 the pairing $\mathcal{A} \otimes \mathcal{A} \to \mathbb{C}$ given by $(a, b) \mapsto f(ab)$ is nondegenerate;
3 $\mathcal{A}f = \mathcal{A}^*$. □

Remark 5.6.2.2 The condition that $\mathcal{A}^* = \mathcal{A} \cdot f$ for some $f \in \mathcal{A}^*$ is called *Gorenstein*. There are numerous definitions of Gorenstein. One that is relevant for Chapter 10 is that $\mathcal{A}$ is Gorenstein if and only if $\mathcal{A}$ is the annihilator of some polynomial D in the dual space, i.e., $D \in \mathbb{C}[\frac{\partial}{\partial x_1}, \ldots, \frac{\partial}{\partial x_n}]$.

Example 5.6.2.3 [Zui15] Consider $\mathcal{A} = \mathbb{C}[x]/(x^2)$, with basis $1, x$, so

$$T_{\mathcal{A}} = 1^* \otimes 1^* \otimes 1 + x^* \otimes 1^* \otimes x + 1^* \otimes x^* \otimes x.$$

Writing $e_0 = 1^*, e_1 = x^*$ in the first two factors and $e_0 = x, e_1 = 1$ in the third,

$$T_{\mathcal{A}} = e_0 \otimes e_0 \otimes e_1 + e_1 \otimes e_0 \otimes e_0 + e_0 \otimes e_1 \otimes e_0.$$

That is, $T_{\mathcal{A}} = T_{WState}$ is a general tangent vector to $Seg(\mathbb{P}A \times \mathbb{P}B \times \mathbb{P}C)$.

More generally, consider $\mathcal{A} = \mathbb{C}[x_1, \ldots, x_n]/(x_1^2, \ldots, x_n^2)$, with basis $x_I = x_{i_1} \cdots x_{i_{|I|}}$, where $1 \leq i_1 < \cdots < i_{|I|} \leq n$, and by convention $x_\emptyset = 1$. Then

$$T_{\mathcal{A}} = \sum_{I, J \subset [n] | I \cap J = \emptyset} x_I^* \otimes x_J^* \otimes x_{I \cup J}.$$

Similar to above, let $e_I = x_I^*$ in the first two factors and $e_I = x_{[n]\setminus I}$ in the third; we obtain

$$T_\mathcal{A} = \sum_{\substack{\{I,J,K\} \\ I \cup J \cup K = [n], \\ |I|+|J|+|K|=n}} e_I \otimes e_J \otimes e_K,$$

so we explicitly see $T_\mathcal{A} \in S^3 \mathbb{C}^{2^n}$.

Exercise 5.6.2.4 (2) Show that for $\mathcal{A} = \mathbb{C}[x_1, \ldots, x_n]/(x_1^2, \ldots, x_n^2)$, $T_\mathcal{A} \simeq T_{WState}^{\otimes n}$, where for $T \in A \otimes B \otimes C$, consider $T^{\otimes n} \in (A^{\otimes n}) \otimes (B^{\otimes n}) \otimes (C^{\otimes n})$ as a three-way tensor.

Exercise 5.6.2.5 (2) Let $\mathcal{A} = \mathbb{C}[x]/(x^n)$. Show that $T_\mathcal{A}(\mathcal{A})T_\mathcal{A}(1)^{-1} \subset End(\mathcal{A})$ corresponds to the centralizer of a regular nilpotent element, so in particular $\underline{\mathbf{R}}(T_\mathcal{A}) = n$ and $\mathbf{R}(T_\mathcal{A}) = 2n - 1$ by Exercise 5.3.1.8 and Proposition 5.1.4.6.

Exercise 5.6.2.6 (2) Fix natural numbers $d_1, \ldots, d_n$. Let $\mathcal{A} = \mathbb{C}[x_1, \ldots, x_n]/(x_1^{d_1}, \ldots, x_n^{d_n})$. Find an explicit identification $\mathcal{A}^* \to \mathcal{A}$ that renders $T_\mathcal{A} \in S^3 \mathcal{A}$.
◎

Example 5.6.2.7 [Zui15] Consider the tensor

$$T_{WState,k} = a_{1,0} \otimes \cdots \otimes a_{k-1,0} \otimes a_{k,1} + a_{1,0} \otimes \cdots \otimes a_{k-2,0} \otimes a_{k-1,1} \otimes a_{k,0} + \cdots$$
$$+ a_{1,1} \otimes a_{2,0} \otimes \cdots \otimes a_{k,0}$$

that corresponds to a general tangent vector to $Seg(\mathbb{P}^1 \times \cdots \times \mathbb{P}^1) \in \mathbb{P}((\mathbb{C}^2)^{\otimes k})$. (Note that $T_{WState} = T_{WState,3}$.) This tensor is called the *generalized W-state* by physicists. Let $\mathcal{A}_{d,N} = (\mathbb{C}[x]/(x^d))^{\otimes N} \simeq \mathbb{C}[x_1, \ldots, x_N]/(x_1^d, \ldots, x_N^d)$.

Exercise 5.6.2.8 (2) Show that $T_{\mathcal{A}_{d,N}} = (T_{WState,d})^{\otimes N}$.

Example 5.6.2.9 (The Coppersmith-Winograd tensor) [LM17b, BL16] Consider the algebra

$$\mathcal{A}_{CW,q} = \mathbb{C}[x_1, \ldots, x_q]/(x_i x_j, x_i^2 - x_j^2, x_i^3, \ i \neq j).$$

Let $\{1, x_i, [x_1^2]\}$ be a basis of $\mathcal{A}$, where $[x_1^2] = [x_j^2]$ for all j. Then

$$T_{\mathcal{A}_{CW,q}} = 1^* \otimes 1^* \otimes 1 + \sum_{i=1}^{q} \left(1^* \otimes x_i^* \otimes x_i + x_i^* \otimes 1^* \otimes x_i \right)$$
$$+ x_i^* \otimes x_i^* \otimes [x_1^2] + 1^* \otimes [x_1^2]^* \otimes [x_1^2] + [x_1^2]^* \otimes 1^* \otimes [x_1^2].$$

Set $e_0 = 1^*$, $e_i = x_i^*$, $e_{q+1} = [x_1^2]^*$ in the first two factors and $e_0 = [x_1^2]$, $e_i = x_i$, $e_{q+1} = 1$ in the third to obtain

$$T_{\mathcal{A}_{CW,q}} = T_{CW,q} = e_0 \otimes e_0 \otimes e_{q+1} + \sum_{i=1}^{q}(e_0 \otimes e_i \otimes e_i + e_i \otimes e_0 \otimes e_i + e_i \otimes e_i \otimes e_0)$$
$$+ e_0 \otimes e_{q+1} \otimes e_0 + e_{q+1} \otimes e_0 \otimes e_0,$$

so we indeed obtain the Coppersmith-Winograd tensor.

Problem 5.6.2.10 When is the structure tensor of $\mathcal{A}_{\mathcal{I}}$ of minimal border rank? Note that if $T \in \mathbb{C}^m \otimes \mathbb{C}^m \otimes \mathbb{C}^m$ is the structure tensor of an algebra $\mathcal{A}$ that is a degeneration of $(\mathbb{C}[x]/(x))^{\oplus m}$ (whose structure tensor is $M_{\langle 1 \rangle}^{\oplus m}$), then $\underline{R}(T) = m$.

5.6.3 The Substitution Method Applied to Structure Tensors of Algebras

Let $\mathcal{A}$ be a finite-dimensional associative algebra. The *radical* of $\mathcal{A}$ is the intersection of all maximal left ideals and denoted Rad($\mathcal{A}$). When $\mathcal{A}$ is abelian, the radical is often call the *nilradical*.

Exercise 5.6.3.1 (2) Show that every element of Rad($\mathcal{A}$) is nilpotent and that if $\mathcal{A}$ is abelian, Rad($\mathcal{A}$) consists exactly of the nilpotent elements of $\mathcal{A}$. (This exercise requires knowledge of standard notions from algebra.) ⊙

Theorem 5.6.3.2 [Blä00, Theorem 7.4] *For any integers $p, q \geq 1$,*

$$\mathbf{R}(T_{\mathcal{A}}) \geq \dim(Rad(\mathcal{A})^p) + \dim(Rad(\mathcal{A})^q) + \dim \mathcal{A} - \dim(Rad(\mathcal{A})^{p+q-1}).$$

For the proof we will need the following lemma, whose proof I skip:

Lemma 5.6.3.3 [Blä00, Lem. 7.3] *Let $\mathcal{A}$ be a finite-dimensional algebra, and let $U, V \subseteq \mathcal{A}$ be vector subspaces such that $U + Rad(\mathcal{A})^p = \mathcal{A}$ and $V + Rad(\mathcal{A})^q = \mathcal{A}$. Then $\langle UV \rangle + Rad(\mathcal{A})^{p+q-1} = \mathcal{A}$.*

Proof of Theorem 5.6.3.2. Use Proposition 5.4.1.2 with

$$\tilde{A} = (Rad(\mathcal{A})^p)^{\perp} \subset \mathcal{A}^*,$$
$$\tilde{B} = (Rad(\mathcal{A})^q)^{\perp} \subset \mathcal{A}^*, \text{ and}$$
$$\tilde{C} = Rad(\mathcal{A})^{p+q-1} \subset \mathcal{A}.$$

Then observe that any $A' \subset \mathcal{A} \backslash Rad(\mathcal{A})^p$, $B' \subset \mathcal{A} \backslash Rad(\mathcal{A})^q$, can play the roles of U, V in the lemma, so $T_{\mathcal{A}}(A', B') \not\subset Rad(\mathcal{A})^{p+q-1}$. Since $C' \subset \mathcal{A}^* \backslash (Rad(\mathcal{A})^{p+q-1})^{\perp}$, we conclude. □

Remark 5.6.3.4 Theorem 5.6.3.2 illustrates the power of the (rank) substitution method over the border substitution method. By merely prohibiting a certain Zariski closed set of degenerations, we can make T_A noncompressible. Without that prohibition, T_A can indeed be compressed in general.

Remark 5.6.3.5 Using similar (but easier) methods, one can show that if $\mathcal{A}$ is simple of dimension $\mathbf{a}$, then $\mathbf{R}(T_A) \geq 2\mathbf{a} - 1$ (see, e.g., [BCS97, Proposition 17.22]). More generally, the Alder-Strassen Theorem [AS81] states that if there are m maximal two-sided ideals in $\mathcal{A}$, then $\mathbf{R}(T_A) \geq 2\mathbf{a} - m$.

Theorem   5.6.3.6   [Bla01a]   *Let* $\mathcal{A}_{trunc,d} := \mathbb{C}[x_1, \ldots, x_n]/(S^d \mathbb{C}^n) = \bigoplus_{j=0}^{d-1} S^j \mathbb{C}^n$. *Then*

$$\mathbf{R}(T_{\mathcal{A}_{trunc,d}}) \geq 3\binom{n+d}{d-1} - \binom{n+\lfloor \frac{d}{2} \rfloor}{\lfloor \frac{d}{2} \rfloor - 1} - \binom{n+\lceil \frac{d}{2} \rceil}{\lceil \frac{d}{2} \rceil - 1}.$$

Proof. Apply Theorem 5.6.3.2. Here $\mathrm{Rad}(\mathcal{A}_{trunc,d})$ is a vector space complement to $\{\mathrm{Id}\}$ in $\mathcal{A}_{trunc,d}$, so it has dimension $\binom{n+d}{d-1} - 1$ and $\mathrm{Rad}(\mathcal{A}_{trunc,d})^k = \sum_{j=k}^{d-1} S^j \mathbb{C}^n$, which has dimension $\binom{n+d}{d-1} - \binom{n+k}{k-1}$. $\qquad\square$

In §5.6.5 we will see that any algebra $\mathbb{C}[x_1, \ldots, x_n]/\mathcal{I}$ where $\mathcal{I}$ is an ideal generated by monomials gives rise to a tensor of minimal border rank. Thus, as was observed by Bläser:

Corollary 5.6.3.7 (Bläser, personal communication) *Let* $d = d(n) < n$ *be an integer valued function of n. Then*

$$\frac{\mathbf{R}(T_{\mathcal{A}_{trunc,d}})}{\underline{\mathbf{R}}(T_{\mathcal{A}_{trunc,d}})} \geq 3 - o(n).$$

If $d = \lfloor \frac{n}{2} \rfloor$, *then the error term is on the order of* $1/\dim \mathcal{A}_{trunc,d}$.

Theorem 5.6.3.8 [Zui15] $\mathbf{R}(T_{WState}^{\otimes n}) = 3 \cdot 2^n - o(2^n)$.

Proof. We have $\mathcal{A} = \mathbb{C}[x_1, \ldots, x_n]/(x_1^2, \ldots, x_n^2)$, so the degree $n - s$ component of $\mathcal{A}$ is $\mathcal{A}_s = \mathrm{span} \bigcup_{S \subset [n]} \{x_1 \cdots \hat{x}_{i_1} \cdots \hat{x}_{i_s} \cdots x_n\} = \mathrm{span} \bigcup_{S \subset [n]} \{\frac{x_1 \cdots x_n}{x_{i_1} \cdots x_{i_s}}\}$. In particular, $\dim \mathcal{A}_s = \binom{n}{s}$.

Note that $\mathrm{Rad}(\mathcal{A})^m = \bigoplus_{j \geq m} \mathcal{A}_j$. Recall that $\sum_{j=0}^{n} \binom{n}{j} = 2^n$. Take $p = q$ in Theorem 5.6.3.2. We have

$$\mathbf{R}(T_A) \geq 2^n + 2\sum_{j=p}^{n} \binom{n}{j} - \sum_{k=2p-1}^{n} \binom{n}{k}$$

$$= 3 \cdot 2^n - 2\sum_{j=0}^{p} \binom{n}{j} - \sum_{k=0}^{n-2p+1} \binom{n}{k}.$$

Write $p = \epsilon n$, for some $0 < \epsilon < 1$. Since $\sum_{j=0}^{\epsilon n} \binom{n}{j} \leq 2^{(-\epsilon \log(\epsilon) - (1-\epsilon)\log(1-\epsilon))n}$ (see §7.5.1), taking, e.g., $\epsilon = \frac{1}{3}$ gives the result. □

Corollary 5.6.3.9 [Zui15] $\frac{\mathbf{R}(T_{WState}^{\otimes n})}{\underline{\mathbf{R}}(T_{WState}^{\otimes n})} \geq 3 - o(1)$, *where the right-hand side is viewed as a function of n.*

More generally, Zuiddam shows, for $T_{WState,k}^{\otimes n} \in (\mathbb{C}^n)^{\otimes k}$:

Theorem 5.6.3.10 [Zui15] $\mathbf{R}(T_{WState,k}^{\otimes n}) = k2^n - o(2^n)$.

Regarding the ratio of rank to border rank, there is the following theorem applicable even to X-rank and X-border rank:

Theorem 5.6.3.11 [BT15] *Let $X \subset \mathbb{P}V$ be a complex projective variety not contained in a hyperplane. Let $\underline{\mathbf{R}}_{X,max}$ denote the maximum X-border rank of a point in $\mathbb{P}V$ and $\mathbf{R}_{X,max}$ the maximum possible X-rank. Then $\mathbf{R}_{X,max} \leq 2\underline{\mathbf{R}}_{X,max}$.*

Proof. Let $U \subset \mathbb{P}V$ be the Zariski dense open subset of points of rank exactly $\underline{\mathbf{R}}_{X,max}$. Let $q \in \mathbb{P}V$ be any point and let p be any point in U. The line L through q and p intersects U at another point p' (in fact, at infinitely many more points). Since p and p' span L, q is a linear combination of p and p', thus $\mathbf{R}_X(q) \leq \mathbf{R}_X(p) + \mathbf{R}_X(p')$. □

Theorem 5.6.3.11 implies that the maximal possible rank of any tensor in $\mathbb{C}^m \otimes \mathbb{C}^m \otimes \mathbb{C}^m$ is at most $2\lceil \frac{m^3-1}{3m-2} \rceil$, so for any concise tensor, the maximal rank to maximal border rank ratio is bounded above by approximately $\frac{2m}{3}$, which is likely far from sharp.

5.6.4 The Border Substitution Method and Tensor Powers of $T_{cw,2}$

Lemma 5.6.4.1 [BL16] *For any tensor $T_1 \in A_1 \otimes B_1 \otimes C_1$, and any $q \geq 2$,*

$$\min_{\alpha \in (A \otimes A_1)^* \setminus \{0\}} (\operatorname{rank}(T_{cw,q} \otimes T_1)\,|_{\alpha \otimes B^* \otimes C^*}) \geq 2\min_{\alpha_1 \in A_1 \setminus \{0\}} (\operatorname{rank}(T_1\,|_{\alpha_1 \otimes B_1^* \otimes C_1^*})).$$

Proof. Write $\alpha = 1 \otimes \alpha_0 + \sum_{j=1}^q e_j^* \otimes \alpha_j \in (A \otimes A_1)^*$ for some $\alpha_0, \alpha_j \in A_1^*$. If all the α_j are zero for $1 \leq j \leq q$, then $T_{cw,q}(e_0^* \otimes \alpha_0)$ is the reordering and grouping of

$$\sum_{i=1}^q (e_i \otimes e_i) \otimes T_1(\alpha_0),$$

which has rank (as a linear map) at least $q \cdot \operatorname{rank}(T_1(\alpha_0))$. Otherwise, without loss of generality, assume $\alpha_1 \neq 0$. Note that $T_{cw,q}(e_1^* \otimes \alpha_1)$ is the reordering and grouping of

$$e_1 \otimes e_0 \otimes T_1(\alpha_1) + e_0 \otimes e_1 \otimes T_1(\alpha_1),$$

which has rank two and is linearly independent of any of the other factors appearing in the image, so the rank is at least $2 \cdot \operatorname{rank}(T_1(\alpha_0))$. $\qquad\square$

Theorem 5.6.4.2 [BL16] *For all $q \geq 2$, consider $T_{cw,q}^{\otimes n} \in \mathbb{C}^{(q+1)^n} \otimes \mathbb{C}^{(q+1)^n} \otimes \mathbb{C}^{(q+1)^n}$. Then $\underline{\mathbf{R}}(T_{cw,q}^{\otimes n}) \geq (q+1)^n + 2^n - 1$.*

Proof. Note that $T_{cw,q}^{\otimes n} = T_{cw,q} \otimes T_{cw,q}^{\otimes(n-1)}$. Apply the lemma iteratively and use Corollary 5.4.1.4. $\qquad\square$

Remark 5.6.4.3 As was pointed out in [BCS97, Remark 15.44], if the asymptotic rank (see Definition 3.4.6.1) of $T_{cw,2}$ is the minimal 3, then the exponent of matrix multiplication is 2. The bound in the theorem does not rule this out.

5.6.5 Smoothable Ideals and Tensors of Minimal Border Rank

In §5.6.1 we saw that classifying 1_A and 1_B generic tensors of minimal border rank is equivalent to the potentially simpler problem of classifying algebras in the $GL_{\mathbf{m}}$-orbit closure of $M_{(1)}^{\oplus \mathbf{m}}$. We can translate this further when the algebras are of the form $\mathbb{C}[x_1, \ldots, x_N]/\mathcal{I}$ for some ideal $\mathcal{I}$. The question then becomes if $\mathcal{I}$ is a degeneration of an ideal whose zero set consists of $\mathbf{m}$ distinct points (counted with multiplicity). Such ideals are said to be *smoothable* (see [RS11]).

The degenerations of ideals have been well studied, and we are interested in the degeneration of the ideal of $\mathbf{m}$ distinct points to other ideals.

For example, the following algebras have the desired property, and thus their structure tensors are of minimal border rank (see [CEVV09]):

- $\dim(\mathcal{A}) \leq 7$,
- $\mathcal{A}$ is generated by two elements,
- the radical of $\mathcal{A}$ satisfies $\dim(\operatorname{Rad}(\mathcal{A})^2/\operatorname{Rad}(\mathcal{A})^3) = 1$, and
- the radical of $\mathcal{A}$ satisfies $\dim(\operatorname{Rad}(\mathcal{A})^2/\operatorname{Rad}(\mathcal{A})^3) = 2$, $\dim \operatorname{Rad}(\mathcal{A})^3 \leq 2$ and $\operatorname{Rad}(\mathcal{A})^4 = 0$.

An ideal $\mathcal{I}$ is a *monomial ideal* if it is generated by monomials (in some coordinate system). Choose an order on monomials such that if $|I| > |J|$, then $x^I < x^J$. Given $f \in \mathbb{C}[x_1, \ldots, x_n]$, define $in(f)$ to be the lowest monomial term of f, the initial term of f. Given an ideal $\mathcal{I}$, define its *initial ideal* (with respect to some chosen order) as $(in(f) \mid f \in \mathcal{I})$. An ideal can be degenerated to its initial ideal.

Proposition 5.6.5.1 [CEVV09] *Monomial ideals are smoothable, so if $\mathcal{I}$ is a monomial ideal, then the structure tensor of $\mathbb{C}[x_1, \ldots, x_n]/\mathcal{I}$ is of minimal border rank.*

Proof. Write $\mathcal{I} = (x^{I_1}, \dots, x^{I_s})$ for the ideal, where $I_\alpha = (i_{\alpha,1}, \dots, i_{\alpha,|I_\alpha|})$, and let $\mathbf{m} = \dim \mathbb{C}[x_1, \dots, x_N]/\mathcal{I}$. Take a sequence $a_1, a_2, \dots$ of distinct elements of $\mathbb{C}$. Define

$$f_q := \Pi_{j=1}^{N}(x_j - a_1)(x_j - a_2) \cdots (x_j - a_{i_{s,q}}).$$

Note that $in(f_q) = x^{I_q}$. Let $\mathcal{J}$ be the ideal generated by the f_q. Then $in(\mathcal{J}) \supset (in(f_1), \dots, in(f_s)) = \mathcal{I}$, so $\dim \mathbb{C}[x_1, \dots, x_N]/\mathcal{J} \leq \mathbf{m}$. But now for any of the $x^{I_q} \in \mathcal{I}$, each f_q vanishes at $(a_{I_{q,1}}, \dots, a_{I_{q,N}}) \in \mathbb{C}^N$. Thus $\mathcal{J}$ must be the radical ideal vanishing at the s points and have initial ideal $\mathcal{I}$, so $\mathcal{I}$ is smoothable. $\square$

6

Valiant's Hypothesis I: Permanent versus Determinant and the Complexity of Polynomials

Recall from the introduction that for a polynomial P, the *determinantal complexity of P*, denoted $\mathrm{dc}(P)$, is the smallest n such that P is an affine linear projection of the determinant, and Valiant's hypothesis 1.2.4.2 that $\mathrm{dc}(\mathrm{perm}_m)$ grows faster than any polynomial in m. In this chapter I discuss the conjecture, progress toward it and its Geometric Complexity Theory (GCT) variant.

I begin, in §6.1, with a discussion of circuits, context for Valiant's hypothesis, definitions of the complexity classes **VP** and **VNP**, and the strengthening of Valiant's hypothesis of [MS01] that is more natural for algebraic geometry and representation theory. In particular, I explain why it might be considered as an algebraic analog of the famous $\mathbf{P} \neq \mathbf{NP}$ conjecture (although there are other conjectures in the Boolean world that are more closely related to Valiant's hypothesis).

Our study of matrix multiplication indicates a strategy for Valiant's hypothesis: look for polynomials on the space of polynomials that vanish on the determinant and not on the permanent, and look for such polynomials with the aid of geometry and representation theory. Here there is extra geometry available: a polynomial $P \in S^d V$ defines a *hypersurface*

$$\mathrm{Zeros}(P) := \{[\alpha] \in \mathbb{P}V^* \mid P(\alpha) = 0\} \subset \mathbb{P}V^*.$$

Hypersurfaces in projective space have been studied for hundreds of years, and much is known about them.

In §6.2 I discuss the simplest polynomials on spaces of polynomials, the *catalecticants*, which date back to Sylvester.

One approach to Valiant's hypothesis discussed at several points in this chapter is to look for pathologies of the hypersurface $\mathrm{Zeros}(\det_n)$ that persist under degeneration and that are not shared by $\mathrm{Zeros}(\ell^{n-m} \mathrm{perm}_m)$. The simplest pathology of a hypersurface is its singular set. I discuss the singular loci of the permanent and determinant and make general remarks on singularities in §6.3.

I then present the classical and recent lower bounds on $dc(perm_m)$ of von zur Gathen and Alper-Bogart-Velasco in §6.3.4. These lower bounds on $dc(perm_m)$ rely on a key regularity result observed by von zur Gathen. These results do not directly extend to the measure $\overline{dc}(perm_m)$ defined in §6.1.6 because of the regularity result.

The best general lower bound on $dc(perm_m)$, namely, $dc(perm_m) \geq \frac{m^2}{2}$, comes from local differential geometry: the study of *Gauss maps*. It is presented in §6.4. This bound extends to $\overline{dc}(perm_m)$ after some work. The extension is presented in §6.5. To better utilize geometry and representation theory, I describe the symmetries of the permanent and determinant in §6.6. Given $P \in S^dV$, let $G_P := \{g \in GL(V) \mid g \cdot P = P\}$ denote the symmetry group of the polynomial P.

Since $\det(AXB) = \det(X)$, if A, B are $n \times n$ matrices with determinant one, and $\det(X^T) = \det(X)$, writing $V = E \otimes F$ with $E, F = \mathbb{C}^n$, we have a map

$$(SL(E) \times SL(F)) \rtimes \mathbb{Z}_2 \to G_{\det_n}$$

where the $\mathbb{Z}_2$ is transpose and $SL(E)$ is the group of linear maps with determinant equal to one.

Similarly, letting $T_E^{SL} \subset SL(E)$ denote the diagonal matrices, we have a map

$$[(T_E^{SL} \rtimes \mathfrak{S}_n) \times (T_F^{SL} \rtimes \mathfrak{S}_n)] \rtimes \mathbb{Z}_2 \to G_{perm_n}.$$

In §6.6, I show that both maps are surjective.

Just as it is interesting and useful to study the difference between rank and border rank, it is worthwhile to study the difference between dc and $\overline{dc}$, which I discuss in §6.7.

One situation where there is some understanding of the difference between $\overline{dc}$ and dc is for cubic surfaces: a smooth cubic polynomial P in three variables satisfies $dc(P) = 3$, and thus every cubic polynomial Q in three variables satisfies $\overline{dc}(Q) = 3$. I give an outline of the proof in §6.8. Finally, although it is not strictly related to complexity theory, I cannot resist a brief discussion of determinantal hypersurfaces – those degree n polynomials P with $dc(P) = n$ – which I also discuss in in §6.8.

In this chapter I emphasize material that is not widely available to computer scientists and do not present proofs that already have excellent expositions in the literature, such as the completeness of the permanent for **VNP**.

This chapter can be read mostly independently of Chapters 2–5.

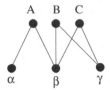

Figure 6.1.1 A bipartite graph. Vertex sets are $\{A, B, C\}$ and $\{\alpha, \beta, \gamma\}$.

6.1 Circuits and Definitions of VP and VNP

In this section I give definitions of **VP** and **VNP** via arithmetic circuits and show $(\det_n) \in$ **VP**. I also discuss why Valiant's hypothesis is a cousin of **P** $\neq$ **NP**, namely, I show that the permanent can compute the number of perfect matchings of a bipartite graph, something considered difficult, while the determinant can be computed by a polynomial size circuit.

6.1.1 The Permanent can Do Things Considered Difficult

A standard problem in graph theory, for which the only known algorithms are exponential in the size of the graph, is to count the number of perfect matchings of a bipartite graph, that is, a graph with two sets of vertices and edges only joining vertices from one set to the other (Figure 6.1.1).

A *perfect matching* is a subset of the edges such that each vertex shares an edge from the subset with exactly one other vertex.

To a bipartite graph, one associates an incidence matrix x_j^i, where $x_j^i = 1$ if an edge joins the vertex i above to the vertex j below and is zero otherwise. (Figure 6.1.1) has incidence matrix

$$\begin{pmatrix} 1 & 1 & 0 \\ 0 & 1 & 1 \\ 0 & 1 & 1 \end{pmatrix}.$$

A perfect matching corresponds to a matrix constructed from the incidence matrix by setting some of the entries to zero so that the resulting matrix has exactly one 1 in each row and column, i.e., is a permutation matrix.

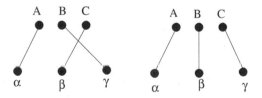

Figure 6.1.2 Two perfect matchings of the graph from Figure 6.1.1.

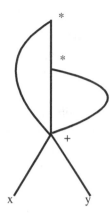

Figure 6.1.3 Circuit for $(x + y)^3$.

Exercise 6.1.1.1 (1) Show that if x is the incidence matrix of a bipartite graph, then $\text{perm}_n(x)$ indeed equals the number of perfect matchings.

For example, $\text{perm}_3 \begin{pmatrix} 1 & 1 & 0 \\ 0 & 1 & 1 \\ 0 & 1 & 1 \end{pmatrix} = 2$.

Thus a classical problem: determine the complexity of counting the number of perfect matchings of a bipartite graph (which is complete for the complexity class $\sharp$**P**, see [BCS97, p. 574]). This classical problem can be studied via algebra – determine the complexity of evaluating the permanent.

6.1.2 Circuits

Definition 6.1.2.1 An *arithmetic circuit* C is a finite, directed, acyclic graph with vertices of in-degree 0 or 2 and exactly one vertex of out-degree 0. The vertices of in-degree 0 are labeled by elements of $\mathbb{C} \cup \{x_1, \ldots, x_n\}$ and called *inputs*. Those of in-degree 2 are labeled with $+$ or $*$ and are called *gates*. If the out-degree of v is 0, then v is called an *output gate*. The *size* of C is the number of edges (Figure 6.1.3).

To each vertex v of a circuit C, associate the polynomial that is computed at v, which will be denoted C_v. In particular, the polynomial associated with the output gate is called the polynomial computed by C.

At first glance, circuits do not look geometrical, as they depend on a choice of coordinates. While computer scientists always view polynomials as being given in some coordinate expression, in geometry, one is interested in properties of objects that are independent of coordinates. These perspectives are compatible because with circuits, one is not concerned with the precise size of a circuit but with its size up to, e.g., a polynomial factor. Reducing the size at worst by a polynomial factor, we can think of the inputs to our circuits as arbitrary affine linear or linear functions on a vector space.

6.1.3 Arithmetic Circuits and Complexity Classes

Definition 6.1.3.1 Let $d(n), N(n)$ be polynomials and let $f_n \in \mathbb{C}[x_1, \ldots, x_{N(n)}]_{\leq d(n)}$ be a sequence of polynomials. We say $(f_n) \in \mathbf{VP}$ if there exists a sequence of circuits $\mathcal{C}_n$ of size polynomial in n computing f_n.

Often the phrase "there exists a sequence of circuits $\mathcal{C}_n$ of size polynomial in n computing f_n" is abbreviated "there exists a polynomial sized circuit computing (f_n)."

The class **VNP**, which consists of sequences of polynomials whose coefficients are "easily" described, has a more complicated definition:

Definition 6.1.3.2 A sequence (f_n) is in **VNP** if there exists a polynomial p and a sequence $(g_n) \in \mathbf{VP}$ such that

$$f_n(x) = \sum_{\epsilon \in \{0,1\}^{p(n)}} g_n(x, \epsilon).$$

One may think of elements of the class VNP as projections of elements of VP, where elements of **VP** are thought of as sequences of maps, say, $g_n : \mathbb{C}^{N(n)} \to \mathbb{C}$, and elements of **VNP** are projections of these maps by eliminating some of the variables by averaging or "integration over the fiber." In algebraic geometry, it is well known that projections of varieties can be far more complicated than the original varieties. See [Bas15] for more on this perspective.

The class **VNP** is sometimes described as the polynomial sequences that can be written down "explicitly." Mathematicians should take note that the computer science definition of explicit is different from what a mathematician might use. For example, as pointed out in [FS13a], roots of unity are not explicit because using them computationally typically requires expanding them as a decimal with exponential precision, which is inefficient. On the other hand, the lexicographically first function $f : \{0, 1\}^{\lfloor \log \log n \rfloor} \to \{0, 1\}$ with the maximum possible circuit complexity among all functions on $\lfloor \log \log n \rfloor$ bits is explicit because, while seemingly unstructured, this function can be written down efficiently via brute force. See [FS13a] for the definition.

Definition 6.1.3.3 One says that a sequence $(g_m(y_1, \ldots, y_{M(m)}))$ can be polynomially *reduced* to $(f_n(x_1, \ldots, x_{N(n)}))$ if there exists a polynomial

$n(m)$ and affine linear functions $X_1(y_1, \ldots, y_M), \ldots, X_N(y_1, \ldots, y_M)$ such that $g_m(y_1, \ldots, y_{M(m)}) = f_n(X_1(y), \ldots, X_{N(n)}(y))$. A sequence (p_n) is *hard* for a complexity class **C** if (p_n) can be reduced to every $(f_m) \in$ **C**, and it is *complete* for **C** if furthermore $(p_n) \in$ **C**.

Exercise 6.1.3.4 (1) Show that every polynomial of degree d can be reduced to x^d.

Theorem 6.1.3.5 *[Valiant]* [Val79] (perm_m) *is complete for* **VNP**.

There are many excellent expositions of the proof, see, e.g., [BCS97] or [Gat87].
Thus Conjecture 1.2.1.1 is equivalent to:

Conjecture 6.1.3.6 *[Valiant]* [Val79] *There does not exist a polynomial size circuit computing the permanent.*

Now for the determinant:

Proposition 6.1.3.7 $(\det_n) \in$ **VP**.

Remark 6.1.3.8 $\det_n$ would be **VP** complete if $\text{dc}(p_m)$ grew no faster than a polynomial for all sequences $(p_m) \in$ **VP**.

One can compute the determinant quickly via Gaussian elimination: one uses the group to put a matrix in a form where the determinant is almost effortless to compute (the determinant of an upper triangular matrix is just the product of its diagonal entries). However, this algorithm as presented is not a circuit (there are divisions, and one needs to check if pivots are zero). After a short detour on symmetric polynomials, I prove Proposition 6.1.3.7 in §6.1.5.

6.1.4 Symmetric Polynomials

An ubiquitous class of polynomials are the *symmetric polynomials*: let $\mathfrak{S}_N$ act on $\mathbb{C}^N$ by permuting basis elements, which induces an action on the polynomial ring $\mathbb{C}[x_1, \ldots, x_N]$. Let $\mathbb{C}[x_1, \ldots, x_N]^{\mathfrak{S}_N}$ denote the subspace of polynomials invariant under this action. What follows are standard facts and definitions about symmetric functions. For proofs, see, e.g., [Mac95, §I.2].

The *elementary symmetric functions* (or elementary symmetric polynomials) are

$$e_n = e_{n,N} = e_n(x_1, \ldots, x_N) := \sum_{J \subset [N] \mid |J| = n} x_{j_1} \cdots x_{j_n}. \qquad (6.1.1)$$

If the number of variables is understood, I write e_n for $e_{n,N}$. They generate the ring of symmetric polynomials. They have the *generating function*

$$E_N(t) := \sum_{k \geq 0} e_k(x_1, \ldots, x_N) t^k = \prod_{i=1}^{N} (1 + x_i t). \qquad (6.1.2)$$

Exercise 6.1.4.1 (1) Verify the coefficient of t^n in $E_N(t)$ is $e_{n,N}$.

The *power sum symmetric functions* are

$$p_n = p_{n,N} = p_{n,N}(x_1, \ldots, x_N) = x_1^n + \cdots + x_N^n. \qquad (6.1.3)$$

They also generate the ring of symmetric polynomials. They have the generating function

$$P_N(t) = \sum_{k \geq 1} p_k t^{k-1} = \frac{d}{dt} \ln \left[\prod_{j=1}^{N} (1 - x_j t)^{-1} \right]. \qquad (6.1.4)$$

Exercise 6.1.4.2 (2) Verify that the coefficient of t^n in $P_N(t)$ is indeed $p_{n,N}$. ⊚

Exercise 6.1.4.3 (2) Show that

$$P_N(-t) = -\frac{E'_N(t)}{E_N(t)}. \qquad (6.1.5)$$

Exercise 6.1.4.3, together with a little more work (see, e.g., [Mac95, p. 28]), shows that

$$p_n = \det{}_n \begin{pmatrix} e_1 & 1 & 0 & \cdots & 0 \\ 2e_2 & e_1 & 1 & \cdots & 0 \\ \vdots & \vdots & \ddots & \ddots & \vdots \\ \vdots & \vdots & \vdots & & 1 \\ ne_n & e_{n-1} & e_{n-2} & \cdots & e_1 \end{pmatrix}. \qquad (6.1.6)$$

Similarly,

$$e_n = \frac{1}{n!} \det{}_n \begin{pmatrix} p_1 & 1 & 0 & \cdots & 0 \\ p_2 & p_1 & 2 & \cdots & 0 \\ \vdots & \vdots & \vdots & \ddots & \vdots \\ p_{n-1} & p_{n-2} & & \cdots & n-1 \\ p_n & p_{n-1} & & \cdots & p_1 \end{pmatrix}. \qquad (6.1.7)$$

6.1.5 Proof of Proposition 6.1.3.7

Here is a construction of a small circuit for the determinant that essentially appeared in [Csa76]:

The determinant of a linear map $f : V \to V$ is the product of its eigenvalues $\lambda_1, \ldots, \lambda_v$, i.e., $e_v(\lambda) = \lambda_1 \cdots \lambda_v$.

On the other hand, trace(f) is the sum of the eigenvalues of f, and more generally, letting f^k denote the composition of f with itself k times,

$$\text{trace}(f^k) = p_k(\lambda) = \lambda_1^k + \cdots + \lambda_v^k.$$

The quantities trace(f^k) can be computed with small circuits.

Exercise 6.1.5.1 (2) Write down a circuit for the polynomial $A \mapsto \text{trace}(A^2)$ when A is an $n \times n$ matrix with variable entries.

Thus we can compute $\det_n$ via small circuits and (6.1.7). While (6.1.7) is still a determinant, it is almost lower triangular and its naïve computation, e.g., with Laplace expansion, can be done with an $O(n^3)$-size circuit and the full algorithm for computing $\det_n$ can be executed with an $O(n^4)$ size circuit.

Remark 6.1.5.2 A more restrictive class of circuits are *formulas* which are circuits that are trees. Let **VP**$_e$ denote the sequences of polynomials that admit a polynomial size formula. The circuit in the proof above is not a formula because results from computations are used more than once. It is known that the determinant admits a *quasi-polynomial* size formula, that is, a formula of size $n^{O(\log n)}$, and it is complete for the complexity class **VQP** $=$ **VP**$_s$ consisting of sequences of polynomials admitting a quasi-polynomial size formula (see, e.g., [BCS97, §21.5]) or equivalently, a polynomial sized "skew" circuit; see [Tod92]). It is not known whether or not the determinant is complete for **VP**.

6.1.6 The Geometric Complexity Theory (GCT) Variant of Valiant's Hypothesis

Recall that when we used polynomials in the study of matrix multiplication, we were proving lower bounds on tensor border rank rather than tensor rank. In the case of matrix multiplication, at least as far as the exponent is concerned, this changed nothing. In the case of determinant versus permanent, *it is not known* if using polynomial methods leads to a stronger separation of complexity classes. In any case, it will be best to clarify the two different types of lower bounds.

I recall from §1.2 that using padded polynomials, one can rephrase Valiant's hypothesis as follows:

Conjecture 6.1.6.1 *[Rephrasing of Valiant's hypothesis] Let ℓ be a linear coordinate on $\mathbb{C}^1$ and consider any linear inclusion $\mathbb{C}^1 \oplus \mathbb{C}^{m^2} \to \mathbb{C}^{n^2}$, so in* *particular $\ell^{n-m} \operatorname{perm}_m \in S^n \mathbb{C}^{n^2}$. Let $n(m)$ be a polynomial. Then, for all sufficiently large m,*

$$[\ell^{n-m} \operatorname{perm}_m] \notin \operatorname{End}(\mathbb{C}^{n^2}) \cdot [\det_{n(m)}].$$

Recall that the formulations are equivalent because if $\operatorname{perm}(y_j^i) = \det_n(\Lambda + \sum_{i,j} A_{ij} y_{i,j})$, then $\ell^{n-m} \operatorname{perm}_m(y_{i,j}) = \det_n(\ell \Lambda + \sum_{i,j} A_{ij} y_{i,j})$. Such an expression is equivalent to setting each entry of the $n \times n$ matrix to a linear combination of the variables $\ell, y_{i,j}$, which is precisely what the elements of rank $m^2 + 1$ in $\operatorname{End}(\mathbb{C}^{n^2})$ can accomplish. Moreover $\ell^{n-m} \operatorname{perm}_m = X \cdot \det_{n(m)}$ for some $X \in \operatorname{End}(\mathbb{C}^{n^2})$ implies X has rank $m^2 + 1$.

Recall the following conjecture, made to facilitate the use of tools from algebraic geometry and representation theory to separate complexity classes:

Conjecture 6.1.6.2 [MS01] *Let ℓ be a linear coordinate on $\mathbb{C}^1$ and consider any linear inclusion $\mathbb{C}^1 \oplus \mathbb{C}^{m^2} \to \mathbb{C}^{n^2}$, so in particular $\ell^{n-m} \operatorname{perm}_m \in S^n \mathbb{C}^{n^2}$. Let $n(m)$ be a polynomial. Then, for all sufficiently large m,*

$$[\ell^{n-m} \operatorname{perm}_m] \notin \overline{GL_{n^2} \cdot [\det_{n(m)}]}.$$

Note that $\overline{GL_{n^2} \cdot [\det_n]} = \overline{\operatorname{End}(\mathbb{C}^{n^2}) \cdot [\det_n]}$. In §6.7.2 I show $\overline{GL_{n^2} \cdot [\det_n]} \supsetneq \operatorname{End}(\mathbb{C}^{n^2}) \cdot [\det_n]$, so Conjecture 6.1.6.2 is a strengthening of Conjecture 6.1.6.1. It will be useful to rephrase the conjecture slightly, to highlight that it is a question about determining whether one orbit closure is contained in another. Let

$$\mathcal{D}et_n := \overline{GL_{n^2} \cdot [\det_n]},$$

and let

$$\mathcal{P}erm_n^m := \overline{GL_{n^2} \cdot [\ell^{n-m} \operatorname{perm}_m]}.$$

Conjecture 6.1.6.3 [MS01] *Let $n(m)$ be a polynomial. Then for all sufficiently large m,*

$$\mathcal{P}erm_{n(m)}^m \not\subset \mathcal{D}et_{n(m)}.$$

The equivalence of Conjectures 6.1.6.3 and 6.1.6.2 follows as $\ell^{n-m} \operatorname{perm}_m \notin \mathcal{D}et_n$ implies $GL_{n^2} \cdot \ell^{n-m} \operatorname{perm}_m \not\subset \mathcal{D}et_n$, and since $\mathcal{D}et_n$ is closed and both sides are irreducible, there is no harm in taking closure on the left-hand side, as you showed in Exercise 3.3.1.1.

Both $\mathcal{P}erm_n^m$ and $\mathcal{D}et_n$ are *invariant* under GL_{n^2}, so their ideals are GL_{n^2}-modules. To separate them, one may look for a GL_{n^2}-module M such that $M \subset I[\mathcal{D}et_n]$ and $M \not\subset I[\mathcal{P}erm_n^m]$.

In §8.8 I explain the original program to solve this conjecture. Although that program cannot work as stated, I believe that the refocusing of a problem of separating complexity classes to questions in algebraic geometry and representation theory could lead to viable paths to resolving Valiant's hypothesis.

6.2 Flattenings: Our First Polynomials on the Space of Polynomials

In this section I discuss the most classical polynomials on the space of polynomials, which were first introduced by Sylvester in 1852 and called *catalecticants* by him. They are also called *flattenings*, and in the computer science literature the polynomials induced by the *method of partial derivatives*.

6.2.1 Three Perspectives on $S^d \mathbb{C}^M$

I review our perspectives on $S^d \mathbb{C}^M$ from §2.3.2. We have seen $S^d \mathbb{C}^M$ is the space of symmetric tensors in $(\mathbb{C}^M)^{\otimes d}$. Given a symmetric tensor $T \in S^d \mathbb{C}^M$, we may form a polynomial P_T on $\mathbb{C}^{M*}$ by, for $v \in \mathbb{C}^{M*}$, $P_T(v) := T(v, \ldots, v)$. I use this identification repeatedly without further mention.

One can also recover T from P_T via *polarization*. Then (up to universal constants) $T(v_{i_1}, \ldots, v_{i_M})$, where $1 \leq i_1 \leq \cdots \leq i_M$ is the coefficient of $t_{i_1} \cdots t_{i_M}$ in $P_T(t_1 v_1 + \cdots + t_M v_M)$. See [Lan12, Chapter 2] for details.

As was mentioned in Exercise 2.3.2.4, we may also think of $S^d \mathbb{C}^M$ as the space of homogeneous differential operators of order d on $Sym(\mathbb{C}^{M*}) := \oplus_{j=0}^{\infty} S^j \mathbb{C}^{M*}$.

Thus we may view an element of $S^d \mathbb{C}^M$ as a homogeneous polynomial of degree d on $\mathbb{C}^{M*}$, a symmetric tensor, and as a homogeneous differential operator of order d on the space of polynomials $Sym(\mathbb{C}^{M*})$.

6.2.2 Catalecticants, aka the Method of Partial Derivatives

Now would be a good time to read §3.1 if you have not already done so. I review a few essential points from it.

The simplest polynomials in $S^n \mathbb{C}^N$ are just the nth powers of linear forms. Their zero set is a hyperplane (counted with multiplicity n). Let $P \in S^n \mathbb{C}^N$. How can one test if P is an nth power of a linear form, $P = \ell^n$ for some $\ell \in \mathbb{C}^N$?

Exercise 6.2.2.1 (1!) Show that $P = \ell^n$ for some $\ell \in \mathbb{C}^N$ if and only if $\dim\langle \frac{\partial P}{\partial x^1}, \ldots, \frac{\partial P}{\partial x^N} \rangle = 1$, where $x^1, \ldots, x^N$ are coordinates on $\mathbb{C}^N$.

Exercise 6.2.2.1 is indeed a polynomial test: the dual space $\mathbb{C}^{N*}$ may be considered as the space of first order homogeneous differential operators on $S^n \mathbb{C}^N$, and the test is that the 2×2 minors of the linear map $P_{1,n-1} : \mathbb{C}^{N*} \to S^{n-1}\mathbb{C}^N$, given by $\frac{\partial}{\partial x^j} \mapsto \frac{\partial P}{\partial x^j}$ are zero.

Exercise 6.2.2.1 may be phrased without reference to coordinates: recall the inclusion $S^n V \subset V \otimes S^{n-1}V = \mathrm{Hom}(V^*, S^{n-1}V)$. For $P \in S^n V$, write $P_{1,n-1} \in \mathrm{Hom}(V^*, S^{n-1}V)$.

Definition 6.2.2.2 I will say P is *concise* if $P_{1,n-1}$ is injective.

In other words, P is concise if every expression of P in coordinates uses all the variables.

Exercise 6.2.2.1 may be rephrased as follows: P is an nth power of a linear form if and only if $\mathrm{rank}(P_{1,n-1}) = 1$.

Recall that the *nth Veronese variety* is

$$v_n(\mathbb{P}V) := \{[P] \in \mathbb{P}S^n V \mid P = \ell^n \text{ for some } \ell \in V\} \subset \mathbb{P}(S^n V).$$

Exercise 6.2.2.1 shows that the Veronese variety is indeed an algebraic variety. It is homogenous, i.e., a single $GL(V)$-orbit.

More generally define the *subspace variety*

$$Sub_k(S^n V) := \mathbb{P}\{P \in S^n V \mid \mathrm{rank}(P_{1,n-1}) \le k\}.$$

Note that $[P] \in Sub_k(S^n V)$ if and only if there exists a coordinate system where P can be expressed using only k of the $\dim V$ variables. The subspace variety $Sub_k(S^n V) \subset \mathbb{P}S^n V$ has the geometric interpretation as the polynomials whose zero sets in projective space are *cones* with a $\mathbf{v} - k$ dimensional vertex. (In affine space the zero set may look like a cylinder, such as the surface $x^2 + y^2 = 1$ in $\mathbb{R}^3$.) Consider the hypersurface $X_P \subset \mathbb{P}^{k-1}$ cut out by restricting P to a subspace L where $(P|_L)_{1,n-1}$ is injective. Then points of $\mathrm{Zeros}(P) \subset \mathbb{P}V^*$ are of the form $[x + y]$ where $x \in \hat{X}_P$ and $y \in \mathbb{P}^{\mathbf{v}-k-1} = \mathbb{P}\ker(P_{1,n-1})$. See §6.4.2 for more details.

The *symmetric rank* of $P \in S^n V^*$, $\mathbf{R}_{v_n(\mathbb{P}V)}(P) = \mathbf{R}_S(P)$, is the smallest r such that $P = \ell_1^n + \cdots + \ell_r^n$ for $\ell_j \in V$. The *symmetric border rank* of P, $\underline{\mathbf{R}}_{v_n(\mathbb{P}V)}(P) = \underline{\mathbf{R}}_S(P)$, is the smallest r such that $[P] \in \sigma_r(v_n(\mathbb{P}V))$, the rth secant variety of the Veronese variety (see §4.7.1). Symmetric rank will appear naturally in the study of Valiant's hypothesis and its variants. In the language of §7.1, $\mathbf{R}_S(P)$ is essentially the size of the smallest homogeneous $\Sigma\Lambda\Sigma$-circuit computing P.

How would one test if P is the sum of two nth powers, $P = \ell_1^n + \ell_2^n$ for some $\ell_1, \ell_2 \in \mathbb{C}^N$?

Exercise 6.2.2.3 (1) Show that $P = \ell_1^n + \ell_2^n$ for some $\ell_j \in \mathbb{C}^N$ implies $\dim \mathrm{span}\{\frac{\partial P}{\partial x^1}, \ldots, \frac{\partial P}{\partial x^N} \mid 1 \le i, j \le N\} \le 2$.

Exercise 6.2.2.4 (2) Show that any polynomial vanishing on all polynomials of the form $P = \ell_1^n + \ell_2^n$ for some $\ell_j \in \mathbb{C}^N$ also vanishes on $x^{n-1}y$. ⊙

Exercise 6.2.2.4 reminds us that $\sigma_2(v_n(\mathbb{P}V))$ also includes points on tangent lines.

The condition in Exercise 6.2.2.3 is not sufficient to determine membership in $\sigma_2(v_n(\mathbb{P}V))$, in other words, $\sigma_2(v_n(\mathbb{P}V)) \subsetneq Sub_2(S^nV)$: consider $P = \ell_1^{n-2}\ell_2^2$. It has $\mathrm{rank}(P_{1,n-1}) = 2$ but $P \notin \sigma_2(v_n(\mathbb{P}V))$ as can be seen by the following exercises:

Exercise 6.2.2.5 (1) Show that $P = \ell_1^n + \ell_2^n$ for some $\ell_j \in \mathbb{C}^N$ implies $\dim \mathrm{span}\{\frac{\partial^2 P}{\partial x^i \partial x^j}\} \leq 2$.

Exercise 6.2.2.6 (1) Show that $P = \ell_1^{n-2}\ell_2^2$ for some distinct $\ell_j \in \mathbb{C}^N$ implies $\dim \mathrm{span}\{\frac{\partial^2 P}{\partial x^i \partial x^j}\} > 2$.

Let $P_{2,n-2} : S^2\mathbb{C}^{N*} \to S^{n-2}\mathbb{C}^N$ denote the map with image $\langle \cup_{i,j} \frac{\partial^2 P}{\partial x^i \partial x^j} \rangle$. Vanishing of the size three minors of $P_{1,n-1}$ and $P_{2,n-2}$ are necessary and sufficient conditions for $P \in \sigma_2(v_n(\mathbb{P}V))$, as was shown in 1886 by Gundelfinger [Gun86].

More generally, one can consider the polynomials given by the minors of the maps $S^k\mathbb{C}^{N*} \to S^{n-k}\mathbb{C}^N$, given by $D \mapsto D(P)$. Write these maps as $P_{k,n-k} : S^kV^* \to S^{n-k}V$. These equations date back to Sylvester [Syl52] and are called the *method of partial derivatives* in the complexity literature, e.g. [CKW10]. The ranks of these maps gives a complexity measure on polynomials.

Let's give a name to the varieties defined by these polynomials: define $Flat_r^{k,d-k}(S^dV) := \{P \in S^dV \mid \mathrm{rank}(P_{k,d-k}) \leq r\}$.

Exercise 6.2.2.7 (1!) What does the method of partial derivatives tell us about the complexity of $x_1 \cdots x_n$, $\det_n$ and perm_n, e.g., taking $k = \lfloor \frac{n}{2} \rfloor$? ⊙

Exercise 6.2.2.7 provides an exponential lower bound for the permanent in the complexity measure of symmetric border rank $\underline{\mathbf{R}}_S$, but we obtain the *same* lower bound for the determinant. Thus this measure will not be useful for separating the permanent from the determinant. It still gives interesting information about other polynomials such as symmetric functions, which we will examine.

The variety of homogeneous polynomials of degree n that are products of linear forms also plays a role in complexity theory. Recall the *Chow variety* of polynomials that decompose into a product of linear forms from §3.1.2:

$$Ch_n(V) := \mathbb{P}\{P \in S^nV \mid P = \ell_1 \cdots \ell_n \text{ for } \ell_j \in V\}.$$

One can define a complexity measure for writing a polynomial as a sum of products of linear forms. The "Zariski closed" version of this condition is membership in $\sigma_r(Ch_n(V))$. In the language of circuits, $\mathbf{R}_{Ch_n(V)}(P)$ is (essentially) the size of the smallest homogeneous $\Sigma\Pi\Sigma$ circuit computing a polynomial P. I discuss this in §7.5.

Exercise 6.2.2.7 gives a necessary test for a polynomial $P \in S^n\mathbb{C}^N$ to be a product of n linear forms, namely, $\mathrm{rank}(P_{\lfloor\frac{n}{2}\rfloor,\lceil\frac{n}{2}\rceil}) \leq \binom{n}{\lfloor\frac{n}{2}\rfloor}$. A question to think about: how would one develop a necessary and sufficient condition to show a polynomial $P \in S^n\mathbb{C}^N$ is a product of n linear forms? See §9.6 for an answer.

Unfortunately we have very few techniques for finding good spaces of polynomials on polynomials. One such that generalizes flattenings, called *Young flattenings*, is discussed in §8.2.

A natural question is whether all flattenings are nontrivial. I address this in §6.2.4 below after defining *conormal spaces*, which will be needed for the proof.

6.2.3 Conormal Spaces

Recall the definition of the tangent space to a point on a variety $X \subset \mathbb{P}V$ or $X \subset V$, $\hat{T}_x X \subset V$, from §3.1.3. The *conormal space* $N_x^* X \subset V^*$ is simply defined to be the annihilator of the tangent space: $N_x^* X = (\hat{T}_x X)^\perp$.

Exercise 6.2.3.1 (2!) Show that in $\hat{\sigma}_r^0(Seg(\mathbb{P}^{u-1} \times \mathbb{P}^{v-1}))$, the space of $u \times v$ matrices of rank r,

$$\hat{T}_M \sigma_r^0(Seg(\mathbb{P}^{u-1} \times \mathbb{P}^{v-1})) = \{X \in Mat_{u\times v} \mid X \ker(M) \subset \mathrm{Image}(M)\}.$$

Give a description of $N_M^* \sigma_r^0(Seg(\mathbb{P}^{u-1} \times \mathbb{P}^{v-1}))$. ⊚

6.2.4 All Flattenings Give Nontrivial Equations

The polynomials obtained from the maximal minors of $P_{i,d-i}$ give nontrivial equations. In other words, let $r_0 = r_0(i, d, \mathbf{v}) = \binom{v+i-1}{i}$. Then I claim that for $i \leq d - i$, $Flat_{r_0-1}^{i,d-i}(S^dV)$ is a proper subvariety of $\mathbb{P}S^dV$.

Exercise 6.2.4.1 (1) Show that if $P_{\lfloor\frac{d}{2}\rfloor,\lceil\frac{d}{2}\rceil}$ is of maximal rank, then all $P_{k,d-k}$ are of maximal rank.

Theorem 6.2.4.2 [Gre78, IE78] *For a general polynomial $P \in S^dV$, all the maps $P_{k,d-k} : S^kV^* \to S^{d-k}V$ are of maximal rank.*

Proof. (Adapted from [IK99]) By Exercise 6.2.4.1, it is sufficient to consider the case $k = \lfloor\frac{d}{2}\rfloor$. For each $0 \leq t \leq \binom{v+\lfloor\frac{d}{2}\rfloor-1}{\lfloor\frac{d}{2}\rfloor}$, let

$$Gor(t) := \left\{ P \in S^dV \mid \mathrm{rank} P_{\lfloor\frac{d}{2}\rfloor,\lceil\frac{d}{2}\rceil} = t \right\}.$$

("Gor" is after Gorenstein; see [IK99].) Note that $S^d V = \sqcup_t Gor(t)$. Since this is a finite union there must be exactly one t_0 such that $\overline{Gor(t_0)} = S^d V$. We want to show that $t_0 = \binom{v + \lfloor \frac{d}{2} \rfloor - 1}{\lfloor \frac{d}{2} \rfloor}$. I will do this by compuiting conormal spaces as $N_P^* Gor(t_0) = 0$ for $P \in Gor(t_0)$. Now, for any t, the subspace $N_P^* Gor(t) \subset S^d V$ satisfies

$$N_P^* Gor(t) \subset N_{P_{\lfloor \frac{d}{2} \rfloor, \lceil \frac{d}{2} \rceil}}^* \sigma_t$$

$$= N_{P_{\lfloor \frac{d}{2} \rfloor, \lceil \frac{d}{2} \rceil}}^* \sigma_t \left(Seg\left(\mathbb{P} S^{\lfloor \frac{d}{2} \rfloor} V \times \mathbb{P} S^{\lceil \frac{d}{2} \rceil} V \right) \right) \subset S^{\lfloor \frac{d}{2} \rfloor} V^* {\otimes} S^{\lceil \frac{d}{2} \rceil} V^*,$$

and $N_P^* Gor(t)$ is simply the image of $N_{P_{\lfloor \frac{d}{2} \rfloor, \lceil \frac{d}{2} \rceil}}^* \sigma_t$ under the multiplication map $S^{\lfloor \frac{d}{2} \rfloor} V^* {\otimes} S^{\lceil \frac{d}{2} \rceil} V^* \to S^d V^*$. On the other hand, by Exercise 6.2.3.1,

$$N_{P_{\lfloor \frac{d}{2} \rfloor, \lceil \frac{d}{2} \rceil}}^* \sigma_t = \ker P_{\lfloor \frac{d}{2} \rfloor, \lceil \frac{d}{2} \rceil} {\otimes} \ker P_{\lceil \frac{d}{2} \rceil, \lfloor \frac{d}{2} \rfloor}.$$

In order for $N_P^* Gor(t)$ to be zero, we need $N_{P_{\lfloor \frac{d}{2} \rfloor, \lceil \frac{d}{2} \rceil}}^* \sigma_t$ to be zero (otherwise there will be something nonzero in the image of the symmetrization map: if d is odd, the two degrees are different and this is clear; if d is even, the conormal space is the tensor product of a vector space with itself), which implies $\ker P_{\lceil \frac{d}{2} \rceil, \lfloor \frac{d}{2} \rfloor} = 0$, and thus $t_0 = \binom{v + \lfloor \frac{d}{2} \rfloor - 1}{\lfloor \frac{d}{2} \rfloor}$. $\qquad\square$

Note that the maximum symmetric border rank (in all but a few known exceptions) is $\lceil \frac{1}{v} \binom{v+d-1}{d} \rceil$, whereas flattenings only give equations up to symmetric border rank $\binom{v + \lfloor \frac{d}{2} \rfloor - 1}{\lfloor \frac{d}{2} \rfloor}$.

Another way to prove the flattenings are all nontrivial is to exhibit, for all d and $\mathbf{v}$, an explicit polynomial $P_{d,\mathbf{v}}$ with $(P_{d,\mathbf{v}})_{\lfloor \frac{d}{2} \rfloor, \lceil \frac{d}{2} \rceil}$ of maximal rank. Several such are known: the complete symmetric polynomials, see [GL17] and in even degree $d = 2k$, the polynomial $(p_{2,\mathbf{v}})^k$ (the second power sum polynomial raised to the k-th power), while in odd degree $d = 2k + 1$, the polynomial $p_{1,\mathbf{v}}(p_{2,\mathbf{v}})^k$. The first is due to Reznick [Ger89], the second in [GL17]. These two are remarkable in that they are in the complexity class $\mathbf{VP}_e$, illustrating a weakness of the method of partial derivatives as a complexity measure.

6.3 Singular Loci and Jacobian Varieties

As mentioned above, the geometry of the hypersurfaces $Zeros(\det_n)$ and $Zeros(\text{perm}_m)$ will aid us in comparing the complexity of the determinant and permanent. A simple invariant that will be useful is the dimension of the singular set of a hypersurface. The definition presented in §3.1.3 of the singular locus results in a singular locus whose dimension is not upper semicontinuous under degeneration. I first give a new definition that is semicontinuous under degeneration.

6.3.1 Definition of the (Scheme Theoretic) Singular Locus

Definition 6.3.1.1 Say a variety $X = \{P_1 = 0, \dots, P_s = 0\} \subset \mathbb{P}V$ has codimension c, using the definition of codimension in §3.1.5. Then $x \in X$ is a *singular point* if $dP_{1,x}, \dots, dP_{s,x}$ fail to span a space of dimension c. Let $X_{sing} \subset X$ denote the singular points of X. In particular, if $X = \mathrm{Zeros}(P)$ is a hypersuface and $x \in X$, then $x \in X_{sing}$ if and only if $dP_x = 0$. Note that X_{sing} is also the zero set of a collection of polynomials.

Warning: This definition is a property of the ideal generated by the polynomials $P_1, \dots, P_s$, not of X as a set. For example, every point of $(x_1^2 + \dots + x_n^2)^2 = 0$ is a singular point. In the language of algebraic geometry, one refers to the singular point of the *scheme* associated to the ideal generated by $\{P_1 = 0, \dots, P_s = 0\}$.

"Most" hypersurfaces $X \subset \mathbb{P}V$ are smooth, in the sense that $\{P \in \mathbb{P}S^dV \mid \mathrm{Zeros}(P)_{sing} \neq \emptyset\} \subset \mathbb{P}S^dV$ is a hypersurface, see, e.g., [Lan12, §8.2.1]. The dimension of $\mathrm{Zeros}(P)_{sing}$ is a measure of the pathology of P.

Singular loci will also be used in the determination of symmetry groups.

6.3.2 Jacobian Varieties

While the ranks of symmetric flattenings are the same for the permanent and determinant, by looking more closely at the maps, we can extract geometric information that distinguishes them.

First, for $P \in S^nV$, consider the images $P_{k,n-k}(S^kV^*) \subset S^{n-k}V$. This is a space of polynomials, and we can consider the ideal they generate, called the *kth Jacobian ideal of P*, and the common zero set of these polynomials, called the *kth Jacobian variety of P*:

$$\mathrm{Zeros}(P)_{Jac,k} := \{[\alpha] \in \mathbb{P}V^* \mid q(\alpha) = 0 \ \forall q \in P_{k,n-k}(S^kV^*)\}.$$

Exercise 6.3.2.1 (1) Show that $\mathrm{Zeros}(\det_n)_{Jac,k}$ is $\sigma_{n-k-1}(Seg(\mathbb{P}^{n-1} \times \mathbb{P}^{n-1}))$, the matrices of rank at most $n - k - 1$.

It is not known what the varieties $\mathrm{Zeros}(\mathrm{perm}_m)_{Jac,k}$ are in general. I explicitly determine $\mathrm{Zeros}(\mathrm{perm}_m)_{Jac,m-2}$ in Lemma 6.3.3.4 below as it is used to prove the symmetries of the permanent are what we expect them to be.

6.3.3 Singularities of $\mathrm{Zeros}(\mathrm{perm}_m)$

In contrast to the determinant, the singular set of the permanent is not understood; even its codimension is not known. The problem is more difficult because, unlike in the determinant case, we do not have normal forms for points on Zeros($perm_m$). In this section I show that $\text{codim}(\text{Zeros}(perm_m)_{sing}) \geq 5$.

Exercise 6.3.3.1 (1!) Show that the permanent admits a "Laplace type" expansion similar to that of the determinant.

Exercise 6.3.3.2 (2) Show that Zeros($perm_m$)$_{sing}$ consists of the $m \times m$ matrices with the property that all size $m - 1$ submatrices of it have permanent zero.

Exercise 6.3.3.3 (1) Show that Zeros($perm_m$)$_{sing}$ has codimension at most $2m$ in $\mathbb{C}^{m^2}$. ⊚

Since Zeros($perm_2$)$_{sing} = \emptyset$, let's start with $perm_3$. Since we will need it later, I prove a more general result:

Lemma 6.3.3.4 *The variety* Zeros($perm_m$)$_{Jac,m-2}$ *is the union of the following varieties:*

1 *Matrices A with all entries zero except those in a single size 2 submatrix, and that submatrix has zero permanent.*
2 *Matrices A with all entries zero except those in the jth row for some j.*
3 *Matrices A with all entries zero except those in the jth column for some j.*

In other words, let $X \subset Mat_m(\mathbb{C})$ *denote the subvariety of matrices that are zero except in the upper* 2×2 *corner and that* 2×2 *submatrix has zero permanent, and let Y denote the variety of matrices that are zero except in the first row, then*

$$\text{Zeros}(perm_m)_{Jac,m-2} = \bigcup_{\sigma \in (\mathfrak{S}_m \times \mathfrak{S}_m) \rtimes \mathbb{Z}_2} \sigma \cdot X \sqcup \sigma \cdot Y. \qquad (6.3.1)$$

Here $\mathfrak{S}_m \times \mathfrak{S}_m$ acts by left and right multiplication by permutation matrices and the $\mathbb{Z}_2$ is generated by sending a matrix to its transpose.

The proof is straightforward. Here is the main idea: take a matrix with entries that don't fit that pattern, e.g., one that begins

$$\begin{array}{ccc} a & b & e \\ * & d & *, \end{array}$$

and note that it is not possible to fill in the two unknown entries and have all size two subpermanents, even in this corner, zero. There are just a few such cases since we are free to act by $(\mathfrak{S}_m \times \mathfrak{S}_m) \rtimes \mathbb{Z}_2 \subset G_{perm_m}$.

Corollary 6.3.3.5

$$\{\mathrm{perm}_3 = 0\}_{sing} = \bigcup_{\sigma \in (\mathfrak{S}_3 \times \mathfrak{S}_3) \rtimes \mathbb{Z}_2} \sigma \cdot X \cup \sigma \cdot Y.$$

In particular, all the irreducible components of $\{\mathrm{perm}_3 = 0\}_{sing}$ have the same dimension and $codim(\{\mathrm{perm}_3 = 0\}_{sing}, \mathbb{C}^9) = 6$.

This equidimensionality property already fails for perm_4: consider

$$\left\{ \begin{pmatrix} x_1^1 & x_2^1 & 0 & 0 \\ x_1^2 & x_2^2 & 0 & 0 \\ 0 & 0 & x_3^3 & x_4^3 \\ 0 & 0 & x_3^4 & x_4^4 \end{pmatrix} \mid x_1^1 x_2^2 + x_1^2 x_2^1 = 0,\; x_3^3 x_4^4 + x_3^4 x_4^3 = 0 \right\}.$$

This defines a six-dimensional irreducible component of $\{\mathrm{perm}_4 = 0\}_{sing}$ which is not contained in either a space of matrices with just two nonzero rows (or columns) or the set of matrices that are zero except for in some 3×3 submatrix which has zero permanent. In [vzG87] von zur Gathen states that all components of $\{\mathrm{perm}_4 = 0\}_{sing}$ are either of dimension six or eight.

Although we do not know the codimension of $\mathrm{Zeros}(\mathrm{perm}_m)_{sing}$, the following estimate will suffice for the application of von zur Gathen's regularity theorem 6.3.4.1 below.

Proposition 6.3.3.6 (von zur Gathen [vzG87])

$$codim(\mathrm{Zeros}(\mathrm{perm}_m)_{sing}, \mathbb{P}^{m^2-1}) \geq 5.$$

Proof. I work by induction on m. Since $\mathrm{Zeros}(\mathrm{perm}_2)$ is a smooth quadric, the base case is established. Let I, J be multi-indices of the same size and let $sp(I|J)$ denote the subpermanent of the $(m - |I|, m - |I|)$ submatrix omitting the index sets (I, J). Let $C \subset \mathrm{Zeros}(\mathrm{perm}_m)_{sing}$ be an irreducible component of the singular set. If $sp(i_1, i_2|j_1, j_2)|_C = 0$ for all $(i_1, i_2|j_1, j_2)$, we are done by induction as then $C \subset \bigcup_{i,j} \mathrm{Zeros}(sp(i|j))_{sing}$. So assume there is at least one size $m - 2$ subpermanent that is not identically zero on C, without loss of generality assume it is $sp(m - 1, m|m - 1, m)$. We have, via permanental Laplace expansions,

$$0 = sp(m, m)|_C$$
$$= \sum_{j-1}^{m-2} x_{m-1}^j sp(i, m|m - 1, m) + x_{m-1}^{m-1} sp(m - 1, m|m - 1, m),$$

so on a Zariski open subset of C, x_{m-1}^{m-1} is a function of the $m^2 - 4$ variables x_t^s, $(s, t) \notin \{(m - 1, m - 1), (m - 1, m), (m, m - 1), (m, m)\}$, Similar expansions give us x_m^{m-1}, x_{m-1}^m, and x_m^m as functions of the other variables, so we conclude

$\dim C \leq m^2 - 4$. We need to find one more nonzero polynomial that vanishes identically on C that does not involve the variables $x_{m-1}^{m-1}, x_{m-1}^{m}, x_{m}^{m-1}, x_{m}^{m}$ to obtain another relation and to conclude $\dim C \leq m^2 - 5$. Consider

$$sp(m-1, m|m-1, m)sp(m-2, m) - sp(m-2, m|m-1, m)sp(m-1, m)$$
$$- sp(m-2, m-1|m-1, m)sp(m, m)$$
$$= -2x_{m-1}^{m-2}sp(m-2, m-1|m-1, m)sp(m-2, m|m-1, m)$$
$$+ \text{terms not involving } x_{m-1}^{m-2},$$

where we obtained the second line by permanental Laplace expansions in the size $m - 1$ subpermanents in the expression, and arranged things such that all terms with $x_{m-1}^{m-1}, x_{m-1}^{m}, x_{m}^{m-1}, x_{m}^{m}$ appearing cancel. Since this expression is a sum of terms divisible by size $m - 1$ subpermanents, it vanishes identically on C. But $2x_{m-1}^{m-2}sp(m-2, m-1|m-1, m)sp(m-2, m|m-1, m)$ is not the zero polynomial, so the whole expression is not the zero polynomial. Thus we obtain another nonzero polynomial that vanishes identically on C and is not in the ideal generated by the previous four as it does not involve any of $x_{m-1}^{m-1}, x_{m-1}^{m}, x_{m}^{m-1}, x_{m}^{m}$. $\qquad\square$

It is embarrassing that the following question is still open:

Question 6.3.3.7 What is $\mathrm{codim}(\mathrm{Zeros}(\mathrm{perm}_m)_{sing})$?

6.3.4 von zur Gathen's Regularity Theorem and Its Consequences for Lower Bounds

Proposition 6.3.4.1 (von zur Gathen [vzG87], also see [ABV15]) *Let $M > 4$, and let $P \in S^m\mathbb{C}^M$ be concise and satisfy $\mathrm{codim}(\{P = 0\}_{sing}, \mathbb{C}^M) \geq 5$. If $P = \det_n \circ \tilde{A}$, where $\tilde{A} = \Lambda + A : \mathbb{C}^M \to \mathbb{C}^{n^2}$ is an affine linear map with Λ constant and A linear, then $\mathrm{rank}(\Lambda) = n - 1$.*

Proof. I first claim that if $\tilde{A}(y) \in \mathrm{Zeros}(\det_n)_{sing}$, then $y \in \mathrm{Zeros}(P)_{sing}$. To see this, note that for any $y \in \mathbb{C}^M$, the differential of P at y satisfies (by the chain rule)

$$dP|_y = d(\det_n \circ \tilde{A})|_y = A^T(d(\det_n)|_{\tilde{A}(y)}),$$

where I have used that $d(\det_n)|_{\tilde{A}(y)} \in T^*_{\tilde{A}(y)}\mathbb{C}^{n^2} \simeq \mathbb{C}^{n^2 *}$ and $A^T : \mathbb{C}^{n^2 *} \to \mathbb{C}^{M*}$ is the transpose of the differential of $\tilde{A}$. In particular, if $d(\det_n)|_{\tilde{A}(y)} = 0$ then $dP_y = 0$, which is what we needed to show.

Now by Theorem 3.1.5.1, the set

$$\tilde{A}(\mathbb{C}^M) \cap \mathrm{Zeros}(\det_n)_{sing} \subset \mathbb{C}^{n^2}$$

is either empty or of dimension at least $\dim(\tilde{A}(\mathbb{C}^M)) + \dim(\text{Zeros}(\det_n)_{sing}) - n^2 = M + (n^2 - 4) - n^2 = M - 4$. (Here $\tilde{A}$ must be injective as P is concise.) The same is true for $\tilde{A}^{-1}(\tilde{A}(\mathbb{C}^M) \cap \text{Zeros}(\det_n)_{sing})$. But this latter set is contained in $\text{Zeros}(P)_{sing}$, which is of dimension at most $M - 5$, so we conclude it is empty.

Thus for all $y \in \mathbb{C}^M$, $\text{rank}(\tilde{A}(y)) \geq n - 1$. In particular $\text{rank}(\tilde{A}(0)) \geq n - 1$, but $\tilde{A}(0) = \Lambda$. Finally equality holds because if Λ had rank n, then $\det(\tilde{A}(\mathbb{C}^M))$ would have a constant term. $\qquad \square$

Exercise 6.3.4.2 (1) Prove that any polynomial $P \in S^d \mathbb{C}^M$ with singular locus of codimension greater than four must have $\text{dc}(P) > d$.

Proposition 6.3.4.3 [Cai90] *Let $F \subset Mat_n(\mathbb{C})$ be an affine linear subspace such that for all $X \in F$, $\text{rank}(F) \geq n - 1$. Then $\dim F \leq \binom{n+1}{2} + 1$.*

For the proof, see [Cai90]. Note that Proposition 6.3.4.3 is near-optimal, as consider F the set of upper triangular matrices with 1s on the diagonal, which has dimension $\binom{n}{2}$.

Exercise 6.3.4.4 (2) Use Proposition 6.3.4.3 to show $\text{dc}(\text{perm}_m) \geq \sqrt{2}m$.

Exercise 6.3.4.5 (2) Let $Q \subset \mathbb{P}^{n+1}$ be a smooth quadric hypersurface of dimension n. Show that the maximum dimension of a linear projective space contained in Q is $\lfloor \frac{n}{2} \rfloor$. ⊚

Theorem 6.3.4.6 (Alper-Bogart-Velasco [ABV15]) *Let $P \in S^d \mathbb{C}^M$ with $d \geq 3$ and such that $codim(\text{Zeros}(P)_{sing}, \mathbb{C}^M) \geq 5$. Then*

$$\text{dc}(P) \geq codim(\text{Zeros}(P)_{sing}, \mathbb{C}^M) + 1.$$

Proof. Let $n = \text{dc}(P)$. Say $P = \det_n \circ \tilde{A}$, with $\tilde{A} = \Lambda + A$. By Proposition 6.3.4.1, $\text{rank}(\Lambda) = n - 1$, and using $G_{\det_n}$, we may assume Λ is normalized to the matrix that is zero everywhere but the diagonal, where it has one's except in the $(1, 1)$-slot where it is zero. Expand $\det(\tilde{A}(y)) = p_0 + p_1 + \cdots + p_n$ as a sum of homogeneous polynomials. Since the right-hand side equals P, we must have $p_j = 0$ for $j < d$. Then $p_0 = \det(\Lambda) = 0$ and $p_1 = A_1^1$. Now $p_2 = \sum_{i=2}^n A_i^1 A_1^i = 0$ and more generally, each p_j is a sum of monomials, each of which contains an element in the first column and an element in the first row of A. Each A_j^i is a linear form on $\mathbb{C}^M$ and as such, we can consider the intersection of their kernels. Write $\Gamma = \cap_{i=1}^{n-1}(\ker A_1^i) \cap (\ker A_i^1)$. Then $\Gamma \subset \text{Zeros}(P)_{sing}$. Consider the A_i^1, A_1^j as coordinates on $\mathbb{C}^{2(n-1)}$, p_2 defines a smooth quadric hypersurface in $\mathbb{P}^{2(n-1)-1}$. By Exercise 6.3.4.5, the maximum dimension of a linear space on such a quadric is $n - 1$, so the rank of the linear

Figure 6.4.1 The shaded area of the surface maps to the shaded area of the sphere.

map $\mathbb{C}^M \to \mathbb{C}^{2(n-1)}$ given by $y \mapsto (A_i^1(y), A_1^j(y))$ is at most $n-1$. But Γ is the kernel of this map. We have

$$n - 1 \geq \mathrm{codim}(\Gamma) \geq \mathrm{codim}(\mathrm{Zeros}(P)_{sing}, \mathbb{C}^M),$$

and recalling that $n = \mathrm{dc}(P)$, we conclude. $\qquad\qquad\square$

Exercise 6.3.4.7 (2) Prove that $\mathrm{codim}((\mathrm{perm}_m)_{sing}) = 2m$ when $m = 3, 4$.

Corollary 6.3.4.8 [ABV15] $\mathrm{dc}(\mathrm{perm}_3) = 7$ *and* $\mathrm{dc}(\mathrm{perm}_4) \geq 9$.

The upper bound for $\mathrm{dc}(\mathrm{perm}_3)$ is from (1.2.3).

Even if one could prove $\mathrm{codim}((\mathrm{perm}_m)_{sing}) = 2m$ for all m, the above theorem would only give a linear bound on $\mathrm{dc}(\mathrm{perm}_m)$. This bound would be obtained from taking one derivative. In the next section, I show that taking two derivatives, one can get a quadratic bound.

6.4 Geometry and the State of the Art Regarding dc(perm$_m$)

In mathematics, one often makes transforms to reorganize information, e.g., the Fourier transform. There are geometric transforms to "reorganize" the information in an algebraic variety. Taking the Gauss image (dual variety) of a hypersurface is one such, as I now describe.

6.4.1 Gauss Maps

A classical construction for the geometry of surfaces in 3-space is the *Gauss map*, which maps a point of the surface to its unit normal vector on the unit sphere, as in Figure 6.4.1.

This Gauss image can be defined for a surface in $\mathbb{P}^3$ without the use of a distance function if one instead takes the union of all *conormal lines* (see §6.2.3) in $\mathbb{P}^{3*}$. Let $S^\vee \subset \mathbb{P}^{3*}$ denote this Gauss image, also called the *dual variety* of S. One loses information in this setting, however one still has the information of the *dimension* of $S^\vee$.

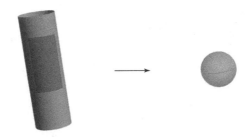

Figure 6.4.2 Lines on the cylinder are collapsed to a point.

This dimension will drop if through all points of the surface there is a curve along which the tangent plane is constant. For example, if M is a cylinder, i.e., the union of lines in three space perpendicular to a plane curve, the Gauss image is a curve (Figure 6.4.2).

The extreme case is when the surface is a plane, then its Gauss image is just a point.

6.4.2 What Do Surfaces with Degenerate Gauss Maps "Look Like"?

Here is a generalization of the cylinder above: consider a curve $C \subset \mathbb{P}^3$, and a point $p \in \mathbb{P}^3$. Define *the cone over C with vertex p*,

$$J(C, p) := \{[x] \in \mathbb{P}^3 \mid x = y + \overline{p} \text{ for some } y \in \hat{C}, \ \overline{p} \in \hat{p}\}.$$

Exercise 6.4.2.1 (1) Show that if $p \neq y$, $\hat{T}_{[\overline{y}+\overline{p}]}J(C, p) = \text{span}\{\hat{T}_y C, \hat{p}\}$.

Thus the tangent space to the cone is constant along the rulings, and the surface only has a curve's worth of tangent (hyper-)planes, so its dual variety is degenerate.

Exercise 6.4.2.2 (2) More generally, let $X \subset \mathbb{P}V$ be an irreducible variety and let $L \subset \mathbb{P}V$ be a linear space. Define $J(X, L)$, the *cone* over X with vertex L analogously. Show that given $x \in X_{smooth}$, with $x \notin L$, the tangent space to $J(X, L)^\vee$ at $[\overline{x} + \overline{\ell}]$ is constant for all $\ell \in L$.

Here is another type of surface with a degenerate Gauss map: consider again a curve $C \subset \mathbb{P}^3$, and this time let $\tau(C) \subset \mathbb{P}^3$ denote the Zariski closure of the union of all points on $\mathbb{P}\hat{T}_x C$ as x ranges over the smooth points of C. The variety $\tau(C)$ is called the *tangential variety* to the curve C.

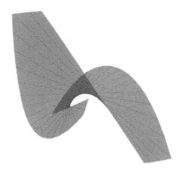

Exercise 6.4.2.3 (2) Show that if $y_1, y_2 \in \tau(C)$ are both on a tangent line to $x \in C$, then $\hat{T}_{y_1} \tau(C) = \hat{T}_{y_2} \tau(C)$, and thus $\tau(C)^{\vee}$ is degenerate. ⊚

In 1910, C. Segre proved that the above two examples are the only surfaces with degenerate dual varieties:

Theorem 6.4.2.4 [Seg10, p. 105] *Let $S^2 \subset \mathbb{P}^3$ be a surface with degenerate Gauss image. Then S is one of the following:*

1 *A linearly embedded $\mathbb{P}^2$,*
2 *A cone over a curve C, or*
3 *A tangential variety to a curve C.*

Case (1) is a special case of both (2) and (3) and is the only intersection of the two.

The proof is differential-geometric; see [IL16b, §4.3].

6.4.3 Dual Varieties

If $X \subset \mathbb{P}V$ is an irreducible hypersurface, the Zariski closure of its Gauss image will be a projective subvariety of $\mathbb{P}V^*$. Gauss images of hypersurfaces are special cases of *dual varieties*. For an irreducible variety $X \subset \mathbb{P}V$, define $X^{\vee} \subset \mathbb{P}V^*$, the *dual variety of X*, by

$$X^{\vee} := \overline{\{H \in \mathbb{P}V^* \mid \exists x \in X_{smooth}, \ \hat{T}_x X \subseteq \hat{H}\}}$$
$$= \overline{\{H \in \mathbb{P}V^* \mid \exists x \in X_{smooth}, \ H \in \mathbb{P}N_x^* X\}}.$$

Here H refers both to a point in $\mathbb{P}V^*$ and the hyperplane in $\mathbb{P}V$ it determines.

That the dual variety is indeed a variety may be seen by considering the following *incidence correspondence*:

$$\mathcal{I} := \overline{\{(x, H) \in X_{smooth} \times \mathbb{P}V^* \mid \mathbb{P}\hat{T}_x X \subseteq H\}} \subset \mathbb{P}V \times \mathbb{P}V^*,$$

and note that its image under the projections to $\mathbb{P}V$ and $\mathbb{P}V^*$ are, respectively, X and $X^\vee$. When X is smooth, $\mathcal{I} = \mathbb{P}N^*X$, the projectivized conormal bundle. Both projections are surjective regular maps, so by Theorem 3.1.4.1, $X^\vee$ is an irreducible variety.

Exercise 6.4.3.1 (2) Show

$$\mathcal{I} = \overline{\{(x, H) \in \mathbb{P}V \times (X^\vee)_{smooth} \mid \mathbb{P}\hat{T}_H X^\vee \subseteq x\}} \subset \mathbb{P}V \times \mathbb{P}V^*$$

and thus $(X^\vee)^\vee = X$. (This is called the *reflexivity theorem* and dates back to C. Segre.) ⊚

For our purposes, the most important property of dual varieties is that for a smooth hypersurface other than a hyperplane, its dual variety is also a hypersurface. This will be a consequence of the B. Segre dimension formula 6.4.5.1 below. If the dual of $X \subset \mathbb{P}V$ is not a hypersurface, one says that *X has a degenerate dual variety*. It is a classical problem to study the varieties with degenerate dual varieties.

Exercise 6.4.2.2 shows that higher-dimensional cones have degenerate dual varieties. Griffiths and Harris [GH79] vaguely conjectured a higher-dimensional generalization of C. Segre's theorem, namely, that a variety with a degenerate dual is "built out of" cones and tangent developables. For example, Zeros($\det_n$) may be thought of as the union of tangent lines to tangent lines to ... to the Segre variety $Seg(\mathbb{P}^{n-1} \times \mathbb{P}^{n-1})$, and we will see that it indeed has a degenerate dual variety.

Segre's theorem indicates that if we take the Zariski closure in $\mathbb{P}S^d V^*$ of the set of irreducible hypersurfaces of degree d with degenerate dual varieties, we will obtain a reducible variety. This will complicate the use of dual varieties for Valiant's hypothesis.

For more on dual varieties, see [Lan12, §8.2].

6.4.4 Zeros($\det_n$)$_{sing}$

As far as singularities are concerned, the determinant is quite pathological: thanks to $G_{\det_n}$, the determination of Zeros($\det_n$)$_{sing}$ is easy to describe. Any point of Zeros($\det_n$) is in the $G_{\det_n}$-orbit of some

$$p_r := \begin{pmatrix} \mathrm{Id}_r & 0 \\ 0 & 0 \end{pmatrix}, \tag{6.4.1}$$

where $1 \leq r \leq n - 1$ and the blocking is $(r, n - r) \times (r, n - r)$. The nature of the singularity of $x \in \text{Zeros}(\det_n)$ is the same as that of the corresponding p_r.

Recall that $\sigma_r = \sigma_r(Seg(\mathbb{P}^{n-1} \times \mathbb{P}^{n-1})) \subset \mathbb{P}(\mathbb{C}^n \otimes \mathbb{C}^n)$ is the set of matrices (up to scale) of rank at most r.

The smooth points of $\text{Zeros}(\det_n) = \sigma_{n-1}$ are those in the $G_{\det_n}$-orbit of p_{n-1}, as shown by the following exercises:

Exercise 6.4.4.1 (1) Show that $d(\det_n)_{p_{n-1}} = dx_n^n$.

Exercise 6.4.4.2 (1) Show that $\text{Zeros}(\det_n)_{sing} = \sigma_{n-2}$.

Exercise 6.4.4.3 (1) Show that $\sigma_r = \text{Zeros}(\det_n)_{Jac,n-r}$.

Exercise 6.2.3.1 implies $\dim \sigma_r(Seg(\mathbb{P}^{u-1} \times \mathbb{P}^{v-1})) = r(u + v - r) - 1$.

6.4.5 What does this have to do with Complexity Theory?

Having a degenerate dual variety is a pathology, and our dimension calculation below will show that if $Q \in S^m \mathbb{C}^M$ is an irreducible polynomial such that Q is an affine linear degeneration of an irreducible polynomial P, then $\dim(\text{Zeros}(Q)^\vee) \leq \dim(\text{Zeros}(P)^\vee)$.

To determine the dual variety of $\text{Zeros}(\det_n) \subset \mathbb{P}(E \otimes F)$, recall that any smooth point of $\text{Zeros}(\det_n)$ is $G_{\det_n}$-equivalent to

$$
p_{n-1} = \begin{pmatrix} 1 & & & \\ & \ddots & & \\ & & 1 & \\ & & & 0 \end{pmatrix} \in \text{Zeros}(\det_n)
$$

and that

$$
N^*_{p_{n-1}} \text{Zeros}(\det_n) = \begin{pmatrix} 0 & 0 & 0 & 0 \\ \vdots & \ddots & \vdots & \vdots \\ 0 & 0 & 0 & 0 \\ 0 & 0 & 0 & * \end{pmatrix}.
$$

Since any smooth point of $\text{Zeros}(\det_n)$ can be moved to p_{n-1} by a change of basis, we conclude that the tangent hyperplanes to $\text{Zeros}(\det_n)$ are parametrized by the rank one matrices $Seg(\mathbb{P}E^* \otimes \mathbb{P}F^*)$, which has dimension $2n - 2$, because they are obtained by multiplying a column vector by a row vector.

Proposition 6.4.5.1 (B. Segre) *Let $P \in S^d V^*$ be irreducible and let $[x] \in \text{Zeros}(P)$ be a general point. Then*

$$\dim \text{Zeros}(P)^\vee = \text{rank}(P_{d-2,2}(x^{d-2})) - 2. \tag{6.4.2}$$

Here $P_{d-2,2}(x^{d-2}) \in S^2V^*$, and we are computing the rank of this symmetric matrix. In coordinates, $P_{d-2,2}$ may be written as a symmetric matrix whose entries are polynomials of degree $d - 2$ in the coordinates of x, and is called the *Hesssian*.

Proof. Let $x \in \hat{\text{Zeros}}(P) \subset V$ be a general point, so $P(x) = \overline{P}(x, \ldots, x) = 0$ and $dP_x = \overline{P}(x, \ldots, x, \cdot) \neq 0$ and take $h = dP_x \in V^*$, so $[h] \in \text{Zeros}(P)^\vee$. Now consider a curve $h_t \subset \hat{\text{Zeros}}(P)^\vee$ with $h_0 = h$. There must be a corresponding (possibly stationary) curve $x_t \in \hat{\text{Zeros}}(P)$ such that $h_t = \overline{P}(x_t, \ldots, x_t, \cdot)$ and thus $h'_0 = (d - 1)\overline{P}(x^{d-2}, x'_0, \cdot)$. Thus the dimension of $\hat{T}_h\text{Zeros}(P)^\vee$ is the rank of $P_{d-2,2}(x^{d-2})$ minus one (we subtract one because we are only allowed to feed in vectors x'_0 that are tangent to $\text{Zeros}(P)$). Now just recall that $\dim Z = \dim \hat{T}_z Z - 1$. We needed x to be general to insure that $[h]$ is a smooth point of $\text{Zeros}(P)^\vee$. $\qquad\square$

Exercise 6.4.5.2 (1) Show that if $Q \in S^m\mathbb{C}^M$ and there exists $\tilde{A} : \mathbb{C}^M \to \mathbb{C}^N$ such that $Q(y) = P(\tilde{A}(y))$ for all $y \in \mathbb{C}^{M*}$, then $\text{rank}(Q_{m-2,2}(y)) \leq \text{rank}(P_{m-2,m}(\tilde{A}(y)))$.

Exercise 6.4.5.3 (1) Show that every $P \in Sub_k(S^dV)$ has $\dim \text{Zeros}(P)^\vee \leq k - 2$.

Exercise 6.4.5.4 (2) Show that $\sigma_3(Ch_n(\mathbb{C}^{n^2})) \not\subset \mathcal{D}et_n$.

Exercise 6.4.5.5 (2) Show that $\sigma_{2n+1}(v_n(\mathbb{P}^{n^2-1})) \not\subset \mathcal{D}et_n$.

Exercise 6.4.5.6 (2) Show that $\{x_1 \cdots x_n + y_1 \cdots y_n = 0\} \subset \mathbb{P}^{2n-1}$ is self-dual, in the sense that it is isomorphic to its own dual variety.

To show a hypersurface has a nondegenerate dual variety, it suffices to find a point where the Hessian of its defining equation has maximal rank.

6.4.6 Permanent Case

Consider the point

$$
y_0 - \begin{pmatrix} 1 - m & 1 & \cdots & 1 \\ 1 & 1 & \cdots & 1 \\ & \vdots & & \\ 1 & 1 & \cdots & 1 \end{pmatrix}.
$$

Exercise 6.4.6.1 (1!) Show $\text{perm}(y_0) = 0$. ◎

Now compute $(\mathrm{perm}_m)_{m-2,2}(y_0)$: first note that

$$\frac{\partial}{\partial y_j^i}\frac{\partial}{\partial y_l^k}\mathrm{perm}_m(y) = \begin{cases} 0 & \text{if } i = k \text{ or } j = l \\ \mathrm{perm}_{m-2}\left(y_{\hat{j}\hat{l}}^{\hat{i}\hat{k}}\right) & \text{otherwise,} \end{cases}$$

where $y_{\hat{j}\hat{l}}^{\hat{i}\hat{k}}$ is the size $(m-2) \times (m-2)$ matrix obtained by removing rows i, k and columns j, l.

Exercise 6.4.6.2 (2) Show that if we order indices $y_1^1, \ldots, y_1^m, y_2^1, \ldots, y_2^m, \ldots, y_m^m$, then the Hessian matrix of the permanent at y_0 takes the form

$$\begin{pmatrix} 0 & Q & Q & \cdots & Q \\ Q & 0 & R & \cdots & R \\ Q & R & 0 & \ddots & \vdots \\ \vdots & \vdots & \ddots & \ddots & R \\ Q & R & \cdots & R & 0 \end{pmatrix}, \tag{6.4.3}$$

where

$$Q = (m-2)\begin{pmatrix} 0 & 1 & \cdots & 1 \\ 1 & 0 & \ddots & \vdots \\ \vdots & \ddots & \ddots & 1 \\ 1 & \cdots & 1 & 0 \end{pmatrix},$$

$$R = \begin{pmatrix} 0 & m-2 & m-2 & \cdots & m-2 \\ m-2 & 0 & -2 & \cdots & -2 \\ m-2 & -2 & 0 & \ddots & \vdots \\ \vdots & \vdots & \ddots & \ddots & -2 \\ m-2 & -2 & \cdots & -2 & 0 \end{pmatrix}.$$

Lemma 6.4.6.3 *Let Q, R be invertible $m \times m$ matrices and let M be an $m^2 \times m^2$ matrix of the form (6.4.3). Then M is invertible.*

Proof. Without loss of generality, we may assume $Q = \mathrm{Id}_m$ by multiplying on the left and right by the block diagonal matrix whose block diagonals are $Q^{-1}, \mathrm{Id}_m, \ldots, \mathrm{Id}_m$. Let $v = (v_1, \ldots, v_m)^T$, where $v_j \in \mathbb{C}^m$, be a vector in the kernel. Then we have the equations

$$v_2 + \cdots + v_m = 0,$$
$$v_1 + Rv_3 + \cdots + Rv_m = 0,$$
$$\vdots$$
$$v_1 + Rv_2 + \cdots + Rv_{m-1} = 0,$$

i.e.,

$$v_2 + \cdots + v_m = 0,$$
$$v_1 - Rv_2 = 0,$$
$$\vdots$$
$$v_1 - Rv_m = 0.$$

Multiply the first line by R to conclude $(m-1)v_1 = 0$ and hence $v_1 = 0$, and the remaining equations imply the other $v_j = 0$. $\qquad\square$

Thus the permanent hypersurface $\mathrm{Zeros}(\mathrm{perm}_m) \subset \mathbb{P}^{m^2-1}$ has a non-degenerate Gauss map. When one includes $\mathbb{C}^{m^2} \subset \mathbb{C}^{n^2}$, so the equation $\mathrm{Zeros}(\mathrm{perm}_m)$ becomes an equation in a space of n^2 variables that only uses m^2 of the variables, one gets a cone with vertex $\mathbb{P}^{n^2-m^2-1}$ corresponding to the unused variables, in particular, the Gauss image will have dimension $m^2 - 2$.

If one makes an affine linear substitution $X = X(Y)$, by the chain rule, the Gauss map of $\{\det(X(Y)) = 0\}$ will be at least as degenerate as the Gauss map of $\{\det(X) = 0\}$ by Exercise 6.4.5.2. Using this, one obtains the following:

Theorem 6.4.6.4 (Mignon-Ressayre [MR04]) *If $n(m) < \frac{m^2}{2}$, then there do not exist affine linear functions $x_j^i(y_t^s)$, $1 \le i, j \le n$, $1 \le s, t \le m$ such that $\mathrm{perm}_m(Y) = \det_n(X(Y))$. I.e., $\mathrm{dc}(\mathrm{perm}_m) \ge \frac{m^2}{2}$.*

Remark 6.4.6.5 We saw a linear lower bound by taking one derivative and a quadratic lower bound by taking two. Unfortunately, it does not appear to be possible to improve the Mignon-Ressayre bound by taking three derivatives.

6.5 Extension of the Mignon-Ressayre Result to $\overline{\mathrm{dc}}$

To extend the Mignon-Ressayre theorem to $\overline{\mathrm{dc}}$, we will need to find polynomials on $\mathbb{P}S^n V$ that vanish on the hypersurfaces with degenerate dual varieties. This was a classically studied question whose answer was known only in a very few number of small cases. In this section I present an answer to the classical question and its application to Conjecture 1.2.5.2.

6.5.1 First Steps Toward Equations

Let $P \in S^d V^*$ be irreducible. Segre's formula (6.4.2) may be restated as follows: $\dim \mathrm{Zeros}(P)^\vee \leq k$ if and only if, for all $w \in V$,

$$P(w) = 0 \;\Rightarrow\; \det_{k+3}(P_{d-2,2}(w^{d-2})|_F) = 0 \;\forall F \in G(k+3, V). \quad (6.5.1)$$

Here $G(k+3, V)$ is the Grassmannian of $(k+3)$-planes through the origin in V (see Definition 2.3.3.1). Equivalently, for any $F \in G(k+3, V)$, the polynomial P must divide $\det_{k+3}(P_{d-2,2}|_F) \in S^{(k+3)(d-2)} V^*$, where $\det_{k+3}$ is evaluated on the $S^2 V^*$ factor in $S^2 V^* \otimes S^{d-2} V^*$.

Thus to find polynomials on $S^d V^*$ characterizing hypersurfaces with degenerate duals, we need polynomials that detect if a polynomial P divides a polynomial Q. Now, $P \in S^d V^*$ divides $Q \in S^e V^*$ if and only if $Q \in P \cdot S^{e-d} V^*$, i.e.,

$$x^{I_1} P \wedge \cdots \wedge x^{I_D} P \wedge Q = 0,$$

where x^{I_j} is a basis of $S^{e-d} V$ (and $D = \binom{v+e-d-1}{e-d}$). Let $\mathcal{D}_{k,d,N} \subset \mathbb{P}S^d \mathbb{C}^N$ denote the zero set of these equations when $Q = \det_{k+3}(P_{d-2,2}|_F)$ as F ranges over $G(k+3, V)$.

Define $Dual_{k,d,N} \subset \mathbb{P}(S^d V^*)$ as the Zariski closure of the set of irreducible hypersurfaces of degree d in $\mathbb{P}V \simeq \mathbb{P}^{N-1}$, whose dual variety has dimension at most k. Our discussion above implies $Dual_{k,d,N} \subseteq \mathcal{D}_{k,d,N}$.

Note that

$$[\det_n] \in Dual_{2n-2,n,n^2} \subseteq \mathcal{D}_{2n-2,n,n^2}. \quad (6.5.2)$$

6.5.2 The Lower Bound on $\overline{dc}(\mathrm{perm}_m)$

The calculation of §6.4.6 shows that $\mathrm{perm}_{m-2,2}(y_0^{m-2})$ is of maximal rank. Here we don't have perm_m but rather $\ell^{n-m} \, \mathrm{perm}_m$.

Proposition 6.5.2.1 [LMR13] *Let* $U = \mathbb{C}^M$, *let* $R \in S^m U^*$ *be irreducible, let* ℓ *be a coordinate on* $L \simeq \mathbb{C}^1$, *let* $U^* \oplus L^* \subset \mathbb{C}^{N*}$ *be a linear inclusion.*

If $[R] \in \mathcal{D}_{\kappa,m,M}$ *and* $[R] \notin \mathcal{D}_{\kappa-1,m,M}$, *then* $[\ell^{d-m} R] \in \mathcal{D}_{\kappa,d,N}$ *and* $[\ell^{d-m} R] \notin \mathcal{D}_{\kappa-1,d,N}$.

Proof. Let $u_1, \ldots, u_M, v, w_{M+2}, \ldots, w_N$ be a basis of $\mathbb{C}^N$ adapted to the inclusions $\mathbb{C}^M \subset \mathbb{C}^{M+1} \subset \mathbb{C}^N$, so $(U^*)^\perp = \langle w_{M+2}, \ldots, w_N \rangle$ and $(L^*)^\perp = \langle u_1, \ldots, u_M, w_{M+2}, \ldots, w_N \rangle$. Let $c = (d-m)(d-m-1)$. In these coordinates, the matrix of $(\ell^{d-m}R)_{d-2,2}$ is in $(M, 1, N - M - 1) \times (M, 1, N - M - 1)$-block form:

$$(\ell^{d-m}R)_{d-2,2} = \begin{pmatrix} \ell^{d-m}R_{m-2,2} & \ell^{d-m-1}R_{m-1,1} & 0 \\ \ell^{d-m-1}R_{m-1,1} & c\ell^{d-m-2}R & 0 \\ 0 & 0 & 0 \end{pmatrix}.$$

First note that $\det_{M+1}((\ell^{d-m}R)_{d-2,2}|_F)$ for any $F \in G(M + 1, \mathbb{C}^N)$ is either zero or a multiple of $\ell^{d-m}R$. If $\dim \mathrm{Zeros}(R)^\vee = M - 2$ (the expected dimension), then for a general $F \in G(M + 1, \mathbb{C}^N)$, $\det_M((\ell^{d-m}R)_{d-2,2}|_F)$ will not be a multiple of $(\ell^{d-m}R)_{d-2,2}$, and more generally if $\dim \mathrm{Zeros}(R)^\vee = \kappa$, then for a general $F \in G(\kappa + 2, \mathbb{C}^N)$, $\det_{\kappa+2}((\ell^{d-m}R)_{d-2,2}|_F)$ will not be a multiple of $\ell^{d-m}R$ but for any $F \in G(\kappa + 3, \mathbb{C}^N)$, $\det_{\kappa+3}((\ell^{d-m}R)_{d-2,2}|_F)$ will be a multiple of $\ell^{d-m}R$. This shows $[R] \notin \mathcal{D}_{\kappa-1,m,M}$, implies $[\ell^{d-m}R] \notin \mathcal{D}_{\kappa-1,d,N}$.

Exercise 6.5.2.2 (1) Show that $[R] \in \mathcal{D}_{\kappa,m,M}$, implies $[\ell^{d-m}R] \in \mathcal{D}_{\kappa,d,N}$. ◎   □

The inclusion (6.5.2) and Proposition 6.5.2.1 imply the following:

Theorem 6.5.2.3 [LMR13] $\mathcal{P}erm_n^m \not\subset \mathcal{D}_{2n-2,n,n^2}$ when $m < \frac{n^2}{2}$. *In particular,* $\overline{dc}(\mathrm{perm}_m) \geq \frac{m^2}{2}$.

On the other hand, by Exercise 6.4.5.3, cones have degenerate duals, so $\ell^{n-m} \mathrm{perm}_m \in \mathcal{D}_{2n-2,n,n^2}$ whenever $m \geq \frac{n^2}{2}$.

The next step from this perspective would be as follows:

Problem 6.5.2.4 Find equations that distinguish cones (e.g. $\mathrm{Zeros}(\ell^{n-m} \mathrm{perm}_m) \subset \mathbb{P}^{n^2-1}$) from tangent developables (e.g., $\mathrm{Zeros}(\det_n) \subset \mathbb{P}^{n^2-1}$). More precisely, find equations that are zero on tangent developables but nonzero on cones.

6.5.3 A Better Module of Equations

The equations above are of enormous degree. I now derive equations of much lower degree. Since $P \in S^d \mathbb{C}^N$ divides $Q \in S^e \mathbb{C}^N$ if and only if for each $L \in G(2, \mathbb{C}^N)$, $P|_L$ divides $Q|_L$, it will be sufficient to solve this problem for polynomials on $\mathbb{C}^2$. This will have the advantage of producing polynomials of much lower degree.

Let $d \leq e$, let $P \in S^d \mathbb{C}^2$ and $Q \in S^e \mathbb{C}^2$. If P divides Q, then $S^{e-d} \mathbb{C}^2 \cdot P$ will contain Q. That is,

$$x^{e-d}P \wedge x^{e-d-1}yP \wedge \cdots \wedge y^{e-d}P \wedge Q = 0.$$

Since dim $S^e\mathbb{C}^2 = e + 1$, these potentially give a $\binom{e+1}{e-d+2}$-dimensional vector space of equations of degree $e - d + 1$ in the coefficients of P and linear in the coefficients of Q.

By taking our polynomials to be $P = P|_L$ and $Q = \det_{k+3}(P_{n-2,2}|_F)|_L$ for $F \in G(k+3, V)$ and $L \in G(2, F)$ (or, for those familiar with flag varieties, better to say $(L, F) \in Flag_{2,k+3}(V)$), we now have equations parametrized by the pairs (L, F). Note that $\deg(Q) = e = (k+3)(d-2)$. These were the polynomials that were used in [LMR13].

Remark 6.5.3.1 More generally, given $P \in S^d\mathbb{C}^2$, $Q \in S^e\mathbb{C}^2$, one can ask if P, Q have at least r roots in common (counting multiplicity). Then P, Q having r points in common says the spaces $S^{e-r}\mathbb{C}^2 \cdot P$ and $S^{d-r}\mathbb{C}^2 \cdot Q$ intersect. That is,

$$x^{e-r}P \wedge x^{e-r-1}yP \wedge \cdots \wedge y^{e-r}P \wedge x^{d-r}Q \wedge x^{d-r-1}yQ \wedge \cdots \wedge y^{d-r}Q = 0.$$

In the case $r = 1$, we get a single polynomial, called the *resultant*, which is of central importance. In particular, the proof of Noether normalization from §3.1.4, that the projection of a projective variety $X \subset \mathbb{P}W$ from a point $y \in \mathbb{P}W$ with $y \notin X$, to $\mathbb{P}(W/\hat{y})$ is still a projective variety, relies on the resultant to produce equations for the projection.

6.6 Symmetries of the Determinant and Permanent

The permanent and determinant both have the property that they are *characterized* by their symmetry groups in the sense described in §1.2.5. I expect these symmetry groups to play a central role in the study of Valiant's hypothesis in future work. For example, the only known exponential separation of the permanent from the determinant in any restricted model (as defined in Chapter 7), is the model of *equivariant determinantal complexity*, which is defined in terms of symmetry groups, see §7.4.1.

6.6.1 Symmetries of the Determinant

Theorem 6.6.1.1 (Frobenius [Fro97]) *Write* $\rho : GL_{n^2} \to GL(S^n\mathbb{C}^{n^2})$ *for the induced action. Let* $\phi \in GL_{n^2}$ *be such that* $\rho(\phi)(\det_n) = \det_n$. *Then, identifying* $\mathbb{C}^{n^2}$ *with the space of* $n \times n$ *matrices,*

$$\phi(z) = \begin{cases} gzh, & \text{or} \\ gz^Th \end{cases}$$

for some $g, h \in GL_n$, *with* $\det_n(g)\det_n(h) = 1$. *Here* z^T *denotes the transpose of* z.

I present the proof from [Die49] below.

Write $\mathbb{C}^{n^2} = E \otimes F = \text{Hom}(E^*, F)$ with $E, F = \mathbb{C}^n$. Let $\mathbb{Z}_n$ denote the cyclic group of order n and consider the inclusion $\mathbb{Z}_n \times \mathbb{Z}_n \subset GL(E) \times GL(F)$ given by the nth roots of unity times the identity matrix. Let μ_n denote the kernel of the product map $(\mathbb{Z}_n)^{\times 2} \to \mathbb{Z}_n$.

Corollary 6.6.1.2 $G_{\det_n} = (SL(E) \times SL(F))/\mu_n \rtimes \mathbb{Z}_2$

To prove the corollary, just note that the $\mathbb{C}^*$ corresponding to $\det(g)$ above and μ_n are the kernel of the map $\mathbb{C}^* \times SL(E) \times SL(F) \to GL(E \otimes F)$.

Exercise 6.6.1.3 (2) Prove the $n = 2$ case of Theorem 6.6.1.1. ⊚

Lemma 6.6.1.4 *Let $U \subset E \otimes F$ be a linear subspace such that $U \subset$ Zeros($\det_n$). Then $\dim U \leq n^2 - n$. The subvariety of the Grassmannian $G(n^2 - n, E \otimes F)$ consisting of maximal linear spaces on Zeros($\det_n$) has two irreducible components, call them Σ_α and Σ_β, where*

$$\Sigma_\alpha = \{X \in G(n^2 - n, E \otimes F) \mid \ker(X) = \hat{L} \text{ for some } L \in \mathbb{P}E^*\} \simeq \mathbb{P}E^* \text{ and}$$
$$(6.6.1)$$

$$\Sigma_\beta = \{X \in G(n^2 - n, E \otimes F) \mid \text{Image}(X) = \hat{H} \text{ for some } H \in \mathbb{P}F^*\} \simeq \mathbb{P}F^*.$$
$$(6.6.2)$$

Here, for $f \in X$, $f : E^* \to F$ is considered as a linear map, $\ker(X)$ means the intersections of the kernels of all $f \in X$, and Image(X) is the span of all the images.

Moreover, for any two distinct $X_j \in \Sigma_\alpha$, $j = 1, 2$, and $Y_j \in \Sigma_\beta$, we have

$$\dim(X_1 \cap X_2) = \dim(Y_1 \cap Y_2) \quad = n^2 - 2n \text{ and} \quad (6.6.3)$$
$$\dim(X_i \cap Y_j) = n^2 - 2n + 1. \quad (6.6.4)$$

Exercise 6.6.1.5 (2) Prove Lemma 6.6.1.4. ⊚

One can say more: each element of Σ_α corresponds to a left ideal and each element of Σ_β corresponds to a right ideal in the space of $n \times n$ matrices.

Proof of theorem 6.6.1.1. Let $\Sigma = \Sigma_\alpha \cup \Sigma_\beta$. Then the automorphism of $G(n^2 - n, E \otimes F)$ induced by ϕ must preserve Σ. By the conditions (6.6.3),(6.6.4) of Lemma 6.6.1.4, to preserve dimensions of intersections, either every $U \in \Sigma_\alpha$ must map to a point of Σ_α, in which case every $V \in \Sigma_\beta$ must map to a point of Σ_β, or every $U \in \Sigma_\alpha$ must map to a point of Σ_β and every $V \in \Sigma_\beta$ must map to a point of Σ_α. If we are in the second case, replace ϕ by $\phi \circ T$, where $T(z) = z^T$, so we may now assume ϕ preserves both Σ_α and Σ_β.

Observe that ϕ induces an algebraic map $\phi_E : \mathbb{P}E^* \to \mathbb{P}E^*$.

Exercise 6.6.1.6 (2) Show that $L_1, L_2, L_3 \in \mathbb{P}E$ lie on a $\mathbb{P}^1$ if and only if then $\dim(U_{L_1} \cap U_{L_2} \cap U_{L_3}) = n^2 - 2n$, where $U_L = \{X \mid \ker(X) = L\}$.

For ϕ to preserve $\dim(U_{L_1} \cap U_{L_2} \cap U_{L_3})$, the images of the L_j under ϕ_E must also lie on a $\mathbb{P}^1$, and thus ϕ_E must take lines to lines (and similarly hyperplanes to hyperplanes). But then, (see, e.g., [Har95, §18, p. 229]) $\phi_E \in PGL(E)$, and similarly, $\phi_F \in PGL(F)$, where $\phi_F : \mathbb{P}F^* \to \mathbb{P}F^*$ is the corresponding map. Here $PGL(E)$ denotes $GL(E)/\mathbb{C}^*$, the image of $GL(E)$ in its action on projective space. Write $\hat{\phi}_E \in GL(E)$, $\hat{\phi}_F \in GL(F)$ for any choices of lifts.

Consider the map $\tilde{\phi} \in GL(E \otimes F)$ given by $\tilde{\phi}(z) = \hat{\phi}_E^{-1} \phi(z) \hat{\phi}_F^{-1}$. The map $\tilde{\phi}$ sends each $U \in \Sigma_\alpha$ to itself as well as each $V \in \Sigma_\beta$, in particular it does the same for all intersections. Hence it preserves $Seg(\mathbb{P}E \times \mathbb{P}F) \subset \mathbb{P}(E \otimes F)$ pointwise, so it is up to scale the identity map because $E \otimes F$ is spanned by points of $\hat{Seg}(\mathbb{P}E \times \mathbb{P}F)$.   □

6.6.2 Symmetries of the Permanent

Write $\mathbb{C}^{n^2} = E \otimes F$. Let $\Gamma_n^E := T_E^{SL} \rtimes \mathfrak{S}_n$, and similarly for F. As discussed in the introduction to this chapter, $(\Gamma_n^E \times \Gamma_n^F) \rtimes \mathbb{Z}_2 \to G_{\mathrm{perm}_n}$, where the nontrivial element of $\mathbb{Z}_2$ acts by sending a matrix to its transpose. We would like to show this map is surjective and determine its kernel. However, it is not when $n = 2$.

Exercise 6.6.2.1 (1) What is G_{perm_2}? ⊚

Theorem 6.6.2.2 [MM62] *For $n \geq 3$, $G_{\mathrm{perm}_n} = (\Gamma_n^E \times \Gamma_n^F)/\mu_n \rtimes \mathbb{Z}_2$.*

Proof. I follow [Ye11]. Recall the description of $\mathrm{Zeros}(\mathrm{perm}_n)_{Jac,n-2}$ from Lemma 6.3.3.4. Any linear transformation preserving the permanent must send a component of $\mathrm{Zeros}(\mathrm{perm}_n)_{Jac,n-2}$ of type (1) to another of type (1). It must send a component C^j either to some C^k or some C_i. But if $i \neq j$, $C^j \cap C^i = 0$ and for all i, j, $\dim(C^i \cap C_j) = 1$. Since intersections must be mapped to intersections, either all components C^i are sent to components C_k or all are permuted among themselves. By composing with an element of $\mathbb{Z}_2$, we may assume all the C^is are sent to C^is and the C_js are sent to C_js. Similarly, by composing with an element of $\mathfrak{S}_n \times \mathfrak{S}_n$, we may assume each C_i and C^j is sent to itself. But then their intersections are sent to themselves. So we have, for all i, j,

$$(x_j^i) \mapsto (\lambda_j^i x_j^i) \tag{6.6.5}$$

for some λ_j^i, and there is no summation in the expression. Consider the image of a size 2 submatrix, e.g.,

$$
\begin{matrix} x_1^1 & x_2^1 \\ x_1^2 & x_2^2 \end{matrix} \mapsto \begin{matrix} \lambda_1^1 x_1^1 & \lambda_2^1 x_2^1 \\ \lambda_1^2 x_1^2 & \lambda_2^2 x_2^2 \end{matrix}.
\tag{6.6.6}
$$

In order that the map (6.6.5) is given by an element of G_{perm_n}, when $(x_j^i) \in$ $\mathrm{Zeros}(\mathrm{perm}_n)_{Jac,n-2}$, the permanent of the matrix on the right-hand side of (6.6.6) must be zero. Using that $x_1^1 x_2^2 + x_2^1 x_1^2 = 0$, the permanent of the right-hand side of (6.6.6) is $\lambda_1^1 \lambda_2^2 x_1^1 x_2^2 + \lambda_1^2 \lambda_2^1 x_2^1 x_1^2 = x_1^1 x_2^2 (\lambda_1^1 \lambda_2^2 - \lambda_1^2 \lambda_2^1)$ which implies $\lambda_1^1 \lambda_2^2 - \lambda_2^1 \lambda_1^2 = 0$, thus all the 2×2 minors of the matrix (λ_j^i) are zero, so it has rank one and is the product of a column vector and a row vector, but then it arises from $x \mapsto txt'$ with t, t' diagonal, and for the permanent to be preserved, $\det(t)\det(t') = 1$. Without loss of generality, we may insist that both determininants equal one. $\square$

6.6.3 Grenet's Decomposition: Symmetry and the Best upper Bound on dc(perm$_m$)

Recall from Chapter 4 that the symmetries of the matrix multiplication tensor appear in the optimal and conjecturally optimal rank expressions for it. Will the same be true for determinantal expressions of polynomials, in particular of the permanent?

The best known determinantal expression of perm_m is of size $2^m - 1$ and is due to Grenet [Gre11]. (Previously Valiant [Val79] had shown there was an expression of size 4^m.) We saw (Corollary 6.3.4.8) that when $m = 3$ this is the best expression. This motivated N. Ressayre and myself to try to understand Grenet's expression. We observed the following *equivariance* property: let $G \subseteq G_{\mathrm{perm}_m}$ I will say a determinantal expression for perm_m is *G-equivariant* if given $g \in G$, there exist $n \times n$ matrices B, C such that $\tilde{A}_{Grenet,m}(g \cdot Y) = B\tilde{A}_{Grenet,m}(Y)C$ or $B\tilde{A}_{Grenet,m}(Y)^T C$. In other words, there exists an injective group homomorphism $\psi : G \to G_{\det_n}$ such that $\tilde{A}_{Grenet,m}(Y) = \psi(g)(\tilde{A}_{Grenet,m}(gY))$.

Proposition 6.6.3.1 [LR15] *Grenet's expressions* $\tilde{A}_{Grenet} : Mat_m(\mathbb{C}) \to$ $Mat_n(\mathbb{C})$ *such that* $\mathrm{perm}_m(Y) = \det_n(\tilde{A}_{Grenet}(Y))$ *are* Γ_m^E-*equivariant.*

For example, let

$$
g(t) = \begin{pmatrix} t_1 & & \\ & t_2 & \\ & & t_3 \end{pmatrix}.
$$

Then $A_{Grenet,3}(g(t)Y) = B(t)A_{Grenet,3}(Y)C(t)$, where

$$B(t) = \begin{pmatrix} t_3 & & & & & \\ & t_1 t_3 & & & & \\ & & t_1 t_3 & & & \\ & & & t_1 t_3 & & \\ & & & & 1 & \\ & & & & & 1 \\ & & & & & & 1 \end{pmatrix} \quad \text{and} \quad C(t) = B(t)^{-1}.$$

Exercise 6.6.3.2 (2) Determine $B(g)$ and $C(g)$ when $g \in \Gamma_3^E$ is the permutation $(1, 2)$.

Via this equivariance, one can give an invariant description of Grenet's expressions, as follows. The space $S^k E$ is an irreducible $GL(E)$-module, but it is not in general irreducible as a Γ_m^E-module. Let $e_1, \dots, e_m$ be a basis of E, and let $(S^k E)_{reg} \subset S^k E$ denote the span of $\prod_{i \in I} e_i$, for $I \subset [m]$ of cardinality k (the space spanned by the square-free monomials, also known as the space of *regular* weights): $(S^k E)_{reg}$ is an irreducible Γ_m^E-submodule of $S^k E$. Moreover, there exists a unique Γ_m^E-equivariant projection π_k from $S^k E$ to $(S^k E)_{reg}$.

For $v \in E$, define $s_k(v) : (S^k E)_{reg} \to (S^{k+1} E)_{reg}$ to be multiplication by v followed by π_{k+1}. Alternatively, $(S^{k+1} E)_{reg}$ is a Γ_m^E-submodule of $E \otimes (S^k E)_{reg}$, and $s_k : E \to (S^k E)_{reg}^* \otimes (S^{k+1} E)_{reg}$ is the unique Γ_m^E-equivariant inclusion.

Fix a basis $f_1, \dots, f_m$ of F^*. If $y = (y_1, \dots, y_m) \in E \otimes F$, let $(s_k \otimes f_j)(y) := s_k(y_j)$.

Proposition 6.6.3.3 [LR15] *The following is Grenet's determinantal representation of* perm_m. *Let* $\mathbb{C}^n = \bigoplus_{k=0}^{m-1} (S^k E)_{reg}$, *so* $n = 2^m - 1$, *and identify* $S^0 E \simeq (S^m E)_{reg}$ *(both are trivial Γ_m^E-modules). Set*

$$\Lambda_0 = \sum_{k=1}^{m-1} \mathrm{Id}_{(S^k E)_{reg}}$$

and define

$$\tilde{A} = \Lambda_0 + \sum_{k=0}^{m-1} s_k \otimes f_{k+1}. \tag{6.6.7}$$

Then $(-1)^{m+1} \mathrm{perm}_m = \det_n \circ \tilde{A}$. *To obtain the permanent exactly, replace* $\mathrm{Id}_{(S^1 E)_{reg}}$ *by* $(-1)^{m+1} \mathrm{Id}_{(S^1 E)_{reg}}$ *in the formula for Λ_0.*
Moreover, the map $\tilde{A}$ is Γ_m^E-equivariant.

I prove Proposition 6.6.3.3 in §8.11.1.

Remark 6.6.3.4 In bases respecting the block decomposition induced from the direct sum, the linear part, other than the last term, which lies in the upper right block, lies just below the diagonal blocks, and all blocks other than the upper right block and the diagonal and subdiagonal blocks, are zero. This expression is better viewed as an iterated matrix multiplication as in §7.3.1: $\mathrm{perm}(y) = (s_{m-1} \otimes f_m(y))(s_{m-2} \otimes f_{m-1}(y)) \cdots (s_0 \otimes f_1(y))$.

6.7 dc versus $\overline{\mathrm{dc}}$

Is conjecture 6.1.6.2 really stronger than Valiant's hypothesis 6.1.6.1? That is, do there exist sequences (P_m) of polynomials with $\overline{\mathrm{dc}}(P_m)$ bounded by a polynomial in m but $\mathrm{dc}(P_m)$ growing superpolynomially?

K. Mulmuley [Mul14] conjectures that this is indeed the case and that the existence of such sequences "explains" why Valiant's hypothesis is so difficult.

Before addressing this conjecture, one should at least find a sequence P_m with $\mathrm{dc}(P_m) > \overline{\mathrm{dc}}(P_m)$. I describe one such sequence in §6.7.2.

6.7.1 On the Boundary of the Orbit of the Determinant

Let $W = \mathbb{C}^{n^2} = E^* \otimes E$ with $E = \mathbb{C}^n$, and let $\sigma_{n^2-1}(Seg(\mathbb{P}W^* \times \mathbb{P}W)) \subset \mathbb{P}(W^* \otimes W)$ be the endomorphisms of W of rank at most $n^2 - 1$. An obvious subset of $\partial \mathcal{D}et_n$ is obtained by $\hat{\sigma}_{n^2-1}(Seg(\mathbb{P}W^* \times \mathbb{P}W)) \cdot \mathrm{det}_n$. This is $\overline{GL(W) \cdot \mathrm{det}_n}|_{(E^* \otimes E)_0}$, the orbit closure of the determinant restricted to the traceless matrices. This description shows it has codimension one in $\mathcal{D}et_n$ and is irreducible, so it is a component of $\partial \mathcal{D}et_n$.

Other components can be found as follows: let $U \subset W$ be a subspace such that $\mathrm{det}_n |_U = 0$, and let V be a complement. Given a matrix M, write $M = M_U \oplus M_V$. Introduce a parameter t and consider $M \mapsto \mathrm{det}_n(M_U + tM_V)$ and expand out in a Taylor series. Say the first nonvanishing term is t^k, then $M \mapsto \overline{\mathrm{det}_n}(M_U, \ldots, M_U, M_V, \ldots, M_V)$, where there are k M_Vs, is a point of $\mathcal{D}et_n$ and it is "usually" a point of $\partial \mathcal{D}et_n$. One can do more complicated constructions by taking more complicated splittings. In all cases, the first step is to find a subspace $U \subset W$ on which the determinant is zero. It is not hard to see that without loss of generality, one can restrict to U that are *unextendable*, i.e., there does not exist any $U' \supset U$ with $\mathrm{det}_n |_{U'} = 0$. For results on such subspaces, see, e.g., [IL99, Atk83, EH88, dSP16, FLR85]. Unfortunately, they are little understood in general. The first interesting such example, when n is odd, is the space of skew-symmetric matrices.

When $n = 3$, the unextendable subspaces have been classified by Atkinson [Atk83]: there are four such up to $GL_3 \times GL_3$-action, namely,

$$\begin{pmatrix} * & * & * \\ * & * & * \\ 0 & 0 & 0 \end{pmatrix}, \begin{pmatrix} * & * & 0 \\ * & * & 0 \\ * & * & 0 \end{pmatrix}, \begin{pmatrix} * & * & * \\ * & 0 & 0 \\ * & 0 & 0 \end{pmatrix}, \left\{ \begin{pmatrix} 0 & \alpha & \beta \\ -\alpha & 0 & \gamma \\ -\beta & -\gamma & 0 \end{pmatrix} \mid \alpha, \beta, \gamma \in \mathbb{C} \right\}.$$

Another way to study the boundary is to consider the rational map

$$\psi : \mathbb{P}(\mathrm{End}(\mathbb{C}^{n^2})) \quad \dashrightarrow \mathcal{D}et_n \tag{6.7.1}$$

$$[X] \quad \mapsto [\det_n \circ X].$$

One could hope to understand the components of the boundary by blowing up the indeterminacy locus, which consists of $X \in \mathrm{End}(\mathbb{C}^{n^2})$ such that $\det_n|_{\mathrm{Image}(X)} = 0$.

6.7.2 A Component via the Skew-Symmetric Matrices

The transposition $\tau \in G_{\det_n}$ allows us to write $\mathbb{C}^{n^2} = E \otimes E = S^2 E \oplus \Lambda^2 E$, where the decomposition is into the ± 1 eigenspaces for τ. For $M \in E \otimes E$, write $M = M_S + M_\Lambda$ reflecting this decomposition.

Define a polynomial $P_\Lambda \in S^n(\mathbb{C}^{n^2})^*$ by

$$P_\Lambda(M) = \overline{\det}_n(M_\Lambda, \dots, M_\Lambda, M_S).$$

Let $\mathrm{Pf}_i(M_\Lambda)$ denote the Pfaffian (see, e.g., [Lan12, §2.7.4] for the definition of the Pfaffian and a discussion of its properties) of the skew-symmetric matrix, obtained from M_Λ by suppressing its ith row and column. Write $M_S = (s_{ij})$.

Exercise 6.7.2.1 (2) Show that

$$P_\Lambda(M) = \sum_{i,j} s_{ij} \, \mathrm{Pf}_i(M_\Lambda) \, \mathrm{Pf}_j(M_\Lambda).$$

In particular, $P_\Lambda = 0$ if n is even, but is not identically zero when n is odd.

Proposition 6.7.2.2 [LMR13] $P_\Lambda \in \mathcal{D}et_n$. *Moreover,* $\overline{GL(W) \cdot P_\Lambda}$ *is an irreducible codimension one component of the boundary of* $\mathcal{D}et_n$, *not contained in* $\mathrm{End}(W) \cdot [\det_n]$. *In particular,* $\overline{dc}(P_\Lambda) = n < dc(P_\Lambda)$.

The proof of Proposition 6.7.2.2 is given in §8.5.1.

Exercise 6.7.2.3 (3) Show that

$$\mathrm{Zeros}(P_\Lambda)^\vee = \overline{\mathbb{P}\{v^2 \oplus v \wedge w \in S^2\mathbb{C}^n \oplus \Lambda^2\mathbb{C}^n, \ v, w \in \mathbb{C}^n\}} \subset \mathbb{P}^{n^2-1}.$$

As expected, $\mathrm{Zeros}(P_\Lambda)^\vee$ resembles $Seg(\mathbb{P}^{n-1} \times \mathbb{P}^{n-1})$.

Remark 6.7.2.4 For those familiar with the notation, $\mathrm{Zeros}(P_\Lambda)$ can be defined as the image of the projective bundle $\pi : \mathbb{P}(\mathcal{E}) \to \mathbb{P}^{n-1}$, where $\mathcal{E} = \mathcal{O}(-1) \oplus \mathcal{Q}$ is the sum of the tautological and quotient bundles on $\mathbb{P}^{n-1}$, by a sublinear system of $\mathcal{O}_E(1) \otimes \pi^*\mathcal{O}(1)$. This sublinear system contracts the divisor $\mathbb{P}(\mathcal{Q}) \subset \mathbb{P}(\mathcal{E})$ to the Grassmannian $G(2, n) \subset \mathbb{P}\Lambda^2\mathbb{C}^n$.

For large n I expect there are many components of the boundary, however, for $n = 3$, we have the following:

Theorem 6.7.2.5 [HL16] *The boundary $\partial \mathcal{D}et_3$ has exactly two irreducible components:* $\overline{GL_9 \cdot P_\Lambda}$ *and* $\overline{GL_9 \cdot \det_3}|_{(E^* \otimes E)_0}$.

The proof has two parts: first they resolve (6.7.1), which can be done with one blow-up (so in terms of a limit above, only $\frac{1}{t}$ need show up). They then analyze each component of Atkinson's classification and identify the component of the boundary it lies in.

6.7.3 Mulmuley's Conjectures on the Wildness of the Boundary

There is scant evidence for or against the conjecture of [Mul14] mentioned above. In §6.8.1 I outline the proof that all $P \in S^3\mathbb{C}^3$ with smooth zero set have $\mathrm{dc}(P) = 3$ and thus for all $Q \in S^3\mathbb{C}^3$, $\overline{\mathrm{dc}(Q)} = 3$. In this one case, there is a big jump between $\overline{\mathrm{dc}}$ and dc, giving some positive news for the conjecture:

Theorem 6.7.3.1 [ABV15] $\mathrm{dc}(x_1^3 + x_2^2 x_3 + x_2 x_4^2) \geq 6$, *and thus when* $n = 3$, $\mathrm{dc}(P_\Lambda) \geq 6$.

The second assertion follows because $x_1^3 + x_2^2 x_3 + x_2 x_4^2$ is the determinant of the degeneration of P_Λ obtained by taking

$$M_\Lambda = \begin{pmatrix} 0 & x_4 & x_2 \\ -x_3 & 0 & x_1 \\ -x_3 & -x_1 & 0 \end{pmatrix}, \quad M_S = \begin{pmatrix} x_1 & 0 & 0 \\ 0 & x_4 & 0 \\ 0 & 0 & x_2 \end{pmatrix}.$$

Exercise 6.7.3.2 (1) Using Theorem 6.3.4.6, prove the first assertion of Theorem 6.7.3.1.

6.8 Determinantal Hypersurfaces

This section uses results from algebraic geometry that we have not discussed. It is not used elsewhere and can be safely skipped.

6.8.1 All Smooth Cubic Surfaces in $\mathbb{P}^3$ are Determinantal

Grassmann [Gra55] showed that all smooth cubic surfaces in $\mathbb{P}^3$ lie in $\mathrm{End}(\mathbb{C}^9) \cdot \det_3$, and thus all cubic surfaces in $\mathbb{P}^3$ lie in $\mathcal{D}et_3$. I give an outline of the proof from [BKs07, Ger89]. Every smooth cubic surface $S \subset \mathbb{P}^3$ arises in the following way. Consider $\mathbb{P}^2$ and distinguish six points not on a conic and with no three colinear. There is a four-dimensional space of cubic polynomials, say, spanned by $F_1, \ldots, F_4 \in S^3\mathbb{C}^3$, that vanish on the six points. Consider the rational map $\mathbb{P}^2 \dashrightarrow \mathbb{P}^3$ defined by these polynomials, i.e., $[y] \mapsto [F_1(y), \ldots, F_4(y)]$, where the map is defined on $\mathbb{P}^2$ minus the six points, and let S denote the closure of the image. (Better, one blows up $\mathbb{P}^2$ at the six points to obtain a surface $\tilde{S}$

and S is the image of the corresponding regular map from $\tilde{S}$.) Give $\mathbb{C}^3$ coordinates x_1, x_2, x_3. By the Hilbert-Burch Theorem (see, e.g., [Eis05, Theorem 3.2]), there exists a 3×4 matrix $L(x_1, x_2, x_3)$, linear in x_1, x_2, x_3, whose size three minors are the F_j. Define a 3×3 matrix $M = M(z_1, \ldots, z_4)$ by

$$M \begin{pmatrix} x_1 \\ x_2 \\ x_3 \end{pmatrix} = L \begin{pmatrix} z_1 \\ z_2 \\ z_3 \\ z_4 \end{pmatrix}.$$

Then $\det(M)$ is the equation of S.

Remark 6.8.1.1 The set of nonequivalent representations of a cubic as a determinant is in one-to-one correspondence with the subsets of six (of the 27) lines of S that do not intersect each other (see [BKs07]). In particular, there are 72 such representations.

6.8.2 Description of the Quartic Hypersurfaces in $\mathbb{P}^3$ that are Determinantal

Classically, there was interest in determining which smooth hypersurfaces of degree d were expressible as a $d \times d$ determinant. The result in the first nontrivial case shows how daunting GCT might be.

Theorem 6.8.2.1 (Letao Zhang and Zhiyuan Li, personal communication) *The variety $\mathbb{P}\{P \in S^4\mathbb{C}^4 \mid [P] \in \mathcal{D}et_4\} \subset \mathbb{P}S^4\mathbb{C}^4$ is a hypersurface of degree* 640, 224.

The rest of this subsection uses more advanced language from algebraic geometry and can be safely skipped.

The following "folklore" theorem was made explicit in [Bea00, Corollary 1.12]:

Theorem 6.8.2.2 *Let $U = \mathbb{C}^{n+1}$, let $P \in S^d U$, and let $Z = \text{Zeros}(P) \subset \mathbb{P}^n$ be the corresponding hypersurface of degree d. Assume Z is smooth, and choose any inclusion $U \subset \mathbb{C}^{d^2}$.*

If $P \in \text{End}(\mathbb{C}^{d^2}) \cdot [\det_d]$, we may form a map between vector bundles $M : \mathcal{O}_{\mathbb{P}^n}(-1)^d \to \mathcal{O}_{\mathbb{P}^n}^d$ whose cokernel is a line bundle $L \to Z$ with the properties

   i $H^i(Z, L(j)) = 0$ *for* $1 \le i \le n-2$ *and all* $j \in \mathbb{Z}$ *and*
   ii $H^0(X, L(-1)) = H^{n-1}(X, L(j)) = 0$

Conversely, if there exists $L \to Z$ satisfying properties (i) and (ii), then Z is determinantal via a map M, as above, whose cokernel is L.

If we are concerned with the hypersurface being in $\mathcal{D}et_n$, the first case where this is not automatic is for quartic surfaces, where it is a codimension one condition:

Proposition 6.8.2.3 [Bea00, Corollary 6.6] *A smooth quartic surface is determinantal if and only if it contains a nonhyperelliptic curve of genus 3 embedded in $\mathbb{P}^3$ by a linear system of degree 6.*

Proof of 6.8.2.1. From Proposition 6.8.2.3, the hypersurface is the locus of quartic surfaces containing a (Brill-Noether general) genus 3 curve C of degree six. This translates into the existence of a lattice polarization

$$
\begin{array}{c|cc}
 & h & C \\
\hline
h & 4 & 6 \\
C & 6 & 4
\end{array}
$$

of discriminant $-(4^2 - 6^2) = 20$. By the Torelli theorems, the $K3$ surfaces with such a lattice polarization have codimension one in the moduli space of quartic $K3$ surfaces.

Let $D_{3,6}$ denote the locus of quartic surfaces containing a genus 3 curve C of degree six in $\mathbb{P}^{34} = \mathbb{P}(S^4\mathbb{C}^4)$. It corresponds to the Noether-Lefschetz divisor NL_{20} in the moduli space of the degree four $K3$ surfaces. Here NL_d denotes the Noether-Lefschetz divisor, parameterizing the degree 4 $K3$ surfaces whose Picard lattice has a rank 2 sublattice containing h with discriminant $-d$ (h is the polarization of the degree four $K3$ surface, $h^2 = 4$).

The Noether-Lefschetz number n_{20}, which is defined by the intersection number of NL_{20} and a line in the moduli space of degree four $K3$ surfaces, equals the degree of $D_{3,6}$ in $\mathbb{P}^{34} = \mathbb{P}(S^4\mathbb{C}^4)$.

The key fact is that n_d can be computed via the modularity of the generating series for any integer d. More precisely, the generating series $F(q) := \sum_d n_d q^{d/8}$ is a modular form of level 8 and can be expressed by a polynomial of $A(q) = \sum_n q^{n^2/8}$ and $B(q) = \sum_n (-1)^n q^{n^2/8}$.

The explicit expression of $F(q)$ is in [MP13, Thm 2]. As an application, the Noether-Lefschetz number n_{20} is the coefficient of the term $q^{20/8} = q^{5/2}$, which is 640, 224. $\qquad\square$

7

Valiant's Hypothesis II: Restricted Models and Other Approaches

This chapter continues the discussion of Valiant's hypothesis and its variants. Chapter 6 described progress via benchmarks such as lower bounds for $dc(perm_m)$. Another approach to these problems is to prove complexity lower bounds under supplementary hypotheses, called *restricted models* in the computer science literature. I begin, in §7.1, with a discussion of the geometry of one of the simplest classes of shallow circuits, the $\Sigma\Lambda\Sigma$-circuits whose complexity essentially measures symmetric tensor rank, and discuss the symmetric tensor rank of the elementary symmetric polynomials. Next, in §7.2, I discuss $\Sigma\Pi\Sigma$ circuits and their relationship to secant varieties of the Chow variety. There are several complexity measures that are equivalent to determinantal complexity, such as *algebraic branching programs* and *iterated matrix multiplication complexity*. These are discussed in §7.3. Additional restricted models are presented in §7.4: Aravind and Joegelkar's *rank k determinantal expressions* of [AJ15], Shpilka's restricted model [Shp02] of *depth-2 symmetric arithmetic circuits*, a result of Glynn [Gly13] on a certain class of expressions for the permanent, Nisan's noncommutative ABPs [Nis91], and the equivariant determinantal complexity of [LR15]. Equivariant determinantal complexity is the only known restricted model that gives an exponential separation between the permanent and determinant.

I devote §7.5 to the restricted models of *shallow circuits* because there is a path to proving Valiant's hypothesis by proving lower bounds that are stronger than superpolynomial for them. The *depth* of a circuit C is the number of edges in the longest path in C from an input to its output. If a circuit has small depth, it is called a *shallow circuit*, and the polynomial it computes can be computed quickly in parallel. The section begins in §7.5.1 with a detour for readers not familiar with big numbers as different levels of superpolynomial growth need to be compared both for statements and proofs. Having already discussed the geometry associated to depth 3 circuits in §7.2, I explain the geometry associated to the depth 4 and 5 circuits that arise in [GKKS13a] in §7.5.3. I discuss the tantalizing lower bounds of [GKKS13a] in §7.6, and analyze the method of proof, *shifted partial derivatives*, in detail. I then show that this method cannot separate the padded permanent from the determinant.

I conclude with a brief discussion of polynomial identity testing (PIT), hitting sets, and effective Noether normalization in §7.7. I believe these topics are potentially of great interest to algebraic geometry.

As pointed out by Shpilka and Yehudayoff in [SY09], restricted circuits of polynomial size only compute polynomials with "simple" structure. Thus to understand them, one needs to determine the precise meaning of "simple" for a given restricted class and then find an "explicit" polynomial without such structure. One could rephrase this geometrically as restricted circuits of a fixed size s define an algebraic variety in $S^n\mathbb{C}^N$ that is the closure of the set of polynomials computable with a restricted circuit of size s. The goal becomes to find an equation of that variety and an explicit polynomial not satisfying that equation.

Recall that computer scientists always work in bases and the inputs to the circuits are constants and variables. For homogeneous circuits, the inputs are simply the variables. The first layer of a $\Sigma\Lambda\Sigma$, $\Sigma\Pi\Sigma$, or $\Sigma\Lambda\Sigma\Lambda\Sigma$ circuit for a polynomial $P \in S^d\mathbb{C}^N$ is just to obtain arbitrary linear forms from these variables, so it plays no role in the geometry, and at worst multiplies the circuit size by N, and often enlarges it by much less. This fact will be used throughout this chapter.

I continue to work exclusively with homogeneous polynomials and over the complex numbers. In particular, for a **v**-dimensional complex vector space V, S^dV denotes the space of homogeneous polynomials of degree d on V^*.

7.1 Waring Rank, Depth Three Powering Circuits, and Symmetric Polynomials

Recall from §6.2.2 that the symmetric tensor rank (Waring rank) of a polynomial $P \in S^dV$, denoted $\mathbf{R}_S(P)$, is the smallest r such that we may write $P = \ell_1^d + \cdots + \ell_r^d$ for some $\ell_j \in V$. As explained in §7.1.1, such P admit $\Sigma\Lambda\Sigma$ circuits of size at most $r(\mathbf{v}+2)$. Although not directly related to Valiant's hypothesis, they are a simple enough class of circuits that one can actually prove lower bounds and they are used as the basis for further lower bound results.

Similarly, the class of elementary symmetric polynomials is a class of polynomials simple enough for one to prove complexity results but rich enough to be of interest. In §7.1.2 I discuss the elementary symmetric function $e_{n,n} = x_1 \cdots x_n$, describing its symmetry group and Waring decomposition. In §7.1.3

I discuss the Waring decompositions of elementary symmetric polynomials in general.

Recall the notation $\sigma_r(v_d(\mathbb{P}V)) = \overline{\mathbb{P}\{P \in S^d V \mid P = \ell_1^d + \cdots \ell_r^d, \ \ell_j \in V\}}$ for the Zariski closure of the set of polynomials in $\mathbb{P}S^d V$ of Waring rank at most r, called the rth secant variety of the Veronese variety, and that $\underline{\mathbf{R}}_S(P)$ denotes the smallest r such that $P \in \sigma_r(v_d(\mathbb{P}V))$.

7.1.1 $\sigma_r(v_d(\mathbb{P}V))$ and $\Sigma\Lambda\Sigma$ Circuits

When one studies circuits of bounded depth, one must allow gates to have an arbitrary number of edges coming in to them, which is called *unbounded fanin*. For such circuits, multiplication by constants is considered free.

A $\Sigma\Lambda^\delta\Sigma$ circuit consists of three layers, the first of addition gates, the second of powering gates, that map $\ell \mapsto \ell^\delta$ (so each gate has a single input and output), and the third a single addition gate. Such circuits are also called *diagonal depth-3 circuits*, or *depth three powering circuits* (see, e.g., [Sax08]).

Proposition 7.1.1.1 *Say $P \in S^d \mathbb{C}^\mathbf{v}$ satisfies $\mathbf{R}_S(P) = r$. Then P admits a $\Sigma\Lambda^d\Sigma$ circuit of size $r(\mathbf{v} + 2)$.*

Proof. We are given that $P = \ell_1^d + \cdots + \ell_r^d$ from some $\ell_j \in \mathbb{C}^\mathbf{v}$. We need at most $\mathbf{v}$ additions to construct each ℓ_j, of which there are r, so $r\mathbf{v}$ edges at the first level. Then there are r powering gates, of one edge each and each of these sends one edge to the final addition gate, for a total of $r\mathbf{v} + r + r$. $\qquad\square$

The following proposition bounds $\Sigma\Lambda\Sigma$ complexity by $\overline{\mathrm{dc}}$:

Proposition 7.1.1.2 *Let $P \in S^m V$ and let $\ell \in V$. Then $\mathrm{dc}(P) \le m\mathbf{R}_S(P) + 1$ and $\overline{\mathrm{dc}}(P) \le m\underline{\mathbf{R}}_S(P) + 1$.*

Exercise 7.1.1.3 (2) Prove Proposition 7.1.1.2. ⊚

7.1.2 The Polynomial $x_1 \cdots x_n$

Consider the polynomial $e_{n,n} := x_1 \cdots x_n \in S^n \mathbb{C}^n$ (the nth elementary symmetric function in n variables). This simple polynomial plays a major role in complexity theory and geometry. Its GL_n-orbit closure has been studied for over a hundred years and is discussed in Chapter 9. In some sense it is the "weakest" polynomial known that requires an exponential size $\Sigma\Lambda\Sigma$-circuit, which will be important in §7.7. I first determine its symmetry group $G_{e_{n,n}}$, which will be used several times in what follows.

It is clear $T_n^{SL} \rtimes \mathfrak{S}_n \subseteq G_{e_{n,n}}$, where T_n^{SL} denotes the diagonal matrices with determinant one (the matrix with $(\lambda_1, \ldots, \lambda_n)$ on the diagonal sends x_j to $\lambda_j x_j$)

and $\mathfrak{S}_n$ acts by permuting the basis vectors. We need to determine if the stabilizer is larger. Let $g \in GL_n$. Then

$$ g \cdot e_{n,n} = \left(\sum_{j_1=1}^{n} g_1^{j_1} x_{j_1} \right) \cdots \left(\sum_{j_n=1}^{n} g_n^{j_n} x_{j_n} \right). $$

In order that this be equal to $x_1 \cdots x_n$, by unique factorization of polynomials, there must be a permutation $\sigma \in \mathfrak{S}_n$ such that for each k, we have $\sum_j g_k^j x_j = \lambda_k x_{\sigma(k)}$ for some $\lambda_k \in \mathbb{C}^*$. Composing with the inverse of this permutation, we have $g_k^j = \delta_k^j \lambda_j$, and finally we see that we must further have $\lambda_1 \cdots \lambda_n = 1$, which means it is an element of T_n^{SL}, so the original g is an element of $T_n^{SL} \rtimes \mathfrak{S}_n$. Thus $G_{e_{n,n}} = T_n^{SL} \rtimes \mathfrak{S}_n$. By the discussion in §4.2, any Waring decomposition of $e_{n,n}$ containing a pinning set can have symmetry group at most $\mathfrak{S}_n$.

The optimal Waring decomposition of $x_1 \cdots x_n$ is

$$ x_1 \cdots x_n = \frac{1}{2^{n-1} n!} \sum_{\substack{\epsilon \in \{-1,1\}^n \\ \epsilon_1=1}} \left[\left(\Pi_{i=1}^n \epsilon_i \sum_{j=1}^n \epsilon_j x_j \right)^n \right], \qquad (7.1.1) $$

a sum with 2^{n-1} terms. It is called *Fischer's formula* in the computer science literature because Fischer wrote it down in 1994 [Fis94]. While similar formulas appeared earlier (e.g., formula (7.1.2) below appeared in 1934), I have not found this precise formula earlier in the literature. I give the proof of its optimality (due to Ranestad and Schreyer [RS11]) in §10.1.2.

Fischer's decomposition transparently has an $\mathfrak{S}_{n-1}$-symmetry. Here is a slightly larger expression that transparently has an $\mathfrak{S}_n$-symmetry:

$$ x_1 \cdots x_n = \frac{1}{2^n n!} \sum_{\epsilon \in \{-1,1\}^n} \left[\Pi_{i=1}^n \epsilon_i \left(\sum_{j=1}^n \epsilon_j x_j \right)^n \right]. \qquad (7.1.2) $$

This formula dates back at least to 1934, where Mazur and Orlicz [MO34] gave it and generalizations.

Remarkably, as was realized by H. Lee [Lee16], Fischer's expression already has an $\mathfrak{S}_n$-symmetry when n is odd.

For example:

$$ xyz = \frac{1}{24}[(x+y+z)^3 - (x+y-z)^3 - (x-y+z)^3 - (-x+y+z)^3]. $$

For an integer set I and an integer i, define

$$ \delta(I, i) = \begin{cases} -1 & i \in I \\ 1 & i \notin I \end{cases}. $$

When $n = 2k + 1$ is odd, rewrite Fischer's formula as

$$x_1 x_2 \cdots x_n = \frac{1}{2^{n-1} n!} \sum_{I \subset [n], |I| \leq k} (-1)^{|I|} (\delta(I, 1)x_1 + \delta(I, 2)x_2 + \cdots + \delta(I, n)x_n)^n.$$

(7.1.3)

When $n = 2k$ is even, the situation is a little more subtle. One may rewrite Fischer's formula as

$$x_1 x_2 \cdots x_n = \frac{1}{2^{n-1} n!} \left[\sum_{I \subset [n], |I| < k} (-1)^{|I|} (\delta(I, 1)x_1 + \delta(I, 2)x_2 + \cdots + \delta(I, n)x_n)^n \right.$$

$$\left. + \sum_{I \subset [n], |I| = k, 1 \in I} \frac{(-1)^k}{2} (\delta(I, 1)x_1 + \delta(I, 2)x_2 + \cdots + \delta(I, n)x_n)^n \right].$$

(7.1.4)

The collection of terms in the second summation is only $\mathfrak{S}_n$-invariant up to sign. In the language of Chapter 4, if we write the decomposition as $\mathcal{S} = \{\ell_1^n, \ldots, \ell_{2^{n-1}}^n\}$, the decomposition $\mathcal{S}$ *is* $\mathfrak{S}_n$-invariant. Moreover, the set $\{[\ell_1], \ldots, [\ell_{2^{n-1}}]\}$ is $\mathfrak{S}_n$-invariant, however, the set $\{\ell_1, \ldots, \ell_{2^{n-1}}\}$ is only $\mathfrak{S}_{n-1}$-invariant (and $\mathfrak{S}_n$-invariant up to sign).

Remark 7.1.2.1 Using the techniques of [RS00], Ranestad (personal communication) has shown that *every* minimal rank decomposition of $x_1 \cdots x_n$ is in the T^{SL_n}-orbit of the the right-hand side of (7.1.1), so in particular, by Proposition 4.1.2.2, every decomposition has $\mathfrak{S}_n$-symmetry.

7.1.3 Symmetric Ranks of Elementary Symmetric Polynomials

Here are generalizations of the Waring expressions for $e_{n,n}$ to all symmetric polynomials due to H. Lee:

Theorem 7.1.3.1 [Lee16] *Let $d = 2k + 1$ and let $N \geq d$. Then*

$$e_{d,N} = \frac{1}{2^{d-1} d!} \sum_{I \subset [N], |I| \leq k} (-1)^{|I|} \binom{N - k - |I| - 1}{k - |I|} (\delta(I, 1)x_1$$

$$+ \delta(I, 2)x_2 + \cdots + \delta(I, N)x_N)^d.$$

In particular, for d odd, $\mathbf{R}_S(e_{d,N}) \leq \sum_{i=0}^{\lfloor \frac{d}{2} \rfloor} \binom{N}{i}$.

This formula nearly appeared in [MO34] in 1934, but just as with Fischer's, there was a doubling of size.

Proof. Working by downward induction, the case $d = N$ is Fischer's formula. Let $d < N$, and let $F_{d,N}$ denote the right-hand side of the expression.

Observe that $F_{d,d} = e_{d,d}$ and $F_{d,N-1} = F_{d,N}(x_1, \ldots, x_{N-1}, 0)$ up to a constant. In particular $F_{d,d} = F_{d,N}(x_1, \ldots, x_d, 0, \ldots, 0)$ up to a constant. The analogous statement holds setting any subset of the variables to zero. This implies that $F_{d,N}$ is an expression that has all the square-free monomials in $e_{d,N}$ appearing in it, all with the same coefficient. Moreover, there are no other monomials appearing in $F_{d,N}$ as otherwise there would be a monomial involving fewer than d variables that would appear in some specialization to some $e_{d,d}$. One concludes by checking the constant is correct.   □

Lee gives a similar formula for d even.

7.2 Depth Three Circuits and Secant Varieties of the Chow Variety

In this section I discuss the *depth three* or $\Sigma\Pi\Sigma$ circuits, which consist of depth three formulas where the first layer of gates consist of additions, the second of multiplications, and the last gate is an addition gate. Remarkably, these circuits are powerful enough to potentially separate **VP** from **VNP**, as is explained in §7.5.

There is a subtlety with these circuits: their homogeneous version, used naïvely, lacks computing power. This can be fixed either by allowing inhomogeneous circuits, which is what is generally done in the computer science literature, or with the help of padding, which I discuss in §7.2.3.

7.2.1 Secant Varieties and Homogeneous Depth Three Circuits

Recall the Chow variety $Ch_n(W) \subset \mathbb{P}S^nW$. When $\mathbf{w} = \dim W \geq n$, it is the orbit closure $\overline{GL(W) \cdot [x_1 \cdots x_n]}$. The set of polynomials of the form $\sum_{i=1}^r \ell_{i,1} \cdots \ell_{i,n}$, where $\ell_{i,j} \in W$ (the *sum-product polynomial* in the computer science literature) is denoted $\sigma_r^0(Ch_n(W))$, and $\sigma_r(Ch_n(W))$ is the Zariski closure in $\mathbb{P}S^nW$ of $\sigma_r^0(Ch_n(W))$, the rth secant variety of the Chow variety.

The relation between secant varieties of Chow varieties and depth three circuits is as follows:

Proposition 7.2.1.1 [Lan15a] *A polynomial $P \in S^nW$ in $\sigma_r^0(Ch_n(W))$ is computable by a homogeneous depth three circuit of size $r + nr(1 + \mathbf{w})$. If $P \notin \sigma_r^0(Ch_n(W))$, then P cannot be computed by a homogeneous depth three circuit of size $n(r + 1) + r + 1$.*

Proof. In the first case, $P = \sum_{j=1}^r (\ell_{1j} \cdots \ell_{nj})$ for some $\ell_{sj} \in W$. Expressed in terms of a fixed basis of W, each ℓ_{sj} is a linear combination of at worst $\mathbf{w}$ basis vectors, thus to create the ℓ_{sj} requires at worst $nr\mathbf{w}$ additions. Then to multiply them in groups of n is nr multiplications, and finally to add these together is r further additions. In the second case, at best P is in $\sigma_{r+1}^0(Ch_n(W))$, in which case, even if each of the ℓ_{sj}'s is a basis vector (so no initial additions are needed), we still must perform $n(r+1)$ multiplications and $r+1$ additions. $\qquad\square$

7.2.2 Why Homogeneous Depth Three Circuits do not Appear Useful at First Glance

Exercise 6.2.2.7 implies that in order that $[\det_n] \in \sigma_r(Ch_n(\mathbb{C}^{n^2}))$, we must have $r\binom{n}{\lfloor\frac{n}{2}\rfloor} \geq \binom{n}{\lfloor\frac{n}{2}\rfloor}^2$, i.e., $r > \binom{n}{\lfloor\frac{n}{2}\rfloor} \sim 2^n/n$ (see §7.5.1).

By Proposition 7.2.1.1, we conclude:

Proposition 7.2.2.1 [NW97] *The polynomial sequences* $\det_n$ *and* perm_n *do not admit homogeneous depth three circuits of size* $2^n/n$.

Remark 7.2.2.2 The proof above follows from considering partial derivatives in middle degree. In [NW97] they consider all partial derivatives of all orders simultaneously to improve the lower bound to 2^n.

Thus homogeneous depth three circuits at first sight do not seem that powerful because a homogeneous depth 3 circuit of size 2^n cannot compute the determinant.

To make matters worse, consider the polynomial corresponding to iterated matrix multiplication of three by three matrices $IMM_k^3 \in S^k(\mathbb{C}^{9k})$. It is complete for the class $\mathbf{VP}_e$ of sequences with polynomial sized formulas discussed in Remark 6.1.5.2 (see [BOC92]) and also has an exponential lower bound for its Chow border rank:

Exercise 7.2.2.3 (2) Use flattenings to show $IMM_k^3 \notin \sigma_{poly(k)}(Ch_k(\mathbb{C}^{9k}))$.

By Exercise 7.2.2.3, sequences of polynomials admitting polynomial size formulas do not in general have polynomial size homogeneous depth three circuits.

7.2.3 Homogeneous Depth Three Circuits for Padded Polynomials

If one works with padded polynomials instead of polynomials (as we did with $\mathcal{D}et_n$), the power of homogeneous depth three circuits increases to the power of arbitrary depth three circuits. The following geometric version of a result of Ben-Or and Cleve (presented below as a corollary) was suggested by K. Efremenko:

Proposition 7.2.3.1 [Lan15a] *Let* $\mathbb{C}^{m+1}$ *have coordinates* $\ell, x_1, \ldots, x_m$ *and let* $e_{k,m} = e_{k,m}(x_1, \ldots, x_m)$ *be the kth elementary symmetric polynomial. For all* $k \leq m$, $\ell^{m-k}e_{k,m} \in \sigma_m^0(Ch_m(\mathbb{C}^{m+1}))$.

Proof. Fix an integer $u \in \mathbb{Z}$, recall the generating function E_m for the elementary symmetric functions from (6.1.2), and define

$$g_u(x, \ell) = (u\ell)^m E_m \left(\frac{1}{u\ell} \right)$$

$$= \prod_{i=1}^{m} (x_i + u\ell)$$

$$= \sum_k u^{m-k} e_{k,m}(x) \ell^{m-k}.$$

The second line shows $g_u(x, \ell) \in Ch_m(\mathbb{C}^{m+1})$. Letting $u = 1, \ldots, m$, we may use the inverse of the Vandermonde matrix to write each $\ell^{m-k} e_{k,m}$ as a sum of m points in $Ch_m(\mathbb{C}^{m+1})$ because

$$\begin{pmatrix} 1^0 & 1^1 & \cdots & 1^m \\ 2^0 & 2^1 & \cdots & 2^m \\ & \vdots & & \\ m^0 & m^1 & \cdots & m^m \end{pmatrix} \begin{pmatrix} \ell^{m-1} e_{1,m} \\ \ell^{m-2} e_{2,m} \\ \vdots \\ \ell^0 e_{m,m} \end{pmatrix} = \begin{pmatrix} g_1(x, \ell) \\ g_2(x, \ell) \\ \vdots \\ g_m(x, \ell) \end{pmatrix}. \qquad \square$$

Corollary 7.2.3.2 [BOC92] $\ell^{m-k} e_{k,m}$ *can be computed by a homogeneous depth three circuit of size $3m^2 + m$.*

Proof. As remarked above, for any point of $\sigma_r(Ch_n(\mathbb{C}^{m+1}))$ one gets a circuit of size at most $r + nr + rn(m + 1)$, but here at the first level all the addition gates have fanin two (i.e., there are two inputs to each addition gate) instead of the possible $m + 1$. $\qquad \square$

Remark 7.2.3.3 The best lower bound for computing the $e_{k,n}$ via a $\Sigma\Pi\Sigma$ circuit is $\Omega(n^2)$ [SW01], so Corollary 7.2.3.2 is very close to (and may well be) sharp.

Proposition 7.2.3.4 [Lan15a] *Say $P \in S^m\mathbb{C}^M$ is computable by a depth three circuit of size s. Then, for some $n < s + m$, $\ell^{n-m}P$ is computable by a homogeneous depth three circuit of size $O(s^2)$.*

Proof. Start with the inhomogeneous circuit computing P. At the first level, add a homogenizing variable ℓ, so that the affine linear outputs become linear in our original variables plus ℓ, the product gates will each produce a homogeneous polynomial. While the different product gates may produce polynomials of different degrees, when we add them up what remains must be a sum of homogeneous polynomials, such that when we set $\ell = 1$, we obtain the desired homogeneous polynomial. Say the largest power of ℓ appearing in this sum is

q. Note that $q < s$. For each other term there is some other power of ℓ appearing, say q_i for the ith term. Then to the original circuit, add $q - q_i$ inputs to the ith product gate, where each input is ℓ. This will not change the size of the circuit by more than $qr < s^2$. Our new homogeneous depth three circuit will output $\ell^q P$. $\square$

7.3 Algebraic Branching Programs

In this section I describe *algebraic branching programs*, a model of computation with complexity equivalent to that of the determinant, as well as two restrictions of it, one (noncommutative ABPs) that has an exponential lower bound for the permanent (but also for the determinant), and another (read once ABPs), where it is possible to carry out deterministic polynomial identity testing as described in §7.7.

7.3.1 Algebraic Branching Programs and Iterated Matrix Multiplication

Definition 7.3.1.1 (Nisan [Nis91]) An *Algebraic Branching Program* (ABP) over $\mathbb{C}$ is a directed acyclic graph Γ with a single source s and a single sink t. Each edge e is labeled with an affine linear function ℓ_e in the variables $\{y_i | 1 \leq i \leq M\}$. Every directed path $p = e_1 e_2 \cdots e_k$ computes the product $\Gamma_p := \prod_{j=1}^{k} \ell_{e_j}$. For each vertex v the polynomial Γ_v is defined as $\sum_{p \in \mathcal{P}_{s,v}} \Gamma_p$ where $\mathcal{P}_{s,v}$ is the set of paths from s to v. We say that Γ_v *is computed by* Γ *at* v. We also say that Γ_t *is computed by* Γ or that Γ_t *is the output of* Γ.

The *size* of Γ is the number of vertices. Let $\mathrm{abpc}(P)$ denote the smallest size of an algebraic branching program that computes P.

An ABP is *layered* if we can assign a layer $i \in \mathbb{N}$ to each vertex such that for all i, all edges from layer i go to layer $i + 1$. An ABP is *homogeneous* if the polynomials computed at each vertex are all homogeneous. A homogeneous ABP Γ is *degree layered* if Γ is layered and the layer of a vertex v coincides with the degree of v. For a homogeneous P let $\mathrm{dlabpc}(P)$ denote the smallest size of a degree layered algebraic branching program that computes P. Of course $\mathrm{dlabpc}(P) \geq \mathrm{abpc}(P)$.

Definition 7.3.1.2 The *iterated matrix multiplication complexity* of a polynomial $P(y)$ in M variables, $\mathrm{immc}(P)$ is the smallest n such that there exists affine linear maps $B_j : \mathbb{C}^M \to \mathrm{Mat}_n(\mathbb{C})$, $j = 1, \ldots, n$, such that $P(y) = \mathrm{trace}(B_n(y) \cdots B_1(y))$. The *homogeneous iterated matrix multiplication complexity* of a degree m homogeneous polynomial $P \in S^m \mathbb{C}^M$, $\mathrm{himmc}(P)$, is the smallest n such that there exist natural numbers $n_1, \ldots, n_m$ with $1 = n_1$, and

$n = n_1 + \cdots + n_m$, and linear maps $A_s : \mathbb{C}^M \to \text{Mat}_{n_s \times n_{s+1}}$, $1 \le s \le m$, with $n_{m+1} = 1$, such that $P(y) = A_m(y) \cdots A_1(y)$.

7.3.2 Determinantal Complexity and ABPs

Two complexity measures m_1, m_2 are *polynomially related* if, for any sequence p_n of polynomials, there exist constants C_1, C_2 such that for all sufficiently large n, $m_1(p_n) \le (m_2(p_n))^{C_1}$ and $m_2(p_n) \le (m_1(p_n))^{C_2}$.

The following folklore theorem was stated explicitly in [IL16a] with precise upper and lower bounds between the various complexity measures:

Theorem 7.3.2.1 [IL16a] *The complexity measures* dc, abpc, immc, dlabpc, *and* himmc *are all polynomially related.*

Additional relations between different models are given in [MP08].

Regarding the geometric search for separating equations, the advantage one gains by removing the padding in the iterated matrix multiplication model is offset by the disadvantage of dealing with the himmc polynomial that for all known equations such as Young flattenings (which includes the method of shifted partial derivatives as a special case) and equations for degenerate dual varieties, behaves far more generically than the determinant.

Work of Mahajan-Vinay [MV97] implies the following:

Proposition 7.3.2.2 [IL16a] $\text{dlabpc}(\det_m) \le \frac{m^3}{3} - \frac{m}{3} + 2$ *and* $\text{himmc}(\det_m) \le \frac{m^3}{3} - \frac{m}{3} + 2$.

Remark 7.3.2.3 For $m < 7$, the size $2^m - 1$ Grenet-like expressions from [LR15] for $\det_m$ give smaller iterated matrix multiplication expressions than the Mahajan-Vinay expressions. This warns us that small cases can be deceptive.

Remark 7.3.2.4 It is an important and perhaps tractable open problem to prove an $\omega(m^2)$ lower bound for $\text{dc}(\text{perm}_m)$. By the more precise version of Theorem 7.3.2.1 in [IL16a], it would suffice to prove an $\omega(m^6)$ lower bound for $\text{himmc}(\text{perm}_m)$.

Here are the size $\frac{m^3}{3} - \frac{m}{3} + 2$ himmc expressions for $\det_m$ when $m = 3, 4, 5$:

$$
\det_3(x) = \left(x_1^2, x_1^3, x_2^2, x_2^3, x_3^3 \right)
\begin{pmatrix}
x_2^2 & x_2^3 & 0 \\
x_3^2 & x_3^3 & 0 \\
-x_1^2 & -x_1^3 & 0 \\
0 & 0 & x_3^2 \\
-x_1^2 & -x_1^3 & -x_2^2
\end{pmatrix}
\begin{pmatrix}
x_2^1 \\
x_3^1 \\
-x_1^1
\end{pmatrix}.
$$

Let $M_1 = (-x_1^2, -x_1^3, -x_1^4, -x_2^2, -x_2^3, -x_2^4, -x_3^3, -x_3^4, -x_4^4)$. Then

$$
\det_4(x) = M_1
\begin{pmatrix}
x_2^2 & x_2^3 & x_2^4 & 0 & 0 & 0 & 0 \\
x_3^2 & x_3^3 & x_3^4 & 0 & 0 & 0 & 0 \\
x_4^2 & x_4^3 & x_4^4 & 0 & 0 & 0 & 0 \\
-x_1^2 & -x_1^3 & -x_1^4 & 0 & 0 & 0 & 0 \\
0 & 0 & 0 & x_3^2 & x_3^3 & x_3^4 & 0 \\
0 & 0 & 0 & x_4^2 & x_4^3 & x_4^4 & 0 \\
-x_1^2 & -x_1^3 & -x_1^4 & -x_2^2 & -x_2^3 & -x_2^4 & 0 \\
0 & 0 & 0 & 0 & 0 & 0 & x_4^3 \\
-x_1^2 & -x_1^3 & -x_1^4 & -x_2^2 & -x_2^3 & -x_2^4 & -x_3^3
\end{pmatrix}
$$

$$
\times
\begin{pmatrix}
x_2^2 & x_2^3 & x_2^4 & 0 \\
x_3^2 & x_3^3 & x_3^4 & 0 \\
x_4^2 & x_4^3 & x_4^4 & 0 \\
-x_1^2 & -x_1^3 & -x_1^4 & 0 \\
0 & 0 & 0 & x_3^2 \\
0 & 0 & 0 & x_4^2 \\
-x_1^2 & -x_1^3 & -x_1^4 & -x_2^2
\end{pmatrix}
\begin{pmatrix}
x_2^1 \\
x_3^1 \\
x_4^1 \\
-x_1^1
\end{pmatrix}.
$$

Let $M_1 = (x_1^2, x_1^3, x_1^4, x_1^5, x_2^2, x_2^3, x_2^4, x_2^5, x_3^3, x_3^4, x_3^5, x_4^4, x_4^5, x_5^5)$,

$$
M_2 =
\begin{pmatrix}
x_2^2 & x_2^3 & x_2^4 & x_2^5 & 0 & 0 & 0 & 0 & 0 & 0 & 0 & 0 \\
x_3^2 & x_3^3 & x_3^4 & x_3^5 & 0 & 0 & 0 & 0 & 0 & 0 & 0 & 0 \\
x_4^2 & x_4^3 & x_4^4 & x_4^5 & 0 & 0 & 0 & 0 & 0 & 0 & 0 & 0 \\
x_5^2 & x_5^3 & x_5^4 & x_5^5 & 0 & 0 & 0 & 0 & 0 & 0 & 0 & 0 \\
-x_1^2 & -x_1^3 & -x_1^4 & -x_1^5 & 0 & 0 & 0 & 0 & 0 & 0 & 0 & 0 \\
0 & 0 & 0 & 0 & x_3^2 & x_3^3 & x_3^4 & x_3^5 & 0 & 0 & 0 & 0 \\
0 & 0 & 0 & 0 & x_4^2 & x_4^3 & x_4^4 & x_4^5 & 0 & 0 & 0 & 0 \\
0 & 0 & 0 & 0 & x_5^2 & x_5^3 & x_5^4 & x_5^5 & 0 & 0 & 0 & 0 \\
-x_1^2 & -x_1^3 & -x_1^4 & -x_1^5 & -x_2^2 & -x_2^3 & -x_2^4 & -x_2^5 & 0 & 0 & 0 & 0 \\
0 & 0 & 0 & 0 & 0 & 0 & 0 & 0 & x_4^3 & x_4^4 & x_4^5 & 0 \\
0 & 0 & 0 & 0 & 0 & 0 & 0 & 0 & x_5^3 & x_5^4 & x_5^5 & 0 \\
-x_1^2 & -x_1^3 & -x_1^4 & -x_1^5 & -x_2^2 & -x_2^3 & -x_2^4 & -x_2^5 & -x_3^3 & -x_3^4 & -x_3^5 & 0 \\
0 & 0 & 0 & 0 & 0 & 0 & 0 & 0 & 0 & 0 & 0 & x_5^4 \\
-x_1^2 & -x_1^3 & -x_1^4 & -x_1^5 & -x_2^2 & -x_2^3 & -x_2^4 & -x_2^5 & -x_3^3 & -x_3^4 & -x_3^5 & -x_4^4
\end{pmatrix},
$$

$$M_3 = \begin{pmatrix}
x_2^2 & x_2^3 & x_2^4 & x_2^5 & 0 & 0 & 0 & 0 & 0 \\
x_3^2 & x_3^3 & x_3^4 & x_3^5 & 0 & 0 & 0 & 0 & 0 \\
x_4^2 & x_4^3 & x_4^4 & x_4^5 & 0 & 0 & 0 & 0 & 0 \\
x_5^2 & x_5^3 & x_5^4 & x_5^5 & 0 & 0 & 0 & 0 & 0 \\
-x_1^2 & -x_1^3 & -x_1^4 & -x_1^5 & 0 & 0 & 0 & 0 & 0 \\
0 & 0 & 0 & 0 & x_3^2 & x_3^3 & x_3^4 & x_3^5 & 0 \\
0 & 0 & 0 & 0 & x_4^2 & x_4^3 & x_4^4 & x_4^5 & 0 \\
0 & 0 & 0 & 0 & x_5^2 & x_5^3 & x_5^4 & x_5^5 & 0 \\
-x_1^2 & -x_1^3 & -x_1^4 & -x_1^5 & -x_2^2 & -x_2^3 & -x_2^4 & -x_2^5 & 0 \\
0 & 0 & 0 & 0 & 0 & 0 & 0 & 0 & x_4^3 \\
0 & 0 & 0 & 0 & 0 & 0 & 0 & 0 & x_5^3 \\
-x_1^2 & -x_1^3 & -x_1^4 & -x_1^5 & -x_2^2 & -x_2^3 & -x_2^4 & -x_2^5 & -x_3^3
\end{pmatrix},$$

$$M_4 = \begin{pmatrix}
x_2^2 & x_2^3 & x_2^4 & x_2^5 & 0 \\
x_3^2 & x_3^3 & x_3^4 & x_3^5 & 0 \\
x_4^2 & x_4^3 & x_4^4 & x_4^5 & 0 \\
x_5^2 & x_5^3 & x_5^4 & x_5^5 & 0 \\
-x_1^2 & -x_1^3 & -x_1^4 & -x_1^5 & 0 \\
0 & 0 & 0 & 0 & x_3^2 \\
0 & 0 & 0 & 0 & x_4^2 \\
0 & 0 & 0 & 0 & x_5^2 \\
-x_1^2 & -x_1^3 & -x_1^4 & -x_1^5 & -x_2^2
\end{pmatrix}, \quad M_5 = \begin{pmatrix}
x_2^1 \\
x_3^1 \\
x_4^1 \\
x_5^1 \\
-x_1^1
\end{pmatrix}.$$

Then $\det_5(x) = M_1 M_2 M_3 M_4 M_5$.

Let $M_1 = (-x_1^2, -x_1^3, -x_1^4, -x_1^5, -x_1^6, -x_2^2, -x_2^3, -x_2^4, -x_2^5, -x_2^6, -x_3^3, -x_3^4, -x_3^5, -x_3^6, -x_4^4, -x_4^5, -x_4^6, -x_5^5, -x_5^6, -x_6^6)$

$$M_2 = \begin{pmatrix}
x_2^2 & x_2^3 & x_2^4 & x_2^5 & x_2^6 & 0 & 0 & 0 & 0 & 0 & 0 & 0 & 0 & 0 & 0 & 0 & 0 & 0 \\
x_3^2 & x_3^3 & x_3^4 & x_3^5 & x_3^6 & 0 & 0 & 0 & 0 & 0 & 0 & 0 & 0 & 0 & 0 & 0 & 0 & 0 \\
x_4^2 & x_4^3 & x_4^4 & x_4^5 & x_4^6 & 0 & 0 & 0 & 0 & 0 & 0 & 0 & 0 & 0 & 0 & 0 & 0 & 0 \\
x_5^2 & x_5^3 & x_5^4 & x_5^5 & x_5^6 & 0 & 0 & 0 & 0 & 0 & 0 & 0 & 0 & 0 & 0 & 0 & 0 & 0 \\
x_6^2 & x_6^3 & x_6^4 & x_6^5 & x_6^6 & 0 & 0 & 0 & 0 & 0 & 0 & 0 & 0 & 0 & 0 & 0 & 0 & 0 \\
-x_1^2 & -x_1^3 & -x_1^4 & -x_1^5 & -x_1^6 & 0 & 0 & 0 & 0 & 0 & 0 & 0 & 0 & 0 & 0 & 0 & 0 & 0 \\
0 & 0 & 0 & 0 & 0 & x_3^2 & x_3^3 & x_3^4 & x_3^5 & x_3^6 & 0 & 0 & 0 & 0 & 0 & 0 & 0 & 0 \\
0 & 0 & 0 & 0 & 0 & x_4^2 & x_4^3 & x_4^4 & x_4^5 & x_4^6 & 0 & 0 & 0 & 0 & 0 & 0 & 0 & 0 \\
0 & 0 & 0 & 0 & 0 & x_5^2 & x_5^3 & x_5^4 & x_5^5 & x_5^6 & 0 & 0 & 0 & 0 & 0 & 0 & 0 & 0 \\
0 & 0 & 0 & 0 & 0 & x_6^2 & x_6^3 & x_6^4 & x_6^5 & x_6^6 & 0 & 0 & 0 & 0 & 0 & 0 & 0 & 0 \\
-x_1^2 & -x_1^3 & -x_1^4 & -x_1^5 & -x_1^6 & -x_2^2 & -x_2^3 & -x_2^4 & -x_2^5 & -x_2^6 & 0 & 0 & 0 & 0 & 0 & 0 & 0 & 0 \\
0 & 0 & 0 & 0 & 0 & 0 & 0 & 0 & 0 & 0 & x_4^3 & x_4^4 & x_4^5 & x_4^6 & 0 & 0 & 0 & 0 \\
0 & 0 & 0 & 0 & 0 & 0 & 0 & 0 & 0 & 0 & x_5^3 & x_5^4 & x_5^5 & x_5^6 & 0 & 0 & 0 & 0 \\
0 & 0 & 0 & 0 & 0 & 0 & 0 & 0 & 0 & 0 & x_6^3 & x_6^4 & x_6^5 & x_6^6 & 0 & 0 & 0 & 0 \\
-x_1^2 & -x_1^3 & -x_1^4 & -x_1^5 & -x_1^6 & -x_2^2 & -x_2^3 & -x_2^4 & -x_2^5 & -x_2^6 & -x_3^3 & -x_3^4 & -x_3^5 & -x_3^6 & 0 & 0 & 0 & 0 \\
0 & 0 & 0 & 0 & 0 & 0 & 0 & 0 & 0 & 0 & 0 & 0 & 0 & 0 & x_5^4 & x_5^5 & x_5^6 & 0 \\
0 & 0 & 0 & 0 & 0 & 0 & 0 & 0 & 0 & 0 & 0 & 0 & 0 & 0 & x_6^4 & x_6^5 & x_6^6 & 0 \\
-x_1^2 & -x_1^3 & -x_1^4 & -x_1^5 & -x_1^6 & -x_2^2 & -x_2^3 & -x_2^4 & -x_2^5 & -x_2^6 & -x_3^3 & -x_3^4 & -x_3^5 & -x_3^6 & -x_4^4 & -x_4^5 & -x_4^6 & 0 \\
0 & 0 & 0 & 0 & 0 & 0 & 0 & 0 & 0 & 0 & 0 & 0 & 0 & 0 & 0 & 0 & 0 & x_6^5 \\
-x_1^2 & -x_1^3 & -x_1^4 & -x_1^5 & -x_1^6 & -x_2^2 & -x_2^3 & -x_2^4 & -x_2^5 & -x_2^6 & -x_3^3 & -x_3^4 & -x_3^5 & -x_3^6 & -x_4^4 & -x_4^5 & -x_4^6 & -x_5^5
\end{pmatrix},$$

$$
M_3 = \begin{pmatrix}
x_2^2 & x_2^3 & x_2^4 & x_2^5 & x_2^6 & 0 & 0 & 0 & 0 & 0 & 0 & 0 & 0 & 0 & 0 \\
x_3^2 & x_3^3 & x_3^4 & x_3^5 & x_3^6 & 0 & 0 & 0 & 0 & 0 & 0 & 0 & 0 & 0 & 0 \\
x_4^2 & x_4^3 & x_4^4 & x_4^5 & x_4^6 & 0 & 0 & 0 & 0 & 0 & 0 & 0 & 0 & 0 & 0 \\
x_5^2 & x_5^3 & x_5^4 & x_5^5 & x_5^6 & 0 & 0 & 0 & 0 & 0 & 0 & 0 & 0 & 0 & 0 \\
x_6^2 & x_6^3 & x_6^4 & x_6^5 & x_6^6 & 0 & 0 & 0 & 0 & 0 & 0 & 0 & 0 & 0 & 0 \\
-x_1^2 & -x_1^3 & -x_1^4 & -x_1^5 & -x_1^6 & 0 & 0 & 0 & 0 & 0 & 0 & 0 & 0 & 0 & 0 \\
0 & 0 & 0 & 0 & 0 & x_3^2 & x_3^3 & x_3^4 & x_3^5 & x_3^6 & 0 & 0 & 0 & 0 & 0 \\
0 & 0 & 0 & 0 & 0 & x_4^2 & x_4^3 & x_4^4 & x_4^5 & x_4^6 & 0 & 0 & 0 & 0 & 0 \\
0 & 0 & 0 & 0 & 0 & x_5^2 & x_5^3 & x_5^4 & x_5^5 & x_5^6 & 0 & 0 & 0 & 0 & 0 \\
0 & 0 & 0 & 0 & 0 & x_6^2 & x_6^3 & x_6^4 & x_6^5 & x_6^6 & 0 & 0 & 0 & 0 & 0 \\
-x_1^2 & -x_1^3 & -x_1^4 & -x_1^5 & -x_1^6 & -x_2^2 & -x_2^3 & -x_2^4 & -x_2^5 & -x_2^6 & 0 & 0 & 0 & 0 & 0 \\
0 & 0 & 0 & 0 & 0 & 0 & 0 & 0 & 0 & 0 & x_4^3 & x_4^4 & x_4^5 & x_4^6 & 0 \\
0 & 0 & 0 & 0 & 0 & 0 & 0 & 0 & 0 & 0 & x_5^3 & x_5^4 & x_5^5 & x_5^6 & 0 \\
0 & 0 & 0 & 0 & 00 & 0 & 0 & 0 & 0 & 0 & x_6^3 & x_6^4 & x_6^5 & x_6^6 & 0 \\
-x_1^2 & -x_1^3 & -x_1^4 & -x_1^5 & -x_1^6 & -x_2^2 & -x_2^3 & -x_2^4 & -x_2^5 & -x_2^6 & -x_3^3 & -x_3^4 & -x_3^5 & -x_3^6 & 0 \\
0 & 0 & 0 & 0 & 0 & 0 & 0 & 0 & 0 & 0 & 0 & 0 & 0 & 0 & x_5^4 \\
0 & 0 & 0 & 0 & 0 & 0 & 0 & 0 & 0 & 0 & 0 & 0 & 0 & 0 & x_6^4 \\
-x_1^2 & -x_1^3 & -x_1^4 & -x_1^5 & -x_1^6 & -x_2^2 & -x_2^3 & -x_2^4 & -x_2^5 & -x_2^6 & -x_3^3 & -x_3^4 & -x_3^5 & -x_3^6 & -x_4^4
\end{pmatrix},
$$

$$
M_4 = \begin{pmatrix}
x_2^2 & x_2^3 & x_2^4 & x_2^5 & x_2^6 & 0 & 0 & 0 & 0 & 0 & 0 \\
x_3^2 & x_3^3 & x_3^4 & x_3^5 & x_3^6 & 0 & 0 & 0 & 0 & 0 & 0 \\
x_4^2 & x_4^3 & x_4^4 & x_4^5 & x_4^6 & 0 & 0 & 0 & 0 & 0 & 0 \\
x_5^2 & x_5^3 & x_5^4 & x_5^5 & x_5^6 & 0 & 0 & 0 & 0 & 0 & 0 \\
x_6^2 & x_6^3 & x_6^4 & x_6^5 & x_6^6 & 0 & 0 & 0 & 0 & 0 & 0 \\
-x_1^2 & -x_1^3 & -x_1^4 & -x_1^5 & -x_1^6 & 0 & 0 & 0 & 0 & 0 & 0 \\
0 & 0 & 0 & 0 & 0 & x_3^2 & x_3^3 & x_3^4 & x_3^5 & x_3^6 & 0 \\
0 & 0 & 0 & 0 & 0 & x_4^2 & x_4^3 & x_4^4 & x_4^5 & x_4^6 & 0 \\
0 & 0 & 0 & 0 & 0 & x_5^2 & x_5^3 & x_5^4 & x_5^5 & x_5^6 & 0 \\
0 & 0 & 0 & 0 & 0 & x_6^2 & x_6^3 & x_6^4 & x_6^5 & x_6^6 & 0 \\
-x_1^2 & -x_1^3 & -x_1^4 & -x_1^5 & -x_1^6 & -x_2^2 & -x_2^3 & -x_2^4 & -x_2^5 & -x_2^6 & 0 \\
0 & 0 & 0 & 0 & 0 & 0 & 0 & 0 & 0 & 0 & x_4^3 \\
0 & 0 & 0 & 0 & 0 & 0 & 0 & 0 & 0 & 0 & x_5^3 \\
0 & 0 & 0 & 0 & 0 & 0 & 0 & 0 & 0 & 0 & x_6^3 \\
-x_1^2 & -x_1^3 & -x_1^4 & -x_1^5 & -x_1^6 & -x_2^2 & -x_2^3 & -x_2^4 & -x_2^5 & -x_2^6 & -x_3^3
\end{pmatrix},
$$

$$
M_5 = \begin{pmatrix}
x_2^2 & x_2^3 & x_2^4 & x_2^5 & x_2^6 & 0 \\
x_3^2 & x_3^3 & x_3^4 & x_3^5 & x_3^6 & 0 \\
x_4^2 & x_4^3 & x_4^4 & x_4^5 & x_4^6 & 0 \\
x_5^2 & x_5^3 & x_5^4 & x_5^5 & x_5^6 & 0 \\
x_6^2 & x_6^3 & x_6^4 & x_6^5 & x_6^6 & 0 \\
-x_1^2 & -x_1^3 & -x_1^4 & -x_1^5 & -x_1^6 & 0 \\
0 & 0 & 0 & 0 & 0 & x_3^2 \\
0 & 0 & 0 & 0 & 0 & x_4^2 \\
0 & 0 & 0 & 0 & 0 & x_5^2 \\
0 & 0 & 0 & 0 & 0 & x_6^2 \\
-x_1^2 & -x_1^3 & -x_1^4 & -x_1^5 & -x_1^6 & -x_2^2
\end{pmatrix}, \quad
M_6 = \begin{pmatrix}
x_2^1 \\
x_3^1 \\
x_4^1 \\
x_5^1 \\
x_6^1 \\
-x_1^1
\end{pmatrix}
$$

Then $\det_6(X) = M_1 M_2 M_3 M_4 M_5 M_6$.

Compare these with the expression from [LR15]:

$$\det_3(x) = \left(x_1^1, x_1^2, x_1^3\right) \begin{pmatrix} x_2^2 & -x_2^3 & 0 \\ -x_2^1 & 0 & x_2^3 \\ 0 & x_2^1 & -x_2^2 \end{pmatrix} \begin{pmatrix} x_3^3 \\ x_3^2 \\ x_3^1 \end{pmatrix}, \qquad (7.3.1)$$

and for $\det_4$, the sizes of the matrices are 1×4, 4×6, 6×4, 4×1.

7.3.3 A Classical Exponential Lower Bound for the Permanent (and Determinant)

Consider a restricted model where one is not allowed to exploit the commutativity of multiplication. Let $\mathbb{C}\{y_1, \ldots, y_N\}$ denote the ring of polynomials in the noncommuting variables $y_1, \ldots, y_N$. Choose an expression for a polynomial P and consider it in this larger ring. The definition of circuits is the same here, just that we cannot assume $ab = ba$ for expressions a and b.

Theorem 7.3.3.1 [Nis91] *The degree homogeneous noncommutative ABP complexity of* $\det_m$ *and* perm_m *are both* $2^m - 1$.

Proof. Choose the representations of the determinant and permanent where the first row comes first, the second comes second, etc. Consider the degree homogeneous ABP Γ with $m + 1$ layers that computes $\det_m$ (or perm_m). Keep the labels from all edges that appear before level s and set the labels on all other layers to constants to see that all terms of the form $\sum_{\sigma \in \mathfrak{S}_m} c_\sigma y_{\sigma(1)}^1 \cdots y_{\sigma(s)}^s$ can be computed by taking linear combinations of the polynomials Γ_v, where v is a vertex in layer s. Since these terms span a vector space of dimension $\binom{m}{s}$ there must be at least $\binom{m}{s}$ linearly independent polynomials Γ_v, so there must be at least $\binom{m}{s}$ vertices on layer s. Summing up the binomial coefficients yields the lower bound.

The Grenet determinantal presentation of perm_m [Gre11] and the regular determinantal presentation of $\det_m$ of [LR15] give rise to column-wise multilinear iterated matrix multiplication presentations, and thus non-commutative ABPs, of size $2^m - 1$. $\qquad \square$

Remark 7.3.3.2 In contrast to ABPs, for general noncommutative circuits, very little is known (see, e.g., [LMS16, HWY10]). There are exponential bounds for skew circuits in [LMS16] (the class of circuits equivalent in power to the determinant).

7.3.4 Read Once ABPs

Another restriction of ABPs is that of *read once oblivious ABPs*, henceforth ROABPs. Here the ABP is layered. The read-once means that the edges at layer i only use a variable x_i. On the other hand, the weights are allowed to be low degree polynomials in the x_i. The word *oblivious* means additionally that an ordering of the variables is fixed in advance. I return to this model in §7.7 because it is restrictive enough that it admits explicit deterministic hitting sets for polynomial identity testing. On the other hand, this model can efficiently simulate depth three powering circuits.

7.4 Additional Restricted Models

The purpose of this section is to survey restricted models that have geometric aspects. Each subsection may be read independently of the others.

7.4.1 Equivariant Determinantal Complexity

Motivated by the symmetry of Grenet's expressions for the permanent discussed in §6.6.3, N. Ressayre and I asked, what happens if one *imposes* the Γ_m^E-equivariance? We found the following:

Theorem 7.4.1.1 [LR15] *Among Γ_m^E-equivariant determinantal expressions for* perm$_m$, *Grenet's size $2^m - 1$ expressions are optimal and unique up to trivialities.*

The Γ_m^E-equivariance is peculiar as it only makes sense for the permanent. To fix this, we defined a complexity measure that could be applied to all polynomials:

Let $P \in S^m \mathbb{C}^M$ have symmetry group G_P, let $A : \mathbb{C}^M \to \mathbb{C}^{n^2}$ be the linear part of a determinantal expression of P with constant term Λ. Let $G_{\det_n, \Lambda} = G_{\det_n} \cap G_\Lambda \subset GL_{n^2}$. Note that $G_P \times G_{\det_n, \Lambda}$ acts on $\mathbb{C}^{M^*} \otimes \mathbb{C}^{n^2}$ by $(g, h)A(y) := h \cdot A(g^{-1}y)$.

Definition 7.4.1.2 Define the *symmetry group of $\tilde{A}$* to be

$$G_{\tilde{A}} := \{(g, h) \in G_P \times G_{\det_n, \Lambda} \mid (g, h) \cdot A = A\}.$$

Call $\tilde{A}$ an *equivariant determinantal expression* for P if the projection from $G_{\tilde{A}}$ to G_P is surjective. Define edc(P) to be the smallest size of an equivariant determinantal expression for P.

If G is a subgroup of G_P, we say that $\tilde{A}$ is *G-equivariant* if $G \subseteq G_{\tilde{A}}$.

Note that if P is a generic polynomial of degree greater than two, $\text{edc}(P) = \text{dc}(P)$, because it will have a trivial symmetry group. One also has $\text{edc}(\det_m) = \text{dc}(\det_m)$, because $A = \text{Id}: \mathbb{C}^{n^2} \to \mathbb{C}^{n^2}$ and $\Lambda = 0$ is an equivariant expression.

Theorem 7.4.1.3 [LR15] *There exists an equivariant determinantal expression for* perm_m *of size* $\binom{2m}{m} - 1$.

Theorem 7.4.1.4 [LR15] *Among equivariant determinatal expressions for* perm_m, *the size* $\binom{2m}{m} - 1$ *expressions are optimal and unique up to trivialities.*

In particular, Valiant's hypothesis holds in the restricted model of equivariant expressions. To my knowledge, *equivariant determinantal complexity is the only restricted model with a known exponential separation of the permanent from the determinant.*

Proofs are outlined in §8.11.2.

Note that $\binom{2m}{m} \sim 4^m$, so the size of the equivariant determinantal expressions are roughly the square of the size of Grenet's expressions. In particular, they are polynomially related in size.

Thus, if one could show either

- there exists an optimal determinantal expression for perm_m with *some* symmetry, or
- there exists an equivariant determinantal expression for perm_m of size polynomial in $\text{dc}(\text{perm}_m)$,

then one would have proven Valiant's hypothesis. I write "some" symmetry, because as is shown in the proof, full Γ_m^E-symmetry is not needed for the exponential lower bound. (I do not know just how large the symmetry group needs to be to obtain an exponential bound.)

Regarding the possibility of proving either of the above, we have seen that the optimal Waring rank expression for $x_1 \cdots x_n$ (and more generally odd degree elementary symmetric functions) have maximal symmetry, as does the optimal rank expression for $M_{\langle 2 \rangle}$.

7.4.2 Elementary Symmetric Polynomial Complexity

Let $P \in S^m \mathbb{C}^k$ and define the *elementary symmetric complexity* of P, $\text{esc}(P)$, to be the smallest N such that there exists a linear inclusion $\mathbb{C}^k \subset \mathbb{C}^n$ with $P \in \text{End}(\mathbb{C}^N) \cdot e_{m,N} =: \hat{\mathcal{E}}lemen^0_{m,N}$, and $\overline{\text{esc}}(P)$ to be the smallest N such that $P \in \text{End}(\mathbb{C}^N) \cdot e_{m,N} = \overline{GL_N \cdot e_{m,N}} =: \hat{\mathcal{E}}lemen_{m,N}$. A. Shpilka [Shp02] refers to $\text{esc}(P)$ as the "size of the smallest depth two circuit with a symmetric gate at the top and plus gates at the bottom."

For any polynomial P, $\text{esc}(P)$ is finite. More precisely:

Proposition 7.4.2.1 [Shp02] $\sigma_r^0(v_m(\mathbb{P}V)) \subset \mathcal{E}lemen_{m,rm}^0$ *and* $\sigma_r(v_m(\mathbb{P}V)) \subset$ $\mathcal{E}lemen_{m,rm}$. *In other words, if* $P \in S^d V$ *is computable by a* $\Sigma\Lambda\Sigma$ *circuit of size* r, *then* $\mathrm{esc}(P) \leq rm$.

Proof. Without loss of generality, assume $\mathbf{v} = r$, and let $y_1, \dots, y_r$ be a basis of V. It will be sufficient to show $\sum y_j^m \in \mathcal{E}lemen_{m,mr}^0$. Let ω be a primitive mth root of unity. Then I claim

$$\sum y_j^m = -e_{m,rm}(y_1, -\omega y_1, -\omega^2 y_1, \dots, \omega^{m-1} y_1, -y_2, -\omega y_2, \dots, -\omega^{m-1} y_r t).$$

To see this, evaluate the generating function

$$
\begin{aligned}
&E_{rm}(t)(y_1, -\omega y_1, -\omega^2 y_1, \dots, \omega^{m-1} y_1, -y_2, -\omega y_2, \dots, -\omega^{m-1} y_r) \\
&= \prod_{i \in [r]} \prod_{s \in [m]} (1 - \omega^s y_i) \\
&= \prod_{i \in [r]} (1 - y_i^m t^m).
\end{aligned}
$$

The coefficient of t^m on the last line is $-\sum_i y_i^m$. $\qquad\square$

Note that $\dim(\mathcal{E}lemen_{m,rm}) \leq r^2 m^2$ while $\dim(\sigma_r(v_m(\mathbb{P}^{rm-1}))) = rm^2 - 1$, so the dimensions differ only by a factor of r. Contrast this with the inclusion implied by Theorem 7.1.3.1 of $\mathcal{E}lemen_{d,N} \subset \sigma_q(v_d(\mathbb{P}^{N-1}))$ with $q = \sum_{j=0}^{\lfloor \frac{d}{2} \rfloor} \binom{N}{j}$, where the second space in general has dimension exponentially larger than the first.

Regarding lower bounds for esc, Corollary 7.2.3.2 implies that $\mathrm{esc}(P)$ is at least the square root of the size of the smallest depth three circuit computing P.

Shpilka proves lower bounds for esc in the same way the first lower bounds for determinantal complexity were found: by considering linear spaces on the zero set $\mathrm{Zeros}(e_{m,N}) \subset \mathbb{P}^{N-1}$.

Theorem 7.4.2.2 [Shp02] *Let* $L \subset \mathrm{Zeros}(e_{m,N}) \subset \mathbb{P}^{N-1}$ *be a linear space. Then* $\dim L \leq \min(\max(N - m, m - 1), \frac{m+N}{2}) - 1$.

Proof. The key to the proof is the algebraic independence of the $e_{j,N}$ (see, e.g., [Mac95, §1.2]). Any linear space of dimension k will have an isomorphic projection onto some coordinate k-plane. Without loss of generality, assume it has an isomorphic projection onto the span of the first k-coordinates, so that $\hat{L} \subset \mathbb{C}^N$ has equations $x_s = \ell_s(x_1, \dots, x_k)$ for $k + 1 \leq s \leq N$. We are assuming $e_{m,N}|_{\hat{L}} = 0$.

Exercise 7.4.2.3 (1) Show that if we have two sets of variables $(x, y) = (x_1, \dots, x_k, y_1, \dots, y_{N-k})$, then $e_{m,N}(x, y) = \sum_{j=0}^m e_{m-j,k}(x) e_{j,N-k}(y)$.

By Exercise 7.4.2.3,

$$0 = e_{m,N}(x, \ell(x))$$

$$= e_{m,k}(x) + \sum_{j=1}^{m} e_{m-j,k}(x)e_{j,N-k}(\ell(x)). \qquad (7.4.1)$$

First assume $k = \dim \hat{L} \geq \max(N - m + 1, m)$. Since $e_{k,u} = 0$ if $k > u$, if $N - k < m$, the sum in (7.4.1) is from 1 to $N - k$.

Let $\Psi : \mathbb{C}[x_1, \ldots, x_k] \to \mathbb{C}[x_1, \ldots, x_k]^{\mathfrak{S}_k}$ denote the symmetrization operator. (Sometimes Ψ is called a *Reynolds operator*.)

Exercise 7.4.2.4 (1) Show that for any functions f, g, $\Psi(f + g) = \Psi(f) + \Psi(g)$.

Exercise 7.4.2.5 (1) Show that if f is a symmetric function and g is a polynomial, then $\Psi(fg) = \Psi(f)\Psi(g)$.

Apply Ψ to (7.4.1) to obtain

$$0 = e_{m,k}(x) + \sum_{j=1}^{N-k} e_{m-j,k}(x)\Psi(e_j(\ell(x))),$$

but this expresses $e_{m,k}$ as a polynomial in symmetric functions of degree less than k, a contradiction.

Now assume $\dim \hat{L} \geq \frac{m+N}{2}$, so

$$0 = e_{m,k}(x) + e_{m,N-k}(\ell(x)) + \sum_{j=1}^{m} e_{m-j,k}(x)e_j(\ell(x)).$$

The idea is again the same, but we must somehow reduce to a smaller space. If we take $D \in \{\ell_1, \ldots, \ell_{N-k}\}^{\perp} \subset \mathbb{C}^N$ and apply it, we can eliminate the $e_{m,N-k}(\ell(x))$ term. But if we take a general such D, we will no longer have symmetric functions. However, one can find a D such that, if we restrict to span of the first $m - 1$ coordinate vectors, call this space $V_{m-1} \subset \mathbb{C}^k \subset \mathbb{C}^N$, then $(De_{r,k})|_{V_{m-1}} = e_{r-1,m-1}$ (see [Shp02]). Unfortunately, this is still not good enough, as letting $x' = (x_1, \ldots, x_{m-1})$, we now have

$$0 = e_{m-1,m-1}(x') + \sum_{j=1}^{m} e_{m-j,k}(x')e_j(\ell(x')).$$

We could argue as before if we could eliminate the $j = 1$ term. A modification of D as described in [Shp02] also satisfies $D(e_{1,k}(x)) = 0$. □

Thus if Zeros(P) has large linear spaces on it, we obtain lower bounds for esc(P). Recall that for a projective subspace $L \subset \mathbb{P}^{N-1}$, $\hat{L} \subset \mathbb{C}^N$ denotes the corresponding linear subspace.

Exercise 7.4.2.6 (1) Show $\overline{esc}(\det_m) \geq 2m^2 - 3m$.

Exercise 7.4.2.7 (1) Show that if $m \geq \frac{N+1}{2}$, there exists a linear space of dimension $m - 2$ on $\text{Zeros}(e_{m,N})$. ⊚

Say m is odd and N is even. Let

$$\hat{L} = \text{span}\{(1, -1, 0, \ldots, 0), (0, 0, 1, -1, 0, \ldots, 0), , \ldots, (0, \ldots, 0, 1, -1)\}.$$

Notice that all odd power sum functions vanish on $\hat{L}$. When we express $e_{m,N}$ in terms of power sum functions, each term will contain an odd degree power sum, so we conclude $e_{m,N}|_{\hat{L}} = 0$. More generally:

Proposition 7.4.2.8 [Shp02] *[attributed to Saks] There exists a* $\mathbb{P}^{\lfloor \frac{N}{q} \rfloor - 1} \subset \text{Zeros}(e_{m,N})$, *where q is the smallest integer such that q does not divide m.*

Exercise 7.4.2.9 (2) Prove Proposition 7.4.2.8. ⊚

Exercise 7.4.2.7 and Proposition 7.4.2.8 show that Theorem 7.4.2.2 is close to being sharp.

The following conjecture appeared in [Shp02] (phrased differently):

Conjecture 7.4.2.10 [Shp02] *There exists a polynomial $r(m)$ such that* $\sigma_{r(m)}(Ch_m(\mathbb{C}^{mr(m)})) \not\subset \mathcal{E}lemen_{m,2^m}$. *One might even be able to take $r(m) \equiv 2$.*

The second assertion is quite strong, as when $r = 1$, there is containment, and when $r = 2$, the left-hand side has dimension about $4m$ and the right-hand side has dimension about 4^m.

Exercise 7.4.2.11 (2) Show that $\sigma_2(Ch_m(\mathbb{C}^{2m})) \not\subset \mathcal{E}lemen_{m, \frac{3}{2}m-3}$.

Question 7.4.2.12 [Shp02] What is the maximal dimension of a linear subspace $L \subset \mathbb{P}^{N-1}$ such that $L \subset \text{Zeros}(e_{m,N})$?

7.4.3 Raz's Theorem on Tensor Rank and Formula Size

In this section I explain Raz's results that if one considers a tensor as a polynomial, lower bounds on the tensor rank have consequences for the formula size of the corresponding polynomial.

Definition 7.4.3.1 A polynomial $P \in S^d V$ is *multilinear* if $V = V_1 \oplus \cdots \oplus V_d$ and $P \in V_1 \otimes \cdots \otimes V_d \subset S^d V$.

The permanent and determinant may be considered as multilinear polynomials (in two different ways). In the literature, e.g., [Raz10b], they do not insist on homogeneous polynomials, so they use the term *set-multilinear* to describe such polynomials where each monomial appearing is multilinear (but does not necessarily use variables from each of the V_j).

Given a tensor $T \in A_1 \otimes \cdots \otimes A_d$, by considering $A_1 \otimes \cdots \otimes A_d \subset S^d(A_1 \oplus \cdots \oplus A_d)$, we may think of T as defining a multilinear polynomial. When I want to emphasize T as a multilinear polynomial, I'll write $P_T \in S^d(A_1 \oplus \cdots \oplus A_d)$.

One can compare the tensor rank of T with the circuit complexity of P_T. Raz compares it with the formula complexity: He shows that super-polynomial lower bounds for multilinear formulas for polynomial sequences P_n where the degree grows slowly, imply superpolynomial lower bounds for general formulas:

Theorem 7.4.3.2 [Raz10b] *Let* $\dim A_j = n$ *and let* $T_n \in A_1 \otimes \cdots \otimes A_d$ *be a sequence of tensors with* $d = d(n)$ *satisfying* $d = O(\frac{\log(n)}{\log(\log(n))})$. *If there exists a formula of size* n^C *for* P_{T_n}, *then* $\mathbf{R}(T_n) \leq n^{d(1-2^{O(C)})}$.

Corollary 7.4.3.3 [Raz10b] *Let* $\dim A_j = n$ *and let* $T_n \in A_1 \otimes \cdots \otimes A_d$ *be a sequence of tensors with* $d = d(n)$ *satisfying* $d = O(\frac{\log(n)}{\log(\log(n))})$. *If* $\mathbf{R}(T_n) \geq n^{d(1-o(1))}$, *then there is no polynomial size formula for* P_T.

These results were extended in [CKSV16].

Via flattenings, one can exhibit explicit tensors with $\underline{\mathbf{R}}(T) \geq n^{\lfloor \frac{d}{2} \rfloor}$. Using the substitution method (see §5.3), that was improved for tensor rank to $2n^{\lfloor \frac{d}{2} \rfloor} + n - O(d \log(n))$ in [AFT11] by a construction generalizing the one described in §5.3.1 for the case $d = 3$.

The idea of proof is as follows: a rank decomposition of T, viewed as a computation of P_T, corresponds to a depth-3 multilinear formula for P_T. Raz shows that for any polynomial sequence P_n, if there is a fanin-2 formula of size s and depth δ for P, then there exists a homogeneous formula of size $O(\binom{\delta+d+1}{d}s)$ for P_n. He then shows that for any multilinear polynomial P_n, if there exists a fanin-2 formula of size s and depth δ, then there exists a multilinear formula of size $O((\delta + 2)^d s)$ for P_n.

7.4.4 Multilinear Formulas

A formula is multilinear if the polynomial computed by each of its subformulas is multilinear. For example, Ryser's formula for the permanent is multilinear. On the other hand, the smallest known formula for the determinant is not multilinear.

In [Raz09], Raz shows that any multilinear arithmetic formula for perm_n or $\det_n$ is of size $n^{\Omega(n)}$. The starting point of the proof is the method of partial derivatives. Then Raz makes certain reductions, called *random restrictions* to reduce to a smaller polynomial that one can estimate more precisely.

7.4.5 Raz's Elusive Functions and Circuit Lower Bounds

Raz defines the following "hay in a haystack" approach to Valiant's hypothesis. Consider a linear projection of a Veronese $proj : \mathbb{P}S^r\mathbb{C}^s \dashrightarrow \mathbb{P}^m$, and let $\Gamma_{r,s} :=$ $proj \circ v_r : \mathbb{P}^{s-1} \dashrightarrow \mathbb{P}^m$ be the composition of the projection with the Veronese map. A map $f : \mathbb{P}^n \to \mathbb{P}^m$ is said to be (r, s)-*elusive* if $f(\mathbb{P}^n)$ is not contained in the image of any such $\Gamma_{r,s}$.

Recall that **VNP** may be thought of as the set of "explicit" polynomial sequences.

Theorem 7.4.5.1 [Raz10a] *Let m be superpolynomial in n, and $s \geq m^{\frac{9}{10}}$. If there exists an explicit $(s, 2)$-elusive $f : \mathbb{P}^n \to \mathbb{P}^m$, then* **VP** $\neq$ **VNP**.

Theorem 7.4.5.2 [Raz10a] *Let $r(n) = \log(\log(n))$, $s(n) = n^{\log(\log(\log(n)))}$, $m = n^r$, and let C be a constant. If there exists an explicit (s, r)-elusive $f : \mathbb{P}^n \to \mathbb{P}^m$, then* **VP** $\neq$ **VNP**.

By a dimension count, a general polynomial in either range will be elusive.

Again, one can approach, e.g., the case where $r = 2$, by finding equations for the variety of all images of projections of the quadratic Veronese, and then finding a polynomial (point) not in the zero set.

In the same paper, Raz constructs an explicit f, whose entries are monomials, that requires circuits of size at least $n^{1+\Omega(\frac{1}{r})}$ to compute.

7.4.6 Glynn's Theorem on Expressions for the Permanent

Recall, for $P \in S^m\mathbb{C}^M$, $\mathbf{R}_{Ch_m(\mathbb{C}^M)}(P)$ is the smallest r such that $P(y_1, \ldots, y_M) = \sum_{s=1}^r \Pi_{u=1}^m \left(\sum_{a=1}^M \lambda_{s,u,a} y_a \right)$ for some constants $\lambda_{s,u,a}$. This corresponds to the smallest homogeneous $\Sigma^r \Pi^m \Sigma^M$ circuit that computes P. If P is multilinear, so $M = mw$, and we may write $y_a = (y_{i\alpha})$, where $1 \leq i \leq m$, $1 \leq \alpha \leq w$, and $P = \sum C_\alpha y_{1\alpha} \cdots y_{m\alpha}$ we could restrict to *multilinear* $\Sigma\Pi\Sigma$ circuits (ML-$\Sigma\Pi\Sigma$ circuits), those of the form $\sum_{s=1}^r \Pi_{i=1}^m \left(\sum_{\alpha=1}^w \lambda_{s,\alpha} y_{i\alpha} \right)$. Write $\mathbf{R}^{ML}_{Ch_m(\mathbb{C}^M)}(P)$ for the smallest multilinear $\Sigma^r \Pi^m \Sigma^w$ circuit for such a P. Consider multilinear $\Sigma\Pi\Sigma$-circuit complexity as a restricted model. In this context, we have the following theorem of D. Glynn:

Theorem 7.4.6.1 [Gly13] $\mathbf{R}^{ML}_{Ch_m(\mathbb{C}^M)}(\text{perm}_m) = \mathbf{R}_S(x_1 \cdots x_m) = 2^{m-1}$.

Moreover, there is a one-to-one correspondence between Waring decompositions of $x_1 \cdots x_m$ and ML $-$ $\Sigma\Pi\Sigma$ decompositions of perm_m. *The correspondence is as follows: constants $\lambda_{s,j}$, $1 \leq s \leq r$, $1 \leq j \leq m$ satisfy*

$$x_1 \cdots x_m = \sum_{s=1}^r \left(\sum_{j=1}^m \lambda_{s,j} x_j \right)^m \tag{7.4.2}$$

if and only if

$$\mathrm{perm}_m(y_{ij}) = m! \sum_{s=1}^{r} \prod_{i=1}^{m} \left(\sum_{j=1}^{m} \lambda_{s,j} y_{ij} \right). \tag{7.4.3}$$

Proof. Given a Waring decomposition (7.4.2) of $x_1 \cdots x_m$, set $x_j = \sum_k y_{jk} z_k$. The coefficient of $z_1 \cdots z_m$ in the resulting expression on the left-hand side is the permanent and the coefficient of $z_1 \cdots z_m$ on the right-hand side is the right-hand side of (7.4.3).

To see the other direction, given an expression (7.4.3), I will specialize to various matrices to show identities among the $\lambda_{s,j}$ that will imply all coefficients but the desired one on the right-hand side of (7.4.2) are zero.

The coefficient of $x_1^{b_1} \cdots x_m^{b_m}$, where $b_1 + \cdots + b_m = m$ in (7.4.2) is $\binom{m}{b_1, \ldots, b_m} \sum_s \lambda_{s,1}^{b_1} \cdots \lambda_{s,m}^{b_m}$.

Let y be a matrix where there are b_j 1s in column j and zero elsewhere. Then unless each $b_j = 1$, $\mathrm{perm}(y) = 0$. But (7.4.3) says that $0 = \mathrm{perm}(y)$ is a nonzero constant times $\sum_s \lambda_{s,1}^{b_1} \cdots \lambda_{s,m}^{b_m}$. Thus all these terms are zero and the only potential nonzero coefficient in the right-hand side of (7.4.2) is the coefficient of $x_1 \cdots x_m$. This coefficient is $m! = \binom{m}{1, \ldots, 1}$ times $\lambda_{s,1} \cdots \lambda_{s,m}$. Plugging in $y = \mathrm{Id}$ shows $1 = m! \lambda_{s,1} \cdots \lambda_{s,m}$. $\square$

Remark 7.4.6.2 As mentioned in Remark 7.1.2.1, all rank 2^{m-1} expressions for $x_1 \cdots x_m$ come from the T^{SL_m} orbit of (7.1.1), so the same holds for size 2^{m-1} $ML - \Sigma\Pi\Sigma$ expressions for perm_m.

7.4.7 Rank k Determinantal Expressions

Restricted models with a parameter k that converge to the original problem as k grows are particularly appealing, as one can measure progress toward the original conjecture. Here is one such: given a polynomial $P \in S^m \mathbb{C}^M$ and determinantal expression $\tilde{A} : \mathbb{C}^M \to \mathbb{C}^{n^2}$, $\tilde{A}(y) = \Lambda + \sum_{j=1}^{M} A_j y_j$ where Λ, A_j are matrices, define the *rank* of $\tilde{A}$ to be the largest rank of the A_js. Note that this depends on the coordinates up to rescaling them, but for the permanent, this is not a problem, as G_{perm_m} defines the coordinates up to scale.

If one could show that perm_m did not admit an expression with rank polynomial in m, then that would trivially prove Valiant's hypothesis.

The notation of rank of a determinantal expression was introduced in [AJ15], as a generalization of the *read* of a determinantal expression, which is the maximal number of nonzero entries of the A_j. As observed by Anderson, Shpilka, and Volk (personal communication from Shpilka), as far as complexity is concerned, the measures are equivalent: if a polynomial P in n variables admits a rank k determinantal expression of size s, then it admits a read-k determinantal expression of size $s + 2nk$.

The state of the art regarding this model is not very impressive:

Theorem 7.4.7.1 [IL16a] *The polynomial* perm_m *does not admit a rank one determinantal expression over* $\mathbb{C}$ *when* $m \geq 3$. *In particular,* perm_m *does not admit a read once regular determinantal expression over* $\mathbb{C}$ *when* $m \geq 3$.

7.5 Shallow Circuits and Valiant's Hypothesis

In this section I discuss three classes of shallow circuits that could be used to prove Valiant's hypothesis. We have already seen the first, the $\Sigma\Pi\Sigma$ circuits. The next is the $\Sigma\Lambda\Sigma\Lambda\Sigma$ circuits, which are depth five circuits where the first layer of gates are additions, the second layer consists of "powering gates," where a powering gate takes f to f^δ for some natural number δ, the third layer addition gates, the fourth layer again powering gates, and the fifth layer is an addition gate. The third is the class of depth four $\Sigma\Pi\Sigma\Pi$ circuits. I describe the associated varieties to these classes of circuits in §7.5.3. A $\Sigma\Lambda^\alpha\Sigma\Lambda^\beta\Sigma$ circuit means the powers are respectively β and α, and other superscripts are to be similarly interpreted.

7.5.1 Detour for those not Familiar with Big Numbers

When dealing with shallow circuits, we will have to distinguish between different rates of superpolynomial growth, both in statements and proofs of theorems. This detour is for those readers not used to comparing large numbers.

All these identities follow from (7.5.1), which follows from *Stirling's formula*, which gives an approximation for the Gamma function, e.g., for $x > 0$,

$$\Gamma(x) = \sqrt{2\pi} x^{x-\frac{1}{2}} e^{-x} e^{\frac{\theta(x)}{12x}},$$

where $0 < \theta(x) < 1$. Stirling's formula may be proved via complex analysis (estimating a contour integral) (see, e.g., [Ahl78, §5.2.5]). Let

$$H_e(x) := -x \ln x - (1 - x) \ln(1 - x)$$

denote the *Shannon entropy*:

$$n! \gtrsim\!\!\!\!\!\sim \sqrt{2\pi n} \left(\frac{n}{e}\right)^n, \tag{7.5.1}$$

$$\ln(n!) = n \ln(n) - O(\ln(n)), \tag{7.5.2}$$

$$\binom{2n}{n} \gtrsim\!\!\!\!\!\sim \frac{4^n}{\sqrt{\pi n}}, \tag{7.5.3}$$

$$\ln \binom{\alpha n}{\beta n} = \alpha H_e \left(\frac{\beta}{\alpha}\right) n - O(\ln n), \tag{7.5.4}$$

$$\binom{\alpha n}{\beta n} = \left[\frac{\alpha^\alpha}{\beta^\beta (\alpha - \beta)^{\alpha - \beta}}\right]^n O\left(\frac{1}{n}\right). \tag{7.5.5}$$

Exercise 7.5.1.1 (1) Show that for $0 < x < 1$, $0 < H_e(x) \leq 1$. For which x is the maximum achieved?

Exercise 7.5.1.2 (1) Show $a^{\log(b)} = b^{\log(a)}$.

Exercise 7.5.1.3 (1!) Consider the following sequences of n:

$$\log_2(n),\ n,\ 100n,\ n^2,\ n^3,\ n^{\log_2(n)},\ 2^{[\log_2(n)]^2},\ n^{\sqrt{\log_2(n)}},\ 2^n,\ \binom{2n}{n},\ n!,\ n^n.$$

In each case, determine for which n, the sequence surpasses the number of atoms in the known universe. (It is estimated that there are between 10^{78} and 10^{82} atoms in the known universe.)

Exercise 7.5.1.4 (1) Compare the growth of $s^{\sqrt{d}}$ and $2^{\sqrt{d \log ds}}$.

Exercise 7.5.1.5 (1!) Compare the growth of $\binom{n^2 + \frac{n}{2} - 1}{\frac{n}{2}}$ and $\binom{n}{\frac{n}{2}}^2$. Compare with your answer to Exercise 6.2.2.7.

7.5.2 Depth Reduction Theorems

A major result in the study of shallow circuits was [VSBR83], where it was shown that if a polynomial of degree d can be computed by a circuit of size s, then it can be computed by a circuit of depth $O(\log d \log s)$ and size polynomial in s. Since then there has been considerable work on shallow circuits. See, e.g., [GKKS17] for a history.

Here are the results relevant for our discussion. They combine results of [Bre74, GKKS13b, Tav15, Koi12, AV08]:

Theorem 7.5.2.1 *Let $N = N(d)$ be a polynomial, and let $P_d \in S^d\mathbb{C}^N$ be a sequence of polynomials that can be computed by a circuit of polynomial size $s = s(d)$. Let $S(d) := 2^{O(\sqrt{d \log(ds)} \log(N))}$.*
Then,

1. *P is computable by a homogeneous $\Sigma\Pi\Sigma\Pi$ circuit of size $S(d)$,*
2. *P is computable by a $\Sigma\Pi\Sigma$ circuit of size of size $S(d)$, and*
3. *P is computable, by a homogeneous $\Sigma\Lambda\Sigma\Lambda\Sigma$ circuit of size $S(d)$, and both powering gates of size $O(\sqrt{d})$.*

Note that $S(d)$ is approximately $s^{\sqrt{d}}$.

Corollary 7.5.2.2 *If perm_m is not computable by one of a homogeneous $\Sigma\Pi\Sigma\Pi$ circuit, a $\Sigma\Pi\Sigma$ circuit, or a homogeneous $\Sigma\Lambda\Sigma\Lambda\Sigma$ circuit of size $2^{\omega(\sqrt{m} \log^{\frac{3}{2}} m)}$, then $\mathbf{VP} \neq \mathbf{VNP}$.*

Here are ideas toward the proof: in [GKKS13b] they prove upper bounds for the size of a depth three circuit computing a polynomial, in terms of the size of an arbitrary circuit computing the polynomial. They first apply the work of [Koi12, AV08], which allows one to reduce an arbitrary circuit of size s computing a polynomial of degree d in N variables to a formula of size $2^{O(\log s \log d)}$ and depth d.

The next step is via the iterated matrix multiplication polynomial. By Theorem 7.3.2.1, formula size is at least as large as iterated matrix multiplication complexity. Say we can compute $f \in S^m \mathbb{C}^M$ via m matrix multiplications of $n \times n$ matrices with linear entries. (Here n will be comparable to s.) Group the entries into groups of $\lceil \frac{m}{a} \rceil$ for some a. To simplify the discussion, assume $\frac{m}{a}$ is an integer. Write

$$X_1 \cdots X_m = \left(X_1 \cdots X_{\frac{m}{a}}\right)\left(X_{\frac{m}{a}+1} \cdots X_{2\frac{m}{a}}\right) \cdots \left(X_{m-\frac{m}{a}+1} \cdots X_m\right).$$

Each term in parenthesis can be computed (using the naïve matrix multiplication algorithm) via a $\Sigma\Pi^{\frac{m}{a}}$-circuit of size $O(n^{\frac{m}{a}})$. After getting the resulting matrices, we can compute the rest via a $\Sigma\Pi^a$ circuit of size $O(n^a)$. This reduces one to a depth four circuit of size $S = 2^{O(\sqrt{d \log d} \log s \log n)}$. Then one can get a depth five powering circuit using (7.1.1). (An alternative, perhaps simpler, proof appears in [Sap, Theorem 5.17].)

The new circuit has size $O(S)$ and is of the form $\Sigma\Lambda\Sigma\Lambda\Sigma$. Finally, they use (6.1.6) to convert the power sums to elementary symmetric functions, which keeps the size at $O(S)$ and drops the depth to three.

7.5.3 Geometry and Shallow Circuits

I first rephrase the depth 3 result:

Proposition 7.5.3.1 [Lan15a] *Let* $d = N^{O(1)}$ *and let* $P \in S^d \mathbb{C}^N$ *be a polynomial that can be computed by a circuit of size* s.
Then $[\ell^{n-d} P] \in \sigma_r(Ch_n(\mathbb{C}^{N+1}))$ *with roughly* $rn \sim s^{\sqrt{d}}$, *more precisely,* $rn = 2^{O(\sqrt{d} \log(N) \log(ds))}$.

Corollary 7.5.3.2 [GKKS13b] $[\ell^{n-m} \det_m] \in \sigma_r(Ch_n(\mathbb{C}^{m^2+1}))$ *where* $rn = 2^{O(\sqrt{m} \log m)}$.

Proof. The determinant admits a circuit of size m^4, so it admits a $\Sigma\Pi\Sigma$ circuit of size

$$2^{O(\sqrt{m} \log(m) \log(m*m^4))} = 2^{O(\sqrt{m} \log m)},$$

so its padded version lies in $\sigma_r(Ch_n(\mathbb{C}^{m^2+1}))$ where $rn = 2^{O(\sqrt{m} \log m)}$. $\square$

Corollary 7.5.3.3 [GKKS13b] *If for all but finitely many m and all r, n with $rn = 2^{\sqrt{m}\log(m)\omega(1)}$, one has $[\ell^{n-m}\operatorname{perm}_m] \not\in \sigma_r(Ch_n(\mathbb{C}^{m^2+1}))$, then there is no circuit of polynomial size computing the permanent, i.e., $\mathbf{VP} \neq \mathbf{VNP}$.*

Proof. One just needs to observe that the number of edges in the first layer (which are invisible from the geometric perspective) is dominated by the number of edges in the other layers. $\qquad\square$

I now reformulate the other shallow circuit results in geometric language. I first give a geometric reformulation of homogeneous $\Sigma\Lambda\Sigma\Lambda\Sigma$ circuits As mentioned previously, the first layer just allows one to work with arbitrary linear forms. The second layer of a $\Sigma\Lambda\Sigma\Lambda\Sigma$ circuit sends a linear form ℓ to ℓ^δ, i.e., it outputs points of $v_\delta(\mathbb{P}V)$. The next layer consists of addition gates, outputting sums of dth powers, i.e., points of $\sigma_r(v_\delta(\mathbb{P}V))$. The next layer Veronese re-embeds and multiplies (i.e., projects $S^{\delta'}(S^\delta V) \to S^{\delta\delta'}V$) these secant varieties to obtain points of $mult(v_{\delta'}(\sigma_r(v_\delta(\mathbb{P}V))))$, and the final addition gate outputs a point of $\sigma_{r'}(mult((v_{\delta'}(\sigma_r(v_\delta(\mathbb{P}V))))))$. In what follows I will simply write $\sigma_{r'}(v_{\delta'}(\sigma_r(v_\delta(\mathbb{P}V))))$ for this variety. Thus we may rephrase Theorem 7.5.2.1(2) of [GKKS13b] as follows:

Proposition 7.5.3.4 [Lan15a] *Let $d = N^{O(1)}$, and let $P_N \in S^d\mathbb{C}^N$ be a polynomial sequence that can be computed by a circuit of size s. Then $[P_N] \in \sigma_{r_1}(v_{\frac{d}{\delta}}(\sigma_{r_2}(v_\delta(\mathbb{P}^{N-1}))))$ with roughly $\delta \sim \sqrt{d}$ and $r_1r_2 \sim s^{\sqrt{d}}$, more precisely $r_1r_2\delta = 2^{O(\sqrt{d\log(ds)}\log(N))}$.*

Corollary 7.5.3.5 [Lan15a] *If for all but finitely many m, $\delta \simeq \sqrt{m}$, and all r_1, r_2 such that $r_1r_2 = 2^{\sqrt{m}\log(m)\omega(1)}$, one has $[\operatorname{perm}_m] \not\in \sigma_{r_1}(v_{m/\delta}(\sigma_{r_2}(v_\delta(\mathbb{P}^{m^2-1}))))$, then there is no circuit of polynomial size computing the permanent, i.e., $\mathbf{VP} \neq \mathbf{VNP}$.*

Problem 7.5.3.6 Find equations in the ideal of $\sigma_{r_1}(v_\delta(\sigma_{r_2}(v_\delta(\mathbb{P}^{m^2-1}))))$.

Y. Guan [Gua15b] has compared the flattening rank of a generic polynomial in $\sigma_{r_1}(v_\delta(\sigma_{r_2}(v_\delta(\mathbb{P}^{m^2-1}))))$ with that of the permanent and showed that

$$\operatorname{perm}_n \not\in \sigma_{2^{\sqrt{n}\log(n)\omega(1)}}\left(v_{\sqrt{n}}\left(\sigma_{2^{2\sqrt{n}-\log(n)\omega(1)}}\left(v_{\sqrt{n}}\left(\mathbb{P}^{n^2-1}\right)\right)\right)\right).$$

Remark 7.5.3.7 The expected dimension of $\sigma_r(Ch_m(W))$ is $rm\mathbf{w} + r - 1$. If we take n and work instead with padded polynomials $\ell^{n-m}P$, the expected dimension of $\sigma_r(Ch_n(W))$ is $rn\mathbf{w} + r - 1$. In contrast, the expected dimension of $\sigma_r(v_{d-a}(\sigma_\rho(v_a(\mathbb{P}W))))$ does not change when one increases the degree, which indicates why padding is so useful for homogeneous depth three circuits but not for $\Sigma\Lambda\Sigma\Lambda\Sigma$ circuits.

I now describe depth four circuits in terms of joins and multiplicative joins. Following [Lan10], for varieties $X \subset \mathbb{P}S^a W$ and $Y \subset \mathbb{P}S^b W$, define the *multiplicative join* of X and Y, $MJ(X, Y) := \{[xy] \mid [x] \in X, \ [y] \in Y\} \subset \mathbb{P}S^{a+b}W$, and define $MJ(X_1, \ldots, X_k)$ similarly. Let $MJ^k(X) = MJ(X_1, \ldots, X_k)$ when all the $X_j = X$, which is a multiplicative analog of the secant variety. Note that $MJ^k(\mathbb{P}W) = Ch_k(W)$. The varieties associated to the polynomials computable by depth $k + 1$ formulas are of the form $\sigma_{r_k}(MJ^{d_{k-1}}(\sigma_{r_{k-2}}(\cdots MJ^{d_1}(\mathbb{P}W)\cdots)))$, and $MJ^{d_k}(\sigma_{r_{k-1}}(MJ^{d_{k-2}}(\sigma_{r_{k-3}}(\cdots MJ^{d_1}(\mathbb{P}W)\cdots))))$. In particular, a $\Sigma^r \Pi^\alpha \Sigma^s \Pi^\beta$ circuit computes (general) points of $\sigma_r(MJ^\alpha(\sigma_s(MJ^\beta(\mathbb{P}W))))$.

7.6 Hilbert Functions of Jacobian Ideals (Shifted Partial Derivatives) and VP versus VNP

The paper [GKKS13a] by Gupta, Kamath, Kayal, and Saptharishi (GKKS) won the best paper award at the 2013 Conference on Computational Complexity (CCC) because it came tantalizingly close to proving Valiant's hypothesis by showing that the permanent does not admit a depth four circuit with top fanin $2^{o(\sqrt{m})}$. Compare this with Theorem 7.5.2.1 that implies to prove **VP** $\neq$ **VNP**, it would be sufficient to show that perm_m is not computable by a homogeneous $\Sigma\Pi^{O(\sqrt{m})}\Sigma\Pi^{O(\sqrt{m})}$ circuit with top fanin $2^{\Omega(\sqrt{m}\log(m))}$.

The caveat is that in the same paper, they proved the same lower bound for the determinant. On the other hand, a key estimate they use (7.6.6) is close to being sharp for the determinant but conjecturally far from being sharp for the permanent.

Their method of proof is via a classical subject in algebraic geometry: the study of *Hilbert functions*, and opens the way for using techniques from commutative algebra (study of *syzygies*) in algebraic complexity theory. I begin, in §7.6.1, with a general discussion on the growth of Hilbert functions of ideals. In §7.6.2, I outline the proof of the above-mentioned GKKS theorem. In §7.6.3, I show that the shifted partial derivative technique alone cannot separated the determinant from the padded permanent. However, more powerful tools from commutative algebra should be useful for future investigations. With this in mind, in §10.4, I discuss additional information about the permanent and determinant coming from commutative algebra.

7.6.1 Generalities on Hilbert Functions

In what follows we will be comparing the sizes of ideals in judiciously chosen degrees. In this section I explain the fastest and slowest possible growth of ideals generated in a given degree.

Theorem 7.6.1.1 (Macaulay, see, e.g., [Gre98]) *Let* $\mathcal{I} \subset Sym(\mathbb{C}^N)$ *be a homogeneous ideal, and let d be a natural number. Write*

$$\dim S^d \mathbb{C}^N / \mathcal{I}_d = \binom{a_d}{d} + \binom{a_{d-1}}{d-1} + \cdots + \binom{a_\delta}{\delta} \qquad (7.6.1)$$

with $a_d > a_{d-1} > \cdots > a_\delta$ *(such an expression exists and is unique). Then*

$$\dim \mathcal{I}_{d+\tau} \geq \binom{N+d+\tau-1}{d+\tau}$$
$$- \left[\binom{a_d+\tau}{d+\tau} + \binom{a_{d-1}+\tau}{d+\tau-1} + \cdots + \binom{a_\delta+\tau}{\delta+\tau} \right]. \qquad (7.6.2)$$

See [Gre98] for a proof.

Corollary 7.6.1.2 *Let* $\mathcal{I}$ *be a homogeneous ideal such that* $\dim \mathcal{I}_d \geq \dim S^{d-q} \mathbb{C}^N = \binom{N+d-q-1}{d-q}$ *for some* $q < d$. *Then*

$$\dim \mathcal{I}_{d+\tau} \geq \dim S^{d-q+\tau} \mathbb{C}^N = \binom{N+\tau+d-q-1}{\tau+d-q}.$$

Proof of Corollary. First use the identity

$$\binom{a+b}{b} = \sum_{j=1}^{q} \binom{a+b-j}{b-j+1} + \binom{a+b-q}{b-q} \qquad (7.6.3)$$

with $a = N - 1$, $b = d$. Write this as

$$\binom{N-1+d}{d} = Q_d + \binom{N-1+d-q}{d-q}.$$

Set

$$Q_{d+\tau} := \sum_{j=1}^{q} \binom{N-1+d+\tau-j}{d+\tau-j+1}.$$

By Macaulay's theorem, any ideal $\mathcal{I}$ with

$$\dim \mathcal{I}_d \geq \binom{N-1+d-q}{d-q}$$

must satisfy

$$\dim \mathcal{I}_{d+\tau} \geq \binom{N-1+d+\tau}{d+\tau} - Q_{d+\tau} = \binom{N-1+d-q+\tau}{d-q+\tau}.$$

$\square$

Gotzman [Got78] showed that if $\mathcal{I}$ is generated in degree at most d, then equality is achieved for all τ in (7.6.2) if equality holds for $\tau = 1$. This is the slowest possible growth of an ideal. Ideals satisfying this minimal growth exist. For example, *lex-segment ideals* satisfy this property, see [Gre98]. These are the ideals, say generated by K elements, where the generators are the first K monomials in lexicographic order. For $1 \leq K \leq M$, the generators are $x_1^d, x_1^{d-1}x_2, \ldots, x_1^{d-1}x_K$. For $M + 1 \leq K \leq 2M$, the generators are $x_1^{d-1}x_j, x_1^{d-2}x_2x_s, 1 \leq j \leq M, 2 \leq s \leq K - M$, etc.

In general, slow growth occurs because there are *syzygies* among the generators of the ideal, that is there are relations of the form $P_1Q_1 + \cdots + P_rQ_r = 0$, where $P_j \in \mathcal{I}$ and the Q_j are polynomials of low degree. For any ideal, one has tautological syzygies, called the *Koszul syzygies* with $r = 2$ and $Q_1 = P_2$ and $Q_2 = -P_1$. Ideals which have only these syzygies grow fast. Explicitly, the fastest possible growth of an ideal generated in degree d by $K < N$ generators is like that of a *complete intersection*: a variety $X \subset \mathbb{P}V$ of codimension c is a complete intersection if its ideal can be generated by c elements. The degree D component of an ideal generated in degree d by K generators that grows like a complete intersection ideal has dimension

$$\sum_{j=1}^{K}(-1)^{j+1}\binom{K}{j}\binom{N + D - jd - 1}{D - jd}. \tag{7.6.4}$$

Fröberg [Frö85] conjectures ideals with this growth exist even when $K > N$ and Iarrobino [Iar97] conjectures further that the ideal generated by $\ell_1^d, \ldots, \ell_K^d$, with the ℓ_j general, has this growth (this is known for $K \leq N$).

Exercise 7.6.1.3 (2) Prove directly that (7.6.4) holds for an ideal generated by ℓ_1^d, ℓ_2^d. ⊚

The study of the growth of ideals is a classical subject in algebraic geometry. The function $\mathrm{HilbF}_t(\mathcal{I}) := \dim \mathcal{I}_t$ is called the *Hilbert function* of the ideal $\mathcal{I} \subset Sym(V)$.

7.6.2 Lower Complexity Bounds for perm_m (and $\det_n$) for Depth Four Circuits

Theorem 7.6.2.1 [GKKS13a] *Any* $\Sigma\Pi^{O(\sqrt{m})}\Sigma\Pi^{O(\sqrt{m})}$ *circuit that computes* perm_m *or* $\det_m$ *must have top fanin at least* $2^{\Omega(\sqrt{m})}$.

In other words $[\mathrm{perm}_m] \notin \sigma_s(MJ^q(\sigma_t(MJ^{m-q}(\mathbb{P}^{m^2-1}))))$, for $s = 2^{o(\sqrt{m})}$ and $q = O(\sqrt{m})$. In fact they show $[\mathrm{perm}_m] \notin \sigma_s(MJ^q(\mathbb{P}S^{m-q}\mathbb{C}^{m^2}))$.

Recall the Jacobian varieties from §6.3.2. The dimension of $\mathrm{Zeros}(P)_{Jac,k}$ is a measure of the nature of the singularities of $\mathrm{Zeros}(P)$. The proof proceeds by comparing the Hilbert functions of Jacobian varieties.

If $P = Q_1 \cdots Q_p$ is the product of p polynomials, and $k \leq p$, then $Z_{Jac,k}$ will be of codimension at most $k+1$ because it contains $\text{Zeros}(Q_{i_1}) \cap \cdots \cap \text{Zeros}(Q_{i_{k+1}})$ for all $(i_1, \ldots, i_{k+1}) \subset [p]$.

Now $\sigma_s(MJ^q(\mathbb{P}S^{m-q}\mathbb{C}^{m^2}))$ does not consist of polynomials of this form, but sums of such. With the sum of m such, we can arrive at a smooth hypersurface. So the goal is to find a pathology of $Q_1 \cdots Q_p$ that persists even when taking sums. (The goal is to find something that persists even when taking a sum of $2^{\sqrt{m}}$ such!)

In this situation, the dimension of the space of partial derivatives (rank of the flattenings) is not small enough to prove the desired lower bounds. However, the image of the flattening map will be of a pathological nature, in that all the polynomials in the image are in an ideal generated by a small number of lower degree polynomials. To see this, when $P = Q_1 \cdots Q_p$, with $\deg(Q_j) = q$, any first derivative is in $\sum_j S^{q-1}V \cdot (Q_1 \cdots \hat{Q}_j \cdots Q_p)$, where the hat denotes omission. The space of kth derivatives, when $k < p$, is in $\sum_{|J|=k} S^{q-k}V \cdot (Q_1 \cdots \hat{Q}_{j_1} \cdots \hat{Q}_{j_k} \cdots Q_p)$. In particular, it has dimension at most

$$\binom{p}{k} \dim S^{q-k}V = \binom{p}{k}\binom{\mathbf{v}+q-k-1}{q-k}. \tag{7.6.5}$$

More important than its dimension, is its structure: the ideal it generates, in a given degree D "looks like" the polynomials of degree $D-k$ times a small fixed space of dimension $\binom{p}{k}$.

This behavior is similar to the lex-segment ideals. It suggests comparing the Hilbert functions of the ideal generated by a polynomial computable by a "small" depth four circuit, i.e., of the form $\sum_{j=1}^{s} Q_{1j} \cdots Q_{pj}$ with the ideal generated by the partial derivatives of the permanent, which are just the subpermanents. As remarked earlier, even the dimension of the zero set of the size k subpermanents is not known in general. Nevertheless, we just need a lower bound on its growth, which we can obtain by degenerating it to an ideal we can estimate.

First we get an upper bound on the growth of the ideal of the Jacobian variety of $Q_1 \cdots Q_m$: by the discussion above, in degree $m-k+\tau$, it has dimension at most

$$\binom{p}{k} \dim S^{q-k+\tau}V = \binom{p}{k}\binom{\mathbf{v}+\tau+q-k-1}{q-k}.$$

To get the lower bound on the growth of the ideal generated by subpermanents we use a crude estimate: given a polynomial f given in coordinates, its *leading monomial* in some order (say lexicographic), is the monomial in its expression that is highest in the order. So if an ideal is generated by $f_1, \ldots, f_q$ in degree d, then in degree $d+\tau$, it is of dimension at most the number of monomials in degree $d + \tau$ divisible by a leading monomial from one of the f_j.

If we order the variables in $\mathbb{C}^{m^2}$ by $y_1^1 > y_2^1 > \cdots > y_m^1 > y_1^2 > \cdots > y_m^m$, then the leading monomial of any subpermanent is the product of the elements on the principal diagonal. Even working with this, the estimate is difficult, so in [GKKS13a] they restrict further to only look at leading monomials among the variables on the diagonal and super diagonal: $\{y_1^1, \ldots, y_m^m, y_2^1, y_3^2, \ldots, y_m^{m-1}\}$. Among these, they compute that the number of leading monomials of degree δ is $\binom{2m-\delta}{\delta}$. In our case, $\delta = m - k$ and $D = \tau + m - k$. Let $I_d^{\text{perm}_m, k} \subset S^d \mathbb{C}^{m^2}$ denote the degree d component of the ideal generated by the order k partial derivatives of the permanent, i.e., the kth Jacobian variety of perm_m. In [GKKS13a], $I_d^{\text{perm}_m, k}$ is denoted $\langle \partial^{=k} \text{perm}_m \rangle_{=d-m+k}$. We have

$$\dim I_{m-k+\tau}^{\text{perm}_m, k} \geq \binom{m+k}{2k}\binom{m^2+\tau-2k}{\tau},\qquad (7.6.6)$$

and

$$\dim I_{m-k+\tau}^{\det_m, k} \geq \binom{m+k}{2k}\binom{m^2+\tau-2k}{\tau}.\qquad (7.6.7)$$

Putting the estimates together, if we want to realize the permanent by size s $\Sigma\Pi^{O(\sqrt{m})}\Sigma\Pi^{O(\sqrt{m})}$ circuit, we need

$$s \geq \frac{\binom{m+k}{2k}\binom{m^2+\tau-2k}{\tau}}{\binom{c\sqrt{m}+k}{k}\binom{m^2+\tau+(\sqrt{m}-1)k}{m^2}}.\qquad (7.6.8)$$

Theorem 7.6.2.1 follows by setting $\tau = m^{\frac{5}{2}}$ and $k = \epsilon m^{\frac{1}{2}}$ where ϵ is a constant defined below. To see this, one calculates (using the estimates of §7.5.1)

$$\ln \frac{\binom{m^2+m^{\frac{5}{2}}-2\epsilon\sqrt{m}}{m^{\frac{5}{2}}}}{\binom{m^2+m^{\frac{5}{2}}+(\sqrt{m}-1)\epsilon\sqrt{m}}{m^2}} = -2\epsilon\sqrt{m}\ln\sqrt{m} - \epsilon\sqrt{m} \pm O(1)$$

$$\ln \frac{\binom{m^2+\epsilon\sqrt{m}}{2\epsilon\sqrt{m}}}{\binom{(c+\epsilon)\sqrt{m}}{\epsilon\sqrt{m}}} = \sqrt{m}2\epsilon\ln\frac{\sqrt{m}}{2\epsilon} + 2\epsilon$$

$$+ (c+\epsilon)\left[\frac{\epsilon}{c+\epsilon}\ln\left(\frac{\epsilon}{c+\epsilon}\right) + \left(1-\frac{\epsilon}{c+\epsilon}\right)\ln\left(1-\frac{\epsilon}{c+\epsilon}\right)\right] + O(\ln m).$$

These imply

$$\ln(s) \geq \epsilon\sqrt{m}\ln\frac{1}{4\epsilon(c+\epsilon)} \pm O(1),$$

so choosing ϵ such that $\frac{1}{4\epsilon(c+\epsilon)} = e$, yields $\ln(s) \geq \Omega(\sqrt{m})$.

7.6.3 Shifted Partial Derivatives cannot Separate
Permanent from Determinant

Recall the notations for a polynomial $P \in S^n V$, that $I_d^{P,k} = \langle \partial^{=k} P \rangle_{=d-n+k}$ is the degree d component of the ideal generated by the order k partial derivatives of P, i.e., the degree d component of the ideal of the kth Jacobian variety of P.

Theorem 7.6.3.1 [ELSW16] *There exists a constant M such that for all $m > M$, every $n > 2m^2 + 2m$, any τ, and any $k < n$,*

$$\dim I_{n+\tau}^{\ell^{n-m} \mathrm{perm}_m, k} < \dim I_{n+\tau}^{\det_n, k}.$$

In other words,

$$\dim \langle \partial^{=k} (\ell^{n-m} \mathrm{perm}_m) \rangle_{=\tau} < \dim \langle \partial^{=k} \det_n \rangle_{=\tau}.$$

The proof of Theorem 7.6.3.1 splits into four cases:

- (C1) Case $k \geq n - \frac{n}{m+1}$. This case has nothing to do with the padded permanent or its derivatives: the estimate is valid for any polynomial in $m^2 + 1$ variables.
- (C2) Case $2m \leq k \leq n - 2m$. This case uses that when $k < n - m$, the Jacobian ideal of *any* padded polynomial $\ell^{n-m} P \in S^n W$ is contained in the ideal generated in degree $n - m - k$ by ℓ^{n-m-k} which has slowest growth by Macaulay's theorem.
- (C3) Case $k < 2m$ and $\tau > \frac{3}{2} n^2 m$. This case is similar to case C2, only a degeneration of the determinant is used in the comparison.
- (C4) Case $k < 2m$ and $\tau < \frac{n^3}{6m}$. This case uses (7.6.7) and compares it with a very crude upper bound for the dimension of the space of the shifted partial derivatives of the permanent.

Note that C1, C2 overlap when $n > 2m^2 + 2m$ and C3, C4 overlap when $n > \frac{m^2}{4}$, so it suffices to take $n > 2m^2 + 2m$.

Case C1

The assumption is $(m + 1)(n - k) \leq n$. It will be sufficient to show that some $R \in \mathrm{End}(W) \cdot \det_n$ satisfies $\dim I_{n-k+\tau}^{\ell^{n-m} \mathrm{perm}_m, k} < \dim I_{n-k+\tau}^{R,k}$. Block the matrix $x = (x_u^s) \in \mathbb{C}^{n^2}$, with $1 \leq s, u \leq n$, as a union of $n - k$ blocks of size $m \times m$ in the upper-left corner plus the remainder, which by our assumption includes at least $n - k$ elements on the diagonal. Set each diagonal block to the matrix (y_j^i), with $1 \leq i, j \leq n$, (there are $n - k$ such blocks), fill the remainder of the diagonal with ℓ (there are at least $n - k$ such terms), and fill the remainder of the matrix with zeros. Let R be the restriction of the determinant to this subspace. Then the space of partials of R of degree $n - k$, $I_{n-k}^{R,k} \subset S^{n-k} \mathbb{C}^{n^2}$ contains a space of polynomials isomorphic to $S^{n-k}\mathbb{C}^{m^2+1}$, and $I_{n-k}^{\ell^{n-m}\,\mathrm{perm}_m,k} \subset S^{n-k}\mathbb{C}^{m^2+1}$, so we conclude.

Example 7.6.3.2 Let $m = 2, n = 6, k = 4$. The matrix is

$$
\begin{pmatrix}
y_1^1 & y_2^1 & & & & \\
y_1^2 & y_2^2 & & & & \\
& & y_1^1 & y_2^1 & & \\
& & y_1^2 & y_2^2 & & \\
& & & & \ell & \\
& & & & & \ell
\end{pmatrix}.
$$

The polynomial $(y_1^1)^2$ is the image of $\frac{\partial^4}{\partial x_2^2 \partial x_4^4 \partial x_5^5 \partial x_6^6}$ and the polynomial $y_2^1 y_2^2$ is the image of $\frac{\partial^4}{\partial x_1^2 \partial x_3^3 \partial x_5^5 \partial x_6^6}$.

Case C2

As long as $k < n - m$, $I_{n-k}^{\ell^{n-m}\,\mathrm{perm}_m,k} \subset \ell^{n-m-k} \cdot S^m W$, so

$$
\dim I_{n-k+\tau}^{\ell^{n-m}\,\mathrm{perm}_m,k} \le \binom{n^2 + m + \tau - 1}{m + \tau}. \tag{7.6.9}
$$

By Corollary 7.6.1.2, with $N = n^2$, $d = n - k$, and $d - q = m$, it will be sufficient to show that

$$
\dim I_{n-k}^{\det_n,k} = \binom{n}{k}^2 \ge \dim S^m W = \binom{n^2 + m - 1}{m}. \tag{7.6.10}
$$

In the range $2m \le k \le n - 2m$, the quantity $\binom{n}{k}$ is minimized at $k = 2m$ and $k = n - 2m$, so it is enough to show that

$$
\binom{n}{2m}^2 \ge \binom{n^2 + m - 1}{m}. \tag{7.6.11}
$$

The estimates of §7.5.1 show that this holds when $\left(\frac{n}{2m} - 1\right)^4 > \left(\frac{n^2}{m} - \frac{m-1}{m}\right)$, which holds for all sufficiently large m when $n > m^2$.

Case C3

Here simply degenerate $\det_n$ to $R = \ell_1^n + \ell_2^n$ by, e.g., setting all diagonal elements to ℓ_1, all the subdiagonal elements to ℓ_2, as well as the $(1, n)$-entry, and setting all other elements of the matrix to zero. Then $I_{n-k}^{R,k} = \mathrm{span}\{\ell_1^{n-k}, \ell_2^{n-k}\}$. Since this is a complete intersection ideal,

$$
\dim I_{n-k+\tau}^{R,k} = 2\binom{n^2 + \tau - 1}{\tau} - \binom{n^2 + \tau - (n-k) - 1}{\tau - (n-k)}. \tag{7.6.12}
$$

Using the estimate (7.6.9) from Case C2, it remains to show

$$2\binom{n^2+\tau-1}{\tau} - \binom{n^2+\tau+m-1}{\tau+m} - \binom{n^2+\tau-(n-k)-1}{\tau-(n-k)} > 0.$$

Divide by $\binom{n^2+\tau-1}{\tau}$. We need

$$2 > \prod_{j=1}^{m}\frac{n^2+\tau+m-j}{\tau+m-j} + \prod_{j=1}^{n-k}\frac{\tau-j}{n^2+\tau-j} \qquad (7.6.13)$$

$$= \prod_{j=1}^{m}\left(1+\frac{n^2}{\tau+m-j}\right) + \prod_{j=1}^{n-k}\left(1-\frac{n^2}{n^2+\tau-j}\right). \qquad (7.6.14)$$

The second line is less than

$$\left(1+\frac{n^2}{\tau}\right)^{m} + \left(1-\frac{n^2}{n^2+\tau-1}\right)^{n-k}. \qquad (7.6.15)$$

Consider (7.6.15) as a function of τ. Write $\tau = n^2 m\delta$, for some constant δ. Then (7.6.15) is bounded above by

$$e^{\frac{1}{\delta}} + e^{\frac{2}{\delta}-\frac{n}{m\delta}}.$$

The second term goes to zero for large m, so we just need the first term to be less than 2, so take, e.g., $\delta = \frac{3}{2}$.

Case C4

Compare (7.6.7) with the very crude estimate

$$\dim I_{n-k+\tau}^{\ell^{n-m}\,\mathrm{perm}_m,k} \le \sum_{j=0}^{k}\binom{m}{j}^{2}\binom{n^2+\tau-1}{\tau},$$

where $\sum_{j=0}^{k}\binom{m}{j}^{2}$ is the dimension of the space of partials of order k of $\ell^{n-m}\,\mathrm{perm}_m$, and the $\binom{n^2+\tau-1}{\tau}$ is what one would have if there were no syzygies. One then concludes using the estimates of §7.5.1, although it is necessary to split the estimates into two subcases: $k \ge \frac{m}{2}$ and $k < \frac{m}{2}$. See [ELSW16] for details.

7.7 Polynomial Identity Testing, Hitting Sets, and Explicit Noether Normalization

I give an introduction to the three topics in the section title. Hitting sets are defined with respect to a coordinate system, however they reflect geometry that is independent of coordinates that merits further study.

For simplicity, I work with homogeneous polynomials, and continue to work exclusively over $\mathbb{C}$.

7.7.1 PIT

If someone hands you a homogeneous polynomial, given in terms of a circuit, or in terms of a sequence of symmetrizations and skew-symmetrizations (as often happens in representation theory), how can you test if it is identically zero?

I will only discuss "black box" polynomial identity testing (henceforth PIT), where one is only given the output of the circuit, as opposed to "white box" PIT where the structure of the circuit may also be examined.

Consider the simplest case: say you are told the polynomial in N-variables is linear. Then it suffices to test it on N points in general linear position in $\mathbb{P}^{N-1}$. Similarly, if we have a conic the projective plane, six general points suffice to test if the conic is zero (and given six points, it is easy to test if they are general enough).

Any $P \in S^d \mathbb{C}^2$ vanishing on any $d+1$ distinct points in $\mathbb{P}^1$ is identically zero. More generally, for $P \in S^d \mathbb{C}^N$, $\binom{N+d-1}{d}$ sufficiently general points in $\mathbb{P}^{N-1}$ suffice to test if P is zero. If N, d are large, this is not feasible. Also, it is not clear how to be sure points are sufficiently general. Fortunately, for a small price, we have the following lemma, which dates back at least to [AT92], addressing the "sufficiently general" issue:

Lemma 7.7.1.1 *Let Σ be a collection of $d+1$ distinct nonzero complex numbers, and let $\Sigma^N = \{(c_1, \ldots, c_N) \mid c_i \in \Sigma\}$. Then any $P \in S^d \mathbb{C}^N$ vanishing on Σ^N is identically zero.*

Proof. Work by induction on N, the case $N = 1$ is clear. Write P as a polynomial in x_N: $P(x_1, \ldots, x_N) = \sum_{j=0}^d P_j(x_1, \ldots, x_{N-1}) x_N^j$, where $P_j \in S^{d-j} \mathbb{C}^{N-1}$, and assume P vanishes on Σ^N. For each $(c_1, \ldots, c_{N-1}) \in \Sigma^{N-1}$, $P(c_1, \ldots, c_{N-1}, x_N)$ is a polynomial in one variable vanishing on Σ^1 and is therefore identically zero. Thus each P_j vanishes identically on Σ^{N-1} and by induction is identically zero. $\square$

Now say we are given a polynomial with extra structure and we would like to exploit the structure to determine if it is nonzero using a smaller set of points than Σ^N. If we are told it is a dth power (or zero), then its zero set is simply a hyperplane, so $N+1$ points in general linear position again suffice. Now say we are told it has low Waring rank. How could we exploit that information to find a small set of points to test?

7.7.2 Hitting Sets

Definition 7.7.2.1 (see, e.g, [SY09, §4.1]) Given a subset $\mathcal{C} \subset \mathbb{C}[x_1, x_2, \ldots, x_N]$, a finite subset $\mathcal{H} \subset \mathbb{C}^N$ is a *hitting set* for $\mathcal{C}$ if for all nonzero $f \in \mathcal{C}$, there exists $\alpha \in \mathcal{H}$ such that $f(\alpha) \neq 0$.

Lemma 7.7.1.1 provides an explicit, size $(d+1)^N$ hitting set for $S^d\mathbb{C}^N$. Call this the *naïve (d, N)-hitting set*.

In geometric language, a hitting set is a subset $\mathcal{H} \subset \mathbb{C}^N$ such that the evaluation map $eval_{\mathcal{H}} : \mathbb{C}^{\binom{n+d}{d}} \to \mathbb{C}^{|\mathcal{H}|}$ satisfies $eval_{\mathcal{H}}^{-1}(0) \cap \mathcal{C} = 0$.

Existence of a hitting set implies black box PIT via the evaluation map.

Lemma 7.7.2.2 [HS82] *There exist hitting sets for*

$$\mathcal{C}_s := \{ f \in S^d\mathbb{C}^n \mid \exists \text{ a size } s \text{ circuit computing } f \},$$

with size bounded by a polynomial in s, d and n.

7.7.3 Waring Rank

Returning to the problem of finding an explicit (in the computer science sense, see §6.1.3) hitting set for polynomials of small Waring rank, recall that we do not know defining equations for $\sigma_r(v_d(\mathbb{P}^{N-1}))$, however, we do have some equations, at least as long as $r < \binom{N+\lfloor \frac{d}{2} \rfloor - 1}{\lfloor \frac{d}{2} \rfloor}$, namely the flattenings. So it is easier to change the question: we simply look for a hitting set for the larger variety $Flat_r^{\lfloor \frac{d}{2} \rfloor, \lceil \frac{d}{2} \rceil}(S^dV) := \{ P \in S^dV \mid \mathrm{rank}(P_{\lfloor \frac{d}{2} \rfloor, \lceil \frac{d}{2} \rceil}) \leq r \}$, where $P_{\lfloor \frac{d}{2} \rfloor, \lceil \frac{d}{2} \rceil} : S^{\lfloor \frac{d}{2} \rfloor}V^* \to S^{\lceil \frac{d}{2} \rceil}V$ is the partial derivative map. We have a considerable amount of information about $Flat_r^{\lfloor \frac{d}{2} \rfloor, \lceil \frac{d}{2} \rceil}(S^dV)$.

Consider the case $r = 2$: our polynomial is of the form $P = (\lambda_1 x_1 + \cdots \lambda_N x_N)^d + (\mu_1 x_1 + \cdots \mu_N x_N)^d$, for some $\lambda_i, \mu_j \in \mathbb{C}$. It is no longer sufficient to check on the N coordinate points, as it could be that $\lambda_j^d + \mu_j^d = 0$ for all j but P is nonzero. On the other hand, there cannot be too much "interference": restrict to the $\binom{N}{2}$ coordinate $\mathbb{P}^1$'s: it is straightforward to see that if all these restrictions are identically zero, then the polynomial must be zero. Moreover, each of those restrictions can be tested to be zero by just checking on $d + 1$ points on a line. Rephrasing geometrically: no point of $\sigma_2(v_d(\mathbb{P}^{N-1}))$ has a zero set that contains the $\binom{N}{2}$ $\mathbb{P}^1$'s spanned by pairs of points from any collection of N points that span $\mathbb{P}^{N-1}$. (Compare with Lemma 2.6.2.1.) In contrast, consider $\ell_1 \cdots \ell_d = 0$: it contains d-hyperplanes!

The general idea is that, if the flattening rank of P is small and P is not identically zero, then for some "reasonably small" k, there cannot be a collection of $\binom{N}{k}$ $\mathbb{P}^{k-1}$'s spanned by k subsets of any set of N points spanning $\mathbb{P}^{N-1}$ in the zero set of P. In coordinates, this means there is a monomial in the expression for P that involves at most k variables, so it will suffice to restrict P to each of the $\binom{N}{k}$ coordinate subspaces and test these restrictions on a naïve (d, k)-hitting set.

From the example of $P = \ell_1 \cdots \ell_d$, we see that "small" means at least that $r < \binom{N}{\lfloor \frac{d}{2} \rfloor}$. In [FS13a], they show that we may take $k = \log(r)$. (Note that if r is close to 2^N, the assertion becomes vacuous as desired.) Explicitly:

Theorem 7.7.3.1 [FS13a] *Let $\mathcal{H}$ consist of the $(d+1)^k \binom{N}{k}$ points of naïve hitting sets on each coordinate $\mathbb{P}^{k-1}$. Then $\mathcal{H}$ is an explicit hitting set for $\{P \in S^d \mathbb{C}^N \mid \mathrm{rank}(P_{\lfloor \frac{d}{2} \rfloor, \lceil \frac{d}{2} \rceil}) < 2^k\}$, in particular for points of $\sigma_{2^k}(v_d(\mathbb{P}^{\mathbb{N}-1}))$.*

An even better hitting set is given in [FSS13].
Recall ROABPs from §7.3.4.

Theorem 7.7.3.2 [FS13b] *Let $\mathcal{C} \subset \mathbb{C}[x_1, \ldots, x_n]$ denote the set of polynomials computable by a depth n, width at most w, degree at most r ROABP. Then $\mathcal{C}$ has an explicit hitting set $\mathcal{H}$ of size $poly(n, w, r)^{O(\log(n))}$ (quasi-polynomial size). Furthermore, one can take $\mathcal{H} \subset \mathbb{Q}^n$.*

7.7.4 Efficient Noether Normalization

One of the difficulties in understanding $\mathcal{D}et_n \subset \mathbb{P}S^n \mathbb{C}^{n^2}$ is that its codimension is of size exponential in n. It would be desirable to have a subvariety of at worst polynomial codimension to work with, as then one could use additional techniques to study its coordinate ring. If one is willing to put up with the destruction of external symmetry, one might simply take a linear projection of $\mathcal{D}et_n$ to a small ambient space. By Noether-Normalization §3.1.4, we know that a "random" linear space of codimension, say $2n^4$ would give rise to an isomorphic projection. However what one would need is an *explicit* such linear space. In [Mul12] Mulmuley considers this problem of explicitness, in the context of separating points of an affine variety (described below) via a small subset of its coordinate ring. Call $\mathcal{S} \subset \mathbb{C}[X]$ a *separating subset* if for all $x, y \in X$, there exists $f \in \mathcal{S}$ that distinguishes them, i.e., $f(x) \neq f(y)$.

Remark 7.7.4.1 In [Mul12] the desired linear projection is referred to as a "normalizing map", which is potentially confusing to algebraic geometers because it is *not* a normalization of the image variety.

Consider $\mathrm{End}(\mathbb{C}^m)^{\oplus r}$, which is an SL_m-variety under the diagonal action. Write $\overline{A} = A_1 \oplus \cdots \oplus A_r \in \mathrm{End}(\mathbb{C}^m)^{\oplus r}$.

Theorem 7.7.4.2 [Raz74, Pro76] *[First fundamental theorem for matrix invariants] $\mathbb{C}[\mathrm{End}(\mathbb{C}^m)^{\oplus r}]^{SL_m}$ is generated by*

$$T_\alpha(\overline{A}) := \mathrm{trace}(A_{\alpha_1} \cdots A_{\alpha_k}), \ k \leq m^2, \ \alpha_1, \ldots, \alpha_k \in [r].$$

It is also known that if one takes $k \leq \lfloor \frac{m^2}{8} \rfloor$ one does not obtain generators. In particular, one has an exponentially large (with respect to m) number of generators.

Put all these polynomials together in a generating function: let $y = (y_j^s)$, $1 \leq j \leq m^2$, $1 \leq s \leq r$ and define

$$T(y, \overline{A}) := \text{trace}\left[\left(\text{Id} + y_1^1 A_1 + \cdots + y_1^k A_k\right) \cdots \left(\text{Id} + y_{m^2}^1 A_1 + \cdots + y_{m^2}^k A_k\right)\right]$$

The right-hand side is an IMM, even a ROABP. Thus all the generating invariants may be read off as the coefficients of the output of an ROABP. This, combined with Theorem 7.7.3.2 implies:

Theorem 7.7.4.3 [FS13a] *There exists a poly$(n, r)^{O(\log(n))}$-sized set $\mathcal{H} \subset \mathbb{C}[\text{End}(\mathbb{C}^m)^{\oplus r}]^{SL_m}$ of separating invariants, with poly(n, r)-explicit ABPs. In other words, for any $\overline{A}, \overline{B} \in \text{End}(\mathbb{C}^m)^{\oplus r}$, there exists $f \in \mathbb{C}[\text{End}(\mathbb{C}^m)^{\oplus r}]^{SL_m}$ with $f(\overline{A}) \neq f(\overline{B})$ if and only if there exists such an $f \in \mathcal{H}$.*

Remark 7.7.4.4 A more geometric way of understanding Theorem 7.7.4.3 is to introduce the *GIT-quotient* $\text{End}(\mathbb{C}^m)^{\oplus r} /\!\!/ SL_m$ (see §9.5.2), which is an affine algebraic variety whose coordinate ring is $\mathbb{C}[\text{End}(\mathbb{C}^m)^{\oplus r}]^{SL_m}$. Then $\mathcal{H}$ is a subset that separates points of the GIT-quotient $\text{End}(\mathbb{C}^m)^{\oplus r} /\!\!/ SL_m$.

The following conjecture appeared in the 2012 version of [Mul12]:

Conjecture 7.7.4.5 [Mul12] *Noether normalization can be performed explicitly for $\text{End}(\mathbb{C}^m)^{\oplus r} /\!\!/ SL_m$ in polynomial time.*

Conjecture 7.7.4.5 motivated the work of [FS13a], as Theorem 7.7.4.3 implies:

Corollary 7.7.4.6 [FS13a] *Noether normalization can be performed explicitly for $\text{End}(\mathbb{C}^m)^{\oplus r} /\!\!/ SL_m$ in quasi-polynomial time.*

Remark 7.7.4.7 The PIT problem is the word problem for the field of rational functions over a set of commuting variables. One can ask the same for the (free) skew field over noncommuting variables. This is answered in [GGOW15] where there are connections to and implications for many areas including PIT, quivers and GIT questions.

8

Representation Theory and Its Uses in Complexity Theory

In this chapter I derive the representation theory of the general linear group $GL(V)$ and give numerous applications to complexity theory. In order to get to the applications as soon as possible, I summarize basic facts about representations of $GL(V)$ in §8.1. The first application, in §8.2, explains the theory of *Young flattenings* underlying the equations that led to the $2\mathbf{n}^2 - \mathbf{n}$ lower bound for the border rank of matrix multiplication (Theorem 2.5.2.6). I also explain how the method of shifted partial derivatives may be viewed as a special case of Young flattenings. Next, in §8.3, I briefly discuss how representation theory has been used to find equations for secant varieties of Segre varieties and other varieties. In §8.4, I describe severe restrictions on modules of polynomials to be useful for the permanent v. determinant problem. In §8.5, I give the proofs of several statements about Det_n from Chapter 7. In §8.6, I begin to develop representation theory via the double commutant theorem, the algebraic Peter-Weyl theorem and Schur-Weyl duality. The reason for this choice of development is that the (finite) Peter-Weyl theorem is the starting point of the Cohn-Umans program of §3.5 and the algebraic Peter-Weyl theorem was the starting point of the program of [MS01, MS08] described in §8.8. The representations of the general linear group are then derived in §8.7. In §8.8 I begin a discussion of the program of [MS01, MS08], as refined in [BLMW11], to separate the permanent from the determinant via representation theory. This is continued in §8.9, which contains a general discussion of plethysm coefficients, and §8.10, which presents results of [IP15] and [BIP16] that show this program cannot work as stated. I then, in §8.11 outline the proofs of Theorems 7.4.1.1 and 7.4.1.4 regarding equivariant determinantal expressions for the permanent. I conclude, in §8.12 with additional theory how to determine symmetry groups of polynomials and illustrate the theory with several examples relevant for complexity theory.

Figure 8.1.1 Young diagram for $\pi = (4, 2, 1)$.

8.1 Representation Theory of the General Linear Group

Irreducible representations of $GL(V)$ in $V^{\otimes d}$ are indexed by partitions of d with length at most **v**, as we will prove in Theorem 8.7.1.2. Let $S_\pi V$ denote the isomorphism class of the irreducible representation associated to the partition π, and let $S_{\overline{\pi}} V$ denote some particular realization of $S_\pi V$ in $V^{\otimes d}$. In particular $S_{(d)} V = S^d V$ and $S_{(1,\dots,1)} V = \Lambda^d V$ where there are d 1's. For a partition $\pi = (p_1, \dots, p_k)$, write $|\pi| = p_1 + \cdots + p_k$ and $l(\pi) = k$. If a number is repeated I sometimes use superscripts to record its multiplicity, for example $(2, 2, 1, 1, 1) = (2^2, 1^3)$.

Define a *Young diagram* associated to a partition π to be a collection of left-aligned boxes with p_j boxes in the the jth row, as in Figure 8.1.1.

Define the *conjugate partition* π' to π to be the partition whose Young diagram is the reflection of the Young diagram of π in the north-west to southeast diagonal, as in Figure 8.1.2.

8.1.1 Lie Algebras

Associated to any Lie group G is a *Lie algebra* $\mathfrak{g}$, which is a vector space that may be identified with $T_{\mathrm{Id}}G$. For basic information on the Lie algebra associated to a Lie group, see any of [Spi79, IL16b, Pro07].

When $G = GL(V)$, then $\mathfrak{g} = \mathfrak{gl}(V) := V^* \otimes V$. If $G \subseteq GL(V)$, so that G acts on $V^{\otimes d}$, there is an induced action of $\mathfrak{g} \subseteq \mathfrak{gl}(V)$ given by, for $X \in \mathfrak{g}$,

$$X.(v_1 \otimes v_2 \otimes \cdots \otimes v_d) = (X.v_1) \otimes v_2 \otimes \cdots \otimes v_d + v_1 \otimes (X.v_2) \otimes \cdots \otimes v_d$$
$$+ \cdots + v_1 \otimes v_2 \otimes \cdots \otimes v_{d-1} \otimes (X.v_d).$$

Figure 8.1.2 Young diagram for $\pi' = (3, 2, 1, 1)$, the conjugate partition to $\pi = (4, 2, 1)$.

To see why this is a natural induced action, consider a curve $g(t) \subset G$ with $g(0) = \text{Id}$ and $X = g'(0)$ and take

$$\frac{d}{dt}\big|_{t=0}\, g(t) \cdot (v_1 \otimes \cdots \otimes v_d) = \frac{d}{dt}\big|_{t=0}\, (g(t) \cdot v_1) \otimes \cdots \otimes (g(t) \cdot v_d).$$

One concludes by applying the Leibnitz rule.

8.1.2 Weights

Fix a basis $e_1, \ldots, e_v$ of V, let $T \subset GL(V)$ denote the subgroup of diagonal matrices, called a *maximal torus*, let $B \subset GL(V)$ be the subgroup of upper triangular matrices, called a *Borel subgroup*, and let $N \subset B$ be the upper triangular matrices with 1's along the diagonal. The Lie algebra $\mathfrak{n}$ of N consists of nilpotent matrices. Call $z \in V^{\otimes d}$ a *weight vector* if $T[z] = [z]$. If

$$\begin{pmatrix} x_1 & & \\ & \ddots & \\ & & x_v \end{pmatrix} z = (x_1)^{p_1} \cdots (x_v)^{p_v} z$$

we say z has *weight* $(p_1, \ldots, p_v) \in \mathbb{Z}^v$.

Call z a *highest weight vector* if $B[z] = [z]$, i.e., if $Nz = z$. If M is an irreducible $GL(V)$-module and $z \in M$ is a highest weight vector, call the weight of z the *highest weight* of M. A necessary condition for two irreducible $GL(V)$-modules to be isomorphic is that they have the same highest weight (because they must also be isomorphic T-modules). The condition is also sufficient, see §8.7.

Exercise 8.1.2.1 (1) Show that z is a highest weight vector if and only if $\mathfrak{n}.z = 0$.

The elements of $\mathfrak{n}$ are often called *raising operators*.

Exercise 8.1.2.2 (1) Show that if $z \in V^{\otimes d}$ is a highest weight vector of weight $(p_1, \ldots, p_v)$, then $(p_1, \ldots, p_v)$ is a partition of d. ⊚

When $G = GL(A_1) \times \cdots \times GL(A_n)$, the maximal torus in G is the product of the maximal tori in the $GL(A_j)$, and similarly for the Borel. A weight is then defined to be an n-tuple of weights etc...

Because of the relation with weights, it will often be convenient to add a string of zeros to a partition to make it a string of v integers.

Exercise 8.1.2.3 (1) Show that the space $S^2(S^2\mathbb{C}^2)$ contains a copy of $S_{(2,2)}\mathbb{C}^2$ by showing that $(x_1^2)(x_2^2) - (x_1x_2)(x_1x_2) \in S^2(S^2\mathbb{C}^2)$ is a highest weight vector.

Exercise 8.1.2.4 (1!) Find highest weight vectors in $V, S^2V, \Lambda^2V, S^3V, \Lambda^3V$ and the kernels of the symmetrization and skew-symmetrization maps $V \otimes S^2V \to S^3V$ and $V \otimes \Lambda^2V \to \Lambda^3V$. Show that both of the last two modules have highest weight $(2, 1)$, i.e., they are realizations of $S_{(2,1)}V$.

Exercise 8.1.2.5 (2) More generally, find a highest weight vector for the kernel of the symmetrization map $V \otimes S^{d-1}V \to S^dV$ and of the kernel of the "exterior derivative" (or "Koszul") map

$$S^kV \otimes \Lambda^tV \to S^{k-1}V \otimes \Lambda^{t+1}V \tag{8.1.1}$$

$$x_1 \cdots x_k \otimes y_1 \wedge \cdots \wedge y_t \mapsto \sum_{j=1}^{k} x_1 \cdots \hat{x}_j \cdots x_k \otimes x_j \wedge y_1 \wedge \cdots \wedge y_t.$$

Exercise 8.1.2.6 (1!) Let $\pi = (p_1, \ldots, p_\ell)$ be a partition with at most $\mathbf{v}$ parts and let $\pi' = (q_1, \ldots, q_{p_1})$ denote the conjugate partition. Show that

$$z_\pi := (e_1 \wedge \cdots \wedge e_{q_1}) \otimes (e_1 \wedge \cdots \wedge e_{q_2}) \otimes \cdots \otimes (e_1 \wedge \cdots \wedge e_{q_{p_1}}) \in V^{\otimes |\pi|} \tag{8.1.2}$$

is a highest weight vector of weight π.

8.1.3 The Pieri Rule

I describe the decomposition of $S_\pi V \otimes V$ as a $GL(V)$-module. Write $\pi' = (q_1, \ldots, q_{p_1})$ and recall z_π from (8.1.2). Consider the vectors:

$$(e_1 \wedge \cdots \wedge e_{q_1} \wedge e_{q_1+1}) \otimes (e_1 \wedge \cdots \wedge e_{q_2}) \otimes \cdots \otimes (e_1 \wedge \cdots \wedge e_{q_{p_1}})$$

$$\vdots$$

$$(e_1 \wedge \cdots \wedge e_{q_1}) \otimes (e_1 \wedge \cdots \wedge e_{q_2}) \otimes \cdots \otimes (e_1 \wedge \cdots \wedge e_{q_{p_1}} \wedge e_{q_{p_1}+1})$$

$$(e_1 \wedge \cdots \wedge e_{q_1}) \otimes (e_1 \wedge \cdots \wedge e_{q_2}) \otimes \cdots \otimes (e_1 \wedge \cdots \wedge e_{q_{p_1}}) \otimes e_1.$$

These are all highest weight vectors obtained by tensoring z_π with a vector in V and skew-symmetrizing appropriately, so the associated modules are contained in $S_\pi V \otimes V$. With a little more work, one can show these are highest weight vectors of all the modules that occur in $S_\pi V \otimes V$. If $q_j = q_{j+1}$ one gets the same module if one inserts e_{q_j+1} into either slot, and its multiplicity in $S_\pi V \otimes V$ is one. More generally one obtains:

Theorem 8.1.3.1 (The Pieri formula) *The decomposition of $S_\pi V \otimes S^d V$ is multiplicity free. The partitions corresponding to modules $S_\mu V$ that occur are those obtained from the Young diagram of π by adding d boxes to the diagram of π, with no two boxes added to the same column.*

Definition 8.1.3.2 Let $\pi = (p_1, \ldots, p_{l(\pi)})$, $\mu = (m_1, \ldots, m_{l(\mu)})$ be partitions with $l(\mu) < l(\pi)$ One says μ *interlaces* π if $p_1 \geq m_1 \geq p_2 \geq m_2 \geq \cdots \geq m_{l(\pi)-1} \geq p_{l(\pi)}$.

Exercise 8.1.3.3 (1) Show that $S_\pi V \otimes S_{(d)} V$ consists of all the $S_\mu V$ such that $|\mu| = |\pi| + d$ and π interlaces μ.

Exercise 8.1.3.4 (1) Show that a necessary condition for $S_\pi V$ to appear in $S^d(S^n V)$ is that $l(\pi) \leq d$.

Although a pictorial proof is possible, the standard proof of the Pieri formula uses a *character* (see §8.6.7) calculation, computing $\chi_\pi \chi_{(d)}$ as a sum of χ_μ's. See, e.g., [Mac95, §I.9]. A different proof, using Schur-Weyl duality is in [GW09, §9.2]. There is an algorithm to compute arbitrary tensor product decompositions called the *Littlewood Richardson Rule*. See, e.g., [Mac95, §I.9] for details.

Similar considerations give:

Theorem 8.1.3.5 *[The skew-Pieri formula] The decomposition of $S_\pi V \otimes \Lambda^k V$ is multiplicity free. The partitions corresponding to modules $S_\mu V$ that occur are those obtained from the Young diagram of π by adding k boxes to the diagram of π, with no two boxes added to the same row.*

8.1.4 The $GL(V)$-Modules not Appearing in the Tensor Algebra of V

The $GL(V)$-module V^* does not appear in the tensor algebra of V. Nor do the one-dimensional representations for $k > 0$, $\det^{-k} : GL(V) \to GL(\mathbb{C}^1)$ given by, for $v \in \mathbb{C}^1$, $\det^{-k}(g)v := \det(g)^{-k}v$.

Exercise 8.1.4.1 (1) Show that if $\pi = (p_1, \ldots, p_v)$ with $p_v > 0$, then $\det^{-1} \otimes S_\pi V = S_{(p_1-1, \ldots, p_v-1)} V$. ⊚

Exercise 8.1.4.2 (1) Show that as a $GL(V)$-module, $V^* = \Lambda^{v-1} V \otimes \det^{-1} = S_{1^{v-1}} V \otimes \det^{-1}$. ⊚

Every irreducible $GL(V)$-module is of the form $S_\pi V \otimes \det^{-k}$ for some partition π and some $k \geq 0$. Thus they may be indexed by nonincreasing sequences of integers $(p_1, \ldots, p_v)$ where $p_1 \geq p_2 \geq \cdots \geq p_v$. Such a module is isomorphic to $S_{(p_1-p_v, \ldots, p_{v-1}-p_v, 0)} V \otimes \det^{p_v}$.

Using

$$S_\pi V \otimes V^* = S_\pi V \otimes \Lambda^{v-1} V \otimes \det^{-1},$$

we may compute the decomposition of $S_\pi V \otimes V^*$ using the skew-symmetric version of the Pieri rule.

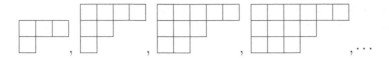

Figure 8.1.3 Young diagrams for SL_3-modules equivalent to $S_{421}\mathbb{C}^3$.

Example 8.1.4.3 Let $\mathbf{w} = 3$, then

$$S_{(32)}W \otimes W^* = S_{(43)}W \otimes \det{}^{-1} \oplus S_{(331)}W \otimes \det{}^{-1} \oplus S_{(421)}W \otimes \det{}^{-1}$$
$$= S_{(43)}W \otimes \det{}^{-1} \oplus S_{(22)}W \oplus S_{(31)}W.$$

The first module does not occur in the tensor algebra but the rest do.

8.1.5 $SL(V)$-Modules in $V^{\otimes d}$

Every $SL(V)$-module is the restriction to $SL(V)$ of some $GL(V)$-module. However distinct $GL(V)$-modules, when restricted to $SL(V)$ can become isomorphic, such as the trivial representation and $\Lambda^{\mathbf{v}}V = S_{(1^{\mathbf{v}})}V = \det^1$.

Proposition 8.1.5.1 *Let $\pi = (p_1, \ldots, p_{\mathbf{v}})$ be a partition. The $SL(V)$-modules in the tensor algebra $V^{\otimes}$ that are isomorphic to $S_\pi V$ are $S_\mu V$ with $\mu = (p_1 + j, p_2 + j, \ldots, p_{\mathbf{v}} + j)$ for $-p_{\mathbf{v}} \leq j < \infty$.*

Exercise 8.1.5.2 (2) Prove Proposition 8.1.5.1. ⊙

For example, as SL_2-modules, $S_{p_1,p_2}\mathbb{C}^2 \simeq S^{p_1-p_2}\mathbb{C}^2$. We conclude:

Corollary 8.1.5.3 *A complete set of the finite-dimensional irreducible representations of SL_2 are the $S^d\mathbb{C}^2$ with $d \geq 0$.*

The $GL(V)$-modules that are $SL(V)$-equivalent to $S_\pi V$ may be visualized as being obtained by erasing or adding columns of size $\mathbf{v}$ from the Young diagram of π, as in Figure 8.1.3.

The Lie algebra of $SL(V)$, denoted $\mathfrak{sl}(V)$, is the set of traceless endomorphisms. One can define weights for the Lie algebra of the torus, which are essentially the logs of the corresponding torus in the group. In particular, vectors of $\mathfrak{sl}$-weight zero have $GL(V)$-weight $(d, \ldots, d) = (d^{\mathbf{v}})$ for some d.

Exercise 8.1.5.4 (1!) Let $T^{SL} \subset SL(V)$ be the diagonal matrices with determinant one. Show that $(V^{\otimes d})^{T^{SL}}$ is zero unless $d = \delta \mathbf{v}$ for some natural number δ and in this case it consists of all vectors of weight $(\delta^{\mathbf{v}})$.

8.2 Young Flattenings

Most known equations for border rank of tensors, i.e., polynomials in the ideal of the variety $\sigma_r(Seg(\mathbb{P}A_1 \times \cdots \times \mathbb{P}A_n))$ and symmetric border rank of polynomials, i.e., polynomials in the ideal of the variety $\sigma_r(v_d(\mathbb{P}V))$, are obtained by taking minors of some auxiliary matrix constructed from the tensor (polynomial). What follows is a general way to use representation theory to find such matrices.

8.2.1 The Case of Polynomials

Let $P \in S^d V$. Recall the flattenings from §6.2: $P_{k,d-k} : S^k V^* \to S^{d-k} V$. Flattenings give rise to a $GL(V)$-module of equations because the inclusion $S^d V \subset S^k V \otimes S^{d-k} V$ is a $GL(V)$-module map. The generalization is similar:

Proposition 8.2.1.1 *Given a linear inclusion $S^d V \subset U \otimes W$, i.e., $S^d V$ is realized as a space of linear maps from U^* to W, say the rank of the linear map associated to ℓ^d is r_0. If the rank of the linear map associated to P is r, then $\underline{\mathbf{R}}_S(P) \geq \frac{r}{r_0}$.*

Exercise 8.2.1.2 (1!) Prove Proposition 8.2.1.1. ⊙

This method works best when r_0 is small. For example in the classical flattening case $r_0 = 1$.

We will take U, W to be $GL(V)$-modules and the linear inclusion a $GL(V)$-module map because $I(\sigma_r(v_d(\mathbb{P}V)))$ is a $GL(V)$-module. It turns out that *we know all such maps*. The Pieri rule §8.1.3 says they are all of the form $S^d V \subset S_\pi V^* \otimes S_\mu V$ where the Young diagram of μ is obtained from the Young diagram of π by adding d boxes, with no two boxes added to the same column. To make this completely correct, we need to consider sequences with negative integers, where e.g., the Young diagram of $(-d)$ should be thought of as $-d$ boxes in a row. Alternatively, one can work with $SL(V)$-modules, as then $\det^{-d} = S_{(-d)}V = S_{(d^{v-1})}V$ as $SL(V)$-modules. For every such pair (π, μ) there is exactly one $GL(V)$-inclusion. Call the resulting linear map a *Young-flattening*.

The classical case is $\pi = (-k)$ and $\mu = (d - k)$, or in terms of $SL(V)$-modules, $\pi = (k^{v-1})$ and $\mu = (k^v, d - k)$. The main example in [LO13], called a (polynomial) *Koszul flattening* was constructed as follows: take the classical flattening $P_{k,d-k} : S^k V^* \to S^{d-k} V$ and tensor it with $\mathrm{Id}_{\Lambda^p V}$ for some p, to get a map $S^k V^* \otimes \Lambda^p V \to S^{d-k} V \otimes \Lambda^p V$. Now include $S^{d-k} V \subset S^{d-k-1} V \otimes V$, to obtain a map $S^k V^* \otimes \Lambda^p V \to S^{d-k-1} V \otimes V \otimes \Lambda^p V$ and finally skew-symmetrize the last two factors to obtain a map

$$P_{k,d-k}^{\wedge p} : S^k V^* \otimes \Lambda^p V \to S^{d-k-1} V \otimes \Lambda^{p+1} V. \tag{8.2.1}$$

If one views this as a map $S^d V \otimes (S^k V^* \otimes \Lambda^p V) \to S^{d-k-1} V \otimes \Lambda^{p+1} V$, it is a $GL(V)$-module map. By the Pieri rule,

$$(S^k V^* \otimes \Lambda^p V)^* = S_{(k,1^{v-p})} V \otimes \det{}^{-1} \oplus S_{(k+1,1^{v-p-1})} V \otimes \det{}^{-1}$$

and

$$S^{d-k-1} V \otimes \Lambda^{p+1} V = S_{(d-k-1,1^{p+1})} V \oplus S_{(d-k,1^p)} V.$$

Although in practice one usually works with the map (8.2.1), the map is zero except restricted to the map between irreducible modules:

$$[S_{(k,1^{v-p})} V^* \otimes \det{}^{-1}]^* \to S_{(d-k,1^p)} V.$$

The method of shifted partial derivatives §7.6 is a type of Young flattening which I will call a *Hilbert flattening*, because it is via Hilbert functions of Jacobian ideals. It is the symmetric cousin of the Koszul flattening: take the classical flattening $P_{k,d-k} : S^k V^* \to S^{d-k} V$ and tensor it with $\mathrm{Id}_{S^\ell V}$ for some ℓ, to get a map $S^k V^* \otimes S^\ell V \to S^{d-k} V \otimes S^\ell V$. Now simply take the projection (multiplication map) $S^{d-k} V \otimes S^\ell V \to S^{d-k+\ell} V$, to obtain a map

$$P_{k,d-k[\ell]} : S^k V^* \otimes S^\ell V \to S^{d-k+\ell} V. \tag{8.2.2}$$

The target is an irreducible $GL(V)$-module, so the pruning is easier here.

8.2.2 The Case of Tensors

Young flattenings can also be defined for tensors. For tensors in $A \otimes B \otimes C$, the Koszul flattenings $T_A^{\wedge p} : \Lambda^p A \otimes B^* \to \Lambda^{p+1} A \otimes C$ used in §2.4 appear to be the only useful cases.

In principle there are numerous inclusions

$$A \otimes B \otimes C \subset (S_\pi A \otimes S_\mu B \otimes S_\nu C)^* \otimes (S_{\tilde\pi} A \otimes S_{\tilde\mu} B \otimes S_{\tilde\nu} C),$$

where the Young diagram of $\tilde\pi$ is obtained from the Young diagram of π by adding a box (and similarly for μ, ν), and the case of Koszul flattenings is where (up to permuting the three factors) $\pi = (1^p)$, $\mu = (1^{\mathbf{b}-1})$ (so $S_\mu B \simeq B^*$ as $SL(B)$-modules) and $\nu = \emptyset$.

Exercise 2.4.1.1 already indicates why symmetrization is not useful, and an easy generalization of it proves this to be the case for Young flattenings of tensors. But perhaps additional skew-symmetrization could be useful. Let $T \in A \otimes B \otimes C$ and consider $T \otimes \mathrm{Id}_{\Lambda^q A} \otimes \mathrm{Id}_{\Lambda^q B} \otimes \mathrm{Id}_{\Lambda^s C}$ as a linear map $B^* \otimes \Lambda^q B^* \otimes \Lambda^p A \otimes \Lambda^s C \to \Lambda^q B^* \otimes \Lambda^p A \otimes A \otimes \Lambda^s C \otimes C$. Now quotient to the exterior powers to get a map:

$$T_{p,q,s} : \Lambda^{q+1} B^* \otimes \Lambda^p A \otimes \Lambda^s C \to \Lambda^q B^* \otimes \Lambda^{p+1} A \otimes \Lambda^{s+1} C.$$

This generalizes the map $T_A^{\wedge p}$ which is the case $q = s = 0$. Claim: this generalization does not give better lower bounds for border rank than Koszul flattenings when $\mathbf{a} = \mathbf{b} = \mathbf{c}$. (Although it is possible it could give better lower bounds for some particular tensor.) If T has rank one, say $T = a \otimes b \otimes c$, the image of $T_{p,q,s}$ is

$$\Lambda^q(b^\perp) \otimes (a \wedge \Lambda^p A) \otimes (c \wedge \Lambda^s C).$$

Here $b^\perp := \{\beta \in B^* \mid \underline{(b)} = 0\}$. The image of $(a \otimes b \otimes c)_{p,q,s}$ has dimension

$$d_{p,q,s} := \binom{\mathbf{b}-1}{q}\binom{\mathbf{a}-1}{p}\binom{\mathbf{c}-1}{s}.$$

Thus the size $rd_{p,q,s} + 1$ minors of $T_{p,q,s}$ potentially give equations for the variety of tensors of border rank at most r. We have nontrivial minors as long as

$$rd_{p,q,s} + 1 \le \min\left\{\dim(\Lambda^q B^* \otimes \Lambda^{p+1} A \otimes \Lambda^{s+1}), \dim(\Lambda^{q+1} B^* \otimes \Lambda^p A \otimes \Lambda^s C)\right\},$$

i.e., as long as

$$r < \min\left\{ \frac{\binom{\mathbf{b}}{q}\binom{\mathbf{a}}{p+1}\binom{\mathbf{c}}{s+1}}{\binom{\mathbf{b}-1}{q}\binom{\mathbf{a}-1}{p}\binom{\mathbf{c}-1}{s}}, \frac{\binom{\mathbf{b}}{q+1}\binom{\mathbf{a}}{p}\binom{\mathbf{c}}{s}}{\binom{\mathbf{b}-1}{q}\binom{\mathbf{a}-1}{p}\binom{\mathbf{c}-1}{s}} \right\},$$

i.e.

$$r < \min\left\{ \frac{\mathbf{abc}}{(\mathbf{b}-q)(p+1)(s+1)}, \frac{\mathbf{abc}}{(q+1)(\mathbf{a}-p)(\mathbf{c}-s)} \right\}.$$

Consider the case $q = 0$, so we need

$$r < \min\left\{ \frac{\mathbf{ac}}{(p+1)(s+1)}, \frac{\mathbf{abc}}{(\mathbf{a}-p)(\mathbf{c}-s)} \right\}.$$

Let's specialize to $\mathbf{a} = \mathbf{c}$, $p = q$, so we need

$$r < \min\left\{ \frac{\mathbf{a}^2}{(p+1)^2}, \frac{\mathbf{a}^2\mathbf{b}}{(\mathbf{a}-p)^2} \right\}.$$

Consider the case $\mathbf{a} = mp$ for some m. Then if m is large, the first term is large, but the second is very close to $\mathbf{b}$. So unless the dimensions are unbalanced, one is unlikely to get any interesting equations out of these Young flattenings.

8.2.3 General Perspective

Let $X \subset \mathbb{P}V$ be a G-variety for some reductive group G, where $V = V_\lambda$ is an irreducible G-module with the highest weight λ.

Proposition 8.2.3.1 *Given irreducible G-modules V_μ, V_ν such that $V_\lambda \subset V_\mu \otimes V_\nu$ and $v \in V$, we obtain a linear map $v_{\mu,\nu} : V_\mu^* \to V_\nu$. Say the maximum* *rank of such a linear map for $x \in X$ is q, then the size $(qr + 1)$-minors of $v_{\mu,\nu}$ test membership in $\sigma_r(X)$.*

8.3 Additional Uses of Representation Theory to Find Modules of Equations

In this section, I briefly cover additional techniques for finding modules of polynomials in ideals of G-varieties. I am brief because either the methods are not used in this book or they are described at length in [Lan12].

8.3.1 A Naïve Algorithm

Let $X \subset \mathbb{P}W$ be a G-variety. We are primarily interested in the cases $X = \sigma_r(Seg(\mathbb{P}A \times \mathbb{P}B \times \mathbb{P}C)) \subset \mathbb{P}(A \otimes B \otimes C)$, where $G = GL(A) \times GL(B) \times GL(C)$ and $X = \mathcal{D}et_n \subset \mathbb{P}S^n\mathbb{C}^{n^2}$, where $G = GL_{n^2}$. Since the ideal of X will be a G-module, we can look for irreducible modules in the ideal of X by testing highest weight vectors. If $U \subset S^dW^*$ is an irreducible G-module with highest weight vector u, then $U \subset I(X)$ if and only if $u \in I(X)$ because if $u \in I(X)$ then $g(u) \in I(X)$ for all $g \in G$ and such vectors span U. Thus in each degree d, we can in principle determine $I_d(X)$ by a finite calculation. In practice we test each highest weight vector u on a "random" point $[x] \in X$. If $u(x) \neq 0$, we know for sure that $U \not\subset I_d(X)$. If $u(x) = 0$, then with extremely high probability (probability one if the point is truly randomly chosen), we have $U \subset I(X)$. After testing several such points, we have high confidence in the result. Once one has a candidate module by such tests, one can often prove it is in the ideal by different methods.

More precisely, if S^dW^* is multiplicity free as a G-module, there are a finite number of highest weight vectors to check. If a given irreducible module has multiplicity m, then we need to take a basis $u_1, \ldots, u_m$ of the highest weight space, test on say $x_1, \ldots, x_q$ with $q \geq m$ if $\sum_j y_j u_j(x_s) = 0$ for some constants $y_1, \ldots, y_m$ and all $1 \leq s \leq q$.

To carry out this procedure in our two cases we would respectively need

- A method to decompose $S^d(A \otimes B \otimes C)^*$ (resp. $S^d(S^n\mathbb{C}^{n^2})$) into irreducible submodules.
- A method to explicitly write down highest weight vectors.

There are several systematic techniques for accomplishing both these tasks that work well in small cases, but as cases get larger one needs to introduce additional methods to be able to carry out the calculations in practice. The first task amounts to the well-studied problem of computing *Kronecker coefficients* defined in §8.8.2. I briefly discuss the second task in §8.7.2.

8.3.2 Enhanced Search Using Numerical Methods

Rather than discuss the general theory, I outline the method used in [HIL13] to find equations for $\sigma_6(Seg(\mathbb{P}^3 \times \mathbb{P}^3 \times \mathbb{P}^3))$. First fix a "random" linear space $L \subset \mathbb{P}^{63}$ of dimension 4 (i.e., $\mathrm{codim}\,\sigma_6(Seg(\mathbb{P}^3 \times \mathbb{P}^3 \times \mathbb{P}^3)))$ and consider the finite set $Z := \sigma_6(Seg(\mathbb{P}^3 \times \mathbb{P}^3 \times \mathbb{P}^3)) \cap L$. The first objective is to compute points in Z, with the goal of computing every point in Z. To this end, first compute one point in Z as follows. One first picks a random point $x^* \in \sigma_6(Seg(\mathbb{P}^3 \times \mathbb{P}^3 \times \mathbb{P}^3))$, which is easy since an open dense subset of $\sigma_6(Seg(\mathbb{P}^3 \times \mathbb{P}^3 \times \mathbb{P}^3))$ is parameterizable. Let $\tilde{L}$ be a system of 59 linear forms whose zero locus is L, and let L_{t,x^*} be the zero locus of $L(x) - t \cdot L(x^*)$. Since $x^* \in \sigma_6(Seg(\mathbb{P}^3 \times \mathbb{P}^3 \times \mathbb{P}^3)) \cap L_{1,x^*}$, a point in Z is the endpoint of the path defined by $\sigma_6(Seg(\mathbb{P}^3 \times \mathbb{P}^3 \times \mathbb{P}^3)) \cap L_{t,x^*}$ at $t = 0$ starting from x^* at $t = 1$.

Even though the above process could be repeated for different x^* to compute points in Z, we instead used *monodromy loops* [SVW01] for generating more points in Z. After performing 21 loops, the number of points in Z that we computed stabilized at 15,456. The *trace test* [SVW02] shows that 15,456 is indeed the degree of $\sigma_6(Seg(\mathbb{P}^3 \times \mathbb{P}^3 \times \mathbb{P}^3))$ thereby showing we had indeed computed Z.

From Z, we performed two computations. The first was the *membership test* of [HS13] for deciding if $M_{(2)} \in \sigma_6(Seg(\mathbb{P}^3 \times \mathbb{P}^3 \times \mathbb{P}^3))$, which requires tracking 15,456 homotopy paths that start at the points of Z and end on a $\mathbb{P}^4$ containing $M_{(2)}$. In this case, each of these 15,456 paths converged to points in $\sigma_6(Seg(\mathbb{P}^3 \times \mathbb{P}^3 \times \mathbb{P}^3))$ distinct from $M_{(2)}$ providing a numerical proof that $M_{(2)} \notin \sigma_6(Seg(\mathbb{P}^3 \times \mathbb{P}^3 \times \mathbb{P}^3))$. The second was to compute the minimal degree of nonzero polynomials vanishing on $Z \subset L$. This sequence of polynomial interpolation problems showed that no nonconstant polynomials of degree ≤ 18 vanished on Z and hence on $\sigma_6(Seg(\mathbb{P}^3 \times \mathbb{P}^3 \times \mathbb{P}^3))$. The 15456×8855 matrix resulting from polynomial interpolation of homogeneous forms of degree 19 in 5 variables using the approach of [GHPS14] has a 64-dimensional null space. Thus, the minimal degree of nonzero polynomials vanishing on $Z \subset L$ is 19, showing $\dim I_{19}(\sigma_6) \leq 64$.

The next objective was to verify that the minimal degree of nonzero polynomials vanishing on the curve $C := \sigma_6(Seg(\mathbb{P}^3 \times \mathbb{P}^3 \times \mathbb{P}^3)) \cap K \subset K$ for a fixed "random" linear space $K \subset \mathbb{P}^{63}$ of dimension 5 was also 19. We used 50,000 points on C and the 50000×42504 matrix resulting from polynomial interpolation of homogeneous forms of degree 19 in 6 variables using the approach of [GHPS14] also has a 64-dimensional null space. With this agreement, we decomposed $S^{19}(\mathbb{C}^4 \otimes \mathbb{C}^4 \otimes \mathbb{C}^4)$ and looked for a 64-dimensional submodule. The only reasonable candidate was to take a copy of

$S_{5554}\mathbb{C}^4 \otimes S_{5554}\mathbb{C}^4 \otimes S_{5554}\mathbb{C}^4$. We found a particular copy that was indeed in the ideal and then proved that $M_{\langle 2 \rangle}$ is not contained in $\sigma_6(Seg(\mathbb{P}^3 \times \mathbb{P}^3 \times \mathbb{P}^3))$ by showing a polynomial in this module did not vanish on it. The evaluation was numerical, so the result was:

Theorem 8.3.2.1 [HIL13] *With extremely high probability, the ideal of $\sigma_6(Seg(\mathbb{P}^3 \times \mathbb{P}^3 \times \mathbb{P}^3))$ is generated in degree* 19 *by the module $S_{5554}\mathbb{C}^4 \otimes S_{5554}\mathbb{C}^4 \otimes S_{5554}\mathbb{C}^4$. This module does not vanish on $M_{\langle 2 \rangle}$.*

In the same paper, a copy of the trivial degree twenty module $S_{5555}\mathbb{C}^4 \otimes S_{5555}\mathbb{C}^4 \otimes S_{5555}\mathbb{C}^4$ is shown to be in the ideal of $\sigma_6(Seg(\mathbb{P}^3 \times \mathbb{P}^3 \times \mathbb{P}^3))$ by symbolic methods, giving a new proof that:

Theorem 8.3.2.2 [Lan06, HIL13] $\underline{\mathbf{R}}(M_{\langle 2 \rangle}) = 7$.

The same methods have shown $I_{45}(\sigma_{15}(Seg(\mathbb{P}^3 \times \mathbb{P}^7 \times \mathbb{P}^8))) = 0$ and that $I_{186,999}(\sigma_{18}(Seg(\mathbb{P}^6 \times \mathbb{P}^6 \times \mathbb{P}^6))) = 0$ (this variety is a hypersurface), both of which are relevant for determining the border rank of $M_{\langle 3 \rangle}$, see [HIL13].

8.3.3 Inheritance

Inheritance is a general technique for studying equations of G-varieties that come in series. It is discussed extensively in [Lan12, §7.4,§16.4].

If $V \subset W$ then $S_{\overline{\pi}}V \subset V^{\otimes d}$ induces a module $S_{\overline{\pi}}W \subset W^{\otimes d}$ by, e.g., choosing a basis of W whose first $\mathbf{v}$ vectors are a basis of V. Then the two modules have the same highest weight vector and one obtains the $GL(W)$-module the span of the $GL(W)$-orbit of the highest weight vector.

Because the realizations of $S_\pi V$ in $V^{\otimes d}$ do not depend on the dimension of V, one can reduce the study of $\sigma_r(Seg(\mathbb{P}A \times \mathbb{P}B \times \mathbb{P}C))$ to that of $\sigma_r(Seg(\mathbb{P}^{r-1} \times \mathbb{P}^{r-1} \times \mathbb{P}^{r-1}))$. As discussed in §3.3.1 this latter variety is an orbit closure, namely the orbit closure of $M_{\langle 1 \rangle}^{\oplus r}$.

Proposition 8.3.3.1 [LM04, Proposition 4.4] *For all vector spaces B_j with $\dim B_j = \mathbf{b}_j \geq \dim A_j = \mathbf{a}_j \geq r$, a module $S_{\overline{\mu}_1}B_1 \otimes \cdots \otimes S_{\overline{\mu}_n}B_n$ such that $l(\mu_j) \leq \mathbf{a}_j$ for all j, is in $I_d(\sigma_r(Seg(\mathbb{P}B_1^* \times \cdots \times \mathbb{P}B_n^*)))$ if and only if $S_{\overline{\mu}_1}A_1 \otimes \cdots \otimes S_{\overline{\mu}_n}A_n$ is in $I_d(\sigma_r(Seg(\mathbb{P}A_1^* \times \cdots \times \mathbb{P}A_n^*)))$.*

Corollary 8.3.3.2 [LM04, AR03] *Let $\dim A_j \geq r$, $1 \leq j \leq n$. The ideal of $\sigma_r(Seg(\mathbb{P}A_1 \times \cdots \times \mathbb{P}A_n))$ is generated by the modules inherited from the ideal of $\sigma_r(Seg(\mathbb{P}^{r-1} \times \cdots \times \mathbb{P}^{r-1}))$ and the modules generating the ideal of $Sub_{r,...,r}(A_1 \otimes \cdots \otimes A_n)$. The analogous scheme and set-theoretic results hold as well.*

8.3.4 Prolongation

Prolongation and multiprolongation provide a systematic method to find equations for secant varieties that is particularly effective for secant varieties of homogeneous varieties. For a general discussion and proofs see [Lan12, §7.5]. For our purposes, we will need the following:

Proposition 8.3.4.1 *Given* $X \subset \mathbb{P}V^*$, $I_{r+1}(\sigma_r(X)) = (I_2(X) \otimes S^{r-1}V) \cap S^{r+1}V$.

Proposition 8.3.4.2 [SS09] *Let* $X \subset \mathbb{P}V$ *be a variety with* $I_{d-1}(X) = 0$. *Then for all* $\delta < (d-1)r$, $I_\delta(\sigma_r(X)) = 0$.

Corollary 8.3.4.3 $I_d(\sigma_d(v_n(\mathbb{P}V))) = 0$.

8.4 Necessary Conditions for Modules of Polynomials to Be Useful for GCT

The polynomial $\ell^{n-m} \operatorname{perm}_m \in S^n \mathbb{C}^{n^2}$ has two properties that can be studied individually: it is *padded*, i.e., it is divisible by a large power of a linear form, and its zero set is a *cone* with a $(n^2 - m^2 - 1)$-dimensional vertex, that is, it only uses $m^2 + 1$ of the n^2 variables in an expression in good coordinates. Both of these properties restrict the types of polynomials we should look for. Equipped with the language of representation theory we can give precise descriptions of the modules we should restrict our attention to, which I call *GCT useful*.

I begin with the study of cones, a classical topic.

8.4.1 Cones

Recall the subspace variety $Sub_k(S^dV) \subset \mathbb{P}S^dV$ from §6.2.2, the polynomials whose associated hypersurfaces are cones with a $(\mathbf{v} - k)$-dimensional vertex.

Proposition 8.4.1.1 $I_\delta(Sub_k(S^dV))$ *consists of the isotypic components of the modules* $S_\pi V^*$ *appearing in* $S^\delta(S^dV^*)$ *such that* $l(\pi) > k$.

Exercise 8.4.1.2 (2!) Prove Proposition 8.4.1.1. ⊚

With just a little more effort, one can prove the degree $k + 1$ equations from Proposition 8.4.1.1 generate the ideal:

Theorem 8.4.1.3 [Wey03, Corollary 7.2.3] *The ideal of* $Sub_k(S^dV)$ *is generated by the image of* $\Lambda^{k+1}V^* \otimes \Lambda^{k+1}S^{d-1}V^* \subset S^{k+1}(V^* \otimes S^{d-1}V^*)$ *in* $S^{k+1}(S^dV^*)$, *the size* $k + 1$ *minors of the* $(k, d - k)$*-flattening.*

Aside 8.4.1.4 Here is further information about the variety $Sub_k(S^dV)$: It is an example of a variety admitting a *Kempf-Weyman desingularization*, a type of desingularization that G-varieties often admit. Rather than discuss the general theory here (see [Wey03] for a full exposition or [Lan12, Chapter 17] for an elementary introduction), I just explain this example, which gives a proof of Theorem 8.4.1.3, although more elementary proofs are possible. As was mentioned in §5.4.3, the Grassmannian $G(k, V)$ has a tautological vector bundle $\pi : \mathcal{S} \to G(k, V)$, where the fiber over a k-plane E is just the k-plane itself. The whole bundle is a subbundle of the trivial bundle $\underline{V}$ with fiber V. Consider the bundle $S^d \mathcal{S} \subset S^d \underline{V}$. We have a projection map $p : S^d \underline{V} \to S^d V$. The image of $S^d \mathcal{S}$ under p is $\hat{S}ub_k(S^d V)$. Moreover, the map is a *desingularization*, that is $S^d \mathcal{S}$ is smooth, and the map to $\hat{S}ub_k(S^d V)$ is generically one to one. In particular, this implies $\dim \hat{S}ub_k(S^d V) = \dim(S^d \mathcal{S}) = \binom{k+d-1}{d} + d(\mathbf{v} - k)$. One obtains the entire minimal free resolution of $Sub_k(S^d V)$ by "pushing down" a tautological resolution "upstairs". From the minimal free resolution one can read off the generators of the ideal.

8.4.2 The Variety of Padded Polynomials

Define the *variety of padded polynomials*

$$\mathrm{Pad}_{n-m}(S^n W)$$
$$:= \mathbb{P}\{P \in S^n W \mid P = \ell^{n-m} h, \text{ for some } \ell \in W, h \in S^m W\} \subset \mathbb{P}S^n W.$$

Note that $\mathrm{Pad}_{n-m}(S^n W)$ is a $GL(W)$-variety.

Proposition 8.4.2.1 [KL14] *Let* $\pi = (p_1, \ldots, p_{\mathbf{w}})$ *be a partition of dn. If* $p_1 < d(n - m)$, *then the isotypic component of* $S_\pi W^*$ *in* $S^d(S^n W^*)$ *is contained in* $I_d(\mathrm{Pad}_{n-m}(S^n W))$.

Proof. Fix a (weight) basis $e_1, \ldots, e_{\mathbf{w}}$ of W with dual basis $x_1, \ldots, x_{\mathbf{w}}$ of W^*. Note any element $\ell^{n-m} h \in \mathrm{Pad}_{n-m}(S^n W)$ is in the $GL(W)$-orbit of $(e_1)^{n-m} \tilde{h}$ for some $\tilde{h}$, so it will be sufficient to show that the ideal in degree d contains the modules vanishing on the orbits of elements of the form $(e_1)^{n-m} h$. The highest weight vector of any copy of $S_{(p_1, \ldots, p_{\mathbf{w}})} W^*$ in $S^d(S^n W^*)$ will be a linear combination of vectors of the form $m_I := (x_1^{i_1^1} \cdots x_{\mathbf{w}}^{i_{\mathbf{w}}^1}) \cdots (x_1^{i_1^d} \cdots x_{\mathbf{w}}^{i_{\mathbf{w}}^d})$, where $i_j^1 + \cdots + i_j^d = p_j$ for all $1 \leq j \leq \mathbf{w}$ and $i_1^k + \cdots + i_{\mathbf{w}}^k = n$ for all $1 \leq k \leq d$ as these are all the vectors of weight π in $S^d(S^n W)$. Each m_I vanishes on any $(e_1)^{n-m} h$ unless $p_1 \geq d(n - m)$. (For a coordinate-free proof, see [KL14].) $\quad\square$

What we really need to study is the variety $\mathrm{Pad}_{n-m}(Sub_k(S^d W))$ of padded cones.

Proposition 8.4.2.2 [KL14] $I_d(\mathrm{Pad}_{n-m}(Sub_k(S^n W^*)))$ *consists of all modules* $S_{\bar{\pi}} W$ *such that* $S_{\bar{\pi}} \mathbb{C}^k$ *is in the ideal of* $\mathrm{Pad}_{n-m}(S^n \mathbb{C}^{k*})$ *and all modules whose associated partition has length at least* $k + 1$.

Exercise 8.4.2.3 (2) Prove Proposition 8.4.2.2.

In summary:

Proposition 8.4.2.4 *In order for a module* $S_{(p_1,\ldots,p_l)}W^*$*, where* $(p_1,\ldots,p_l)$ *is a partition of* dn *to be GCT-useful for showing* $\ell^{n-m}\,\mathrm{perm}_m \notin \overline{GL_{n^2} \cdot \det_n}$ *we must have*

- $l \leq m^2 + 1$*, and*
- $p_1 > d(n-m)$.

8.5 Representation Theory and $\mathcal{D}et_n$

8.5.1 Proof of Proposition 6.7.2.2

Recall $P_\Lambda(M) = \overline{\det}_n(M_\Lambda,\ldots,M_\Lambda,M_S)$ from §6.7.1 where $M = M_\Lambda + M_S$ is the decomposition of the matrix M into its skew-symmetric and symmetric components. We need to show $\overline{GL_{n^2} \cdot [P_\Lambda]}$ has codimension one in $\mathcal{D}et_n$ and is not contained in $\mathrm{End}(\mathbb{C}^{n^2}) \cdot [\det_n]$. We compute the stabilizer of P_Λ inside $GL(E{\otimes}E)$, where $E = \mathbb{C}^n$. The action of $GL(E)$ on $E{\otimes}E$ by $M \mapsto gMg^T$ preserves P_Λ up to scale, and the Lie algebra of the stabilizer of $[P_\Lambda]$ is a $GL(E)$ submodule of $\mathrm{End}(E{\otimes}E)$. Note that $\mathfrak{sl}(E) = S_{(21^{n-2})}E$ and $\mathfrak{gl}(E) = \mathfrak{sl}(E) \oplus \mathbb{C}$. Decompose $\mathrm{End}(E{\otimes}E)$ as a $SL(E)$-module:

$$\mathrm{End}(E{\otimes}E) = \mathrm{End}(\Lambda^2 E) \oplus \mathrm{End}(S^2 E) \oplus \mathrm{Hom}(\Lambda^2 E, S^2 E) \oplus \mathrm{Hom}(S^2 E, \Lambda^2 E)$$

$$= \Lambda^2 E {\otimes} \Lambda^2 E^* \oplus S^2 E {\otimes} S^2 E^* \oplus \Lambda^2 E^* {\otimes} S^2 E \oplus S^2 E^* {\otimes} \Lambda^2 E$$

$$= (\mathfrak{gl}(E) \oplus S_{2^2,1^{n-2}}E) \oplus (\mathfrak{gl}(E) \oplus S_{4,2^{n-1}}E)$$

$$\oplus (\mathfrak{sl}(E) \oplus S_{3,1^{n-2}}E) \oplus (\mathfrak{sl}(E) \oplus S_{3^2,2^{n-2}}E) \tag{8.5.1}$$

By testing highest weight vectors, one concludes the Lie algebra of G_{P_Λ} is isomorphic to $\mathfrak{gl}(E) \oplus \mathfrak{gl}(E)$, which has dimension $2n^2 = \dim G_{\det_n} + 1$, implying $\overline{GL(W) \cdot P_\Lambda}$ has codimension one in $\overline{GL(W) \cdot [\det_n]}$. Since it is not contained in the orbit of the determinant, it must be an irreducible component of its boundary. Since the zero set is not a cone, P_Λ cannot be in $\mathrm{End}(W) \cdot \det_n$ which consists of $GL(W) \cdot \det_n$ plus polynomials whose zero sets are cones, as any element of $\mathrm{End}(W)$ either has a kernel or is invertible.

Exercise 8.5.1.1 (3) Verify by testing on highest weight vectors that the only summands in (8.5.1) annihilating P_Λ are those in $\mathfrak{gl}(E) \oplus \mathfrak{gl}(E)$. Note that as a $\mathfrak{gl}(E)$-module, $\mathfrak{gl}(E) = \mathfrak{sl}(E) \oplus \mathbb{C}$ so one must test the highest weight vector of $\mathfrak{sl}(E)$ and $\mathbb{C}$.

8.5.2 The Module Structure of the Equations for Hypersurfaces with Degenerate Duals

Recall the equations for $\mathcal{D}_{k,d,N} \subset \mathbb{P}(S^d\mathbb{C}^{N*})$ that we found in §6.5.3. In this subsection I describe the module structure of those equations. It is technical and can be skipped on a first reading.

Write $P = \sum_J \tilde{P}_J x^J$ with the sum over $|J| = d$. The weight of a monomial $\tilde{P}_{J_0} x^{J_0}$ is $J_0 = (j_1, \dots, j_n)$. Adopt the notation $[i] = (0, \dots, 0, 1, 0, \dots, 0)$ where the 1 is in the ith slot and similarly for $[i, j]$ where there are two 1's. The entries of $P_{d-2,2}$ are, for $i \neq j$, $(P_{d-2,2})_{i,j} = P_{I+[i,j]} x^I$, and for $i = j$, $P_{I+2[i]} x^I$, where $|I| = d - 2$, and P_J is $\tilde{P}_J$ with the coefficient adjusted, e.g., $P_{(d,0,\dots,0)} = d(d-1)\tilde{P}_{(d,0,\dots,0)}$ etc.. (This won't matter because we are only concerned with the weights of the coefficients, not their values.) To determine the highest weight vector, take $L = \text{span}\{e_1, e_2\}$, $F = \text{span}\{e_1, \dots, e_{k+3}\}$. The highest weight term of

$$(x_1^{e-d}P|_L) \wedge (x_1^{e-d-1}x_2 P|_L) \wedge \cdots \wedge (x_2^{e-d}P|_L) \wedge (\det_{k+3}(P_{d-2,2}\,|_F))|_L$$

is the coefficient of $x_1^e \wedge x_1^{e-1}x_2 \wedge \cdots \wedge x_1^{e-(e-d+2)}x_2^{e-d+2}$. It will not matter how we distribute these for the weight, so take the coefficient of x_1^e in $(\det_{k+3}(P_{d-2,2}\,|_F))|_L$. It has leading term

$$P_{(d,0,\dots,0)}P_{(d-2,2,0,\dots,0)}P_{(d-2,0,2,0,\dots,0)} \cdots P_{(d-2,0,\dots,0,2,0,\dots,0)}$$

which is of weight $(d + (k+2)(d-2), 2^{k+2})$. For each $(x_1^{e-d-s}x_2^s P|_L)$ take the coefficient of $x_1^{e-s-1}x_2^{s+1}$ which has the coefficient of $P_{(d-1,1,0,\dots,0)}$ each time, to get a total weight contribution of $((e-d+1)(d-1), (e-d+1), 0, \dots, 0)$ from these terms. Adding the weights together, and recalling that $e = (k+3)(d-2)$, the highest weight is

$$(d^2k + 2d^2 - 2dk - 4d + 1, dk + 2d - 2k - 3, 2^{k+1}),$$

which may be written as

$$((k+2)(d^2 - 2d) + 1, (k+2)(d-2) + 1, 2^{k+1}).$$

In summary:

Theorem 8.5.2.1 [LMR13] *The ideal of the variety* $\mathcal{D}_{k,d,N} \subset \mathbb{P}(S^d\mathbb{C}^{N*})$ *contains a copy of the* GL_N*-module* $S_{\pi(k,d)}\mathbb{C}^N$, *where*

$$\pi(k,d) = ((k+2)(d^2 - 2d) + 1, d(k+2) - 2k - 3, 2^{k+1}).$$

Since $|\pi| = d(k+2)(d-1)$, *these equations have degree* $(k+2)(d-1)$.

Observe that the module $\pi(2n-2,n)$ indeed satisfies the requirements to be $(m, \frac{m^2}{2})$-GCT useful, as $p_1 = 2n^3 - 2n^2 + 1 > n(n-m)$ and $l(\pi(2n-2,n)) = 2n+1$.

8.5.3 $Dual_{k,d,N}$ versus $\mathcal{D}_{k,d,N}$

Recall that $Dual_{k,d,N} \subset \mathbb{P}S^d\mathbb{C}^{N*}$ is the Zariski closure of the irreducible polynomials whose hypersurfaces have k-dimensional dual varieties. The following more refined information may be useful for studying permanent v. determinant:

Proposition 8.5.3.1 [LMR13] *As subsets of* $S^d\mathbb{C}^{N*}$, $Dual_{k,d,N}$ *intersected with the irreducible hypersurfaces equals* $\mathcal{D}_{k,d,N}$ *intersected with the irreducible hypersurfaces.*

Proof. Let $P \in \mathcal{D}_{k,d,N}$ be irreducible. For each $(L, F) \in G(2, F) \times G(k+3, V)$ one obtains set-theoretic equations for the condition that $P|_L$ divides $Q|_L$, where $Q = \det(P_{d-2,2}|_F)$. But P divides Q if and only if restricted to each plane P divides Q, so these conditions imply that the dual variety of the irreducible hypersurface $\text{Zeros}(P)$ has dimension at most k. $\qquad\square$

Theorem 8.5.3.2 [LMR13] $\mathcal{D}et_n$ *is an irreducible component of* $\mathcal{D}_{2n-2,n,n^2}$

The proof of Theorem 8.5.3.2 requires familiarity with Zariski tangent spaces to schemes. Here is an outline: Given two schemes, X, Y with X irreducible and $X \subseteq Y$, an equality of Zariski tangent spaces, $T_xX = T_xY$ for some $x \in X_{smooth}$, implies that X is an irreducible component of Y (and in particular, if Y is irreducible, that $X = Y$). The following theorem is a more precise version:

Theorem 8.5.3.3 [LMR13] *The scheme* $\mathcal{D}_{2n-2,n,n^2}$ *is smooth at* $[\det_n]$, *and* $\mathcal{D}et_n$ *is an irreducible component of* $\mathcal{D}_{2n-2,n,n^2}$

The idea of the proof is as follows: We need to show $T_{[det_n]}\mathcal{D}_{n,2n-2,n^2} = T_{[det_n]}\mathcal{D}et_n$. We already know $T_{[det_n]}\mathcal{D}et_n \subseteq T_{[det_n]}\mathcal{D}_{n,2n-2,n^2}$. Both of these vector spaces are G_{det_n}-submodules of $S^n(E \otimes F)$. In 8.7.1.3 you will prove the *Cauchy formula* that $S^n(E \otimes F) = \bigoplus_{|\pi|=n} S_\pi E \otimes S_\pi F$.

Exercise 8.5.3.4 (2) Show that $[\det_n] = S_{1^n}E \otimes S_{1^n}F$ and $\hat{T}_{det_n}\mathcal{D}et_n = S_{1^n}E \otimes S_{1^n}F \oplus S_{2,1^{n-1}}E \otimes S_{2,1^{n-1}}F$. ⊚

So as a $GL(E) \times GL(F)$-module, $T_{[det_n]}\mathcal{D}et_n = S_{2,1^{n-2}}E \otimes S_{2,1^{n-2}}F$. The problem now becomes to show that none of the other modules in $S^n(E \otimes F)$ are in $T_{[det_n]}\mathcal{D}_{n,2n-2,n^2}$. To do this, it suffices to check a single point in each module. A first guess would be to check highest weight vectors, but these are not so easy to write down in any uniform manner. Fortunately in this case there is another choice, namely the *immanants* IM_π defined by Littlewood [Lit06], the unique trivial representation of the diagonal $\mathfrak{S}_n$ in the weight $((1^n), (1^n))$ subspace of $S_\pi E \otimes S_\pi F$, and the proof in [LMR13] proceeds by checking that none of these other than $IM_{2,1^{n-2}}$ are contained in $T_{[\det_n]}\mathcal{D}_{n,2n-2,n^2}$.

Theorem 8.5.3.3 implies that the $GL(W)$-module of highest weight $\pi(2n - 2, n)$ given by Theorem 8.5.2.1 gives local equations at $[\det_n]$ of $\mathcal{D}et_n$, of degree $2n(n-1)$. Since $Sub_k(S^n\mathbb{C}^N) \subset Dual_{k,n,N}$, the zero set of the equations is strictly larger than $\mathcal{D}et_n$. Recall that $\dim Sub_k(S^n\mathbb{C}^{n^2}) = \binom{k+n+1}{n} + (k+2)(N-k-2) - 1$. For $k = 2n - 2$, $N = n^2$, this is larger than the dimension of the orbit of $[\det_n]$, and therefore $Dual_{2n-2,n,n^2}$ is not irreducible.

8.6 Double-Commutant and Algebraic Peter-Weyl Theorems

I now present the theory that will enable proofs of the statements in §8.1 and §3.5.

8.6.1 Algebras and Their Modules

For an algebra $\mathcal{A}$, and $a \in \mathcal{A}$ the space $\mathcal{A}a$ is a left ideal and a (left) $\mathcal{A}$-module.

Let G be a finite group. Recall from §3.5.1 the notation $\mathbb{C}[G]$ for the space of functions on G, and $\delta_g \in \mathbb{C}[G]$ for the function such that $\delta_g(h) = 0$ for $h \neq g$ and $\delta_g(g) = 1$. Define a representation $L : G \to GL(\mathbb{C}[G])$ by $L(g)\delta_h = \delta_{gh}$ and extending the action linearly. Define a second representation $R : G \to GL(\mathbb{C}[G])$ by $R(g)\delta_h = \delta_{hg^{-1}}$. Thus $\mathbb{C}[G]$ is a $G \times G$-module under the representation (L, R), and for all $c \in \mathbb{C}[G]$, the ideal $\mathbb{C}[G]c$ is a G-module under the action L.

A representation $\rho : G \to GL(V)$ induces an algebra homomorphism $\mathbb{C}[G] \to \mathrm{End}(V)$, and it is equivalent that V is a G-module or a left $\mathbb{C}[G]$-module.

A module M (for a group, ring, or algebra) is *simple* if it has no proper submodules. The module M is *semi-simple* if it may be written as the direct sum of simple modules. An algebra is *completely reducible* if all its modules are semi-simple. For groups alone I will continue to use the terminology *irreducible* for a simple module, *completely reducible* for a semi-simple module, and *reductive* for a group such that all its modules can be decomposed into a direct sum of irreducible modules.

Exercise 8.6.1.1 (2) Show that if $\mathcal{A}$ is completely reducible, V is an $\mathcal{A}$-module with an $\mathcal{A}$-submodule $U \subset V$, then there exists an $\mathcal{A}$-invariant complement to U in V and a projection map $\pi : V \to U$ that is an $\mathcal{A}$-module map. ⊚

8.6.2 The Double-Commutant Theorem

Our sought-after decomposition of $V^{\otimes d}$ as a $GL(V)$-module will be obtained by exploiting the fact that the actions of $GL(V)$ and $\mathfrak{S}_d$ on $V^{\otimes d}$ commute. In this subsection I discuss commuting actions in general, as this is also the basis of the generalized DFT used in the Cohn-Umans method §3.5, and the starting point of the program of [MS01, MS08]. References for this section are [Pro07, Chapter 6] and [GW09, §4.1.5]. Let $S \subset \text{End}(V)$ be any subset. Define the *centralizer* or *commutator* of S to be

$$S' := \{X \in \text{End}(V) \mid Xs = sX \; \forall s \in S\}$$

Proposition 8.6.2.1 1 $S' \subset \text{End}(V)$ *is a subalgebra.*
               2 $S \subset (S')'$.

Exercise 8.6.2.2 (1!) Prove Proposition 8.6.2.1.

Theorem 8.6.2.3 *[Double-Commutant Theorem] Let $\mathcal{A} \subset \text{End}(V)$ be a completely reducible associative algebra. Then $\mathcal{A}'' = \mathcal{A}$.*

There is an ambiguity in the notation S' as it makes no reference to V, so instead introduce the notation $\text{End}_S(V) := S'$.

Proof. By Proposition 8.6.2.1, $\mathcal{A} \subseteq \mathcal{A}''$. To show the reverse inclusion, say $T \in \mathcal{A}''$. Fix a basis $v_1, \ldots, v_{\mathbf{v}}$ of V. Since the action of T is determined by its action on a basis, we need to find $a \in \mathcal{A}$ such that $av_j = Tv_j$ for $j = 1, \ldots, \mathbf{v}$. Let $w := v_1 \oplus \cdots \oplus v_{\mathbf{v}} \in V^{\oplus \mathbf{v}}$ and consider the submodule $\mathcal{A}w \subseteq V^{\oplus \mathbf{v}}$. By Exercise 8.6.1.1, there exists an $\mathcal{A}$-invariant complement to this submodule and an $\mathcal{A}$-equivariant projection $\pi : V^{\oplus \mathbf{v}} \to \mathcal{A}w \subset V^{\oplus \mathbf{v}}$, that is, a projection π that commutes with the action of $\mathcal{A}$, i.e., $\pi \in \text{End}_{\mathcal{A}}(V^{\oplus \mathbf{v}})$. Since $T \in \text{End}_{\mathcal{A}}(V)$ and the action on $V^{\oplus \mathbf{v}}$ is diagonal, $T \in \text{End}_{\mathcal{A}}(V^{\oplus \mathbf{v}})$. We have $\pi(Tw) = T(\pi(w))$ but $T(\pi(w)) = T(w) = Tv_1 \oplus \cdots \oplus Tv_{\mathbf{v}}$. But since $\pi(Tw) \in \mathcal{A}w$, there must be some $a \in \mathcal{A}$ such that $aw = T(w)$, i.e., $av_1 \oplus \cdots \oplus av_{\mathbf{v}} = Tv_1 \oplus \cdots \oplus Tv_{\mathbf{v}}$, i.e., $av_j = Tv_j$ for $j = 1, \ldots, \mathbf{v}$. $\qquad\square$

Burnside's theorem, stated in §3.5, has a similar proof:

Theorem 8.6.2.4 *[Burnside] Let $\mathcal{A} \subseteq \text{End}(V)$ be a finite-dimensional simple subalgebra of $\text{End}(V)$ (over $\mathbb{C}$) acting irreducibly on a finite-dimensional vector space V. Then $\mathcal{A} = \text{End}(V)$. More generally, a finite-dimensional semisimple associative algebra $\mathcal{A}$ over $\mathbb{C}$ is isomorphic to a direct sum of matrix algebras:*

$$\mathcal{A} \simeq Mat_{d_1 \times d_1}(\mathbb{C}) \oplus \cdots \oplus Mat_{d_q \times d_q}(\mathbb{C})$$

for some $d_1, \ldots, d_q$.

Proof. For the first assertion, we need to show that given $X \in \mathrm{End}(V)$, there exists $a \in \mathcal{A}$ such that $av_j = Xv_j$ for $v_1, \ldots, v_v$ a basis of V. Now just imitate the proof of Theorem 8.6.2.3. For the second assertion, note that $\mathcal{A}$ is a direct sum of simple algebras.   □

Remark 8.6.2.5 A pessimist could look at this theorem as a disappointment: all kinds of interesting looking algebras over $\mathbb{C}$, such as the group algebra of a finite group, are actually just plain old matrix algebras in disguise. An optimist could view this theorem as stating there is a rich structure hidden in matrix algebras. We will determine the matrix algebra structure explicitly for the group algebra of a finite group.

8.6.3 Consequences for Reductive Groups

Let S be a group or algebra and let V, W be S-modules, adopt the notation $\mathrm{Hom}_S(V, W)$ for the space of S-module maps $V \to W$, i.e.,

$$\mathrm{Hom}_S(V, W) := \{ f \in \mathrm{Hom}(V, W) \mid s(f(v)) = f(s(v)) \; \forall \, s \in S, \; v \in V \}$$
$$= (V^* \otimes W)^S.$$

Theorem 8.6.3.1 *Let G be a reductive group and let V be a G-module. Then*

1 *The commutator $\mathrm{End}_G(V)$ is a semi-simple algebra.*
2 *The isotypic components of G and $\mathrm{End}_G(V)$ in V coincide.*
3 *Let U be one such isotypic component, say for irreducible representations A of G and B of $\mathrm{End}_G(V)$. Then, as a $G \times \mathrm{End}_G(V)$-module,*

$$U = A \otimes B,$$

as an $\mathrm{End}_G(V)$-module

$$B = \mathrm{Hom}_G(A, U),$$

and as a G-module

$$A = \mathrm{Hom}_{\mathrm{End}_G(V)}(B, U).$$

In particular, $\mathrm{mult}(A, V) = \dim B$ *and* $\mathrm{mult}(B, V) = \dim A$.

Example 8.6.3.2 Below we will see that $\mathrm{End}_{GL(V)}(V^{\otimes d}) = \mathbb{C}[\mathfrak{S}_d]$. As an $\mathfrak{S}_3 \times GL(V)$-module, we have the decomposition $V^{\otimes 3} = ([3] \otimes S^3 V) \oplus ([2, 1] \otimes S_{21} V) \oplus ([1, 1, 1] \otimes \Lambda^3 V)$ which illustrates Theorem 8.6.3.1.

To prove the theorem, we will need the following lemma:

Lemma 8.6.3.3 *For $W \subset V$ a G-submodule and $f \in \mathrm{Hom}_G(W, V)$, there exists $a \in \mathrm{End}_G(V)$ such that $a|_W = f$.*

Proof. Consider the diagram

$$
\begin{array}{ccc}
\mathrm{End}(V) & \longrightarrow & \mathrm{Hom}(W, V) \\
\downarrow & & \downarrow \\
\mathrm{End}_G(V) & \longrightarrow & \mathrm{Hom}_G(W, V)
\end{array}
$$

The vertical arrows are G-equivariant projections, and the horizontal arrows are restriction of domain of a linear map. The diagram is commutative. Since the vertical arrows and upper horizontal arrow are surjective, we conclude the lower horizontal arrow is surjective as well. $\qquad\square$

Proof of Theorem 8.6.3.1. I first prove (3): The space $\mathrm{Hom}_G(A, V)$ is an $\mathrm{End}_G(V)$-module because for $s \in \mathrm{Hom}_G(A, V)$ and $a \in \mathrm{End}_G(V)$, the composition $as : A \to V$ is still a G-module map. We need to show (i) that $\mathrm{Hom}_G(A, V)$ is an irreducible $\mathrm{End}_G(V)$-module and (ii) that the isotypic component of A in V is $A \otimes \mathrm{Hom}_G(A, V)$.

To show (i), it is sufficient to show that for all nonzero $s, t \in \mathrm{Hom}_G(A, V)$, there exists $a \in \mathrm{End}_G(V)$ such that $at = s$. Since tA and sA are isomorphic G-modules, by Lemma 8.6.3.3, there exists $a \in \mathrm{End}_G(V)$ extending an isomorphism between them, so $a(tA) = sA$, i.e., $at : A \to sA$ is an isomorphism. Consider the isomorphism $S : A \to sA$, given by $a \mapsto sa$, so $S^{-1}at$ is a nonzero scalar c times the identity. Then $\tilde{a} := \frac{1}{c}a$ has the property that $\tilde{a}t = s$.

To see (ii), let U be the isotypic component of A, so $U = A \otimes B$ for some vector space B. Let $b \in B$ and define a map $\tilde{b} : A \to V$ by $a \mapsto a \otimes b$, which is a G-module map where the action of G on the target is just the action on the first factor. Thus $B \subseteq \mathrm{Hom}_G(A, V)$. Any G-module map $A \to V$ by definition has image in U, so equality holds.

(3) implies (2).

To see (1), note that $\mathrm{End}_G(V)$ is semi-simple because if the irreducible $G \times \mathrm{End}_G(V)$-components of V are U_i, then $\mathrm{End}_G(V) = \oplus_i \mathrm{End}_G(U_i) = \oplus_i \mathrm{End}_G(A_i \otimes B_i) = \oplus_i \mathrm{End}(B_i)$. $\qquad\square$

8.6.4 Matrix Coefficients

For affine algebraic reductive groups, one can obtain all their (finite-dimensional) irreducible representations from the ring of regular functions on G, denoted $\mathbb{C}[G]$. Here G is an *affine algebraic variety*, i.e., a subvariety of $\mathbb{C}^N$ for some N, so $\mathbb{C}[G] = \mathbb{C}[x_1, \ldots, x_N]/I(G)$.

Exercise 8.6.4.1 (1!) Show that GL_n is an affine algebraic subvariety of $\mathbb{C}^{n^2+1}$ with coordinates (x_j^i, z) by considering the polynomial $z \det_n(x_j^i) - 1$.

Thus $\mathbb{C}[GL(W)]$ may be defined to be the restriction of polynomial functions on $\mathbb{C}^{n^2+1}$ to the subvariety isomorphic to $GL(W)$. (For a finite group, all complex-valued functions on G are algebraic, so this is consistent with our earlier notation.) If $G \subset GL(W)$ is defined by algebraic equations, this also enables us to define $\mathbb{C}[G]$ because $G \subset GL(W)$ is a subvariety. In this section and the next, we study the structure of $\mathbb{C}[G]$ as a G-module.

Let G be an affine algebraic group. Let $\rho : G \to GL(V)$ be a finite-dimensional representation of G. Define a map $i_V : V^* \otimes V \to \mathbb{C}[G]$ by $i_V(\alpha \otimes v)(g) := \alpha(\rho(g)v)$. The space of functions $i_V(V^* \otimes V)$ is called the *space of matrix coefficients of V*.

Exercise 8.6.4.2 (1)

   i Show i_V is a $G \times G$-module map.

   ii Show that if V is irreducible, i_V is injective. ⊙

   iii If we choose a basis $v_1, \ldots, v_{\mathbf{v}}$ of V with dual basis $\alpha^1, \ldots, \alpha^{\mathbf{v}}$, then $i_V(\alpha^i \otimes v_j)(g)$ is the (i, j)th entry of the matrix representing $\rho(g)$ in this basis (which explains the name "matrix coefficients").

   iv Compute the matrix coefficient basis of the three irreducible representations of $\mathfrak{S}_3$ in terms of the standard basis $\{\delta_\sigma \mid \sigma \in \mathfrak{S}_3\}$.

   v Let $G = GL_2\mathbb{C}$, write $g = \begin{pmatrix} a & b \\ c & d \end{pmatrix} \in G$, and compute the matrix coefficient basis as functions of a, b, c, d when $V = S^2\mathbb{C}^2, S^3\mathbb{C}^2$ and $\Lambda^2\mathbb{C}^2$.

Theorem 8.6.4.3 *Let G be an affine algebraic group and let V be an irreducible G-module. Then $i_V(V^* \otimes V)$ equals the isotypic component of type V in $\mathbb{C}[G]$ under the action L and the isotypic component of V^* in $\mathbb{C}[G]$ under the action R.*

Proof. It suffices to prove one of the assertions, consider the action L. Let $j : V \to \mathbb{C}[G]$ be a G-module map under the action L. We need to show $j(V) \subset i_V(V^* \otimes V)$. Define $\alpha \in V^*$ by $\alpha(v) := j(v)(\mathrm{Id}_G)$. Then $j(v) = i_V(\alpha \otimes v)$, as $j(v)g = j(v)(g \cdot \mathrm{Id}_G) = j(gv)(\mathrm{Id}_G) = \alpha(gv) = i_V(\alpha \otimes v)g$. □

8.6.5 Application to Representations of Finite Groups

Theorem 8.6.4.3 implies:

Theorem 8.6.5.1 *Let G be a finite group, then as a $G \times G$-module under the action (L, R) and as an algebra,*

$$\mathbb{C}[G] = \bigoplus_i V_i \otimes V_i^* \tag{8.6.1}$$

where the sum is over all the distinct irreducible representations of G.

Exercise 8.6.5.2 (1!) Let G be a finite group and H a subgroup. For the homogeneous space G/H, show that $\mathbb{C}[G/H] = \bigoplus_i V_i^* \otimes (V_i)^H$ as a G-module under the action L.

8.6.6 The Algebraic Peter-Weyl Theorem

Theorem 8.6.5.1 generalizes to reductive algebraic groups. The proof is unchanged, except that one has an infinite sum:

Theorem 8.6.6.1 *Let G be a reductive algebraic group. Then there are only countably many nonisomorphic finite-dimensional irreducible G-modules. Let Λ_G^+ denote a set indexing the irreducible G-modules, and for $\lambda \in \Lambda_G^+$, let V_λ denote the irreducible module associated to λ. Then, as a $G \times G$-module*

$$\mathbb{C}[G] = \bigoplus_{\lambda \in \Lambda_G^+} V_\lambda \otimes V_\lambda^*.$$

Corollary 8.6.6.2 *Let $H \subset G$ be a closed subgroup. Then, as a G-module, the coordinate ring of the homogeneous space G/H is*

$$\mathbb{C}[G/H] = \mathbb{C}[G]^H = \bigoplus_{\lambda \in \Lambda_G^+} V_\lambda \otimes (V_\lambda^*)^H = \bigoplus_{\lambda \in \Lambda_G^+} V_\lambda^{\oplus \dim(V_\lambda^*)^H}. \qquad (8.6.2)$$

Here G acts on the V_λ and $(V_\lambda^*)^H$ is just a vector space whose dimension records the multiplicity of V_λ in $\mathbb{C}[G/H]$.

Exercise 8.6.6.3 (2!) Use Corollary 8.6.6.2 to determine $\mathbb{C}[v_d(\mathbb{P}V)]$ (even if you already know it by a different method).

8.6.7 Characters and Representations of Finite Groups

Let $\rho : G \to GL(V)$ be a representation. Define a function $\chi_\rho : G \to \mathbb{C}$ by $\chi_\rho(g) = \text{trace}(\rho(g))$. The function χ_ρ is called the *character* of ρ.

Exercise 8.6.7.1 (1) Show that χ_ρ is constant on conjugacy classes of G.

A function $f : G \to \mathbb{C}$ such that $f(hgh^{-1}) = f(g)$ for all $g, h \in G$ is called a *class function*.

Exercise 8.6.7.2 (1) For representations $\rho_j : G \to GL(V_j)$, show that $\chi_{\rho_1 \oplus \rho_2} = \chi_{\rho_1} + \chi_{\rho_2}$.

Exercise 8.6.7.3 (1) Given $\rho_j : G \to GL(V_j)$ for $j = 1, 2$, define $\rho_1 \otimes \rho_2 : G \to GL(V_1 \otimes V_2)$ by $\rho_1 \otimes \rho_2(g)(v_1 \otimes v_2) = \rho_1(g)v_1 \otimes \rho_2(g)v_2$. Show that $\chi_{\rho_1 \otimes \rho_2} = \chi_{\rho_1} \chi_{\rho_2}$.

Theorem 8.6.5.1 is not yet useful, as we do not yet know what the V_i are. Let $\mu_i : G \to GL(V_i)$ denote the representation. It is not difficult to show that the functions χ_{μ_i} are linearly independent in $\mathbb{C}[G]$. (One uses a G-invariant Hermitian inner-product $\langle \chi_V, \chi_W \rangle := \frac{1}{|G|} \sum_{g \in G} \chi_V(g)\overline{\chi_W(g)}$ and shows that they are orthogonal with respect to this inner-product, see, e.g., [FH91, §2.2].) On the other hand, we have a natural basis of the class functions, namely the δ-functions on each conjugacy class. Let C_j be a conjugacy class of G and define $\delta_{C_j} := \sum_{g \in C_j} \delta_g$. It is straightforward to see, via the DFT (§3.5.1), that the span of the δ_{C_j}'s equals the span of the χ_{μ_i}'s, that is *the number of distinct irreducible representations of G equals the number of conjugacy classes* (see, e.g., [FH91, §2.2] for the standard proof using the Hermitian inner-product on class functions and [GW09, §4.4] for a DFT proof).

Remark 8.6.7.4 The classical Heisenberg uncertainty principle from physics, in the language of mathematics, is that it is not possible to localize both a function and its Fourier transform. A discrete analog of this uncertainty principle holds, in that the transforms of the delta functions have large support in terms of matrix coefficients and vice versa. In particular, the relation between these two bases can be complicated.

8.6.8 Representations of $\mathfrak{S}_d$

When $G = \mathfrak{S}_d$, we get lucky: one may associate irreducible representations directly to conjugacy classes.

The conjugacy class of a permutation is determined by its decomposition into a product of disjoint cycles. The conjugacy classes of $\mathfrak{S}_d$ are in 1-1 correspondence with the set of partitions of d: to a partition $\pi = (p_1, \ldots, p_r)$ one associates the conjugacy class of an element with disjoint cycles of lengths $p_1, \ldots, p_r$. Let $[\pi]$ denote the isomorphism class of the irreducible $\mathfrak{S}_d$-module associated to the partition π. In summary:

Proposition 8.6.8.1 *The irreducible representations of $\mathfrak{S}_d$ are indexed by partitions of d.*

Thus as an $\mathfrak{S}_d \times \mathfrak{S}_d$ module under the (L, R)-action:

$$\mathbb{C}[\mathfrak{S}_d] = \bigoplus_{|\pi|=d} [\pi]_L \otimes [\pi]_R^*. \tag{8.6.3}$$

We can say even more: as $\mathfrak{S}_d$ modules, $[\pi]$ is isomorphic to $[\pi]^*$. This is usually proved by first noting that for any finite group G, and any irreducible representation μ, $\chi_{\mu^*} = \overline{\chi_\mu}$ where the overline denotes complex conjugate and then observing that the characters of $\mathfrak{S}_d$ are all real-valued functions. Thus we may rewrite (8.6.3) as

$$\mathbb{C}[\mathfrak{S}_d] = \bigoplus_{|\pi|=d} [\pi]_L \otimes [\pi]_R. \qquad (8.6.4)$$

Exercise 8.6.8.2 (1) Show $[d] \subset [\pi] \otimes [\mu]$ if and only if $\pi = \mu$. ⊚

Exercise 8.6.8.3 (1) Show that moreover $[d] \subset [\pi] \otimes [\pi]$ with multiplicity one. ⊚

8.7 Representations of $\mathfrak{S}_d$ and $GL(V)$

In this section we finally obtain our goal of the decomposition of $V^{\otimes d}$ as a $GL(V)$-module.

8.7.1 Schur-Weyl Duality

We have already seen that the actions of $GL(V)$ and $\mathfrak{S}_d$ on $V^{\otimes d}$ commute.

Proposition 8.7.1.1 $\mathrm{End}_{GL(V)}(V^{\otimes d}) = \mathbb{C}[\mathfrak{S}_d]$.

Proof. We will show that $\mathrm{End}_{\mathbb{C}[\mathfrak{S}_d]}(V^{\otimes d})$ is the algebra generated by $GL(V)$ and conclude by the double commutant theorem. Since

$$\mathrm{End}(V^{\otimes d}) = V^{\otimes d} \otimes (V^{\otimes d})^*$$
$$\simeq (V \otimes V^*)^{\otimes d}$$

under the reordering isomorphism, $\mathrm{End}(V^{\otimes d})$ is spanned by elements of the form $X_1 \otimes \cdots \otimes X_d$ with $X_j \in \mathrm{End}(V)$, i.e., elements of $\hat{Seg}(\mathbb{P}(\mathrm{End}(V)) \times \cdots \times \mathbb{P}(\mathrm{End}(V)))$. The action of $X_1 \otimes \cdots \otimes X_d$ on $v_1 \otimes \cdots \otimes v_d$ induced from the $GL(V)^{\times d}$-action is $v_1 \otimes \cdots \otimes v_d \mapsto (X_1 v_1) \otimes \cdots \otimes (X_d v_d)$. Since $g \in GL(V)$ acts by $g \cdot (v_1 \otimes \cdots \otimes v_d) = gv_1 \otimes \cdots \otimes gv_d$, the image of $GL(V)$ in $(V \otimes V^*)^{\otimes d}$ lies in $S^d(V \otimes V^*)$, in fact it is a Zariski open subset of $\hat{v}_d(\mathbb{P}(V \otimes V^*))$ which spans $S^d(V \otimes V^*)$. In other words, the algebra generated by $GL(V)$ is $S^d(V \otimes V^*) \subset \mathrm{End}(V^{\otimes d})$. But by definition $S^d(V \otimes V^*) = [(V \otimes V^*)^{\otimes d}]^{\mathfrak{S}_d}$ and we conclude. □

Theorem 8.6.3.1 and Proposition 8.7.1.1 imply:

Theorem 8.7.1.2 *[Schur-Weyl duality] The irreducible decomposition of $V^{\otimes d}$ as a $GL(V) \times \mathbb{C}[\mathfrak{S}_d]$-module (equivalently, as a $GL(V) \times \mathfrak{S}_d$-module) is*

$$V^{\otimes d} = \bigoplus_{|\pi|=d} S_\pi V \otimes [\pi], \qquad (8.7.1)$$

where $S_\pi V := \mathrm{Hom}_{\mathfrak{S}_d}([\pi], V^{\otimes d})$ is an irreducible $GL(V)$-module.

Note that as far as we know, $S_\pi V$ could be zero. (It will be zero whenever $l(\pi) \geq \dim V$.)

Exercise 8.7.1.3 (2) Show that as a $GL(E) \times GL(F)$-module, $S^d(E \otimes F) = \bigoplus_{|\pi|=d} S_\pi E \otimes S_\pi F$. This is called the *Cauchy formula*. ⊚

8.7.2 Explicit Realizations of Representations of $\mathfrak{S}_d$ and $GL(V)$

By Theorem 8.6.5.1 we may explicitly realize each irreducible $\mathfrak{S}_d$-module via some projection from $\mathbb{C}[\mathfrak{S}_d]$. The question is, which projections?

Given π we would like to find elements $c_{\overline{\pi}} \in \mathbb{C}[\mathfrak{S}_d]$ such that $\mathbb{C}[\mathfrak{S}_d]c_{\overline{\pi}}$ is isomorphic to $[\pi]$. I write $\overline{\pi}$ instead of just π because the elements are far from unique; there is a vector space of dimension $\dim[\pi]$ of such projection operators by Theorem 8.6.5.1, and the overline signifies a specific realization. In other words, the $\mathfrak{S}_d$-module map $RM_{c_{\overline{\pi}}} : \mathbb{C}[\mathfrak{S}_d] \to \mathbb{C}[\mathfrak{S}_d], f \mapsto fc_{\overline{\pi}}$ should kill all $\mathfrak{S}_d^R$-modules not isomorphic to $[\pi]_R$, and the image should be $[\pi]_L \otimes z$ for some $z \in [\pi]_R$. If this works, as a bonus, the map $c_{\overline{\pi}} : V^{\otimes d} \to V^{\otimes d}$ induced from the $\mathfrak{S}_d$-action will have image $S_{\overline{\pi}}V \otimes z \simeq S_{\overline{\pi}}V$ for the same reason, where $S_{\overline{\pi}}V$ is some realization of $S_\pi V$ and $z \in [\pi]$.

Here are projection operators for the two representations we understand well:

When $\pi = (d)$, there is a unique up to scale $c_{\overline{(d)}}$ and it is easy to see it must be $c_{\overline{(d)}} := \sum_{\sigma \in \mathfrak{S}_d} \delta_\sigma$, as the image of $RM_{c_{\overline{(d)}}}$ is clearly the line through $c_{\overline{(d)}}$ on which $\mathfrak{S}_d$ acts trivially. Note further that $c_{\overline{(d)}}(V^{\otimes d}) = S^d V$ as desired.

When $\pi = (1^d)$, again we have a unique up to scale projection, and its clear we should take $c_{\overline{(1^d)}} = \sum_{\sigma \in \mathfrak{S}_d} \text{sgn}(\sigma)\delta_\sigma$ as the image of any δ_τ will be $\text{sgn}(\tau)c_{\overline{(1^d)}}$, and $c_{\overline{(1^d)}}(V^{\otimes d}) = \Lambda^d V$.

The only other representation of $\mathfrak{S}_d$ that we have a reasonable understanding of is the standard representation $\pi = (d-1, 1)$ which corresponds to the complement of the trivial representation in the permutation action on $\mathbb{C}^d$. A basis of this space could be given by $e_1 - e_d, e_2 - e_d, \ldots, e_{d-1} - e_d$. Note that the roles of $1, \ldots, d-1$ in this basis are the "same" in that if one permutes them, one gets the same basis, and that the role of d with respect to any of the other e_j is "skew" in some sense. To capture this behavior, consider

$$c_{\overline{(d-1,1)}} := (\delta_{\text{Id}} - \delta_{(1,d)}) \left(\sum_{\sigma \in \mathfrak{S}_{d-1}[d-1]} \delta_\sigma \right)$$

where $\mathfrak{S}_{d-1}[d-1] \subset \mathfrak{S}_d$ is the subgroup permuting the elements $\{1, \ldots, d-1\}$. Note that $c_{\overline{(d-1,1)}}\delta_\tau = c_{\overline{(d-1,1)}}$ for any $\tau \in \mathfrak{S}_{d-1}[d-1]$ so the image is of dimension at most $d = \dim(\mathbb{C}[\mathfrak{S}_d]/\mathbb{C}[\mathfrak{S}_{d-1}])$.

Exercise 8.7.2.1 (2) Show that the image is $d-1$-dimensional.

Now consider $RM_{c_{(d-1,1)}}(V^{\otimes d})$: after reorderings, it is the image of the composition of the maps

$$V^{\otimes d} \to V^{\otimes d-2} \otimes \Lambda^2 V \to S^{d-1}V \otimes V.$$

In particular, in the case $d = 3$, it is the image of

$$V \otimes \Lambda^2 V \to S^2 V \otimes V,$$

which is isomorphic to $S_{21}V$, as was mentioned in in §4.1.5.

Here is the general recipe to construct an $\mathfrak{S}_d$-module isomorphic to $[\pi]$: fill the Young diagram of a partition π of d with integers $1, \ldots, d$ from top to bottom and left to right. For example let $\pi = (4, 2, 1)$ and write:

$$
\begin{array}{|c|c|c|c|}
\hline
1 & 4 & 6 & 7 \\
\hline
2 & 5 \\
\cline{1-2}
3 \\
\cline{1-1}
\end{array}
\tag{8.7.2}
$$

Define $\mathfrak{S}_{\overline{\pi}'} \simeq \mathfrak{S}_{q_1} \times \cdots \times \mathfrak{S}_{q_{p_1}} \subset \mathfrak{S}_d$ to be the subgroup that permutes elements in each column and $\mathfrak{S}_{\overline{\pi}}$ is the subgroup of $\mathfrak{S}_d$ that permutes the elements in each row.

Explicitly, writing $\pi = (p_1, \ldots, p_{q_1})$ and $\pi' = (q_1, \ldots, q_{p_1})$, $\mathfrak{S}_{q_1}$ permutes the elements of $\{1, \ldots, q_1\}$, $\mathfrak{S}_{q_2}$ permutes the elements of $\{q_1 + 1, \ldots, q_1 + q_2\}$ etc.. Similarly, $\mathfrak{S}_{\overline{\pi}} \simeq \mathfrak{S}_{p_1} \times \cdots \times \mathfrak{S}_{p_\ell} \subset \mathfrak{S}_d$ is the subgroup where $\mathfrak{S}_{p_1}$ permutes the elements $\{1, q_1 + 1, q_1 + q_2 + 1, \ldots, q_1 + \cdots + q_{p_1-1} + 1\}$, $\mathfrak{S}_{p_2}$ permutes the elements $\{2, q_1 + 2, q_1 + q_2 + 2, \ldots, q_1 + \cdots + q_{p_1-1} + 2\}$ etc..

Define two elements of $\mathbb{C}[\mathfrak{S}_d]$: $s_{\overline{\pi}} := \sum_{\sigma \in \mathfrak{S}_{\overline{\pi}}} \delta_\sigma$ and $a_{\overline{\pi}} := \sum_{\sigma \in \mathfrak{S}_{\overline{\pi}'}} \operatorname{sgn}(\sigma) \delta_\sigma$. Fact: Then $[\pi]$ is the isomorphism class of the $\mathfrak{S}_d$-module $\mathbb{C}[\mathfrak{S}_d]a_{\overline{\pi}}s_{\overline{\pi}}$. (It is also the isomorphism class of $\mathbb{C}[\mathfrak{S}_d]s_{\overline{\pi}}a_{\overline{\pi}}$, although these two realizations are generally distinct.)

Exercise 8.7.2.2 (1) Show that $[\pi'] = [\pi] \otimes [1^d]$ as $\mathfrak{S}_d$-modules. ⊚

The action on $V^{\otimes d}$ is first to map it to $\Lambda^{q_1} V \otimes \cdots \otimes \Lambda^{q_{p_1}} V$, and then the module $S_\pi V$ is realized as the image of a map from this space to $S^{p_1} V \otimes \cdots \otimes S^{p_{q_1}} V$ obtained by reordering then symmetrizing. So despite their original indirect definition, we may realize the modules $S_\pi V$ explicitly simply by skew-symmetrizations and symmetrizations.

Other realizations of $S_\pi V$ (resp. highest weight vectors for $S_\pi V$, in fact a basis of them) can be obtained by letting $\mathfrak{S}_d$ act on $RM_{c_{\overline{\pi}}} V^{\otimes d}$ (resp. the highest weight vector of $RM_{c_{\overline{\pi}}} V^{\otimes d}$).

Example 8.7.2.3 Consider $c_{\overline{(2,2)}}$, associated to

$$
\begin{array}{|c|c|}
\hline
1 & 3 \\
\hline
2 & 4 \\
\hline
\end{array}
\tag{8.7.3}
$$

which realizes a copy of $S_{(2,2)}V \subset V^{\otimes 4}$. It first maps $V^{\otimes 4}$ to $\Lambda^2 V \otimes \Lambda^2 V$ and then maps that to $S^2 V \otimes S^2 V$. Explicitly, the maps are

$$
a\otimes b\otimes c\otimes c \mapsto (a\otimes b - b\otimes a)\otimes(c\otimes d - d\otimes c)
$$

$$
= a\otimes b\otimes c\otimes d - a\otimes b\otimes d\otimes c - b\otimes a\otimes c\otimes d + b\otimes a\otimes d\otimes c
$$

$$
\mapsto (a\otimes b\otimes c\otimes d + c\otimes b\otimes a\otimes d + a\otimes d\otimes c\otimes b + c\otimes d\otimes a\otimes b)
$$

$$
- (a\otimes b\otimes d\otimes c + d\otimes b\otimes a\otimes c + a\otimes c\otimes d\otimes b + d\otimes c\otimes a\otimes b)
$$

$$
- (b\otimes a\otimes c\otimes d + c\otimes a\otimes b\otimes d + b\otimes d\otimes c\otimes a + c\otimes d\otimes b\otimes a)
$$

$$
+ (b\otimes a\otimes d\otimes c + d\otimes a\otimes b\otimes c + b\otimes c\otimes d\otimes a + d\otimes c\otimes b\otimes a)
$$

Exercise 8.7.2.4 (2) Show that a basis of the highest weight space of $[2,1]\otimes S_{21}V \subset V^{\otimes 3}$ is $v_1 = e_1 \wedge e_2 \otimes e_1$ and $v_2 = e_1 \otimes e_1 \wedge e_2$. Let $\mathbb{Z}_3 \subset \mathfrak{S}_3$ be the cyclic permutation of the three factors in $V^{\otimes 3}$ and show that $\omega v_1 \pm \omega^2 v_2$ are eigenvectors for this action with eigenvalues ω, ω^2, where $\omega = e^{\frac{2\pi i}{3}}$.

8.8 The Program of [MS01, MS08]

Algebraic geometry was used successfully in [Mul99] to prove lower bounds in the "PRAM model without bit operations" (the model is defined in [Mul99]), and the proof indicated that algebraic geometry, more precisely invariant theory, could be used to resolve the **P** v. **NC** problem (a cousin of permanent v. determinant). This was investigated further in [MS01, MS08] and numerous sequels. In this section I present the program outlined in [MS08], as refined in [BLMW11].

Independent of its viability, I expect the ingredients that went into the program of [MS01, MS08] will play a role in future investigations regarding Valiant's conjecture and thus are still worth studying.

8.8.1 Preliminaries

Let $W = \mathbb{C}^{n^2}$. Recall $\mathbb{C}[\hat{\mathcal{D}et}_n] := Sym(S^n W^*)/I(\mathcal{D}et_n)$, the homogeneous coordinate ring of the (cone over) $\mathcal{D}et_n$. This is the space of polynomial functions on $\hat{\mathcal{D}et}_n$ inherited from polynomials on the ambient space.

Since $I(\mathcal{D}et_n) \subset Sym(S^n W^*)$ is a $GL(W)$-submodule, and since $GL(W)$ is reductive, we obtain the following splitting as a $GL(W)$-module:

$$
Sym(S^n W^*) = I(\mathcal{D}et_n) \oplus \mathbb{C}[\hat{\mathcal{D}et}_n].
$$

In particular, if a module $S_\pi W^*$ appears in $Sym(S^n W^*)$ and it does not appear in $\mathbb{C}[\hat{\mathcal{D}et}_n]$, it must appear in $I(\mathcal{D}et_n)$.

Now consider

$$\mathbb{C}[GL(W) \cdot \det_n] = \mathbb{C}[GL(W)/G_{\det_n}] = \mathbb{C}[GL(W)]^{G_{\det_n}}.$$

There is an injective map

$$\mathbb{C}[\hat{\mathcal{D}et}_n] \to \mathbb{C}[GL(W) \cdot \det_n]$$

given by restriction of functions. The map is an injection because any function identically zero on a Zariski open subset of an irreducible variety is identically zero on the variety.

Corollary 8.6.6.2 in principle gives a recipe to determine the modules in $\mathbb{C}[GL(W) \cdot \det_n]$, which motivates the following plan:

Plan : *Find a module $S_\pi W^*$ not appearing in $\mathbb{C}[GL(W)/G_{\det_n}]$ that does appear in $Sym(S^n W^*)$.*

By the above discussion such a module must appear in $I(\mathcal{D}et_n)$.

Definition 8.8.1.1 An irreducible $GL(W)$-module $S_\pi W^*$ appearing in $Sym(S^n W^*)$ and not appearing in $\mathbb{C}[GL(W)/G_{\det_n}]$ is called an *orbit occurrence obstruction*.

The precise condition a module must satisfy in order to not occur in $\mathbb{C}[GL(W)/G_{\det_n}]$ is explained in Proposition 8.8.2.2. The discussion in §8.4 shows that in order to be useful, π must have a large first part and few parts.

One might object that, as $GL(W)$-modules, the coordinate rings of different orbits could coincide, or at least be very close. Indeed this is the case for generic polynomials, but in GCT one generally restricts to polynomials whose symmetry groups *characterize* the orbit in the sense of Definition 1.2.5.3. We have seen in §6.6 that both the determinant and permanent polynomials are characterized by their stabilizers.

Corollary 8.6.6.2 motivates the study of polynomials characterized by their stabilizers: if $P \in V$ is characterized by its stabilizer, then $G \cdot P$ is the unique orbit in V with coordinate ring isomorphic to $\mathbb{C}[G \cdot P]$ as a G-module. Thus one can think of polynomial sequences that are complete for their complexity classes and are characterized by their stabilizers as "best" representatives of their class.

Remark 8.8.1.2 All $GL(W)$-modules $S_{(p_1,\dots,p_w)}W$ may be graded using $p_1 + \cdots + p_w$ as the grading. One does not have such a grading for $SL(W)$-modules, which makes their use in GCT more difficult. In [MS01, MS08], it was proposed to use the $SL(W)$-module structure because it had the advantage that the

SL-orbit of $\det_n$ is already closed. The disadvantage from the lack of a grading appears to outweigh this advantage.

8.8.2 The Coordinate Ring of $GL_{n^2} \cdot \det_n$

Write $\mathbb{C}^{n^2} = E \otimes F$, with $E, F = \mathbb{C}^n$. I first compute the $SL(E) \times SL(F)$-invariants in $S_\pi(E \otimes F)$ where $|\pi| = d = \underline{n}$. Recall from §8.7.1 that by definition, $S_\pi W = \mathrm{Hom}_{\mathfrak{S}_d}([\pi], W^{\otimes d})$. Thus

$$S_\pi(E \otimes F) = \mathrm{Hom}_{\mathfrak{S}_d}([\pi], E^{\otimes d} \otimes F^{\otimes d})$$

$$= \mathrm{Hom}_{\mathfrak{S}_d}\left([\pi], \left(\bigoplus_{|\mu|=d} [\mu] \otimes S_\mu E \right) \otimes \left(\bigoplus_{|\nu|=d} [\nu] \otimes S_\nu F \right) \right)$$

$$= \bigoplus_{|\mu|=|\nu|=d} \mathrm{Hom}_{\mathfrak{S}_d}([\pi], [\mu] \otimes [\nu]) \otimes S_\mu E \otimes S_\nu F$$

The vector space $\mathrm{Hom}_{\mathfrak{S}_d}([\pi], [\mu] \otimes [\nu])$ simply records the multiplicity of $S_\mu E \otimes S_\nu F$ in $S_\pi(E \otimes F)$. The numbers $k_{\pi,\mu,\nu} = \dim \mathrm{Hom}_{\mathfrak{S}_d}([\pi], [\mu] \otimes [\nu])$ are called *Kronecker coefficients*.

Exercise 8.8.2.1 (2) Show that

$$k_{\pi,\mu,\nu} = \mathrm{Hom}_{\mathfrak{S}_d}([d], [\pi] \otimes [\mu] \otimes [\nu]) = \mathrm{mult}(S_\pi A \otimes S_\mu B \otimes S_\nu C, S^d(A \otimes B \otimes C)).$$

In particular, $k_{\pi,\mu,\nu}$ is independent of the order of π, μ, ν.

Recall from §8.1.5 that $S_\mu E$ is a trivial $SL(E)$ module if and only if $\mu = (\delta^n)$ for some $\delta \in \mathbb{Z}$. Thus so far, we are reduced to studying the Kronecker coefficients $k_{\pi,\delta^n,\delta^n}$. Now take the $\mathbb{Z}_2$ action given by exchanging E and F into account. Write $[\mu] \otimes [\mu] = S^2[\mu] \oplus \Lambda^2[\mu]$. The first module will be invariant under $\mathbb{Z}_2 = \mathfrak{S}_2$, and the second will transform its sign under the transposition. So define the *symmetric Kronecker coefficients* $sk^\pi_{\mu,\mu} :=$ $\dim(\mathrm{Hom}_{\mathfrak{S}_d}([\pi], S^2[\mu]))$.

We conclude:

Proposition 8.8.2.2 [BLMW11] *Let* $W = \mathbb{C}^{n^2}$. *The coordinate ring of the* $GL(W)$-orbit of $\det_n$ is

$$\mathbb{C}[GL(W) \cdot \det_n] = \bigoplus_{d \subset \mathbb{Z}} \bigoplus_{\pi \mid |\pi|=nd} (S_\pi W^*)^{\oplus sk^\pi_{d^n,d^n}}.$$

While Kronecker coefficients were studied classically (if not the symmetric version), unfortunately very little is known about them. In the next section I describe a geometric method used to study them.

8.9 Plethysm Coefficients, Kronecker Coefficients, and Geometry

A basic, if not *the* basic problem in representation theory is: given a group G, an irreducible G-module U, and a subgroup $H \subset G$, decompose U as an H-module. The determination of Kronecker coefficients can be phrased this way with $G = GL(V \otimes W)$, $U = S_\lambda(V \otimes W)$ and $H = GL(V) \times GL(W)$. The determination of plethysm coefficients may be phrased as the case $G = GL(S^nV)$, $U = S^d(S^nV)$ and $H = GL(V)$.

I briefly discuss a geometric method of L. Manivel and J. Wahl [Wah91, Man97, Man98, Man15b, Man15a] based on the *Bott-Borel-Weil theorem* that allows one to gain asymptotic information about such decomposition problems.

The Bott-Borel-Weil theorem realizes modules as spaces of sections of vector bundles on homogeneous varieties. The method studies sequences of such sections. It has the properties: (i) the vector bundles come with filtrations that allow one to organize information, (ii) the sections of the associated graded bundles can be computed explicitly, giving one bounds for the coefficients, and (iii) Serre's theorem on the vanishing of sheaf cohomology tells one that the bounds are achieved eventually, and gives an upper bound for when stabilization occurs.

I now discuss the decomposition of $S^d(S^nV)$.

8.9.1 Asymptotics of Plethysm Coefficients

We want to decompose $S^d(S^nV)$ as a $GL(V)$-module, or more precisely, to obtain qualitative asymptotic information about this decomposition. Note that $S^{dn}V \subset S^d(S^nV)$ with multiplicity one. Beyond that the decomposition gets complicated. Let $x_1, \ldots, x_\mathbf{v}$ be a basis of V, so $((x_1)^n)^d$ is the highest highest weight vector in $S^d(S^nV)$.

Define the *inner degree lifting map* $\mathfrak{m}_{x_1} = \mathfrak{m}_{x_1}^{d,m,n} : S^d(S^mV) \to S^d(S^nV)$ on basis elements by

$$\left(x_1^{i_1^1} x_2^{i_2^1} \cdots x_d^{i_d^1}\right) \cdots \left(x_1^{i_1^d} \cdots x_d^{i_d^d}\right) \mapsto \left(x_1^{i_1^1+(n-m)} x_2^{i_2^1} \cdots x_d^{i_d^1}\right) \cdots \left(x_1^{i_1^d+(n-m)} \cdots x_d^{i_d^d}\right) \tag{8.9.1}$$

and extend linearly. Here $i_1^j + \cdots + i_d^j = m$ for all j.

A vector of weight $\mu = (q_1, q_2, \ldots, q_d)$ is mapped under $\mathfrak{m}_{x_1}$ to a vector of weight $\pi = (p_1, \ldots, p_d) := \mu + (d(n-m)) = (q_1 + d(n-m), q_2, \ldots, q_d)$ in $S^d(S^nV)$.

Define the *outer degree lifting map* $\mathfrak{o}_{x_1} = \mathfrak{o}_{x_1}^{\delta,d,n} : S^\delta(S^nV) \to S^d(S^nV)$ on basis elements by

$$(x_{i_{1,1}} \cdots x_{i_{1,n}}) \cdots (x_{i_{\delta,1}} \cdots x_{i_{\delta,n}}) \mapsto (x_{i_{1,1}} \cdots x_{i_{1,n}}) \cdots (x_{i_{\delta,1}} \cdots x_{i_{\delta,n}})(x_1^n) \cdots (x_1^n) \tag{8.9.2}$$

and extend linearly. A vector of weight $\mu = (q_1, q_2, \ldots, q_d)$ is mapped under $\mathfrak{o}_{x_1}$ to a vector of weight $\pi = (p_1, \ldots, p_d) := \mu + ((d - \delta)n) = (q_1 + (d - \delta)n, q_2, \ldots, q_d)$ in $S^d(S^n V)$.

Both $\mathfrak{m}_{x_1}$ and $\mathfrak{o}_{x_1}$ take highest weight vectors to highest weight vectors, as Lie algebra raising operators annihilate x_1.

This already shows qualitative behavior if we allow the first part of a partition to grow. More generally, one has:

Theorem 8.9.1.1 [Man97] *Let μ be a fixed partition. Then* mult$(S_{(dn-|\mu|,\mu)}V, S^d(S^n V))$ *is a nondecreasing function of both d and n that is constant as soon as $d \geq |\mu|$ or $n \geq l(\mu)$.*

More precisely, the inner and outer degree lifting maps $\mathfrak{m}_{x_1}$ and $\mathfrak{o}_{x_1}$ are both injective and eventually isomorphisms on highest weight vectors of isotypic components of partitions $(p_1, \ldots, p_v)$ with $(p_2, \ldots, p_v)$ fixed and p_1 growing.

There are several proofs of the stability. The precise stabilization is proved by computing the space of sections of homogeneous vector bundles on $\mathbb{P}V$ via an elementary application of *Bott's theorem* (see, e.g., [Wey03, §4.1] for an exposition of Bott's theorem).

One way to view what we just did was to write $V = x_1 \oplus T$, so

$$S^n(x_1 \oplus T) = \bigoplus_{j=0}^{n} x_1^{n-j} \otimes S^j T. \tag{8.9.3}$$

Then decompose the dth symmetric power of $S^n(x_1 \oplus T)$ and examine the stable behavior as we increase d and n. One could think of the decomposition (8.9.3) as the osculating sequence of the nth Veronese embedding of $\mathbb{P}V$ at $[x_1^n]$ and the further decomposition as the *osculating sequence* (see, e.g., [IL16b, Chapter 4]) of the dth Veronese reembedding of the ambient space refined by (8.9.3).

For Kronecker coefficients and more general decomposition problems the situation is more complicated in that the ambient space is no longer projective space, but a homogeneous variety, and instead of an osculating sequence, one examines *jets* of sections of a vector bundle.

8.9.2 A Partial Converse to Proposition 8.4.2.1

Proposition 8.9.2.1 [KL14] *Let $\pi = (p_1, \ldots, p_w)$ be a partition of dn. If $p_1 \geq \min\{d(n - 1), dn - m\}$, then $I_d(\mathrm{Pad}_{n-m}(S^n W))$ does not contain a copy of $S_\pi W^*$.*

Proof. The image of the space of highest weight vectors for the isotypic component of $S_\mu W^*$ in $S^d(S^m W^*)$ under $\mathfrak{m}_{x_1}^{d,m,n}$ will be in $\mathbb{C}[\mathrm{Pad}_{n-m}(S^n W)]$ because, for example, such a polynomial will not vanish on $(e_1)^{n-m}[(e_1)^{i_1^1} \cdots (e_d)^{i_d^1} + \cdots + (e_1)^{i_1^d} \cdots (e_d)^{i_d^d}]$, but if $p_1 \geq d(n-1)$ we are in the stability range.

For the sufficiency of $p_1 \geq dn - m$, note that if $p_1 \geq (d-1)n + (n-m) = dn - m$, then in an element of weight π, each of the exponents $i_1^1, \ldots, i_1^d$ of x_1 must be at least $n - m$. So there again exists an element of $\mathrm{Pad}_{n-m}(S^n W)$ such that a vector of weight π does not vanish on it.   □

8.10 Orbit Occurrence Obstructions Cannot Separate $\mathcal{P}erm_n^m$ from $\mathcal{D}et_n$

I present an outline of the proof [IP15, BIP16] that the program of [MS01, MS08] cannot work as originally proposed, or even the refinement discussed in [BLMW11]. Despite this negative news, the program has opened several promising directions, and inspired perspectives that have led to concrete advances such as [LR15] as described in §7.4.1.

Throughout this section, set $W = \mathbb{C}^{n^2}$.

8.10.1 Occurrence Obstructions Cannot Separate

The program of [MS01, MS08] proposed to use orbit occurrence obstructions to prove Valiant's conjecture. In [IP15] they show that this cannot work. Furthermore, in [BIP16] they prove that one cannot even use the following relaxation of orbit occurrence obstructions:

Definition 8.10.1.1 An irreducible $GL(W)$-module $S_\lambda W^*$ appearing in $Sym(S^n W^*)$ and not appearing in $\mathbb{C}[\hat{\mathcal{D}et}_n]$ is called an *occurrence obstruction*.

The extension is all the more remarkable because they essentially prove that occurrence obstructions cannot even be used to separate any degree m polynomial padded by ℓ^{n-m} in m^2 variables from

$$MJ(v_{n-k}(\mathbb{P}W), \sigma_r(v_k(\mathbb{P}W))) = \overline{GL(W) \cdot [\ell^{n-k}(x_1^k + \cdots + x_r^k)]} \quad (8.10.1)$$

for certain k, r with $kr \leq n$. Here MJ is the multiplicative join of §7.5.3.

First I show that the variety (8.10.1) is contained in $\mathcal{D}et_n$. I will use the following classical result:

Theorem 8.10.1.2 *[Valiant [Val79], Liu-Regan [LR06]] Every $f \in \mathbb{C}[x_1, \ldots, x_n]$ of formula size u is a projection of $\det_{u+1}$. In other words $f \in \mathrm{End}(\mathbb{C}^{(u+1)^2}) \cdot \det_{u+1}$.*

Note that the formula size of $x_1^k + \cdots + x_r^k$ is at most rk.

Corollary 8.10.1.3 *[BIP16] If $rk < n$ then $[\ell^{n-k}(x_1^k + \cdots + x_r^k)] \in \mathcal{D}et_n$ and thus $\overline{GL(W) \cdot [\ell^{n-k}(x_1^k + \cdots + x_r^k)]} \subset \mathcal{D}et_n$.*

Their main theorem is:

Theorem 8.10.1.4 [BIP16] *Let* $n > m^{25}$. *Let* $\pi = (p_1, \ldots, p_\ell)$ *be a partition of dn such that* $\ell \leq m^2 + 1$ *and* $p_1 \geq d(n - m)$. *If a copy of* $S_\pi W^*$ *occurs in* $S^d(S^n W^*)$ *then a copy also occurs in some* $\mathbb{C}[GL(W) \cdot [\ell^{n-k}(x_1^k + \cdots + x_r^k)]]$ *for some r, k with rk $< n$.*

By the above discussion, this implies occurrence obstructions cannot be used to separate the permanent from the determinant.

The proof is done by splitting the problem into three cases:

1. $d \leq \sqrt{\frac{n}{m}}$,

2. $d > \sqrt{\frac{n}{m}}$ and $p_1 > dn - m^{10}$, and

3. $d > \sqrt{\frac{n}{m}}$ and $p_1 \leq dn - m^{10}$.

The first case is an immediate consequence of the prolongation property §8.3.4: take $r = d$ and $k = m$.

The second reduces to the first by two applications of Manivel's stability theorem:

Proposition 8.10.1.5 [BIP16, Proposition 5.2] *Let* $|\pi| = dn$, $l(\pi) \leq m^2 + 1$, $p_2 \leq k$, $m^2 k^2 \leq n$ *and* $m^2 k \leq d$. *If a copy of* $S_\pi W$ *occurs in* $S^d(S^n W)$, *then a copy also occurs in* $\mathbb{C}[GL(W) \cdot [\ell^{n-k}(x_1^k + \cdots + x_{m^2k}^k)]]$.

Proof. For a partition $\mu = (m_1, \ldots, m_l)$, introduce the notation $\bar{\mu} = (m_2, \ldots, m_l)$ First note that the inner degree lifting map (8.9.1) $\mathrm{m}_\ell^{d,k,n}$: $S^d(S^k W^*) \to S^d(S^n W^*)$ is an isomorphism on highest weight vectors in this range because d is sufficiently large, so there exists μ with $|\mu| = dk$ and $\bar{\pi} = \bar{\mu}$. Moreover, if v_μ is a highest weight vector of weight μ, then $\mathrm{m}_\ell^{d,k,n}(v_\mu)$ is a highest weight vector of weight π. Since $m^2 k$ is sufficiently large, there exists v with $|v| = m^2 k^2 = (m^2 k)k$, with $\bar{v} = \bar{\mu}$ such that $v_\mu = \mathfrak{o}_{x_1}(w_v)$, where w_v is a highest weight vector of weight v in $S^{m^2 k}(S^k W^*)$. Since $I_{m^2 k}(\sigma_{m^2 k}(v_k(\mathbb{P}W))) = 0$, we conclude that a copy of $S_v W^*$ is in $\mathbb{C}[\sigma_{m^2 k}(v_k(\mathbb{P}W))]$ and then by the discussion above the modules corresponding to μ and π are respectively in the coordinate rings of $MJ([\ell^{d-m^2k}], \sigma_{m^2 k}(v_k(\mathbb{P}W)))$ and $MJ([\ell^{n-k}], \sigma_{m^2 k}(v_k(\mathbb{P}W)))$. Since $(m^2 k)k \leq n$, the result follows by prolongation. $\square$

The third case relies on a building block construction made possible by the following exercise:

Exercise 8.10.1.6 (1!) Show that if V is a $GL(W)$-module and $Q \in S_\lambda W \subset S^d V$ and $R \in S_\mu W \subset S^\delta V$ are both highest weight vectors, then $QR \in S_{\lambda+\mu} W \subset S^{d+\delta} V$ is also a highest weight vector.

Exercise 8.10.1.6, combined with the fact that for an irreducible variety X, if $Q, R \in \mathbb{C}[X]$, then $QR \in \mathbb{C}[X]$ enables the building block construction assuming $n > m^{25}$. I will show (Corollary 9.4.1.2) that for n even, there exists a copy of $S_{(n^d)}W$ in $\mathbb{C}[\sigma_d(v_n(\mathbb{P}W))]$, providing one of the building blocks. The difficulty in their proof lies in establishing the other base building block cases. See [BIP16] for the details.

Remark 8.10.1.7 In [IP15] the outline of the proof is similar, except there is an interesting argument by contradiction: they show that in a certain range of n and m, if an orbit occurrence obstruction exists, then the same is true for larger values of n with the same m. But this contradicts Valiant's result (see §6.6.3) that if $n = 4^m$, then $\ell^{n-m} \operatorname{perm}_m \in \mathcal{D}et_n$.

It is conceivably possible to carry out a modification of the program, either taking into account information about multiplicities, or with the degree m iterated matrix multiplication polynomial IMM_n^m in place of the determinant, as the latter can be compared to the permanent without padding.

8.11 Equivariant Determinantal Complexity

The GCT perspective of focusing on symmetry groups led to the discovery of symmetry in Grenet's expression for the permanent, as well as the restricted model of equivariant determinantal complexity. In this section I first give a geometric description of Grenet's expressions in the IMM model, and then outline the proof that the equivariant determinantal complexity of perm_m is $\binom{2m}{m} - 1$.

8.11.1 Geometric Description of Grenet's Expression

I now describe Grenet's size $2^m - 1$ determinantal expression for perm_m from a geometric perspective. The matrix $A_{Grenet}(y)$ in Grenet's expression is in block format, and taking $\det(\tilde{A}_{Grenet}(y))$ amounts to the matrix multiplication of these blocks (see, e.g., the expression (1.2.3) compared with (7.3.1)), and so are more naturally described as a homogeneous iterated matrix multiplication. Recall that for $P \in S^m \mathbb{C}^N$, this is a sequence of matrices $M_1(y), \ldots, M_m(y)$, with M_j of size $m_{j-1} \times m_j$ and $m_0 = m_m = 1$, such that $P(y) = M_1(y) \cdots M_m(y)$. View this more invariantly as

$$U_m = \mathbb{C} \xrightarrow{M_m(y)} U_{m-1} \xrightarrow{M_{m-1}(y)} \cdots \to U_1 = \mathbb{C},$$

where M_j is a linear map $\mathbb{C}^N \to U_j^* \otimes U_{j-1}$. Such a presentation is G-*equivariant*, for some $G \subseteq G_P$, if there exist representations $\rho_j : G \to GL(U_j)$, with dual representations $\rho_j^* : G \to GL(U_j^*)$, such that for all $g \in G$, $(\rho_j^* \otimes \rho_{j+1})(g)M_j(g \cdot y) = M(y)$.

Write $\text{perm}_m \in S^m(E \otimes F)$. In the case of Grenet's presentation, we need each U_j to be a $\Gamma^E = (T^{SL(E)} \rtimes \mathfrak{S}_m)$-module and $M_1(y) \cdots M_m(y)$ to equal the permanent.

Let $(S^k E)_{reg}$ denote the span of the square free monomials, which I will also call the *regular weight space*. It is the span of all vectors of weight $(a_1, \ldots, a_m)$ with $a_j \in \{0, 1\}$ and $\sum_{a_j} = k$. This is an irreducible Γ^E-module. Note that $(S^m E)_{reg}$ is a one-dimensional vector space, and $\text{perm}_m \in (S^m E)_{reg} \otimes (S^m F)_{reg} \subset S^m E \otimes S^m F \subset S^m(E \otimes F)$, which characterizes perm_m up to scale (and the scale can be fixed e.g., by evaluating on the identity matrix).

Note that $E \subset \text{Hom}((S^j E)_{reg}, (S^{j+1} E)_{reg})$ via the composition

$$E \otimes (S^j E)_{reg} \to S^{j+1} E \to (S^{j+1} E)_{reg} \qquad (8.11.1)$$

where the first map is multiplication and the second projection onto the regular weight space. This inclusion is as a Γ^E-module. Fix a basis $f_1, \ldots, f_m$ of F. Consider the spaces $U_j := (S^j E)_{reg} \otimes S^j F$, and the inclusions $E \otimes f_j \subset \text{Hom}((S^j E)_{reg} \otimes S^j F, (S^{j+1} E)_{reg} \otimes S^{j+1} F)$ where the E side is mapped via (8.11.1) and the F side is multiplied by the vector f_j.

Taking the chain of maps from U_0 to U_m, by construction our output polynomial lies in $(S^m E)_{reg} \otimes S^m F$, but the weight on the second term is $(1, \ldots, 1)$ so it must lie in the one-dimensional space $(S^m E)_{reg} \otimes (S^m F)_{reg}$. Finally we check that it is indeed the permanent by evaluating on the identity matrix.

Remark 8.11.1.1 The above construction is a symmetric cousin of a familiar construction in algebra, namely the *Koszul maps*:

$$\Lambda^0 E \xrightarrow{\wedge y_1} \Lambda^1 E \xrightarrow{\wedge y_2} \Lambda^2 E \xrightarrow{\wedge y_3} \cdots \xrightarrow{\wedge y_m} \Lambda^m E.$$

If we tensor this with exterior multiplication by basis vectors of F, we obtain a $SL(E)$-equivariant homogeneous iterated matrix multiplication of $\det_m \in \Lambda^m E \otimes \Lambda^m F$ of size $2^m - 1$.

(Note that both the Koszul maps and (8.11.1) give rise to complexes, i.e., if we multiply by the same vector twice we get zero.)

This IMM realization of the determinant is related to the IMM version of Grenet's realization of the permanent via the *Howe-Young duality functor*: The involution on the space of symmetric functions (see [Mac95, §I.2]) that exchanges elementary symmetric functions with complete symmetric functions, (and, for those familiar with the notation, takes the Schur function s_π to $s_{\pi'}$) extends to modules of the general linear group. This functor exchanges symmetrization and skew-symmetrization. For more explanations, see §10.4.4, where it plays a central role. I expect it will be useful for future work regarding permanent v. determinant. It allows one to transfer knowledge about the well-studied determinant, to the less understood permanent.

One can have a full G_{perm_m}-equivariant expression by considering the inclusions

$$E \otimes F \subset \text{Hom}((S^j E)_{reg} \otimes (S^j F)_{reg}, (S^{j+1} E)_{reg} \otimes (S^{j+1} F)_{reg}). \qquad (8.11.2)$$

(The transpose invariance is possible because transposing the matrices in the sequence M_{m-j} is sent to M_j^T and $(M_{m-j}(y^T))^T = M_j(y)$.)

Exercise 8.11.1.2 (1) Show that (8.11.2) gives rise to a size $\binom{2m}{m}$ IMM expression for perm_m. ⊙

Remark 8.11.1.3 One similarly obtains a size $\binom{2m}{m}$ $G_{\det_m}$-equivariant IMM presentation of $\det_m$.

8.11.2 Outline of Proofs of Lower Bounds

Recall the lower bound theorems:

Theorem 8.11.2.1 [LR15] *Assume $m \geq 3$.*

- $\text{edc}(\text{perm}_m) = \binom{2m}{m} - 1$ *with equality given by the determinantal expression obtained from* (8.11.2).
- *The smallest size of a Γ^E-equivariant determinantal expression for perm_m is $2^m - 1$ and is given by $\tilde{A}_{Grenet}$.*

Ideas toward the proofs are as follows: Write $\mathbb{C}^{n^2} = B \otimes C$. Without loss of generality, one takes the constant part Λ of $\tilde{A}$ to be the diagonal matrix with zero in the $(1, 1)$-slot and 1's on the remaining diagonal entries. Then Λ determines a splitting $B \otimes C = (B_1 \oplus B_2) \otimes (C_1 \oplus C_2)$ with $\dim B_1 = \dim C_1 = 1$. Consider the linear part of an expression $A : E \otimes F \to B \otimes C$. We have already seen (in the proof of Theorem 6.3.4.6) the component in $B_1 \otimes C_1$ (i.e., the $(1, 1)$ slot in the matrix $A(y)$) must be zero. Thus in order for the expression not to be identically zero, we must have the components of $A(y)$ in $B_1 \otimes C_2$ and $B_2 \otimes C_1$ nonzero (i.e., other entries in the first row and column must be nonzero). Focus on the Γ^E-equivariant case for simplicity of exposition. As a Γ^E-module, $E \otimes F = E^{\oplus m}$. By Γ^E-equivariance, $B_1 \otimes C_2$ must contain at least one copy of E, write the submodule as $B_1 \otimes C_{2,1} \simeq E^{\oplus j}$. For simplicity of discussion, assume $j = 1$. Also for simplicity, assume the one-dimensional space B_1 is a trivial Γ^E-module, so $C_{2,1} \simeq E$ as a Γ^E-module. Since Γ^E is reductive, we have a splitting $C_2 = C_{2,1} \oplus C_2'$. In order that there is no degree two component appearing, we must have the map to $C_{2,1}^* \otimes B_1^*$ be zero. The picture of what we have reduced to so far looks like this:

$$\begin{pmatrix} 0 & C_{2,1}^* \otimes B_1^* & * \\ B_1 \otimes C_{2,1} & \text{Id} & * \\ * & ? & * \end{pmatrix}.$$

Now in order that the determinant is not identically zero, the ? block cannot be identically zero, so there must be some $B_{2,1} \subset B_2$, such that $C_{2,1}^* \otimes B_2 \simeq E^* \otimes B_{2,1}$ contains a copy of E.

Fact: the minimum dimension of a Γ^E-module M such that $E \subset E^* \otimes M$ is $\binom{m}{2}$ and the corresponding module is (up to tensoring with a one-dimensional representation) $(S^2 E)_{reg}$.

Remark 8.11.2.2 Were we constructing a $SL(E)$-equivariant regular determinantal presentation of the determinant, we would need an $SL(E)$-module M such that $E \subset E^* \otimes M$. By the Pieri rule, the admissible M correspond to Young diagrams with two boxes, i.e., $S^2 E$ and $\Lambda^2 E$. Note that $\dim(\Lambda^2 E) = \binom{m}{2}$. This "coincidence" of dimensions is attributable to the Howe-Young duality endofunctor.

Continuing, we need some $B_{2,2}$ such that $E \subset (S^2 E)_{reg}^* \otimes B_{2,2}$, and the smallest such is $B_{2,2} = (S^3 E)_{reg}$ (just as in the skew case, one needs a Young diagram with three boxes, the smallest such module is $\Lambda^3 E$).

One continues until arriving at $B = \bigoplus_{j=0}^{m-1} (S^j E)_{reg}$ and one concludes.

Remark 8.11.2.3 In the above discussion I swept two important complications under the rug. First, we don't really have $\Gamma^E \subset G_{\det_n, \Lambda}$, but rather a group $G \subset G_{\det_n, \Lambda}$ that has a surjective map onto Γ^E. This problem is dealt with by observing that the modules for any such G can be labeled using the labels from Γ^E-modules. Second, since Γ^E is not connected, we need to allow the possibility that the $\mathbb{Z}_2 \subset G_{\det_n, \Lambda}$ is part of the equivariance. This second problem is dealt with by restricting to the alternating group. For details, see [LR15].

8.12 Symmetries of Additional Polynomials Relevant for Complexity Theory

A central insight from GCT is that polynomials that are determined by their symmetry groups should be considered preferred representatives of their complexity classes. This idea has already guided several results: (i) the symmetries of the matrix multiplication tensor have given deep insight into its decompositions, (ii) these symmetries were critical for proving its border rank lower bounds, and (iii) the above results on equivariant determinantal complexity. We have already determined the symmetry groups of the determinant, permanent, and $x_1 \cdots x_n$. In this section I present the symmetry groups of additional polynomials relevant for complexity theory and techniques for determining them.

Throughout this section $G = GL(V)$, $\dim V = n$, and I use index ranges $1 \leq i, j, k \leq n$.

8.12.1 The Fermat

This example follows [CKW10]. Let $\mathrm{fermat}_n^d := x_1^d + \cdots + x_n^d \in S^d \mathbb{C}^n$. The GL_n-orbit closure of $[\mathrm{fermat}_n^d]$ is the nth secant variety of the Veronese variety $\sigma_n(v_d(\mathbb{P}^{n-1})) \subset \mathbb{P}S^d \mathbb{C}^n$. It is clear $\mathfrak{S}_n \subset G_{\mathrm{fermat}}$, as well as the diagonal matrices whose entries are dth roots of unity. We need to see if there is anything else. The first idea, to look at the singular locus, does not work, as the zero set is smooth, so consider $(\mathrm{fermat}_n^d)_{2,d-2} = x_1^2 \otimes x^{d-2} + \cdots + x_n^2 \otimes x^{d-2}$. Write the further polarization $(\mathrm{fermat}_n^d)_{1,1,d-2}$ as a symmetric matrix whose entries are homogeneous polynomials of degree $d-2$ (the Hessian matrix):

$$\begin{pmatrix} x_1^{d-2} & & \\ & \ddots & \\ & & x_n^{d-2} \end{pmatrix}.$$

Were the determinant of this matrix $GL(V)$-invariant, we could proceed as we did with $e_{n,n}$, using unique factorization. Although it is not, it is close enough as follows:

Recall that for a linear map $f : W \to V$, where $\dim W = \dim V = n$, we have $f^{\wedge n} \in \Lambda^n W^* \otimes \Lambda^n V$ and an element $(h, g) \in GL(W) \times GL(V)$ acts on $f^{\wedge n}$ by $(h, g) \cdot f^{\wedge n} = (\det(h))^{-1}(\det(g))f^{\wedge n}$. In our case $W = V^*$ so $P_{2,d-2}^{\wedge n}(x) = \det(g)^2 P_{2,d-2}^{\wedge n}(g \cdot x)$, and the polynomial obtained by the determinant of the Hessian matrix is invariant up to scale.

Arguing as in §7.1.2, $\sum_{i,j} (g_1^{j_1} x_{j_1})^{d-2} \cdots (g_n^{j_n} x_{j_n})^{d-2} = x_1^{d-2} \cdots x_n^{d-2}$ and we conclude again by unique factorization that g is in $\mathfrak{S}_n \ltimes T_n$. Composing with a permutation matrix to make $g \in T$, we see that, by acting on the Fermat itself, that the entries on the diagonal are dth roots of unity.

In summary:

Proposition 8.12.1.1 $G_{x_1^d + \cdots + x_n^d} = \mathfrak{S}_n \ltimes (\mathbb{Z}_d)^{\times n}$.

Exercise 8.12.1.2 (2) Show that the Fermat is characterized by its symmetries.

8.12.2 The Sum-Product Polynomial

The polynomial

$$SP_r^n := \sum_{i=1}^{r} \Pi_{j=1}^n x_{ij} \in S^n(\mathbb{C}^{nr}),$$

called the *sum-product polynomial* in the CS literature, was used in our study of depth three circuits. Its $GL(rn)$-orbit closure is the rth secant variety of the Chow variety $\sigma_r(Ch_n(\mathbb{C}^{nr}))$.

Exercise 8.12.2.1 (2) Determine $G_{SP_r^n}$ and show that SP_r^n is characterized by its symmetries.

8.12.3 Further Techniques

One technique for determining G_P is to form auxiliary objects from P which have a symmetry group H that one can compute, and by construction H contains G_P. Usually it is easy to find a group H' that clearly is contained in G_P, so if $H = H'$, we are done.

Recall that we have already used auxiliary varieties such as $\text{Zeros}(P)_{Jac,k}$ and $\text{Zeros}(P)^\vee$ in determining the symmetry groups of perm_n and det_n.

One can determine the connected component of the stabilizer by a Lie algebra calculation: If we are concerned with $p \in S^d V$, the connected component of the identity of the stabilizer of p in $GL(V)$ is the connected Lie group associated to the Lie subalgebra of $\mathfrak{gl}(V)$ that annihilates p. (The analogous statement holds for tensors.) To see this, let $\mathfrak{h} \subset \mathfrak{gl}(V)$ denote the annihilator of p and let $H = exp(\mathfrak{h}) \subset GL(V)$ the corresponding Lie group. Then it is clear that H is contained in the stabilizer as $h \cdot p = exp(X) \cdot p = (\text{Id} + X + \frac{1}{2}XX + \cdots)p$ the first term preserves p and the remaining terms annihilate it. Similarly, if H is the group preserving p, taking the derivative of any curve in H through Id at $t = 0$ gives $\frac{d}{dt}|_{t=0}h(t) \cdot p = 0$.

To recover the full stabilizer from knowledge of the connected component of the identity, we have the following observation, the first part comes from [BGL14]:

Proposition 8.12.3.1 *Let V be an irreducible $GL(W)$-module. Let G_v^0 be the identity component of the stabilizer G_v of some $v \in V$ in $GL(W)$. Then G_v is contained in the normalizer $N(G_v^0)$ of G_v^0 in $GL(W)$. If G_v^0 is semi-simple and $[v]$ is determined by G_v^0, then up to scalar multiples of the identity in $GL(W)$, G_v and $N(G_v^0)$ coincide.*

Proof. First note that for any group H, the full group H normalizes H^0. (If $h \in H^0$, take a curve h_t with $h_0 = \text{Id}$ and $h_1 = h$, then take any $g \in H$, the curve gh_tg^{-1} connects gh_1g^{-1} to the identity.) So G_v is contained in the normalizer of G_v^0 in $GL(W)$.

For the second assertion, let $h \in N(G_v^0)$ be in the normalizer. We have $h^{-1}ghv = g'v = v$ for some $g' \in G_v^0$, and thus $g(hv) = (hv)$. But since $[v]$ is the unique line preserved by G_v^0 we conclude $hv = \lambda v$ for some $\lambda \in \mathbb{C}^*$. $\qquad\square$

Here is a lemma for those familiar with roots and weights:

Lemma 8.12.3.2 [BGL14, Proposition 2.2] *Let G^0 be semi-simple and act irreducibly on V. Then its normalizer $N(G^0)$ is generated by G^0, the scalar matrices, and a finite group constructed as follows: Assume we have chosen a Borel for G^0, and thus have distinguished a set of simple roots Δ and a group homomorphism $Aut(\Delta) \to GL(V)$. Assume $V = V_\lambda$ is the irreducible representation with highest weight λ of G^0 and consider the subgroup $Aut(\Delta, \lambda) \subset Aut(\Delta)$ that fixes λ. Then $N(G^0) = ((\mathbb{C}^* \times G^0)/Z) \rtimes Aut(\Delta, \lambda)$.*

For the proof, see [BGL14].

8.12.4 Iterated Matrix Multiplication

Let $IMM_n^k \in S^n(\mathbb{C}^{k^2 n})$ denote the iterated matrix multiplication operator for $k \times k$ matrices, $(X_1, \dots, X_n) \mapsto \mathrm{trace}(X_1 \cdots X_n)$. Letting $V_j = \mathbb{C}^k$, invariantly

$$IMM_n^k = \mathrm{Id}_{V_1} \otimes \cdots \otimes \mathrm{Id}_{V_n} \in (V_1 \otimes V_2^*) \otimes (V_2 \otimes V_3^*) \otimes \cdots \otimes (V_{n-1} \otimes V_n^*) \otimes (V_n \otimes V_1^*)$$
$$\subset S^n((V_1 \otimes V_2^*) \oplus (V_2 \otimes V_3^*) \oplus \cdots \oplus (V_{n-1} \otimes V_n^*) \oplus (V_n \otimes V_1^*)),$$

and the connected component of the identity of $G_{IMM_n^k} \subset GL(\mathbb{C}^{k^2 n})$ is $GL(V_1) \times \cdots \times GL(V_n)$.

The case of IMM_n^3 is important as this sequence is complete for the complexity class $\mathbf{VP}_e$, of sequences of polynomials admitting polynomial size formulas, see [BOC92]. Moreover IMM_n^n is complete for the same complexity class as the determinant, namely $\mathbf{VQP} = \mathbf{VP}_s$, see [Blä01b].

The first equality in the following theorem for the case $k = 3$ appeared in [dG78, Thms. 3.3,3.4] and [Bur15, Proposition 4.7] with ad hoc proofs.

Theorem 8.12.4.1 [Ges16] $G_{IMM_n^k} = (GL_k^{\times n}/\mathbb{C}^*) \rtimes D_n$, where $D_n = \mathbb{Z}_n \rtimes \mathbb{Z}_2$ is the dihedral group. The $\mathbb{Z}_n$ corresponds to cyclic permutation of factors, and the $\mathbb{Z}_2$ is generated by $(X_1, \dots, X_k) \mapsto (X_k^T, \dots, X_1^T)$.

A "hands on" elementary proof is possible, see, e.g. [Bur15, Proposition 4.7]. Here is an elegant proof for those familiar with Dynkin diagrams from [Ges16] in the special case of $M_{\langle \mathbf{n} \rangle}$, i.e., $k = \mathbf{n}$ and $n = 3$.

Proof. It will be sufficient to show the second equality because the $(\mathbb{C}^*)^{\times 2}$ acts trivially on $A \otimes B \otimes C$. For polynomials, the method of [BGL14, Proposition 2.2] adapts to reducible representations. A straightforward Lie algebra calculation shows the connected component of the identity of $\tilde{G}_{M_{\langle \mathbf{n} \rangle}}$ is $\tilde{G}_{M_{\langle \mathbf{n} \rangle}}^0 = (\mathbb{C}^*)^{\times 2} \times PGL_n^{\times 3}$. As was observed in [BGL14], the full stabilizer group must be contained in its normalizer $N(\tilde{G}_{M_{\langle \mathbf{n} \rangle}}^0)$, see Proposition 8.12.3.1. But the normalizer of $\tilde{G}^0_{M_{(n)}}$ quotiented by $\tilde{G}^0_{M_{(n)}}$ is the automorphism group of the marked Dynkin diagram for $A \oplus B \oplus C$, which is

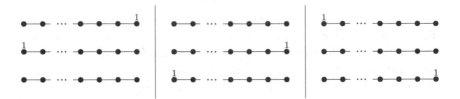

There are three triples of marked diagrams. Call each column consisting of 3 marked diagrams a group. The automorphism group of the picture is $\mathbb{Z}_3 \rtimes \mathbb{Z}_2$, where the $\mathbb{Z}_2$ may be seen as flipping each diagram, exchanging the first and third diagram in each group, and exchanging the first and second group. The $\mathbb{Z}_3$ may be seen as cyclically permuting each group and the diagrams within each group. $\qquad \square$

Problem 8.12.4.2 Find equations in the ideal of $\overline{GL_{9n} \cdot IMM_n^3}$. Determine lower bounds for the inclusions $\mathcal{P}erm_m \subset \overline{GL_{9n} \cdot IMM_n^3}$ and study common geometric properties (and differences) of $\mathcal{D}et_n$ and $\overline{GL_{9n} \cdot IMM_n^3}$.

8.12.5 The Pascal Determinant

Let k be even, and let $A_j = \mathbb{C}^n$. Define the k-factor *Pascal determinant* $PD_{k,n}$ to be the unique up to scale element of $\Lambda^n A_1 \otimes \cdots \otimes \Lambda^n A_k \subset S^n(A_1 \otimes \cdots \otimes A_k)$. Choose the scale such that if $X = \sum x_{i_1,\dots,i_k} a_{1,i_1} \otimes \cdots \otimes a_{k,i_k}$ with $a_{\alpha,j}$ a basis of A_α, then

$$PD_{k,n}(X) = \sum_{\sigma_2,\dots,\sigma_k \in \mathfrak{S}_n} \mathrm{sgn}(\sigma_2 \cdots \sigma_k) x_{1,\sigma_2(1),\dots,\sigma_k(1)} \cdots x_{n,\sigma_2(n),\dots,\sigma_k(n)} \qquad (8.12.1)$$

This expression, for fixed k, shows that $(PD_{k,n}) \in \mathbf{VNP}$.

Proposition 8.12.5.1 (Gurvits) *The sequence* $(PD_{4,n})$ *is* **VNP** *complete.*

Proof. It remains to show **VNP**-hardness. Set $x_{ijkl} = 0$ unless $i = j$ and $k = l$. Then $x_{i,\sigma_2(i),\sigma_3(i),\sigma_4(i)} = 0$ unless $\sigma_2(i) = i$ and $\sigma_3(i) = \sigma_4(i)$ so the only nonzero monomials are those where $\sigma_2 = \mathrm{Id}$ and $\sigma_3 = \sigma_4$. Since the sign of σ_3 is squared, the result is the permanent. $\qquad \square$

Thus we could just as well work with the sequence $PD_{4,n}$ as the permanent. Since $\det_n = PD_{2,n}$, and the symmetry groups superficially resemble each other, it is an initially appealing substitute.

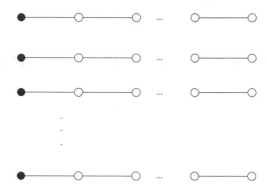

Figure 8.12.1 Marked Dynkin diagram for V.

It is clear the identity component of the stabilizer includes $(SL(A_1) \times \cdots \times SL(A_k))/\mu_{n,k}$ where μ_n is as in §6.6.1, and a straightforward Lie algebra calculation confirms this is the entire identity component. (Alternatively, one can use Dynkin's classification [Dyn52] of maximal subalgebras.) It is also clear that $\mathfrak{S}_k$ preserves $PD_{n,k}$ by permuting the factors.

Theorem 8.12.5.2 (Garibaldi, personal communication) *For all k even*

$$G_{PD_{k,n}} = SL_n^{\times k}/\mu_{n,k} \rtimes \mathfrak{S}_k$$

Note that this includes the case of the determinant, and gives a new proof. The result will follow from the following Lemma and Proposition 8.12.3.1.

Lemma 8.12.5.3 *[Garibaldi, personal communication] Let $V = A_1 \otimes \cdots \otimes A_k$. The normalizer of $SL_n^{\times k}/\mu_n$ in $GL(V)$ is $(GL_n^{\times k}/\mu_k) \rtimes \mathfrak{S}_k$, where μ_k denotes the kernel of the product map $(\mathbb{C}^*)^{\times k} \to \mathbb{C}^*$.*

Proof of Lemma 8.12.5.3. We use Lemma 8.12.3.2. In our case, the Dynkin diagram for (Δ, λ) is and $Aut(\Delta, \lambda)$ is clearly $\mathfrak{S}_k$, as in Figure 8.12.1. $\square$

The theorem follows.

9

The Chow Variety of Products of Linear Forms

In the GCT approach to Valiant's conjecture, one wants to understand the GL_{n^2}-module structure of $\mathbb{C}[\overline{GL_{n^2} \cdot [\det_n]}]$ via $\mathbb{C}[GL_{n^2} \cdot [\det_n]]$. In this chapter I discuss a "toy" problem that turns out to be deep, subtle and have surprising connections with several different areas of mathematics: the orbit closure $\overline{GL_n \cdot [x_1 \cdots x_n]} = Ch_n(\mathbb{C}^n) \subset \mathbb{P}S^n\mathbb{C}^n$. This subject has a remarkable history beginning over 100 years ago, with work of Brill, Gordan, Hermite and Hadamard. The history is rife with rediscoveries and errors that only make the subject more intriguing.

I begin, in §9.1 describing the Hermite-Hadamard-Howe map h_n that has been discovered and rediscovered numerous times. Its kernel is the ideal of the Chow variety. I also state the main results regarding this map: the Black-List propagation theorem and Brion's asymptotic surjectivity theorem. In §9.2 I rederive the map from a GCT perspective that compares the coordinate ring of the orbit to that of its closure. In §9.3 I define a map of modules for the permutation group $\mathfrak{S}_{dn}$ that contains equivalent information to the original map. This map was originally defined in a different manner by Black and List as a path to prove a celebrated conjecture of Foulkes that I also explain in the section. Via a variant of this $\mathfrak{S}_{dn}$-map, I give the proof of the Black-List propagation theorem from [Ike15], which is a geometric reinterpretation of the proof in [McK08]. In §9.4 I illustrate the subtlety of determining the rank of h_n by explaining how a very special case of the problem is equivalent to a famous conjecture in combinatorics due to Alon and Tarsi. In §9.5, I give yet another derivation of the map h_n via algebraic geometry due to Brion. If one is content with set-theoretic equations for the Chow variety, such equations were discovered over a hundred years ago by Brill and Gordan. I give a modern presentation of these equations in §9.6. I conclude in §9.7 with the proof of Brion's asymptotic surjectivity theorem. This last proof requires more advanced results in algebraic geometry

264

and commutative algebra, and should be skipped by readers unfamiliar with the relevant notions.

9.1 The Hermite-Hadamard-Howe Map

I begin with the first description of the ideal of $Ch_n(V^*)$, due to Hadamard (1897).

9.1.1 The Hermite-Hadamard-Howe Map and the Ideal of the Chow Variety

The following linear map was first defined when dim $V = 2$ by Hermite (1854), and in general independently by Hadamard (1897), and Howe (1988).

Definition 9.1.1.1 The *Hermite-Hadamard-Howe map* $h_{d,n} : S^d(S^nV) \to S^n(S^dV)$ is defined as follows: First include $S^d(S^nV) \subset V^{\otimes nd}$. Next, reorder the copies of V from d blocks of n to n blocks of d and symmetrize the blocks of d to obtain an element of $(S^dV)^{\otimes n}$. Finally, thinking of S^dV as a single vector space, symmetrize the n blocks.

For example, putting subscripts on V to indicate position:

$$S^2(S^3V) \subset V^{\otimes 6} = V_1 \otimes V_2 \otimes V_3 \otimes V_4 \otimes V_5 \otimes V_6$$
$$\to (V_1 \otimes V_4) \otimes (V_2 \otimes V_5) \otimes (V_3 \otimes V_6)$$
$$\to S^2V \otimes S^2V \otimes S^2V$$
$$\to S^3(S^2V)$$

Note that $h_{d,n}$ is a $GL(V)$-module map.

Example 9.1.1.2 For $(xy)^2 = (xy)(xy) \in S^2(S^2\mathbb{C}^2)$, here is $h_{2,2}((xy)^2)$:

$$(xy)^2 = \frac{1}{4}[(x \otimes y + y \otimes x) \otimes (x \otimes y + y \otimes x)]$$
$$= \frac{1}{4}[x \otimes y \otimes x \otimes y + x \otimes y \otimes y \otimes x + y \otimes x \otimes x \otimes y + y \otimes x \otimes y \otimes x]$$
$$\mapsto \frac{1}{4}[x \otimes x \otimes y \otimes y + x \otimes y \otimes y \otimes x + y \otimes x \otimes x \otimes y + y \otimes y \otimes x \otimes x]$$
$$\mapsto \frac{1}{4}[2(x^2) \otimes (y^2) + 2(xy) \otimes (xy)]$$
$$\mapsto \frac{1}{2}[(x^2)(y^2) + (xy)(xy)].$$

Exercise 9.1.1.3 (1!) Show that $h_{d,n}((x_1)^n \cdots (x_d)^n) = (x_1 \cdots x_d)^n$.

Theorem 9.1.1.4 (Hadamard [Had97]) $\ker h_{d,n} = I_d(Ch_n(V^*))$.

Proof. Given $P \in S^d(S^n V)$, we determine if P vanishes on $Ch_n(V^*)$. Since $Seg(v_n(\mathbb{P}V) \times \cdots \times v_n(\mathbb{P}V))$ spans $(S^n V)^{\otimes d}$, its projection to $S^d(S^n V)$ also spans, so we may write $P = \sum_j (x_{1j})^n \cdots (x_{dj})^n$ for some $x_{\alpha,j} \in V$. Let $\ell^1, \ldots, \ell^n \in V^*$. Recall $\overline{P}$ is P considered as a linear form on $(S^n V^*)^{\otimes d}$. In what follows I use $\langle -, - \rangle$ to denote the pairing between a vector space and its dual.

$$
\begin{aligned}
P(\ell^1 \cdots \ell^n) &= \langle \overline{P}, (\ell^1 \cdots \ell^n)^d \rangle \\
&= \sum_j \langle (x_{1j})^n \cdots (x_{dj})^n, (\ell^1 \cdots \ell^n)^d \rangle \\
&= \sum_j \langle (x_{1j})^n, (\ell^1 \cdots \ell^n) \rangle \cdots \langle (x_{dj})^n, (\ell^1 \cdots \ell^n) \rangle \\
&= \sum_j \Pi_{s=1}^n \Pi_{i=1}^d x_{ij}(\ell_s) \\
&= \sum_j \langle x_{1j} \cdots x_{dj}, (\ell^1)^d \rangle \cdots \langle x_{1j} \cdots x_{dj}, (\ell^n)^d \rangle \\
&= \langle \overline{h_{d,n}(P)}, (\ell^1)^d \cdots (\ell^n)^d \rangle.
\end{aligned}
$$

If $h_{d,n}(P)$ is nonzero, there will be some monomial of the form $(\ell^1)^d \cdots (\ell^n)^d$ it will pair with to be nonzero (using the spanning property in $S^n(S^d V^*)$). On the other hand, if $h_{d,n}(P) = 0$, then $\overline{P}$ annihilates all points of $Ch_n(V^*)$. $\square$

9.1.2 Information on the Rank of $h_{d,n}$

Exercise 9.1.2.1 (2) Show that $h_{d,n} : S^d(S^n V) \to S^n(S^d V)$ is "self-dual" in the sense that $h_{d,n}^T = h_{n,d} : S^n(S^d V^*) \to S^d(S^n V^*)$. Conclude that $h_{d,n}$ surjective if and only if $h_{n,d}$ is injective.

Exercise 9.1.2.2 (1) Show that if $h_{d,n} : S^d(S^n \mathbb{C}^m) \to S^n(S^d \mathbb{C}^m)$ is not surjective, then $h_{d,n} : S^d(S^n \mathbb{C}^k) \to S^n(S^d \mathbb{C}^k)$ is not surjective for all $k > m$, and that the partitions corresponding to highest weights of the modules in the kernel are the same in both cases if $d \leq m$. ⊚

Exercise 9.1.2.3 (1) Show that if $h_{d,n} : S^d(S^n \mathbb{C}^m) \to S^n(S^d \mathbb{C}^m)$ is surjective, then $h_{d,n} : S^d(S^n \mathbb{C}^k) \to S^n(S^d \mathbb{C}^k)$ is surjective for all $k < m$.

Example 9.1.2.4 (The case $\dim V = 2$) When $\dim V = 2$, every polynomial decomposes as a product of linear factors, so the ideal of $Ch_n(\mathbb{C}^2)$ is zero. We recover the following theorem of Hermite:

Theorem 9.1.2.5 (Hermite reciprocity) *The map $h_{d,n} : S^d(S^n \mathbb{C}^2) \to S^n(S^d \mathbb{C}^2)$ is an isomorphism for all d, n. In particular $S^d(S^n \mathbb{C}^2)$ and $S^n(S^d \mathbb{C}^2)$ are isomorphic GL_2-modules.*

Often in modern textbooks (e.g., [FH91]) only the "In particular" is stated.

Originally Hadamard thought the maps $h_{d,n}$ were always of maximal rank, but later he realized he did not have a proof. In [Had99] he did prove:

Theorem 9.1.2.6 (Hadamard [Had99]) *The map* $h_{3,3} : S^3(S^3V) \to S^3(S^3V)$ *is an isomorphism.*

Proof. By Exercise 9.1.2.2, we may assume $\mathbf{v} = 3$ and $x_1, x_2, x_3 \in V^*$ are a basis. Say we had $P \in \ker(h_{3,3}) = I_3(Ch_3(V^*))$. Consider P restricted to the line in $\mathbb{P}(S^3V^*)$ spanned by $x_1^3 + x_2^3 + x_3^3$ and $x_1x_2x_3$. Write $P(\mu, \nu) := P(\mu(x_1^3 + x_2^3 + x_3^3) - \lambda x_1 x_2 x_3)$ as a cubic polynomial on $\mathbb{P}^1$ with coordinates $[\mu, \lambda]$. Note that $P(\mu, \nu)$ vanishes at the four points $[0, 1], [1, 3], [1, 3\omega], [1, 3\omega^2]$ where ω is a primitive third root of unity. A cubic polynomial on $\mathbb{P}^1$ vanishing at four points is identically zero, so the whole line is contained in $\text{Zeros}(P)$. In particular, $P(1, 0) = 0$, i.e., P vanishes on $x_1^3 + x_2^3 + x_3^3$. Since $\sigma_3(v_3(\mathbb{P}^2))$ is a GL_3-variety, P must vanish identically on $\sigma_3(v_3(\mathbb{P}^2))$. But $I_3(\sigma_3(v_3(\mathbb{P}^2))) = 0$, see, e.g., Corollary 8.3.4.3. (In fact $\sigma_3(v_3(\mathbb{P}^2)) \subset \mathbb{P}S^3\mathbb{C}^3$ is a hypersurface of degree four.) $\qquad\square$

In the same paper, he posed the question:

Question 9.1.2.7 Is $h_{d,n}$ always of maximal rank?

Howe [How87] also investigated the map $h_{d,n}$ and wrote "it is reasonable to expect" that $h_{d,n}$ is always of maximal rank.

Remark 9.1.2.8 The above proof is due to A. Abdesselam (personal communication). It is a variant of Hadamard's original proof, where instead of $x_1^3 + x_2^3 + x_3^3$ one uses an arbitrary cubic f, and generalizing $x_1x_2x_3$ one uses the determinant of the Hessian $\det_3(H(f))$. Then the curves $f = 0$ and $\det_3(H(f)) = 0$ intersect in 9 points (the nine flexes of $f = 0$) and there are four groups of three lines going through these points, i.e., four places where the polynomial becomes a product of linear forms.

Theorem 9.1.2.9 [BL89] *[also see* [McK08, Theorem 8.1] *and* [Ike15]*] If* $h_{d,n}$ *is surjective, then* $h_{d',n}$ *is surjective for all* $d' > d$. *Equivalently, if* $h_{d,n}$ *is injective, then* $h_{d,n'}$ *is injective for all* $n' > n$.

The proof is outlined in §9.3. The following two theorems were shown by a computer calculation:

Theorem 9.1.2.10 [MN05] *The map* $h_{4,4}$ *is an isomorphism.*

The results above imply $h_{d,n}$ is of maximal rank for all $n \leq 4$ and all d.

Theorem 9.1.2.11 [MN05] *The map $h_{5,5}$ is not surjective.*

Remark 9.1.2.12 In [MN05] they showed the map $h_{5,5:0}$ defined in §9.3 below is not injective. A. Abdessalem realized their computation showed the map $h_{5,5}$ is not injective and pointed this out to them. Evidently there was some miscommunication because in [MN05] they mistakenly say the result comes from [Bri02] rather than their own paper.

The $GL(V)$-module structure of the kernel of $h_{5,5}$ was determined by M-W Cheung, C. Ikenmeyer and S. Mkrtchyan as part of a 2012 AMS MRC program:

Proposition 9.1.2.13 [CIM17] *The kernel of* $h_{5,5} : S^5(S^5\mathbb{C}^5) \to S^5(S^5\mathbb{C}^5)$ *consists of irreducible modules corresponding to the following partitions:*

$$\{(14, 7, 2, 2), (13, 7, 2, 2, 1), (12, 7, 3, 2, 1), (12, 6, 3, 2, 2),$$
$$(12, 5, 4, 3, 1), (11, 5, 4, 4, 1), (10, 8, 4, 2, 1), (9, 7, 6, 3)\}.$$

All these occur with multiplicity one in the kernel, but not all occur with multiplicity one in $S^5(S^5\mathbb{C}^5)$. *In particular, the kernel is not a sum of isotypic components.*

It would be interesting to understand if there is a pattern to these partitions. Their Young diagrams are:

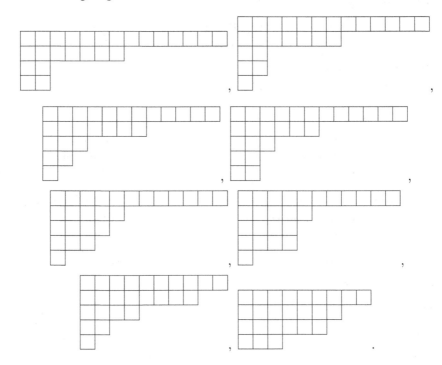

While the Hermite-Hadamard-Howe map is not always of maximal rank, it is "eventually" of maximal rank:

Theorem 9.1.2.14 [Bri93, Bri97] *The Hermite-Hadamard-Howe map*

$$h_{d,n} : S^d(S^n V^*) \to S^n(S^d V^*)$$

is surjective for d sufficiently large, in fact for $d \gtrsim n^2 \binom{n+d}{d}$.

I present the proof of Theorem 9.1.2.14 in §9.5.2.

Problem 9.1.2.15 (The Hadamard-Howe Problem) Determine the function $d(n)$ such that $h_{d,n}$ is surjective for all $d \geq d(n)$.

A more ambitious problem would be:

Problem 9.1.2.16 Determine the kernel of $h_{d,n}$.

A less ambitious problem is:

Problem 9.1.2.17 Improve Brion's bound to, say, a polynomial bound in n.

Another apparently less ambitious problem is the following conjecture:

Conjecture 9.1.2.18 (Kumar [Kum15]) *Let n be even, then $S_{(n^n)}\mathbb{C}^n \not\subset \ker h_{n,n}$, i.e., $S_{(n^n)}\mathbb{C}^n \subset \mathbb{C}[Ch_n(\mathbb{C}^n)]$.*

Kumar conjectures further that for all $d \leq n$, $S_{(n^d)}\mathbb{C}^n \not\subset \ker h_{d,n}$, i.e., $S_{(n^d)}\mathbb{C}^n \subset \mathbb{C}[Ch_n(\mathbb{C}^n)]$, but Conjecture 9.1.2.18 is the critical case. By Corollary 9.2.2.2 below, when n is even, the module $S_{(n^d)}\mathbb{C}^n$ occurs in $S^d(S^n\mathbb{C}^n)$ with multiplicity one.

I discuss Conjecture 9.1.2.18 in §9.4. It turns out to be equivalent to a famous conjecture in combinatorics.

9.2 The GCT Perspective

In this section, in the spirit of GCT, I compare $\mathbb{C}[Ch_n(V^*)] = \mathbb{C}[\overline{GL(V) \cdot (x_1 \cdots x_n)}]$ with $\mathbb{C}[GL(V) \cdot (x_1 \cdots x_n)]$. Throughout this section, assume $\dim V = n$.

9.2.1 Application of the Algebraic Peter-Weyl Theorem

Let $x_1, \ldots, x_n \in V^*$ be a basis. Recall from §7.1.2 that the symmetry group of $x_1 \cdots x_n$ is $\Gamma_n := T^{SL_n} \rtimes \mathfrak{S}_n$. Also recall that for any orbit, G/H, the algebraic Peter-Weyl theorem (see §8.6) implies $\mathbb{C}[G/H] = \bigoplus_{\lambda \in \Lambda_G^+} V_\lambda \otimes (V_\lambda^*)^H$, so

$$\mathbb{C}[GL(V) \cdot (x_1 \cdots x_n)] = \bigoplus_{l(\pi) \leq n} (S_\pi V)^{\oplus \dim(S_\pi V^*)^{\Gamma_n}}, \qquad (9.2.1)$$

where here $\pi = (p_1, \ldots, p_n)$ with $p_j \in \mathbb{Z}$ satisfies $p_1 \geq p_2 \geq \cdots \geq p_n$. (Note that the p_j are allowed to be negative.) We break up the determination of $(S_\pi V^*)^{\Gamma_n}$ into two problems: first determine the T^{SL_n}-invariants, and then the $\mathfrak{S}_n$ invariants inside the T^{SL_n}-invariants. By Exercise 8.1.5.4, the T^{SL_n}-invariants are the weight $(s, \ldots, s) = (s^n)$ subspaces, so in particular $|\pi| = sn$ for some $s \in \mathbb{Z}$. Let $(S_\pi V^*)_0$ denote the space of T^{SL_n}-invariants. The notation is chosen because this is the $\mathfrak{sl}(V)$-weight zero subspace.

It remains to determine $(S_\pi V^*)_0^{\mathfrak{S}_n}$. This is not known. In the next subsection, I relate it to another unknown quantity. Remarkably, this will enable us to get a satisfactory answer.

9.2.2 Plethysm and the Double Commutant Theorem

The group $\mathfrak{S}_n$ acts on the $\mathfrak{sl}$-weight zero subspace by permuting basis vectors. (This is an example of a *Weyl group* action.) The following theorem is proved using the Double Commutant Theorem 8.6.2.3.

Theorem 9.2.2.1 [Gay76] *Let μ be a partition of $n\delta$ (so that $(S_\mu V)_0 \neq 0$). Suppose that the decomposition of $(S_\mu V)_0$ into irreducible $\mathfrak{S}_n$-modules is*

$$(S_\mu V)_0 = \bigoplus_{|\pi|=n} [\pi]^{\oplus s_{\mu,\pi}}.$$

Then the decomposition of $S_\pi(S^\delta V)$ as a $GL(V)$-module is

$$S_\pi(S^\delta V) = \bigoplus_{|\mu|=\delta n} (S_\mu V)^{\oplus s_{\mu,\pi}}.$$

In particular, for $\delta = 1$, i.e., $|\mu| = n$, $(S_\mu V)_0 = [\mu]$.

Corollary 9.2.2.2 *For any partition π of dn,*

$$\mathrm{mult}(S_\pi V, S^n(S^d \mathbb{C}^n)) = \mathrm{mult}([n], (S_\pi \mathbb{C}^n)_0).$$

9.2.3 Back to the Coordinate Ring

Now specialize to the case of modules appearing in $Sym(S^n V)$. Introduce the notation $M_{poly} \subset M$ where M is a $GL(V)$-module and M_{poly} is the submodule of the isotypic components of all $S_\pi V$ in M where π is a partition. (I.e., here I do require the parts of π to be nonnegative. The notation is used because these are the polynomial $GL(V)$-modules.) If we consider all the π's together, Corollary 9.2.2.2 combined with Equation (9.2.1) implies the following the equality of $GL(V)$-modules:

$$\mathbb{C}[GL(V) \cdot (x_1 \cdots x_n)]_{poly} = \bigoplus_s S^n(S^s V).$$

In particular, $\bigoplus_s S^n(S^s V)$ inherits a graded ring structure. We'll return to this in §9.5.2. If X is an irreducible affine variety and $X^0 \subset X$ is a Zariski open subset (so $X = \overline{X^0}$), one has an injection

$$\mathbb{C}[X] \to \mathbb{C}[X^0]$$

by restriction of functions. We thus have a sequence of $GL(V)$-module maps

$$\mathbb{C}[S^n V^*] \to \mathbb{C}[Ch_n(V^*)] \to \mathbb{C}[GL(V) \cdot (x_1 \cdots x_n)]_{poly} = \bigoplus_s S^n(S^s V),$$

with the first surjective and the second injective. Their composition is a map

$$h_n : Sym(S^n(V)) \to \mathbb{C}[GL(V) \cdot (x_1 \cdots x_n)]_{poly}$$

with kernel $I(Ch_n(V^*))$. It should come as no surprise that in degree d, h_n is $h_{d,n}$. A proof is given in §9.5. This gives us a second, GCT interpretation of the Hadamard-Howe map.

9.3 $\mathfrak{S}_{dn}$-Formulation of the Hadamard-Howe Problem

I now give an interpretation of the Hadamard-Howe problem in terms of maps of $\mathfrak{S}_{dn}$-modules.

9.3.1 The Black-List Map

The dimension of V, as long as it is at least d, is irrelevant for the $GL(V)$-module structure of the kernel of $h_{d,n}$. *In this section assume* $\dim V = dn$.

If one restricts $h_{d,n}$ to the $\mathfrak{sl}(V)$-weight zero subspace, since the permutation of basis vectors commutes with $h_{d,n}$, one obtains a $\mathfrak{S}_{dn}$-module map

$$h_{d,n:0} : S^d(S^n V)_0 \to S^n(S^d V)_0. \tag{9.3.1}$$

Let $\mathfrak{S}_n \wr \mathfrak{S}_d \subset \mathfrak{S}_{dn}$ denote the *wreath product*, which, by definition, is the normalizer of $\mathfrak{S}_n^{\times d}$ in $\mathfrak{S}_{dn}$. It is the semidirect product of $\mathfrak{S}_n^{\times d}$ with $\mathfrak{S}_d$, where $\mathfrak{S}_d$ acts by permuting the factors of $\mathfrak{S}_n^{\times d}$, see e.g., [Mac95, p 158]. The action of the group $\mathfrak{S}_n \wr \mathfrak{S}_d$ on $V^{\otimes dn}$ induced from the $\mathfrak{S}_{dn}$-action is as follows: consider $V^{\otimes dn}$ as $(V^{\otimes n})^{\otimes d}$, d blocks of n-copies of V, permuting the n copies of V within each block as well as permuting the blocks. Thus $S^d(S^n V) = (V^{\otimes dn})^{\mathfrak{S}_n \wr \mathfrak{S}_d}$.

Notice that

$$(V^{\otimes dn})^{\mathfrak{S}_n \wr \mathfrak{S}_d} = \left(\bigoplus_{|\pi| = dn} [\pi] \otimes S_\pi V \right)^{\mathfrak{S}_n \wr \mathfrak{S}_d} = \bigoplus_{|\pi| = dn} [\pi]^{\mathfrak{S}_n \wr \mathfrak{S}_d} \otimes S_\pi V,$$

so

$$\mathrm{mult}(S_\pi V, S^d(S^n V)) = \dim[\pi]^{\mathfrak{S}_n \wr \mathfrak{S}_d}.$$

Unfortunately the action of $\mathfrak{S}_n \wr \mathfrak{S}_d$ is difficult to analyze.

In other words, recalling the discussion in §9.2.2, as a $\mathfrak{S}_{dn}$-module map, (9.3.1) is

$$h_{d,n:0} : \operatorname{Ind}_{\mathfrak{S}_n \wr \mathfrak{S}_d}^{\mathfrak{S}_{dn}} \text{triv} \to \operatorname{Ind}_{\mathfrak{S}_d \wr \mathfrak{S}_n}^{\mathfrak{S}_{dn}} \text{triv} . \qquad (9.3.2)$$

Call $h_{d,n:0}$ the *Black-List map*. Since every irreducible module appearing in $S^d(S^n V)$ has a nonzero weight zero subspace, $h_{d,n}$ is the unique $GL(V)$-module extension of $h_{d,n:0}$.

The above discussion shows that one can deduce the kernel of $h_{d,n}$ from that of $h_{d,n:0}$ and vice versa. In particular, one is injective if and only if the other is, giving us our third interpretation of the Hadamard-Howe problem.

The map $h_{d,n:0}$ was defined purely in terms of combinatorics in [BL89] as a path to try to prove the following conjecture of Foulkes:

Conjecture 9.3.1.1 [Fou50] *Let $d > n$, let π be a partition of dn and let $[\pi]$ denote the corresponding $\mathfrak{S}_{dn}$-module. Then,*

$$\operatorname{mult}\left([\pi], \operatorname{Ind}_{\mathfrak{S}_n \wr \mathfrak{S}_d}^{\mathfrak{S}_{dn}} \text{triv}\right) \geq \operatorname{mult}\left([\pi], \operatorname{Ind}_{\mathfrak{S}_d \wr \mathfrak{S}_n}^{\mathfrak{S}_{dn}} \text{triv}\right).$$

Equivalently,

$$\operatorname{mult}(S_\pi V, S^d(S^n V)) \geq \operatorname{mult}(S_\pi V, S^n(S^d V)). \qquad (9.3.3)$$

Theorem 8.9.1.1 shows that equality holds asymptotically in (9.3.3), and Theorem 9.1.2.10 shows it holds for $d \leq 4$. In [CIM17] they show it also holds for $d = 5$ by showing $h_{6,5}$ is surjective. Conjecture 9.3.1.1 is still open in general.

9.3.2 Outline of Proof of Theorem 9.1.2.9

I prove that if $h_{d,n-1}$ is injective, then $h_{d,n}$ is injective. I follow the proof in [Ike15]. Write $W = E \oplus F$ with $\dim E = d$ and $\dim F = n$. Give E a basis $e_1, \ldots, e_d$ and F a basis $f_1, \ldots, f_n$ inducing a basis of W ordered $(e_1, e_2, \ldots, f_n)$. For a $GL(E) \times GL(F)$-weight $\alpha = (a_1, \ldots, a_d)$, $\beta = (b_1, \ldots, b_n)$, let $(W^{\otimes dn})_{(\alpha,\beta)}$ denote the (α, β) weight subspace of $W^{\otimes dn}$. Define the lowering map

$$\phi_{i,j} : (W^{\otimes dn})_{(\alpha,\beta)} \to (W^{\otimes dn})_{(a_1,\ldots,a_{i-1},(a_i-1),a_{i+1},\ldots,a_d),\beta=(b_1,\ldots,(b_j+1),\ldots,b_n)}$$

induced from the map $W \to W$ that sends e_i to f_j and maps all other basis vectors to themselves. It is straightforward to see the $\phi_{i,j}$ commute. Let $\phi_{d\times n} : (W^{\otimes dn})_{(n^d,(0))} \to (W^{\otimes dn})_{((0),d^n)}$ denote the composition of $\phi_{1,1} \cdots \phi_{d,b}$ restricted to $(W^{\otimes dn})_{(n^d,(0))}$.

Call $\phi_{d\times n}$ the *McKay map*.

Proposition 9.3.2.1 *As* $\mathfrak{S}_{dn}$*-module maps,* $\phi_{d \times n} = h_{d,n;0}$*, i.e., as maps of* $\mathfrak{S}_{dn}$*-modules, the McKay map is equivalent to the Black-List map.*

The proof is indirect, by showing that the spaces coincide and the kernels are isomorphic $\mathfrak{S}_{dn}$-modules. More precisely:

Proposition 9.3.2.2 *[Ikenmeyer, personal communication]*

> i $\mathrm{mult}([\pi], (W^{\otimes dn})_{(n^d,(0))}) = \mathrm{mult}(S_\pi W, S^d(S^n W))$
> ii $\mathrm{mult}([\pi], \phi_{d \times n}((W^{\otimes dn})_{(n^d,(0))})) = \mathrm{mult}(S_\pi W, h_{d,n}(S^d(S^n W)))$.

Ikenmeyer proves Proposition 9.3.2.2 with explicit bases of both spaces defined via tableau. *A posteriori* this shows $(W^{\otimes dn})_{(n^d,(0))} = \mathrm{Ind}_{\mathfrak{S}_n \wr \mathfrak{S}_d}^{\mathfrak{S}_{dn}} \mathrm{triv}$ as $\mathfrak{S}_{dn}$-modules and $h_{d,n;0} = \phi_{d \times n}$.

Now for the proof of Theorem 9.1.2.9: We need to show $\phi_{d \times (n-1)}$ injective implies $\phi_{d \times n}$ is injective.

Reorder and decompose

$$\phi_{d \times n} = (\phi_{1,1} \cdots \phi_{1,n-1} \phi_{2,1} \cdots \phi_{d,n-1}) \cdot (\phi_{1,n} \cdots \phi_{d,n})$$

and call the first term the left factor and the second the right factor. Each term in the left factor is injective by assumption. It remains to show injectivity of each $\phi_{i,n}$. I will show injectivity of $\phi_{i,n}$ restricted to each $(((n-1)^{i-1}, n^{d-i}), (0^{n-1}, i-1))$ weight space. Each of these restrictions just involves a raising operator in the $\mathbb{C}^2$ with basis e_i, f_n, so we need to see the lowering map $((\mathbb{C}^2)^{\otimes n+i-1})_{(n,i-1)} \to ((\mathbb{C}^2)^{\otimes n+i-1})_{(n-1,i)}$ is injective. Decompose

$$(\mathbb{C}^2)^{\otimes n+i-1} = \bigoplus_{p_2=0}^{\lfloor \frac{n+i-1}{2} \rfloor} S_{n+i-1-p_2,p_2} \mathbb{C}^2.$$

The weight $(n-1, i)$ vector in each space may be written as $(e_i \wedge f_n)^{\otimes p_2} \otimes (e_i^{n-p_2} f_n^{i-1-p_2})$. The lowering operator is zero on the first factor so this vector maps to $(e_i \wedge f_n)^{\otimes p_2} \otimes (e_i^{n-p_2-1} f_n^{i-p_2})$ which is a basis vector in the target.

9.4 Conjecture 9.1.2.18 and a Conjecture in Combinatorics

For any even n, the one-dimensional module $S_{(n^d)} \mathbb{C}^d$ occurs with multiplicity one in $S^d(S^n \mathbb{C}^d)$ (cf. [How87, Proposition 4.3]). Let $P \in S_{n^d}(\mathbb{C}^d) \subset S^d(S^n \mathbb{C}^d)$ be nonzero. Conjecture 9.1.2.18 and its generalizations may be stated as $P((x_1 \cdots x_n)^d) \neq 0$. Our first task is to obtain an expression for P.

9.4.1 Realization of the Module

Let $V = \mathbb{C}^d$. Fix a nonzero basis element $\det_d \in \Lambda^d V$.

Proposition 9.4.1.1 [KL15] *Let n be even. The unique (up to scale) element* $P \in S_{(n^d)}V \subset S^d(S^nV)$ *evaluated on*

$$x = \left(v_1^1 \cdots v_n^1\right)\left(v_1^2 \cdots v_n^2\right) \cdots \left(v_1^d \cdots v_n^d\right) \in S^d(S^nV^*), \quad \text{for any } v_j^i \in V^*,$$

is

$$\langle P, x \rangle = \sum_{\sigma_1,\dots,\sigma_d \in \mathfrak{S}_n} \det_d \left(v_{\sigma_1(1)}^1 \wedge \cdots \wedge v_{\sigma_d(1)}^d\right) \cdots \det_d \left(v_{\sigma_1(n)}^1 \wedge \cdots \wedge v_{\sigma_d(n)}^d\right).$$

$$(9.4.1)$$

Proof. Let $\tilde{P}(x)$ denote the right-hand side of (9.4.1), so $\tilde{P} \in (V)^{\otimes nd}$. It suffices to check that

   i $\tilde{P} \in S^d(S^nV)$,
   ii $\tilde{P}$ is $SL(V)$ invariant, and
   iii $\tilde{P}$ is not identically zero.

Observe that (iii) follows from the identity (9.4.1) by taking $v_j^i = x_i$ where $x_1, \dots, x_d$ is a basis of V^*, and (ii) follows because $SL(V)$ acts trivially on $\det_d$.

To prove (i), I show (ia) $\tilde{P} \in S^d(V^{\otimes n})$ and (ib) $\tilde{P} \in (S^nV)^{\otimes d}$ to conclude. To see (ia), it is sufficient to show that exchanging two adjacent factors in parentheses in the expression of x will not change (9.4.1). Exchange v_j^1 with v_j^2 in the expression for $j = 1, \dots, n$. Then, each individual determinant will change sign, but there are an even number of determinants, so the right-hand side of (9.4.1) is unchanged. To see (ib), it is sufficient to show the expression is unchanged if we swap v_1^1 with v_2^1 in (9.4.1). If we multiply by $n!$, we may assume $\sigma_1 = \mathrm{Id}$, i.e.,

$$\langle \tilde{P}, x \rangle = n! \sum_{\sigma_2,\dots,\sigma_d \in \mathfrak{S}_n} \det_d \left(v_1^1, v_{\sigma_2(1)}^2, \dots, v_{\sigma_d(1)}^d\right)$$
$$\det_d \left(v_2^1 \wedge v_{\sigma_2(2)}^2 \wedge \cdots \wedge v_{\sigma_d(2)}^d\right) \cdots \det_d \left(v_n^1 \wedge v_{\sigma_2(n)}^2 \wedge \cdots \wedge v_{\sigma_d(n)}^d\right).$$

With the two elements v_1^1 and v_2^1 swapped, we get

$$n! \sum_{\sigma_2,\dots,\sigma_d \in \mathfrak{S}_n} \det_d \left(v_2^1 \wedge v_{\sigma_2(1)}^2 \wedge \cdots \wedge v_{\sigma_d(1)}^d\right)$$
$$\det_d \left(v_1^1 \wedge v_{\sigma_2(2)}^2 \wedge \cdots \wedge v_{\sigma_d(2)}^d\right) \cdots \det_d \left(v_n^1 \wedge v_{\sigma_2(n)}^2 \wedge \cdots \wedge v_{\sigma_d(n)}^d\right). \quad (9.4.2)$$

Now right compose each σ_s in (9.4.2) by the transposition $(1, 2)$. The expressions become the same. $\quad\square$

Corollary 9.4.1.2 *The unique (up to scale) polynomial* $P \in S_{(n^d)}V \subset S^d(S^nV)$ *when n is even, is nonzero on* $(y_1)^n + \cdots + (y_d)^n$ *if the* y_j *are linearly independent. In particular,* $S_{n^d}V \subset \mathbb{C}[\sigma_d(v_n(\mathbb{P}V^*))]$ *whenever* $\dim V \geq d$.

Proof. The monomial $(y_1)^n \cdots (y_d)^n$ appears in $((y_1)^n + \cdots + (y_d)^n)^d$ and all other monomials appearing pair with P to be zero. □

Now specialize to the critical case $d = n$ and evaluate on $(x_1 \cdots x_n)^n$, where $x_1, \ldots, x_n$ is a basis of V^* such that $\det_n(x_1 \wedge \cdots \wedge x_n) = 1$.

$$\langle P, (x_1 \cdots x_n)^n \rangle = \sum_{\sigma_1,\ldots,\sigma_n \in \mathfrak{S}_n} \det_d(x_{\sigma_1(1)}, \ldots, x_{\sigma_n(1)}) \cdots \det_d(x_{\sigma_1(n)}, \ldots, x_{\sigma_n(n)}).$$

$$(9.4.3)$$

For a fixed $(\sigma_1, \ldots, \sigma_n)$ the contribution will either be 0, 1 or -1. The contribution is zero unless for each j, the indices $\sigma_1(j), \ldots, \sigma_n(j)$ are distinct. Arrange these numbers in an array:

$$\begin{pmatrix} \sigma_1(1) & \cdots & \sigma_n(1) \\ & \vdots & \\ \sigma_1(n) & \cdots & \sigma_n(n) \end{pmatrix}$$

The contribution is zero unless the array is a *Latin square*, i.e., an $n \times n$ matrix such that each row and column consists of the integers $\{1, \ldots, n\}$. If it is a Latin square, the rows correspond to permutations, and the contribution of the term is the product of the signs of these permutations. Call this the *row sign* of the Latin square. The products of both the signs of the row permutations and the column permutations is called the *sign* of the Latin square:

Conjecture 9.4.1.3 (Alon-Tarsi [AT92]) *Let n be even. The number of sign -1 Latin squares of size n is not equal to the number of sign $+1$ Latin squares of size n.*

Conjecture 9.4.1.3 is known to be true when $n = p \pm 1$, where p is an odd prime; in particular, it is known to be true up to $n = 24$ [Gly10, Dri97].

On the other hand, in [Alp17, CW16] they show that the ratio of the number of sign -1 Latin squares of size n to the number of sign $+1$ Latin squares of size n tends to one as n goes to infinity.

In [HR94], Huang and Rota showed:

Theorem 9.4.1.4 *[HR94, Identities 8,9] The difference between the number of row even Latin squares of size n and the number of row odd Latin squares of size n equals the difference between the number of even Latin squares of size n and the number of odd Latin squares of size n, up to sign.*

In particular, the Alon-Tarsi conjecture holds for n if and only if the row-sign Latin square conjecture holds for n. Thus

Theorem 9.4.1.5 [KL15] *The Alon-Tarsi conjecture holds for n if and only if* $S_{(n^n)}(\mathbb{C}^n) \in \mathbb{C}[Ch_n(\mathbb{C}^n)]$.

In [KL15] several additional statements equivalent to the conjecture were given. In particular, for those familiar with integration over compact Lie groups, the conjecture holds for n if and only if

$$\int_{(g^i_j) \in SU(n)} \prod_{1 \leq i, j \leq n} g^i_j d\mu \neq 0$$

where $d\mu$ is Haar measure.

9.5 Algebraic Geometry Derivation of the Hadamard-Howe Map

9.5.1 Preliminaries from Algebraic Geometry

In modern geometry, one studies a space by the functions on it. The general definition of an affine variety over $\mathbb{C}$ can be made without reference to an ambient space. It corresponds to a finitely generated ring over $\mathbb{C}$ with no nilpotent elements (see, e.g., [Har95, Lect. 5]), as these are the rings that are realizable as the ring of regular functions of a subvariety of affine space. In this section we will deal with two affine varieties that are presented to us in terms of their rings of regular functions, the *normalization* of an affine variety and the *GIT quotient* of an affine variety with an algebraic group action.

If R, S are rings with $R \subset S$, $s \in S$ is *integral* over R if it satisfies a monic polynomial with coefficients in R: $s^d + r_1 s^{d-1} + \cdots + r_d = 0$ for some $r_i \in R$, and S is integral over R if every element of S is integral over R.

A regular map (see §3.1.4) between affine varieties $f : X \to Y$ such that $f(X)$ is dense in Y is said to be *finite* if $\mathbb{C}[X]$ is *integral* over $\mathbb{C}[Y]$ (see, e.g. [Sha07, §I.5.3]).

An affine variety Z is *normal* if $\mathbb{C}[Z]$ is integrally closed, that is if every element of $\mathbb{C}(Z)$, the field of fractions of $\mathbb{C}[Z]$, that is integral over $\mathbb{C}[Z]$ is in $\mathbb{C}[Z]$. To every affine variety Z one may associate a unique normal affine variety $Nor(Z)$, called the *normalization* of Z, such that there is a generically one to one finite map $\pi : Nor(Z) \to Z$. If Z is smooth then $Nor(Z) = Z$, and more generally π is one to one over the smooth points of Z. For details see [Sha07, §II.5].

Exercise 9.5.1.1 (1) Show that if Z is a G-variety, then $Nor(Z)$ is too.

Recall from Exercise 3.1.4.6 the inclusion $\mathbb{C}[Z] \to \mathbb{C}[Nor(Z)]$ given by pullback of functions. If the nonnormal points of Z form a finite set, then the cokernel of this inclusion is finite-dimensional.

9.5.2 Coordinate Ring of the Normalization of the Chow Variety

In this section I work in affine space and follow [Bri93]. The normalization of the (cone over the) Chow variety and its coordinate ring have a simple description that I now explain. The cone $\hat{C}h_n(V^*) \subset S^nV^*$ is the image of the following map:

$$\phi_n : V^{*\times n} \to S^nV^*$$

$$(u_1, \dots, u_n) \mapsto u_1 \cdots u_n.$$

Note that ϕ_n is $GL(V)$-equivariant.

For any affine algebraic group Γ and any affine Γ-variety Z, define the *GIT quotient* $Z \mathbin{/\!\!/} \Gamma$ to be the affine algebraic variety whose coordinate ring is $\mathbb{C}[Z]^\Gamma$. (When Γ is finite, this is just the usual set-theoretic quotient. In the general case two Γ-orbits will be identified under the quotient map $Z \to Z \mathbin{/\!\!/} \Gamma$ when there is no Γ-invariant regular function that can distinguish them.)

Exercise 9.5.2.1 (2!) Consider the space of $n \times n$ matrices Mat_n with the action of GL_n via conjugation. Give an explicit description of the map $Mat_n \to Mat_n \mathbin{/\!\!/} GL_n$. ⊚

Exercise 9.5.2.2 (2) Show that if Z is normal, then so is $Z \mathbin{/\!\!/} \Gamma$. ⊚

In our case $V^{*\times n}$ is an affine $\Gamma_n := T^{SL_n} \rtimes \mathfrak{S}_n$-variety, where a diagonal matrix in T^{SL_n} with entries λ_j acts on $V^{*\times n}$ by $(\alpha_1, \dots, \alpha_n) \mapsto (\lambda_1\alpha_1, \dots, \lambda_n\alpha_n)$. The map ϕ_n factors through the GIT quotient because it is Γ_n-equivariant, giving a map

$$\psi_n : V^{*\times n} \mathbin{/\!\!/} \Gamma_n \to S^nV^*, \tag{9.5.1}$$

whose image is $\hat{C}h_n(V^*)$. By unique factorization, ψ_n is generically one to one. Elements of $V^{*\times n}$ of the form $(0, u_2, \dots, u_n)$ cannot be distinguished from $(0, \dots, 0)$ by Γ_n-invariant functions, so they are identified with $(0, \dots, 0)$ in the quotient, which is consistent with the fact that $\phi_n(0, u_2, \dots, u_n) = 0$.

Consider the induced map on coordinate rings:

$$\psi_n^* : \mathbb{C}[S^nV^*] \to \mathbb{C}[V^{*\times n}] \mathbin{/\!\!/} \Gamma_n] = \mathbb{C}[V^{*\times n}]^{\Gamma_n}.$$

For affine varieties, $\mathbb{C}[Y \times Z] = \mathbb{C}[Y] \otimes \mathbb{C}[Z]$ (see e.g., [Sha07, §2.2 Ex.1.10]), so

$$\mathbb{C}[V^{*\times n}] = \mathbb{C}[V^*]^{\otimes n}$$
$$= Sym(V) \otimes \cdots \otimes Sym(V)$$
$$= \bigoplus_{i_1, \dots, i_n \in \mathbb{Z}_{\geq 0}} S^{i_1}V \otimes \cdots \otimes S^{i_n}V.$$

Taking T^{SL_n} invariants gives

$$\mathbb{C}[V^{*\times n}]_n^{T_n^{SL}} = \bigoplus_{i \geq 0} S^i V \otimes \cdots \otimes S^i V,$$

and finally

$$\left(\mathbb{C}[V^{*\times n}]_n^{T_n^{SL}}\right)^{\mathfrak{S}_n} = \bigoplus_{i \geq 0} S^n(S^i V).$$

The map

$$\tilde{h}_n := \psi_n^* : Sym(S^n V) \rightarrow \oplus_i(S^n(S^i V)),$$

respects GL-degree, so it gives rise to maps $\tilde{h}_{d,n} : S^d(S^n V) \rightarrow S^n(S^d V)$.

Proposition 9.5.2.3 $\tilde{h}_{d,n} = h_{d,n}$.

Proof. Since elements of the form $x_1^n \cdots x_d^n$ span $S^d(S^n V)$ it will be sufficient to prove the maps agree on such elements. By Exercise 9.1.1.3, $h_{d,n}(x_1^n \cdots x_d^n) = (x_1 \cdots x_d)^n$. On the other hand, in the algebra $\mathbb{C}[V^*]^{\otimes n}$, the multiplication is $(f_1 \otimes \cdots \otimes f_n) \odot (g_1 \otimes \cdots \otimes g_n) = f_1 g_1 \otimes \cdots \otimes f_n g_n$ and this descends to the algebra $(\mathbb{C}[V^*]^{\otimes n})^{\Gamma_n}$ which is the target of the algebra map $\tilde{h}_n$, i.e.,

$$\begin{aligned}
\tilde{h}_{d,n}\left(x_1^n \cdots x_d^n\right) &= \psi_n^*\left(x_1^n \cdots x_d^n\right) \\
&= \psi_n^*\left(x_1^n\right) \odot \cdots \odot \psi_n^*\left(x_d^n\right) \\
&= x_1^n \odot \cdots \odot x_d^n \\
&= (x_1 \cdots x_d)^n.
\end{aligned}$$

$\square$

Proposition 9.5.2.4 $\psi_n : V^{*\times n} /\!\!/ \Gamma_n \rightarrow \hat{C}h_n(V^*)$ *is the normalization of* $\hat{C}h_n(V^*)$.

I prove Proposition 9.5.2.4 in §9.7. Thus we get a fourth formulation of the Hadamard-Howe problem: Determine the cokernel of the natural inclusion map

$$\mathbb{C}[\hat{C}h(V^*)] \rightarrow \mathbb{C}[Nor(\hat{C}h(V^*))].$$

This is equivalent to the other formulations because the cokernel of $\tilde{h}_n$ is also the cokernel of the composition $Sym(S^n V) \rightarrow \mathbb{C}[\hat{C}h_n(V^*)] \rightarrow \mathbb{C}[Nor(\hat{C}h_n(V^*))]$. The proof of Proposition 9.5.2.4 and the qualitative assertion of Theorem 9.1.2.14 will hinge on exploiting that the only nonnormal point of $\hat{C}h(V^*)$ is the origin. Since it involves more advanced results from algebraic geometry, I postpone the proofs until the end of this chapter.

9.6 Brill's Equations

Set theoretic equations of $Ch_d(V^*)$ have been known since 1894. Here is a modern presentation elaborating the presentation in [Lan12, §8.6], which was suggested by E. Briand.

9.6.1 Preliminaries

Our goal is a polynomial test to determine if $f \in S^d V^*$ is a product of linear factors. We can first try to just determine if f is divisible by a power of a linear form. The discussion in §8.4.2 will not be helpful as the conditions there are vacuous when $n - m = 1$. We could proceed as in §6.5.1 and check if $\ell x^{I_1} \wedge \cdots \wedge \ell x^{I_D} \wedge f = 0$ where the x^{I_j} are a basis of $S^{d-1} V^*$, but in this case there is a simpler test to see if a given linear form ℓ divides f:

Consider the map $\pi_{d,d} : S^d V^* \otimes S^d V^* \to S_{(d,d)} V^*$ obtained by projection. (By the Pieri rule 8.1.3.1, $S_{(d,d)} V^* \subset S^d V^* \otimes S^d V^*$ with multiplicity one.)

Lemma 9.6.1.1 *Let $\ell \in V^*$, $f \in S^d V^*$. Then $f = \ell h$ for some $h \in S^{d-1} V^*$ if and only if $\pi_{d,d}(f \otimes \ell^d) = 0$.*

Proof. Since $\pi_{d,d}$ is linear, it suffices to prove the lemma when $f = \ell_1 \cdots \ell_d$. In that case $\pi_{d,d}(f \otimes \ell^d)$, up to a constant, is $(\ell_1 \wedge \ell) \cdots (\ell_d \wedge \ell)$. $\qquad\square$

We would like a map that sends $\ell_1 \cdots \ell_d$ to $\sum_j \ell_j^d \otimes stuff_j$, as then we could apply $\pi_{d,d} \otimes \mathrm{Id}$ to f tensored with the result of our desired map to obtain equations. I construct such a map in several steps.

The maps $f \mapsto f_{j,d-j}$ send $(\ell_1 \cdots \ell_d)$ to $\sum_{|K|=j} \ell_K \otimes \ell_{K^c}$ where $\ell_K = \ell_{k_1} \cdots \ell_{k_j}$ and K^c denotes the complementary index set in $[d]$. The ℓ_K are monomials appearing in elementary symmetric functions and the idea is to convert this to power sums by the conversion formula obtained from the relation between generating functions (6.1.5):

$$
p_d = \mathcal{P}_d(e_1, \ldots, e_d) := \det \begin{pmatrix} e_1 & 1 & 0 & \cdots & 0 \\ 2e_2 & e_1 & 1 & \cdots & 0 \\ \vdots & \vdots & \vdots & & \vdots \\ de_d & e_{d-1} & e_{d-2} & \cdots & e_1 \end{pmatrix}. \qquad (9.6.1)
$$

The desired term comes from the diagonal e_1^d and the rest of the terms kill off the unwanted terms of e_1^d. This idea almost works – the only problem is that our naïve correction terms have the wrong degree on the right-hand side. For example, when $d = 3$, naïvely using $p_3 = e_1^3 - 3e_1 e_2 + 3e_3$ would give, for the first term, degree $6 = 2 + 2 + 2$ on the right-hand side of the tensor product, the second degree $3 = 2 + 1$ and the third degree zero. In general, the right-hand side of the e_1^d term would have degree $(d-1)^d$, whereas the de_d term would have degree zero. In addition to fixing the degree mismatch, we need to formalize how we will treat the right-hand sides.

Define maps

$$E_j : S^\delta V^* \to S^j V^* \otimes S^{\delta-1} V^* \tag{9.6.2}$$
$$f \mapsto f_{j,\delta-j} \odot (1 \otimes f^{j-1}),$$

where $\odot$ is the multiplication introduced in the proof of Proposition 9.5.2.3. The $(1 \otimes f^{j-1})$ fixes our degree problem. If $j > \delta$ define $E_j(f) = 0$.

Our desired map is

$$Q_d : S^d V^* \to S^d V^* \otimes S^{d(d-1)} V^* \tag{9.6.3}$$
$$f \mapsto \mathcal{P}_d(E_1(f), \dots, E_d(f)).$$

9.6.2 Statement and Proof of Brill's Equations

Define *Brill's map*

$$\mathcal{B} : S^d V^* \to S_{d,d} V^* \otimes S^{d^2-d} V^* \tag{9.6.4}$$
$$f \mapsto (\pi_{d,d} \otimes \mathrm{Id}_{S^{d^2-d}V^*})[f \otimes Q_d(f)].$$

Theorem 9.6.2.1 (Brill [Bri93], Gordan [Gor94], Gelfand-Kapranov-Zelevinski [GKZ94], Briand [Bri10]) $[f] \in Ch_d(V^*)$ *if and only if* $\mathcal{B}(f) = 0$.

The proof will be by an induction argument that will require a generalization of Q_d. Define

$$Q_{d,\delta} : S^\delta V^* \to S^d V^* \otimes S^{d(\delta-1)} V^* \tag{9.6.5}$$
$$f \mapsto \mathcal{P}_d(E_1(f), \dots, E_d(f)).$$

Lemma 9.6.2.2 *If* $f_1 \in S^\delta V^*$ *and* $f_2 \in S^{d'-\delta} V^*$, *then*

$$Q_{d,d'}(f_1 f_2) = \left(1 \otimes f_1^d\right) \odot Q_{d,d'-\delta}(f_2) + \left(1 \otimes f_2^d\right) \odot Q_{d,\delta}(f_1).$$

Assume Lemma 9.6.2.2 for the moment.

Proof of Theorem 9.6.2.1. Say $f = \ell_1 \cdots \ell_d$. First note that for $\ell \in V^*$, $E_j(\ell^j) = \ell^j \otimes \ell^{j-1}$ and $Q_{d,1}(\ell) = \ell^d \otimes 1$. Next, compute $E_1(\ell_1 \ell_2) = \ell_1 \otimes \ell_2 + \ell_2 \otimes \ell_1$ and $E_2(\ell_1 \ell_2) = \ell_1 \ell_2 \otimes \ell_1 \ell_2$, so $Q_{2,2}(\ell_1 \ell_2) = \ell_1^2 \otimes \ell_2^2 + \ell_2^2 \otimes \ell_1^2$. By induction and Lemma 9.6.2.2,

$$Q_{d,\delta}(\ell_1 \cdots \ell_\delta) = \sum_j \ell_j^d \otimes \left(\ell_1^d \cdots \ell_{j-1}^d \ell_{j+1}^d \cdots \ell_\delta^d\right).$$

We conclude $Q_d(f) = \sum_j \ell_j^d \otimes (\ell_1^d \cdots \ell_{j-1}^d \ell_{j+1}^d \cdots \ell_d^d)$ and $\pi_{d,d}(\ell_1 \cdots \ell_d, \ell_j^d) = 0$ for each j by Lemma 9.6.1.1.

Now assume $\mathcal{B}(f) = 0$ and we will see $[f] \in Ch_d(V^*)$. Compute $Q_d(f) = (E_1(f))^d + \sum \mu_j \otimes \psi_j$ where $\psi_j \in S^{d^2-d}V^*$, $\mu_j \in S^d V^*$ and f divides ψ_j for each j because $E_1(f)^d$ occurs as a monomial in the determinant (9.6.1) and all the other terms contain an $E_j(f)$ with $j > 1$, and so are divisible by f.

First assume f is reduced, i.e., has no repeated factors, then every component of Zeros(f) contains a smooth point. Let $z \in$ Zeros(f)$_{smooth}$. Thus $\mathcal{B}(f)(\cdot, z) = \pi_{d,d}(f \otimes (df_z)^d)$ because $E_1(f)^d = (f_{1,d-1})^d$ and $f_{1,d-1}(\cdot, z) = df_z$, and all the $\psi_j(z)$ are zero. By Lemma 9.6.1.1, df_z divides f for all $z \in$ Zeros(f). But this implies the tangent space to f is constant in a neighborhood of z, i.e., that the component containing z is a linear space. So when f is reduced, Zeros(f) is a union of hyperplanes, which is what we set out to prove.

Finally, say $f = g^k h$ where g is irreducible of degree q and h is of degree $d - qk$ and is relatively prime to g. Apply Lemma 9.6.2.2:

$$Q_d(g(g^{k-1}h)) = (1 \otimes g^d) \odot Q_{d,d-q}(g^{k-1}h) + (1 \otimes (g^{k-1}h)^d) \odot Q_{d,q}(g).$$

A second application gives

$$\begin{aligned} Q_d(g^k h) = (1 \otimes g^d) &\odot [(1 \otimes g^d) \odot Q_{d,d-2q}(g^{k-2}h) \\ &+ (1 \otimes (g^{k-2}h)^d) \odot Q_{d,q}(g) + (1 \otimes (g^{k-2}h)^d) \odot Q_{d,q}(g)]. \end{aligned}$$

After $k - 1$ applications one obtains:

$$Q_d(g^k h) = (1 \otimes g^{d(k-1)}) \odot [k(1 \otimes h^d) \odot Q_{d,q}(g) + (1 \otimes g^d) \odot Q_{d,d-qk}(h)]$$

and $(1 \otimes g^{d(k-1)})$ will also factor out of $\mathcal{B}(f)$. Since $\mathcal{B}(f)$ is identically zero but $g^{d(k-1)}$ is not, we conclude

$$0 = \pi_{d,d} \otimes \mathrm{Id}_{S^{d^2-d}V^*} f \otimes [k(1 \otimes h^d) \odot Q_{d,q}(g) + (1 \otimes g^d) \odot Q_{d,d-qk}(h)].$$

Let $w \in$ Zeros(g) be a general point, so in particular $h(w) \neq 0$. Evaluating at (z, w) with z arbitrary gives zero on the second term and the first implies $\pi_{d,d} \otimes \mathrm{Id}_{S^{d^2-d}V^*}(f \otimes Q_{d,q}(g)) = 0$ which implies dg_w divides g, so g is a linear form. Applying the argument to each nonreduced factor of f we conclude. $\square$

Proof of Lemma 9.6.2.2. Define, for $u \in Sym(V^*) \otimes Sym(V^*)$,

$$\Delta_u : Sym(V^*) \rightarrow Sym(V^*) \otimes Sym(V^*)$$
$$f \mapsto \sum_j u^j \odot f_{j,\deg(f)-j}.$$

Exercise 9.6.2.3 (2) Show that $\Delta_u(fg) = (\Delta_u f) \odot (\Delta_u g)$, and that the generating series for the $E_j(f)$ may be written as

$$\mathcal{E}_f(t) = \frac{1}{1 \otimes f} \odot \Delta_{t(1 \otimes f)} f.$$

Note that $(1 \otimes f)^{\odot s} = 1 \otimes f^s$ and $(1 \otimes fg) = (1 \otimes f) \odot (1 \otimes g)$. Thus

$$\mathcal{E}_{fg}(t) = \left[\frac{1}{1 \otimes f} \odot \Delta_{[t(1 \otimes g)](1 \otimes f)}(f) \right] \odot \left[\frac{1}{1 \otimes g} \odot \Delta_{[t(1 \otimes f)](1 \otimes g)}(g) \right],$$

and taking the logarithmic derivative (recalling Equation (6.1.5)) we conclude.

$\square$

Remark 9.6.2.4 There was a gap in the argument in [Gor94], repeated in [GKZ94], when proving the "only if" part of the argument. They assumed that the zero set of f contains a smooth point, i.e., that the differential of f is not identically zero. This gap was fixed in [Bri10]. In [GKZ94] they use $G_0(d, \dim V^*)$ to denote $Ch_d(V^*)$.

9.6.3 Brill's Equations as Modules

Brill's equations are of degree $d+1$ on $S^d V^*$. (The total degree of $S_{d,d} V \otimes S^{d^2-d} V$ is $d(d+1)$ which is the total degree of $S^{d+1}(S^d V)$.) Consider the $GL(V)$-module map

$$S_{(d,d)} V \otimes S^{d^2-d} V \to S^{d+1}(S^d V) \qquad (9.6.6)$$

whose image consists of Brill's equations. The irreducible components of the target are not known in general and the set of modules present grows extremely fast. One can use the Pieri formula 8.1.3.1 to get the components of the domain. Using the Pieri formula, we conclude:

Proposition 9.6.3.1 *As a $GL(V)$-module, Brill's equations are multiplicity free.*

Exercise 9.6.3.2 (2) Write out the decomposition and show that only partitions with three parts appear as modules in Brill's equations. $\odot$

Not all partitions with three parts appear:

Theorem 9.6.3.3 [Gua15a] *As a $GL(V)$-module, Brill's equations are:*

$$S_{(732)} V \text{ when } d = 3, \text{ and}$$

$$\bigoplus_{j=2}^{d} S_{(d^2-d,d,j)} V \text{ when } d > 3.$$

The proof is given by explicitly writing out highest weight vectors and determining their image under (9.6.6).

Remark 9.6.3.4 If $d < \mathbf{v} = \dim V^*$, then $Ch_d(V^*) \subset Sub_d(S^d V^*)$ so $I(Ch_d(V^*)) \supset \Lambda^{d+1} V \otimes \Lambda^{d+1}(S^{d-1} V)$. J. Weyman (in unpublished notes from 1994) observed that these equations are not in the ideal generated by Brill's equations. More precisely, the ideal generated by Brill's equations does not include modules $S_\pi V$ with $l(\pi) > 3$ in degree $d + 1$, so it does not cut out $Ch_d(V^*)$ scheme theoretically when $d < \mathbf{v}$. By Theorem 9.1.2.11 the same conclusion holds for $Ch_5(\mathbb{C}^5)$ and almost certainly holds for all $Ch_n(\mathbb{C}^n)$ with $n \geq 5$.

9.7 Proofs of Proposition 9.5.2.4 and Theorem 9.1.2.14

9.7.1 Proof of Proposition 9.5.2.4

Lemma 9.7.1.1 *Let X, Y be affine varieties equipped with polynomial $\mathbb{C}^*$-actions with unique fixed points $0_X \in X$, $0_Y \in Y$, and let $f : X \to Y$ be a $\mathbb{C}^*$-equivariant morphism such that as sets, $f^{-1}(0_Y) = \{0_X\}$. Then f is finite.*

Assume Lemma 9.7.1.1 for the moment.

Proof of Proposition 9.5.2.4. Since $V^{\times n} /\!\!/ \Gamma_n$ is normal and ψ_n of (9.5.1) is regular and generically one to one, it just remains to show ψ_n is finite.

Write $[0] = [0, \ldots, 0]$. To show finiteness, by Lemma 9.7.1.1, it is sufficient to show $\psi_n^{-1}(0) = [0]$ as a set, as $[0]$ is the unique $\mathbb{C}^*$ fixed point in $V^{\times n} /\!\!/ \Gamma_n$, and every $\mathbb{C}^*$ orbit closure contains $[0]$. Now $u_1 \cdots u_n = 0$ if and only if some $u_j = 0$, say $u_1 = 0$. The T^{SL_n}-orbit closure of $(0, u_2, \ldots, u_n)$ contains the origin so $[0, u_2, \ldots, u_n] = [0]$. $\square$

Sketch of Proof of Lemma 9.7.1.1. $\mathbb{C}[X]$, $\mathbb{C}[Y]$ are $\mathbb{Z}_{\geq 0}$-graded, and the hypothesis $f^{-1}(0_Y) = \{0_X\}$ states that

$$\mathbb{C}[X]/(f^*(\mathbb{C}[Y]_{>0}))$$

is a finite-dimensional vector space. We want to show that $\mathbb{C}[X]$ is integral over $\mathbb{C}[Y]$. This follows from a graded version of Nakayama's Lemma (the algebraic implicit function theorem). $\square$

The condition $f^{-1}(0_Y) = \{0_X\}$ as sets in Lemma 9.7.1.1 says that the only maximal ideal of $\mathbb{C}[X]$ containing the ideal generated by $f^*\mathbb{C}[Y]_{>0}$ is $\mathbb{C}[X]_{>0}$.

If R is a finitely generated ring with no nilpotents, the points of the associated affine variety are in one to one correspondence with the maximal ideals of R and the prime ideals correspond to the irreducible subvarieties. For any ring R let

$Spec(R)$ denote the set of prime ideals of R, called the *affine scheme* associated to R. See [Sha13, §5.1] for an introduction.

Here are more details for the proof of Lemma 9.7.1.1 (see, e.g. [Kum13, Lemmas 3.1,3.2], or [Eis95, p136, Ex. 4.6a]):

Lemma 9.7.1.2 *Let R, S be $\mathbb{Z}_{\geq 0}$-graded, finitely generated domains over $\mathbb{C}$ such that $R_0 = S_0 = \mathbb{C}$, and let $f^* : R \to S$ be an injective graded algebra homomorphism. If $S_{>0}$ is the only maximal ideal of S containing the ideal generated by $f^*(R_{>0})$, then S is a finitely generated R-module. In particular, it is integral over R.*

Proof. Let $\mathfrak{m}$ be the ideal generated by $f^*(R_{>0})$, so the radical of $\mathfrak{m}$ equals $S_{>0}$, and in particular $S_{>0}^d$ must be contained in it for all $d > d_0$, for some d_0. So $S/\mathfrak{m}$ is a finite-dimensional vector space, and by the next lemma, S is a finitely generated R-module.   □

Lemma 9.7.1.3 *Let S be as above, and let M be a $\mathbb{Z}_{\geq 0}$-graded S-module. Assume $M/(S_{>0} \cdot M)$ is a finite-dimensional vector space over $S/S_{>0} \simeq \mathbb{C}$. Then M is a finitely generated S-module.*

Proof. Choose a set of homogeneous generators $\{\bar{x}_1, \ldots, \bar{x}_n\} \subset M/(S_{>0} \cdot M)$ and let $x_j \in M$ be a homogeneous lift of $\bar{x}_j$. Let $N \subset M$ be the graded S-submodule $Sx_1 + \cdots + Sx_n$. Then $M = S_{>0}M + N$, as let $a \in M$, consider $\bar{a} \in M/(S_{>0}M)$ and lift it to some $b \in N$, so $a - b \in S_{>0}M$, and $a = (a - b) + b$. Now quotient by N to obtain

$$S_{>0} \cdot (M/N) = M/N. \qquad (9.7.1)$$

If $M/N \neq 0$, let d_0 be the smallest degree such that $(M/N)^{d_0} \neq 0$. But $S_{>0} \cdot (M/N)^{\geq d_0} \subset (M/N)^{\geq d_0+1}$ so there is no way to obtain $(M/N)^{d_0}$ on the right-hand side. Contradiction.   □

9.7.2 Proof of the Qualitative Assertion in Theorem 9.1.2.14

Theorem 9.7.2.1 [Bri93] *For all $n \geq 1$, ψ_n restricts to a map*

$$\psi_n^o : (V^{*\times n} \, /\!/ \, \Gamma_n)\backslash[0] \to S^n V^*\backslash 0 \qquad (9.7.2)$$

such that $\psi_n^{o*} : \mathbb{C}[S^n V^*\backslash 0] \to \mathbb{C}[(V^{*\times n} \, /\!/ \, \Gamma_n)\backslash[0]]$ is surjective.

Corollary 9.7.2.2 [Bri93] *The Hermite-Hadamard-Howe map*

$$h_{d,n} : S^d(S^n V) \to S^n(S^d V)$$

is surjective for d sufficiently large.

Proof of Corollary. Theorem 9.7.2.1 implies $h_{d,n} = (\psi_n^*)_d$ is surjective for d sufficiently large, because the cokernel of ψ_n^* is supported at a point and thus must vanish in large degree.   □

The proof of Theorem 9.7.2.1 will give a second proof that the kernel of ψ_n^* equals the ideal of $Ch_n(V^*)$.

Proof of Theorem 9.7.2.1. Since ψ_n is $\mathbb{C}^*$-equivariant, we can consider the quotient map to projective space

$$\underline{\psi}_n : ((V^{*\times n} /\!\!/ \Gamma_n)\backslash[0])/\mathbb{C}^* \to (S^n V^*\backslash 0)/\mathbb{C}^* = \mathbb{P}S^n V^*$$

and show that $\underline{\psi}_n^*$ is surjective. Note that $((V^{*\times n} /\!\!/ \Gamma_n)\backslash[0])/\mathbb{C}^*$ is $GL(V)$-isomorphic to $(\mathbb{P}V^*)^{\times n}/\mathfrak{S}_n$, as

$$(V^{*\times n} /\!\!/ \Gamma_n)\backslash[0] = (V^*\backslash 0)^{\times n}/\Gamma_n$$

and $\Gamma_n \times \mathbb{C}^* = (\mathbb{C}^*)^{\times n} \rtimes \mathfrak{S}_n$. So we may write

$$\underline{\psi}_n : (\mathbb{P}V^*)^{\times n}/\mathfrak{S}_n \to \mathbb{P}S^n V^*.$$

It will be sufficient to show $\underline{\psi}_n^*$ is surjective on affine open subsets that cover the source and target. Let $w_1, \dots, w_{\mathbf{v}}$ be a basis of V^* and consider the affine open subset of $\mathbb{P}V^*$ given by elements where the coordinate on w_1 is nonzero, and the corresponding induced affine open subsets of $(\mathbb{P}V^*)^{\times n}$ and $\mathbb{P}S^n V^*$, call these $(\mathbb{P}V^*)_1^{\times n}$ and $(\mathbb{P}S^n V^*)_1$. I will show that the algebra of $\mathfrak{S}_n$-invariant functions on $(\mathbb{P}V^*)_1^{\times n}$ is in the image of $(\mathbb{P}S^n V^*)_1$. The restriction of the quotient by $\mathfrak{S}_n$ of $(\mathbb{P}V^*)^{\times n}$ composed with $\underline{\psi}_n$ to these open subsets in coordinates is

$$\left(\left(w_1 + \sum_{s=2}^{\mathbf{v}} x_s^1 w_s \right), \dots, \left(w_1 + \sum_{s=2}^{\mathbf{v}} x_s^{\mathbf{v}} w_s \right) \right) \mapsto \prod_{i=1}^n \left(w_1 + \sum_{s=2}^{\mathbf{v}} x_s^i w_s \right).$$

The coefficients appearing on the right-hand side are the *elementary multisymmetric polynomials* (also called the elementary symmetric vector polynomials). These generate the algebra of multisymmetric polynomials, i.e., the algebra of $\mathfrak{S}_n$-invariant functions in the n sets of variables $(x_s^i)_{i=1,\dots,n}$. For a proof see [Wey97, §II.3] or [GKZ94, §4, Theorem 2.4]. The proof proceeds by first showing the power sum multisymmetric polynomials generate the algebra and then showing one can express the power sum multisymmetric polynomials in terms of the elementary ones.   □

Note that the proof also shows that $(\mathbb{P}V^*)^{\times n}/\mathfrak{S}_n$ is isomorphic to $Ch_n(V^*)$ as a projective variety, which is also shown in [GKZ94, §4 Theorem 2.2].

For any orbit closure $\overline{G \cdot v}$ in affine space (where $v \in V$ and V is a G-module), we always have an inclusion $\mathbb{C}[Nor(\overline{G \cdot v})] \subseteq \mathbb{C}[G \cdot v]_{poly}$ because $G \cdot v$ is also a Zariski open subset of the normalization, as it is contained in the smooth points of $\overline{G \cdot v}$. In our situation $\mathbb{C}[Nor(\hat{Ch}_n(V^*))] = \mathbb{C}[GL(V) \cdot (x_1 \cdots x_n)]_{poly}$. This gives a second proof that $\psi_n^* = h_n$.

Remark 9.7.2.3 Given the above situation, I had asked: Under what circumstances is $\mathbb{C}[Nor(\overline{GL(V) \cdot w})] = \mathbb{C}[GL(V) \cdot w]_{poly}$ when W is a polynomial $GL(V)$-module, $w \in W$, and G_w is reductive? In [Hü17] Hüttenhain answers this question: A simple necessary condition is that $End(V) \cdot w = \overline{GL(V) \cdot w}$. A necessary and sufficient condition is that for all $X \in End(W)$ such that $w \in \ker(X)$, the zero endomorphism lies in $\overline{G_w \cdot X} \subset End(W)$. A simple example where this fails is the cubic $w = x^3 + y^3 + z^3 \in S^3\mathbb{C}^3$, whose orbit closure is the degree four hypersurface $\sigma_3(v_3(\mathbb{P}^2))$. By this result and the boundary component of §6.7.1, we know that the coordinate ring of the normalization of $\mathcal{D}et_n$ and the polynomial part of the coordinate ring of the orbit do not agree.

9.7.3 Proof of Brion's Quantitative Theorem 9.1.2.14

We have a ring map

$$h_n : Sym(S^n V) \to \bigoplus_i S^n(S^i V) \qquad (9.7.3)$$

The proof has three steps:

1. Show $\mathbb{C}[Nor(Ch_n(V^*))]$ is generated in degree at most $(n-1)(\mathbf{v}-1)$ via vanishing of cohomology (Castelnuovo-Mumford regularity, see, e.g., [Eis05, Chapter 4]).
2. Show that $h_n((v^n)^{d(n-1)} \cdot \mathbb{C}[Nor(Ch_n(V^*))]) \subset \mathbb{C}[Ch_n(V^*)]$ via a localization argument to reduce to a question about multisymmetric functions.
3. Use that Zariski open subset of the polynomials of degree n in $\mathbf{v}$ variables can be written as a sum of r_0 nth powers, where $r_0 \sim \frac{1}{n}\binom{\mathbf{v}+n-1}{n}$ (The Alexander-Hirschowitz theorem [AH95], see [BO08] for a detailed exposition of the proof or [Lan12, Chapter 15] for an overview of the proof).

Then we conclude that for $d \geq (n-1)(\mathbf{v}-1)(r_0(n-1)+n)$ that $h_{d,n}$ is surjective.

Proof of Step 1. Recall that $\mathbb{C}[Nor(Ch_n(V^*))] = (\mathbb{C}[V^{*\times n}]^{T^{SL_n}})^{\mathfrak{S}_n}$ so it will be sufficient to show that $\mathbb{C}[V^{*\times n}]^{T^{SL_n}}$ is generated in degree at most

$(n-1)(\mathbf{v}-1)$. This translates into a sheaf cohomology problem:

$$\mathbb{C}[V^{*\times n}]^{T_n} = \bigoplus_{d=0}^{\infty} H^0(\mathbb{P}V^{*\times n}, \mathcal{O}_{\mathbb{P}V^*}(d)^{\times n})$$

$$= \bigoplus_{d=0}^{\infty} H^0(\mathbb{P}S^nV^*, proj_*\mathcal{O}_{\mathbb{P}V^*}(d)^{\times n}),$$

where $proj : \mathbb{P}V^{*\times n} \to \mathbb{P}(S^nV^*)$ is the projection map. We want an upper bound on the degrees of the generators of the graded $Sym(S^nV)$-module associated to the sheaf $proj_*\mathcal{O}_{\mathbb{P}V^*}^{\times n}$. Castelnuovo-Mumford regularity [Mum66, Lect. 14] gives a bound in terms of vanishing of sheaf cohomology groups. Here we are dealing with groups we can compute: $H^j(\mathbb{P}V^{*\times n}, \mathcal{O}(d-j)^{\times n})$, and the result follows from this computation.   □

Proof of Step 2. Let $v = v_{\mathbf{v}} \in V \backslash 0$, and let $v_1, \ldots, v_{\mathbf{v}}$ be a basis of V, which may also be considered as linear forms on V^*, so $x_i := \frac{v_i}{v}$ makes sense. Consider the localization of the coordinate ring of the normalization at v^n, the degree zero elements in the localization of $\mathbb{C}[Nor(Ch_n(V^*))][\frac{1}{v^n}]$:

$$\mathbb{C}[Nor(Ch_n(V^*))]_{v^n} := \bigcup_{d\geq 0} S^n(S^dV)(v^n)^{-d}$$

$$= S^n(\bigcup_{d\geq 0}(S^dV)(v^n)^{-d}$$

$$= S^n\mathbb{C}[x_1, \ldots, x_{\mathbf{v}-1}] =: S^n\mathbb{C}[\bar{x}]$$

$$= [(\mathbb{C}[\bar{x}])^{\otimes n}]^{\mathfrak{S}_n}$$

$$= (\mathbb{C}[\overline{x_1}, \ldots, \overline{x_n}])^{\mathfrak{S}_n},$$

where $\overline{x_j} = (x_{1,j}, \ldots, x_{\mathbf{v}-1,j})$.
    Similarly

$$Sym(S^nV)_{v^n} = \bigcup_{d\geq 0} S^d(S^nV)(v^n)^{-d}$$

$$= Sym(S^nV/v^n)$$

$$= Sym\left(\bigoplus_{i=1}^{n}\mathbb{C}[\bar{x}]_i\right).$$

We get a localized graded algebra map h_{n,v^n} between these spaces. Hence it is determined in degree one, where the map

$$\bigoplus_{i=1}^{n}\mathbb{C}[\bar{x}]_i \to \mathbb{C}[\overline{x_1}, \ldots, \overline{x_n}]^{\mathfrak{S}_n}$$

takes the degree at most n monomial $x_1^{a_1} \cdots x_{d-1}^{a_{d_1}}$ to the coefficient of $t_1^{a_1} \cdots t_{d-1}^{a_{d-1}}$ in the expansion of

$$\Pi_{i=1}^n (1 + \overline{x_{i1}} t_1 + \cdots + \overline{x_{id-1}} t_{d-1})$$

Again we obtain elementary multisymmetric functions which generate the ring of multisymmetric functions $\mathbb{C}[\overline{x_1}, \ldots, \overline{x_n}]^{\mathfrak{S}_n}$. Thus h_{n,v^n} is surjective.

Moreover, if $f \in \mathbb{C}[\overline{x_1}, \ldots, \overline{x_n}]^{\mathfrak{S}_n}$ has all its partial degrees at most d, then the total degree of f is at most dn in the $\overline{x_j}$'s, so it is a polynomial of degree at most dn in the elementary multisymmetric functions. In other words, the map

$$S^{dn}(S^n V)(v^n)^{-dn} \to S^n(S^d V)(v^n)^{-d}$$

is surjective, so $h_n((v^n)^{d(n-1)} \mathbb{C}[Nor(Ch_n(V))] \subset \mathbb{C}[Ch_n(V)]$. $\qquad\square$

We conclude by appeal to the Alexander-Hirschowitz theorem [AH95].

10

Topics Using Additional Algebraic Geometry

This chapter covers four mostly independent topics: §10.1 presents symmetric (Waring) rank lower bounds for polynomials, §10.2 explains limits of determinantal methods (such as the method of partial derivatives, of shifted partial derivatives and Koszul flattenings) for proving lower complexity bounds for tensors and polynomials, §10.3 shows that the singularities of the varieties $\mathcal{D}et_n$ and $\mathcal{P}erm_n^m$ make their study more difficult (they are not normal varieties), and §10.4 discusses further commutative algebra results that might be useful in future study of Valiant's hypothesis (syzygies of Jacobian loci of det_n and $perm_m$). Other than §10.2, they can be read independently, and §10.2 only requires §10.1.

In §10.1, I introduce the language of zero-dimensional schemes to state and prove the *Apolarity Lemma*, an important tool for proving symmetric rank lower bounds. This section does not assume any algebraic geometry beyond what was discussed in Chapters 1–8. It will hopefully motivate computer scientists to learn about zero-dimensional schemes and show algebraic geometers interesting applications of the subject to complexity. I introduce the *cactus variety*, as the apolarity method generally also proves lower bounds on the cactus rank. In §10.2, the cactus variety is shown to be a major obstruction to proving superlinear border rank lower bounds for tensors: all known equations for lower bounds also give lower bounds for the cactus variety, but tensors in $\mathbb{C}^m \otimes \mathbb{C}^m \otimes \mathbb{C}^m$ never have cactus border rank above **6m**.

In §10.3 I present Kumar's proof that $\mathcal{D}et_n$ is not a normal variety. This section does not assume anything beyond what was introduced in Chapters 1–9.

I conclude, in §10.4, with Lascoux's derivation [Las78], as made explicit by Weyman [Wey03], of the minimal free resolution of the ideal generated by the size k minors of a matrix of indeterminants and briefly compare it with the ideal generated by subpermanents. The exposition indicates how tools from commutative algebra might be helpful in proving lower bounds on $\overline{\mathrm{dc}}(\mathrm{perm}_m)$. Parts of this section assume additional background in algebraic geometry and representation theory.

10.1 Rank and Cactus Rank of Polynomials

This section and the next deal with two complexity issues using zero-dimensional schemes: lower bounds on the symmetric rank of polynomials and the limits of determinantal methods for proving border rank lower bounds. In this section I discuss lower bounds on rank. I begin, in §10.1.1, by introducing the language of affine and projective schemes and defining *cactus varieties*, a generalization of secant varieties. In §10.1.2 I introduce apolarity as a tool for proving symmetric rank (and cactus rank) lower bounds. The key to using apolarity is *Bezout's theorem*, a classical theorem in algebraic geometry. I state and prove a version sufficient for our purposes in in §10.1.3. With this, the Ranestad-Schreyer results [RS11] on the ranks of monomials follow, in particular, that $\mathbf{R}_S(x_1 \cdots x_n) = 2^{n-1}$. This is presented in §10.1.4. Bezout's theorem similarly enables Lee's lower bounds [Lee16] on the symmetric ranks of elementary symmetric functions, which are tight in odd degree and presented in §10.1.5.

To facilitate the distinction between elements of $Sym(V)$ and $Sym(V^*)$, I will use lower case letters for elements of $Sym(V)$ and either upper case letters or differential operator notation for elements of $Sym(V^*)$, e.g., $f \in S^d V$, $P \in S^e V^*$, $\frac{\partial}{\partial x_n} \in V^*$.

10.1.1 Language from Algebraic Geometry

As mentioned in §9.7, affine varieties correspond to finitely generated algebras over $\mathbb{C}$ with no nilpotent elements and *affine schemes* similarly correspond to finitely generated rings. Given a finitely generated algebra, the corresponding scheme is the set of its prime ideals (endowed with a topology that generalizes the Zariski topology for varieties). This enables us to "remember" nonreduced structures. For example, $\mathbb{C}[x]/(x)^2$ defines a scheme which we think of as the origin in $\mathbb{A}^1$ with multiplicity two. An affine scheme Z is *zero-dimensional* if the corresponding ring (called the ring of regular functions on Z) is a finite-dimensional vector space over $\mathbb{C}$. If a variety is a collection of d distinct points, its corresponding coordinate ring is a d-dimensional vector space. The *length* or *degree* of a zero-dimensional affine scheme is the dimension of the corresponding ring as a $\mathbb{C}$-vector space. If Z denotes a zero-dimensional affine scheme, where the corresponding ring is a quotient ring of $\mathbb{C}[x_1, \ldots, x_n]$, i.e., $\mathbb{C}[Z] = \mathbb{C}[x_1, \ldots, x_n]/\mathcal{I}$, we consider Z as a subscheme of the affine space $\mathbb{A}^n$.

A homogeneous ideal $I \subset Sym(V^*)$ is *saturated* if every $P \in Sym(V^*)$ such that for all $L \in V^*$, there exists a δ such that $PL^\delta \in I$ satisfies $P \in I$. A *projective scheme* corresponds to a graded ring $S = Sym(V^*)/I$ with I a saturated homogeneous ideal not equal to $Sym(V^*)_{>0}$, and the associated projective scheme is the set of homogeneous prime ideals of S, excluding $\oplus_{d>0} S_d$, see, e.g., [Har77, §II.2]. The corresponding scheme is denoted Proj(S). I continue to use the notation Zeros(I) for the zero set of an ideal I. One says $X = \text{Proj}(Sym(V^*)/I)$ is a subscheme of $\mathbb{P}V$ and writes $X \subset \mathbb{P}V$ and I is called the ideal of X. More generally, for schemes $X, Y \subset \mathbb{P}V$ defined by ideals $I(X)$ and $I(Y)$, $X \subset Y$ means $I(Y) \subset I(X)$. The *support* of a scheme determined by an ideal I is Zeros(I). Define the *span* of X, $\langle X \rangle$ to be the linear space $\text{Zeros}(I(X)_1) \subset \mathbb{P}V$.

Definition 10.1.1.1 [BB14] Let $X \subset \mathbb{P}V$ be a projective variety and let $y \in \mathbb{P}V$. Define the *X-cactus rank* of y to be the smallest r such that there exists a zero-dimensional scheme $Z \subset X$ of length r such that $y \in \langle Z \rangle$. Write $\mathfrak{cr}_X(y) = r$. (The usual case of X-rank is when Z consists of r distinct points.) Define the rth *cactus variety* of X to be

$$ \mathfrak{k}_r(X) := \overline{\{y \in \mathbb{P}V \mid \mathfrak{cr}_X(y) \leq r\}} $$

and define the *cactus border rank* of y, $\underline{\mathfrak{cr}}_X(y)$ to be the smallest r such that $y \in \mathfrak{k}_r(X)$.

By definition, $\mathfrak{cr}_X(y) \leq \mathbf{R}_X(y)$ and $\underline{\mathfrak{cr}}_X(y) \leq \underline{\mathbf{R}}_X(y)$, i.e., $\sigma_r(X) \subseteq \mathfrak{k}_r(X)$, and strict inequality can occur in both cases. The cactus rank was originally defined for polynomials in [Iar95], where it was called *scheme length*, and in general in [BB14]. We will be mostly concerned with the cactus rank of polynomials with respect to $X = v_d(\mathbb{P}V)$. For $f \in S^d V$, write $\mathfrak{cr}_S(f) := \mathfrak{cr}_{v_d(\mathbb{P}V)}(f)$. If $Y \subset v_d(\mathbb{P}V)$, then since the Veronese map is an embedding, there exists a subscheme $Z \subset \mathbb{P}V$ such that $Y = v_d(Z)$. It will be more convenient to write $v_d(Z)$ for a subscheme of $v_d(\mathbb{P}V)$ in what follows.

Exercise 10.1.1.2 (1!) Show that for any subscheme $Z \subset \mathbb{P}V$, $(I(Z))_e = \langle v_e(Z) \rangle^\perp \subset S^e V^*$, where $\perp$ denotes the annihilator in the dual space. In particular, $I(v_d(Z))_1 = I(Z)_d$.◎

10.1.2 The Apolar Ideal

For $f \in S^d V$, recall from §6.2 the flattening (catalecticant) maps $f_{j,d-j} : S^j V^* \to S^{d-j} V$ given by $D \mapsto D(f)$. Define the *annihilator of f* or *apolar ideal* *of f, $f^{ann} \subset Sym(V^*)$* by

$$f^{ann} := \bigoplus_{j=1}^{d} \ker f_{j,d-j} \oplus \bigoplus_{k=d+1}^{\infty} S^k V^*$$

$$= \{P \in Sym(V^*) \mid P(f) = 0\}.$$

Given a (not necessarily homogeneous) polynomial $f \in \mathbb{C}[x_1, \ldots, x_n]$, define $f^{ann} := \{P \in \mathbb{C}[\frac{\partial}{\partial x_1}, \ldots, \frac{\partial}{\partial x_n}] \mid P(f) = 0\}$.

I will also use the notation $\text{Partials}(f) := \{P(f) \mid P \in Sym(V^*)\} \subset Sym(V)$.

Exercise 10.1.2.1 (1) Show that if $e < d$, and $P \in S^e V^*$ satisfies $P(f) \neq 0$, then there exists $L \in V^*$ such that $(LP)(f) \neq 0$. Show more generally that for any $\delta \leq d - e$ there exists $Q \in S^\delta V^*$ with $QP(f) \neq 0$.

The following lemma is critical:

Lemma 10.1.2.2 *[Apolarity Lemma] A finite subscheme $Z \subset \mathbb{P}V$ satisfies $f \in \langle v_d(Z) \rangle = \text{Zeros}(I(Z)_d)$ if and only if $I(Z) \subseteq f^{ann}$. In particular, $f \in \text{span}\{\ell_1^d, \ldots, \ell_r^d\} \subset S^d V$ if and only if $f^{ann} \supseteq I(\{[\ell_1], \ldots, [\ell_r]\})$.*

If Z satisfies the conditions of the Apolarity Lemma, we say Z is *apolar* to $f \in S^d V$.

Proof. The "if" is clear. To prove the other direction, consider $I(Z)_e$. When $e > d$, $f^{ann} = S^e V^*$. When $e = d$, it is the hypothesis. For $e < d$, let $P \in I(Z)_e$. Then $S^{d-e} V^* \cdot P \subset I(Z)_d \subset (f^{ann})_d$, so $(QP)(f) = 0$ for all $Q \in S^{d-e} V^*$, which implies $P(f) = 0$ by Exercise 10.1.2.1, which is what we wanted to prove. $\square$

10.1.3 Bezout's Theorem

Given a graded ring R, define its *Hilbert function* $\text{HilbF}_k(R) := \dim(R_k)$. If $R = Sym(V^*)/I$ for some homogeneous ideal $I \subset Sym(V^*)$, then there exists a polynomial, called the *Hilbert polynomial* of R, $\text{HilbP}_z(R)$ in a variable z such that for k sufficiently large $\text{HilbF}_k(R) = \text{HilbP}_k(R)$, see, e.g., [Sha13, §6.4.2]. For a projective scheme X defined by an ideal $I \subset Sym(V^*)$, one may define its dimension as $\dim(X) := \deg(\text{HilbP}_z(Sym(V^*)/I))$, which agrees with our previous definition for varieties. One writes $\text{HilbF}_k(X)$ and $\text{HilbP}_z(X)$ for the Hilbert functions and polynomials of the coordinate ring of X.

Exercise 10.1.3.1 (1) Let $X = \mathbb{P}^{\ell-1} \subseteq \mathbb{P}V$ be a linear space. Show $\text{HilbP}_z(X) = \frac{1}{(\ell-1)!} z^{\ell-1} + O(z^{\ell-2})$.

Exercise 10.1.3.2 (1) Let $\text{Zeros}(P) \subseteq \mathbb{P}V$ be a hypersurface of degree d. Show $\text{HilbP}_z(\text{Zeros}(P)) = \frac{d}{(\mathbf{v}-2)!} z^{\mathbf{v}-2} + O(z^{\mathbf{v}-3})$.

The above exercise suggests that one may define deg(X), the degree of a projective scheme X, to be the coefficient of $z^{\dim(X)}$ in HilbP$_z(X)$ times dim(X)!, which indeed agrees with our previous definition of degree for a projective variety (see, e.g., [Har95, Lect. 14]) and for a zero-dimensional scheme (in this case the Hilbert polynomial is constant).

Definition 10.1.3.3 Given an ideal $I \subset Sym(V^*)$ and $G \in S^e V^*$, say G is *transverse* to I if the multiplication map

$$Sym(V^*)/I \xrightarrow{\cdot G} Sym(V^*)/I \qquad (10.1.1)$$

given by $P \mapsto GP$ is injective.

We will need a corollary of the following classical theorem:

Theorem 10.1.3.4 (Bezout's Theorem) *Let $I \subset Sym(V^*)$ be a homogeneous ideal, and let $G \in S^e V^*$ be transverse to I. Write* HilbP$_z(Sym(V^*)/I) = \frac{d}{n!}z^n + O(z^{n-1})$ *and assume $n \geq 1$. Then* HilbP$_z(Sym(V^*)/(I + (G))) = \frac{ed}{(n-1)!}z^{n-1} + O(z^{n-2})$.

Proof. Consider the exact sequence

$$0 \to Sym(V^*)/I \xrightarrow{\cdot G} Sym(V^*)/I \to Sym(V^*)/(I + (G)) \to 0.$$

This is an exact sequence of graded $Sym(V^*)$-modules, i.e., for all δ, the sequence

$$0 \to S^{\delta-e}V^*/I_{\delta-e} \xrightarrow{\cdot G} S^\delta V^*/I_\delta \to S^\delta V^*/(I + (G))_\delta \to 0$$

is exact, so

$$\dim(S^\delta V^*/(I + (G))_\delta) = \dim(S^\delta(V^*)/I_\delta) - \dim(S^{\delta-e}(V^*)/I_{\delta-e}).$$

Thus

$$\mathrm{HilbP}_z(Sym(V^*)/(I + (G))) = \mathrm{HilbP}_z(Sym(V^*)/I) - \mathrm{HilbP}_{z-e}(Sym(V^*)/I).$$

Write HilbP$_z(Sym(V^*)/I) = \frac{d}{n!}z^n + cz^{n-1} + O(z^{n-2})$, so

$$\mathrm{HilbP}_{z-e}(Sym(V^*)/I) = \frac{d}{n!}(z-e)^n + c(z-e)^{n-1} + O(z^{n-2})$$

and

$$\mathrm{HilbP}_z(Sym(V^*)/(I + (G))) = \frac{ed}{(n-1)!}z^{n-1} + O(z^{n-2}). \qquad \square$$

Corollary 10.1.3.5 *Let $I \subset Sym(V^*)$ be a homogeneous ideal defining a zero-dimensional scheme in $\mathbb{P}V$, and let $G \in S^e V^*$ be transverse to I. Then $\dim(Sym(V^*)/(I(Z) + (G))) = \delta \deg(Z)$.*

Proof. First consider the one-dimensional affine scheme defined by $I(Z)$ in the affine space V. To return to the projective setting (so that one can apply Theorem 10.1.3.4), consider $V \subset \mathbb{P}^v$ as an affine open subset, e.g., the subset $[1, x_1, \ldots, x_v]$. Then $I(Z) + (G)$ cuts out a zero-dimensional subscheme of $\mathbb{P}^v$ supported at the point $[1, 0, \ldots, 0]$, and we can use Bezout's theorem on $\mathbb{P}^v$ to conclude $\dim(S^D(\mathbb{C}^{v+1*})/(I(Z) + (G))_D) = \delta \deg(Z)$ for D sufficiently large. (Here the Hilbert polynomial is a constant.) But this implies $\dim(Sym(V^*)/(I(Z) + (G))) = \delta \deg(Z)$. □

10.1.4 Lower Bounds on Cactus Rank

Theorem 10.1.4.1 [RS11] *Let $f \in S^d V$ and say f^{ann} is generated in degrees at most δ. Then*

$$\mathfrak{cr}_S(f) \geq \frac{1}{\delta} \dim(Sym(V^*)/f^{ann}) = \frac{1}{\delta} \sum_{j=0}^{d} \operatorname{rank} f_{j,d-j} = \frac{1}{\delta} \dim(\text{Partials}(f)).$$

Proof. Let $f \in S^d V$, and let $Z \subset \mathbb{P}V$ be a zero-dimensional projective scheme of minimal degree satisfying $I(Z) \subseteq f^{ann}$ (i.e., $f \in \langle v_d(Z) \rangle$), so $\mathfrak{cr}_S(f) = \deg(Z)$. There exists $G \in (f^{ann})_\delta$ such that G is transverse to $I(Z)$ because in degrees $e > d$, $(f^{ann})_e = S^e V^*$, so there must be some polynomial in the ideal transverse to $I(Z)$, and since the ideal is generated in degrees at most δ, there must be such a polynomial in degree δ. By Corollary 10.1.3.5, $\dim(Sym(V^*)/(I(Z) + (G))) = \delta \deg(Z)$.

Finally, $\dim(Sym(V^*)/(I(Z) + (G))) \geq \dim(Sym(V^*)/f^{ann})$. □

For example, if $f = xyz$, then $\operatorname{rank}(f_{3,0}) = 1$, $\operatorname{rank}(f_{2,1}) = 3$, $\operatorname{rank}(f_{1,2}) = 3$, $\operatorname{rank}(f_{0,3}) = 1$, and f^{ann} is generated in degree two, so $\mathfrak{cr}_S(xyz) \geq 4$. On the other hand, f^{ann} is generated by $\frac{\partial^2}{(\partial x)^2}, \frac{\partial^2}{(\partial y)^2}, \frac{\partial^2}{(\partial z)^2}$, and the scheme with the ideal generated by any two of these has length four, so equality holds.

Exercise 10.1.4.2 (1) Prove that $\mathbf{R}_S(x_1 \cdots x_n) = \mathfrak{cr}_S(x_1 \cdots x_n) = 2^{n-1}$, which was first shown in [RS11].

Exercise 10.1.4.3 (2) Prove that more generally, for a monomial $x_1^{d_1} \cdots x_n^{d_n}$ with $d_1 < d_2 < \cdots \leq d_n$, $\mathbf{R}_S(x_1^{d_1} \cdots x_n^{d_n}) \geq \mathfrak{cr}_{v_d(\mathbb{P}V)}(x_1^{d_1} \cdots x_n^{d_n}) = (d_1 + 1) \cdots (d_{n-1} + 1)$. This was also first shown in [RS11]. ⊙

Remark 10.1.4.4 L. Oeding [Oed16], using Young flattenings, has shown that $\underline{\mathbf{R}}_S(x_1 \cdots x_n) = 2^{n-1}$, and using a generalization of them, for $d_1 \leq d_2 \leq \cdots \leq d_n$, that $\underline{\mathbf{R}}_S(x_1^{d_1} \cdots x_n^{d_n}) = (d_1 + 1) \cdots (d_{n-1} + 1)$.

10.1.5 Waring ranks of Elementary Symmetric Functions

For ideals $I, J \subset Sym(V^*)$, introduce the *colon ideal*

$$I : J := \{P \in Sym(V^*) \mid PJ \subseteq I\}.$$

Exercise 10.1.5.1 (1) Prove that if $I, J \subset Sym(V^*)$ are saturated homogeneous ideals such that $Sym(V^*)/I$ and $Sym(V^*)/J$ contain no nilpotent elements, then $I : J$ is the ideal of polynomials vanishing on the components of $Zeros(I)$ that are not contained in $Zeros(J)$.

Exercise 10.1.5.2 (1) Show that for $D \in Sym(V^*)$, $f^{ann} : D = (D(f))^{ann}$.

Theorem 10.1.5.3 [CCC$^+$15a] *For $f \in S^d V$, and sufficiently general $P \in S^e V^*$,*

$$\mathbf{R}_S(f) \geq \frac{1}{e} \dim \left(\frac{Sym(V^*)}{f^{ann} : (P) + (P)} \right).$$

Proof. Say $f = \ell_1^d + \cdots + \ell_r^d$ is a minimal rank decomposition of f, so by the Apolarity Lemma 10.1.2.2, $f^{ann} \supseteq I(\{[\ell_1], \ldots, [\ell_r]\})$. Take P such that for $1 \leq j \leq r, P(\ell_j) \neq 0$. (Note that a Zariski open subset of $S^e V^*$ has this property, explaining the "sufficiently general" condition.) Let $J = I(\{[\ell_1], \ldots, [\ell_r]\})$: (P), and let $Proj(J)$ be the corresponding projective scheme. Our choice of P insures that the multiplication map $Sym(V^*)/J \xrightarrow{\cdot P} Sym(V^*)/J$ is injective. To see this, say $H \notin J$ and $H \cdot P \in J$. Then $H \cdot P^2 \in I(\{[\ell_1], \ldots, [\ell_r]\})$, but $I(\{[\ell_1], \ldots, [\ell_r]\})$ is reduced so $H \cdot P \in I(\{[\ell_1], \ldots, [\ell_r]\})$, which means $H \in J$. Corollary 10.1.3.5 applies to show $e \cdot \deg(Proj(J)) = \dim(Sym(V^*)/(J + (P)))$.

The genericity condition also implies $\deg(Proj(J)) = \deg(\{[\ell_1], \ldots, [\ell_r]\}) = r = \mathbf{R}_S(f)$. Furthermore, since $J \subseteq f^{ann} : (P)$,

$$\dim \left(\frac{Sym(V^*)}{f^{ann} : (P) + (P)} \right) \leq \dim \left(\frac{Sym(V^*)}{J + (P)} \right),$$

and we conclude. $\qquad \square$

Corollary 10.1.5.4 [Lee16, CCC$^+$15a] *Let $f \in S^d V$ be concise, and let $L \in V^* \backslash 0$ be arbitrary. Then*

$$\mathbf{R}_S(f) \geq \dim \left(\frac{Sym(V^*)}{f^{ann} : (L) + (L)} \right).$$

Proof. The ideal $I(\{[\ell_1], \ldots, [\ell_r]\})$ is reduced and empty in degree one. Thus L is not a zero divisor in $I(\{[\ell_1], \ldots, [\ell_r]\}) : L$, so Theorem 10.1.5.3 applies with $P = L$. $\qquad \square$

Let $f = e_{d,n} \in S^d\mathbb{C}^n$ be the dth elementary symmetric function. Take $L = \frac{\partial}{\partial x_n} \in S^1\mathbb{C}^{n*}$ and apply Corollary 10.1.5.4. Exercise 10.1.5.2 implies

$$(e_{d,n})^{ann} : \frac{\partial}{\partial x_n} + \left(\frac{\partial}{\partial x_n}\right) = \left(\frac{\partial}{\partial x_n}e_{d,n}\right)^{ann} + \left(\frac{\partial}{\partial x_n}\right)$$

$$= e_{d-1,n-1}^{ann,\mathbb{C}^n} + \left(\frac{\partial}{\partial x_n}\right),$$

where $e_{d-1,n-1}^{ann,\mathbb{C}^n}$ is the annihilator of $e_{d-1,n-1}$ considered as a function of n variables that does not involve x_n. Now

$$\frac{Sym(\mathbb{C}^{n*})}{e_{d-1,n-1}^{ann,\mathbb{C}^n} + \left(\frac{\partial}{\partial x_n}\right)} \simeq \frac{Sym(\mathbb{C}^{(n-1)*})}{e_{d-1,n-1}^{ann,\mathbb{C}^{n-1}}}.$$

Exercise 10.1.5.5 (1) Show that for $t \leq \frac{\delta}{2}$, $(Sym(\mathbb{C}^{k*})/e_{\delta,k}^{ann})_t$ is the span of the square free monomials, so it is of dimension $\binom{k}{t}$. By symmetry, for $\frac{\delta}{2} \leq t \leq \delta$, $\dim((Sym(\mathbb{C}^{k*})/e_{\delta,k}^{ann})_t) = \binom{k}{\delta-t}$. Finally, it is zero for $t > \delta$.

Putting it all together:

Theorem 10.1.5.6 [Lee16] *For all n, and even d,*

$$\sum_{j=0}^{\frac{d}{2}}\binom{n}{j} - \binom{n-1}{\frac{d}{2}} \leq \mathbf{R}_S(e_{d,n}) \leq \sum_{j=0}^{\frac{d}{2}}\binom{n}{j}.$$

For all n, and odd d,

$$\mathbf{R}_S(e_{d,n}) = \sum_{j=0}^{\frac{d-1}{2}}\binom{n}{j}.$$

Proof. Let $d = 2k + 1$ By Exercise 10.1.5.5 and the discussion above,

$$\mathbf{R}_S(e_{d,n}) \geq 2\sum_{j=0}^{\frac{d-1}{2}}\binom{n-1}{j}$$

$$= \binom{n-1}{0} + \sum_{j=1}^{k}\left[\binom{n-1}{j} + \binom{n-1}{j-1}\right]$$

$$= 1 + \sum_{j=1}^{k}\binom{n}{j}.$$

But this is the upper bound of Theorem 7.1.3.1. The even case is similar. $\square$

10.2 Cactus Varieties and Secant Varieties

Recall that $\sigma_r(X) \subseteq \mathfrak{k}_r(X)$. Cactus border rank might appear to be just a curiosity, but the cactus variety turns out to be *the* obstruction to proving further lower bounds with current technology for $\underline{\mathbf{R}}(M_{\langle \mathbf{n} \rangle})$ and places limits on the utility of lower bound techniques arising from determinantal equations. As I explain in §10.2.1, *almost all the equations discussed in this book (method of partial derivatives Koszul flattenings, method of shifted partial derivatives, etc.) are equations for the cactus variety.* Thus our border rank and symmetric border rank lower bounds are actually cactus border rank lower bounds. The reason this is a problem is explained in §10.2.2: the cactus varieties fill the ambient space much faster than the secant varieties. What is particularly surprising is that the cactus analog of the greater areole of §5.4.4 already fills the ambient space.

10.2.1 Young-Flattenings and the Cactus Variety

Recall the variety $Flat_r^{i,d-i}(V) := \mathbb{P}\{P \in S^d V \mid \operatorname{rank}(P_{i,d-i}) \leq r\}$ from §6.2.2.

Proposition 10.2.1.1 [IK99, Theorem 5.3D] *(also see [BB14]) For all r, d, i,*
$$\mathfrak{k}_r(v_d(\mathbb{P}V)) \subseteq Flat_r^{i,d-i}(V).$$

Proof. Say $[f] \in \langle v_d(Z) \rangle$ for a zero-dimensional subscheme $Z \subset \mathbb{P}V$ of degree at most r, i.e., $\hat{f} \subset I(Z)_d^\perp$. We need to show $[f] \in Flat_r^{i,d-i}(V)$. We have $\hat{f}(S^i V^*) \subset I(Z)_d^\perp(S^i V^*)$. By the same argument as in the proof of the Apolarity Lemma, $I(Z)_d^\perp(S^i V^*) \subset I(Z)_{d-i}^\perp$. By Exercise 10.1.1.2, $I(Z)_{d-i}^\perp = \langle v_{d-i}(Z) \rangle$ and $\dim \langle v_{d-i}(Z) \rangle \leq \deg(Z)$. $\square$

More generally, Galcazka [Gal17] shows that for any variety X, $\mathfrak{k}_r(X)$ is in the zero set of any equations for $\sigma_r(X)$ arising from minors of a map between ~~vector bundles. In particular:~~

Theorem 10.2.1.2 [Gal17] *The equations from Koszul flattenings for $\sigma_r(Seg(\mathbb{P}A_1 \times \cdots \times \mathbb{P}A_k))$ and the equations from Koszul and Hilbert flattenings for $\sigma_r(v_d(\mathbb{P}V))$ are equations for the corresponding cactus varieties.*

In the next section I explain how the cactus varieties fill the ambient space much faster than the secant varieties.

10.2.2 Local Cactus Rank and the Local Cactus Variety

Let $X \subset \mathbb{P}V$ be a variety. Fix $x \in X$, and define the *local X-cactus rank of $y \in \mathbb{P}V$ based at x*, denoted $\mathfrak{lcr}_{X,x}(y)$, to be the smallest r such that there exists a length r zero-dimensional scheme $Z \subset X$, with the support of Z equal to $\{x\}$, such that $y \in \langle Z \rangle$.

Define the *local cactus variety of X based at x* to be

$$\mathfrak{lc}_r(X, x) := \overline{\bigcup_{\substack{Z \subset X, \deg(Z) \le r, \\ \text{support}(Z) = x}} \langle Z \rangle} \subset \mathbb{P}V.$$

Of course, $\mathfrak{lc}_r(X, x) \subseteq \mathfrak{c}_r(X)$. Compare the local cactus variety with the greater areole of §5.4.4.

Given $f \in S^d \mathbb{C}^n$, define the dehomogenization $f_{x_n} := f(x_1, \ldots, x_{n-1}, 1) \in \mathbb{C}[x_1, \ldots, x_{n-1}]$ of f with respect to x_n.

Theorem 10.2.2.1 [BR13] *Let $f \in S^d \mathbb{C}^n$. Then*

$$\mathfrak{crs}(f) \le \mathfrak{lcr}_S\left(f, \left[x_n^d\right]\right) \le \dim(\text{Partials}(f_{x_n})).$$

Proof. The ideal defined by $(f_{x_n})^{ann}$ in $\mathbb{C}\left[\frac{\partial}{\partial x_1}, \ldots, \frac{\partial}{\partial x_{n-1}}\right]$ may be homogenized to define a homogeneous ideal in $\mathbb{C}\left[\frac{\partial}{\partial x_1}, \ldots, \frac{\partial}{\partial x_n}\right]$. Consider the subscheme of $\mathbb{P}^{n-1}$ defined by this homogeneous ideal. It has degree equal $\dim(\text{Partials}(f_{x_n}))$ and support $\{[0, \ldots, 0, 1]\}$. Assume f is concise. (If it is not, just start over in the smaller space.) I next show the homogenized $(f_{x_n})^{ann}$ is contained in f^{ann}.

Let $G \in (f_{x_n})^{ann} \subset \mathbb{C}\left[\frac{\partial}{\partial x_1}, \ldots, \frac{\partial}{\partial x_{n-1}}\right]$. Write $G = G_1 + \cdots + G_r$, where $\deg(G_j) = j$. (Note that $G_0 = 0$ in order that $G(f_{x_n}) = 0$.) Similarly, write $f_{x_n} = f_0 + \cdots + f_d$. Then $G(f_{x_n}) = 0$ says that for all $e \in \{0, \ldots, d-1\}$, $\sum_j G_j(f_{j+e}) = 0$. Let G^h be the homogenization of G, i.e., $G^h = (\frac{\partial}{\partial x_n})^{r-1} G_1 + (\frac{\partial}{\partial x_n})^{r-2} G_2 + \cdots + G_r$. Then, since $f = x_n^d f_0 + x_n^{d-1} f_1 + \cdots + f_d$,

$$G^h(f) = 0$$

if and only if

$$\sum_e \sum_j x_n^{d-r-e} G_j(f_{e+j}) = \sum_e x_n^{d-r-e} \sum_j G_j(f_{e+j}) = 0.$$

Thus the homogenization of $(f_{x_n})^{ann}$ is contained in f^{ann}, and $\mathfrak{lcr}(f, [x_n^d])$ is at most the degree of the scheme defined by f_{x_n}, which is $\dim(\text{Partials}(f_{x_n}))$. $\square$

Corollary 10.2.2.2 *Set $N_{n,d} = \sum_{j=0}^d \binom{n-1+j-1}{j}$. Then $\mathfrak{lc}_{N_{n,d}}(v_d(\mathbb{P}^{n-1}), [x_n^d]) = \mathfrak{c}_{N_{n,d}}(v_d(\mathbb{P}^{n-1})) = \mathbb{P}S^d \mathbb{C}^n$.*

Note that $N_{n,d} \sim 2\binom{n+\lceil \frac{d}{2} \rceil}{d} \ll \frac{1}{n}\binom{n+d-1}{d} =: r_{n,d}$, the latter being the smallest r such that $\sigma_r(v_d(\mathbb{P}^{n-1})) = \mathbb{P}S^d \mathbb{C}^n$ (except for a few exceptions where $r_{n,d}$ is even larger [AH95]; see [Lan12, §5.4.1] for a discussion).

So, for example, if $n = 2k + 1$ is odd, then the upper bound for cactus rank in $S^n \mathbb{C}^{n^2}$ grows as $2\binom{4k^2+5k}{k} \simeq 2(2k)^{2k}$ plus lower order terms, while the border rank upper bound is $\binom{4k^2+6k+1}{2k+1}/(2k+1)^2 \simeq (2k)^{4k}$ plus lower order terms. The even case is similar.

For $S^3\mathbb{C}^n$, we have the more precise result:

Theorem 10.2.2.3 [BR13] $\mathfrak{k}_{2n}(v_3(\mathbb{P}^{n-1})) = \mathbb{P}S^3\mathbb{C}^n$.

Compare this with the secant variety $\sigma_r(v_3(\mathbb{P}^{n-1}))$, which equals $\mathbb{P}S^3\mathbb{C}^n$ when $r = r_{n,3} = \lceil \frac{1}{n}\binom{n+2}{3} \rceil \sim \frac{n^2}{6}$.

For tensors, the same methods show $\mathfrak{k}_{2(\mathbf{a}+\mathbf{b}+\mathbf{c}-2)}(Seg(\mathbb{P}A \times \mathbb{P}B \times \mathbb{P}C), [a{\otimes}b{\otimes}c]) = \mathbb{P}(A{\otimes}B{\otimes}C)$ (J. Buczynski, personal communication). The precise filling r for the cactus variety is not known. However, since for $\mathbb{C}^m{\otimes}\mathbb{C}^m{\otimes}\mathbb{C}^m$, it is at most $6\mathbf{m}-4$, one will never prove superlinear border rank bounds for tensors with determinantal equations.

10.3 Nonnormality of $\mathcal{D}et_n$

We have already seen that $Ch_n(V)$ is not normal but that the coordinate ring of the normalization, the coordinate ring of the orbit $GL(V) \cdot [x_1 \cdots x_n]$, and the coordinate ring of $Ch_n(V)$ are all closely related. For the determinant we know far less. Not surprisingly, $\mathcal{D}et_n$ is not normal. I explain the proof in this section, which unfortunately is indirect, so it does not indicate relations between the three rings. By Remark 9.7.2.3 and the boundary component of §6.7.1, we know that the coordinate ring of the normalization of $\mathcal{D}et_n$ and the polynomial part of the coordinate ring of the orbit do not agree, but we know little about their difference. Here I at least show that the normalization is distinct from $\mathcal{D}et_n$.

I begin with generalities on $GL(W)$-orbits of points $P \in V$ with closed $SL(W)$-orbit. By a theorem of Kempf [Kem78, Corollary 5.1], the $SL(W)$-orbit of P is closed if the $SL(W)$-isotropy group is not contained in any proper parabolic subgroup of $SL(W)$, which is the case for the $SL(W)$-stabilizers of perm_n and $\det_n$.

I follow [Lan15a] in this section, which gives an exposition of the results of [Kum13].

10.3.1 Generalities on $GL(W)$-Orbit Closures

Throughout this section I make the following assumptions and adopt the following notation:

Set up:

- V is a $GL(W)$-module, and $P \in V$.
- $\mathcal{P}^0 := GL(W) \cdot P$ and $\mathcal{P} := \overline{GL(W) \cdot P}$, respectively, denote the $GL(W)$-orbit and $GL(W)$-orbit closure of P, and $\partial\mathcal{P} = \mathcal{P}\backslash\mathcal{P}^0$ denotes the boundary, which is assumed to be more than zero (otherwise $[\mathcal{P}]$ is homogeneous).

Assumptions: (10.3.1)

1 $P \in V$ is such that the $SL(W)$-orbit of P is closed.
2 The stabilizer $G_P \subset GL(W)$ is reductive, which is equivalent (by a theorem of Matsushima [Mat60]) to requiring that $\mathcal{P}^0$ is an affine variety.

This situation holds when $V = S^n W$, $\dim W = n^2$ and $P = \det_n$ or perm_n as well as when $\dim W = rn$ and $P = S_n^r := \sum_{j=1}^r x_1^j \cdots x_n^j$, the sum-product polynomial, in which case $\mathcal{P} = \hat{\sigma}_r(Ch_n(W))$.

Lemma 10.3.1.1 [Kum13] *Assumptions as in* (10.3.1). *Let* $M \subset \mathbb{C}[\mathcal{P}]$ *be a nonzero* $GL(W)$-*module, and let* $\operatorname{Zeros}(M) = \{y \in \mathcal{P} \mid f(y) = 0 \ \forall f \in M\}$ *denote its zero set. Then* $0 \subseteq \operatorname{Zeros}(M) \subseteq \partial \mathcal{P}$.

If, moreover, $M \subset I(\partial \mathcal{P})$, *then as sets,* $\operatorname{Zeros}(M) = \partial \mathcal{P}$.

Proof. Since $\operatorname{Zeros}(M)$ is a $GL(W)$-stable subset, if it contains a point of $\mathcal{P}^0$, it must contain all of $\mathcal{P}^0$, and thus M vanishes identically on $\mathcal{P}$, which cannot happen as M is nonzero. Thus $\operatorname{Zeros}(M) \subseteq \partial \mathcal{P}$. For the second assertion, since $M \subset I(\partial \mathcal{P})$, we also have $\operatorname{Zeros}(M) \supseteq \partial \mathcal{P}$.   □

Proposition 10.3.1.2 [Kum13] *Assumptions as in* (10.3.1). *The space of* $SL(W)$-*invariants of positive degree in the coordinate ring of* $\mathcal{P}$, $\mathbb{C}[\mathcal{P}]_{>0}^{SL(W)}$, *is nonempty and contained in* $I(\partial \mathcal{P})$. *Moreover,*

1 *any element of* $\mathbb{C}[\mathcal{P}]_{>0}^{SL(W)}$ *cuts out* $\partial \mathcal{P}$ *set-theoretically, and*
2 *the components of* $\partial \mathcal{P}$ *all have codimension one in* $\mathcal{P}$.

Proof. To study $\mathbb{C}[\mathcal{P}]^{SL(W)}$, consider the GIT quotient $\mathcal{P} /\!\!/ SL(W)$ whose coordinate ring, by definition, is $\mathbb{C}[\mathcal{P}]^{SL(W)}$. It parametrizes the closed $SL(W)$-orbits in $\mathcal{P}$, so it is nonempty. Thus $\mathbb{C}[\mathcal{P}]^{SL(W)}$ is nontrivial.

Claim: every $SL(W)$-orbit in $\partial \mathcal{P}$ contains $\{0\}$ in its closure, i.e., $\partial \mathcal{P}$ maps to zero in the GIT quotient. This will imply any $SL(W)$-invariant of positive degree is in $I(\partial \mathcal{P})$ because any nonconstant function on the GIT quotient vanishes on the inverse image of [0]. Thus (1) follows from Lemma 10.3.1.1. The zero set of a single polynomial, if it is not empty, has codimension one, which implies the components of $\partial \mathcal{P}$ are all of codimension one, proving (2).

Let $\rho : GL(W) \to GL(V)$ denote the representation. It remains to show $\partial \mathcal{P}$ maps to zero in $\mathcal{P} /\!\!/ SL(W)$. This GIT quotient inherits a $\mathbb{C}^*$ action via $\rho(\lambda \operatorname{Id})$, for $\lambda \in \mathbb{C}^*$. The normalization of $\mathcal{P} /\!\!/ SL(W)$ is just the affine line $\mathbb{A}^1 = \mathbb{C}$. To see this, consider the $\mathbb{C}^*$-equivariant map $\sigma : \mathbb{C} \to \mathcal{P}$ given by $z \mapsto \rho(z \operatorname{Id}) \cdot P$, which descends to a map $\overline{\sigma} : \mathbb{C} \to \mathcal{P} /\!\!/ SL(W)$. Since the $SL(W)$-orbit of P is closed, for any $\lambda \in \mathbb{C}^*$, $\rho(\lambda \operatorname{Id})P$ does not map to zero in the GIT quotient, so $\overline{\sigma}^{-1}([0]) = \{0\}$ as a set. Lemma 9.7.1.1 applies, so $\overline{\sigma}$ is finite and gives the normalization. Finally, were there a closed nonzero orbit in $\partial\mathcal{P}$, it would have to equal $SL(W) \cdot \sigma(\lambda)$ for some $\lambda \in \mathbb{C}^*$ since $\overline{\sigma}$ is surjective. But $SL(W) \cdot \sigma(\lambda)$ is contained in the image of $\mathcal{P}^0$ in $\mathcal{P} /\!/ SL(W)$. $\square$

Remark 10.3.1.3 That each irreducible component of $\partial\mathcal{P}$ is of codimension one in $\mathcal{P}$ is due to Matsushima [Mat60]. It is a consequence of his result that $\mathcal{P}^0$ is an affine variety if and only if the stabilizer is reductive.

The key to proving nonnormality of $\hat{\mathcal{D}et}_n$ and $\hat{\mathcal{P}erm}_n^n$ is to find an $SL(W)$-invariant in the coordinate ring of the normalization (which has a $GL(W)$-grading), which does not occur in the corresponding graded component of the coordinate ring of S^nW, so it cannot occur in the coordinate ring of any $GL(W)$-subvariety.

Lemma 10.3.1.4 *Assumptions as in* (10.3.1). *Let $V = S^nW$, and let d be the smallest positive $GL(W)$-degree such that $\mathbb{C}[\mathcal{P}^0]_d^{SL(W)} \neq 0$. If n is even (resp. odd) and $d < n\mathbf{w}$ (resp. $d < 2n\mathbf{w}$), then $\mathcal{P}$ is not normal.*

Proof. Since $\mathcal{P}^0 \subset \mathcal{P}$ is a Zariski open subset, we have the equality of $GL(W)$-modules $\mathbb{C}(\mathcal{P}) = \mathbb{C}(\mathcal{P}^0)$. By restriction of functions $\mathbb{C}[\mathcal{P}] \subset \mathbb{C}[\mathcal{P}^0]$ and thus $\mathbb{C}[\mathcal{P}]^{SL(W)} \subset \mathbb{C}[\mathcal{P}^0]^{SL(W)}$. Now $\mathcal{P}^0 /\!/ SL(W) = \mathcal{P}^0/SL(W) \simeq \mathbb{C}^*$ because $SL(W) \cdot P$ is closed, so $\mathbb{C}[\mathcal{P}^0]^{SL(W)} \simeq \bigoplus_{k \in \mathbb{Z}} \mathbb{C}\{z^k\}$. Under this identification, z has $GL(W)$-degree d. By Proposition 10.3.1.2, $\mathbb{C}[\mathcal{P}]^{SL(W)} \neq 0$. Let $h \in \mathbb{C}[\mathcal{P}]^{SL(W)}$ be the smallest element in positive degree. Then $h = z^k$ for some k. Were $\mathcal{P}$ normal, we would have $k = 1$.

But now we also have a surjection $\mathbb{C}[S^nW] \rightarrow \mathbb{C}[\mathcal{P}]$, and by [How87, Proposition 4.3a], the smallest possible $GL(W)$-degree of an $SL(W)$-invariant in $\mathbb{C}[S^nW]$ when n is even (resp. odd) is $\mathbf{w}n$ (resp. $2\mathbf{w}n$) which would occur in $S^{\mathbf{w}}(S^nW)$ (resp. $S^{2\mathbf{w}}(S^nW)$). We obtain a contradiction. $\square$

10.3.2 Case of $P = \det_n$ and $P = \text{perm}_n$

Theorem 10.3.2.1 (Kumar [Kum13]) *For all $n \geq 3$, $\mathcal{D}et_n = \overline{GL_{n^2} \cdot [\det_n]}$ and $\mathcal{P}erm_n^n = \overline{GL_{n^2} \cdot [\text{perm}_n]}$ are not normal. For all $n \geq 2m$ (the range of interest), $\mathcal{P}erm_n^m = \overline{GL_{n^2} \cdot [\ell^{n-m}\text{perm}_m]}$ is not normal.*

I give the proof for $\mathcal{D}et_n$, the case of $\mathcal{P}erm_n^n$ is an easy exercise. Despite the variety $\text{Zeros}(\ell^{n-m}\text{perm}_m)$ being much more singular than $\text{Zeros}(\text{perm}_n)$, the proof for $\mathcal{P}erm_n^m$ is more difficult; see [Kum13].

Proof. Let $\mathbb{C}[\mathcal{D}et_n^0]_{k-GL}^{SL(W)}$ denote the degree k GL-degree component of $\mathbb{C}[\mathcal{D}et_n^0]^{SL(W)}$ as defined in the proof of Lemma 10.3.1.4. I will show that when n is congruent to 0 or 1 mod 4, $\mathbb{C}[\mathcal{D}et_n^0]_{n-GL}^{SL(W)} \neq 0$ and when n is congruent to 2 or 3 mod 4, $\mathbb{C}[\mathcal{D}et_n^0]_{2n-GL}^{SL(W)} \neq 0$. Since $n, 2n < (n^2)n$, Lemma 10.3.1.4 applies.

The $SL(W)$-trivial modules are $(\Lambda^{n^2} W)^{\otimes s} = S_{(s^{n^2})}W$. Write $W = E \otimes F$. We want to determine the lowest degree trivial $SL(W)$-module that has a $G_{\det_n} = (SL(E) \times SL(F)/\mu_n) \rtimes \mathbb{Z}_2$ invariant. We have the decomposition $(\Lambda^{n^2} W)^{\otimes s} = (\bigoplus_{|\pi|=n^2} S_\pi E \otimes S_{\pi'} F)^{\otimes s}$, where π' is the conjugate partition to π. Thus $(\Lambda^{n^2} W)^{\otimes s}$ is the trivial $SL(E) \times SL(F)$ module $(S_{(n^n)}E \otimes S_{(n^n)}F)^{\otimes s} = S_{((sn)^n)}E \otimes S_{((sn)^n)}F$. Now consider the effect of the $\mathbb{Z}_2 \subset G_{\det_n}$ with generator $\tau \in GL(W)$. It sends $e_i \otimes f_j$ to $e_j \otimes f_i$, so acting on W, it has $+1$ eigenspace $\{e_i \otimes f_j + e_j \otimes f_i \mid i \leq j\}$ and -1 eigenspace $\{e_i \otimes f_j - e_j \otimes f_i \mid 1 \leq i < j \leq n\}$. Thus it acts on the one-dimensional vector space $(\Lambda^{n^2} W)^{\otimes s}$ by $((-1)^{\binom{n}{2}})^s$, i.e., by -1 if $n \equiv 2, 3$ mod 4 and s is odd and by 1 otherwise. We conclude that there is an invariant as needed for Lemma 10.3.1.4.   □

Remark 10.3.2.2 In the language of §8.8.2, in the proof above we saw $k_{s^{n^2}, (sn)^n, (sn)^n} = 1$, $sk_{(sn)^n, (sn)^n}^{s^{n^2}} = 1$ for all s when $\binom{n}{2}$ is even, and $sk_{(sn)^n, (sn)^n}^{s^{n^2}} = 1$ for even s when $\binom{n}{2}$ is odd and is zero for odd s.

Exercise 10.3.2.3 (2) Write out the proof of the nonnormality of $\mathcal{P}erm_n^n$.

Exercise 10.3.2.4 (2) Show the same method gives another proof that $Ch_n(W)$ is not normal.

Exercise 10.3.2.5 (2) Show a variant of the above holds for any reductive group with a nontrivial center (one gets a $\mathbb{Z}^k$-grading of modules if the center is k-dimensional), in particular it holds for $G = GL(A) \times GL(B) \times GL(C)$. Use this to show that $\sigma_r(Seg(\mathbb{P}A \times \mathbb{P}B \times \mathbb{P}C))$ is not normal when $\dim A = \dim B = \dim C = r > 2$.

10.4 The Minimal Free Resolution of the Ideal Generated by Minors of Size $r + 1$

I give an exposition of Lascoux's computation of the minimal free resolution of the ideals of the varieties of matrices of rank at most r from [Las78]. I expect it will be useful for the study of Valiant's hypothesis, as from it one can extract numerous algebraic properties of the determinant polynomial.

I follow the exposition in [ELSW15], which is based on the presentation in [Wey03].

10.4.1 Statement of the Result

Let $E, F = \mathbb{C}^n$, give $E \otimes F$ coordinates (x^i_j), with $1 \leq i, j \leq n$. Let $\hat{\sigma}_r = \hat{\sigma}_r(Seg(\mathbb{P}^{n-1} \times \mathbb{P}^{n-1})) \subset \mathbb{C}^n \otimes \mathbb{C}^n = E^* \otimes F^*$ denote the variety of $n \times n$ matrices of rank at most r. By "degree $S_\pi E$", I mean $|\pi| = p_1 + \cdots + p_n$, where $\pi = (p_1, \ldots, p_n)$. Write $\pi + \tilde{\pi} = (p_1 + \tilde{p}_1, \ldots, p_n + \tilde{p}_n)$.

Recall from §8.1.2 that the weight (under $GL(E) \times GL(F)$) of a monomial $x^{i_1}_{j_1} \cdots x^{i_q}_{j_q} \in S^q(E \otimes F)$ is given by a pair of n-tuples $((w^E_1, \ldots, w^E_n), (w^F_1, \ldots, w^F_n))$, where w^E_s is the number of i_α's equal to s and w^F_t is the number of j_α's equal to t.

Theorem 10.4.1.1 [Las78] *Let* $0 \to F_N \to \cdots \to F_1 \to Sym(E \otimes F) = F_0 \to \mathbb{C}[\hat{\sigma}_r] \to 0$ *denote the minimal free resolution of* $\mathbb{C}[\hat{\sigma}_r]$*. Then*

1. $N = (n - r)^2$*, i.e.,* $\hat{\sigma}_r$ *is arithmetically Cohen-Macaulay.*
2. $\hat{\sigma}_r$ *is Gorenstein, i.e.,* $F_N \simeq Sym(E \otimes F)$*, generated by* $S_{(n-r)^n}E \otimes S_{(n-r)^n}F$*. In particular* $F_{N-j} \simeq F_j$ *as* $SL(E) \times SL(F)$*-modules, although they are not isomorphic as* $GL(E) \times GL(F)$*-modules.*
3. *For* $1 \leq j \leq N - 1$*, the space* F_j *has generating modules of degree* $sr + j$*, where* $1 \leq s \leq \lfloor\sqrt{j}\rfloor$*. The modules of degree* $r + j$ *form the generators of the linear strand of the minimal free resolution.*
4. *The generating module of* F_j *is multiplicity free.*
5. *Let* α, β *be (possibly zero) partitions such that* $l(\alpha), l(\beta) \leq s$*. Independent of the lengths (even if they are zero), write* $\alpha = (\alpha_1, \ldots, \alpha_s)$*,* $\beta = (\beta_1, \ldots, \beta_s)$*. The space of degree* $sr + j$ *generators of* F_j*, for* $1 \leq j \leq N$ *is the module*

$$M_{j,rs+j} = \bigoplus_{\substack{|\alpha|+|\beta|=j-s^2 \\ l(\alpha),l(\beta) \leq s}} S_{(s^{r+s})+(\alpha,0^r,\beta')}E \otimes S_{(s^{r+s})+(\beta,0^r,\alpha')}F. \qquad (10.4.1)$$

The Young diagrams of the modules are depicted in Figure 10.4.1.

6. *In particular, the generator of the linear component of* F_j *is*

$$M_{j,j+r} = \bigoplus_{a+b=j-1} S_{a+1,1^{r+b}}E \otimes S_{b+1,1^{r+a}}F. \qquad (10.4.2)$$

Remark 10.4.1.2 The module $M_{j,j+r}$ admits a basis as follows: form a size $r + j$ submatrix using $r + b + 1$ distinct rows, repeating a subset of a rows to have the correct number of rows and $r + a + 1$ distinct columns, repeating a subset of b columns, and then performing a "tensor Laplace expansion" as described below.

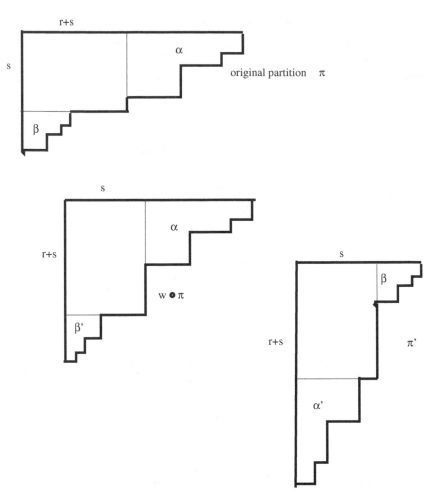

Figure 10.4.1 Partition π and pairs of partitions $(s^{r+s}) + (\alpha, 0^r, \beta') = w \cdot \pi$ and $(s^{r+s}) + (\beta, 0^r, \alpha') = \pi'$ it gives rise to in the resolution (see §10.4.5 for explanations).

10.4.2 The Koszul Resolution

The minimal free resolution of $Sym(V)_{>0}$ is given by the exact complex

$$\cdots \to S^{q-1}V \otimes \Lambda^{p+2}V \to S^q V \otimes \Lambda^{p+1}V \to S^{q+1}V \otimes \Lambda^p V \to \cdots \quad (10.4.3)$$

The maps are given by the transpose of exterior derivative (Koszul) map $d_{p,q} : S^q V^* \otimes \Lambda^{p+1}V^* \to S^{q-1}V^* \otimes \Lambda^{p+2}V^*$. Write $d_{p,q}^T : S^{q-1}V \otimes \Lambda^{p+2}V \to S^q V \otimes \Lambda^{p+1}V$. The Pieri rule (§8.1.3) implies the $GL(V)$-decomposition

$S^q V \otimes \Lambda^{p+1} V = S_{(q,1^{p+1})} V \oplus S_{(q+1,1^p)} V$, so the kernel of $d_{p,q}^T$ is the first module, which also is the image of $d_{p+1,q-1}^T$.

Explicitly, $d_{p,q}^T$ is the composition of polarization ($\Lambda^{p+2} V \to \Lambda^{p+1} V \otimes V$) and multiplication:

$$S^{q-1} V \otimes \Lambda^{p+2} V \to S^{q-1} V \otimes \Lambda^{p+1} V \otimes V \to S^q V \otimes \Lambda^{p+1} V.$$

For the minimal free resolution of any ideal, the linear strand will embed inside (10.4.3).

10.4.3 Geometry of the Terms in the Linear Strand

For $T \in S^\kappa V \otimes V^{\otimes j}$, and $P \in S^\ell V$, introduce notation for multiplication on the first factor, $T \cdot P \in S^{\kappa+\ell} V \otimes V^{\otimes j}$. Write $F_j = M_j \cdot Sym(V)$. As always, $M_0 = \mathbb{C}$. Note that $F_1 = M_1 \cdot Sym(E \otimes F)$, where $M_1 = M_{1,r+1} = \Lambda^{r+1} E \otimes \Lambda^{r+1} F$, the size $r+1$ minors which generate the ideal. The syzygies among the elements of F_1 are generated by

$$M_2 = M_{2,r+2} := S_{1^{r+2}} E \otimes S_{21^r} F \oplus S_{21^r} E \otimes S_{1^{r+2}} F \subset I(\sigma_r)_{r+2} \otimes V$$

(i.e., $F_2 = M_2 \cdot Sym(E \otimes F)$), where elements in the first module may be obtained by choosing $r+1$ rows and $r+2$ columns, forming a size $r+2$ square matrix by repeating one of the rows, then doing a "tensor Laplace expansion" as follows:

In the case $r=1$ the highest weight vector of M_2 is

$$\begin{aligned} S_{123}^{1|12} :&= \left(x_2^1 x_3^2 - x_2^2 x_3^1 \right) \otimes x_1^1 - \left(x_1^1 x_3^2 - x_1^2 x_3^1 \right) \otimes x_2^1 + \left(x_1^1 x_2^2 - x_2^1 x_1^2 \right) \otimes x_3^1 \\ &= M_{23}^{12} \otimes x_1^1 - M_{13}^{12} \otimes x_2^1 + M_{12}^{12} \otimes x_3^1, \end{aligned} \qquad (10.4.4)$$

a tensor Laplace expansion of a 3×3 matrix with first row repeated. In general, M_J^I will denote the minor obtained from the submatrix with indices I, J. To see (10.4.4) is indeed a highest weight vector, first observe that it has the correct weights in both E and F, and that in the F-indices $\{1, 2, 3\}$ it is skew and that in the first two E indices it is also skew. Finally, to see it is a highest weight vector, note that any raising operator sends it to zero. Also note that under the multiplication map $S^2 V \otimes V \to S^3 V$, the element maps to zero, because the map corresponds to converting a tensor Laplace expansion to an actual one, but the determinant of a matrix with a repeated row is zero.

In general, a basis of $S_\pi E \otimes S_\mu F$ is indexed by pairs of semistandard Young tableau in π and μ. In the linear strand, all partitions appearing are hooks, a basis of $S_{a,1^b} E$ is given by two sequences of integers taken from $[n]$, one weakly increasing of length a and one strictly increasing of length b, where the first integer in the first sequence is at least the first integer in the second sequence.

A highest weight vector in $S_{21^r} E \otimes S_{1^{r+2}} F$ is

$$S_{1,\dots,r+2}^{1|1,\dots,r+1} = M_{2,\dots,r+2}^{1,\dots,r+1} \otimes x_1^1 - M_{1,3,\dots,r+1}^{1,\dots,r+1} \otimes x_2^1 + \cdots + (-1)^r M_{1,\dots,r+1}^{1,\dots,r+1} \otimes x_{r+2}^1,$$

a tensor Laplace expansion of a size $r + 2$ matrix with repeated first row. The same argument as above shows it has the desired properties. Other basis vectors are obtained by applying lowering operators to the highest weight vector, so their expressions will be more complicated.

Remark 10.4.3.1 If we chose a size $r + 2$ submatrix, and perform a tensor Laplace expansion of its determinant about two different rows, the difference of the two expressions corresponds to a linear syzygy, but such linear syzygies are in the span of M_2. These expressions are important for comparison with the permanent, as they are the only linear syzygies for the ideal generated by the size $r + 1$ subpermanents, where one takes the permanental Laplace expansion.

Continuing, F_3 is generated by the module

$$M_{3,r+3} = S_{1^{r+3}} E \otimes S_{3,1^r} F \oplus S_{2,1^{r+1}} E \otimes S_{2,1^{r+1}} F \oplus S_{3,1^r} E \otimes S_{1^{r+3}} F \subset M_2 \otimes V.$$

These modules admit bases of double tensor Laplace type expansions of a square submatrix of size $r + 3$. In the first case, the highest weight vector is obtained from the submatrix whose rows are the first $r + 3$ rows of the original matrix, and whose columns are the first r-columns with the first column occurring three times. For the second module, the highest weight vector is obtained from the submatrix whose rows and columns are the first $r + 2$ such, with the first row and column occuring twice. A highest weight vector for $S_{3,1^r} E \otimes S_{1^{r+3}} F$ is

$$S_{1,\dots,r+3}^{11|1,\dots,r+1} = \sum_{1 \leq \beta_1 < \beta_2 \leq r+3} (-1)^{\beta_1 + \beta_2} M_{1,\dots,\hat{\beta_1},\dots,\hat{\beta_2},\dots,r+3}^{1,\dots,r+1} \otimes \left(x_{\beta_1}^1 \wedge x_{\beta_2}^1 \right)$$

$$= \sum_{\beta=1}^{r+3} (-1)^{\beta+1} S_{1,\dots,\hat{\beta},\dots,r+3}^{1|1,\dots,i_{r+1}} \otimes x_\beta^1.$$

Here $S_{1,\dots,\hat{\beta},\dots,r+3}^{1|1,\dots,i_{r+1}}$ is defined in the same way as the highest weight vector.

A highest weight vector for $S_{2,1^{r+1}}E \otimes S_{2,1^{r+1}}F$ is

$$S_{1|1,\ldots,r+2}^{1|1,\ldots,r+3} = \sum_{\alpha,\beta=1}^{r+3} (-1)^{\alpha+\beta} M_{1,\ldots,\beta,\ldots,i+2}^{1,\ldots,\hat{\alpha},\ldots,r+2} \otimes \left(x_1^{\alpha} \wedge x_{\beta}^1\right)$$

$$= \sum_{\beta=1}^{r+3}(-1)^{\beta+1} S_{1|1,\ldots,\hat{\beta},\ldots,r+2}^{1,\ldots,r+2} \otimes x_{\beta}^1 - \sum_{\alpha=1}^{r+3}(-1)^{\alpha+1} S_{1,\ldots,r+2}^{1|1,\ldots,\hat{\alpha},\ldots,r+3} \otimes x_1^{\alpha}.$$

Here $S_{1|1,\ldots,\hat{\beta},\ldots,r+2}^{1,\ldots,r+2}$, $S_{1,\ldots,r+2}^{1|1,\ldots,\hat{\alpha},\ldots,r+3}$ are defined in the same way as the corresponding highest weight vectors.

Proposition 10.4.3.2 *The highest weight vector of* $S_{p+1,1^{r+q}}E \otimes S_{q+1,1^{r+p}}F \subset M_{p+q+1,r+p+q+1}$ *is*

$$S_{1^q|1,\ldots,r+p+1}^{1^p|1,\ldots,r+q+1} =$$

$$\sum_{\substack{I \subset [r+q+1],|I|=q, \\ J \subset [r+p+1],|J|=p}} (-1)^{|I|+|J|} M_{1,\ldots,\hat{j}_1,\ldots,\hat{j}_p,\ldots,(r+p+1)}^{1,\ldots,\hat{i}_1,\ldots,\hat{i}_q,\ldots,(r+q+1)} \otimes \left(x_{j_1}^1 \wedge \cdots \wedge x_{j_p}^1 \wedge x_1^{i_1} \wedge \cdots \wedge x_1^{i_q}\right).$$

A hatted index is one that is omitted from the summation.

Proof. It is clear the expression has the correct weight and is a highest weight vector and that it lies in $S^{r+1}V \otimes \Lambda^{p+q}V$. I now show it maps to zero under the differential.

Under the map $d^T : S^{r+1}V \otimes \Lambda^{p+q}V \to S^rV \otimes \Lambda^{p+q+1}V$, the element $S_{1^q|1,\ldots,r+p+1}^{1^p|1,\ldots,r+q+1}$ maps to

$$\sum_{\substack{I \subset [r+q+1],|I|=q, \\ J \subset [r+p+1],|J|=p}} (-1)^{|I|+|J|}$$

$$\left[\sum_{\alpha \in I} (-1)^{p+\alpha} M_{1,\ldots,\hat{j}_1,\ldots,\hat{j}_p,\ldots,(r+p+1)}^{1,\ldots,\hat{i}_1,\ldots,\hat{i}_q,\ldots,(r+q+1)} x_1^{i_{\alpha}} \otimes \left(x_{j_1}^1 \wedge \cdots \wedge x_{j_p}^1 \wedge x_1^{i_1} \wedge \cdots \wedge \hat{x}_1^{i_{\alpha}} \wedge \cdots \wedge x_1^{i_q}\right) \right.$$

$$\left. + \sum_{\beta \in J} (-1)^{\beta} M_{1,\ldots,\hat{j}_1,\ldots,\hat{j}_p,\ldots,(r+p+1)}^{1,\ldots,\hat{i}_1,\ldots,\hat{i}_q,\ldots,(r+q+1)} x_{j_{\beta}}^1 \otimes \left(x_{j_1}^1 \wedge \cdots \wedge \hat{x}_{j_{\beta}}^1 \wedge \cdots \wedge x_{j_p}^1 \wedge x_1^{i_1} \wedge \cdots \wedge x_1^{i_q}\right) \right].$$

Fix I and all indices in J but one, call the resulting index set J', and consider the resulting term

$$\sum_{\beta \in [r+p+1] \backslash J'} (-1)^{f(\beta,J')} M_{1,\ldots,\hat{j}_1,\ldots,\hat{j}_{p-1},\ldots,(r+p+1)}^{1,\ldots,\hat{i}_1,\ldots,\hat{i}_q,\ldots,(r+q+1)} x_{\beta}^1 \otimes \left(x_{j_1'}^1 \wedge \cdots \wedge x_{j_{p-1}'}^1 \wedge x_1^{i_1} \wedge \cdots \wedge x_1^{i_q}\right),$$

where $f(\beta,J')$ equals the number of $j' \in J$ less than β. This term is the Laplace expansion of the determinant of a matrix of size $r+1$, which has its first row appearing twice, and is thus zero. $\square$

Notice that if $q, p > 0$, then $S_{1^q|1,\ldots,r+p+1}^{1^p|1,\ldots,r+q+1}$ is the sum of terms including $S_{1^{q-1}|1,\ldots,r+p+1}^{1^p|1,\ldots,r+q} \otimes x_1^{r+q+1}$ and $S_{1^q|1,\ldots,r+p}^{1^{p-1}|1,\ldots,r+q+1} \otimes x_{r+p+1}^1$. This implies the following corollary:

Corollary 10.4.3.3 (Roberts [Rob17]) *Each module $S_{a,1^{r+b}}E \otimes S_{b,1^{r+a}}F$, where $a + b = j$ that appears with multiplicity one in $F_{j,j+r}$, appears with multiplicity two in $F_{j-1,j+r}$ if $a, b > 0$, and multiplicity one if a or b is zero. The map $F_{j,j+r+1} \to F_{j-1,j+r+1}$ restricted to $S_{a,1^{r+b}}E \otimes S_{b,1^{r+a}}F$, maps nonzero to both $(S_{a-1,1^{r+b}}E \otimes S_{b,1^{r+a-1}}F) \cdot E \otimes F$ and $(S_{a,1^{r+b-1}}E \otimes S_{b-1,1^{r+a}}F) \cdot E \otimes F$.*

Proof. The multiplicities and realizations come from applying the Pieri rule. (Note that if a is zero, the first module does not exist, and if b is zero, the second module does not exist.) That the maps to each of these is nonzero follows from the observation above. □

Remark 10.4.3.4 In [Rob17] it is proven more generally that all the natural realizations of the irreducible modules in M_j have nonzero maps onto every natural realization of the module in F_{j-1}. Moreover, the constants in all the maps are determined explicitly.

10.4.4 Comparison with the Ideal Generated by Subpermanents

Let $E, F = \mathbb{C}^n$, $V = E \otimes F$, let $I_\kappa^{\mathrm{perm}_n, \kappa} \subset S^\kappa(E \otimes F)$ denote the span of the subpermanents of size κ, and let $I^{\mathrm{perm}_n, \kappa} \subset Sym(E \otimes F)$ denote the ideal it generates. Note that $\dim(I_\kappa^{\mathrm{perm}_n, \kappa}) = \binom{n}{\kappa}^2$. Fix complete flags $0 \subset E_1 \subset \cdots \subset E_n = E$ and $0 \subset F_1 \subset \cdots \subset F_n = F$. Write $\mathfrak{S}_{E_j}$ for the copy of $\mathfrak{S}_j$ acting on E_j and similarly for F.

Write $T_E \subset SL(E)$ for the maximal torus (diagonal matrices). Recall from Theorem 6.6.2.2 that G_{perm_n} is $[(T_E \times \mathfrak{S}_E) \times (T_F \times \mathfrak{S}_F)] \rtimes \mathbb{Z}_2$, divided by the nth roots of unity.

Introduce the notation $\tilde{\mathfrak{S}}_\kappa = \mathfrak{S}_\kappa \times \mathfrak{S}_{n-\kappa} \subset \mathfrak{S}_n$, and if π is a partition of κ, write $[\widetilde{\pi}] = [\pi] \times [n - \kappa]$ for the $\tilde{\mathfrak{S}}_\kappa$-module that is $[\pi]$ as an $\mathfrak{S}_\kappa$-module and trivial as an $\mathfrak{S}_{n-\kappa}$-module. For finite groups $H \subset G$, and an H-module W, $Ind_H^G W = \mathbb{C}[G] \otimes_{\mathbb{C}[H]} W$ is the induced G-module, which has dimension equal to $(\dim W)|G|/|H|$ (see, e.g., [FH91, §3.4]), and that $\dim[\pi]$ is given by the hook-length formula (see, e.g., [FH91, p. 50]). These two facts give the dimensions asserted below.

As an $\mathfrak{S}_{E_n} \times \mathfrak{S}_{F_n}$ module the space $I_\kappa^{\mathrm{perm}_n, \kappa}$ decomposes as

$$Ind_{\tilde{\mathfrak{S}}_{E_\kappa} \times \tilde{\mathfrak{S}}_{F_\kappa}}^{\mathfrak{S}_{E_n} \times \mathfrak{S}_{F_n}} ([\widetilde{\kappa}]_{E_\kappa} \otimes [\widetilde{\kappa}]_{F_\kappa}) = ([n]_E \oplus [n-1, 1]_E \oplus \cdots \oplus$$

$$[n - \kappa, \kappa]_E) \otimes ([n]_F \oplus [n-1, 1]_F \oplus \cdots \oplus [n - \kappa, \kappa]_F). \quad (10.4.5)$$

The space of linear syzygies $M_{2,\kappa+1} := \ker(I_\kappa^{\mathrm{perm}_n,\kappa} \otimes V \to S^{\kappa+1}V)$ is the $\mathfrak{S}_{E_n} \times \mathfrak{S}_{F_n}$-module

$$M_{2,\kappa+1} = Ind_{\tilde{\mathfrak{S}}_{E_{\kappa+1}} \times \tilde{\mathfrak{S}}_{F_{\kappa+1}}}^{\mathfrak{S}_{E_n} \times \mathfrak{S}_{F_n}} (\widetilde{[\kappa+1]}_{E_{\kappa+1}} \otimes \widetilde{[\kappa,1]}_{F_{\kappa+1}} \oplus \widetilde{[\kappa,1]}_{E_{\kappa+1}} \otimes \widetilde{[\kappa+1]}_{F_{\kappa+1}}).$$

This module has dimension $2\kappa\binom{n}{\kappa+1}^2$. A spanning set for it may be obtained geometrically as follows: for each size $\kappa+1$ submatrix, perform the permanental tensor Laplace expansion along a row or column, then perform a second tensor Laplace expansion about a row or column and take the difference. An independent set of such for a given size $\kappa+1$ submatrix may be obtained from the expansions along the first row minus the expansion along the jth for $j = 2, \ldots, \kappa+1$, and then from the expansion along the first column minus the expansion along the jth, for $j = 2, \ldots, \kappa+1$.

Remark 10.4.4.1 Compare this with the space of linear syzygies for the determinant, which has dimension $\frac{2\kappa(n+1)}{n-\kappa}\binom{n}{\kappa+1}^2$. The ratio of their sizes is $\frac{n+1}{n-\kappa}$, so, e.g., when $\kappa \sim \frac{n}{2}$, the determinant has about twice as many linear syzygies, and if κ is close to n, one gets nearly n times as many.

Theorem 10.4.4.2 [ELSW15] $\dim M_{j+1,\kappa+j} = \binom{n}{\kappa+j}^2\binom{2(\kappa+j-1)}{j}$. As an $\mathfrak{S}_E \times \mathfrak{S}_F$-module,

$$M_{j+1,\kappa+j} = Ind_{\tilde{\mathfrak{S}}_{E_{\kappa+j}} \times \tilde{\mathfrak{S}}_{F_{\kappa+j}}}^{\mathfrak{S}_{E_n} \times \mathfrak{S}_{F_n}} \left(\bigoplus_{a+b=j} \widetilde{[\kappa+b, 1^a]}_{E_{\kappa+j}} \otimes \widetilde{[\kappa+a, 1^b]}_{F_{\kappa+j}} \right). \quad (10.4.6)$$

The $\binom{n}{\kappa+j}^2$ is just the choice of a size $\kappa+j$ submatrix, the $\binom{2(\kappa+j-1)}{j}$ comes from choosing a set of j elements from the set of rows union columns. Naïvely, there are $\binom{2(\kappa+j)}{j}$ choices, but there is redundancy as with the choices in the description of M_2.

The proof proceeds in two steps. As described below, one first gets "for free" the minimal free resolution of the ideal generated by $S^\kappa E \otimes S^\kappa F$. Write the generating modules of this resolution as $\tilde{M}_j$. One then locates the generators of the linear strand of the minimal free resolution of the ideal, whose generators I denote $M_{j+1,\kappa+j}$, inside $\tilde{M}_{j+1,\kappa+j}$ and proves the assertion.

To obtain $\tilde{M}_{j+1}$, use the Howe-Young endofunctor mentioned in §8.11.1.1 that comes from the involution on symmetric functions that takes the Schur function s_π to $s_{\pi'}$ (see, e.g., [Mac95, §I.2]). This involution extends to an endofunctor of $GL(V)$-modules and hence of $GL(E) \times GL(F)$-modules, taking $S_\lambda E \otimes S_\mu F$ to $S_{\lambda'} E \otimes S_{\mu'} F$ (see [AW07, §2.4]). This is only true as long as the dimensions of the vector spaces are sufficiently large, so to properly define it, one passes to countably infinite-dimensional vector spaces.

Applying this functor to the resolution (10.4.1), one obtains the resolution of the ideal generated by $S^\kappa E \otimes S^\kappa F \subset S^\kappa (E \otimes F)$. The $GL(E) \times GL(F)$-modules generating the linear component of the jth term in this resolution are

$$\tilde{M}_{j,j+\kappa-1} = \bigoplus_{a+b=j-1} S_{(a,1^{\kappa+b})} E \otimes S_{(b,1^{\kappa+a})} F \qquad (10.4.7)$$

$$= \bigoplus_{a+b=j-1} S_{(\kappa+b+1,1^{a-1})} E \otimes S_{(\kappa+a+1,1^{b-1})} F.$$

Moreover, by Corollary 10.4.3.3 and functoriality, the map from $S_{(\kappa+b+1,1^{a-1})} E \otimes S_{(\kappa+a+1,1^{b-1})} F$ into $\tilde{M}_{j-1,j+\kappa-1}$ is nonzero to the copies of $S_{(\kappa+b+1,1^{a-1})} E \otimes S_{(\kappa+a+1,1^{b-1})} F$ in

$$(S_{\kappa+b,1^{a-1}} E \otimes S_{\kappa+a+1,1^{b-2}} F) \cdot (E \otimes F) \text{ and } (S_{\kappa+b+1,1^{a-2}} E \otimes S_{\kappa+a,1^{b-1}} F) \cdot (E \otimes F),$$

when $a, b > 0$.

Inside $S^\kappa E \otimes S^\kappa F$ is the ideal generated by the subpermanents (10.4.5) which consists of the regular weight spaces $(p_1, \ldots, p_n) \times (q_1, \ldots, q_n)$, where all p_i, q_j are either zero or one. (Each subpermanent has such a weight, and, given such a weight, there is a unique subpermanent to which it corresponds.) The set of regular vectors in any $E^{\otimes m} \otimes F^{\otimes m}$ spans a $\mathfrak{S}_E \times \mathfrak{S}_F$-submodule.

The linear strand of the jth term in the minimal free resolution of the ideal generated by (10.4.5) is thus a $\mathfrak{S}_E \times \mathfrak{S}_F$-submodule of $\tilde{M}_{j,j+\kappa-1}$. I claim this submodule is the span of the regular vectors. In other words:

Lemma 10.4.4.3 [ELSW15] $M_{j+1,\kappa+j} = (\tilde{M}_{j+1,\kappa+j})_{reg}$.

For the proof, see [ELSW15]. Theorem 10.4.4.2 follows because if π is a partition of $\kappa + j$, then the weight $(1, \ldots, 1)$ subspace of $S_\pi E_{\kappa+j}$, considered as an $\mathfrak{S}_{E_{\kappa+j}}$-module, is $[\pi]$ by Theorem 9.2.2.1, and the space of regular vectors in $S_\pi E \otimes S_\mu F$ is $Ind_{\mathfrak{S}_{E_{\kappa+j}} \times \mathfrak{S}_{F_{\kappa+j}}}^{\mathfrak{S}_E \times \mathfrak{S}_F} ([\tilde{\pi}]_E \otimes [\tilde{\mu}]_F)$.

10.4.5 Proof of Theorem 10.4.1.1

The variety $\hat{\sigma}_r$ admits a desingularization by the geometric method of [Wey03], namely, consider the Grassmannian $G(r, E^*)$ and the vector bundle $p : S \otimes F \to G(r, E^*)$ whose fiber over $x \in G(r, E^*)$ is $x \otimes F$. (Although I am breaking symmetry here, it will be restored in the end.) The total space admits the interpretation as the incidence variety

$$\{(x, \phi) \in G(r, E^*) \times \text{Hom}(F, E^*) \mid \phi(F) \subseteq x\},$$

and the projection to $\text{Hom}(F, E^*) = E^* \otimes F^*$ has image $\hat{\sigma}_r$. One also has the exact sequence

$$0 \to \mathcal{S} \otimes F^* \to \underline{E^* \otimes F^*} \to \mathcal{Q} \otimes F^* \to 0,$$

where $\underline{E^* \otimes F^*}$ denotes the trivial bundle with fiber $E^* \otimes F^*$ and $\mathcal{Q} = \underline{E^*}/\mathcal{S}$ is the quotient bundle. As explained in [Wey03], letting $q : \mathcal{S} \otimes F^* \to E^* \otimes F^*$ denote the projection, q is a desingularization of $\hat{\sigma}_r$, the higher direct images $\mathcal{R}_i q^* (\mathcal{O}_{\mathcal{S} \otimes F^*})$ are zero for $i > 0$, and so by [Wey03, Theorems 5.12,5.13] one concludes $F_i = M_i \cdot Sym(E \otimes F)$, where

$$M_i = \bigoplus_{j \geq 0} H^j(G(r, E^*), \Lambda^{i+j}(\mathcal{Q}^* \otimes F))$$

$$= \bigoplus_{j \geq 0} \bigoplus_{|\pi|=i+j} H^j(G(r, E^*), S_\pi \mathcal{Q}^*) \otimes S_{\pi'} F.$$

One now uses the Bott-Borel-Weil theorem to compute these cohomology groups. Homogeneous vector bundles on the Grassmannian $G(r, n)$ are indexed by sequences $(k_1, \ldots, k_n)$, where $k_1 \geq k_2 \cdots \geq k_r$ and $k_{r+1} \geq k_{r+2} \geq \cdots \geq k_n$. An algorithm for implementing the Bott-Borel-Weil theorem is given in [Wey03, Rem. 4.1.5]: if $\pi = (p_1, \ldots, p_q)$ (where we must have $p_1 \leq n$ to have $S_{\pi'} F$ nonzero, and $q \leq n - r$ as rank $\mathcal{Q} = n - r$), then $S_\pi \mathcal{Q}^*$ is the vector bundle corresponding to the sequence

$$(0^r, p_1, \ldots, p_{n-r}). \tag{10.4.8}$$

The dotted Weyl action by $\sigma_i = (i, i+1) \in \mathfrak{S}_n$ is

$$\sigma_i \cdot (\alpha_1, \ldots, \alpha_n) = (\alpha_1, \ldots, \alpha_{i-1}, \alpha_{i+1} - 1, \alpha_i + 1, \alpha_{i+2}, \ldots, \alpha_n),$$

and one applies simple reflections to try to transform α to a partition until one either gets a partition after u simple reflections, in which case, the cohomology group $H^u(G(r, E^*), S_\pi \mathcal{Q}^*)$ is equal to the module associated to the partition one ends up with and all other cohomology groups are zero, or one ends up on a wall of the Weyl chamber, i.e., at one step one has $(\beta_1, \ldots, \beta_n)$ with some $\beta_{i+1} = \beta_i + 1$, in which case, there is no cohomology.

In our case, we need to move p_1 over to the first position in order to obtain a partition, which means we need $p_1 \geq r + 1$, and then if $p_2 < 2$, we are done; otherwise, we need to move it, etc. The upshot is we can get cohomology only if there is an s such that $p_s \geq r + s$ and $p_{s+1} < s + 1$, in which case we get

$$S_{(p_1-r, \ldots, p_s-r, s^r, p_{s+1}, \ldots, p_{n-r})} E \otimes S_{\pi'} F$$

contributing to $H^{rs}(G(r, E^*), S_\pi \mathcal{Q}^*)$. Say we are in this situation; then write $(p_1 - r - s, \ldots, p_s - r - s) = \alpha$, $(p_{s+1}, \ldots, p_{n-r}) = \beta'$, so

$$(p_1 - r, \ldots, p_s - r, s^r, p_{s+1}, \ldots, p_{n-r}) = (s^{r+s}) + (\alpha, 0^r, \beta'),$$

and moreover, we may write

$$\pi' = (s^{r+s}) + (\beta, 0^r, \alpha'),$$

proving Theorem 10.4.1.1. The case $s = 1$ gives the linear strand of the resolution.

Hints and Answers to Selected Exercises

Chapter 1

1.1.15.1 In general, the trilinear map associated to a bilinear form is $(u, v, \gamma) \mapsto \gamma(T(u, v))$. Let z_v^{*u} denote the linear form that eats a matrix and returns its (u, v)th entry. Since $(XY)_k^i = \sum_j x_j^i y_k^j$, the associated trilinear map is $(X, Y, z_v^{*u}) \mapsto \sum_j x_j^u y_v^j$. On the other hand, $\text{trace}(XYZ) = \sum_{i,j,k} x_j^i y_k^j z_i^k$. Now observe that both these agree, e.g., on basis vectors.

Chapter 2

2.1.1.4 For the second assertion, a generic matrix will have nonzero determinant. For the last assertion, first say $\text{rank}(f) = r' \le r$ and let $v_1, \ldots, v_{\mathbf{v}}$ be a basis of V such that the kernel is spanned by the last $\mathbf{v} - r'$ vectors. Then the matrix representing f will be nonzero only in the upper $r' \times r'$ block and thus all minors of size greater than r' will be zero. Next say $\text{rank}(f) = s > r$. In the same manner, we see the upper right size s submatrix will have a nonzero determinant. Taking a Laplace expansion, we see at least one size $r + 1$ minor of it is nonzero. In any other choice of basis minors expressed in the new basis are linear combinations of minors expressed in the old, so we conclude. For the last assertion, since polynomials are continuous, if f_t is in the zero set of all size $(r + 1)$ minors, so will its continous limit f.

2.1.1.5 $v \in V$ goes to the map $\beta \mapsto \beta(v)$.

2.1.2.1 A multilinear map is determined by its action on bases of $A_1^*, \ldots, A_n^*$.

2.1.2.4 See (4.1.1).

2.1.5.2 Write an arbitrary rank two tensor as $(\alpha_1 a_1 + \alpha_2 a_2) \otimes (\beta_1 b_1 + \beta_2 b_2) \otimes (\gamma_1 c_1 + \gamma_1 c_2) + (\alpha_1' a_1 + \alpha_2' a_2) \otimes (\beta_1' b_1 + \beta_2' b_2) \otimes (\gamma_1' c_1 + \gamma_1' c_2)$ where the Greek letters are arbitrary constants and show they cannot be chosen to make the tensor equal to $a_1 \otimes b_1 \otimes c_2 + a_1 \otimes b_2 \otimes c_1 + a_2 \otimes b_1 \otimes c_1$.

2.1.5.4 See §3.1.6.

2.1.6.1 For example, take $a_1 \otimes b_1 \otimes c_2 + a_1 \otimes b_2 \otimes c_1 + a_2 \otimes b_1 \otimes c_1 + \sum_{j=3}^{r} a_j \otimes b_j \otimes c_j$.

2.1.6.2 If $T = \sum_{i=1}^{r} a_i \otimes b_i \otimes c_i$, then, letting $\pi_A : A \to A/(A')^{\perp}$ be the projection, and similarly for B, C, $T_{A' \otimes B' \otimes C'} = \sum_{i=1}^{r} \pi_A(a_i) \otimes \pi_B(b_i) \otimes \pi(c_i)$.

2.1.7.2 First assume $\underline{\mathbf{R}}(T) = \mathbf{R}(T)$ and write $T = a_1 \otimes b_1 \otimes c_1 + \cdots + a_r \otimes b_r \otimes c_r$. Then $T(A^*) = \mathrm{span}\{b_1 \otimes c_1, \ldots, b_r \otimes c_r\}$, so $\underline{\mathbf{R}}(T) \geq \mathrm{rank} T_A$. Now use that ranks of linear maps are determined by polynomials (the minors of the entries) to conclude.

2.2.1.2 Say $T = \sum_{j=1}^{\mathbf{b}} a_j \otimes b_j \otimes c_j$ and this is an optimal expression. Since T_A is injective, the a_j must be a basis. Let α^j be the dual basis, so $T(\alpha^j) = b_j \otimes c_j$ has rank one. These span. In the other direction, say the image is $\mathrm{span}\{b_1 \otimes c_1, \ldots, b_{\mathbf{b}} \otimes c_{\mathbf{b}}\}$. Then, for each j, there must be some $\alpha^j \in A^*$ with $T(\alpha^j) = b_j \otimes c_j$. Since T_A is injective, these form a basis of A, so we must have $T = \sum_{j=1}^{\mathbf{b}} a_j \otimes b_j \otimes c_j$ with a_j the dual basis vectors.

2.2.2.2 Use Exercise 2.1.7.4, taking three matrices in A^*, e.g., Id, a matrix with all 1s just below the diagonal and zero elsewhere and a matrix with 1s just above the diagonal and zeros elsewhere.

2.3.3.2 First assume $T = e_I = e_{i_1} \wedge \cdots \wedge e_{i_k}$ and take $\mu = e^L$ and $\zeta = e^J$. Then

$$\mu \lrcorner T = \begin{cases} e_{I \setminus L} & \text{if} \quad L \subset I \\ 0 \text{ if } L \not\subset I \end{cases}$$

$$\zeta \lrcorner T = \begin{cases} e^{J \setminus I} & \text{if} \quad I \subset J \\ 0 \text{ if } I \not\subset J \end{cases}$$

and $\langle e^{J \setminus I}, e_{I \setminus L} \rangle = 0$, because they have no indices in common. By linearity we get zero for any linear combination of such e^J, e_L's so we see that $G(k, V)$ is in the zero set of the equations. (Any element of $G(k, V)$ is equivalent to $[e_I]$ after a change of basis and our equations are independent of the choice of basis.)

Now for simplicity assume $T = e_{I_1} + e_{I_2}$, where I_1, I_2 have at least two indices different. Take $\zeta = e^{I_1 \cup F}$ where $F \subseteq I_2$, $F \not\subset I_1$ and $I_2 \not\subset I_1 \cup F$. Then $\zeta \lrcorner T = e^F$. Take $\mu = e^{I_2 \setminus F}$ so $\mu \lrcorner T = e_F$. We conclude.

Any element of $\Lambda^k V$ not in $\hat{G}(k, V)$ can be degenerated to be of the form T, so we conclude in general.

2.4.2.2 Show that for $X \in \Lambda^{p-1}A \otimes B^*$, $T_A^{\wedge p}(a \wedge X) = -a \wedge T_A^{\wedge p-1}(X)$. It is sufficient to consider the case $q = p - 1$. Say $X \in \ker(T_A^{\wedge p-1})$. Then $a \wedge X \in \ker(T_A^{\wedge p})$ so $a \wedge X = 0$ for all $a \in A$. But this is not possible.

2.5.1.4 trace(f).

2.5.1.5 Use Exercise 2.5.1.2.

2.5.2.2 Extend the a_j to a basis of A and consider the induced basis of $\Lambda^{q+1}A$. Write out $X_j \wedge a_j$ with respect to the induced basis and compare coefficients.

2.5.2.3 Use a variant of Lemma 2.5.2.1.

2.5.3.2 Apply the proof of Theorem 2.5.2.6 to $M_{\langle p,p,2 \rangle}$.

Chapter 3

3.1.4.2 By the first part of the exercise, every point on the Chow variety is a projection of a point of the form $v_1 \otimes \cdots \otimes v_d$, for some $v_j \in V$, but the projection of $v_1 \otimes \cdots \otimes v_d$ is $v_1 \cdots v_d$.

3.1.4.3 The ideal is generated by $p_3^2 - p_2 p_4$, $p_2^2 - p_0 p_4$. Note that we simply are throwing away the polynomials with p_1. The point p_3, corresponding to the polynomial $x^3 y$ is on a tangent line to $v_4(\mathbb{P}^1)$, while the point p_{22}, corresponding to the polynomial $x^2 y^2$ is not.

3.1.4.5 The ideal is generated by $p_2^2 - p_1 p_3$, $p_1 p_2 - p_0 p_3$, $p_1^2 - p_0 p_2$.

3.1.4.8 Say $f(X) = Z_1 \cup Z_2$ and note that $X = f^{-1}(Z_1) \cup f^{-1}(Z_2)$.

3.2.1.4 Recall from Exercise 2.5.1.9 that $\otimes_j M_{\langle l_j, m_j, n_j \rangle} = M_{\langle \Pi_j l_j, \Pi_k m_k, \Pi_l n_l \rangle}$. Set $N = \mathbf{nml}$ and consider $M_{\langle N \rangle} = M_{\langle \mathbf{m}, \mathbf{n}, \mathbf{l} \rangle} \otimes M_{\langle \mathbf{n}, \mathbf{l}, \mathbf{m} \rangle} \otimes M_{\langle \mathbf{l}, \mathbf{m}, \mathbf{n} \rangle}$.

3.2.2.1 Consider

3.3.1.3 Since the border rank of points in $GL(A) \times GL(B) \times GL(C) \cdot T$ equals the border rank of T, the border rank of points in the closure cannot increase.

3.4.6.3 Use Proposition 3.2.1.7.

3.4.9.3 Instead of the curve $a_0 + t a_1$, use $a_0 + t a_1 + t^2 a_{q+1}$, and similarly for b, c.

3.5.3.3 If $\mathbf{R}_h(T) = \underline{\mathbf{R}}(T)$, then when writing $T = \lim_{t \to 0} T(t)$, we may take $t \in \mathbb{Z}_{h+1}$.

3.5.3.4 If we are multiplying polynomials of degrees d_1 and d_2, then their product has degree $d_1 d_2$, so the answer is the same as if we were working over $\mathbb{Z}_{d_1 d_2}$.

Chapter 4

4.1.1.1 If one uses the images of the standard basis vectors, one gets

$$M_{(2)} = \begin{pmatrix} 0 & -1 \\ 1 & -1 \end{pmatrix}^{\otimes 3} + \begin{pmatrix} 1 & 0 \\ 0 & 0 \end{pmatrix}^{\otimes 3} + \begin{pmatrix} 0 & 1 \\ 0 & 1 \end{pmatrix}^{\otimes 3} + \begin{pmatrix} 0 & 0 \\ -1 & 1 \end{pmatrix}^{\otimes 3}$$
$$+ \left\langle \begin{pmatrix} 0 & 1 \\ 0 & 0 \end{pmatrix} \otimes \begin{pmatrix} 0 & 0 \\ 1 & 0 \end{pmatrix} \otimes \begin{pmatrix} 1 & -1 \\ 1 & -1 \end{pmatrix} \right\rangle_{\mathbb{Z}_3}.$$

4.2.2.2 $(1, -\frac{1}{2})$, $(-\frac{1}{2}, 1)$, $(-\frac{1}{2}, -\frac{1}{2})$.

4.5.2.1 $\begin{pmatrix} * & 0 & 0 \\ * & * & * \\ 0 & 0 & * \end{pmatrix}$.

4.7.5.1 If a line goes through $[a \otimes b \otimes c]$, then it must be contained in $\mathbb{P}\hat{T}_{[a \otimes b \otimes c]} Seg(\mathbb{P}A \times \mathbb{P}B \times \mathbb{P}C)$.

Chapter 5

5.1.4.5 First note that if x is generic, it is diagonalizable with distinct eigenvalues, so if x is generic, then $\dim C(x) = \mathbf{b}$. Then observe that $\dim(C(x))$ is semicontinuous as the set $\{y \mid \dim C(y) \le p\}$ is an algebraic variety. Alternatively, and more painfully, compute the centralizer of elements in Jordan canonical form.

5.2.1.1 See the proof of Proposition 5.2.1.2 in the case $k = 1$.

5.3.1.4 For the lower bound, use Koszul flattenings; for the upper, write T as the sum of the first AFT tensor and the remainder and bound the border rank of each.

5.3.1.8 For the lower bound, use the substitution method. For the upper, consider the rank decomposition of the structure tensor of $\mathbb{C}[\mathbb{Z}_{2m-1}]$, which, using the DFT, has rank and border rank $\mathbf{m}$. Show that this tensor degenerates to the tensor corresponding to the centralizer of a regular nilpotent element.

5.4.3.5 $\overline{G \cdot x}$ is a union of orbits, so the boundary is a union of orbits all of dimension strictly less than $\dim(G \cdot x)$.

5.4.4.3 For any $z \subset v_n(Seg(\mathbb{P}E \times \mathbb{P}F))$, $G_{\det_n, z}$, the group preserving both $\det_n$ and z, is isomorphic to $P_E \times P_F$, where P_E, P_F are the parabolic subgroups of matrices with zero in the first column except the $(1, 1)$-slot and z is in the $G_{\det_n, z}$-orbit closure of any $q \in v_n(\mathbb{P}W)$.

5.4.4.4 Notice that fixing $k = [(\mu \otimes v) \otimes (v \otimes w) \otimes (\omega \otimes u)]$ is equivalent to fixing a partial flag in each U, V, and W consisting of a line and a hyperplane containing it. Let $[a \otimes b \otimes c] \in Seg(\mathbb{P}A \times \mathbb{P}B \times \mathbb{P}C)$. If $[a] \notin Seg(\mathbb{P}U^* \times \mathbb{P}V)$ then the orbit is not closed, even under the torus action on V or U^* that is compatible with the flag. So without loss of generality, we may assume $[a \otimes b \otimes c] \in Seg(\mathbb{P}U^* \times \mathbb{P}V \times \mathbb{P}V^* \times \mathbb{P}W \times \mathbb{P}W^* \times \mathbb{P}U)$. Write $a \otimes b \otimes c = (\mu' \otimes v') \otimes (v' \otimes w') \otimes (\omega' \otimes u')$. If, for example, $v' \neq v$, we may act with an element of $GL(V)$ that preserves the partial flag and sends v' to $v + \epsilon v'$. Hence v is in the closure of the orbit of v'. As $G_{M_{(U,V,W)},k}$ preserves v, we may continue, reaching k in the closure.

5.4.5.2 $\binom{n+j-2}{j-1} = \dim S^{j-1} \mathbb{C}^{n-1}$, so the sum may be thought of as computing the dimension of $S^{m-1} \mathbb{C}^n$, where each summand represents basis vectors (monomials) where, e.g., x_1 appears to the power $m - j$.

5.4.5.3 Without loss of generality, assume $2 \leq i \leq j$. For $j = 2, 3$ the inequality is straightforward to check, so assume $j \geq 4$. Prove the inequality 5.4.3 by induction on $\mathbf{n}$: for $\mathbf{n} = ij$, the inequality follows from the combinatorial interpretation of binomial coefficients and the fact that the middle one is the largest. We have $\binom{\mathbf{n}+1-1+ij-1}{ij-1} = \binom{\mathbf{n}-1+ij-1}{ij-1} \frac{\mathbf{n}-1+ij}{\mathbf{n}}$, $\binom{\mathbf{n}+1-j+i-1}{i-1} = \binom{\mathbf{n}-j+i-1}{i-1} \frac{\mathbf{n}-j+i}{\mathbf{n}-j+1}$ and $\binom{\mathbf{n}+1-i+j-1}{j-1} = \binom{\mathbf{n}-i+j-1}{j-1} \frac{\mathbf{n}-i+j}{\mathbf{n}-i+1}$. By induction, it is enough to prove that

$$\frac{\mathbf{n} - 1 + ij}{\mathbf{n}} \geq \frac{\mathbf{n} - j + i}{\mathbf{n} - j + 1} \frac{\mathbf{n} - i + j}{\mathbf{n} - i + 1}. \tag{10.4.9}$$

This is equivalent to

$$ij - 1 \geq \frac{\mathbf{n}(i-1)}{\mathbf{n}-j+1} + \frac{\mathbf{n}(j-1)}{\mathbf{n}-i+1} + \frac{\mathbf{n}(i-1)(j-1)}{(\mathbf{n}-j+1)(\mathbf{n}-i+1)}.$$

As the left-hand side is independent from $\mathbf{n}$ and each fraction on the right-hand side decreases with growing $\mathbf{n}$, we may set $\mathbf{n} = ij$ in inequality 10.4.9. Thus it is enough to prove

$$2 - \frac{1}{ij} \geq \left(1 + \frac{i-1}{ij-j+1}\right)\left(1 + \frac{j-1}{ij-i+1}\right).$$

Then the inequality is straightforward to check for $i = 2$, so assume $i \geq 3$.

5.6.2.6 $\mathcal{A}$ has basis $x_J := x_1^{j_1} \cdots x_n^{j_n}$ with $0 \leq j_s < a_s$. Let e_J be the dual basis. Then $T_A = \sum_{i_s + j_s < a_s} e_I \otimes e_J \otimes x_{I+J}$. Write $x_K^* = x_1^{a_1 - k_1 - 1} \cdots x_n^{a_n - k_n - 1}$. Then $T_A = \sum_{i_s + j_s + k_s < a_s} e_I \otimes e_J \otimes e_K$.

5.6.3.1 Show that if $n \in \text{Rad}(\mathcal{A})$ is not nilpotent, then there is some prime ideal of $\mathcal{A}$ not containing n.

Chapter 6

6.1.4.2 Use that $\frac{1}{1-\lambda t} = \sum_j \lambda^j t^j$.

6.2.2.4 Consider $\lim_{\epsilon \to 0} \frac{1}{\epsilon}((x + \epsilon y)^n - x^n)$.

6.2.2.7 Respectively, taking $k = \lfloor \frac{n}{2} \rfloor$, one gets that the ranks are $\binom{n}{\lfloor \frac{n}{2} \rfloor}$, $\binom{n}{\lfloor \frac{n}{2} \rfloor}^2$, and $\binom{n}{\lfloor \frac{n}{2} \rfloor}^2$.

6.2.3.1 $N^*_M \sigma^0_r = \ker M \otimes (\text{Image } M)^{\perp} = \ker M \otimes \ker M^T \subset U \otimes V^*$. The second equality holds because for a linear map $f : V \to W$, $\text{Image}(f)^{\perp} = \ker(f^T)$.

6.3.3.3 The space of matrices with last two columns equal to zero is contained in $Z(\text{perm}_m)_{sing}$.

6.3.4.5 Let $\hat{Q} \in S^2 V$ be the corresponding quadratic form (defined up to scale). Take a basis $e_1, \ldots, e_v$ of V such that $e_1, \ldots, e_k$ correspond to a linear space on Q, so $Q(e_s, e_t) = 0$ for $0 \le s, t \le k$. But Q being smooth says $\hat{Q}$ is nondegenerate, so for each e_s, there must be some $e_{f(s)}$ with $Q(e_s, e_{f(s)}) \ne 0$.

6.4.2.3 Parametrize C by a parameter s and $\tau(C)$ by s and a parameter t for the line, then differentiate.

6.4.3.1 Consider a curve $([\overline{x}(t)], [\overline{H}(t)]) \in \mathcal{I}$. Note that $\langle \overline{x}(t), \overline{H}(t) \rangle \equiv 0$ where $\langle \cdot, \cdot \rangle : V \times V^* \to \mathbb{C}$ is the pairing. Now consider $\frac{d}{dt}|_{t=0} \langle \overline{x}(t), \overline{H}(t) \rangle$.

6.4.6.1 First note that perm_m evaluated on a matrix whose entries are all one is $m!$. Then perform a permanental Laplace expansion about the first row.

6.5.2.2 Note that $\frac{\partial R}{\partial x_i} = \sum_j \frac{\partial^2 R}{\partial x_i \partial x_j}$, and now consider the last nonzero column.

6.6.1.3 In this case the determinant is a smooth quadric.

6.6.1.5 Linear spaces on a variety X through a point $x \in X$ must be contained in $\mathbb{P}\hat{T}_x X$.

6.6.2.1 $\{\text{perm}_2 = 0\}$ is a smooth quadric.

Chapter 7

7.1.1.3 Consider (where blank entries are zero)

$$\det \begin{pmatrix} 0 & x_1 & & x_2 & & x_3 & \\ x_1 & \ell & & & & & \\ & x_1 & \ell & & & & \\ x_2 & & & \ell & & & \\ & & & x_2 & \ell & & \\ x_3 & & & & & \ell & \\ & & & & & x_3 & \ell \end{pmatrix} = \ell^{7-3}(x_1^3 + x_2^3 + x_3^3).$$

7.4.2.7 Take $x_m = x_{m+1} = \cdots = x_N = 0$.

7.4.2.9 Let ω be a primitive qth root of unity. Let $x_1, \ldots, x_N$ denote the standard basis of $\mathbb{C}^N$. Consider the vector $(1, \omega, \omega^2, \ldots, \omega^{q-1}, 0, \ldots, 0)$ and its shifts by zeros.

7.6.1.3 In degree $d + \tau$, this ideal consists of all polynomials of the form $\ell_1^d Q_1 + \ell_2^d Q_2$ with $Q_1, Q_2 \in S^\tau \mathbb{C}^{n^2}$, which has dimension $2\dim S^\tau \mathbb{C}^{n^2} - \dim S^{\tau-(d)} \mathbb{C}^{n^2}$, because the polynomials of the form $\ell_1^d \ell_2^d Q_3$ with $Q_3 \in S^{\tau-(d)} \mathbb{C}^{n^2}$ appear in both terms.

Chapter 8

8.1.2.2 Say we have a weight vector $z \in V^{\otimes d}$ weight $(j_1, \ldots, j_{\mathbf{v}})$ with $j_i < j_{i+1}$. Consider the matrix g that is the identity plus a vector with one nonzero entry in the $(i, i+1)$ slot. Then gz is a nonzero vector of weight $(j_1, \ldots, j_{i-1}, j_i + 1, j_{i+1} - 1, \ldots, j_{\mathbf{v}})$.

8.1.4.1 The weight of the one-dimensional representation $\det^{-1}$ is $(-1, \ldots, -1)$.

8.1.4.2 Consider the linear form $v \mapsto \det_{\mathbf{v}}(v_1, \ldots, v_{\mathbf{v}-1}, v)$.

8.1.5.2 $g \cdot e_1 \wedge \cdots \wedge e_{\mathbf{v}} = \det(g) e_1 \wedge \cdots \wedge e_{\mathbf{v}}$

8.2.1.2 By linearity, for any P_1, P_2, the rank of the linear map $U^* \to W$ associated to $P_1 + P_2$ is at most the sum of the ranks of the maps associated to P_1 and P_2.

8.4.1.2 A highest weight vector of any copy of $S_\pi V^*$ is constructed skew-symmetrizing over $l(\pi)$ vectors. For the other direction, the zero set of any $P \in S^\delta(S^d \mathbb{C}^k)$ is a proper subvariety of $S^d \mathbb{C}^k$.

8.5.3.4 Under the action of a basis vector in $\mathfrak{gl}(E \otimes F)$, since it is by Leibnitz rule, at most one variable in each monomial can be changed. So whatever highest weight vectors appear in the tangent space, their weight can differ by at most one in each of E, F from $((1^n), (1^n))$. But there is only one partition pair with this property that occurs in $S^n(E \otimes F)$, namely, $(2, 1^{n-1}), (2, 1^{n-1}))$.

8.6.1.1 Prove an algebra version of Schur's Lemma.

8.6.4.2 If V is an irreducible G-module, then $V^* \otimes V$ is an irreducible $G \times G$-module.

8.6.8.2 We need $\mathrm{Hom}_{\mathfrak{S}_d}([\pi]^*, [\mu]) \neq 0$. But $[\pi]^* \simeq [\pi]$. By Schur's Lemma, $\mathrm{Hom}_{\mathfrak{S}_d}([\pi], [\mu]) \neq 0$ if and only if $[\pi] = [\mu]$.

8.6.8.3 If the multiplicity were greater than one, π would not be irreducible by Schur's Lemma.

8.7.1.3

$$
\begin{aligned}
S^d(E \otimes F) &= [(E \otimes F)^{\otimes d}]^{\mathfrak{S}_d} \\
&= (E^{\otimes d} \otimes F^{\otimes d})^{\mathfrak{S}_d} \\
&= [(\oplus_{|\pi|=d} S_\pi E \otimes [\pi])) \otimes (\oplus_{|\mu|=d} S_\mu F \otimes [\mu]))]^{\mathfrak{S}_d} \\
&= \oplus_{|\mu|,|\pi|=d} S_\pi E \otimes S_\mu F \otimes ([\pi] \otimes [\mu])^{\mathfrak{S}_d}.
\end{aligned}
$$

Now use Exercise 8.6.8.2.

8.7.2.2 $c_{\pi'} = \sum_{\sigma \in \mathfrak{S}_{\pi'}} \delta_\sigma \sum_{\sigma \in \mathfrak{S}_\pi} \mathrm{sgn}(\sigma) \delta_\sigma$. Now show $c_{(1^d)} c_\pi = c_{\pi'}$.

8.11.1.2 $\sum_{j=0}^{m} \binom{m}{j}^2 = \binom{2m}{m}$ as $\Lambda^m(E \oplus F) = \sum_j \Lambda^j E \otimes \Lambda^{m-j} F$.

Chapter 9

9.1.2.2 Highest weight vectors here correspond to partitions with at most d parts.

9.5.2.1 The map $Mat_n \to Mat_n /\!\!/ GL_n$ sends a matrix to the coefficients of its characteristic polynomial, i.e., the elementary symmetric functions of its eigenvalues.

9.5.2.2 Say $P \in \mathbb{C}(Nor(Z /\!\!/ \Gamma))$ satifies a monic polynomial with coefficients in $\mathbb{C}[Nor(Z /\!\!/ \Gamma)]$. Note that $\mathbb{C}(Nor(Z /\!\!/ \Gamma)) \subset \mathbb{C}(Z)^\Gamma$, and of course, $\mathbb{C}[Nor(Z /\!\!/ \Gamma)] \subset \mathbb{C}[Z]$, so by the normality of Z, $P \in \mathbb{C}[Z]$, but $\mathbb{C}[Nor(Z /\!\!/ \Gamma)] = \mathbb{C}[Z] \cap \mathbb{C}(Z)^\Gamma$.

9.6.3.2 By the Pieri formula, one can have at most three parts. On the other hand, $Ch_d(\mathbb{C}^2) = \mathbb{P}S^d\mathbb{C}^2$.

Chapter 10

10.1.1.2 For $P \in S^e V^*$, $P(x) = 0$ is equivalent to $\langle \overline{P}, x^e \rangle = 0$.

10.1.4.3 Consider R with $I_R = (x_1^{d_1+1}, \ldots, x_{n-1}^{d_{n-1}+1})$.

Bibliography

[ABV15] J. Alper, T. Bogart, and M. Velasco, *A lower bound for the determinantal complexity of a hypersurface*, to appear in FOCM **17** (2017), no. 3, pp. 829–836.

[AFLG15] Andris Ambainis, Yuval Filmus, and François Le Gall, *Fast matrix multiplication: limitations of the Coppersmith-Winograd method (extended abstract)*, Symposium on Theory of Computing, ACM, New York, 2015, pp. 585–593. MR 3388238

[AFT11] Boris Alexeev, Michael A. Forbes, and Jacob Tsimerman, *Tensor rank: some lower and upper bounds*, 26th Annual Conference on Computational Complexity, IEEE, Los Alamitos, CA, 2011, pp. 283–291. MR 3025382

[AH95]   J. Alexander and A. Hirschowitz, *Polynomial interpolation in several variables*, J. Algebraic Geom. **4** (1995), no. 2, 201–222. MR 96f:14065

[Ahl78] Lars V. Ahlfors, *Complex Analysis*, 3rd ed., McGraw-Hill, New York, 1978.

[AJ15]   N. R. Aravind and Pushkar S. Joglekar, *On the expressive power of read-once determinants*, Fundamentals of computation theory, Lecture Notes in Comput. Sci., vol. 9210, Springer, Cham, 2015, pp. 95–105. MR 3440499

[Alp17] Levent Alpoge, *Square-root cancellation for the signs of Latin squares*, Combinatorica **37** (2017), no. 2, 137–142. MR 3638338

[AR03]   Elizabeth S. Allman and John A. Rhodes, *Phylogenetic invariants for the general Markov model of sequence mutation*, Math. Biosci. **186** (2003), no. 2, 113–144. MR 2 024 609

[Aro58] S. Aronhold, *Theorie der homogenen Functionen dritten Grades von drei Veränderlichen*, J. Reine Angew. Math. **55** (1858), 97–191. MR 1579064

[AS81]   A. Alder and V. Strassen, *On the algorithmic complexity of associative algebras*, Theoret. Comput. Sci. **15** (1981), no. 2, 201–211. MR MR623595 (82g:68038)

[AS13]   V. B. Alekseev and A. V. Smirnov, *On the exact and approximate bilinear complexities of multiplication of 4×2 and 2×2 matrices*, Proc. Steklov Inst. Math. **282** (2013), no. 1, 123–139.

[AT92]   N. Alon and M. Tarsi, *Colorings and orientations of graphs*, Combinatorica **12** (1992), no. 2, 125–134. MR 1179249

[Atk83] M. D. Atkinson, *Primitive spaces of matrices of bounded rank. II*, J. Austral. Math. Soc. Ser. A **34** (1983), no. 3, 306–315. MR 695915

[AV08]   M. Agrawal and V. Vinay, *Arithmetic circuits: A chasm at depth four*, Proc. 49th IEEE Symposium on Foundations of Computer Science (2008), 67–75.

[AW07]   Kaan Akin and Jerzy Weyman, *Primary ideals associated to the linear strands of Lascoux's resolution and syzygies of the corresponding irreducible representations*

          of the Lie superalgebra $\mathbf{gl}(m|n)$, J. Algebra **310** (2007), no. 2, 461–490. MR
          2308168 (2009c:17007)

[Bar77]   W. Barth, *Moduli of vector bundles on the projective plane*, Invent. Math. **42** (1977),
          63–91. MR MR0460330 (57 #324)

[Bas15]   Saugata Basu, *A complexity theory of constructible functions and sheaves*, Found.
          Comput. Math. **15** (2015), no. 1, 199–279. MR 3303696

[BB]   Austin R. Benson and Grey Ballard, *A framework for practical parallel fast matrix
          multiplication*, arXiv:1409.2908 (2014).

[BB14]   Weronika Buczyńska and Jaroslaw Buczyński, *Secant varieties to high degree
          Veronese reembeddings, catalecticant matrices and smoothable Gorenstein
          schemes*, J. Algebraic Geom. **23** (2014), no. 1, 63–90. MR 3121848

[BCRL79] Dario Bini, Milvio Capovani, Francesco Romani, and Grazia Lotti, $O(n^{2.7799})$
          complexity for $n \times n$ *approximate matrix multiplication*, Inform. Process. Lett. **8**
          (1979), no. 5, 234–235. MR MR534068 (80h:68024)

[BCS97]   Peter Bürgisser, Michael Clausen, and M. Amin Shokrollahi, with Thomas
          Lickteig, *Algebraic complexity theory*, Grundlehren der mathematischen Wis-
          senschaften [Fundamental Principles of Mathematical Sciences], vol. 315,
          Springer, Berlin, 1997. MR 99c:68002

[BDHM15] A. Bernardi, N. S. Daleo, J. D. Hauenstein, and B. Mourrain, *Tensor decomposition
          and homotopy continuation*, ArXiv e-prints (2015).

[Bea00]   Arnaud Beauville, *Determinantal hypersurfaces*, Mich. Math. J. **48** (2000), 39–64.
          MR 1786479 (2002b:14060)

[BGL13]   Jaroslaw Buczyński, Adam Ginensky, and J. M. Landsberg, *Determinantal equa-
          tions for secant varieties and the Eisenbud-Koh-Stillman conjecture*, J. Lond. Math.
          Soc. (2) **88** (2013), no. 1, 1–24. MR 3092255

[BGL14]   H. Bermudez, S. Garibaldi, and V. Larsen, *Linear preservers and representations
          with a 1-dimensional ring of invariants*, Trans. Am. Math. Soc. **366** (2014), no. 9,
          4755–4780. MR 3217699

[BILR]   Grey Ballard, Christian Ikenmeyer, J. M. Landsberg, and Nick Ryder, *The geometry
          of rank decompositions of matrix multiplication ii: 3x3 matrices*, preprint.

[Bin80]   D. Bini, *Relations between exact and approximate bilinear algorithms. Applica-
          tions*, Calcolo **17** (1980), no. 1, 87–97. MR 605920 (83f:68043b)

[BIP16]   Peter Bürgisser, Christian Ikenmeyer, and Greta Panova, *No occurrence obstruc-
          tions in geometric complexity theory*, CoRR **abs/1604.06431** (2016).

[BKs07]   Anita Buckley and Tomaž Košir, *Determinantal representations of smooth cubic
          surfaces*, Geom. Dedicata **125** (2007), 115–140. MR 2322544

[BL89]   S. C. Black and R. J. List, *A note on plethysm*, Eur. J. Combin. **10** (1989), no. 1,
          111–112. MR 977186 (89m:20011)

[BL14]   Jaroslaw Buczyński and J. M. Landsberg, *On the third secant variety*, J. Algebraic
          Combin. **40** (2014), no. 2, 475–502. MR 3239293

[BL16]   M. Bläser and V. Lysikov, *On degeneration of tensors and algebras*, 41st Inter-
          national Symposium on Mathematical Foundations of Computer Science (MFCS
          2016), LIPIcs (2016), 58:19:1–19:11.

[Blä00]   Markus Bläser, *Lower bounds for the bilinear complexity of associative algebras*,
          Comput. Complexity **9** (2000), no. 2, 73–112. MR 1809686

[Bla01a] Markus Bläser, *Improvements of the Alder-Strassen bound: algebras with nonzero
          radical*, Automata, Languages and Programming, Lecture Notes in Comput. Sci.,
          vol. 2076, Springer, Berlin, 2001, pp. 79–91. MR 2065853

[Blä01b] Markus Bläser, *Complete problems for Valiant's class of qp-computable fami-
          lies of polynomials*, Computing and Combinatorics (Guilin, 2001), Lecture Notes
          in Comput. Sci., vol. 2108, Springer, Berlin, 2001, pp. 1–10. MR 1935355
          (2003j:68051)

[Blä03]   ———, *On the complexity of the multiplication of matrices of small formats*, J. Complexity **19** (2003), no. 1, 43–60. MR MR1951322 (2003k:68040)

[Blä13]   Markus Bläser, *Fast matrix multiplication*, Graduate Surveys, no. 5, Theory of Computing Library, 2013.

[Blä14]   Markus Bläser, *Explicit tensors*, Perspectives in Computational Complexity, Springer, New York, 2014, pp. 117–130.

[BLMW11]   Peter Bürgisser, J. M. Landsberg, Laurent Manivel, and Jerzy Weyman, *An overview of mathematical issues arising in the geometric complexity theory approach to* VP $\neq$ VNP, SIAM J. Comput. **40** (2011), no. 4, 1179–1209. MR 2861717

[BLR80]   Dario Bini, Grazia Lotti, and Francesco Romani, *Approximate solutions for the bilinear form computational problem*, SIAM J. Comput. **9** (1980), no. 4, 692–697. MR MR592760 (82a:68065)

[BO08]   Maria Chiara Brambilla and Giorgio Ottaviani, *On the Alexander-Hirschowitz theorem*, J. Pure Appl. Algebra **212** (2008), no. 5, 1229–1251. MR 2387598 (2008m:14104)

[BOC92]   Micheal Ben Or and Richard Cleve, *Computing algebraic formulas using a constant number of registers*, SIAM J. Comput. **21** (1992), no. 21, 54–58.

[BR13]   Alessandra Bernardi and Kristian Ranestad, *On the cactus rank of cubics forms*, J. Symbolic Comput. **50** (2013), 291–297. MR 2996880

[Bre70]   R. P. Brent, *Algorithms for matrix multiplication*, Technical Report TR-CS-70-157 DCS, Stanford (1970), 1–52.

[Bre74]   Richard P. Brent, *The parallel evaluation of general arithmetic expressions*, J. Assoc. Comput. Mach. **21** (1974), 201–206. MR 0660280 (58 #31996)

[Bri93]   A. Brill, *Über symmetrische functionen von variabelnpaaren*, Nachrichten von der Königlichen Gesellschaft der Wissenschaften und der Georg-Augusts-Universität zu Göttingen **20** (1893), 757–762.

[Bri93]   Michel Brion, *Stable properties of plethysm: on two conjectures of Foulkes*, Manuscripta Math. **80** (1993), no. 4, 347–371. MR MR1243152 (95c:20056)

[Bri97]   ———, *Sur certains modules gradués associés aux produits symétriques*, Algèbre non commutative, groupes quantiques et invariants (Reims, 1995), Sémin. Congr., vol. 2, Soc. Math. France, Paris, 1997, pp. 157–183. MR 1601139 (99e:20054)

[Bri02]   Emmanuel Briand, *Polynômes multisymétriques*, Ph.D. thesis, Université de Rennes 1 et Universidad de Cantabria, 2002.

[Bri10]   ———, *Covariants vanishing on totally decomposable forms*, Liaison, Schottky problem and invariant theory, Progr. Math., vol. 280, Birkhäuser Verlag, Basel, 2010, pp. 237–256. MR 2664658

[Bsh98]   Nader H. Bshouty, *On the direct sum conjecture in the straight line model*, J. Complexity **14** (1998), no. 1, 49–62. MR 1617757 (99c:13056)

[BT15]   Grigoriy Blekherman and Zach Teitler, *On maximum, typical and generic ranks*, Math. Ann. **362** (2015), no. 3-4, 1021–1031. MR 3368091

[Bur14]   Vladimir P. Burichenko, *On symmetries of the strassen algorithm*, CoRR **abs/1408.6273** (2014).

[Bur15]   ———, *Symmetries of matrix multiplication algorithms. I*, CoRR **abs/1508.01110** (2015).

[Cai90]   Jin-Yi Cai, *A note on the determinant and permanent problem*, Inform. and Comput. **84** (1990), no. 1, 119–127. MR MR1032157 (91d:68028)

[CCC+15a]   E. Carlini, M. V. Catalisano, L. Chiantini, A. V. Geramita, and Y. Woo, *Symmetric tensors: rank, Strassen's conjecture and e-computability*, ArXiv e-prints (2015).

[CCC15b]   Enrico Carlini, Maria Virginia Catalisano, and Luca Chiantini, *Progress on the symmetric Strassen conjecture*, J. Pure Appl. Algebra **219** (2015), no. 8, 3149–3157. MR 3320211

[CEVV09]   Dustin A. Cartwright, Daniel Erman, Mauricio Velasco, and Bianca Viray, *Hilbert schemes of 8 points*, Algebra Number Theory **3** (2009), no. 7, 763–795. MR 2579394

[CHI$^+$]   Luca Chiantini, Jon Hauenstein, Christian Ikenmeyer, J. M. Landsberg, and Giorgio Ottaviani, *Polynomials and the exponent of matrix multiplication*, in preparation.

[CILO16]   Luca Chiantini, Christian Ikenmeyer, J. M. Landsberg, and Giorgio Ottaviani, *The geometry of rank decompositions of matrix multiplication I: 2x2 matrices*, CoRR **abs/1610.08364** (2016).

[CIM17]   Man-Wai Cheung, Christian Ikenmeyer, and Sevak Mkrtchyan, *Symmetrizing tableaux and the 5th case of the Foulkes conjecture*, J. Symbolic Comput. **80** (2017), part 3, 833–843. MR 3574536

[CKSU05]   H. Cohn, R. Kleinberg, B. Szegedy, and C. Umans, *Group-theoretic algorithms for matrix multiplication*, Proceedings of the 46th Annual Symposium on Foundations of Computer Science (2005), 379–388.

[CKSV16]   S. Chillara, M. Kumar, R. Saptharishi, and V Vinay, *The chasm at depth four, and tensor rank: old results, new insights*, ArXiv e-prints (2016).

[CKW10]   Xi Chen, Neeraj Kayal, and Avi Wigderson, *Partial derivatives in arithmetic complexity and beyond*, Found. Trends Theor. Comput. Sci. **6** (2010), no. 1–2, front matter, 1–138 (2011). MR 2901512

[Com02]   P. Comon, *Tensor decompositions, state of the art and applications*, Mathematics in Signal Processing V (J. G. McWhirter and I. K. Proudler, eds.), Clarendon Press, Oxford, 2002, arXiv:0905.0454v1, pp. 1–24.

[Csa76]   L. Csanky, *Fast parallel matrix inversion algorithms*, SIAM J. Comput. **5** (1976), no. 4, 618–623. MR 0455310 (56 #13549)

[CU03]   H. Cohn and C. Umans, *A group theoretic approach to fast matrix multiplication*, Proceedings of the 44th Annual Symposium on Foundations of Computer Science (2003), no. 2, 438–449.

[CU13]   ———, *Fast matrix multiplication using coherent configurations*, Proceedings of the 24th Annual ACM-SIAM Symposium on Discrete Algorithms (2013), no. 2, 1074–1087.

[CW82]   D. Coppersmith and S. Winograd, *On the asymptotic complexity of matrix multiplication*, SIAM J. Comput. **11** (1982), no. 3, 472–492. MR 664715 (83j:68047b)

[CW90]   Don Coppersmith and Shmuel Winograd, *Matrix multiplication via arithmetic progressions*, J. Symbolic Comput. **9** (1990), no. 3, 251–280. MR 91i:68058

[CW16]   Nicholas J. Cavenagh and Ian M. Wanless, *There are asymptotically the same number of Latin squares of each parity*, Bull. Austr. Math. Soc. **FirstView** (2016), 1–8.

[dG78]   Hans F. de Groote, *On varieties of optimal algorithms for the computation of bilinear mappings. I. The isotropy group of a bilinear mapping*, Theoret. Comput. Sci. **7** (1978), no. 1, 1–24. MR 0506377 (58 #22132)

[Die49]   Jean Dieudonné, *Sur une généralisation du groupe orthogonal à quatre variables*, Arch. Math. **1** (1949), 282–287. MR 0029360 (10,586l)

[Dri97]   Arthur A. Drisko, *On the number of even and odd Latin squares of order $p + 1$*, Adv. Math. **128** (1997), no. 1, 20–35. MR 1451417 (98e:05018)

[DS13]   A. M. Davie and A. J. Stothers, *Improved bound for complexity of matrix multiplication*, Proc. R. Soc. Edinburgh Sect. A **143** (2013), no. 2, 351–369. MR 3039815

[dSP16]   Clément de Seguins Pazzis, *Large spaces of bounded rank matrices revisited*, Linear Algebra Appl. **504** (2016), 124–189. MR 3502533

[Dyn52]   E. B. Dynkin, *Maximal subgroups of the classical groups*, Trudy Moskov. Mat. Obšč. **1** (1952), 39–166. MR 0049903 (14,244d)

[EH88]   David Eisenbud and Joe Harris, *Vector spaces of matrices of low rank*, Adv. Math. **70** (1988), no. 2, 135–155. MR 954659

[Eis95]   David Eisenbud, *Commutative Algebra*, Graduate Texts in Mathematics, vol. 150, Springer, New York, 1995. MR MR1322960 (97a:13001)

[Eis05]   ———, *The Geometry of Syzygies*, Graduate Texts in Mathematics, vol. 229, Springer, New York, 2005. MR 2103875 (2005h:13021)

[ELSW15]   K. Efremenko, J. M. Landsberg, H. Schenck, and J. Weyman, *On minimal free resolutions of sub-permanents and other ideals arising in complexity theory*, ArXiv e-prints (2015).

[ELSW16]   ———, *The method of shifted partial derivatives cannot separate the permanent from the determinant*, ArXiv e-prints, to appear in MCOM (2016).

[FH91]   William Fulton and Joe Harris, *Representation Theory*, Graduate Texts in Mathematics, vol. 129, Springer, New York, 1991. MR 1153249 (93a:20069)

[Fis94]   Ismor Fischer, *Sums of like powers of multivariate linear forms*, Math. Mag. **67** (1994), no. 1, 59–61. MR 1573008

[FLR85]   P. Fillmore, C. Laurie, and H. Radjavi, *On matrix spaces with zero determinant*, Linear Multilinear Algebra **18** (1985), no. 3, 255–266. MR 828407

[Fou50]   H. O. Foulkes, *Concomitants of the quintic and sextic up to degree four in the coefficients of the ground form*, J. London Math. Soc. **25** (1950), 205–209. MR MR0037276 (12,236e)

[Fro97]   G. Frobenius, *Über die Darstellung der endlichen Gruppen durch lineare Substitutionen*, Sitzungsber Deutsch. Akad. Wiss. Berlin (1897), 994–1015.

[Frö85]   Ralf Fröberg, *An inequality for Hilbert series of graded algebras*, Math. Scand. **56** (1985), no. 2, 117–144. MR 813632 (87f:13022)

[FS13a]   Michael A. Forbes and Amir Shpilka, *Explicit Noether normalization for simultaneous conjugation via polynomial identity testing*, Approximation, Randomization, and Combinatorial Optimization, Lecture Notes in Comput. Sci., vol. 8096, Springer, Heidelberg, 2013, pp. 527–542. MR 3126552

[FS13b]   ———, *Quasipolynomial-time identity testing of non-commutative and read-once oblivious algebraic branching programs*, 54th annual symposium on Foundations of Computer Science, IEEE, Los Alamitos, CA, 2013. MR 3246226

[FSS13]   Michael A. Forbes, Ramprasad Saptharishi, and Amir Shpilka, *Pseudorandomness for multilinear read-once algebraic branching programs, in any order*, CoRR **abs/1309.5668** (2013).

[FW84]   Ephraim Feig and Shmuel Winograd, *On the direct sum conjecture*, Linear Algebra Appl. **63** (1984), 193–219. MR 766508 (86h:15022)

[Gal17]   Maciej Gałczaka, *Vector bundles give equations of cactus varieties*, Linear Algebra Appl. **521** (2017), 254–262. MR 3611482

[Gat87]   Joachim von zur Gathen, *Feasible arithmetic computations: Valiant's hypothesis*, J. Symbolic Comput. **4** (1987), no. 2, 137–172. MR MR922386 (89f:68021)

[Gay76]   David A. Gay, *Characters of the Weyl group of SU(n) on zero weight spaces and centralizers of permutation representations*, Rocky Mountain J. Math. **6** (1976), no. 3, 449–455. MR MR0414794 (54 #2886)

[Ger61]   Murray Gerstenhaber, *On dominance and varieties of commuting matrices*, Ann. Math. **73** (1961), 324–348. MR 0132079 (24 #A1926)

[Ger89]   Anthony V. Geramita (ed.), *The Curves Seminar at Queen's. Vol. VI*, Queen's Papers in Pure and Applied Mathematics, vol. 83, Queen's University, Kingston, ON, 1989, Papers from the seminar held at Queen's University, Kingston, Ontario, 1989. MR 1036030

[Ges16]   Fulvio Gesmundo, *Geometric aspects of iterated matrix multiplication*, J. Algebra **461** (2016), 42–64. MR 3513064

[GGOW15]   A. Garg, L. Gurvits, R. Oliveira, and A. Wigderson, *A deterministic polynomial time algorithm for non-commutative rational identity testing with applications*, ArXiv e-prints (2015).

[GH79]   Phillip Griffiths and Joseph Harris, *Algebraic geometry and local differential geometry*, Ann. Sci. École Norm. Sup. **12** (1979), no. 3, 355–452. MR 81k:53004

[GHIL16]   Fulvio Gesmundo, Jonathan D. Hauenstein, Christian Ikenmeyer, and J. M. Landsberg, *Complexity of linear circuits and geometry*, Found. Comput. Math. **16** (2016), no. 3, 599–635. MR 3494506

[GHPS14]   Zachary A. Griffin, Jonathan D. Hauenstein, Chris Peterson, and Andrew J. Sommese, *Numerical computation of the Hilbert function and regularity of a zero dimensional scheme*, Connections between algebra, combinatorics, and geometry, Springer Proc. Math. Stat., vol. 76, Springer, New York, 2014, pp. 235–250. MR 3213522

[GKKS13a]   Ankit Gupta, Pritish Kamath, Neeraj Kayal, and Ramprasad Saptharishi, *Approaching the chasm at depth four*, Proceedings of the Conference on Computational Complexity (CCC) (2013).

[GKKS13b]   ———, *Arithmetic circuits: A chasm at depth three*, Electronic Colloquium on Computational Complexity (ECCC) **20** (2013), 26.

[GKKS17]   ———, *Unexpected power of low-depth arithmetic circuits*, preprint, to appear in CACM (2017).

[GKZ94]   I. M. Gel′fand, M. M. Kapranov, and A. V. Zelevinsky, *Discriminants, resultants, and multidimensional determinants*, Mathematics: Theory & Applications, Birkhäuser, Boston, MA, 1994. MR 95e:14045

[GL17]   Gesmundo, Fulvio and Landsberg, J.M., *Explicit polynomial sequences with maximal spaces of partial derivatives and a question of K. Mulmuley* arXiv:1705.03866.

[Gly10]   David G. Glynn, *The conjectures of Alon-Tarsi and Rota in dimension prime minus one*, SIAM J. Discrete Math. **24** (2010), no. 2, 394–399. MR 2646093 (2011i:05034)

[Gly13]   ———, *Permanent formulae from the Veronesean*, Des. Codes Cryptogr. **68** (2013), no. 1–3, 39–47. MR 3046335

[GM16]   J. A. Grochow and C. Moore, *Matrix multiplication algorithms from group orbits*, ArXiv e-prints (2016).

[Gor94]   P. Gordan, *Das Zerfallen der Curven in gerade Linien*, Math. Ann. **45** (1894), no. 3, 410–427. MR 1510871

[Got78]   Gerd Gotzmann, *Eine Bedingung für die Flachheit und das Hilbertpolynom eines graduierten Ringes*, Math. Z. **158** (1978), no. 1, 61–70. MR 0480478 (58 #641)

[Gra55]   H. Grassmann, *Die stereometrischen Gleichungen dritten Grades, und die dadurch erzeugten Oberflächen*, J. Reine Angew. Math. **49** (1855), 47–65. MR 1578905

[Gre78]   Edward L. Green, *Complete intersections and Gorenstein ideals*, J. Algebra **52** (1978), no. 1, 264–273. MR 0480472

[Gre98]   Mark L. Green, *Generic initial ideals*, Six lectures on commutative algebra (Bellaterra, 1996), Progr. Math., vol. 166, Birkhäuser, Basel, 1998, pp. 119–186. MR 1648665 (99m:13040)

[Gre11]   Bruno Grenet, *An Upper Bound for the Permanent versus Determinant Problem*, manuscript (submitted), 2011.

[Gri86]   B. Griesser, *A lower bound for the border rank of a bilinear map*, Calcolo **23** (1986), no. 2, 105–114 (1987). MR 88g:15021

[Gua15a]   Y. Guan, *Brill's equations as a GL(V)-module*, ArXiv e-prints (2015).

[Gua15b]   ———, *Flattenings and Koszul Young flattenings arising in complexity theory*, ArXiv e-prints (2015).

[Gun86]   S. Gundelfinger, *Zur theorie der binären formen*, J. Reine Angew. Math. **100** (1886), 413–424.

[GW09]   Roe Goodman and Nolan R. Wallach, *Symmetry, representations, and invariants*, Graduate Texts in Mathematics, vol. 255, Springer, Dordrecht, 2009. MR 2522486

[Had97]   J. Hadamard, *Mémoire sur l'élimination*, Acta Math. **20** (1897), no. 1, 201–238. MR 1554881

[Had99]   _____, *Sur les conditions de décomposition des formes*, Bull. Soc. Math. France **27** (1899), 34–47. MR 1504330

[Har77]   Robin Hartshorne, *Algebraic geometry*, Graduate Texts in Mathematics, No. 52 Springer, New York, 1977, MR MR0463157 (57 #3116)

[Har95]   Joe Harris, *Algebraic geometry*, Graduate Texts in Mathematics, vol. 133, Springer, New York, 1995. MR 1416564 (97e:14001)

[HIL13]   Jonathan D. Hauenstein, Christian Ikenmeyer, and J. M. Landsberg, *Equations for lower bounds on border rank*, Exp. Math. **22** (2013), no. 4, 372–383. MR 3171099

[HL16]   Jesko Hüttenhain and Pierre Lairez, *The boundary of the orbit of the 3-by-3 determinant polynomial*, C. R. Math. Acad. Sci. Paris **354** (2016), no. 9, 931–935. MR 3535348

[How87]   Roger Howe, $(\mathrm{GL}_n, \mathrm{GL}_m)$-*duality and symmetric plethysm*, Proc. Ind. Acad. Sci. Math. Sci. **97** (1987), no. 1–3, 85–109 (1988). MR MR983608 (90b:22020)

[HR94]   Rosa Huang and Gian-Carlo Rota, *On the relations of various conjectures on Latin squares and straightening coefficients*, Discrete Math. **128** (1994), no. 1–3, 225–236. MR 1271866 (95i:05036)

[HS82]   J. Heintz and C.-P. Schnorr, *Testing polynomials which are easy to compute*, Logic and algorithmic (Zurich, 1980), Monograph. Enseign. Math., vol. 30, Univ. Genève, Geneva, 1982, pp. 237–254. MR 648305

[HS13]   Jonathan D. Hauenstein and Andrew J. Sommese, *Membership tests for images of algebraic sets by linear projections*, Appl. Math. Comput. **219** (2013), no. 12, 6809–6818. MR 3027848

[Hü17]   Jesko Hüttenhain, *A Note on normalizations of orbit closures*, Commun. Algebra **45** (2017), no. 9, 3716–3723. MR 3627624

[HWY10]   Pavel Hrubes, Avi Wigderson, and Amir Yehudayoff, *Relationless completeness and separations*, 25th annual Conference on Computational Complexity—CCC 2010, IEEE Computer Soc., Los Alamitos, CA, 2010, pp. 280–290. MR 2932363

[Iar95]   A. Iarrobino, *Inverse system of a symbolic power. II. The Waring problem for forms*, J. Algebra **174** (1995), no. 3, 1091–1110. MR 1337187

[Iar97]   _____, *Inverse system of a symbolic power. III. Thin algebras and fat points*, Compositio Math. **108** (1997), no. 3, 319–356. MR 1473851 (98k:13017)

[IE78]   A. Iarrobino and J. Emsalem, *Some zero-dimensional generic singularities; finite algebras having small tangent space*, Compositio Math. **36** (1978), no. 2, 145–188. MR 515043

[IK99]   Anthony Iarrobino and Vassil Kanev, *Power sums, Gorenstein algebras, and determinantal loci*, Lecture Notes in Mathematics, vol. 1721, Springer, Berlin, 1999, Appendix C by Iarrobino and Steven L. Kleiman. MR MR1735271 (2001d:14056)

[Ike15]   C. Ikenmeyer, *On McKay's propagation theorem for the Foulkes conjecture*, ArXiv e-prints (2015).

[IL99]   Bo Ilic and J. M. Landsberg, *On symmetric degeneracy loci, spaces of symmetric matrices of constant rank and dual varieties*, Math. Ann. **314** (1999), no. 1, 159–174. MR MR1689267 (2000e:14091)

[IL16a]   C. Ikenmeyer and J. M. Landsberg, *On the complexity of the permanent in various computational models*, ArXiv e-prints, to appear in JPAA (2016).

[IL16b]   Thomas A. Ivey and J. M. Landsberg, *Cartan for beginners: differential geometry via moving frames and exterior differential systems, second edition*, Graduate Studies in Mathematics, vol. 175, American Mathematical Society, Providence, RI, 2016.

[IM05]   Atanas Iliev and Laurent Manivel, *Varieties of reductions for* $\mathfrak{gl}_n$, Projective varieties with unexpected properties, Walter de Gruyter, Berlin, 2005, pp. 287–316. MR MR2202260 (2006j:14056)

[IP15]   C. Ikenmeyer and G. Panova, *Rectangular Kronecker coefficients and plethysms in geometric complexity theory*, 2016 IEEE 57th Annual Symposium on Foundations of Computer Science (2015).

[JM86]   Rodney W. Johnson and Aileen M. McLoughlin, *Noncommutative bilinear algorithms for* 3 × 3 *matrix multiplication*, SIAM J. Comput. **15** (1986), no. 2, 595–603. MR 837607

[JT86]   Joseph Ja'Ja' and Jean Takche, *On the validity of the direct sum conjecture*, SIAM J. Comput. **15** (1986), no. 4, 1004–1020. MR MR861366 (88b:68084)

[Kem78]   George R. Kempf, *Instability in invariant theory*, Ann. Math. **108** (1978), no. 2, 299–316. MR MR506989 (80c:20057)

[KL14]   Harlan Kadish and J. M. Landsberg, *Padded polynomials, their cousins, and geometric complexity theory*, Comm. Algebra **42** (2014), no. 5, 2171–2180. MR 3169697

[KL15]   Shrawan Kumar and J. M. Landsberg, *Connections between conjectures of Alon-Tarsi, Hadamard-Howe, and integrals over the special unitary group*, Discrete Math. **338** (2015), no. 7, 1232–1238. MR 3322811

[KLPSMN09]   Abhinav Kumar, Satyanarayana V. Lokam, Vijay M. Patankar, and Jayalal Sarma M. N., *Using elimination theory to construct rigid matrices*, Foundations of software technology and theoretical computer science—FSTTCS 2009, LIPIcs. Leibniz Int. Proc. Inform., vol. 4, Schloss Dagstuhl. Leibniz-Zent. Inform., Wadern, 2009, pp. 299–310. MR 2870721

[Koi12]   Pascal Koiran, *Arithmetic circuits: the chasm at depth four gets wider*, Theoret. Comput. Sci. **448** (2012), 56–65. MR 2943969

[Kum13]   Shrawan Kumar, *Geometry of orbits of permanents and determinants*, Comment. Math. Helv. **88** (2013), no. 3, 759–788. MR 3093509

[Kum15]   _____, *A study of the representations supported by the orbit closure of the determinant*, Compos. Math. **151** (2015), no. 2, 292–312. MR 3314828

[Lad76]   Julian D. Laderman, *A noncommutative algorithm for multiplying* 3 × 3 *matrices using* 23 *muliplications*, Bull. Am. Math. Soc. **82** (1976), no. 1, 126–128. MR MR0395320 (52 #16117)

[Lan06]   J. M. Landsberg, *The border rank of the multiplication of* 2 × 2 *matrices is seven*, J. Am. Math. Soc. **19** (2006), no. 2, 447–459. MR 2188132 (2006j:68034)

[Lan10]   _____, *P versus NP and geometry*, J. Symbolic Comput. **45** (2010), no. 12, 1369–1377. MR 2733384 (2012c:68065)

[Lan12]   _____, *Tensors: geometry and applications*, Graduate Studies in Mathematics, vol. 128, American Mathematical Society, Providence, RI, 2012. MR 2865915

[Lan14]   _____, *New lower bounds for the rank of matrix multiplication*, SIAM J. Comput. **43** (2014), no. 1, 144–149. MR 3162411

[Lan15a]   _____, *Geometric complexity theory: an introduction for geometers*, Ann. Univ. Ferrara Sez. VII Sci. Mat. **61** (2015), no. 1, 65–117. MR 3343444

[Lan15b]   _____, *Nontriviality of equations and explicit tensors in* $\mathbb{C}^m \otimes \mathbb{C}^m \otimes \mathbb{C}^m$ *of border rank at least* $2m - 2$, J. Pure Appl. Algebra **219** (2015), no. 8, 3677–3684. MR 3320240

[Las78]   Alain Lascoux, *Syzygies des variétés déterminantales*, Adv. in Math. **30** (1978), no. 3, 202–237. MR 520233 (80j:14043)

[Lee16]   Hwangrae Lee, *Power sum decompositions of elementary symmetric polynomials*, Linear Algebra Appl. **492** (2016), 89–97. MR 3440150

[Lei16]   Arielle Leitner, *Limits under conjugacy of the diagonal subgroup in* $SL_n(\mathbb{R})$, Proc. Am. Math. Soc. **144** (2016), no. 8, 3243–3254. MR 3503693

[LG14]   François Le Gall, *Powers of tensors and fast matrix multiplication*, ISSAC 2014—Proceedings of the 39th International Symposium on Symbolic and Algebraic Computation, ACM, New York, 2014, pp. 296–303. MR 3239939

[Lic84] Thomas Lickteig, *A note on border rank*, Inform. Process. Lett. **18** (1984), no. 3, 173–178. MR 86c:68040

[Lic85] ———, *Typical tensorial rank*, Linear Algebra Appl. **69** (1985), 95–120. MR 87f:15017

[Lit06] Dudley E. Littlewood, *The theory of group characters and matrix representations of groups*, AMS Chelsea, Providence, RI, 2006, reprint of the second (1950) edition. MR MR2213154 (2006m:20013)

[LM04] J. M. Landsberg and Laurent Manivel, *On the ideals of secant varieties of Segre varieties*, Found. Comput. Math. **4** (2004), no. 4, 397–422. MR MR2097214 (2005m:14101)

[LM08a] J. M. Landsberg and L. Manivel, *Generalizations of Strassen's equations for secant varieties of Segre varieties*, Comm. Algebra **36** (2008), no. 2, 405–422. MR 2387532 (2009f:14109)

[LM08b] J. M. Landsberg and Laurent Manivel, *Generalizations of Strassen's equations for secant varieties of Segre varieties*, Comm. Algebra **36** (2008), no. 2, 405–422. MR MR2387532

[LM15] J. M. Landsberg and M. Michalek, *Abelian Tensors*, ArXiv e-prints, to appear in JMPA (2015).

[LM17a] ———, *A $2n^2 - log(n) - 1$ lower bound for the border rank of matrix multiplication*, Int Math Res Notices (2017).

[LM17b] J. M. Landsberg and Mateusz Michalek, *On the Geometry of Border Rank Decompositions for Matrix Multiplication and Other Tensors with Symmetry*, SIAM J. Appl. Algebra Geom. **1** (2017), no. 1, 2–19. MR 3633766

[LMR13] Joseph M. Landsberg, Laurent Manivel, and Nicolas Ressayre, *Hypersurfaces with degenerate duals and the geometric complexity theory program*, Comment. Math. Helv. **88** (2013), no. 2, 469–484. MR 3048194

[LMS16] Nutan Limaye, Guillaume Malod, and Srikanth Srinivasan, *Lower bounds for non-commutative skew circuits*, Theory Comput. **12** (2016), Paper No. 12, 38. MR 3546728

[LO13] J. M. Landsberg and Giorgio Ottaviani, *Equations for secant varieties of Veronese and other varieties*, Ann. Mat. Pura Appl. (4) **192** (2013), no. 4, 569–606. MR 3081636

[LO15] Joseph M. Landsberg and Giorgio Ottaviani, *New lower bounds for the border rank of matrix multiplication*, Theory Comput. **11** (2015), 285–298. MR 3376667

[Lok08] Satyanarayana V. Lokam, *Complexity lower bounds using linear algebra*, Found. Trends Theor. Comput. Sci. **4** (2008), no. 1–2, front matter, 1–155 (2009). MR 2539154 (2011c:68060)

[LR06] Hong Liu and Kenneth W. Regan, *Improved construction for universality of determinant and permanent*, Inform. Process. Lett. **100** (2006), no. 6, 233–237. MR 2270826 (2007f:68084)

[LR15] J. M. Landsberg and N. Ressayre, *Permanent v. determinant: an exponential lower bound assuming symmetry and a potential path towards Valiant's conjecture*, ArXiv e-prints, to appear in DGA special issue on Geometry and complexity (2015).

[LR17] J. M. Landsberg and Nicholas Ryder, *On the Geometry of Border Rank Algorithms for $n \times 2$ by 2×2 Matrix Multiplication*, Exp. Math. **26** (2017), no. 3, 275–286. MR 3642105

[Mac95] I. G. Macdonald, *Symmetric functions and Hall polynomials*, second ed., Oxford Mathematical Monographs, Clarendon Press, New York, 1995, with contributions by A. Zelevinsky, Oxford Science Publications. MR 1354144 (96h:05207)

[Man97] Laurent Manivel, *Applications de Gauss et pléthysme*, Ann. Inst. Fourier (Grenoble) **47** (1997), no. 3, 715–773. MR MR1465785 (98h:20078)

[Man98]   ———, *Gaussian maps and plethysm*, Algebraic geometry (Catania, 1993/ Barcelona, 1994), Lecture Notes in Pure and Appl. Math., vol. 200, Dekker, New York, 1998, pp. 91–117. MR MR1651092 (99h:20070)

[Man15a]   ———, *On the asymptotics of Kronecker coefficients*, J. Algebraic Combin. **42** (2015), no. 4, 999–1025. MR 3417256

[Man15b]   ———, *On the asymptotics of Kronecker coefficients, 2*, Sém. Lothar. Combin. **75** (2015), Art. B75d, 13. MR 3461556

[Mat60]   Yozô Matsushima, *Espaces homogènes de Stein des groupes de Lie complexes*, Nagoya Math. J **16** (1960), 205–218. MR MR0109854 (22 #739)

[McK08]   Tom McKay, *On plethysm conjectures of Stanley and Foulkes*, J. Algebra **319** (2008), no. 5, 2050–2071. MR 2394689 (2008m:20023)

[MM61]   Marvin Marcus and Henryk Minc, *On the relation between the determinant and the permanent*, Illinois J. Math. **5** (1961), 376–381. MR 0147488 (26 #5004)

[MM62]   Marvin Marcus and F. C. May, *The permanent function*, Can. J. Math. **14** (1962), 177–189. MR MR0137729 (25 #1178)

[MN05]   Jurgen Müller and Max Neunhöffer, *Some computations regarding Foulkes' conjecture*, Exp. Math. **14** (2005), no. 3, 277–283. MR MR2172706 (2006e:05186)

[MO34]   S. Mazur and W. Orlicz, *Grundlegende eigenschaften der polynomischen operationen*, Studia Math. **5** (1934), 50–68.

[MP08]   G. Malod and N. Portier, *Characterizing Valiant's algebraic complexity classes*, J. Complexity **24** (2008), 16–38.

[MP13]   Davesh Maulik and Rahul Pandharipande, *Gromov-Witten theory and Noether-Lefschetz theory*, A celebration of algebraic geometry, Clay Math. Proc., vol. 18, Amer. Math. Soc., Providence, RI, 2013, pp. 469–507. MR 3114953

[MR04]   Thierry Mignon and Nicolas Ressayre, *A quadratic bound for the determinant and permanent problem*, Int. Math. Res. Not. (2004), no. 79, 4241–4253. MR MR2126826 (2006b:15015)

[MR13]   Alex Massarenti and Emanuele Raviolo, *The rank of $n \times n$ matrix multiplication is at least $3n^2 - 2\sqrt{2}n^{\frac{3}{2}} - 3n$*, Linear Algebra Appl. **438** (2013), no. 11, 4500–4509. MR 3034546

[MS01]   Ketan D. Mulmuley and Milind Sohoni, *Geometric complexity theory. I. An approach to the P vs. NP and related problems*, SIAM J. Comput. **31** (2001), no. 2, 496–526 (electronic). MR MR1861288 (2003a:68047)

[MS08]   ———, *Geometric complexity theory. II. Towards explicit obstructions for embeddings among class varieties*, SIAM J. Comput. **38** (2008), no. 3, 1175–1206. MR MR2421083

[Mul99]   Ketan Mulmuley, *Lower bounds in a parallel model without bit operations*, SIAM J. Comput. **28** (1999), no. 4, 1460–1509 (electronic). MR 1681069

[Mul12]   Ketan Mulmuley, *Geometric complexity theory V: equivalence between blackbox derandomization of polynomial identity testing and derandomization of noether's normalization lemma*, CoRR **abs/1209.5993** (2012).

[Mul14]   K. Mulmuley, *The GCT chasm*, lecture (2014).

[Mum66]   David Mumford, *Lectures on curves on an algebraic surface*, with a section by G. M. Bergman. Annals of Mathematics Studies, No. 59, Princeton University Press, Princeton, N. J., 1966. MR 0209285

[Mum95]   ———, *Algebraic geometry. I*, Classics in Mathematics, Springer, Berlin, 1995, Complex projective varieties, reprint of the 1976 edition. MR 1344216 (96d:14001)

[MV97]   Meena Mahajan and V. Vinay, *Determinant: combinatorics, algorithms, and complexity*, Chicago J. Theoret. Comput. Sci. (1997), Article 5, 26 pp. (electronic). MR 1484546 (98m:15016)

[Nis91]   Noam Nisan, *Lower bounds for non-commutative computation*, Proceedings of the 23rd annual Symposium on Theory of Computing, ACM, New York, 1991, pp. 410–418.

[NR16]   J. F. Nash and M. T. Rassias, *Open problems in mathematics*, Springer International, Berlin, 2016.

[NW97]   Noam Nisan and Avi Wigderson, *Lower bounds on arithmetic circuits via partial derivatives*, Comput. Complexity **6** (1996/97), no. 3, 217–234. MR 1486927 (99f:68107)

[Oed16]   L. Oeding, *Border ranks of monomials*, ArXiv e-prints (2016).

[Ott07]   Giorgio Ottaviani, *Symplectic bundles on the plane, secant varieties and Lüroth quartics revisited*, Vector bundles and low codimensional subvarieties: state of the art and recent developments, Quad. Mat., vol. 21, Dept. Math., Seconda Univ. Napoli, Caserta, 2007, pp. 315–352. MR 2554725

[Pan66]   V. Ja. Pan, *On means of calculating values of polynomials*, Uspehi Mat. Nauk **21** (1966), no. 1 (127), 103–134. MR 0207178

[Pan78]   V. Ya. Pan, *Strassen's algorithm is not optimal. Trilinear technique of aggregating, uniting and canceling for constructing fast algorithms for matrix operations*, 19th annual Symposium on Foundations of Computer Science, IEEE, Long Beach, CA, 1978, pp. 166–176. MR 539838

[Pra94]   V. V. Prasolov, *Problems and theorems in linear algebra*, Translations of Mathematical Monographs, vol. 134, American Mathematical Society, Providence, RI, 1994, translated from the Russian manuscript by D. A. Leĭtes. MR 1277174

[Pro76]   C. Procesi, *The invariant theory of n × n matrices*, Adv. Math. **19** (1976), no. 3, 306–381. MR 0419491

[Pro07]   Claudio Procesi, *Lie groups*, Universitext, Springer, New York, 2007. MR MR2265844 (2007j:22016)

[Raz74]   Ju. P. Razmyslov, *Identities with trace in full matrix algebras over a field of characteristic zero*, Izv. Akad. Nauk SSSR Ser. Mat. **38** (1974), 723–756. MR 0506414

[Raz09]   Ran Raz, *Multi-linear formulas for permanent and determinant are of super-polynomial size*, J. ACM **56** (2009), no. 2, Art. 8, 17. MR 2535881

[Raz10a]   _____ , *Elusive functions and lower bounds for arithmetic circuits*, Theory Comput. **6** (2010), 135–177. MR 2719753

[Raz10b]   _____ , *Tensor-rank and lower bounds for arithmetic formulas*, Proceedings of the 2010 International Symposium on Theory of Computing, ACM, New York, 2010, pp. 659–666. MR 2743315 (2011i:68044)

[Rob17]   P. Roberts, *A minimal free complex associated to the minors of a matrix*, JCA, to appear (2017).

[RS00]   Kristian Ranestad and Frank-Olaf Schreyer, *Varieties of sums of powers*, J. Reine Angew. Math. **525** (2000), 147–181. MR MR1780430 (2001m:14009)

[RS11]   _____ , *On the rank of a symmetric form*, J. Algebra **346** (2011), 340–342. MR 2842085 (2012j:13037)

[Sap]   R. Saptharishi, *A survey of lower bounds in arithmetic circuit complexity*, https://github.com/dasarpmar/lowerbounds-survey/releases.

[Sax08]   Nitin Saxena, *Diagonal circuit identity testing and lower bounds*, Automata, languages and programming. Part I, Lecture Notes in Comput. Sci., vol. 5125, Springer, Berlin, 2008, pp. 60–71. MR 2500261

[Sch81]   A. Schönhage, *Partial and total matrix multiplication*, SIAM J. Comput. **10** (1981), no. 3, 434–455. MR MR623057 (82h:68070)

[Seg10]   C. Segre, *Preliminari di una teoria delle varieta luoghi di spazi*, Rend. Circ. Mat. Palermo XXX (1910), 87–121.

[Sha07]   Igor R. Shafarevich, *Basic algebraic geometry. 1*, 3rd ed. Springer, Heidelberg, 2013, translated from the 2007 third Russian edition by Miles Reid.

[Sha13]   _____, *Basic algebraic geometry. 2*, 3rd ed., Springer, Heidelberg, 2013, Schemes and complex manifolds, translated from the 2007 third Russian edition by Miles Reid. MR 3100288

[Shp02]   Amir Shpilka, *Affine projections of symmetric polynomials*, J. Comput. System Sci. **65** (2002), no. 4, 639–659, special issue on complexity, 2001 (Chicago, IL). MR 1964647

[Sip92]   Michael Sipser, *The history and status of the p versus np question*, Proceedings of the 24th annual Symposium on Theory of Computing, ACM, 1992, pp. 603–618.

[Smi13]   A. V. Smirnov, *The bilinear complexity and practical algorithms for matrix multiplication*, Comput. Math. Math. Phys. **53** (2013), no. 12, 1781–1795. MR 3146566

[Spi79]   Michael Spivak, *A comprehensive introduction to differential geometry. Vol. I*, 2nd ed., Publish or Perish Inc., Wilmington, DE, 1979. MR MR532830 (82g:53003a)

[SS42]   R. Salem and D. C. Spencer, *On sets of integers which contain no three terms in arithmetical progression*, Proc. Natl. Acad. Sci. U. S. A. **28** (1942), 561–563. MR 0007405

[SS09]   Jessica Sidman and Seth Sullivant, *Prolongations and computational algebra*, Can. J. Math. **61** (2009), no. 4, 930–949. MR 2541390

[Sto]   A. Stothers, *On the complexity of matrix multiplication*, PhD thesis, University of Edinburgh, 2010.

[Str69]   Volker Strassen, *Gaussian elimination is not optimal*, Numer. Math. **13** (1969), 354–356. MR 40 #2223

[Str73]   _____, *Vermeidung von Divisionen*, J. Reine Angew. Math. **264** (1973), 184–202. MR MR0521168 (58 #25128)

[Str83]   V. Strassen, *Rank and optimal computation of generic tensors*, Linear Algebra Appl. **52/53** (1983), 645–685. MR 85b:15039

[Str87]   _____, *Relative bilinear complexity and matrix multiplication*, J. Reine Angew. Math. **375/376** (1987), 406–443. MR MR882307 (88h:11026)

[Str91]   _____, *Degeneration and complexity of bilinear maps: some asymptotic spectra*, J. Reine Angew. Math. **413** (1991), 127–180. MR 92m:11038

[SVW01]   A. J. Sommese, J. Verschelde, and C. W. Wampler, *Using monodromy to decompose solution sets of polynomial systems into irreducible components*, Applications of algebraic geometry to coding theory, physics and computation (Eilat, 2001), NATO Sci. Ser. II Math. Phys. Chem., vol. 36, Kluwer Academic, Dordrecht, 2001, pp. 297–315. MR 1866906

[SVW02]   Andrew J. Sommese, Jan Verschelde, and Charles W. Wampler, *Symmetric functions applied to decomposing solution sets of polynomial systems*, SIAM J. Numer. Anal. **40** (2002), no. 6, 2026–2046 (2003). MR 1974173

[SW01]   Amir Shpilka and Avi Wigderson, *Depth-3 arithmetic circuits over fields of characteristic zero*, Comput. Complexity **10** (2001), no. 1, 1–27. MR 1867306 (2003a:68048)

[SY09]   Amir Shpilka and Amir Yehudayoff, *Arithmetic circuits: a survey of recent results and open questions*, Found. Trends Theor. Comput. Sci. **5** (2009), no. 3–4, 207–388 (2010). MR 2756166

[Syl52]   J. J. Sylvester, *On the principles of the calculus of forms*, Cambridge and Dublin Math. J. (1852), 52–97.

[Tav15]   Sébastien Tavenas, *Improved bounds for reduction to depth 4 and depth 3*, Inf. Comput. **240** (2015), 2–11. MR 3303254

[Ter11]   A. Terracini, *Sulla v_k per cui la varietà degli $s_h(h + 1)$-seganti ha dimensione minore dell'ordinario*, Rend. Circ. Mat. Palermo **31** (1911), 392–396.

[Tod92]   S. Toda, *Classes of arithmetic circuits capturing the complexity of computing the determinant*, IEICE Trans. Inf. Syst. **E75-D** (1992), 116–124.

[Toe77]   Emil Toeplitz, *Ueber ein Flächennetz zweiter Ordnung*, Math. Ann. **11** (1877), no. 3, 434–463. MR 1509924

[Tra84]   B. A. Trakhtenbrot, *A survey of Russian approaches to perebor (brute-force search) algorithms*, Ann. Hist. Comput. **6** (1984), no. 4, 384–400. MR 763733

[Val77]   Leslie G. Valiant, *Graph-theoretic arguments in low-level complexity*, Mathematical foundations of computer science (Proc. Sixth Sympos., Tatranská Lomnica, 1977), Springer, Berlin, 1977, pp. 162–176. Lecture Notes in Comput. Sci., Vol. 53. MR 0660702 (58 #32067)

[Val79]   Leslie G. Valiant, *Completeness classes in algebra*, Proceedings of the 11th STOC, ACM, 1979, pp. 249–261.

[VSBR83]   L. G. Valiant, S. Skyum, S. Berkowitz, and C. Rackoff, *Fast parallel computation of polynomials using few processors*, SIAM J. Comput. **12** (1983), no. 4, 641–644. MR 721003 (86a:68044)

[vzG87]   Joachim von zur Gathen, *Permanent and determinant*, Linear Algebra Appl. **96** (1987), 87–100. MR MR910987 (89a:15005)

[Wah91]   Jonathan Wahl, *Gaussian maps and tensor products of irreducible representations*, Manuscripta Math. **73** (1991), no. 3, 229–259. MR 1132139 (92m:14066a)

[Wey97]   Hermann Weyl, *The classical groups*, Princeton Landmarks in Mathematics, Princeton University Press, Princeton, NJ, 1997, Their invariants and representations, 15th printing, Princeton Paperbacks. MR 1488158 (98k:01049)

[Wey03]   Jerzy Weyman, *Cohomology of vector bundles and syzygies*, Cambridge Tracts in Mathematics, vol. 149, Cambridge University Press, Cambridge, 2003. MR MR1988690 (2004d:13020)

[Wil]   Virginia Williams, *Breaking the coppersimith-winograd barrier*, preprint.

[Win71]   S. Winograd, *On multiplication of* 2×2 *matrices*, Linear Algebra and Appl. **4** (1971), 381–388. MR 45 #6173

[Ye11]   Ke Ye, *The stabilizer of immanants*, Linear Algebra Appl. **435** (2011), no. 5, 1085–1098. MR 2807220 (2012e:15017)

[Zui15]   J. Zuiddam, *A note on the gap between rank and border rank*, ArXiv e-prints (2015).

Index